Guatemala, Belize & Yucatán
La Ruta Maya
a Lonely Planet travel survival kit
Tom Brosnahan

Guatemala, Belize & Yucatán – La Ruta Maya

2nd edition

Published by

Lonely Planet Publications

Head Office: PO Box 617, Hawthorn, Vic 3122, Australia
Branches: PO Box 2001A, Berkeley, CA 94702, USA
10 Barley Mow Passage, Chiswick, London W4 4PH, UK
71 bis rue du Cardinal Lemoine, 75005 Paris, France

Printed by

Colorcraft Ltd, Hong Kong

Photographs by

Tom Brosnahan (TB)
Greg Elms (GE)
James Lyon (JL)
Paul Wentford (PW)
Tony Wheeler (TW)

Front cover: Church, Izamel, Yucatán, Mexico (Charles Place), The Image Bank

First Published

October 1991

This Edition

September 1994

Although the authors and publisher have tried to make the information as accurate as possible, they accept no responsibility for any loss, injury or inconvenience sustained by any person using this book.

National Library of Australia Cataloguing in Publication Data

Brosnahan, Tom
Guatemala, Belize & Yucatán – a travel survival kit.

2nd ed.
Includes index.
ISBN 0 86442 220 2.

1. Yucatán Peninsula – Guidebooks. 2. Guatemala – Guidebooks. 3. Belize – Guidebooks. I. Brosnahan, Tom. Ruta Maya, Yucatán, Guatemala & Belize. II. Title. III. Title: Guatemala, Belize & Yucatán. IV. Title: Ruta Maya, Yucatán, Guatemala & Belize.

917.28

text & maps © Lonely Planet 1994
photos © photographers as indicated 1994
climate charts compiled from information supplied by Patrick J Tyson, © Patrick J Tyson, 1994

Tom Brosnahan

Tom Brosnahan was born and raised in Pennsylvania, went to college in Boston, then set out on the road. After travelling in Europe he joined the Peace Corps, and saw Mexico for the first time as part of the Peace Corps training programme. A short term of teaching English in a Mexico City school whetted his appetite for more exploration. After graduate school he travelled throughout Mexico, Guatemala and Belize writing travel articles and guidebooks for various publishers, and in the past two decades his 20 books covering numerous destinations have sold over two million copies in twelve languages.

Ever since he first saw Yucatán, Guatemala and Belize, Tom had a dream of returning to follow in the footsteps of John L Stephens and write an authoritative guidebook to the Mayan lands. *La Ruta Maya – a travel survival kit*, published in 1991, was the fulfilment of that dream. This second edition, under the new title of *Guatemala, Belize & Yucatán*, continues to share that fulfilment with the increasing number of travellers to the region.

Dedication

For Lydia Celestia, who's Mayan, in a way.

From the Author

I know of no more fascinating places, or better places to explore, than southern Mexico, Guatemala and Belize. Though their fascination is eternal, their exchange rates and economies are not. I've done my best to provide detailed, exact and complete information on accommodation, meals, transportation, etc. But a swing in the world price of oil, or an economic policy decision made in Mexico City, Guatemala City or Belize City can change all of my carefully recorded information in a day. If this happens, please rest assured that the establishments recommended will still offer the best value for the price, whether that price is higher or lower than noted in this guide.

When you return from your journey through the region, I'm sure you'll have suggestions, recommendations and perhaps

even criticisms. Please write and let me know about them so that I can improve the next edition of this guide. You'll be helping many thousands of faithful Lonely Planet readers to enjoy Guatemala, Belize and southern Mexico as you have. I'm very grateful for letters – I read each one and I reply as soon as I can. The names of the travellers who have written in are listed at the back of the book.

A surer way to get a quick reply is to send me electronic mail. Contact me on CompuServe at 76400,3110; on America Online at Tbros; or on the Internet at 76400.3110 @compuserve.com. You can also obtain the latest news and tips on travel in the region by having your computer modem dial my electronic information service in the USA on ☎ (508) 287 0660. (This number is for computer access only; it will not work for voice communication.)

If you have problems with any establishment mentioned in this guide, please write to me so that I can reassess it or remove it and save future travellers from similar problems. Establishments recommended in this guide must provide you, the reader, with good, honest, courteous service at fair prices. If I receive complaints about any establishment, it will be removed from this guide.

Acknowledgements

Thanks and gratitude to the staff and members of the Belize Tourism Industry Association who provided much valuable information and support: Maria Vega, President; Sylvano Guerrero, Executive Director; and special thanks to Alicia Gonzalez, whose efficient and energetic efforts helped to make this a better book. Thanks also to Alan Auil of Budget Rent a Car in Belize City; to Karen Pasquariello, an excellent expedition guide based at the Belize Biltmore Hotel in Belize City; to Tropic Air, and especially Captain Armando Ramirez who made some wonderful aerial photographs possible; and to Continental Airlines, which proved to me that it has the best connections to Belize. Andy Alpers of L Martinez Associates Inc in Miami provided his usual genial and indispensible assistance; as did the staff of the Instituto Guatemalteco de Turismo (INGUAT).

For this edition, the sections covering Chiapas and Tabasco were competently and amiably researched by my friend Sam Whitney, a travel writer with many published travel stories to her credit. When not hopping on planes or writing for various publishers, Sam lives among the mountains of Wyoming, where she leads hiking and skiing expeditions for fun and profit.

For courage through what seemed an endless task I must thank, as always, Jane Fisher, my wife.

From the Publisher

This second edition was edited by David Lowe and Alison White. Thanks to Greg Alford for proofing and map-checking, Kristin Odijk for production and Caroline Williamson for editorial guidance. Thanks also to Rob Flynn for computer stuff and to Sharon Wertheim for indexing. Maps and design are the work of Greg Herriman, with some additional maps from Jane Hart, Louise Keppie, Indra Kilfoyle, Chris Lee Ack, Sandra Smythe and Sally Woodward. Illustrations are by Trudie Canavan and Tamsin Wilson is responsible for cover design.

Warning & Request

Things change – prices go up, schedules change, good places go bad and bad places go bankrupt – nothing stays the same. So if you find things better or worse, recently opened or long since closed, please write and tell us and help make the next edition better.

Your letters will be used to help update future editions and, where possible, important changes will also be included in a Stop Press section in reprints.

We greatly appreciate all information that is sent to us by travellers. Back at Lonely Planet we employ a hard-working readers' letters team to sort through the many letters we receive. The best ones will be rewarded with a free copy of the next edition or another Lonely Planet guide if you prefer. We give away lots of books, but, unfortunately, not every letter/postcard receives one.

Contents

INTRODUCTION 11

FACTS ABOUT THE REGION 13

History 13   People 24   Religion 31
Ecology 21   Architecture 25   Mayan Calendar System 33
Flora & Fauna........... 21   Culture 28   Language....................... 36

FACTS FOR THE VISITOR 41

Suggested Itineraries 41   Electricity.................... 50   Dangers & Annoyances 63
Documents...................... 42   Laundry....................... 50   Work............................ 64
Customs........................ 42   Weights & Measures........ 50   Activities....................... 65
Money.......................... 42   Books & Maps................ 50   Highlights...................... 65
Climate & When to Go........ 44   Media.......................... 54   Accommodation............... 66
What to Bring 46   Radio & TV 54   Food............................ 67
Festivals & Holidays 46   Film & Photography 54   Drinks.......................... 68
Post & Telecommunications..... 48   Health......................... 54   Entertainment................. 70
Time............................ 50   Women Travellers........... 63   Things to Buy.................. 70

GETTING THERE & AWAY 72

Air............................ 72   Land 77   Tours........................... 79

GETTING AROUND.. 80

Air............................ 80   Car............................ 81   Local Transport................ 82
Bus............................ 80   Hitching 81
Train.......................... 81   Boat........................... 81

GUATEMALA

FACTS ABOUT GUATEMALA 84

History 85   Government 88   People........................... 89
Geography 87   Economy 88

FACTS FOR THE VISITOR 90

Visas & Embassies 90   Business Hours 92   Dangers & Annoyances 93
Money.......................... 91   Post & Telecommunications..... 92   Food 94
Climate & When to Go........... 92   Media.......................... 93   Getting There & Around.......... 94

GUATEMALA CITY 95

History 95   Zona 4 102   Places to Stay.................. 104
Orientation.................... 95   Zona 9 102   Places to Eat.................. 106
Information.................... 99   Zona 10 103   Entertainment................. 107
Zona 1......................... 101   Zona 13 103
Zona 2......................... 102   Kaminaljuyú 103

GUATEMALA'S HIGHLANDS 112

Antigua Guatemala 113   Los Encuentros 127   **Quiché 136**
Around Antigua Guatemala 124   Sololá......................... 127   Chichicastenango 137
Lago de Atitlán................. 125 Sololá to Panajachel 128   Santa Cruz del Quiché 142
Tecpán Guatemala.............. 125   Panajachel 128   Nebaj........................... 144
Iximché........................ 125   Around Lago de Atitlán 134

SOUTH-WESTERN HIGHLANDS 145

Cuatro Caminos 145
Totonicapán 145
Quetzaltenango 146
Around Quetzaltenango 153
Huehuetenango 156
La Mesilla 160
Todos Santos Cuchumatán 160

GUATEMALA'S PACIFIC SLOPE 162

Ciudad Tecún Umán 162
El Carmen 162
Coatepeque 164
El Zarco Junction 164
Retalhuleu 164
Around Retalhuleu 166
Champerico 166
Mazatenango 166
Santa Lucía Cotzumalguapa ...166
La Democracia 170
Around La Democracia 171
Escuintla 171
Puerto San José, Likín & Iztapa 171
Monterrico 172
Lago de Amatitlán 172

CENTRAL & EASTERN GUATEMALA 173

Salamá 173
Around Salamá 175
Biotopo del Quetzal 175
Cobán 176
Around Cobán 179
Río Hondo 180
Estanzuela 181
Zacapa 181
Chiquimula 181
Esquipulas 183
Copán (Honduras) 186
Quiriguá 194
Lago de Izabal 197
The Road to Flores 197
Puerto Barrios 198
Lívingston 202

EL PETÉN 205

Flores & Santa Elena 206
El Remate 211
Tikal 213
Uaxactún 221
Eastwards to Belize 221
From El Petén to Chiapas (Mexico) 223
Sayaxché & Ceibal 223

BELIZE

FACTS ABOUT BELIZE 226

History 226
Geography 228
Government 229
Economy 229
Population & People 229
Language 230

FACTS FOR THE VISITOR 231

Visas & Embassies 231
Money 232
Climate & When to Go 232
Tourist Offices 233
Business Hours 233
Post & Telecommunications ...233
Media 234
Food 234

GETTING THERE & AROUND 235

Getting There & Away 235
Air 235
Bus 235
Boat 235
Getting Around 235
Air 235
Bus 236
Car 237
Motorbike & Bicycle 238

BELIZE CITY 240

Orientation 240
Information 240
Walking Tour 242
Places to Stay 243
Places to Eat 248
Entertainment 249
Getting There & Away 249
Getting Around 249

THE CAYES 250

Caye Caulker 250
Ambergris Caye & San Pedro ...255
Other Cayes 262

NORTHERN BELIZE 263

Bermudian Landing Community Baboon Sanctuary 263
Altun Ha & Maruba 264
Crooked Tree Wildlife Sanctuary 265
Lamanai 266
Orange Walk 267
Corozal Town 269

SOUTHERN BELIZE 273

Hummingbird Highway 273
Dangriga 273
Southern Cayes 276

Southern Highway 276
Placencia 277
Punta Gorda 280

Around Punta Gorda 283

WESTERN BELIZE 285

Belize Zoo 285
Banana Bank Lodge 286
Guanacaste Park 286
Belmopan 286

Central Farm 288
San Ignacio (Cayo) 289
Mountain Pine Ridge 293
Xunantunich 296

Benque Viejo del Carmen 297
West to Guatemala 299

YUCATÁN

FACTS ABOUT YUCATÁN 302

History 302
Geography 303

Government 304
Economy 304

People 305

FACTS FOR THE VISITOR 306

Visas & Embassies 306
Money 308
Climate & When to Go 309

Tourist Offices 309
Business Hours 310
Post & Telecommunications ... 310

Media 311
Food 311

GETTING THERE & AROUND 313

Air 313

Land 313

CANCÚN & ISLA MUJERES 315

Cancún 315

Isla Mujeres 327

Around Isla Mujeres 334

CENTRAL & NORTHERN YUCATÁN 335

Valladolid 335
Ekbalam 339
Tizimin 340

Río Lagartos 341
San Felipe 342
Isla Holbox 343

Chichén Itzá 343
Izamal 351

MÉRIDA 353

Around Mérida 368
Dzibilchaltún 368

Progreso 369
Celestún 371

UXMAL & THE PUUC ROUTE 372

Uxmal 374
Puuc Route 379
Uxmal to Campeche 382

Ticul 384
Mérida to Ticul via Acanceh
& Mayapán 385

Mérida to Campeche – short
route (Highway 180) 387

CAMPECHE 388

Campeche 389
Around Campeche 395

Escárcega 395
Escárcega to Chetumal 395

Escárcega to Palenque 396

YUCATÁN'S CARIBBEAN COAST 397

Puerto Morelos (Km 328) 397
Playa del Carmen 399
Cozumel 402
Around Isla Cozumel 409
Tulum 413

Tulum to Boca Paila & Punta
Allen 417
Cobá 418
Felipe Carrillo Puerto 420
Laguna Bacalar 421

Chetumal 422
Around Chetumal 426
South to Belize 427

TABASCO **428**

Villahermosa 428   Around Villahermosa 439

LOWLAND CHIAPAS **441**

Palenque 441   Bonampak & Yaxchilán 452
Río Usumacinta 452   Palenque to San Cristóbal 455

HIGHLAND & PACIFIC CHIAPAS **460**

Villarhermosa to Tuxtla   Comitán 485   Tapachula 492
Gutiérrez 460   Lagos de Montebello 488   Around Tapachula 495
Tuxtla Gutiérrez 461   Motozintla 491   Talismán & Ciudad Hidalgo
Around Tuxtla Gutiérrez 467   Guatemalan Border – Ciudad   (Guatemalan Border) 495
San Cristóbal de Las Casas 469   Cuauhtémoc 491
Around San Cristóbal 482   The Soconusco 491

GLOSSARY **497**

MENU TRANSLATOR **499**

INDEX **502**

Maps 502   Text 502

Map Legend

BOUNDARIES

...............International Boundary
...............Internal Boundary

ROUTES

...............Freeway
...............Highway
...............Major Road
...............Unsealed Road or Track
...............City Road
...............City Street
...............Railway
...............Underground Railway
...............Tram
...............Walking Track
...............Walking Tour
...............Ferry Route
...............Cable Car or Chairlift

AREA FEATURES

...............Park, Gardens
...............National Park
...............Built-Up Area
...............Pedestrian Mall
...............Market
...............Cemetery
...............Reef
...............Beach or Desert
...............Rocks

HYDROGRAPHIC FEATURES

...............Coastline
...............River, Creek
...............Intermittent River or Creek
...............Lake, Intermittent Lake
...............Canal
...............Swamp

SYMBOLS

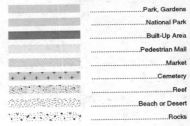

✪ CAPITAL		...............National Capital
◉ Capital		...............State Capital
◍ CITY		...............Major City
● City		...............City
● Town		...............Town
● Village		...............Village
■		...............Place to Stay
▼		...............Place to Eat
◙		...............Bar
✉	☎	...............Post Office, Telephone
❶	⑤	...............Tourist Information, Bank
◉	℗	...............Transport, Parking
⛩	⛫	...............Museum, Youth Hostel
⛺	⚐	Caravan Park, Camping Ground
†	✠	†	...............Church, Cathedral
☪	✡	...............Mosque, Synagogue
⚖	⚜	Buddhist Temple, Hindu Temple

✚	★	...............Hospital, Police Station
✈	✝	...............Airport, Airfield
▣	✿	...............Swimming Pool, Gardens
◆	🐘	...............Shopping Centre, Zoo
⛱	⛽	...............Picnic Site, Petrol Station
←	A25	One Way Street, Route Number
	∴	...............Archaeological Site or Ruins
🏛	⚑	...............Stately Home, Monument
⛩	▣	...............Castle, Tomb
⌂	⌂	...............Cave, Hut or Chalet
▲	✳	...............Mountain or Hill, Lookout
⚓	⚓	...............Lighthouse, Shipwreck
)(	⚭	...............Pass, Spring
		...............Ancient or City Wall
		...............Rapids, Waterfalls
		...............Cliff or Escarpment, Tunnel
		...............Railway Station

Note: not all symbols displayed above appear in this book

Introduction

The Mayan lands of southern Mexico, Guatemala and Belize were home to the western hemisphere's greatest ancient civilisation. Travellers who come to this region today want to see the huge pyramids and temples, the great stelae covered in hieroglyphic inscriptions, and the broad ball courts where mysterious athletic contests were held.

But Mayan lore is more than the forgotten culture of a long-dead empire. As you travel here, the Maya are all around you. Modern descendants of the ancient Maya drive your bus, catch the fish you dine upon, work in the bank where you change money, and greet you as you trudge up the side of a smoking volcano. The Mayan kingdoms may be dead, but the Maya – some two million of them – are very much alive in their ancient land.

The land is exceptionally varied, from the flat limestone shelf of Yucatán to the cool pine-clad mountains of Chiapas and Guatemala, from the steamy jungles of El Petén, rich with tropical birdlife, to the swamps and fens of northern Belize. It is also threatened. Pressured by rapid population growth, development and exploitation, it is in danger of overuse and consequent ecological destruction. The dense rainforest is disappearing at an alarming rate as farmers and ranchers, responding to personal need and world market conditions, slash and burn to carve out new fields for subsistence farming or pastureland for high-profit herds of beef cattle.

The rich heritage of Mayan civilisation and its environment has its defenders, however. Both governments and private

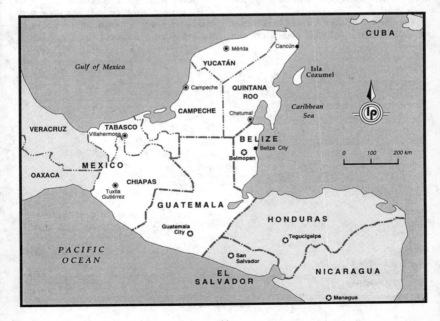

organisations are instituting programmes to preserve and protect both the Mayan heritage and its natural setting. Tourism is one of the most important forces in these plans.

LA RUTA MAYA

La Ruta Maya (The Mayan Route) was a plan conceived and championed by Wilbur E Garrett, former editor of the US *National Geographic* magazine. The concept of La Ruta Maya provides for carefully controlled touristic development with minimal adverse impact on the land, the people and the Maya's heritage. Income from increased tourism may be used to preserve and protect Mayan archaeological sites and jungle biosphere reserves; it may also offer an alternative source of income to those now destroying the forests. The governments of Mexico, Guatemala, Belize, Honduras and El Salvador have subscribed to the plan and have established an intergovernmental organisation called El Mundo Maya to make tourism work to the benefit of the Maya and their land.

The purpose of the La Ruta Maya plan is to highlight the cultural, ecological and archaeological significance of the Maya's lands, to provide direction and resources for protection and conservation, and to help the Maya preserve their ancient culture while improving the conditions under which they live.

The plan envisions not one but many travel routes and circuits throughout the region, encompassing seaside resorts such as Cancún and Cozumel, jungle preserves in Chiapas, Quintana Roo, El Petén and Belize, Spanish colonial cities, and most archaeological sites, excavated and unexcavated.

This guidebook, while emphasising Mayan culture both ancient and modern, also gives complete information for those going to Mexico's Caribbean coast or to Belize's offshore islands for sun, sand, surf and snorkelling, and for those interested in Mérida's beautiful colonial architecture, Campeche's pirate history, and climbable volcanoes near Guatemala's Lake Atitlán. In short, it is a complete guide to the lands of the Maya, ancient and modern.

For more information and some suggested itineraries, see under Facts for the Visitor at the beginning of this book.

Facts about the Region

HISTORY
Timeline

The history of the Maya and their predecessors stretches back over 4000 years. The following timeline may help you to keep track of what was happening when and where. The division of historical periods for Mayan civilisation is that used by Professor Michael D Coe (author of *The Maya*). I've added notes in brackets on contemporary historical events in the Old World so you can compare developments.

13,000 to 2000 BC Archaic Period Hunting and gathering for food. After the end of the Ice Age (7500 BC), primitive agriculture begins.

2000 to 800 BC Early Preclassic Period In a few Mayan regions, formation of fishing and farming villages producing primitive crops. Early Olmec civilisation flourishes (1200 to 900 BC) at San Lorenzo, Veracruz; Teotihuacán culture flourishes in central Mexico. (Old Testament times of Abraham, Isaac and Jacob; Israel escapes from Egypt and crosses Jordan into the Promised Land; reigns of King David, King Solomon, Tutankhamen and Nefertiti. Invention of the alphabet.)

800 to 300 BC Middle Preclassic Period Larger towns; Olmec civilisation reaches its height at La Venta, Tabasco. Great increase in Mayan population. (Flowering of classical Hellenic culture and art around the Aegean Sea.)

300 BC to 250 AD Late Preclassic Period Mayan cities have large but simple temples and pyramids; pottery and decoration become elaborate. (Alexander the Great's conquests; Ptolemies in Egypt; Roman republic and early empire; life of Jesus.)

250 to 600 Early Classic Period Use of the Long Count calendar. In the highlands of Guatemala and Chiapas, great temples are built around spacious plazas; Mayan art is technically excellent. (Founding of Constantinople and building of Hagia Sophia; Huns invade Europe; Vandals sack Rome, beginning of Middle (or Dark) Ages in Europe; Saxons invade Britain.)

600 to 900 Late Classic Period High Mayan civilisation moves from the western highlands to the lowlands of Petén and Yucatán. Mayan art at its most sensitive and refined. (Life of Mohammed; rise of the Arab Empire; Dome of the Rock built in Jerusalem; Harun al-Rashid sends an ambassador to the court of Charlemagne.)

900 to 1200 Early Post-Classic Period Population growth, food shortages, decline in trade, military campaigns, revolutions and migrations cause the swift collapse of Classic Mayan culture. In central Mexico, Toltecs flourish at Tula, later abandon it and invade Yucatán, establishing their capital at Chichén Itzá. (Europe's Dark Ages continue; Norman invasion of Britain; Crusades.)

1200 to 1530 Late Post-Classic Period Toltec civilisation collapses mysteriously, and the Itzaes move from Campeche to El Petén, then to Belize, and finally dominate northern Yucatán. (Magna Carta; Mongol invasion of Eastern Europe under Genghis Khan; Gothic architecture; fall of Constantinople; reigns of Süleyman the Magnificent, Henry VIII, Charles V; European Renaissance; rise of the Inca Empire in Peru.)

1530 to 1821 Colonial Period Francisco de Montejo conquers Yucatán, and Pedro de Alvarado subdues Chiapas and Guatemala, but harsh colonial rule leads to frequent Mayan rebellions.

1821 to Present Independence Period Yucatán declares independence from Spain, and soon after joins the Mexican union. United Provinces of Central America proclaims independence, later divides into separate countries.

Archaic Period (13,000 to 2000 BC)

The great glaciers which blanketed northern Europe, Asia and North America in the Pleistocene Epoch robbed earth's oceans of a lot of water, lowering the sea level. The receding waters exposed enough land so that wandering bands of Asiatic men and women could find their way on dry land from Siberia to Alaska, and then southwards through the western hemisphere.

They made this journey some 13,000 years ago, and in the next 4000 years found their way to every part of North and South America, to the Straits of Magellan. When

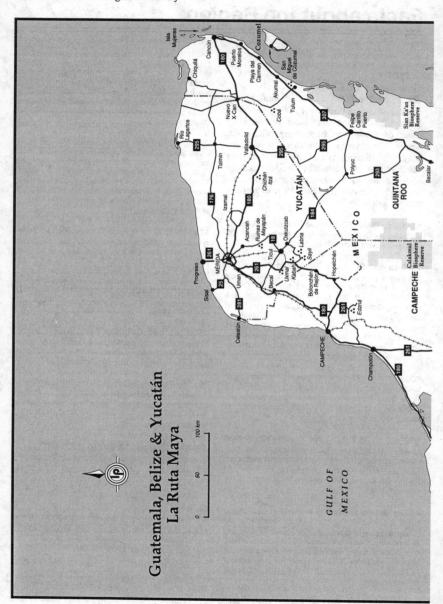

Guatemala, Belize & Yucatán
La Ruta Maya

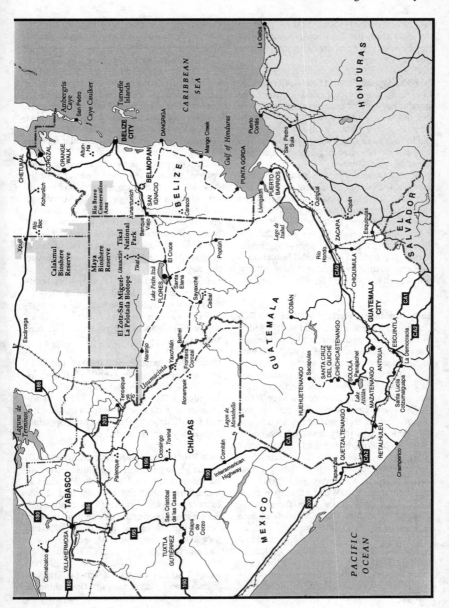

the glaciers melted (about 7000 BC) and the sea level rose, the land bridge over which they crossed was submerged beneath what is now the Bering Strait.

The early inhabitants hunted mammoths, fished and gathered wild foods. After the Ice Age came a hot, dry period in which the mammoths' natural pastureland disappeared and the wild harvests of nuts and berries became scarce. The primitive inhabitants had to find some other way to get by, so they sought out favourable microclimates and invented agriculture.

Beans, tomatoes and squash (marrow) were cultivated, but these took second place to maize (corn), which was nurtured, by hybridisation, from a wild grass into the Mayan staff of life, a status which it enjoys to this day. Baskets were woven to carry in the crops, and turkeys and dogs were domesticated for food. These early homebodies used crude stone tools and primitive pottery, and shaped simple clay fertility figurines.

Early Preclassic Period (2000 to 800 BC)
The improvement in the food supply led to an increase in population, a higher standard of living, and more time to fool around with such things as decorating pots and growing ever-plumper ears of corn. Even at the beginning of the Early Preclassic period, people here spoke an early form of the Mayan language. These early Maya also decided that living in caves and under palm fronds was old-fashioned, so they invented the *na*, or thatched Mayan hut, which is still used today, some 4000 years later, throughout much of the region. Where spring floods were a problem, a family would build its *na* on a mound of earth. When a family member died, burial took place right there in the living room, and the Dear Departed attained the rank of honoured ancestor.

The Copán Valley (in present-day Honduras) had its first proto-Mayan settlers by about 1100 BC, and a century later the settlements on the Pacific coast of what is now Guatemala were developing a hierarchical society.

Olmecs Without question, the most significant happening of the Early Preclassic period took place about 1000 BC, not in the traditional Mayan lands, but in nearby Tabasco and Veracruz (both in modern Mexico). The mysterious Olmec people developed a writing system of hieroglyphics, perhaps based on knowledge borrowed from the Zapotecs of Oaxaca. They also developed what is known as the Vague Year calendar of 365 days (see The Mayan Calendar System below).

The Olmecs' jaguar god art became widespread through Mesoamerica ('middle America'). Their huge, mysterious basalt-carved heads weighing up to 60 tonnes were sculpted with characteristic 'jaguar mouths' and Negroid features. How the heads were hewn without metal tools and moved some 100 km from basalt quarries to the Olmecs' capital city of La Venta remains a mystery to this day.

It's assumed that the Olmecs were trampled by waves of invaders, but aspects of their culture lived on among their neighbours, paving the way for the later accomplishments of Mayan art, architecture and science.

Middle Preclassic Period (800 to 300 BC)
By this time there were rich villages in Honduras' Copán Valley, and settlers had founded villages at Tikal. Trade routes developed, with coastal peoples exchanging salt for highland tribes' tool-grade obsidian. Everybody happily traded pots.

Late Preclassic Period (300 BC to 250 AD)
As the Maya got better at agriculture they got richer, and could then afford such luxuries as a class of scribes and nobility, and all the extravagances which these classes demand. Among the luxuries demanded were temples consisting of raised platforms of earth topped by a thatch-roofed shelter very much like a normal *na*. Pyramid E-VII-sub, of the Chicanel culture at Uaxactún, is a good example of this; others are found at Tikal, El Mirador and Lamanai, sites flourishing in this period. As with a *na*, the local potentate

was buried beneath the shelter. In the lowlands, where limestone was abundant, they began to build platform temples from stone. As each succeeding local potentate had to have a bigger temple, more and larger platforms were put over other platforms, forming huge step pyramids with a na-style shelter on top, with the potentate buried deep within the stack of platforms. Sometimes the pyramids were decorated with huge stylised masks.

More and more pyramids were built around large plazas, much as the common people clustered their thatched houses in family compounds facing a common open space. The stage was set for the flourishing of classic Mayan civilisation.

Early Classic Period (250 to 600)

Armies from Teotihuacán (near modern Mexico City) invaded the Mayan highlands, conquered the Maya and imposed their rule and their culture for a time, but were finally absorbed into Mayan daily life. The so-called Esperanza culture, a blend of Mexican and Mayan elements, was born of this conquest.

The great ceremonial centres at Copán, Tikal, Yaxchilán, Palenque and especially Kaminaljuyú (near present-day Guatemala City) flourished during this time. Mayan astronomers used the elaborate Long Count calendar to date all of human history.

Late Classic Period (600 to 900)

At its height, the Mayan lands were ruled not as an empire but as a collection of independent but also interdependent city-states. Each city-state had its noble house, headed by a king who was the social, political and religious centre of the city's life. The king propitiated the gods by shedding his blood in ceremonies where he pierced his tongue and/or penis with a sharp instrument. He also led his city's soldiers into battle against rival cities, capturing prisoners for use in human sacrifices. Many a king perished in a battle which he was too old to fight; but the king, as sacred head of the community, was

required to lead in battle for religious as well as military reasons.

King Pacal ruled at Palenque and King Bird-Jaguar at Yaxchilán during the early part of this period, marking the height of civilisation and power in these two cities. Mayan civilisation in Tikal was also at its height during the Late Classic period. By the end of the period, however, the great Mayan cities of Tikal, Yaxchilán, Copán, Quiriguá, Piedras Negras and Caracol had reverted to little more than minor towns, or even villages. The focus of Mayan civilisation then shifted to northern Yucatán, where a new civilisation developed at Chichén Itzá, Uxmal and Labná, giving us the artistic styles known as Maya-Toltec, Puuc, Chenes and Río Bec.

Early Post-Classic Period (900 to 1200)

The collapse of classic Mayan civilisation is as surprising as it was sudden. It seems as though the upper classes demanded ever more servants, acolytes and labourers, and though the Mayan population was growing rapidly, it did not furnish enough farmers to feed everyone. Thus weakened, the Maya were prey to the next wave of invaders from central Mexico.

The Toltecs of Tula (near Mexico City) conquered Teotihuacán, then marched and sailed eastwards to Yucatán. They were an extremely warlike people and human sacrifice was a regular practice. The Toltecs were led by a fair-haired, bearded king named Quetzalcóatl (Plumed Serpent), who established himself in Yucatán at Uucil-abnal (Chichén Itzá). He left behind in Mexico, and then in Yucatán, a legend that he would one day return from the direction of the rising sun. The culture at Uucil-abnal flourished after the late 800s, when all of the great buildings were constructed, but by 1200 the city was abandoned.

Late Post-Classic Period (1200 to 1530)

Itzaes After the abandonment of Toltec Uucil-abnal, the site was occupied by a people called the Itzaes. Probably of Mayan race, the Itzaes had lived among the Putun

Maya near Champoton in Tabasco until the early 13th century. They were forced to leave their traditional homeland by other invaders, and headed south-east into El Petén to the lake which became known as Petén Itzá after their arrival. Some continued to Belize, later making their way north along the coast and into northern Yucatán, where they settled at Uucil-abnal. The Itzá leader styled himself Kukulcán, as had the city's Toltec founder, and recycled lots of other Toltec lore as well. But the Itzaes strengthened the belief in sacred cenotes (the natural limestone caves which provided the Maya with their water supply on the riverless plains of the northern Yucatán Peninsula), and they even named their new home Chichén Itzá (At the Mouth of the Well of the Itzaes).

Hernán Cortés 1485-1547

From Chichén Itzá, the ruling Itzaes travelled westwards and founded a new capital city at Mayapán (built 1263-83), which dominated the political life of northern Yucatán for several centuries. The Cocom lineage of the Itzaes ruled a fractious collection of Yucatecan city-states from Mayapán until the mid-1400s, when a subject people called the Xiú, from Uxmal, revolted and overthrew Cocom power. Mayapán was pillaged, ruined and never repopulated. For the next century, until the coming of the conquistadors, northern Yucatán was alive with battles and power struggles among its city-states.

The Coming of the Spaniards The Spaniards had been in the Caribbean since Christopher Columbus arrived in 1492, with their main bases on the islands of Santo Domingo (modern Haiti and the Dominican Republic) and Cuba. Realising that they had not reached the East Indies, they began looking for a passage through the land mass to their west but were distracted by tales of gold, silver and a rich empire. Trading, slaving and exploring expeditions from Cuba were led by Francisco Hernández de Córdoba in 1517 and Juan de Grijalva in 1518 but didn't penetrate inland from Mexico's Gulf coast, where they were driven back by hostile natives.

In 1518 the governor of Cuba, Diego Velázquez, asked Hernán Cortés to lead a new expedition westward. As Cortés gathered ships and men, Velázquez became uneasy about the costs of the venture and about Cortés' questionable loyalty, so he cancelled the expedition. Cortés ignored the governor and set sail on 15 February 1519 with 11 ships, 550 men and 16 horses.

The story of the confrontation between Spaniards and Aztecs is one of the most bizarre in history. Aztec legends predicted the 'return' of fair-skinned gods from the east at just about the time of Cortés' arrival. Thrown off guard by these legends, the rulers of the mighty Aztec empire were overthrown by the small Spanish expeditionary force. A detailed first-hand account may be found in the *True History of the Conquest of New Spain* by one of Cortés' soldiers, Bernal Díaz del Castillo.

Landing first at Cozumel off the Yucatán, the Spaniards were joined by Jerónimo de Aguilar, a Spaniard who had been shipwrecked there several years earlier. With Aguilar acting as translator and guide, Cortés' force moved west along the coast to Tabasco. There they defeated some hostile Indians and Cortés delivered the first of many lectures to the Indians on the importance of Christianity and the greatness of King Carlos V of Spain. Cortés went on to conquer central Mexico, after which he turned his attentions – and his armies – to Yucatán.

The Cocoms and the Xiús were still battling when the conquistadors arrived. Yucatán's Maya could not present a united front to the invaders, and the invaders triumphed. In less than a century after the fall of Mayapán, the conquistadors conquered the Aztec capital of Tenochtitlán (1521; it's now Mexico City), founded Guatemala City (1527) and Mérida (1542), and controlled most of the formerly Mayan lands.

Colonial Period (1530 to 1821)

Yucatán Despite the political infighting among the Yucatecan Maya, conquest by the Spaniards was not easy. The Spanish monarch commissioned Francisco de Montejo (El Adelantado, the Pioneer) with the task, and he set out from Spain in 1527 accompanied by his son, also named Francisco de Montejo. Landing first at Cozumel on the Caribbean coast, then at Xel-ha on the mainland, the Montejos discovered (perhaps not to their surprise) that the local people wanted nothing to do with them. The Maya made it quite clear that they should go conquer somewhere else.

Montejo *père et fils* then sailed around the peninsula, conquered Tabasco (1530), and established their base near Campeche, which could be easily supplied with necessities, arms and new troops from New Spain (central Mexico). They pushed inland to conquer, but after four long, difficult years were forced to retreat and to return to Mexico City in defeat.

The younger Montejo (El Mozo, The Lad) took up the cause again, with his father's support, and in 1540 he returned to Campeche with his cousin named (guess what?) – Francisco de Montejo. The two Francisco de Montejos pressed inland with speed and success, allying themselves with the Xiús against the Cocoms, defeating the Cocoms and gaining the Xiús as converts to Christianity.

When the Xiú leader was baptised, he had to take a Christian name, and it must have seemed to him that there was only one choice, for he became – believe it or not – Francisco de Montejo Xiú.

The Montejos founded Mérida in 1542, and within four years had almost all of Yucatán subjugated to Spanish rule. The once proud and independent Maya became peons, working for Spanish masters without hope of deliverance except in heaven. The attitude of the conquerors toward the indigenous peoples is graphically depicted in the reliefs on the façade of the Montejo mansion in Mérida: in one scene, armour-clad conquistadors are shown with their feet holding down ugly, hairy, club-wielding savages.

Chiapas & Guatemala The conquest of Chiapas and Guatemala fell to Pedro de Alvarado (1485-1541), a clever but cruel soldier who had been Cortés' lieutenant at the conquest of Aztec Tenochtitlán. Several towns in highland Guatemala had sent embassies to Cortés, offering to submit to his control and protection. In response, Cortés dispatched Alvarado in 1523, and his armies roared through Chiapas and the highland kingdoms of the Quiché and Cakchiquel Maya, crushing them. The Mayan lands were divided into large estates or *encomiendas*, and the Maya living on the lands were mercilessly exploited by the landowning *encomenderos*.

With the coming of the Dominican Friar Bartolomé de las Casas, and groups of Franciscan and Augustinian friars, things got a bit better for the Maya. However, while in many cases the friars were able to protect the local people from the worst abuses, exploitation was still the rule.

The capital city of the Captaincy-General of Guatemala was founded as Santiago de los Caballeros de Guatemala at the site now called Ciudad Vieja, near Antigua (also known as Antigua Guatemala), in 1527. Destroyed by a mudslide less than two decades later, the capital was then moved to Antigua (1543). After a devastating earthquake (1773), the capital was moved to the present site of Guatemala City.

Friar Diego de Landa The Maya recorded

lots of information about their history, customs and ceremonies in beautiful 'painted books' made of beaten-bark paper coated with fine lime. These 'codices' must have numbered in the hundreds when the conquistadors and missionary friars first arrived in the Mayan lands. But because the ancient rites of the Maya were seen as a threat to their adoption and retention of Christianity, the priceless books were destroyed upon the orders of the Franciscans. Only a handful of painted books survive, but these provide much insight into ancient Mayan life.

Among those Franciscans directly responsible for the burning of the Mayan books was Friar Diego de Landa who, in July of 1562 at Maní (near present-day Ticul in Yucatán), ordered the destruction of 27 'hieroglyphic rolls' and 5000 idols. Landa went on to become Bishop of Mérida from 1573 until his death in 1579.

Ironically, it was Friar Diego de Landa who wrote the most important book on Mayan customs and practices, the source for very much of what we know about the Maya. Landa's book, *Relacion de las Cosas de Yucatán*, was written in about 1565. It covers virtually every aspect of Mayan life as it was in the 1560s, from the climate, Mayan houses, food and drink, wedding and funeral customs, to the calendar and the counting system. In a way, Landa atoned for the cultural destruction for which he was responsible.

Landa's book is available in English as *Yucatán Before and After the Conquest*, translated by William Gates and first published in 1937; it was republished in 1978 by Dover Publications, 31 E 2nd St, Mineola, NY 11501-3382, USA. You can buy the book in a number of bookshops and shops at archaeological sites in Yucatán and Guatemala.

The Last Mayan Kingdom The last region of Mayan sovereignty was the city-state of Tayasal in Guatemala's department of El Petén. Making their way southwards after being driven out of Chichén Itzá, a group of Itzaes settled on an island in Lago Petén Itzá, at what is now the town of Flores. They founded a city named Tayasal, and enjoyed independence for over a century after the fall of Yucatán. The intrepid Cortés visited Tayasal in 1524 while on his way to conquer Honduras, but did not make war against King Canek, who greeted him peacefully. Only in the latter years of the 17th century did the Spanish decide that this last surviving Mayan state must be brought within the Spanish Empire, and in 1697 Tayasal fell to the latter-day conquistadors, some 2000 years after the founding of the first important Mayan city-states in the Late Preclassic period.

It's interesting to consider that the last independent Mayan king went down to defeat only a decade before the union of England and Scotland (1707), and at a time when Boston, New York and Philadelphia were small but thriving seaport towns.

Independence Period

During the colonial period, society in Spain's New World colonies was rigidly and precisely stratified, with Spanish natives at the very top; next were the creoles, people born in the New World of Spanish stock; below them were the *ladinos* or *mestizos*, people of mixed Spanish and Indian blood; and at the bottom were the Indians and Blacks of pure race. Only the native Spaniards had real power, a fact deeply resented by the creoles.

The harshness of Spanish rule resulted in frequent revolts, none of them successful for very long. Mexico's Miguel Hidalgo y Costilla gave the Grito de Dolores, the 'Cry (of Independence) at Dolores', at his church near Guanajuato in 1810, inciting his parishioners to revolt. With his lieutenant, a mestizo priest named José María Morelos, he brought large areas of central Mexico under his control. But this rebellion, like earlier ones, failed. The power of Spain was too great.

Napoleon's conquests in Europe changed all that, and destabilised the Spanish Empire to its very foundations. When the French emperor deposed Spain's King Ferdinand

VII and put his brother Joseph Bonaparte on the throne of Spain (1808), creoles in many New World colonies took the opportunity to rise in revolt. By 1821 both Mexico and Guatemala had proclaimed their independence. As with the American Revolution of 1776, the Latin American movements were conservative in nature, preserving control of politics, the economy and the military for the upper classes of Spanish blood.

Independent Mexico urged the peoples of Yucatán, Chiapas and Central America to join it in the formation of one large new state. At first Yucatán and Chiapas refused and Guatemala accepted, but all later changed their minds. Yucatán and Chiapas joined the Mexican union, and Guatemala led the formation of the United Provinces of Central America (1 July 1823), with El Salvador, Nicaragua, Honduras and Costa Rica. Their union, torn by civil strife from the beginning, lasted only until 1840 before breaking up into its constituent states.

Central American independence has been marred from the beginning by civil war and by conflicts among the various countries of the region, a condition which persists today.

Though independence brought new prosperity to the creoles, it worsened the lot of the Maya. The end of Spanish rule meant that the Crown's few liberal safeguards, which had afforded the Indians minimal protection from the most extreme forms of exploitation, were abandoned. Mayan claims to ancestral lands were largely ignored and huge plantations were created for the cultivation of tobacco, sugar cane and henequen (agave rope fibre). The Maya, though legally free, were enslaved by debt peonage to the great landowners.

Modern Nations

Following independence from Spanish colonial rule, each of the countries in the region went its own way. For the histories of these modern nations, see the beginning of each country's section in this book.

ECOLOGY

Tropical forests have been called the 'lungs of the planet', converting carbon dioxide into oxygen, purifying and enriching the air we breathe. Besides acting as the planet's lungs, tropical forests are a storehouse of chemical and biological substances and gene materials which has yet to be extensively explored. The thousands of organisms in the forest may contain the materials needed to cure dreaded diseases and develop new forms of life. But if the forests disappear – and they are disappearing at an alarming rate worldwide – humankind will lose this great storehouse, and may not be able to breathe.

The bad news is that the destruction of tropical forests throughout the region is progressing at an alarming rate. One visit to the countryside around Palenque will confirm this. Huge tracts of land still smoulder from the fires that clear the forest for the farmer's plough and the herder's cattle.

The good news is that preliminary steps have been taken to preserve vast tracts of tropical forest. *Biotopos*, or biosphere reserves, have been established in Mexico, Guatemala and Belize. The restrictions in these reserves vary, but in general the cutting or burning of forest and the hunting of animals is forbidden or controlled.

Of the many biosphere reserves, the most impressive is the vast multinational reserve formed by the juxtaposing of three large national reserves along the joint borders of Mexico, Guatemala and Belize. The large Calakmul Reserve in the southern part of the Yucatán peninsula adjoins the enormous Maya Biosphere Reserve which covers all of the northern Petén in Guatemala. Adjoining to the east is Belize's Río Bravo Conservation Area, over 1000 sq km of tropical forests, rivers, ponds and Mayan archaeological sites.

FLORA & FAUNA

As you might expect, the lush jungles of Chiapas, Guatemala and Belize are teeming with fascinating animals and plants. But the drier forests of Yucatán also provide habitats for a surprising number and variety of beasts.

The Maya call Yucatán 'The Land of the Pheasant and the Deer'. These two animals formed the basis for countless legends – and delicious meals – among the ancient Maya. The legends are still alive, and the animals are still on the menu today.

Birds

As you might imagine, birds are numerous and varied throughout the region. In fact, bird-watching in itself is enough reason to plan an extended stay here. In addition to the more well-known species listed below, the region's habitats harbour such ornithological wonders as the the acorn woodpecker and keel-billed toucan, the endangered horned guan and an abundance of macaws, parrots, forest songbirds and aquatic birds – there are 500 recorded species on the Yucatán Peninsula alone, though habitat destruction is taking its steady toll. In Guatemala, for instance, the giant pie-billed grebe once endemic to the shores of Lago de Atitlán is now believed to be extinct.

Turkey The 'pheasant' of Mayan lore is actually the ocellated turkey, a beautiful bird which reminds one of a peacock. Originally, turkeys were native to New England and the Middle Atlantic states in the USA, and to Yucatán, not to Turkey. The birds got their odd Middle Eastern name when they were shipped from New England and Yucatán to the West Indies in the Triangle Trade, from where they then continued their journey to Europe. They were transshipped at Genoa onto English merchant ships returned from the Ottoman Empire; because they arrived in England aboard the 'Turkey boats' they were known as Turkey-birds. In Turkey, by the way, they're called *hindi* (Indian bird), because they came from the (West) Indies; the French name *dinde* (from India) derives from the same source.

Flamingo These long, lanky but graceful birds inhabit certain areas of northern Yucatán, principally the wetlands near the towns of Río Lagartos (north-eastern Yucatán) and Celestun (north-western Yucatán). Flamingoes can be white, pink or salmon-coloured. It's the pink and salmon ones which draw the oohs and ahhs. Look for them when the rainy season begins in late May.

In addition to the flamingo, other long-

Ocellated Turkey

legged birds such as the heron, snowy egret and white ibis often visit Yucatán and Belize. The egrets are especially easy to see in cattle pastures.

Quetzal The gorgeous quetzal, its long, curving tailfeathers iridescent with blue and green (the colours associated with the Mayan world-tree), was highly valued by the ancient Maya for its incomparably beautiful plumage: quetzal feathers were important to the costumes of Mayan royalty. The quetzal is the national bird of Guatemala. It is also nearly extinct.

As the quetzal becomes scarcer, its value rises; and as the rainforests are slashed and burned, its habitat disappears. Still, there are quetzals to be seen, and you may be lucky enough to see one if you work at it. The places to look are in the jungles of Chiapas, in the highlands of Guatemala, or at Tikal National Park. The Guatemalans have established a special quetzal forest reserve (Biotopo del Quetzal) on the road to Cobán, capital of the department of Alta Verapaz. But the bird is shy and elusive, and establishing a reserve does not guarantee that there will be birds in abundance for you to see.

Cats

Mayan culture, and that of the Olmecs which preceded it, could hardly get along without the jaguar, symbol of power, stealth, determination – and bloodletting. Jaguars still roam the forests of the Mayan lands. You are unlikely to see one except in a cage (there's one in Villahermosa's Parque Museo La Venta), but that won't change your opinion of it. You'll realise at once that the jaguar is an animal worthy of respect.

The jaguar lives on deer, peccary and tapir, which may explain why the tapir, when attacked, runs blindly in any direction – anything to get away.

The ocelot and puma also live in the jungles here, but are just as rare as the jaguar these days. Other seldom-seen cat species include the jaguarundi and the margay.

Deer

Deer are plentiful enough in Yucatán for deer hunting to be still popular both as sport and as a way of getting a cheap dinner. Venison appears on many restaurant menus in the tourist resorts (those that serve more than hamburgers or steak and lobster). Deer multiply rapidly, they love eating corn and they don't seem to be in danger of depopulation.

Reptiles

Iguana One animal you can see at any Yucatecan archaeological site is the iguana, a harmless lizard of fearsome appearance. There are many different kinds of iguanas, but most are green with black bands encircling the body. Iguanas can grow to one metre in length, including their long, flat tails, though most of the ones you'll see will be shorter than 30 cm (about one foot). Iguanas love to bask in the sun on the warm rocks of old Mayan temples, but they'll shoot away from their comfy perches and hide if you approach them.

Sea Turtle Giant sea turtles are found in the waters off Yucatán and Belize. They're protected by law, especially during mating and nesting seasons. Though there are legal methods for hunting small numbers of the turtles, most of the casualties come as the result of poaching and of egg-hunting, as sea turtle eggs are believed by the uninformed to be an aphrodisiac. You may see turtle on a menu. It may have been taken legally. Then again, who knows? My feeling is that it's best to discourage trade in any endangered species, even 'controlled' trade.

Other Reptiles Yucatán is home to several varieties of snakes, including the very deadly coral snakes, the fer-de-lance and tropical rattlesnakes. These beasts do not look for trouble, and will slither away from you if they can. It's unlikely that you'll meet one, and if you do, it's unlikely that you'll do something to anger it, and if you do it's unlikely that you'll get bitten. But if you do, you'll need help quickly as they are deadly poisonous. Watch where you step.

Another dangerous reptile is the cayman, a sort of crocodile, found mostly near the town of Río Lagartos on the northern coast of Yucatán. These beasts are fascinating to look at but unpleasant, even deadly, to meet up close. Keep your distance.

Armadillos & Anteaters

Armadillos are creatures about 25 to 30 cm long with prominent ears, snouts, tails, and hard bony coverings for protection. Though they look fearsome, they are dangerous only to insects, which is what they live on. Their sharp claws help them to dig for fat, tasty grubs, and also to hollow out underground burrows, which is where they live. You might see armadillos in northern Yucatán, most likely as road kill, unfortunately.

The anteater is a cousin of the armadillo, though it's difficult to see the resemblance. There are several species, all with very long, flexible snouts and sharp-clawed shovel-like front paws, the two tools needed to seek out and enjoy ants and other insects. Unlike the armadillo, the anteater is covered in hair, with a long bushy tail. Its slow gait and poor eyesight makes it another common road victim.

Tapirs & Peccaries

Short of leg and tail, stout of build, small of eye, ear and intelligence, the tapir eats plants, bathes daily and runs like mad when approached. If you're wandering the leafy paths of Tikal and you hear something crashing through the underbrush nearby, you've probably frightened a tapir. Or it could have been a peccary, a sort of wild pig that can grow to 30 kg (66 lb) or more in weight. If the crashing has been particularly noisy, it's probably peccaries as they tend to travel in groups.

PEOPLE

Many of the Maya you meet today are the direct descendants of the people who built the marvellous temples and pyramids. To confirm this, all you need to do is compare their appearance with that of the ancient Maya shown in inscriptions and drawings.

Farm boys from Todos Santos Cuchuman

For information on the people of each part of the region, see the introduction to each country's section.

Popular Attitudes

With only a few exceptions, the people you encounter throughout the region will be friendly, good-humoured and willing to help. Language difficulties can obscure this fact. Some people are shy or will ignore you because they haven't encountered foreigners before and don't imagine a conversation is possible. But just a few words of Spanish will often bring you smiles and warmth, not to mention lots of questions. Then someone who speaks a few words of English will pluck up the courage to try them out on you, and conversation is under way.

Some Indian peoples adopt a cool attitude to visitors; they have learned to mistrust outsiders after five centuries of exploitation by Spaniards and mestizos. They don't like being gaped at by crowds of tourists and can be sensitive about cameras, particularly in churches and at religious festivals.

If you have a white skin and speak a foreign language, you'll be referred to as a *gringo* or *gringa*, depending upon whether you're male or female, and you'll be assumed to be a citizen of the USA. Your presence may provoke any reaction from curiosity or wonder to reticence or, occasionally, hostility. If you're not a citizen of the USA and you make it known, you may get little reaction at all, or you may be treated as an even greater curiosity, perhaps even as a freak of nature.

The classic Mexican attitude to the USA is a combination of the envy and resentment that a poorer, weaker neighbour feels for a richer, more powerful one. The *norteamericanos* have also committed the sin of sending their soldiers into Mexican territory three times.

Any hostility towards individual Americans usually evaporates as soon as you show that you're human too. And while 'gringo' isn't exactly a compliment – you may hear it in an annoying undertone after you've walked past someone – it can also be used with a brusque friendliness.

In Guatemala and Belize, however, it's Mexico that's the richer, more powerful 'neighbour to the north'. Guatemalan and Belizean attitudes towards North Americans are usually more intensely friendly when they're friendly, and more intensely hostile when they're hostile.

ARCHITECTURE

Mayan architecture is amazing for its achievements, but perhaps even more amazing because of what it did not achieve. Mayan architects never seem to have understood or to have used the true arch (a rounded arch with a keystone), and they never thought to put wheels on boxes and use them as wagons to move the thousands of tonnes

of construction materials needed in their tasks. They had no metal tools – they were technically in a Stone Age culture – yet they could build breathtaking temple complexes and align them so precisely that windows and doors were used as celestial observatories of great accuracy.

The arch used in most Mayan buildings is the corbelled vault (or corbelled arch), which consisted of large flat stones on either side set at an angle inward and topped by capstones. This arch served the purpose, but limited severely the amount of open space beneath. In effect, Mayan architects were limited to long, narrow vaulted rooms. True (Roman) arches and Gothic-style vaulting would have allowed them to build stone roofs above far larger halls.

Another important element lacking to them was draught animals (horses, donkeys, mules, oxen). All the work had to be done by humans, on their feet, with their arms and with their backs, without wagons or even wheelbarrows.

The Celestial Plan

In Mayan architecture there was always a celestial plan. Temples were aligned in such a manner as to enhance celestial observation, whether of the sun, moon, or certain stars, especially Venus. The alignment might not be apparent except at certain conjunctions of the celestial bodies (ie at Venus Rising, or at an eclipse), but the Maya knew each building was properly 'placed', and that this enhanced its sacred character.

Temples usually had other features which linked them to the stars. The doors and windows might be aligned in order to sight a celestial body at a certain exact point in its course on a certain day of a certain year. This is the case with the Governor's Palace at Uxmal, which is aligned in such a way that, from the main doorway, Venus would have been visible exactly on top of a small mound some 3.5 km away, in the year 750 AD. You may notice when you visit Uxmal that all the buildings at the site are aligned on the same pattern except for the Governor's Palace. Venus is the reason why.

At Chichén Itzá the observatory building called El Caracol was aligned in order to sight Venus exactly in the year 1000 AD.

Furthermore, the main door to a temple might be decorated to resemble a huge mouth, signifying entry to Xibalba (the secret world or underworld). Other features might have significance in terms of the numbers of the Calendar Round, as at Chichén Itzá's El Castillo. This pyramid has 364 stairs to the top; with the top platform this makes 365, the number of days in the Mayan Vague Year. On the sides of the pyramid are 52 panels, signifying the 52-year cycle of the Calendar Round. The terraces on each side of each stairway total 18 (nine on either side), signifying the 18 'months' of the solar Vague Year. The alignment of El Castillo catches the sun and turns it into a sacred sky-serpent descending into the earth on the vernal equinox (21 March) each year. The serpent is formed perfectly only on that day, and descends during a short period of only 34 minutes.

As mentioned in the section on Religion, Mayan temples were often built on top of smaller, older temples. This increased their sacredness and preserved the temple complex's alignment.

Mayan Architectural Styles

Mayan architecture's 1500-year history has seen a fascinating progression of styles. The style of architecture changed not just with the times, but with the particular geographic area of Mesoamerica in which the architects worked.

Late Preclassic Late Preclassic architecture is perhaps best exhibited at Uaxactún, north of Tikal in Guatemala's Petén department. At Uaxactún, Pyramid E-VII-sub is a fine example of how the architects of what is known as the Chicanel culture designed their pyramid-temples in the time from around 100 BC to 250 AD. E-VII-sub is a square stepped-platform pyramid with central stairways on each of the four sides, each stairway flanked by large jaguar masks. The entire platform was covered in fine white stucco.

The top platform is flat, and probably bore a temple na made of wooden poles topped with palm thatch. This temple was well preserved because others had been built on top of it; these later structures were ruined by the ages, and were cleared away to reveal E-VII-sub. Chicanel-style temples similar to this one were built at Tikal, El Mirador and Lamanai (in Belize) as well.

By the end of the Late Preclassic period, simple temples such as E-VII-sub were being aligned and arranged around plazas, and all was prepared for the next phase of Mayan architecture.

Early Classic The Esperanza culture typifies this phase. In Esperanza-style temples, the king was buried in a wooden chamber beneath the main staircase of the temple; successive kings were buried in similar places in the pyramids built on top of the first one. Among the largest Early Classic Esperanza sites is Kaminaljuyú in Guatemala City; unfortunately, most of the site was destroyed by construction crews or covered by their buildings, and urban sprawl engulfed the site before archaeologists could complete their work.

Of the surviving Early Classic pyramids, perhaps the best example is the step-pyramid at Acanceh, a few km south of Mérida.

Late Classic The most important Classic sites flourished during the latter part of the period, the so-called Late Classic. By this time the Mayan temple-pyramid had a masonry building on top, replacing the na of wood poles and thatch. Numbers of pyramids were built close together, sometimes forming contiguous or even continuous structures. Near them, different structures now called palaces were built. These palaces sat on lower platforms and held many more rooms, perhaps a dozen or more.

In addition to pyramids and palaces, Classic sites have carved stelae and round 'altar-stones' set in the plaza in front of the pyramids. Another feature of the Classic and later periods is the ball court, with sloping playing surfaces of stone covered in stucco.

Among the purest of the Classic sites is Copán in Honduras, which can be reached on a day's excursion from Guatemala's Motagua Valley. Along the eastern reaches of the Motagua is Quiriguá (Guatemala), where the pyramids are unremarkable but the towering stelae and mysterious zoomorphs are unique.

Of all the Classic sites, however, Tikal is the grandest yet uncovered and restored. Here the pyramids reached their most impressive heights, and were topped by superstructures (called roofcombs by archaeologists) which made them even taller. As in earlier times, these monumental structures were used as the burial-places of kings.

If Tikal is the most impressive Classic Mayan city, Palenque (Chiapas) is certainly the most beautiful. Mansard roofs and large relief murals characterise the great palace, with its unique watchtower, and the harmonious Temple of the Inscriptions. Palenque exhibits the perfection of the elements of the Classic Mayan architectural style. The great stairways, the small sanctuaries on top of pyramids, the lofty roofcombs were all brought to their finest proportions here. The tomb of King Pacal in the Temple of the Inscriptions, reached by a buried staircase, is unique in its Egyptian-like qualities: a secret chamber accessible without dismantling the pyramid, and a great carved slab covering the sarcophagus.

Puuc, Chenes & Río Bec Among the most distinctive of the Late Classic Mayan architectural styles are those which flourished in the western and southern regions of the Yucatán Peninsula. These styles valued exuberant display and architectural bravado more than they did proportion and harmony.

The Puuc style, named for the low Puuc Hills near Uxmal, used facings of thin limestone 'tiles' to cover the rough stone walls of buildings. The tiles were worked into geometric designs and stylised figures of monsters and serpents. Minoan-style columns and rows of engaged columns (half-round cylinders) were also a prominent feature of the style, and were used to good effect on façades of buildings at Uxmal and at the Puuc Route sites of Kabah, Sayil, Xlapak and Labná. Puuc architects were crazy about Chac, the rain god, and stuck his grotesque face on every temple, many times. At Kabah, the façade of the Codz Poop temple is completely covered in Chac masks.

The Chenes style, prevalent in areas to the south of the Puuc Hills in Campeche, is very similar to the Puuc style, but Chenes architects seem to have enjoyed putting huge masks as well as smaller ones on their façades.

The Río Bec style, epitomised in the richly decorated temples at the Río Bec archaeological site on the highway between Escárcega and Chetumal, used lavish decoration as in the Puuc and Chenes styles, but added huge towers to the corners of its low buildings, just for show. Río Bec buildings look like a combination of the Governor's Palace of Uxmal and Temple I at Tikal.

Early Post-Classic The collapse of Classic Mayan civilisation created a power vacuum which was filled by the invasion of the Toltecs from central Mexico. The Toltecs brought with them their own architectural ideas, and in the process of conquest these ideas were assimilated and merged with those of the Puuc style.

The foremost example of what might be called the Toltec-Maya style is Chichén Itzá. Elements of Puuc style – the large masks and decorative friezes – coexist with Toltec Atlantean warriors and *chac-mools*, the odd reclining statues that are purely Toltec, and have nothing to do with Mayan art. Platform pyramids with very broad bases and spacious top platforms, such as the Temple of the Warriors, look as though they might have been imported from the ancient Toltec capital of Tula (near Mexico City), or by way of Teotihuacán, with its broad-based pyramids of the sun and moon. Because Quetzalcóatl (Kukulcán in Mayan) was so important to the Toltecs, feathered serpents are used quite extensively as architectural decoration.

Late Post-Classic After the Toltecs came the Itzaes, who established their capital at Mayapán, south of Mérida, and ruled a confederation of Yucatecan states. After the golden age of Tikal and Palenque, even after the martial architecture of Chichén Itzá, the architecture of Mayapán is a disappointment. The pyramids and temples are small and crude compared to the glorious Classic structures. Mayapán's only architectural distinction comes from its vast defensive city wall, one of the few such walls ever discovered in a Mayan city. The fact that the wall exists testifies to the weakness of the Itzá rulers and the unhappiness of their subject peoples.

Tulum, another walled city, is also a product of this time. The columns of the Puuc style are used here, and the painted decoration on the temples must have been colourful, but there is nothing to rival the Classic age.

Cobá has the finest architecture of this otherwise decadent period. The stately pyramids here had new little temples built atop them in the style of Tulum, the walled seaport town on the coast east of Cobá.

In Guatemala, the finest and best preserved Late Post-Classic sites are: Mixco Viejo, north of Guatemala City; Utatlán (or K'umarcaaj), the old Quiché Maya capital on the outskirts of Santa Cruz del Quiché; and Iximché, the last Cakchiquel capital on the Pan American Highway near Tecpan. All of these sites show pronounced central Mexican influences in their twin temple complexes, which probably descend from similar structures at Teotihuacán.

Colonial Architecture

The conquistadors, Franciscans and Dominicans brought with them the architecture of their native Spain, and adapted it to the conditions they met in the Mayan lands. Churches in the largest cities were decorated with baroque elements, but in general the churches are simple and fortress-like. The exploitation of the Maya by the Spaniards led to frequent rebellions, and the strong, high stone walls of the churches worked well in protecting the upper classes from the wrath of the indigenous people.

As you travel through the region, you'll be surprised to find so many very plain churches – plain outside, and plain inside. The crude and simple borrowings from Spanish architecture are eclipsed by the richness of the religious pageantry that takes place inside the buildings: such as the half Mayan-half Catholic processions, decorations and costumes in the churches of Yucatán, or the crowds of the faithful sitting among hundreds of lighted candles on the floor of the small church of Santo Tomás in Chichicastenango, Guatemala, inhaling the thick incense and scattering flower petals in offering to their ancestral spirits.

CULTURE
Traditional Dress

One of the most intriguing aspects of Indian life throughout the Mayan lands is the colourful, usually handmade traditional clothing. This comes in infinite and exotic variety, often differing dramatically from village to village. Under the onslaught of modernity, such clothing is less common in everyday use than a few decades ago, but in some areas – notably around San Cristóbal in Chiapas – it's actually becoming more popular as Mayan pride reasserts itself and the commercial potential of handicrafts is developed. In general, Mayan women have kept to traditional dress longer than men.

Some styles still in common use go back to precolonial times. Among these (all worn by women) are the *huipil*, a long, sleeveless tunic; the *quechquémitl*, a shoulder cape; and the *enredo*, a wraparound skirt. Blouses are colonial innovations. Mayan men's garments owe more to Spanish influence; nudity was discouraged by the church, so shirts, hats and *calzones*, long baggy shorts, were introduced.

What's most eye-catching about these costumes is their colourful embroidery – often entire garments are covered in a multicoloured web of stylised animal, human, plant and mythical shapes which can take months to complete. Each garment identifies

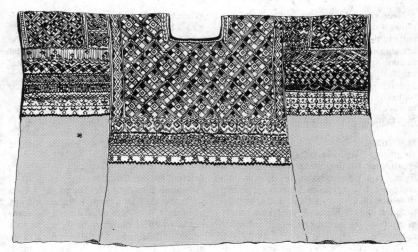

Huipil

the group and village from which its wearer comes. *Fajas*, waist sashes, which bind the garments and also hold what we would put in pockets, are also important in this respect.

The designs often have multiple religious or magical meanings. In some cases the exact significance has been forgotten, but in others the traditional associations are still alive. To the Mayan weavers of Chiapas, diamond shapes represent the universe (the ancient Maya believed the earth was a cube), while wearing a garment with saint figures on it is a form of prayer.

Materials and techniques are changing but the pre-Hispanic back-strap loom is still widely used. The warp (long) threads are stretched between two horizontal bars, one of which is fixed to a post or tree, while the other is attached to a strap which goes round the weaver's lower back. The weft (cross) threads are then woven in.

Yarn is hand-spun in many villages. Vegetable dyes are not yet totally out of use, and natural indigo is employed in several areas. Red dye from cochineal insects and purple dye from sea snails are used by some groups. Modern luminescent dyes go down very well with the Maya, who are happily addicted to bright colours, as you will see.

The variety of techniques, materials, styles and designs is bewildering. (For more on clothing and other handicrafts, see Things to Buy in the introductory Facts for the Visitor chapter.)

Music & Dance

You're likely to hear live music at any time on streets, plazas or even buses. The musicians are playing for their living and range from marimba teams (with big wooden 'xylophones') and mariachi bands (violinists, trumpeters, guitarists and a singer, all dressed in 'cowboy' costume) to ragged lone buskers with out-of-tune guitars and hoarse voices. Marimbas are particularly popular in Guatemala's highlands and on Mexico's Gulf coast.

Music and traditional dances are important parts of the many colourful festivals on the Mayan calendar. Performances honour Christian saints, but in many cases they have pre-Hispanic roots and retain traces of ancient ritual. There are hundreds of traditional dances: some are popular in many parts of the country, others can be seen only in a single town or village. Nearly all of them feature special costumes, often including masks. Some dances tell stories of clear Spanish or colonial origin. Moros y Cristianos is a fairly widespread one which re-enacts the victory of Christians over Moors in medieval Spain.

The Bullfight

To gringo eyes, the bullfight is not very sporting or, for that matter, even much of a fight. Local people, however, see it as both and more. It's a traditional spectacle, more a ritualistic dance than a fight, that originated in Spain and readily lends itself to a variety of symbolic interpretations, mostly related to machismo.

Traditionally, the *corrida de toros* or bullfight begins promptly on Sundays at 4 pm in the winter and 5 pm in the summer with the presentation of the matador and his assistants. Everyone leaves the ring except for the matador and his 'cape men', before the first of six bulls is released from its pen. The cape men try to tire the bull by working him around the ring.

After a few minutes, a trumpet sounds to mark the beginning of the first of three parts *(tercios)* of each 'fight'. Two men called *picadores* enter the ring on thickly padded horses carrying long lances and trot around until they are close enough to the bull to stick their lances into its shoulder muscles. Their main objective is to weaken the bull just enough to make him manageable, but not enough to kill him.

The second tercio begins after the picadores leave the ring. Men with *banderillas*, one-metre-long stilettos, then enter the ring on foot. Their objective is to jam three pairs of banderillas into the bull's shoulders without impaling themselves on the bull's horns.

With that done, the third tercio – the part everyone has been waiting for – begins. The matador has exactly 16 minutes to kill the bull by first tiring him with fancy cape-work.

When he feels the time is right, the matador trades his large cape for a smaller one (the *muleta)* and takes up a sword. He baits the bull, lures it towards him and gives it what he hopes will be the death blow, the final *estocada* or lunge from the sword. If the matador succeeds, and he usually does, you can expect a quick and bloody end.

The bull collapses and an assistant dashes into the ring to slice its jugular and chop off an ear or two and sometimes the tail for the matador, if the spectators indicate that he deserves these honours.

Ancient Mayan Customs

Personal Beauty Friar Diego de Landa wrote that the Maya of the 16th century, just as in the Classic period, flattened the foreheads of their children by tying boards tightly to them, a flat forehead being a mark of beauty. Crossed eyes were another mark of beauty, and to encourage it parents would tie a bead of wax so as to dangle between the child's eyes. Young boys had scalding-hot cloths placed on their faces to discourage the growth of beards, which were considered ugly by the Maya.

Both men and women made cuts in their skin so as to get much-desired scar markings, and both were enthusiastic about getting tattoos. Women sharpened their teeth to points, another mark of beauty which, for all we know, may have helped them to keep the men in line. And both men and women dyed their bodies red, though women refrained from dyeing their faces. Beauty was certainly a different thing among the ancient Maya.

Clothing As for clothing, in the old days the men wrapped long cloths around their loins, with the ends hanging in front and at the back; a square cape was worn on the shoulders, and leather sandals on the feet. Though this sort of clothing has long since disappeared, the men in many Guatemalan highland villages still wrap cloths around them to make a sort of skirt; they wear trousers underneath. Everybody still wears sandals, or goes barefoot.

The women wore huipiles, embroidered dresses that must have looked very much like the huipiles which are still worn by Mayan women in Yucatán, Chiapas and Guatemala today.

Food & Drink Landa tells us that the Maya loved to give banquets for one another, offering roast meat, stews with vegetables, corn cakes (perhaps tortillas or tamales), and cocoa, not to mention lots of alcoholic beverages. The lords got so drunk at these banquets that their wives had to come and drag them home, a condition which still exists. The 'banquets' today are cantinas, and the 'lords' are workmen, but the dragging remains the same. The attitude of the drinkers is aptly expressed in the name of a bar in Acanceh, south of Mérida: *Aquí me queda*, 'Here I stay'.

Sport The recreation most favoured by the Maya was hip-ball. Using a hard rubber ball on stone courts, players tried to stop the ball from hitting the ground, keeping it airborne by batting it with any part of their body other than their hands, head or feet. A wooden bat may have been used. In some regions, a team was victorious if one òf its players hit the ball through stone rings with holes little larger than the ball itself.

The ball game was taken quite seriously and often used to settle disputes between tribes. On occasion, it is thought that the captain of the losing team was punished by the forfeiture of his life.

RELIGION
World-Tree & Xibalba
For the Maya, the world, the heavens and the mysterious 'unseen world' or underworld called Xibalba (shee-bahl-BAH) were all one great unified structure which operated according to the laws of astrology and ancestor worship. The towering *ceiba* tree was considered sacred, for it symbolised the Wacah Chan, or world-tree which united the 13 heavens, the surface of the earth, and the nine levels of the underworld of Xibalba.

The world-tree had a sort of cruciform shape, and was associated with the colour blue-green. In the 16th century, when the Franciscans friars came bearing a cross and required the Indians to venerate it, the symbolism meshed easily with established Maya beliefs.

Points of the Compass
In Mayan cosmology, each point of the compass had special religious significance. East was most important, as it was where the sun was reborn each day; its colour was red. West was black, because it was where the sun disappeared. North was white, and was the direction from which the all-important rains came, beginning in May. South was yellow because it was the 'sunniest' point of the compass.

Everything in the Mayan world was seen in relation to these cardinal points, with the world-tree at the centre; but the cardinal points were only the starting point for the all-important astronomical and astrological observations which determined fate. (See The Mayan Calendar System later in this section for more on Mayan astrology.)

Bloodletting & Human Sacrifice
Humans had certain roles to play within this great system. Just as the great cosmic dragon shed its blood which fell as rain to the earth, so humans had to shed blood to link themselves with Xibalba.

Bloodletting ceremonies were the most important religious ceremonies, and the blood of kings was seen as the most acceptable for these rituals. Thus when the friars said that the blood of Jesus, the King of the Jews, had been spilled for the common people, the Maya could easily understand the symbolism.

Sacred Places
Mayan ceremonies were performed in natural sacred places as well as their human-made equivalents. Mountains, caves, lakes, cenotes (natural limestone cavern pools), rivers and fields were all sacred, and had

special importance in the scheme of things. Pyramids and temples were thought of as stylised mountains; sometimes these 'mountains' had secret chambers within them, which were like the caves in a mountain. A cave was the mouth of the creature which represented Xibalba, and to enter it was to enter the spirit of the secret world. This is why some Mayan temples have doorways surrounded by huge masks: as you enter the door of this 'cave' you are entering the mouth of Xibalba.

The plazas around which the pyramids were placed symbolised the open fields, or the flat land of the tropical forest. What we call stelae were to the Maya 'tree-stones', that is, sacred tree-effigies echoing the sacredness of the world-tree. These tree-stones were often carved with the figures of great Mayan kings, for the king was the world-tree of Mayan society.

As these places were sacred, it made sense for succeeding Mayan kings to build new and ever grander temples directly over older temples, as this enhanced the sacred character of the spot. The temple being covered over was not seen as mere rubble to be exploited as building material, but as a sacred artefact to be preserved. Certain features of these older temples, such as the large masks on the façade, were carefully padded and protected before the new construction was placed over them.

Ancestor worship and genealogy were very important to the Maya, and when they buried a king beneath a pyramid, or a commoner beneath the floor or courtyard of his na, the sacredness of the location was increased.

The Mayan 'Bible'

Of the painted books destroyed by Friar Landa and other Franciscans, no doubt some of them were books of sacred legends and stories similar to the Bible. Such sacred histories and legends provide a world-view to believers, and guidance in belief and daily action.

One such Mayan book, the *Popol Vuh* (or *Wuh*), survived not as a painted book but as a transcription into the Latin alphabet of a Mayan narrative text; that is, it was written in Quiché Maya, but in Latin characters, not hieroglyphs. The *Popol Vuh* was apparently written by Quiché Maya Indians of Guatemala who had learned Spanish and the Latin alphabet from the Dominican friars. The authors showed their book to Francisco Ximénez, a Dominican who lived and worked in Chichicastenango from 1701 to 1703. Friar Ximénez copied the Indians' book word for word, then translated it into Spanish. Both his copy and the Spanish translation survive, but the Indian original has been lost.

For a translation of the Spanish version into English, see *Popol Wuh: Ancient Stories of the Quiche Indians of Guatemala*, by Albertina Saravia E (Guatemala City: Editorial Piedra Santa, 1987), on sale in many bookshops in Guatemala for about US$4.

According to the *Popol Vuh* , the great god K'ucumatz created humankind first from earth (mud), but these 'earthlings' were weak and dissolved in water, so he/she tried again using wood. The wood people had no hearts or minds, and could not praise their Creator, so they were destroyed, all except the monkeys who live in the forest, who are the descendants of the wood people. The Creator tried once again, this time successfully, using substances recommended by four animals – the grey fox, the coyote, the parrot and the crow. The substance was white and yellow corn, ground into meal to form the flesh, and stirred into water to make the blood.

After the devastating earthquake of 1976 in Guatemala, the government rebuilding programme included the printing and distribution of posters bearing a picture of an ear of corn and the words *Hombre de maís, levantate!* (Man of corn, arise!).

The *Popol Vuh* legends include some elements which made it easier for the Maya to understand certain aspects of Christian belief, including virgin birth and sacrificial death followed by a return to life.

Shamanism & Catholicism

The ceiba tree's cruciform shape was not the

Top: Market day, Sololá, Guatemala (PW)
Middle: Window display, Mérida, Yucatán, Mexico (GE)
Bottom: Corn drying, Zunil, Guatemala (PW)

Top: Boating, Isla Mujeres, Mexico (GE)
Bottom: 'Go Slow', Caye Caulker, Belize (TB)

only correspondence the Maya found between their animist beliefs and Christianity. Both traditional Mayan animism and Catholicism have rites of baptism and confession, days of fasting and other forms of abstinence, religious partaking of alcoholic beverages, burning of incense and the use of altars.

Today, the Mayan practice of Catholicism is a fascinating fusion of shamanist-animist and Christian ritual. The traditional religious ways are so important that often a Maya will try to recover from a malady by seeking the advice of a religious shaman rather than a medical doctor. Use of folk remedies linked with animist tradition is widespread in Mayan areas.

MAYAN CALENDAR SYSTEM

In some ways, the ancient Mayan calendar is more accurate than the Gregorian calendar we use today. Without sophisticated technol-

ogy, Mayan astronomers were able to ascertain the length of the solar year, the lunar month and the Venus year. Their calculations enabled them to pinpoint eclipses with uncanny accuracy; their lunar cycle was a mere seven minutes off today's sophisticated technological calculations, and their Venus cycle errs by only two hours for periods covering 500 years.

Time and the calendar, in fact, were the basis of the Mayan religion, which resembled modern astrology in some aspects. Astronomical observations played such a pivotal role in Mayan life that astronomy and religion were linked, and the sun and moon were worshipped. Most Mayan cities were constructed in strict accordance with celestial movements. One remarkable example of this is Chichén Itzá. During equinoxes, the sun illuminates a stairway of El Castillo, turning it into a sacred serpent which 'penetrates' the earth.

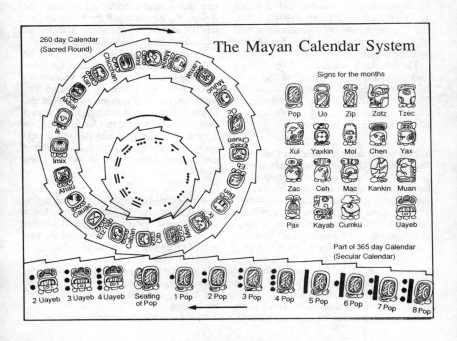

The Mayan Calendar System

260 day Calendar (Sacred Round)

Signs for the months

Pop   Uo   Zip   Zotz   Tzec
Xul   Yaxkin   Mol   Chen   Yax
Zac   Ceh   Mac   Kankin   Muan
Pax   Kayab   Cumku   Uayeb

Part of 365 day Calendar (Secular Calendar)

2 Uayeb 3 Uayeb 4 Uayeb Seating of Pop 1 Pop 2 Pop 3 Pop 4 Pop 5 Pop 6 Pop 7 Pop 8 Pop

How the Calendar Worked

Perhaps the best analogue to the Mayan calendar is in the gears of a mechanical watch, where small wheels mesh with larger wheels which in turn mesh with other sets of wheels to record the passage of time.

Tonalamatl or Tzolkin The two smallest wheels in this Mayan calendar 'watch' were two cycles of 13 days and 20 days. Each of the 13 days bore a number from one to 13; each of the 20 days bore a name such as Imix, Ik, Akbal or Xan. As these two 'wheels' meshed, the passing days received unique names. For example, Day 1 of the 13-day cycle meshed with the day named Imix in the 20-day cycle to produce the day named 1 Imix. Next came 2 Ik, then 3 Akbal, 4 Xan, etc. After 13 days, the first cycle began again at one, even though the 20-day name cycle still had seven days to run, so the 14th day was 1 Ix, then 2 Men, 3 Cib, etc. When the 20-day name cycle was finished, it began again with 8 Imix, 9 Ik, 10 Akbal, 11 Xan, etc. The permutations continued for a total of 260 days, ending on 13 Ahau, before beginning again on 1 Imix.

The two small 'wheels' of 13 and 20 days thus created a larger 'wheel' of 260 days, called a *tonalamatl* or *tzolkin*. Let's leave the 13-day and 20-day 'wheels' and the larger 260-day wheel whirling as we look at another set of gears in the watch.

Vague Year (Haab) Another set of wheels in the Mayan calendar watch were the 18 'months' of 20 days each, which formed the basis of the Mayan solar Vague Year calendar, or *haab*. Each month had a name – Pop, Uo, Zip, Zotz, Tzec, etc and each day had a number from zero (the first day or 'seating' of the month) to 19, much as our Gregorian solar calendar does. There was 0 Pop (the 'seating' of the month Pop), 1 Pop, 2 Pop, etc to 19 Pop, then 0 Uo, 1 Uo, and so forth.

Eighteen months, each of 20 days, equals 360 days; the Maya added a special omen-filled five-day period called the *uayeb* at the end of this cycle in order to produce a solar calendar of 365 days. Anthropologists today call this the Vague Year, its vagueness coming from the fact that the solar year is actually 365.24 days long. To account for this extra quarter-day, we add an extra day to our Gregorian calendars every four years in Leap Year. The Maya did not do this.

Calendar Round The huge wheels of the tzolkin and the haab also meshed, so that each day actually had two names and two numbers, a tzolkin name-number and a haab name-number, used together: 1 Imix 5 Pop, 2 Ik 6 Pop, 3 Akbal 7 Pop, and so on. By the time the huge 260-day wheel of the tzolkin and 365-day wheel of the Vague Year had meshed completely, exhausting all the 18,980 day-name permutations, a period of 52 solar years had passed.

This bewilderingly complex meshing of the tzolkin and the haab is called the Calendar Round, and it was the dating system used throughout Mesoamerica by the Olmecs, the Aztecs, the Zapotecs and the Maya. In fact, it is still in use in some traditional mountain villages of Chiapas and highland Guatemala.

Though fascinating in its complexity, the Calendar Round has its limitations, the greatest being that it only goes for 52 years. After that, it starts again, and it provides no way for Maya ceremony planners (or modern historians) to distinguish a day named 1 Imix 5 Pop in this 52-year Calendar Round cycle from the identically named day in the next cycle, or in the cycle after that, or a dozen cycles later. Thus the need for the Long Count.

Long Count As Mayan civilisation developed, Mayan scientists recognised the limits of a calendar system which could not run more than 52 solar years without starting over, so they developed the so-called Long Count or Great Cycle, a system of distinguishing the 52-year Calendar Round cycles from one another. The Long Count came into use during the Classic period of Mayan civilisation.

The Long Count system modified the

Mayan Time Divisions			
Unit	*Same as*	*Days*	*Gregorian Years**
Kin	–	1	–
Uinal	20 kins	20	–
Tun	20 uinals	360	0.99
Katun	20 tuns	7200	19.7
Baktun	20 katuns	14,000	394
(Great Cycle)	13 baktuns	1.872 million	5125
Pictun	20 baktuns	2.88 million	7885
Calabtun	20 pictuns	57.6 million	157,705
Kinchiltun	20 calabtuns	1.152 billion	3,154,091
Alautun	20 kinchiltuns	23.04 billion	63,081,809

* Approximate

Vague Year solar mechanism, then added yet another set of wheels to the already complex mechanism of Mayan time.

In place of the Vague Year of 365 days, the Long Count uses the *tun*, the 18 months of 20 days each, and ignores the final five-day period. In Long Count terminology, a day was a *kin* (meaning 'sun'). A 20-kin 'month' is called a *uinal*, and 18 uinals make a tun. Thus the 360-day tun replaced the Vague Year in the Long Count system.

The time wheels added by the Long Count were huge. The names of all the time divisions are shown in the table above.

In practice, the gigantic units above baktun (pictun, calabtun, etc) were not used except for grandiose effect, as when a very self-important king wanted to note exactly when his extremely important reign took place in the awesome expanse of time. The largest unit in use in monument inscriptions was usually the baktun. There were 13 baktuns (1,872,000 days, or 5125 Gregorian solar years) in a Great Cycle.

When a Great Cycle was completed a new one would begin, but for the Maya of the Classic period this was unimportant as Classic Mayan civilisation died out long before the end of the first Great Cycle. For them, the Great Cycle began on 11 August 3114 BC (some authorities say 13 August), and it will end on 23 December 2012 AD. The end of a Great Cycle was a time fraught with great significance – usually fearsome.

Keep that date in mind, and let's see how this Great Cycle finishes up!

Even the awesome alautun was not the largest unit used in the Long Count. In order to date everything in proper cosmic style, one date found at Cobá is equivalent to 41,341,050,000,000,000,000,000,000,000,000 of our years! (In comparison, the Big Bang said to have formed our universe is estimated to be a mere 15,000,000,000 years ago.)

It's important to remember that to the Maya, time was not a continuum but a cycle, and even this incomprehensibly large cycle of years would be repeated, over and over, infinitely, in infinitely larger cycles. In effect, the Mayan 'watch' had an unlimited number of gear wheels, and they kept ticking around and around forever.

Mayan Counting System

The Mayan counting system was elegantly simple: dots were used to count from one to four; a horizontal bar signified five; a bar with one dot above it was six, with two dots was seven, etc. Two bars signified 10, three bars 15. Nineteen, the highest common number, was three bars stacked up and topped by four dots.

To signify larger numbers the Maya used positional numbers, a fairly sophisticated system similar to the one we use today, and much more advanced than the crude additive numbers used in the Roman Empire.

In positional numbers, the position of a

sign as well as the sign's value determine the number. For example, in our decimal system the number '23' is made up of two signs: a '2' in the 'tens' position and a '3' in the 'ones' position: two tens plus three ones equals 23.

The Maya used not a decimal system (base 10) but a vigesimal system, that is, a system with base 20; and positions of increasing value went not right to left (as ours do) but from bottom to top. So the bottom position showed values from one to 19, the next position up showed values from 20 to 380. The bottom and upper positions together could show up to 19 twenties plus 19 ones (ie 399). The third position up showed values from one 400 to 19 four hundreds (ie 7600). The three positions together could signify numbers up to 7999. By adding more positions one could count as high as needed.

Such positional numbers depend upon the concept of zero, a concept the Romans never developed, but which the Maya did. The zero in Mayan numbering was represented by a stylised picture of a shell or some other object – anything except a bar or a dot.

The Mayan counting system was used by merchants and others who had to tot up lots of things, but its most important use – and the one you will encounter during your travels – was in writing calendar dates.

LANGUAGE

Spanish is the most commonly spoken language of the countries of La Ruta Maya. English is the official language of Belize although both Spanish and a local Creole are widely spoken.

For a thorough list of useful Spanish words and phrases try Lonely Planet's *Latin American Spanish Phrasebook*.

Spanish

Groups of people in the region speak native Indian languages and dialects; Spanish, however, is the predominant language.

Hints for the Traveller

Fortunately, Spanish is a relatively easy language for an English speaker to learn. If you have no background in the language, you could begin by taking an evening class, or by borrowing a record/cassette course from the local library. Try to find a Spanish speaker to practise with.

There are a few places, notably Antigua Guatemala, that specialize in Spanish language courses. A few weeks spent studying Spanish in Antigua at the beginning of your trip could make an enormous difference in your experience of Central America, and any other Spanish-speaking countries you may ever visit.

A pocket-sized book of Spanish grammar and phrases can help you tremendously. Lonely Planet's *Latin American Spanish phrasebook* is very useful and compact.

Also be sure to take along a pocket-sized Spanish-English dictionary. Many are available, so you might want to compare several. It's best to bring your own as they are not widely available in Central America, though you might find one in an occasional bookstore, or in the gift shop of a major hotel.

Spanish-speakers often have a remarkable patience with those who are attempting to learn the language. Even if you feel like an idiot at first, your efforts to communicate in Spanish will most often be met with smiles and helpfulness by local people.

Pronunciation

Most of the sounds in Spanish have equivalents in English, and written Spanish is largely phonetic. Once you've learnt how to pronounce all the letters, and certain groups of letters, and you know which syllable to stress, you can read any word or sentence and pronounce it more or less correctly.

Stress As a general rule the stress goes on the second last syllable of a word. Words ending in an 'r' (usually verbs) have the stress on the last syllable. If there is an accent on any vowel, the stress is on that syllable:

amigo – a-MI-go
comer – com-ER
aquí – a-QUI

Greetings & Civilities Greetings are used more frequently in Latin America than in English-speaking countries. For example, it is polite to greet people when you walk into a shop or a bar.

Hello.	Hola.
Good morning.	Buenos días.
Good afternoon.	Buenas tardes.
Good evening or good night.	Buenas noches.

The last three are frequently shortened to *buenos/as*. This is used a lot in Central America, accompanied by a slight nod of the head.

How are you?
   ¿Cómo está? (formal)
   or *¿Cómo estás?* (informal)
How are things going?
   ¿Qué tal?
Well, thanks.
   Bien, gracias.
Very well.
   Muy bien.
Very badly.
   Muy mal.
Goodbye.
   Adiós (rarely used).
Bye, see you soon.
   Hasta luego (sometimes just 'sta luego').

please	por favor
thank you	gracias
many thanks	muchas gracias
you're welcome	de nada
excuse me	permiso
sorry	perdón
excuse me, forgive me	disculpe, discúlpame
Good luck!	¡Buena suerte!

Mr, Sir	Señor (formal)
Madam, Mrs	Señora (formal)
unmarried woman	Señorita
pal, friend	compañero/a, amigo/a

More Useful Words & Phrases The following brief guide should help you cope in the lands of the Maya.

I'd like to introduce you to ...
   Le presento a ...
A pleasure (to meet you).
   Mucho gusto.
What is your name?
   ¿Cómo se llama usted? (formal)
   ¿Cómo te llamas? (informal)
My name is ...
   Me llamo ...
Where are you from?
   ¿De dónde es usted? (formal)
   ¿De dónde vienes? (familiar)

I am from ...	Soy de ...
Australia	Australia
Canada	Canadá
England	Inglaterra
Germany	Alemania
Israel	Israel
Italy	Italia
Japan	Japón
New Zealand	Nueva Zelanda
Norway	Noruega
Scotland	Escocia
Sweden	Suecia
the United States	los Estados Unidos

Can I take a photo?
   ¿Puedo sacar una foto?
Of course/Why not/Sure.
   Por supuesto/Cómo no/Claro.
How old are you?
   ¿Cuántos años tiene?
Do you speak English?
   ¿Habla inglés?
I speak a little Spanish.
   Hablo un poquito de español.
I don't understand.
   No entiendo.
Could you repeat that?
   ¿Puede repetirlo?
Could you speak more slowly please?
   ¿Puede hablar más despacio por favor?
How does one say ...?
   ¿Cómo se dice ...?

What does ... mean?
¿Que significa ...?

Where is ...?	*¿Dónde hay ...?*
a hotel	*un hotel*
a boarding house	*una pensión*
a guesthouse	*un hospedaje*
I am looking for ...	*Estoy buscando ...*
a cheap hotel	*un hotel barato*
a good hotel	*un hotel bueno*
a nearby hotel	*un hotel cercano*
a clean hotel	*un hotel limpio*

Are there any rooms available?
¿Hay habitaciones libres?
Where are the toilets?
¿Dónde están los servicios/baños?

I would like a ...	*Quisiera un ...*
single room	*cuarto sencillo*
double room	*cuarto doble*
room with a bath	*cuarto con baño*

Can I see it?	*¿Puedo verlo?*
Are there others?	*¿Hay otros?*
How much is it?	*¿Cuánto cuesta?*
It's too expensive.	*Es demasiado caro.*

your name	*su nombre*
your surname	*su apellido*
your room number	*el número de su cuarto*
Where is ...?	*¿Dónde está ...?*
the central bus station	*la estación central de autobuses*
the railway station	*la estación de trenes*
the airport	*el aeropuerto*
the ticket office	*la boletería*
bus	*autobús/camión*
bus (long-distance)	*flota/bus*

When does the bus/train/plane leave?
¿Cuándo sale el autobus/tren/avión?
I want to go to ...
Quiero ir a ...
What time do they leave?
¿A qué hora salen?
Can you take me to ...?
¿Puede llevarme a ...?

Could you tell me where ... is?
¿Podría decirme dónde está ...?
Is it far?
¿Está lejos?
Is it close to here?
¿Está cerca de aquí?

I'm looking for ...	*Estoy buscando ...*
the post office	*el correo*
the ... embassy	*la embajada de ...*
the museum	*el museo*
the police	*la policía*
the market	*el mercado*
the bank	*el banco*

| Stop! | *¡Pare!* |
| Wait! | *¡Espera!* |

I want to change some money.
Quiero cambiar dinero.
I want to change travellers' cheques.
Quiero cambiar cheques viajeros.
What is the exchange rate?
¿Cuál es el tipo de cambio?
How many colones/pesos/quetzales per dollar?
¿Cuántos colones/pesos/quetzales por dólar?

cashier	*caja*
credit card	*tarjeta de crédito*
the black market	*el mercado negro*
bank notes	*billetes de banco*
exchange houses	*casas de cambio*

Watch out!	*¡Cuidado!*
Help!	*¡Socorro!*
	¡Auxilio!
Fire!	*¡Fuego!*
Thief!	*¡Ladrón!*
I've been robbed.	*Me han robado.*
They took ...	*Se llevaron ...*
my money	*mi dinero*
my passport	*mi pasaporte*
my bag	*mi bolsa*
Where is ...?	*¿Dónde hay ...?*
a policeman	*un policía*
a doctor	*un doctor*
a hospital	*un hospital*
Leave me alone!	*¡Déjeme!*

Don't bother me!	¡No me moleste!	50	cincuenta
Get lost!	¡Váyase!	60	sesenta
		70	setenta
today	hoy	80	ochenta
this morning	esta mañana	90	noventa
this afternoon	esta tarde	100	cien, when followed by
tonight	esta noche		a noun, ciento
yesterday	ayer	101	ciento uno
tomorrow	mañana	102	ciento dos
week/month/year	semana/mes/año	200	doscientos
last week	la semana pasada	300	trescientos
next month	el próximo mes	500	quinientos
always	siempre	600	seiscientos
it's early/late	es temprano/tarde	900	novecientos
now	ahora	1000	mil
before/after	antes/después	2000	dos mil
		100,000	cien mil
What time is it?		1,000,000	un millón
¿Qué hora es?		2,000,000	dos millones

It is 1 o'clock.

Es la una.

It is 7 o'clock.

Son las siete.

0	cero	first	primero
1	uno, una	second	segundo
2	dos	third	tercero
3	tres	fourth	cuarto
4	cuatro	fifth	quinto
5	cinco	sixth	sexto
6	seis	seventh	séptimo
7	siete	eighth	octavo
8	ocho	ninth	noveno, nono
9	nueve	tenth	décimo
10	diez	eleventh	undécimo
11	once	twelfth	duodécimo
12	doce	twentieth	vigésimo
13	trece		
14	catorce		
15	quince		
16	dieciséis		
17	diecisiete		
18	dieciocho		
19	diecinueve		
20	veinte		
21	veintiuno		
22	veintidós		
30	treinta		
31	treinta y uno		
40	cuarenta		

Ancient Mayan

During the Classic period the Mayan lands were divided into two linguistic areas. In the Yucatán Peninsula and Belize, people spoke Yucatecan, and in the highlands and Motagua Valley of Guatemala they spoke a related language called Cholan. People in El Petén were likely to speak both languages, as this was where the linguistic regions overlapped. Yucatecan and Cholan were quite similar – about as similar as Spanish and Italian – a fact which facilitated trade and cultural exchange.

In addition, both Yucatecan and Cholan were written using the same hieroglyphic system, so a written document or inscription could be understood by literate members of either language group.

The written language of the Classic Maya was very complex: glyphs could signify a whole word, or just a syllable, and the same glyph could be drawn in a variety of ways. Sometimes extra symbols were appended to a glyph to help indicate pronunciation. To read ancient Mayan inscriptions and texts accurately takes a great deal of training and experience. In fact, many aspects of the written language are not fully understood even by the experts. In Classic Mayan times it was the same way, as only the nobility would have been able to understand the inscriptions and codices completely.

Modern Mayan

Since the Classic period, these two languages (Yucatecan and Cholan) have subdivided into 35 separate Mayan languages (Yucatec, Chol, Chorti, Tzeltal, Tzotzil, Lacandon, Mam, Quiché, Cakchiquel, etc), some of them unintelligible to speakers of others. Writing today is in the Latin alphabet brought by the conquistadors – what writing there is. Most literate Maya are literate in Spanish, the language of the government, the school, the church, the radio and TV, and the newspapers; they may not be literate in Mayan.

Pronounciation There are several rules to remember when pronouncing Mayan words and place names. Mayan vowels are pretty straightforward; it's the consonants which give problems. Remember that:

c is always hard, like 'k'
j is always an aspirated 'h' sound. So *jipijapa* is pronounced HEE-pee-HAA-pah, and *abaj* is pronounced ah-BAHH; to get the 'HH' sound, take the 'h' sound from 'half' and put it at the end of ah-BAHH.
u is 'oo' except when it begins or ends a word, in which case it is like English 'w'. Thus 'baktun' is 'bahk-TOON', but 'Uaxactún' is 'wah-shak-TOON' and 'ahau' is ah-HAW.
x is like 'sh'

Mayan glottalised consonants, those followed by an apostrophe (b', ch', k', p', t') are similar to normal consonants, but pronounced more forcefully and 'explosively'. An apostrophe following a *vowel* signifies a glottal stop, *not* a more forceful vowel.

Another rule to remember is that in most Mayan words the stress falls on the last syllable. Sometimes this is indicated by an acute accent, sometimes not. Here are some pronunciation examples:

Abaj Takalik	ah-BAHH tah-kah-LEEK
Acanceh	ah-kahn-KEH
Ahau	ah-HAW
Dzibilchaltún	dzee-beel-chahl-TOON
Kaminaljuyú	kah-mee-nahl-hoo-YOO
Oxcutzkab	ohsh-kootz-KAHB
Pacal	pah-KAHL
Pop	pope
Tikal	tee-KAHL
Uaxactún	wah-shahk-TOON
Xcaret	sh-kah-REHT
Yaxchilán	yahsh-chee-LAHN

Facts for the Visitor

SUGGESTED ITINERARIES

In just the last few years, travel throughout southern Mexico, the Yucatán Peninsula, Guatemala and Belize has become considerably easier. More archaeological sites have been opened to visitors, roads and bus services have been improved and expanded, and new air services have made it possible for those with time constraints to see all of the major sights in less time. For the adventurous, new routes by bus and boat through the jungle provide both convenient short cuts and low-budget trekking experiences. In the future, as regional cooperation develops, we can expect even more travel possibilities.

One could easily spend months travelling the region. The lucky few who have a month or more to spend can see and do it all, but the rest of us must make the best use of the short time available to us.

Most travellers arrive at Cancún, as that resort city has the busiest airport and the most frequent, far-reaching and cheap air services. Other possible approaches are via Mexico City, Guatemala City or Belize City. See the Getting There & Away chapter.

The Top Sights in a Week

It is possible to see the top archaeological sites – Chichén Itzá, Uxmal and Tikal – on day trips or overnight excursions by air from Cancún. If you're addicted to the beaches, or if you've signed up for a package vacation which provides a hotel in Cancún, you may want to see them that way. If not, here's what to do:

Spend your first night in Cancún or Isla Mujeres, changing money, getting used to Mexico and enjoying the beaches. Start for Chichén Itzá on the morning of the second day, visit the ancient city, and spend the night in the nearby town of Piste. On the third day return to the ruins in the relative cool of the morning, then drive to Mérida for the afternoon and overnight. On the fourth day visit Uxmal, south of Mérida, either staying over-

night at the ruins or returning to Mérida. On the fifth day head back towards Cancún, via Valladolid or via Felipe Carrillo Puerto and Tulum; spend the night in either of these cities, or in Cancún. On the sixth or seventh day, take a flight from Cancún to Tikal, Guatemala, for a visit to the most magnificent of Mayan cities; stay overnight in nearby Flores, returning to Cancún the following day.

This itinerary is rushed, and you may want to go by rented car rather than by bus to make it more comfortable. The rented car and the flights make it quite expensive, but it does allow you to see the top sights – Cancún, Chichén Itzá, Mérida, Uxmal, Tulum, Tikal – and a good deal of the countryside in the shortest possible time.

Two Weeks

This itinerary gives you a good look at the Mayan sites in Mexico, the highlands of Guatemala, the fabulous ruins of Tikal, and a glimpse of Belize, all in 14 or 15 days. It includes one or two flights, but the rest can be done by bus. If you have 15 or 16 days, or if you move at a slightly faster pace, you can do it all by bus, which brings the cost down considerably.

Day 1 Cancún or Isla Mujeres, arrive and find your hotel
Day 2 Ride to Chichén Itzá, visit the ruins and stay overnight
Day 3 To Mérida and overnight
Day 4 Spend another day in Mérida if you like, or take a day trip to Dzibilchaltún and Progreso, or head south to Mayapán, Ticul and Uxmal
Day 5 Uxmal; overnight near the ruins
Day 6 Visit Kabah on the Puuc Route, and perhaps Sayil, then on to Campeche for the night; or, if you like, directly to Palenque
Day 7 To Palenque and overnight
Day 8 Visit the ruins at Palenque, then onwards to San Cristóbal de las Casas
Day 9 From San Cristóbal, cross the border into Guatemala and get as far as Huehuetenango, or preferably Quetzaltenango

Day 10 If it's Wednesday or Saturday, go to Chichicastenango and find a hotel room in preparation for the market (Thursday and Sunday). If it's Tuesday or Friday go to Sololá and catch the market there before continuing to Panajachel on Lago de Atitlán for the night.

Day 11 Depending upon market days, visit Chichicastenango, Sololá, or Antigua (markets every day, but especially Monday, Thursday and Saturday)

Day 12 Start early from Antigua to the airport at Guatemala City for a flight to Flores, then on to Tikal

Day 13 Visit Tikal. Return to Flores for the night, or to Guatemala City

Day 14 From Flores, fly to Guatemala City or to Belize City for a flight back to Cancún, or fly directly home

Day 15 If you have an extra day, go by bus from Flores to Belize City on Day 14, then from Belize City to Chetumal and back to Cancún on Day 15. This is a lot of bus time, but it saves the cost of a flight and gives you a look at Belize.

Three Weeks
An itinerary of three weeks would follow the same general course as the one for two weeks, but would include more time in several spots. You'd have time to see all the Puuc Route sites including Kabah, Sayil, Labná, Xlapak and the Grutas de Loltún, and you could take a detour to Villahermosa to visit the Parque Museo La Venta. You would also have time for visits to Quiriguá on Guatemala's Atlantic Highway, and to Copán, in Honduras, as well as more time in Belize. Three weeks also gives you an extra day or two at the beach, whether on the Belizean cayes, Mexico's Caribbean coast, Cozumel or Cancún.

Four Weeks
A month is enough time to include interesting but seldom-visited places in your itinerary, places such as Toniná, near Ocosingo in Chiapas; Cobá, inland from Tulum; Kohunlich near Chetumal; Lago de Bacalar, the gorgeous and virtually untouristed lake just north of Chetumal; Mountain Pine Ridge in Belize, as well as the southern part of that country. You'd have lots of time for treks on horseback into the forests surrounding San Cristóbal de las Casas, time

to look for pink flamingoes at Río Lagartos in northern Yucatán, and time to relax in a cabaña on the beach south of Tulum. In fact, one could easily spend months travelling the lands of the Maya.

DOCUMENTS
If you are travelling the region by private car, you will need motor vehicle insurance and a valid import permit. See the Getting There & Away chapter for details.

CUSTOMS
Customs officers only get angry and excited about a few things: drugs, weapons, large amounts of currency, automobiles and other expensive items which might be sold while you're in the country. Don't take illegal drugs or any sort of firearm across these borders. If you want to take a hunting rifle across a border, get a permit from the country's diplomatic mission in advance.

Luggage Inspection
Normally the customs officer will not look seriously in your luggage, and may not look at all. At some border points the amount of search is inversely proportional to the amount of 'tip' you have provided; that is, big tip no search, no tip big search. As for valuable items, if you have an expensive camera, or electronic gizmo, or jewellery, there is a risk that they may be seen as leverage, or be deemed as liable for duty at Customs' discretion. Be prepared and be firm but flexible. (See the section on Crossing Borders in the introductory Getting There & Away chapter for more information.) Whatever you do, keep it all formal and polite. Anger, surliness or impoliteness can get you thrown out of the country, or into jail, or worse.

Importing Motor Vehicles
See the introductory Getting There & Away chapter for details

MONEY
When travelling in the region, it's useful to carry your money in US dollars or US dollar

travellers' cheques. Though you should be able to change other sorts of currency (especially Canadian dollars) in major banks in large cities, it can require some time-consuming hassles, and may be supremely difficult in smaller cities and towns. In many parts of the region (especially Mexico) it can take a lot of time just to change US dollars, let alone some currency that is, to a local bank teller, highly exotic.

ATMs (automatic teller machines) can now be found in cities along La Ruta Maya, especially in Mexico. They often provide instructions in English as well as Spanish, and issue local currency debited against your home account. Look for them. They offer fast, hassle-free service at exchange rates better than most banks or casas de cambio.

Try to spend all of your local currency before you cross a border because the exchange rates between countries are often terrible. For example, if you exchange pesos for quetzals in Guatemala the rate will be very low; the same thing happens if you exchange quetzals for pesos in Mexico, and ditto for quetzals or pesos to Belizean dollars.

It is often difficult or impossible to exchange travellers' cheques on weekends. Friday should be one of your routine moneychanging days so that you'll be supplied with cash for the weekend.

For details on the currency of Guatemala, Belize and Mexico, see Money in the Facts for the Visitor chapter of each country.

Exchange Rates

The Guatemalan quetzal (Q) has been devalued regularly over the past few years, and you'll probably get more quetzals for your

Foreign	Mexico	Guatemala	Belize
US$1	N$3.00	Q5.00	BZ$2.00
CN$1	N$2.58	Q4.25	BZ$1.72
UK£1	N$5.91	Q9.80	BZ$3.94
A$1	N$2.31	Q3.85	BZ$1.54
NZ$1	N$1.80	Q3.00	BZ$1.20
DM1	N$2.04	Q3.50	BZ$1.36
L100	N$2.31	Q3.85	BZ$1.54

dollar as time passes. The Belizean dollar (B$) is closely linked to the US dollar, and thus the rate of exchange will probably remain the same over time. The Mexican New Peso (N$) has been stable for several years, but is now seriously overvalued. There may be a substantial devaluation in the future.

Costs

For the very budget-conscious traveller, Guatemala offers the best bargains on accommodation, food, transportation and things to buy. Mexico is next, with low prices in the smaller towns but surprisingly higher prices in resorts such as Cancún and Cozumel. Belize, in general, is unusually expensive, especially considering what you get for your money. Though a middle-range traveller can do all right in Belize, the low-budget person may find money disappearing at an alarming rate. See the Facts for the Visitor chapters for each country for more information.

Tipping

In general, staff in the smaller, cheaper places don't expect much in the way of tips, while those in the expensive resort establishments expect you to be lavish in your largesse. Tipping in Cancún and Cozumel is up to US standards of 15% to 20%; elsewhere, 10% is usually sufficient; in a small eatery you can get away without a tip.

Bargaining

Though you can attempt to haggle down the price of a hotel room, these rates are usually set and fairly firm, especially during the busy winter season. Off-season price reductions are sometimes negotiable.

For handicrafts and other souvenirs, and for anything in an open-air market, bargaining is the rule, and you may pay many times the going price if you pay the first price quoted. The exception to this rule comes when you buy handicrafts from some Chiapan and Guatemalan artisans' cooperatives, which use fixed prices.

CLIMATE & WHEN TO GO

You can travel the region at any time of year; there is no off season. The Caribbean's pellucid waters are always invitingly warm, the beaches always good for sunning. But the topography of the region is varied, from low-lying Yucatán to the lofty volcanoes of Chiapas and Guatemala, so you will encounter a variety of climatic conditions whenever you go.

The height of the tourist season is in winter, from Christmas to the end of March; the other high-season month is August. You should reserve middle and top-end hotel rooms in advance for Mérida, Uxmal, Cancún, Cozumel, Isla Mujeres, the resorts of Mexico's Caribbean coast, and Belize's cayes during these times. For bottom-end rooms, try to get to your destination as early in the day as possible so you can nail down a room at the price you want.

The hottest month in the region is April, the coolest is February. The most rain falls in June. Hurricane season in the Caribbean, including Cancún, Cozumel, Isla Mujeres, Mexico's Caribbean coast, and all of the Belizean coast and its cayes, is from July to November, with most of the activity from mid-August to mid-September. Normally there are at least a few tropical storms in the

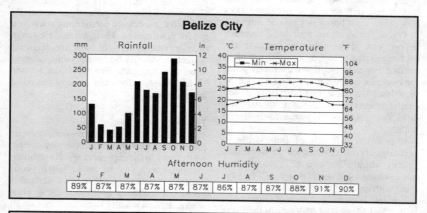

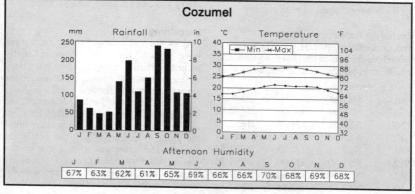

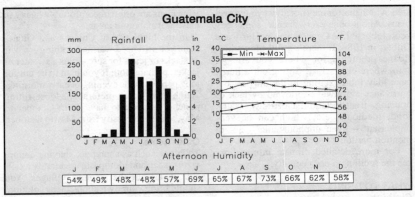

Guatemala City

Rainfall

mm / in

J	F	M	A	M	J	J	A	S	O	N	D

Temperature

°C / °F — Min ─ Max

Afternoon Humidity

J	F	M	A	M	J	J	A	S	O	N	D
54%	49%	48%	48%	57%	69%	65%	67%	73%	66%	62%	58%

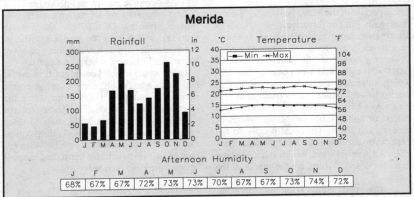

Merida

Rainfall

mm / in

Temperature

°C / °F — Min ─ Max

Afternoon Humidity

J	F	M	A	M	J	J	A	S	O	N	D
68%	67%	67%	72%	73%	73%	70%	67%	67%	73%	74%	72%

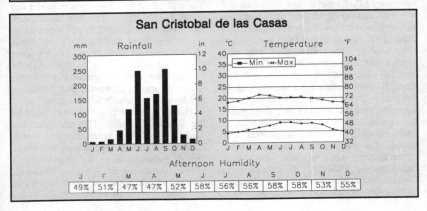

San Cristobal de las Casas

Rainfall

mm / in

Temperature

°C / °F — Min ─ Max

Afternoon Humidity

J	F	M	A	M	J	J	A	S	O	N	D
49%	51%	47%	47%	52%	58%	56%	56%	58%	58%	53%	55%

area, which may or may not affect your travel plans. About once every decade, somebody gets clobbered, as Cancún was by Hurricane Gilbert in 1988. If there's a full-blown hurricane predicted for where you are, go somewhere else – fast! Sitting out a hurricane may look exciting in the movies, but hurricanes are always followed by lack of housing, transportation, electricity, water, food, medicine, etc, which can be very unpleasant – even unphotogenic – not to mention perilous.

For more detailed climate information, see the section on each country.

WHAT TO BRING
Clothing
Local people of the Maya lands tend to dress informally but conservatively. Most men of all classes, from taxi drivers to business executives, wear long trousers and sports shirts or *guayaberas*, the fancy shirts decorated with tucks and worn outside the belt, which substitute for jacket and tie in this warm climate. Women dress traditionally, in long white Mayan dresses with embroidered collars or bodices, or stylishly in dresses or blouses and skirts. The local people do not expect you to dress in the same manner. They allow for foreign ways, but you should know that shorts and T-shirts are the marks of the tourist.

In lowland areas such as Yucatán, Tabasco, El Petén and Belize, both men and women should always have a hat, sunglasses and sunblock cream. If your complexion is particularly fair or if you burn easily, consider wearing light cotton shirts with long sleeves and light cotton slacks. Otherwise, men can wear light cotton trousers or shorts, tennis shoes or sandals and T-shirts, although more conservative wear is in order when visiting churches. Women can dress similarly except off the beaten track in villages unaccustomed to tourists. In general, it is better for women to dress somewhat more conservatively when in town – no shorts, tank tops, etc. Cancún is the exception; in Cancún, wear whatever you like. Bring a light sweater or jacket for evening boat rides.

Blue jeans are often uncomfortably heavy in these warm, humid areas.

In the highlands of Chiapas and Guatemala you will need warmer clothing – a pair of slacks or jeans for sure – plus a sweater or jacket, perhaps both if you plan to be out for long periods in the evening or early morning. A light rain-jacket, preferably a loose-fitting poncho, is good to have from October to May, and is a necessity from May to October.

Other Items
Toiletries such as shampoo, shaving cream, razors, soap and toothpaste are readily available in all but the smallest villages. You should bring your own contact lens solution, tampons, contraceptives and deodorant.

Don't forget the all-important insect repellent containing DEET (see the Health section), which may be easier to find at home. Besides, if you buy it before you leave home, you'll have it when you need it.

Other items which you might find useful are: flashlight (torch) for exploring caves, pyramids, and your hotel room when the electricity fails, disposable lighter (for the same reasons), pocket knife, two to three metres of cord, diving or snorkelling equipment, fishing equipment, a small sewing kit, money belt or pouch, lip balm, and a small Spanish-English dictionary.

FESTIVALS & HOLIDAYS
You will notice that Sunday is indeed a day of rest. Local people put on their best clothes, go to church, then spend the afternoon relaxing in the parks or strolling along the streets. Most businesses are closed, though some towns and villages have Sunday markets. Bus services may be curtailed. In the big resorts (Cancún, Cozumel, Isla Mujeres), Sundays are not observed so strictly.

The big national holidays are dictated by the Roman Catholic Church calendar. Christmas and Holy Week (Semana Santa), leading up to Easter, are the most important, though the celebrations are often as much Mayan shamanist in spirit as Christian. Hotels and buses are very busy in Mexico and packed throughout Guatemala during

Holy Week, especially in the towns which have particularly elaborate and colourful celebrations, such as Antigua.

January

Though the first two weeks of January see somewhat fewer hordes of tourists flocking to Cancún after the Christmas rush, the busy winter sun-and-fun season begins in earnest by mid-January. The weather is dry.

1 January – New Year's Day is a legal holiday in Mexico, Guatemala and Belize.

6 January – Día de los Reyes Magos, or Day of the Three Wise Men. Mexicans exchange Christmas presents on this day, in memory of the kings who brought gifts to baby Jesus.

Last Sunday in January – Día de la Inmaculada Concepción, or Festival of the Immaculate Conception. In Yucatán, nine days of devotions lead up to a secular festival including a dance which features a pig's head decorated with offerings of flowers, ribbons, bread, liquor and cigarettes. The traditional Yucatecan *jaranas* dances are usually performed as well.

February

Height of the tourist season, with most hotel rooms filled, most rental cars rented, and most other activities in full swing.

Religious Holidays – Late February or early March is when Carnival comes, preceding Lent, the start of which is determined by the date of Easter. Carnival festivities are important throughout the region, and include parades with fantastic floats, folk dancing, athletic competitions and everybody dressing up in costumes. Carnival begins in earnest on the weekend preceding the beginning of Lent. The final day of Carnival is often called Mardi Gras (Fat Tuesday), the last day on which observant Catholics are allowed to eat meat. Fat Tuesday is followed by Ash Wednesday, first of the 40 days of Lent leading up to Easter. On Ash Wednesday the Carnival party is over; fasting and prayers are the rule. In 1995, Fat Tuesday is on 28 February. It falls on 20 February 1996, 11 February 1997 and 24 February 1998.

5 February – Constitution Day, a legal holiday in Mexico.

March

The tourist season continues at its height.

Religious Holidays – Carnival (see February) usually falls in early March.

9 March – Baron Bliss Day, a legal holiday in Belize. It honours the English nobleman who dropped anchor in Belizean waters in the 1920s, fell in love with the place, and willed his considerable fortune (several million dollars) to the people of Belize. His bequest, held in trust and earning interest, has been funding worthwhile projects such as roads, schools, market halls, etc ever since.

21 March – Birthday of Benito Juárez, a legal holiday in Mexico, celebrates the plucky Indian president who fought off the French intervention headed by Emperor Maximilian of Hapsburg in the 1860s. Also on 20 or 21 March is the vernal equinox, celebrated at Chichén Itzá as the sun strikes the 'serpent' on the stairway of El Castillo (see the section on Chichén Itzá for details).

April

The rainy season may start by late April. The few weeks before it does are often the hottest of the year. Everyone and everything swelters in the lowlands, while up in the mountains the weather is delightful.

Religious Holidays – During Holy Week, the week before Easter Sunday, things are especially busy in the lands of the Maya, and particularly in the towns of highland Guatemala. Holy Week is 9-15 April in 1995, 31 March-6 April in 1996 and 5-11 April in 1997. The Friday before Easter Sunday (Good Friday), Holy Saturday and Easter Sunday are official holidays in all three countries. Holy Thursday is a holiday in Guatemala; Easter Monday is a holiday in Belize.

21 April – Queen's Birthday, a legal holiday in Belize.

May

The rainy season begins in earnest, with heavy rains during the first few weeks after the season begins. No place escapes the rains, though they are heaviest to the west, in Chiapas and in Guatemala's highlands. In Yucatán the rains may be limited to an hour's downpour in the afternoon.

1 May – Labour Day, a legal holiday in Mexico, Guatemala and Belize.

5 May – Cinco de Mayo, a legal holiday in Mexico commemorating the Battle of Puebla (1862), when Juárez's forces defeated French armies of Maximilian of Hapsburg decisively, ending the European-sponsored occupation of Mexico.

24 May – Commonwealth Day, a legal holiday in Belize.

June

Rains may continue to be heavy during June.

30 June – Army Day and commemoration of the revolution of 1871, a legal holiday in Guatemala.

July

Rains are less bothersome, and the summer tourist season is in full swing. The hurricane season officially begins in July, though historically there are few storms this month. Summer visitors are usually more interested in archaeology and local culture than the sun-and-sea crowd that comes in winter.

August

The summer tourist season peaks, and rooms in some places may be difficult to find. Hurricane season comes to the Caribbean; this is one of the most active months for tropical storms.

15 August – Festival of Guatemala in Guatemala City; offices and shops close for the day.

29 August – Postal Workers' Holiday; all post offices closed in Guatemala.

September

The summer crowd thins out, but it's still quite hot and humid. Hurricane season continues, another active month for tropical storms.

Religious Holidays – El Señor de las Ampollas, a festival in Mérida celebrating the 'Christ of the Blisters' in the cathedral, runs from the end of September into mid-October.

1 September – President's Message to Congress (Mexico).

10 September – Belize National Day, a legal holiday in Belize. It commemorates the Battle of St George's Caye fought in 1798 between British buccaneers and Spanish naval forces. The victory prize was Belize itself. The British won. Celebrations begin today, and continue until Independence Day on the 21st.

15 September – Independence Day, a legal holiday in Guatemala.

16 September – Independence Day, a legal holiday in Mexico.

21 September – Independence Day, a legal holiday in Belize. The colony of British Honduras gained its independence from the UK in 1981.

October

The rains cease sometime during October, as does most danger of hurricanes. The number of visitors drops off, facilities are less crowded, and there are many bargains to be had. It's a great time to travel here.

Religious Holidays – The festival of las Ampollas continues in Mérida (see September). In late October (18 to 28) Izamal (east of Mérida) is the place to be. The Día del Cristo de Sitilpech is celebrated as a venerated statue of Christ comes in procession from the village of Sitilpech to the great monastic church in Izamal. On the evenings of 25 and 28 October, jaranas (Yucatecan dances) are performed in the plazas.

12 October – 'Day of the Race' (Mexico); Columbus Day (Belize), a legal holiday.

20 October – Commemoration of the revolution of 1944 (Guatemala).

31 October – On the eve of Todos Santos (All Saints' Day) in Mexico, visitors place flowers on graves of the deceased, and light candles in their memory.

November

A low season for travel, it's wonderful for the person who wants uncrowded beaches, empty hotels, quiet restaurants, an unhurried pace and discount travel-service prices. Hurricane season officially comes to an end.

1 November – Todos Santos, or All Saints' Day (Guatemala). In Mexico, celebrations and observances continue until 8 November, the Day of the Dead.

19 November – Garifuna Settlement Day (Belize), commemorating when the Garinagus (Black Caribs) arrived to settle in Belize in 1823.

20 November – Anniversary of the Mexican Revolution (Mexico).

December

Until the Christmas rush to the resorts begins, December is an excellent month to visit, with little rain, good temperatures, low prices, and uncrowded facilities. The crowds begin to arrive – and prices rise substantially – after 15 December.

8 December – Feast of the Immaculate Conception in many towns of Mexico and Guatemala. The festivities in Izamal, Yucatán, are particularly lively.

11-12 December – Day of the Virgin of Guadalupe, Mexico's patron saint, a legal holiday in Mexico.

24-25 December – Christmas Eve is a holiday in the afternoon in Mexico and Guatemala; Christmas Day is a holiday in all three countries.

26 December – Boxing Day, a legal holiday in Belize.

31 December – New Year's Eve afternoon is a holiday in Guatemala.

POST & TELECOMMUNICATIONS

Almost every city and town (but not villages) has an Oficina de Correos (post office) where you can buy postage stamps and send or receive mail. Belize has the traditional red pillar boxes familiar to the British.

Sending Mail

If you are sending something by air mail from Mexico or Guatemala, be sure to clearly mark it with the words 'Por Avión'. An airmail letter sent from this part of the world to Canada or the USA may take anywhere from four to 14 days. Airmail letters to Europe can take anywhere from one to three weeks.

Receiving Mail

Receiving mail in Guatemala and Belize is simple: have mail addressed to Poste Restante, and take your passport when you go to pick up mail.

Mexico, however, can be tricky. You can send or receive letters and packages care of a post office if they're addressed as follows:

Jane SMITH (last name should be capitalised)
a/c Lista de Correos
Mérida, Yucatán
(numerical postal code if possible) MEXICO

When the letter arrives at the post office, the name of the addressee is placed on an alphabetical list called the Lista de Correos which is updated daily. If you can, check the list yourself because the letter might be listed under your first name instead of your last.

To claim your mail, present your passport or other identification; there's no charge. The snag is that many post offices only hold Lista mail for 10 days before returning it to the sender. If you think you're going to pick mail up more than 10 days after it has arrived, have it sent to you at Poste Restante, Correo Central, Town/City, State, Mexico. Poste restante usually holds mail for up to a month but no list of what has been received is posted. Again, there's no charge for collection.

If you can arrange for a private address to receive mail, do so. There's less chance of

your mail getting put aside, lost or returned to the sender if you're late in picking it up.

Telephone

Local calls are cheap. International calls are generally very expensive. Don't go to the post office looking for telephones, as telephone companies in these countries are quasi-independent corporations separate from the post office. For details on calling from each country, see that country's section.

Calling from Abroad To call establishments listed in this guide from your home, follow the international calling procedures for your home telephone company, which will include dialling an access code for international service, then the country code, the area or city code, and the local number. City codes are given for most telephone numbers in this guide. Country codes are (52) for Mexico, (502) for Guatemala, and (501) for Belize.

Country Codes Here are some useful country codes:

Country	Code	Country	Code
Australia	61	Israel	972
Austria	43	Italy	39
Belgium	32	Japan	81
Belize	501	Mexico	52
Canada	1	Netherlands	31
Costa Rica	506	New Zealand	64
Denmark	45	Nicaragua	505
Eire	353	Norway	47
El Salvador	503	Portugal	351
Finland	358	South AFrica	27
France	33	Spain	34
Germany	49	Sweden	46
Guatemala	502	Switzerland	41
Honduras	504	UK	44
India	91	USA	1

Fax, Telex & Telegraph

Fax Many middle-range and most top-end hotels have facsimile machines, as do airlines, car rental companies, tourist offices and other businesses. When making reservations or asking for information, a fax is often the cheapest and most efficient way of going about it. The recipient will get written instructions, which makes translations easier and minimises the chance for errors. Also, faxes usually take less time than voice calls, saving you money on telephone tolls. If you don't have access to a fax machine for free at a friend's office, contact one of the many businesses which will send your fax for a fee.

Telex In this age of the fax machine, telexes are used less often as they are slower, and the number of telex machines is fewer. However, you can send telexes to most top-end hotels and to many travel agencies.

Telegraph Many towns have *telégrafos*, offices from which you can send domestic and international telegrams – a simple but not always very quick or cheap means of communication. Fax is usually preferable.

TIME
North American Central Standard Time (GMT/UTC minus six hours) is used in all parts of the region. Daylight saving (or 'summer') time is not used. Here's the time in some other cities when it's noon in Cancún, Mérida, Belize City, Guatemala City, or any other part of the region:

City	Summer	Winter
Paris, Rome	8 pm	7 pm
London	7 pm	6 pm
GMT	6 pm	6 pm
New York, Toronto	2 pm	1 pm
Chicago, New Orleans	1 pm	noon
San Francisco, LA	11 am	10 am
Perth, Hong Kong	3 am*	2 am*
Sydney, Melbourne	5 am*	4 am*
Auckland	6 am*	7 am*
*next day		

ELECTRICITY
Electrical current, plugs and sockets (points) are the same as in the USA and Canada: 115 to 125 V, 60 Hz, with flat-pronged plugs.

LAUNDRY
The larger cities and towns have modern laundries and dry-cleaning shops where you can leave your clothes to be cleaned. Often you can have your laundry back in a day; dry cleaning usually takes at least overnight.

Addresses of convenient laundries are given in this guidebook for each city which has them.

WEIGHTS & MEASURES
Guatemala, Belize and Mexico use the metric system. For conversion information, see the back of this book. Because of the great commercial influence of the USA, you may find that ounces *(onzas)*, pounds *(libras)*, feet *(pies)*, miles *(millas)* and US gallons *(galones)* are used informally, at village markets, for instance. Officially, however, everything's metric.

BOOKS & MAPS
Many aspects of Mayan life and culture remain shrouded in mystery. New discoveries are being made every year by Mayanists and released to the world in books and magazine articles.

Mayan Life & Culture
In preparation for your journey, find a copy of *Maya: The Riddle and Rediscovery of a Lost Civilization* (Penguin Books, 3rd rev. edn, 1987) by Charles Gallenkamp, the best general introduction to Mayan life and culture. Equally good, but more scholarly, is *The Maya*, by the eminent Mayanist Michael D Coe (New York and London: Thames & Hudson, 1987, 4th rev edn; paperback).

Another entertaining and academically accurate book is *A Forest of Kings: The Untold Story of the Ancient Maya*, by Linda Schele & David Freidel (New York: Morrow, 1990; hardback), a much more detailed look at Mayan history and beliefs.

Much of what we know about Mayan life and culture is derived from Friar Diego de Landa's book, translated as *Yucatan Before and After the Conquest* (Mineola, NY: Dover Publications, 1978; paperback). You can find this in numerous bookshops within the region, or order it from your bookshop at home, or directly from the publisher, Dover Publications, 31 E 2nd St, Mineola, NY 11501-3582 USA.

If you have access to back issues of the *National Geographic Magazine* published in

Washington, get hold of 'La Ruta Maya' and related articles, Volume 176, No 4 (October 1989), pp 424-505, for the best short introduction to the concept of La Ruta Maya. Other *National Geographic* articles worth reading are 'Jade, Stone of Heaven' and 'Exploring a Vast Maya City, El Mirador', Volume 172, No 3 (September 1987), pp 282-339.

Travel Guides

Other guidebooks published by Lonely Planet cover areas adjacent to southern Mexico, Guatemala and Belize. The encyclopedic *Mexico – a travel survival kit* covers the entire country in great detail. *Central America on a shoestring* is the guide you want if you're travelling through the rest of the region on a tight budget. *Costa Rica – a travel survival kit* provides full information on that other top Central American destination.

The Complete Visitor's Guide to Mesoamerican Ruins by Joyce Kelly (University of Oklahoma Press, 1982; hardback) gives good directions on how to reach some of the remoter sites, but would be cumbersome to carry along on your trip.

Tikal: A Handbook of the Ancient Maya Ruins, by William R Coe (Philadelphia: The University Museum of the University of Pennsylvania, 1967; paperback) is available at Tikal for US$6, but may be cheaper if you buy it at home before you leave. If you expect to spend several days exploring Tikal, you'll want William Coe's excellent guide.

Backpacking in Mexico & Central America by Hilary Bradt & Rob Rachowiecki (Bradt Enterprises, Cambridge, Mass, and Chalfont St Peter, Bucks, England, 1982) covers only a few hikes in Mexico but has some useful general information plus details of hikes in all the other Central American countries.

Maps

One of the best overall maps of Mexico is published by Bartholomew in its World Travel Map series at a scale of 1:3 million – which means that it folds out to about 1.2 by

0.8 metres. It shows altitudes, rivers, cities and towns, roads, railways and state boundaries clearly and accurately. You can also get a good 1:3.5 million *Tourist Road Map* of the country, which includes good street plans of some cities, free from many tourist offices. For motorists in Mexico, the best road atlas is generally reckoned to be the *Pemex Atlas de Carreteras*, available from some Pemex petrol stations.

International Travel Map Productions, PO Box 2290, Vancouver, BC V6B 3W5, Canada, publishes a series of Traveller's Reference Maps. Titles include *Guatemala-El Salvador* (1:500,000), which also covers neighbouring portions of Chiapas, Tabasco, Belize and Honduras; *Yucatán Peninsula* (1:1 million), which includes Tabasco, Chiapas, Guatemala's Petén and Belize; and *Belize* (1:350,000).

A letter to the Instituto Guatemalteco de Turismo (INGUAT, 7 Avenida 1-17, Zona 4, Guatemala City), sent well in advance of your departure, will yield a useful map of the country with city street plans, but the scale is fairly small. The same map, called the *Mapa Vial Turístico*, may be bought in Guatemala at shops or from street vendors for several dollars (you can bargain with vendors).

For Belize, the *Belize Facilities Map* issued by the Belize Tourist Board, PO Box 325, Belize City, has plans of all major towns in Belize, a road map, plans of the archaeological sites at Altun-ha and Xunantunich, and a list of facts about Belize. If you write to the Board in advance you may be able to get one for free; in Belizean shops the map is sold for US$4.

Travelogues

Most important of all are the delightful travel books written more than 150 years ago by John L Stephens and beautifully illustrated by Frederick Catherwood. Stephens, a New York lawyer, sometime diplomat and amateur archaeologist, and Catherwood, a patient and skilled draughtsman, travelled extensively in the Mayan lands in the mid-19th century. The descriptions of their journeys, published soon after their return, were instant transatlantic best-sellers, entertaining readers throughout North America and Britain. More than just travelogues, their discoveries and painstaking explorations produced the first extensive and serious look at many Mayan archaeological sites. Their detailed descriptions and drawings are now the only evidence we have for some features of the sites which have been lost, destroyed or stolen.

The books, *Incidents of Travel in Central America, Chiapas and Yucatan*, in two volumes (1969 and later reprints of the original 1841 edition), and *Incidents of Travel in Yucatan*, in two volumes (1963 and later reprints of the 1843 edition), by John L Stephens are available in paperback at some bookshops in the region, from many bookshops in the USA and elsewhere with good selections of travel literature, and also directly from the publisher, Dover Publications, 31 East Second St, Mineola, NY 11501-3582 USA.

Aldous Huxley travelled through Mexico too; *Beyond the Mexique Bay*, first published in 1934, has interesting observations on the Maya. Equally interesting is Graham Greene's *The Lawless Roads*, chronicling the writer's travels through Chiapas and Tabasco in 1938.

Contemporary writers have also found the lands of the Maya to be inspiring. *So Far from God: A Journey to Central America* by Patrick Marnham (New York: Viking, 1985 and now in a Penguin paperback) was the winner of the 1985 Thomas Cook Travel Book Award. It's an insightful and often amusing account of a leisurely meander from Texas down to Mexico City and on through Oaxaca and San Cristóbal de las Casas into Central America.

Time Among the Maya: Travels in Belize, Guatemala, and Mexico, by Ronald Wright (New York: Weidenfeld & Nicolson, 1989; hardback) is a thoughtful account of numerous journeys made in recent years among the descendants of the ancient Maya, and will

UXMAL.
Front of the Casa de Las Tortugas.

An engraving of one of Frederick Catherwood's sketches of Uxmal, published in John L Stephens'
Incidents of Travel in Yucatan (1843).

certainly help you to 'feel' Mayan culture as you travel the region. Highly recommended.

Paul Theroux rides the rails through Mexico on *The Old Patagonian Express*, also available in paperback.

History

There are various worthwhile books on the pre-Hispanic period, on the Spanish conquest and its aftermath, and on recent events in Mexico. Starting at the beginning of the Mexican story there's Nigel Davies' *The Ancient Kingdoms of Mexico* (Allen Lane, London, 1982; also available in Pelican paperback). This is a succinct but scholarly study of four of Mexico's ancient civilisations: the Olmecs, the builders of Teotihuacán, the Toltecs and the Aztecs. Diagrams, illustrations, plans and maps complement the text.

Atlas of Ancient America by Michael Coe, Dean Snow & Elizabeth Benson (Facts on File, New York and Oxford, 1986) covers North, South and the rest of Central America as well as Mexico. It's too big to carry in a backpack but is a fascinating, superbly illustrated book. The whole course of ancient Mexico is charted and there are maps showing the areas controlled by the different Mayan cities and the expansion of the Teotihuacán, Toltec and Aztec empires.

Ambivalent Conquests: Maya and Spaniard in Yucatan, 1517-1570 by Inga Clendinnen (Cambridge, New York, Melbourne, Sydney: Cambridge University Press, 1987; paperback) covers the formative years of the relationship between the Maya and their Spanish overlords, years which set the tone of Indian-Hispanic relations for the rest of Yucatecan history.

The multivolume *Handbook of Middle American Indians* (University of Texas Press, Austin, 1964-76), edited by Robert Wauchope, is an encyclopedic work which covers both the pre-Hispanic and more recent stages of Indian history and culture in great detail.

Culture, Art & Architecture

The basic text of Mayan religion is the *Popol*

Vuh (or *Popol Wuh*), which recounts the Mayan creation myths. A version easily available in Guatemala is *Popol Wuh: Ancient Stories of the Quiche Indians of Guatemala*, by Albertina Saravia E (Guatemala City: Editorial Piedra Santa, 1987; paperback).

The Flayed God: The Mythology of Mesoamerica, by Roberta H Markman and Peter T Markman (New York: Harper Collins, 1992) is a fascinating exploration of the religious and cultural myths of the Maya from the earliest times to the present day.

Mexico's post-1521 architectural heritage is documented in *Art & Time in Mexico* by Elizabeth Wilder Weismann & Judith Hancock Sandoval (Harper & Row), a good, fairly handy, recent book on colonial architecture, with many photos.

Maya Missions: Exploring the Spanish Colonial Churches of Yucatan, by Richard and Rosalind Perry (Santa Barbara, Ca: Espadaña Press, 1988) is an excellent guide to the more prominent fortress-like churches of Yucatán. Order it (US$12.95 + shipping) through your bookstore, or from the publisher at PO Box 31067, Santa Barbara, CA 93130, USA.

Chloë Sayer's *Mexican Costume* (London: British Museum Publications, 1985) traces the designs, materials and techniques of the country's highly colourful and varied costumes from pre-Hispanic times to the present. The same author has also written *Crafts of Mexico* (Aldus Books).

The Blood of Kings: Dynasty & Ritual in Maya Art by Linda Schele & Mary Ellen Miller (New York: George Braziller, 1986) is a heavily illustrated guide to the art and culture of the Mayan period with particular emphasis on sacrifices, bloodletting, torture of captives, the ball game and other macabre aspects of Mayan culture. The illustrated analyses of Mayan art are fascinating.

The incredibly complex and portentous Mayan calendrical system makes a fascinating study. *The Book of the Year: Middle American Calendrical Systems*, by Munro S Edmonson (Salt Lake City: University of

Utah Press, 1988; hardback), is an excellent but fairly expensive book.

MEDIA
Newspapers & Magazines
Some major US newspapers such as *USA Today*, the *Miami Herald* and the *Los Angeles Times* are on sale in luxury-hotel newsstands and some big-city and airport bookshops in the region. *Newsweek* and *Time* magazines are also sometimes available, along with the *New York Times* and the *Wall Street Journal*. The better hotel shops also have good selections of European newspapers and magazines in French, German, Italian and Spanish.

For more information on media, see each country's section.

Radio & TV
Local radio broadcasting, both AM and FM, is all in Spanish except in Belize and for a few hours of English programming each day in Cancún. In the evening you may be able to pick up US stations on the AM (medium wave) band.

Many middle-range hotel rooms in Yucatán have TV sets, often with satellite hookups which can receive some US stations. Most popular are ESPN (the sports channel) and UNO, the Spanish-language US network. Local Spanish-language programming includes hours and hours of talk shows and soap operas, some sports, and reruns of old US movies dubbed in Spanish. The situation is similar in Guatemala.

In Belize, the local station is in English, so you can easily understand the news programmes, and you needn't read subtitles while watching the old movies.

FILM & PHOTOGRAPHY
In general, you are allowed to bring in no more than one camera and 12 rolls of film. I have never heard of this ever being enforced. Camera stores, pharmacies and hotels are the most common outlets for buying film. Be suspicious of film that is being sold at prices lower than what you might pay in North America – it is often outdated.

Print film, both B&W and colour, is easily found, though you may not find the brand you like without a search. Processing is not particularly expensive, and can be done in a day or two, even quicker in the large cities. Print film prices are US$1 or US$2 higher than in the USA.

Slide (transparency) film may be more difficult to find in Mexico, especially in smaller locales, and certain types are impossible to find in Guatemala and Belize. Kodachrome, for example, is not sold in these countries because they have no facilities to process it. Ektachrome slide film can be found, but it is very expensive.

Most people in the region do not mind having their photographs taken. Indeed, the children may joyously pester you to take theirs. Of course one must use common sense and decency: ask permission before snapping away at anything military, religious, or close-up personal. And keep in mind that there are a few locations – the village of San Juan Chamula outside San Cristóbal de las Casas, other villages nearby, the church of Santo Tomás in Chichicastenango – where photography is strictly forbidden or frowned upon. If local people make any sign of being offended, you should put your camera away and apologise immediately, both out of decency and for your own safety.

HEALTH
Predeparture Preparations
Ideally, you should make sure you're as healthy as possible before you start travelling. If you're going for more than a couple of weeks, make sure your teeth are OK; there are lots of places in the region where a visit to the dentist would be the last thing you'd want to do. If you wear glasses, take a spare pair and your prescription. Losing your glasses can be a real problem, although in many places you can get new spectacles made up quickly cheaply and competently.

Health Insurance A travel insurance policy to cover theft, loss and medical problems is a wise idea. There are a wide variety of policies and your travel agent will have recommendations. The international student travel policies handled by STA Travel or other student travel organisations are usually good value.

Check the small print. Some policies offer lower and higher medical expenses options. Some policies specifically exclude 'dangerous activities' which can include scuba diving, motorcycling, even trekking. If such activities are on your agenda you don't want that sort of policy. A locally acquired motorcycle licence may not be valid under your policy, so bikers should check this too.

You may prefer a policy which pays doctors or hospitals direct rather than you having to pay on the spot and claim later. If you have to claim later make sure you keep all documentation. Some policies ask you to call back (reverse charges) to a centre in your home country where an immediate assessment of your problem is made.

Check also whether the policy covers ambulances or an emergency flight home. If you have to stretch out you will need two seats and somebody has to pay for them!

Medical Kit It is always a good idea to travel with a small first-aid kit. Some of the items that should be included are: adhesive bandages, a sterilised gauze bandage, cotton wool, a fever thermometer, tweezers and scissors.

You may wish to include the following medication: an antiseptic agent (Dettol or Betadine), burn cream (Caladryl is good for sunburn, minor burns and itchy bites), Panadol or aspirin for pain or fever, insect repellent containing DEET, and multivitamins. Antihistamine (such as Benadryl) is useful as a decongestant for colds and allergies, also to ease the itch from insect bites and stings or to help prevent motion sickness. If you're travelling with children, a rehydration mixture for treatment of severe diarrhoea is particularly important, but recommended for everyone.

Don't forget a full supply of any medication you're already taking; the prescription might be difficult to match abroad. If you're travelling off the beaten track to some of the more remote areas covered in this guide, it may be wise to include antibiotics, which must be prescribed – make sure you carry the prescription with you. Some individuals are allergic to commonly prescribed antibiotics such as penicillin or sulfa drugs. It would be sensible to always carry this information when travelling.

Illness Prevention Specific immunisations are not normally required for travel anywhere in Guatemala, Mexico and Belize. All the same, it's a good idea to be up to date on your tetanus, typhoid-paratyphoid and polio immunisations; if you were born after 1957 you should also make sure that you're immune to measles (ask your doctor). If you plan to stay for more than a few weeks in the region, and you're adventurous in your eating, an immune globulin shot is also recommended for protection against infectious hepatitis. You only need a yellow fever certificate to enter the country if, within the last six months, you have been to a country where yellow fever is present.

Food spoils easily in the tropics, mosquitoes roam freely and sanitation is not always the best, so you must take special care to protect yourself from illness. The most important steps you can take are to be careful about what you eat and drink, to stay away from mosquitoes (or at least make them stay away from you), and to practise safe sex. These measures are particularly important for adventurous travellers who enjoy getting off the beaten track, mingling with the locals and trekking into remote areas.

Before I begin on this somewhat disturbing catalogue of potential illnesses, let me say that after dozens of journeys in every region of these countries in every season of the year, climbing pyramids in remote jungle sites, camping out, staying in cheap hotels and eating in all sorts of markets and restaurants, I have never got anything more serious than traveller's diarrhoea (but I've got that frequently!). I have rarely taken medicines to help get rid of diarrhoea, instead preferring to let my body heal itself. I have not taken malaria prevention medicine or immune globulin, and I have not come down with malaria or hepatitis. Thus I believe that travel in the region is not a particularly perilous activity. But I have known people who have got dengue fever and typhoid fever, so I know that it can happen.

If you come down with a serious illness, be very careful to find a competent doctor, and don't be afraid to get second opinions. You may want to telephone your doctor at home for consultation as well. In some cases it may be best to end your trip and fly home for treatment, difficult as this may be. A friend of mine who contracted typhoid fever in Mexico went to the local hospital where a sympathetic doctor strongly recommended that she and her husband fly home to the USA and go to the hospital there, which she did. Medical practice in the region is not always the exact science it should be.

Basic Rules

Food & Water Food can be contaminated by bacteria, viruses and/or parasites when it is harvested, shipped, handled, washed (if the water is contaminated) or prepared. Cooking, peeling and/or washing food in pure water is the way to get rid of the germs. To avoid gastrointestinal diseases, avoid salads, uncooked vegetables and unpasteurised milk or milk products (including cheese). Make sure the food you eat has been freshly cooked and is still hot. Do not eat raw or rare meat, fish or shellfish. Peel fruit yourself with clean hands and a clean knife.

As for beverages, don't trust any water except that which has been boiled for 20 minutes, or treated with purifiers, or comes in an unopened bottle labelled *agua purificada*. Most hotels have large bottles of purified water from which you can fill your carafe or canteen; some will put smaller capped bottles of purified water in your room. Local people may drink the water from the tap or from the well, and their systems may be used to it; or they may have chronic gastric diseases! Cancún supposedly has purified tap water safe to drink. All the

same, I drink bottled water there, as I do everywhere else in the region. Purified water and ice are available from supermarkets, small grocery stores *(tiendas)* and liquor stores *(licorerías* or *vinos y licores)*.

Use only pure water for drinking, washing food, brushing your teeth, and ice. Tea, coffee, and other hot beverages should be made with boiled water. If the waiter swears that the ice in your drink is made from agua purificada, you may feel you can take a chance with it.

Canned or bottled carbonated beverages, including carbonated water, are usually safe, as are beer, wine and liquor. If you plan to travel off the main roads and into the middle of nowhere, a water purification system is recommended as bottled water may not be readily available outside of touristed areas. Your water purification method might be one of these:

Tincture of iodine 2% *(yodo)* sold in chemist's shops/pharmacies: add about seven drops per litre of clear water; strain cloudy water through a clean cloth first, then add 14 drops of iodine per litre.

Water purification drops or tablets containing tetraglycine hydroperiodide or hydroclonazone, sold under brand names such as Globaline, Potable-Agua or Coughlan's in pharmacies and sporting goods stores in the USA. Within the region, ask for *gotas* (drops) or *pastillas* (tablets) *para purificar agua*, sold in pharmacies and supermarkets.

Boiled water: bringing it to a rolling boil will kill most germs, but you must boil it for at least 20 minutes to kill parasites.

A portable water filter which eliminates bacteria. Compact units are available from major camping supply stores in the USA such as Recreational Equipment, Inc (REI) (☎ (206) 431-5804), PO Box C-88126, Seattle, Washington 98188; and Mountain Equipment Inc (MEI) (☎ (800) 344-7422), 1636 South Second St, Fresno, California 93702, and through outfitters such as Eddie Bauer and L L Bean.

Protection against Mosquitoes Many serious tropical diseases are spread by infected mosquitoes. If you protect yourself against mosquito bites, your travels will be both safer and more enjoyable.

Some mosquitoes feed during the day, others at night. In general, they're most bothersome when the sun is not too hot, in the evening and early morning, and on overcast days. There are many more mosquitoes in lowland and coastal regions and in the countryside than there are in cities or in highland areas, and many more during the rainy season (May to October) than during the dry (October to May). Avoid going to mosquito-infested places during these times and seasons if you can.

Mosquitoes seem to be attracted more to dark colours than to light, so in mosquito-infested areas wear light-coloured long trousers, socks, a long-sleeved shirt and a hat. Clothing should be loose-fitting, as mosquitoes can drill right through the weave of a tight T-shirt. Mosquitoes also seem to be attracted by scents such as those in perfume, cologne, lotions, hair spray etc, so avoid using these cosmetics if possible. Sleep in screened rooms or beneath mosquito netting after you have disposed of the little suckers who have somehow got in there with you. Check to make sure screens are intact, and that all openings to the outside are either screened or blocked.

Use insect repellent which has at least a 20% but no more than a 30% concentration of DEET (N,N diethyl-meta-toluamide) on clothing and exposed skin. Repellents with higher concentrations of DEET work longer, but are also more likely to cause allergic reactions.

It's best to buy repellent before leaving home as repellents bought in Mexico, Guatemala or Belize may or may not have this most effective ingredient. To avoid reactions to the repellent, apply it sparingly only to exposed skin or to clothing, don't inhale the stuff or get it in your eyes or mouth or on broken or irritated skin, and wash it off after you enter a mosquito-free area.

Be particularly careful with children: don't apply it to infants or young children; don't put it on hands which may be put in the mouth or eyes, use as little as possible; and wash it off as soon as you're in a mosquito-free area.

Medical Problems & Treatment

Traveller's Diarrhoea The food and water in a different country has different bacteria from what your digestive system is used to – germs that your immune system may not be prepared to combat. If you plunge right into the local culture and eat lots of food with high concentrations of these different bacteria, your body's natural defences will be overwhelmed and you may get sick.

Travellers to many less developed countries suffer from what is known medically as traveller's diarrhoea (TD) and informally as Montezuma's revenge, *turista*, or the trots, a condition defined as having twice as many (or more) unformed bowel movements as normal; typically, one has four or five watery stools per day.

Symptoms In addition to frequent watery stools, other possible symptoms include abdominal cramps, nausea, fever, malaise, a bloated feeling and urgency of bowel movements. The disease usually hits within the first week of travel, but may hit at any time, and may hit more than once during a trip. A bout of TD typically lasts three or four days, but may be shorter or longer. It seems to affect younger travellers more than older ones, which may be due to lack of caution among the young, or acquired immunity among the old.

Prevention Epidemiologists recommend that you do *not* take medicines for TD prophylaxis; that is, don't take any medicine just in the hope that it will prevent a case of the disease. Taking prophylactic medicines such as antibiotics, bismuth subsalicylate (Pepto-Bismol), or difenoxine (Lomotil) can actually make it *easier* for you to get the disease later on by killing off the benign digestive bacteria which help to protect you from the 'foreign' bacteria. These strong drugs can also cause side effects (some of them serious) such as photosensitivity, a condition in which your skin is temporarily oversensitive to sunlight (in the sunny tropics!).

Instead, observe the rules of safe eating

and drinking, and don't overdo it early in your trip. For the first week after arrival, be extremely careful and conservative in your eating habits, avoid overeating, or eating heavy or spicy food, don't get overtired, and don't drink lots of alcoholic beverages or coffee.

Treatment If you come down with a case of TD, take it easy, with no physical exertion; stay in bed if you can. Be especially careful to replace fluids and electrolytes (potassium, sodium, etc) by drinking caffeine-free soft drinks or glasses of fruit juice (high in potassium) with honey and a pinch of salt added, plus a glass of pure water with a quarter teaspoon of sodium bicarbonate (baking soda) added; weak tea, preferably unsweetened and without milk, is all right. Avoid dairy products. Eat only salted crackers or dry toast for a day or so. After that, eat easily digested foods that are not fatty or overly acid. Yoghurt with live cultures is particularly good as it helps to repopulate the bowel with benign digestive organisms. When you feel better, be particularly careful about what you eat and drink from then on.

As for medications, it's best if you cure yourself without them. If you must have some chemical help, go to a doctor, who may recommend one of the following treatments as described in the US Public Health Service's book, *Health Information for International Travel*. Treatments and dosages should be determined by a competent medical doctor who can tell you about side effects and contraindications; those noted here are the normal ones for otherwise healthy adults (*not* children), and are for information only:

Bismuth subsalicylate (Pepto-Bismol) – One ounce of liquid or the equivalent in tablets every half-hour for four hours. This treatment is not recommended if symptoms last more than more than 48 hours, or if you have high fever, blood in the stool, kidney problems or are allergic to salicylates. Children under the age of two should not be given this medicine. Your tongue may turn black after taking Pepto-Bismol. This is a harmless, though frightening, side effect.

Diphenoxylate and loperamide (Lomotil, Imodium) – These are antimotility agents made from synthetic opiate derivatives. They temporarily slow down the diarrhoea but do not cure it, they increase the risk of getting TD again, and they can make you sluggish or sleepy. They should not be used if you have a high fever, or blood in the stool, or are driving a motor vehicle or operating machinery (your alertness is impaired). In any case, don't use them for longer than two full days.

Doxycycline (100 mg twice daily); or trimethoprim (200 mg twice daily); or trimethoprim (160 mg)/sulfamethoxazole (800 mg, once daily), known as TMP/SMX and sold in Mexico as Bactrim F (Roche) – These are antibiotics which may be indicated if there are three or more loose stools in an eight-hour period, especially with nausea, vomiting, abdominal cramps and fever.

It bears repeating: traveller's diarrhoea is self-limiting, and you're usually better off if you can get through it without taking strong drugs. If you feel that you need medication, go to a doctor. Make sure that you have TD and not some other gastrointestinal ailment for which the treatment may be very different.

Medicines Not to Take You can walk into a chemist's/pharmacy in Mexico, Guatemala or Belize and buy medicines – often without a prescription – which might be banned for good reason in your home country. Well-meaning but incompetent doctors or chemists/pharmacists might recommend such medicines for gastrointestinal ailments, but such medicines may be worse than no medicine at all. Though they may bring some relief from the symptoms of TD, they may cause other sorts of harm such as neurological damage. Medicines called halogenated hydroxyquinoline derivatives are among these, and may bear the chemical names clioquinol or iodoquinol, or brand names EnteroVioform, Mexaform or Intestopan, or something similar. It's best not to take these medicines without consulting a trusted physician, preferably your regular doctor at home.

Heatstroke Only slightly less common than traveller's diarrhoea are the illnesses caused by excessive heat and dehydration. These are more dangerous because they display fewer symptoms.

Symptoms If you exercise excessively in hot regions such as Yucatán, Belize and the low-lying regions of Guatemala, or if you fail to replace lost fluids and electrolytes (salt, potassium, etc), you can suffer from dizziness, weakness, headaches, nausea, and greater susceptibility to other illnesses such as traveller's diarrhoea. This is heat exhaustion, heat prostration or, in severe cases, heatstroke. In this last case, exposure to intense heat can cause convulsions and coma.

Prevention Protect yourself against heat-related diseases by taking special care to drink lots of fluids. If you urinate infrequently and in small amounts, you're not drinking enough fluids. If you feel tired and have a headache, you're not drinking enough fluids. Don't just drink when you're thirsty; make it a habit to drink frequently, whether you're thirsty or not. It's so easy to prevent dehydration that you should feel foolish if you succumb to it.

Alcohol, coffee and tea are diuretics – they make you urinate and lose fluids. They are not a cure for dehydration, they're part of the problem. Drink pure water, fruit juices and soft drinks instead; go easy on the beer. Salty food is good to eat as the salt helps your body to retain fluids.

Other measures to take against the heat: don't overdo it. Take it easy climbing pyramids and trekking through the jungle. Wear light cotton clothing that breathes and cools you; wear a hat and sunglasses. Allow yourself frequent rest breaks in the shade, and give your body a chance to balance itself. Use sunblock to prevent bad sunburn. Be doubly cautious if you spend time near or on the water, as the sun's glare from sand and water can double your exposure to the sun. You may want to swim or go boating wearing a T-shirt and hat.

Fungal Infections Hot weather fungal infections are most likely to occur on the scalp, between the toes or fingers (athlete's foot), in the groin (jock itch or crotch rot) and on the body (ringworm). You get ringworm (which is a fungal infection, not a worm) from infected animals or by walking on damp areas, like shower floors.

Other Illnesses Though you're unlikely to contract anything more than an unpleasant bout of traveller's diarrhoea, you should be informed about the symptoms and treatments of these other diseases just in case.

Cholera This serious disease has spread into Central America. Like dysentery, it is a disease of poor sanitation and spreads quickly in areas, urban and rural, where sewerage and water supplies are rudimentary. It can also be spread in foods which are uncooked or parcooked, such as the popular *ceviche* which is made from marinaded raw fish, as well as salads and raw vegetables.

The disease is characterised by a sudden onset of acute diarrhoea with 'rice water' stools, vomiting, muscular cramps and extreme weakness. You need medical help – but first treat for dehydration, which can be extreme, and if there is an appreciable delay in getting to the hospital, then begin taking tetracycline (adults one 250 mg capsule four times a day, children half this dose; if they are under eight, one third). The disease does respond to treatment if caught early.

Dengue Fever Symptoms include the fast onset of high fever, severe frontal headache, and pain in muscles and joints; there may be nausea and vomiting, and a skin rash may develop about three to five days after the first symptoms, spreading from the torso to arms, legs and face. It is possible to have subclinical dengue (that is, a 'mild' case of it), and also to contract dengue haemorraghic fever (DHF), a very serious and potentially fatal disease.

Dengue is spread by mosquitoes. Risk of contraction, though low for the average traveller, is highest during the summer (July to September), several hours after daybreak and before dusk, and on overcast days. There are four different dengue viruses, but no medicines to combat them.

There is no effective treatment for dengue. The disease is usually self-limiting, which means that the body cures itself. If you are generally healthy and have a healthy immune system, the disease may be unpleasant but it is rarely serious. To prevent against getting dengue, see the section on Protection against Mosquitoes.

Dysentery There are two types of dysentery, both of which are characterised by diarrhoea containing blood and/or mucus. You require a stool test to determine which type you have.

Bacillary dysentery, the most common variety, is short, sharp and nasty but rarely persistent. It hits suddenly and lays you out with fever, nausea, cramps and diarrhoea, but it is self-limiting. Treatment is the same as for traveller's diarrhoea; as it's caused by bacteria, the disease responds well to antibiotics if needed.

Amoebic dysentery is caused by amoebic parasites and is more dangerous. It builds up slowly, cannot be starved out and if untreated will get worse and can permanently damage your intestines. Do not have anyone other than a doctor diagnose your symptoms and administer treatment.

Giardiasis This is caused by a parasite named *Giardia lamblia*, contracted by eating faecally contaminated food or beverages or by contact with a surface which has been similarly contaminated. Symptoms usually last for more than five days (perhaps months!), may be mild or serious, and may include diarrhoea, abdominal cramps, fatigue, weight loss, flatulence, anorexia and/or nausea. If you have gastrointestinal gripes for a length of time, talk to a doctor and have a stool sample analysed for giardia. Medicine is available to rid you of this unpleasant little bug easily and safely.

Hepatitis Hepatitis A (formerly called infectious hepatitis) is the most common travel-acquired illness which can be prevented by vaccination. Protection can be provided in two ways - either with the antibody gammaglobulin or with a new vaccine called Havrix.

Havrix provides long-term immunity (possibly more than 10 years) after an initial course of two injections and a booster at one year. It may be more expensive than gammaglobulin (also called immune globulin or IG) but certainly has many advantages, including length of protection and ease of administration. It is important to know that being a vaccine it will take about three weeks to provide satisfactory protection - hence the need for careful planning prior to travel.

Gammaglobulin is not a vaccination but a ready-made antibody which has proven very successful in reducing the chances of hepatitis infection. Because it may interfere with the development of immunity, it should not be given until at least 10 days after administration of the last vaccine needed; it should also be given as close as possible to departure because it is at its most effective in the first few weeks after administration and the effectiveness tapers off gradually between three and six months.

The risk is only moderate in Mexico, Guatemala and Belize, and is low for the average, careful traveller. But with good water and adequate sewage disposal in most industrialised countries since the 1940s, very few young Western adults now have any natural immunity and must be protected.

The disease is spread by contaminated food or water. The symptoms are fever, chills, headache, fatigue, feelings of weakness and aches and pains, followed by loss of appetite, nausea, vomiting, abdominal pain, dark urine, light coloured faeces, jaundiced skin and the whites of the eyes may turn yellow. In some cases you may feel unwell, tired, have no appetite, experience aches and pains and be jaundiced. You should seek medical advice, but in general there is not much you can do apart from rest, drink lots of fluids, eat lightly and avoid fatty foods. People who have had hepatitis must forego alcohol for six months after the illness, as hepatitis attacks the liver and it needs that amount of time to recover.

Hepatitis B, which used to be called serum hepatitis, is spread through contact with infected blood, blood products or bodily fluids, for example through sexual contact, unsterilised needles and blood transfusions. Other risk situations include having a shave or tattoo in a local shop, or having your ears pierced. The symptoms of type B are much the same as type A except that they are more severe and may lead to irreparable liver damage or even liver cancer.

Although there is no treatment for hepatitis B, an effective prophylactic vaccine is readily available in most countries. The immunisation schedule requires two injections at least a month apart followed by a third dose five months after the second. Persons who should receive a hepatitis B vaccination include anyone who anticipates contact with blood or other bodily secretions, either as a health care worker or through sexual contact with the local population, particularly those who intend to stay in the country for a long period of time.

Hepatitis Non-A Non-B is a blanket term formerly used for several different strains of hepatitis, which have now been separately identified. Hepatitis C is similar to B but is less common. Hepatitis D (the 'delta particle') is also similar to B and always occurs in concert with it; its occurrence is currently limited to IV drug users. Hepatitis E, however, is similar to A and is spread in the same manner, by water or food contamination.

Tests are available for these strands, but are very expensive. Travellers shouldn't be too paranoid about this apparent proliferation of hepatitis strains; they are fairly rare (so far) and following the same precautions as for A and B should be all that's necessary to avoid them.

Sexually Transmitted Diseases Sexual contact with an infected sexual partner spreads these diseases. While abstinence is the only 100 % preventative, using condoms is also effective. Gonorrhoea and syphilis are the most common of these diseases: sores, blisters or rashes around the genitals, discharges or pain when urinating are common symptoms. Symptoms may be less marked or not observed at all in women. Syphilis symptoms eventually disappear completely but the disease continues and can cause severe problems in later years. The treatment of gonorrhoea and syphilis is by antibiotics.

There are numerous other sexually transmitted diseases, for most of which effective treatment is available. However, there is no cure for herpes and there is also no cure for AIDS. Abstinence is the only effective preventative; using condoms is next best.

AIDS can be spread through infected blood transfusions; most developing countries cannot afford to screen blood for transfusions properly. AIDS can also be spread by dirty needles – vaccinations, acupuncture and tattooing can potentially be as dangerous as intravenous drug use if the equipment is not clean. If you do need an injection it may be a good idea to buy a new syringe from a pharmacy and ask the doctor to use it.

Malaria This is the one disease that everyone fears, and the one about which you must make an important decision.

Symptoms may include jaundice (a yellow cast to the skin and/or eyes), general malaise, headaches, fever and chills, bed sweats and anaemia. Symptoms of the disease may appear as early as eight days after infection, or as late as several months after you return from your trip. You can contract malaria even if you've taken medicines to protect yourself.

Malaria is spread by mosquitoes which bite mostly between dusk and dawn. Risk of infection is low in the major resort areas and in the highlands and lower in the dry season (October to May) than in the rainy season (May to October). But it is fair to say that somewhere in the region you will encounter mosquitoes. They may or may not carry infectious diseases. Mexico, Guatemala and Belize do not have chloroquine-resistant strains of *Anopheles* mosquitoes, so chloroquine medicines do help to prevent infection.

The best way to protect yourself against malaria is to protect yourself against mosquito bites (see that section). You can also take medicines to protect against malarial infection, usually chloroquine phosphate (Aralen) or hydroxychloroquine sulphate (Plaquenil), though other medicines may be indicated for specific individuals. You must consult a doctor on the use of these medicines, and get a prescription to buy them. Begin taking the medicine *one or two weeks before you arrive* in a malarial area, continue taking it while you're there, and also for a month after you leave the area, according to your doctor's instructions. Taking medicine does not absolutely guarantee that you will not contract malaria, though.

The choice you must make is whether or not to take preventive medicine. As an adventurous traveller, you are more at risk than a person who buys a package tour to Cancún. Although most visitors to Mexico, Guatemala and Belize do not take malaria medicine, and most do not get malaria, you must decide for yourself. Talk to your doctor. Call a hospital or clinic which specialises in tropical diseases (London Hospital for Tropical Diseases in the UK; in the USA, call the Center for Disease Control's telephone information system toll-free ☎ (800) 526-6367, or the CDC Malaria Hotline, ☎ (404) 332-4555). Whether or not you take medicine, do be careful to protect yourself against mosquito bites.

Rabies The rabies virus is spread through bites by infected animals, or (rarely) through broken skin (scratches, licks) or the mucous membranes (as from breathing rabid-bat-contaminated air in a cave, for instance). Typical signs of a rabid animal are mad or uncontrolled behaviour, inability to eat, biting at anything and everything and frothing at the mouth.

If any animal (but especially a dog) bites you, assume you have been exposed to rabies until you are certain this is not the case – there are no second chances. First,

immediately wash the wound with lots of soap and water – this is very important! If it is possible, and safe to do so, try to capture the animal alive, and give it to local health officials who can determine whether or not it's rabid. Begin rabies immunisation shots as soon as possible; if you are taking antimalarial medicine, be sure to mention this to the doctor because antimalarial medicines can interfere with the effectiveness of rabies vaccine. Rabies is a potentially fatal disease, but it can be cured by prompt and proper treatment.

Schistosomiasis A parasitic worm that makes its way into the bodies of certain tiny freshwater snails and then into humans swimming, wading or otherwise touching the infected fresh water in pools, ponds or cenotes. Two or three weeks after your dip you may experience fever, weakness, headache, loss of appetite, loss of weight, pain in the gut and/or pain in the joints and muscles. You may have nausea and/or coughing. Six to eight weeks after infection, evidence of the worm can be found in the stools.

After this very unpleasant month or two, diagnosis can correctly identify schistosomiasis as the culprit, and you can get rid of it quickly and effectively by taking an inexpensive medicine. To guard against the illness, don't swim in fresh water that may be infected by sewage or other pollution. If you expose your skin to schistosomiasis-infected water, rub the skin vigorously with a towel, and/or rub alcohol on it.

Typhoid Fever This serious disease is spread by contaminated food and beverages, and has symptoms similar to those of traveller's diarrhoea. If you get it, you should have close supervision by a competent doctor for a while, and perhaps a short time in the hospital. Inoculation can give you some protection, but is not 100% effective. If diagnosed and treated early, typhoid can be treated effectively.

Typhus If you go to a mountain town and get head lice, they can give you typhus;

otherwise, risk is extremely low. Typhus is treated by taking antibiotics.

Hospitals & Clinics

Almost every town and city now has either a hospital or medical clinic and Red Cross (Cruz Roja) emergency facilities, all of which are indicated by road signs which show a red cross. Hospitals are generally inexpensive for typical ailments (diarrhoea, dysentery) and minor surgery (stitches, sprains). Clinics are often too understaffed and overburdened with local problems to be of much help, but they are linked by a government radio network to emergency services.

If you must use these services, try to ascertain the competence of the staff treating you. Compare their diagnoses and prescriptions to the information in this section. If you have questions, call your embassy and get a referral for a doctor, or call home and have your doctor advise you.

By the way, Guatemalans and Belizeans with serious illnesses often go to Mexican cities (Chetumal, Mérida, Cancún, Villahermosa, or even Mexico City) for treatment in better medical facilities. People from all three countries look upon Miami, New Orleans and Houston as the medical centres of last resort.

Women's Health

Gynaecological problems, poor diet, lowered resistance due to the use of antibiotics for stomach upsets and even contraceptive pills can lead to vaginal infections when travelling in hot climates. Keeping the genital area clean, and wearing skirts or loose-fitting trousers and cotton underwear will help to prevent infections.

Yeast infections, characterised by a rash, itch and discharge, can be treated with a vinegar or even lemon-juice douche or with yoghurt. Nystatin suppositories are the usual medical prescription. Trichomonas is a more serious infection; symptoms are a discharge and a burning sensation when urinating. Male sexual partners must also be treated, and if a vinegar-water douche is not effective

medical attention should be sought. Flagyl is the prescribed drug.

Pregnancy Most miscarriages occur during the first three months of pregnancy, so this is the most risky time to travel. The last three months should also be spent within reasonable distance of good medical care, as quite serious problems can develop at this time. Pregnant women should avoid all unnecessary medication, but vaccinations and malarial prophylactics should still be taken where possible. Additional care should be taken to prevent illness and particular attention should be paid to diet and nutrition.

WOMEN TRAVELLERS

In general, the local men aren't great believers in the equality of the sexes (what would you expect from the home of machismo?), and women alone have to expect numerous attempts to chat them up. It's commonly believed that foreign women without male companions are easy game for local men. This can get tiresome at times; the best discouragement is a cool, unsmiling but polite initial response and a consistent firm 'No'.

Avoid situations in which you might find yourself alone with one or more strange men, at remote archaeological sites, on empty city streets, or on secluded stretches of beach.

DANGERS & ANNOYANCES
Safety

Adventurous travellers especially should be aware that certain areas have been and may still be the scene of political and military conflict, and even attacks on foreign tourists. These incidents occur at random and are not predictable.

Don't let vague fears or rumours of trouble scare you off, as these areas offer exceptional travel experiences which you should not miss. Your best defences against trouble are up-to-date information and reasonable caution. You should take the trouble to contact your government and enquire about current conditions and trouble spots, and follow the advice offered. Up-to-date travel advisories are available from the US Department of State's Citizens Emergency Center (☎ (202) 647-5225), and the UK Foreign Office's Travel Advisory Service (☎ (071) 270-3000). Or call the US Department of State's electronic Consular Affairs Bulletin Board (CABB) in Washington DC: have your computer modem (8-N-1, up to 14,400 bps) dial ☎ (202) 647-9225.

If you plan to travel by road in the Guatemalan Highlands or El Petén, you should also ask as many other travellers as possible about current conditions. Don't rely on local newspapers, governmental officials or business people as your sole sources of information, as they often cover up 'unpleasant' incidents which might result in the loss of tourist revenues. If you speak Spanish, ask local children, who will not be as reticent as their parents to pass on 'bad' news. Your home country's government, however, is the most reliable source as it has an interest in protecting the lives of its citizens.

Robbery & Theft

Robbery is a danger in Guatemala City, Antigua, Chichicastenango and Belize City. Theft, particularly pocket-picking and purse-snatching, is also not unusual in cities such as Mérida and Antigua, and in beach areas. Foreign tourists are particularly singled out for theft as they are presumed to be 'wealthy' and to be carrying valuables.

To protect yourself, take these commonsense precautions:

- Unless you have immediate need of them, leave most of your cash, travellers' cheques, passport, jewellery (earrings, necklaces, bracelets), airline tickets, credit cards, expensive watch, etc (and perhaps your camera) in a sealed, signed envelope in your hotel's safe; obtain a receipt for the envelope. Virtually all hotels except the very cheapest provide safe-keeping for guests' valuables. You may have to provide the envelope (buy some at a papelería, or stationer's shop). Your signature on the envelope and a receipt from the hotel clerk help to insure that hotel staff won't pilfer your things.
- Leaving valuable items in a locked suitcase in your hotel room is often safer than carrying them with you on the streets of Guatemala City.

- Have a money-belt or a pouch on a string around your neck, place your remaining valuables in it, and wear it *underneath your clothing*. You can carry a small amount of ready money in a pocket or bag.
- Be aware that any purse or bag in plain sight may be slashed or grabbed. Often two thieves work together, one cutting the strap, the other grabbing the bag in a lunge past you, even as you walk along a street or stand at a bus stop. At ticket counters in airports and bus stations, keep your bag between your feet, particularly when you're busy talking to a ticket agent.
- Do not wander alone in empty city streets or isolated areas, particularly at night.
- Do not leave any valuables visible in your vehicle when you park it in a city, unless it is in a guarded car park.
- On beaches and in the countryside, do not camp overnight in lonely places unless you can be sure it's safe.

Reporting a Robbery or Theft There's little point in going to the police after a robbery unless your loss is insured, in which case you'll need a statement from the police to present to your insurance company. You'll probably have to communicate with them in Spanish, so if your own is poor take a more fluent speaker along. Say *Yo quisiera poner una acta de un robo* (I'd like to report a robbery). This should make it clear that you merely want a piece of paper and aren't going to ask the police to do anything inconvenient like look for the thieves or attempt to recover your goods. With luck you should get the required piece of paper without too much trouble. You may have to write it up yourself, then present it for official stamp and signature.

Guatemala suffers from a long-standing guerilla conflict. See the Guatemala section for details.

WORK

According to law you must have a work permit to work in any of these countries. In practice you may get paid under the table, or through some bureaucratic loophole, if you can find suitable work. The most plentiful work for native English speakers is of course teaching their language. Consult the classi-

Top: Palace, Palenque Ruins, Chiapas, Mexico (TW)
Left: Stela A on the Great Plaza at Copán, Honduras (TB)
Right: El Castilo, Chichén Itzá, Yucatán, Mexico (TB)

Top: Pyramid of Kukulcán, Chichén Itzá, Yucatán (TW)
Bottom: Stela, Copán, Honduras (PW)

fied advertisements in local newspapers (both English and Spanish-language), browse the bulletin boards in spots where gringos gather, and ask around. Big cities offer the best possibilities, of course. Pay may be very low, but it's better than a negative cash flow.

More lucrative teaching is to tutor business and bank executives. It takes a while to establish a network of contacts and referrals, so you should not plan to tutor for just a month or two. If you get a good reputation, however, it can pay quite well as your students are among the commercial élite.

ACTIVITIES

Mayan culture, art and archaeology are of prime interest and anyone visiting this area would want to spend some time exploring these. There are many other things to do as well. Some of them have a Mayan connection, some do not.

Water Sports

The Caribbean coast from Cancún and Isla Mujeres in the north to the Belizean cayes in the south is a paradise for water sports, including swimming, snorkelling, scuba diving, fishing, sailing and sailboarding. Cancún has the most water sports facilities, but Cozumel and the Belizean cayes have the barrier reef and thus the best diving to look at tropical fish, coral and undersea flora. If you plan to dive, bring evidence of your certification to show the dive shop people, and check the rental equipment over carefully before you dive.

Guatemala's Pacific coast is relatively undeveloped, and water sports possibilities are not nearly as attractive as they are along the Caribbean. Likewise, the beaches and waters along Mexico's Gulf coast often leave something to be desired (usually cleanliness). The north coast of the Yucatán peninsula has some beaches, most notably at Progreso, but it also has mangrove swamps, shallow waters, and – in certain places – crocodile-like beasts called caymans.

Hiking & Climbing

Much of the region is flat, flat, flat, and tropical jungle to boot, not the most interesting trekking country. The exceptions are the highlands of Chiapas and Guatemala, which have excellent hiking possibilities and many picturesque volcanoes to climb. The best base for hikes into the forests and jungles of Chiapas is San Cristóbal de las Casas. Treks on horseback may be organised here as well. In Guatemala you can climb the volcanoes bordering Lago de Atitlán, though caution is in order as rural areas hereabouts harbour guerrillas and robbers. The volcanoes near Antigua in Guatemala also offer excellent possibilities, but see the warning in the Guatemala's Highlands chapter for information on how to find out whether or not it is currently safe to climb.

Language Courses

Spanish-language courses are given in San Cristóbal de las Casas, Chiapas (Mexico), and in Antigua (Guatemala), both of which are delightful cities in which to spend some time. I have not sampled the instruction in either place, and thus do not feel that I should recommend any particular school or course. Write in advance to the tourist offices in both cities, asking for brochures and information on the courses available. If you discover a course or school which offers good value – or is to be avoided – please write and let me know so that I can advise other readers.

HIGHLIGHTS

The top sights of La Ruta Maya are among the most fascinating on the planet, but some of the most enjoyable and memorable travel experiences happen in small towns and villages off the beaten track, places like Cobán, Guatemala, or San Ignacio, Belize, or Isla Mujeres, Quintana Roo. Just because these lesser known spots are not mentioned below does not mean they are unworthy of your time.

Cities & Towns

The first rank for charm, ambience and interesting things to do includes Mérida, San

Cristóbal de las Casas and Antigua Guatemala (usually just called Antigua). If you want to spend some time in cities, these are the ones to spend it in. They are, however, all on the tourist track. Should you want to get off it, spend a few days in Campeche, an attractive, authentic, very untouristy place with a rich history, beautiful architecture and low prices. Another good choice would be Valladolid, on the highway between Cancún and Chichén Itzá.

Pleasant small towns? First has to be Panajachel, on Guatemala's Lago de Atitlán, in the highlands. It's very touristy, and for good reason: the lake is breathtakingly beautiful, and the villages on its shores offer fascinating possibilities for meeting and getting to know the modern Maya. In Belize, the most pleasant place to spend a few days – apart from the wonderful cayes – is San Ignacio, on the banks of a peaceful river in the forests of the Maya Mountains.

Mayan Archaeological Sites

Without a doubt the top three sites are Chichén Itzá and Uxmal in Yucatán, and Tikal in Guatemala. If I had to name a fourth it would be Palenque, Chiapas, near the city of Villahermosa. These sites have the tallest pyramids, the most buildings, the boldest architecture and the best restoration. They are also the most visited.

If you enjoy having archaeological sites more or less to yourself, consider my favourites among the 'second rank': Kabah, Sayil and Xlapak on the Puuc Route south of Uxmal; Cobá, inland from Tulum; Edzná, near Campeche; Uaxactún, north of Tikal; and Quiriguá off Guatemala's Carretera al Atlantico (Atlantic Highway). Copán, just across the border from Guatemala in Honduras, is among the most important Mayan sites, and falls somewhere in between the first and second rank.

Museums

As for museums, the only top-class museums are the ones in Villahermosa, Tabasco and Guatemala City.

For Olmec lore – including the enormous basalt heads – the Parque Museo La Venta is worth the detour if you get as far as Palenque, only an hour or so east of Villahermosa by bus. And while you're in Villahermosa, take a tour through the good Museo Regional de Antropología Carlos Pellicer Cámara, which offers a competent introduction to Olmec and Mayan culture.

In Guatemala City, don't miss the Museo Popol Vuh, a superb private collection of pre-Columbian and colonial artefacts given to the university; also the Museo Ixchel, famous for its displays of exquisite traditional hand-woven textiles and other crafts still thriving in Guatemala.

ACCOMMODATION

Accommodation ranges from luxury resort hotels, tourist vacation hotels, budget hotels and motels to *casas de huéspedes* (guesthouses) and *albergues de la juventud* (youth hostels).

Hotels & Motels

The luxury resort hotels are mainly found in Cancún, though there are upper-class hostelries in Villahermosa, Guatemala City and Belize City as well. Some of the resorts on the Belizean cayes are positively sybaritic, with prices to match. They are all expensive but most offer excellent value for what you get compared to establishments of a similar class at home. Double room rates start at about US$80 per night and go beyond US$250. Most of the guests at these palatial places do not pay these 'rack rates', however, but are booked on package tours which offer far better value.

In the middle range are comfortable hotels and motels, some with appealing colonial ambience, others quite modern with green lawns, tropical flowers and swimming pools shaded by palm trees; still others are urban high-rise buildings with many services and comforts. These range in price from US$25 to US$80 or so, the higher prices being charged in the major cities.

Budget lodgings, those costing US$6 to US$25 a double, come in many varieties and degrees of comfort and cleanliness. Guatemala has the cheapest and simplest budget hotels and pensions, although as the country becomes more popular prices are rising; Belize has the most expensive ones, with quality not much higher than the Guatemalan ones. Mexico has a good range of options in all price ranges.

Casas de Huéspedes

The next cheapest option is the casa de huéspedes ('guesthouse'), a home converted into simple guest lodgings. A double can cost anywhere from US$10 to US$20 with or without meals.

Youth Hostels

Mexico's government-run albergues de la juventud or youth hostels are associated with the International Youth Hostel Association (IYHA). IYHA cards can be used for admission. The charge is US$6 to US$8 per night. Guatemala and Belize do not really have any usable official hostels.

Camping

You can camp for free on most beaches, though you must be careful to pick a safe place far from thieves. Wherever facilities are available for campers, though, expect to pay from US$3 to US$15 per night, depending upon the facilities and the choiceness of the location. Most equipped campgrounds are trailer parks designed for motor homes.

Cabañas & Hammocks

These are the two cheapest forms of accommodation, usually found in low-key beach spots. Cabañas are palm huts, sometimes with a dirt floor and nothing inside but a bed, other times more solidly built with electric light, mosquito nets, fans, even a cooker. Prices range from US$5 up to US$20 or even more for the most luxurious in the choicest spots.

You can rent a hammock and a place to hang it for less than US$4 in some beach places – usually under a palm roof outside a small casa de huéspedes or a fishing family's hut. If you bring your own hammock the cost may be even less. It's easy enough to buy hammocks in Mexico; Mérida has many shops specialising in them, and they are widely available in other towns throughout Yucatán as well.

FOOD

There are similarities among the cuisines throughout the region but there are also differences. Yucatecan cuisine is quite different from what is served in the rest of Mexico, with several distinctive ingredients such as turkey and venison. Guatemalan cooking, though derived from the same roots as Mexican, has regional specialities and variations. Belizean cooking tends to the rough and ready, reflecting its roots.

There are three meals a day: breakfast (el desayuno), lunch (la comida) and supper (la cena). Each includes one or more of three traditional staples:

Tortillas are thin round patties of pressed corn (maize) dough cooked on griddles. Tortillas may be wrapped around or topped with various foods. Fresh handmade tortillas are best, followed by fresh machine-made ones bought at a tortillería. Usually what one finds are fairly fresh ones kept warm in a hot, moist cloth. These are all right, but they take on a rubbery quality. Worst are old tortillas left to dry out; their edges curl and dry out while the centre could be used to patch a tyre. But don't confuse old tortillas with toasted, thoroughly dried, crisp tortillas, which are another thing altogether, and very good.

Frijoles are beans eaten boiled, fried, refried, in soups, spread on tortillas or with eggs. If you simply order frijoles they may come in a bowl swimming in their own dark sauce, as a runny mass on a plate, or as a thick and almost black paste. No matter how they come, they're usually delicious and very nutritious. The only bad ones are refried beans which have been fried using too much or low-quality oil.

Chillis (peppers) come in many varieties and are consumed in hundreds of ways. Some chillis such as the habanero and serrano are always spicy-hot while others such as the poblano vary in spiciness according to when they were picked. If you are unsure about your tolerance for hot chillis, ask if the chilli is *picante* (spicy-hot) or *muy picante* (very spicy-hot).

For full lists of menu items with translations, see the Menu Translator at the back of this book.

Meals

Breakfast This can be either continental or US-style. A light, continental-style breakfast can be made of sweet rolls *(pan dulce)* or toast and coffee. Often a basket of pan dulce will be placed on your breakfast table when your coffee is served. When the time comes to pay, you tell the clerk how many you have eaten.

US-style breakfasts are always available: bacon or sausage and eggs, hot cakes (called just that: *hot cakes* in Mexico, *panqueques* in Guatemala), cold cereal such as corn flakes or hot cereal such as oatmeal, cream of wheat, fruit juice and coffee. You may order eggs in a variety of ways (see the Menu Translator).

Lunch This, the biggest meal of the day, is served about 1 or 2 pm. In restaurants which do not cater primarily to tourists, menus might change every day, every week or not at all. Meals might be ordered à la carte or table d'hôte. A fixed-price meal of several courses called a *comida corrida* (the bargain or daily special meal) is sometimes offered, and may include from one to five or six courses; choices and price are often displayed near the front door of the restaurant. Simple comidas corridas may consist of a plain soup or pasta, a garnished main course plate and coffee; more expensive versions may have a fancy soup or ceviche, a choice main course such as steak or fish, salad, dessert and coffee.

Supper La cena is a lighter version of lunch served about 7.30 pm. In beach resorts the evening meal tends to be the big one, as everyone is out at the beach during the day, and they hardly want to drag themselves inside for a big meal.

Local Cuisine

For details on each country's cuisine, see under Food in the Facts for the Visitor chapter of each country.

DRINKS

Because of the hot climate in many parts of the region, you will find yourself drinking lots of fluids. Indeed, you must remember to drink even if you don't feel particularly thirsty in order to prevent dehydration and heat exhaustion (see the Health section in this chapter).

Water & Soft Drinks

Bottled or purified water is widely available in hotels and shops (see Food & Water in the Health section). You can also order safe-to-drink fizzy mineral water by saying 'soda'.

Besides the easily recognisable and internationally known brands of *refrescos* (soft drinks) such as Coca-Cola, Pepsi and Seven-Up, you will find interesting local flavours. Orange *(naranja)* flavoured soda is very popular, and grapefruit *(toronja)* is even better, though less readily available. Squirt (pronounced SKWEERT) is a Mexican brand of lemon-flavoured soda which is a bit drier than Seven-Up. Also in Mexico, try the two apple-flavoured drinks named Sidral and Manzanita.

Coffee, Tea & Cocoa The Soconusco region along the Pacific slope of Chiapas and Guatemala has many large coffee plantations which produce excellent beans, including those typed as Guatemalan Antigua and Maragogipes. Some hotels in Antigua have coffee bushes growing right on their grounds (so to speak). Coffee is available everywhere, strong and flavourful in Mexico, surprisingly weak and sugary in some parts of Guatemala.

Black tea *(té negro)*, usually made from bags (often locally produced Lipton), tends to be a disappointment to devoted tea drinkers. It's best to bring your own supply of loose tea and a tea infuser, then just order *una taza de agua caliente* (a cup of hot water) and brew your own.

Herbal teas are much better. Camomile tea *(té de manzanilla)* is a common item on restaurant and café menus, and is a specific remedy for queasy stomach and gripy gut.

Hot chocolate or cocoa was the royal stimulant during the Classic period of Mayan civilisation, being drunk on ceremonial occasions by the kings and nobility. Their version was unsweetened and dreadfully bitter. Today it's sweetened and, if not authentic, at least more palatable.

Fruit & Vegetable Juices

Fresh fruit and vegetable juices *(jugos)*, milkshakes *(licuados)* and flavoured waters *(aguas frescas)* are popular drinks, but particularly in Mexico. Almost every town has a stand serving one or more of these, and Mérida seems to have one every few blocks. All of the fruits and a few of the squeezable vegetables mentioned are used either individually (as in jugos or aguas frescas) or in some combination (as in licuados).

The basic licuado is a blend of fruit or juice with water and sugar. Other items can be added or substituted: raw egg, milk, ice, flavourings such as vanilla or nutmeg. The delicious combinations are practically limitless.

Aguas frescas are made by mixing fruit juice or a syrup made from mashed grains or seeds with sugar and water. You will usually see them in big glass jars on the counters of juice stands. Try the *agua fresca de arroz* (literally rice water) which has a sweet nutty taste.

Alcohol

Supermarkets, grocery shops and liquor stores stock both beer and wine, both imported and locally made. Some of the local stuff is quite good. You certainly won't go thirsty, and drinking won't bust your budget. But remember that excessive alcohol intake is a very efficient way to become dehydrated in the hot climate of the region. If you want to get drunk, make sure you take in plenty of non-alcoholic fluids as well.

Beer Breweries were first established in Mexico and Guatemala by German immigrants in the late 19th century. European techniques and technology have been used ever since the beginning, which may explain why Mexico has so many delicious beers, both light and dark. Most beers *(cervezas)* are light lagers, served cold from bottles or cans, but there are also a few flavourful dark beers such as Modelo Negro (Mexico) and Moza (Guatemala).

Mexico's breweries now produce more than 25 brands of beer including major labels such as Modelo, Superior, Corona, Bohemia and Carta Blanca. Local beers made in Yucatán include the lagers Carta Clara and Montejo, and the dark León Negro.

Guatemala's two nationally distributed beers are Gallo (GAH-yoh, rooster) and Cabro (goat). The distribution prize goes to Gallo – you'll find it everywhere.

In Belize, Belikin beer is the cheapest, most popular local brew. Belikin Export, the premium version, comes in a larger bottle, is much tastier, costs more, and is worth it. When you get sick of Belikin you can readily find US and European beers (Heineken, Löwenbrau, etc), but they cost considerably more.

In restaurants and bars unaccustomed to tourists, beer is sometimes served at room temperature. If you want to be sure of getting a cold beer, ask for *una cerveza fría*. Sometimes the waiter or bartender will hand you the bottle or can and let you feel it for proper coldness. This usually means it's not very cold, and your choice is then the dismal one of 'this beer or no beer at all'.

Wine Wine is not the local drink of choice. That distinction goes to beer and liquor made from sugar cane, by far. But as foreign wine lovers spread through the region, so does the availability of wine.

Mexico has three big wineries producing very drinkable vintages: Industrias Vinicolas Domecq, Formex-Ybarra and Bodegas de Santo Tomás.

Domecq is renowned in Mexico for its Los Reyes table wines. Formex has more than 800 acres of vineyards in the Valle de Guadalupe and is known for its Terrasola table wine. Santo Tomás hopes eventually to produce wines which can compete with California's, including varietal wines such as Pinot Noir, Chardonnay and Cabernet Sauvignon.

The situation in Guatemala and Belize is much worse. Local wines are no thrill to drink, and imported wines are fairly expensive, but at least they're available. In all but the best places you may have to specify that you want your red wine at room temperature and your white wine chilled.

Spirits The traditional Mayan ardent spirit in Yucatán is *xtabentún* (SHTAH-behn-TOON), an anise-flavoured brandy which, when authentic, is made by fermenting honey. The modern version has a goodly proportion of grain neutral spirits, however. It is made to be either dry *(seco)* or sweet *(crema)*. The seco tastes much like the Greek ouzo or French pastis; the crema is like the sweeter Italian Sambuca. It is served in some restaurants as an after dinner drink; you can find it readily in many liquor shops in Mérida, Cancún, and other Yucatecan towns.

Many other famous liquors, liqueurs and brandies are made in Mexico: Bacardi rum, Pedro Domecq brandy, Controy (orange liqueur, a knock-off Cointreau), Kahlua (coffee-flavoured liqueur) and Oso Negro vodka. All are of good quality and quite inexpensive. Tequila and mezcal, made from the maguey plant, come from 'mainland' Mexico (outside Yucatán).

Rum and *aguardiente* (sugar cane liquor) are the favourite strong drinks in Guatemala and Belize as well, and though most are of low price and matching quality, some local products are exceptionally fine. Zacapa Centenario is a very smooth Guatemalan rum made in Zacapa, off the Atlantic Highway. Aged 23 years, it should be sipped slowly, neat, like fine cognac. Cheaper rums and brandies are often mixed with soft drinks to make potent but cooling drinks like the *Cuba libre* of rum and Coke.

Other drinks include gin, mixed with tonic water, ice and lime juice to make what many consider the perfect drink for the hot tropics, and whisky, mostly from the USA.

ENTERTAINMENT

Cancún offers lots of nightclubs, bars, dancing places, spectacles, booze cruises and razzamatazz, all slickly packaged and marketed to the one-week tour crowd. Prices are high (for Mexico), but most people feel they get their money's worth, because the staff are certainly experienced at what they do. Some of the middle-range restaurants in Ciudad Cancún also provide entertainment – a pair of troubadours, a trio of mariachis, a lasso twirler – at no extra cost.

The only other place in the entire region with good nightclubs is Guatemala City. In smaller cities and towns it is not unusual to find a strolling guitarist or other musician(s) entertaining in the better restaurants.

Cinemas are located in the larger cities. Except in Belize, virtually all movies are in Spanish.

THINGS TO BUY

Most *artesanías* (handicrafts) originated in objects made for everyday use or for specific occasions such as festivals. Today many objects are made simply to sell as 'folk art' – some purely decorative, others with a useful function – but that doesn't necessarily reduce their quality. Although traditional materials, particularly textiles, are rarer than they used to be, some artisans have used the opportunity to develop their artistic talents to high levels.

The places where crafts are made aren't always the best places to buy them. There's wide trade in artesanías and you'll often find a better selection in shops and markets in towns and cities than in the original villages. Nor do prices necessarily get much higher in the bigger centres. Indeed, the artisans who make these crafts have learned that the real markets for their wares are in cities such as Mérida, San Cristóbal de las Casas, Panajachel and Antigua Guatemala where there are lots of appreciative tourists interested in buying.

You can get a good overview of the best

that's available and an idea of prices by looking round some of the city stores devoted to these products. Buying in these places also saves the time and effort of seeking out the sometimes remote towns and villages where items are made. The government-run shops in several cities usually have good ranges of high-quality stock at decent prices.

Hammocks

Whether or not you plan to follow the Yucatecan custom of bedding down in a hammock, you should plan to take one home for lazy summer afternoons. Yucatecan hammocks are woven of fine cotton string, natural in tone or dyed in pale colours. With their hundreds of strings they are supremely comfortable and cool, and very cheap. For details, refer to the Mérida chapter, as that city is the centre of the hammock trade.

Textiles

Colourful hand-woven and embroidered Indian costumes come in a number of basic shapes and as many designs as there are weavers. Chiapas and the Guatemalan highland towns have the best work and the widest selection. Some of the finest huipiles are made in the villages around Lago de Atitlán and in the villages near Antigua. Cheaper than the fairly pricey huipiles are the colourful waist sashes (fajas).

Other Woven Goods

Many goods are woven all over the country from palm, straw, reeds or sisal (rope made from the henequen plant). Mérida is a centre for sisal mats, hammocks, bags and hats.

Pottery

This comes in a huge variety of local forms. There are basically two types – unglazed earthenware and sturdier, Spanish-influenced, often highly decorated glazed ware. You can pick up attractive items for a couple of dollars or less in many places. The village of Amatenango del Valle turns out earthenware jugs, vases and animals, fired not in kilns but in open fires, and painted in pleasing 'natural' colours.

Wooden Masks

Ceremonial masks are fascinating, eye-catching, and still in regular use. You'll see them in the markets in San Cristóbal de Las Casas, Panajachel, Sololá, Chichicastenango and Antigua.

Getting There & Away

The easiest approach to the region, and the one most travellers use, is by air. The region's major international airports are at Cancún and Guatemala City, with a small but growing amount of international traffic heading for Belize City. Mexico City also receives a large number of flights from all parts of the world, with connecting flights to points along La Ruta Maya.

Approaches by road from Mexico and Central America (El Salvador and Honduras) are easy, with fairly good roads, and frequent service in comfortable (though not luxurious) buses.

Amtrak and Southern Railways trains approach the US-Mexican border along the Rio Grande, and there are some good Mexican trains from border towns southwards to Mexico City. But beyond the Isthmus of Tehuantepec train service is slow, unreliable, uncomfortable and often unsafe. There is no passenger train service connecting Guatemala with the rest of Central America.

There is no regular car or passenger ferry service between the region and the USA or Central America.

AIR
Routes
International air routes are structured so that virtually all flights into the region from the rest of the world pass through half a dozen 'hub' cities: Dallas/Fort Worth, Houston, Los Angeles, Miami, Mexico City or San Salvador. If you begin your trip in any other city you will probably find yourself stopping in one of these hub cities to change planes, and perhaps airlines, before continuing to your destination.

Mayan Route Tickets
Several of the Central American airlines such as Aviateca, Lacsa and Sahsa offer special combination tickets. Such a ticket

allows you to fly from a gateway (usually Miami, New Orleans or Houston) to the region, make stops in several places, then fly home. Sahsa's US$400 Mayan Tour ticket is one such; the US$500 Eco-Tour ticket includes Costa Rica as well as the other Central American countries. Aviateca's Mayan Path fares are similar. Call the airlines or your travel agent for details on current pricing.

Discount Tickets
Buying airline tickets these days is like shopping for a car, a stereo or a camera – five different travel agents will quote you five different prices. Rule number one if you're looking for a cheap ticket is to go to an agent, not directly to the airline. The airline can only quote you the absolutely straight-up-and-down, by-the-rule-book regular fare. An agent, on the other hand, can offer all sorts of special deals, particularly on competitive routes.

Ideally an airline would like to fly all their flights with every seat in use and every passenger paying the highest fare possible. Fortunately life usually isn't like that and airlines would rather have a half-price passenger than an empty seat. Since the airline itself can't very well offer seats at two different prices, what they do when faced with the problem of too many seats is let agents sell them at cut prices.

Of course what's available and what it costs depends on what time of year it is, what route you're flying and which airline you're flying. If you want to visit the region at the most popular time of year you'll probably have to pay more. If you're flying on a popular route or one where the choice of flights is very limited, then the fare is likely to be higher or there may be nothing available but the official fare.

Similarly, the dirt-cheap fares are likely to be less conveniently scheduled, go by a less convenient route or with a less popular airline.

Round-the-World Tickets

Round-the-World (RTW) tickets are very popular. Should you be coming to the region from far away, you might just want to keep going and circle the globe. Often the cost is not much different from a long return fare.

The official airline RTW tickets are usually put together by a combination of two airlines, and permit you to fly anywhere you want on their route systems so long as you do not backtrack. Other restrictions are that you (usually) must book the first sector in advance and cancellation penalties then apply. There may be restrictions on how many stops you are permitted and usually the tickets are valid from 90 days up to a year. Typical prices for these RTW tickets are from £1400 to £1700 or US$2500 to US$3000.

An alternative type of RTW ticket is one put together by a travel agent using a combination of discounted tickets. A UK agent like Trailfinders can put together interesting London to London RTW combinations for £850 to £1000.

To/From North America

American, Continental, Delta, Northwest and United are the US airlines with the most service to La Ruta Maya. Aeroméxico, Aeroquetzal, Aeronica, Aviateca, Belize Trans Air, COPA, LACSA, Mexicana and TACA are the Latin American airlines with flights to the USA.

You can fly nonstop to Cancún from any of these North American cities: Baltimore, Chicago, Dallas/Fort Worth, Denver, Detroit, Houston, Los Angeles, Miami, New Orleans, New York, Philadelphia, San Francisco, Tampa/St Petersburg and Washington, DC.

Fares There are dozens of airfares which apply to any given air route. They vary with each company, class of service, season of the year, length of stay, dates of travel, date of purchase and reservation. Your ticket may cost more or less depending upon the flexibility you are allowed in changing your plans. The price of the ticket is even affected by how you buy it and from whom.

Travel agents are the first people to consult about fares and routes. Once you've discovered the basics of the airlines flying, the routes taken and the various discounted tickets available, you can consult your favourite bucket shop, consolidator or charter airline to see if their fares are better. Here are some sample fixed-date return fares (also called excursion fares) from various cities to Cancún:

Chicago	US$427
Dallas/Fort Worth	US$350
Los Angeles	US$350
Miami	US$229
New York	US$446
Toronto	US$399

Besides these excursion fares, there are many package tours from the USA which typically provide a round-trip (return) airfare, transfers and accommodation for a few days or a week. These are by far the most economical way to visit Cancún. Some of these tour packages allow you to extend your stay in order to tour the region on your own.

These package tours change in price and features as the seasons change. For a cheap flight to Cancún, read the advertisements in the travel section of your local newspaper and call a package tour operator, or a travel agent who sells such tours, and ask if you can buy 'air only' (just the round-trip air transportation, not the hotel or other features). Often this is possible, and usually it is cheaper than buying a discounted excursion ticket. Sometimes, though, the difference between air-only and a tour package with hotels is so small that it makes sense just to accept the hotel along with the flight. To a limited extent, this is also true of package tours to Guatemala and Belize.

Consolidators are organisations that buy

bulk seats from airlines at considerable discounts and then resell them to the public, usually through travel agents. Though there are some shady dealers, many consolidators are quite legitimate. Consolidators in North America are similar to bucket shops in Europe. Ask your travel agent about buying a consolidator ticket, or look for the consolidator adverts in the travel section of the newspaper (they're the ones with tables of destinations and fares and a toll-free '800' number to call).

Cancún is easy to reach cheaply; it's a bit more difficult to find air-only fares to Guatemala City and Belize.

To/From Canada

Japan Airlines' one-month excursion return fare between Vancouver and Mexico City is good value at US$399. Aeroméxico has non-

---

Air Travel Glossary

Apex Apex, or 'advance purchase excursion' is a discounted ticket which must be paid for in advance. There are penalties if you wish to change it.

Baggage Allowance This will be written on your ticket: usually one 20 kg item to go in the hold, plus one item of hand luggage.

Bucket Shop An unbonded travel agency specialising in discounted airline tickets.

Bumped Just because you have a confirmed seat doesn't mean you're going to get on the plane - see Overbooking.

Cancellation Penalties If you have to cancel or change an Apex ticket there are often heavy penalties involved, insurance can sometimes be taken out against these penalties. Some airlines impose penalties on regular tickets as well, particularly against 'no show' passengers.

Check In Airlines ask you to check in a certain time ahead of the flight departure (usually 1½ hours on international flights). If you fail to check in on time and the flight is overbooked the airline can cancel your booking and give your seat to somebody else.

Confirmation Having a ticket written out with the flight and date you want doesn't mean you have a seat until the agent has checked with the airline that your status is 'OK' or confirmed. Meanwhile you could just be 'on request'.

Discounted Tickets There are two types of discounted fares - officially discounted (see Promotional Fares) and unofficially discounted. The lowest prices often impose drawbacks like flying with unpopular airlines, inconvenient schedules, or unpleasant routes and connections. A discounted ticket can save you other things than money - you may be able to pay Apex prices without the associated Apex advance booking and other requirements. Discounted tickets only exist where there is fierce competition.

Full Fares Airlines traditionally offer first class (coded F), business class (coded J) and economy class (coded Y) tickets. These days there are so many promotional and discounted fares available from the regular economy class that few passengers pay full economy fare.

Lost Tickets If you lose your airline ticket an airline will usually treat it like a travellers' cheque and, after inquiries, issue you with another one. Legally, however, an airline is entitled to treat it like cash and if you lose it then it's gone forever. Take good care of your tickets.

No Shows No shows are passengers who fail to show up for their flight, sometimes due to unexpected delays or disasters, sometimes due to simply forgetting, sometimes because they made more than one booking and didn't bother to cancel the one they didn't want. Full fare passengers who fail to turn up are sometimes entitled to travel on a later flight. The rest of us are penalised (see Cancellation Penalties).

On Request An unconfirmed booking for a flight, see Confirmation.

stop flights between Acapulco and Montréal and Toronto.

To/From Central & South America & the Caribbean

Aeroméxico flies between Mexico City and Panama City, Caracas and Bogotá. Mexicana links Mexico City with Guatemala City, San Juan (Puerto Rico), Havana (Cuba) and San José (Costa Rica); it also has flights between San Juan and Cancún, and Havana and

Mérida. Avianca, the Colombian airline, also links Mexico with South America. Cubana flies between Havana and Mexico City.

To/From Europe

Few European airlines fly directly to points within the region. Most take you to one of the US hub cities, where you change to a plane of a US, Mexican, Guatemalan or other Central American airline. Your flight then continues to Cancún, Chetumal, Cozumel,

---

Open Jaws A return ticket where you fly out to one place but return from another. If available this can save you backtracking to your arrival point.

Overbooking Airlines hate to fly empty seats and since every flight has some passengers who fail to show up (see No Shows) airlines often book more passengers than they have seats. Usually the excess passengers balance those who fail to show up but occasionally somebody gets bumped. If this happens guess who it is most likely to be? The passengers who check in late.

Promotional Fares Officially discounted fares like Apex fares which are available from travel agents or direct from the airline.

Reconfirmation At least 72 hours prior to departure time of an onward or return flight you must contact the airline and 'reconfirm' that you intend to be on the flight. If you don't do this the airline can delete your name from the passenger list and you could lose your seat. You don't have to reconfirm the first flight on your itinerary or if your stopover is less than 72 hours. It doesn't hurt to reconfirm more than once. [Restrictions] Discounted tickets often have various restrictions on them - advance purchase is the most usual one (see Apex). Others are restrictions on the minimum and maximum period you must be away, such as a minimum of 14 days or a maximum of one year. See Cancellation Penalties.

Standby A discounted ticket where you only fly if there is a seat free at the last moment. Standby fares are usually only available on domestic routes.

Tickets Out An entry requirement for many countries is that you have an onward or return ticket, in other words, a ticket out of the country. If you're not sure what you intend to do next, the easiest solution is to buy the cheapest onward ticket to a neighbouring country or a ticket from a reliable airline which can later be refunded if you do not use it.

Transferred Tickets Airline tickets cannot be transferred from one person to another. Travellers sometimes try to sell the return half of their ticket, but officials can ask you to prove that you are the person named on the ticket. This is unlikely to happen on domestic flights, on an international flight tickets may be compared with passports.

Travel Agencies Travel agencies vary widely and you should ensure you use one that suits your needs. Some simply handle tours while full-service agencies handle everything from tours and tickets to car rental and hotel bookings. A good one will do all these things and can save you a lot of money but if all you want is a ticket at the lowest possible price, then you really need an agency specialising in discounted tickets. A discounted ticket agency, however, may not be useful for other things, like hotel bookings.

Travel Periods Some officially discounted fares, Apex fares in particular, vary with the time of year. There is often a low (off-peak) season and a high (peak) season. Sometimes there's an intermediate or shoulder season as well. At peak times, when everyone wants to fly, not only will the officially discounted fares be higher but so will unofficially discounted fares or there may simply be no discounted tickets available. Usually the fare depends on your outward flight - if you depart in the high season and return in the low season, you pay the high-season fare. ■

Guatemala City, Mérida, Tuxtla Gutiérrez or Villahermosa.

The most common types of ticket from Europe to the region are one ways, fixed-date returns, open returns, circle trips and ticketed surface sectors. Most of them are available at discount rates from cheap ticket agencies in Europe's bargain flight centres like London, Amsterdam, Paris and Frankfurt.

Fixed-date returns require you to decide dates of travel when you buy the ticket. Open tickets allow you to choose your dates later; they're usually valid for 180 days or a year and are a bit more expensive than fixed-date returns. Circle trips and surface sectors are useful if you want to travel from one part of the region to another, or between points within the region and elsewhere on the American continent, without backtracking.

On both you usually depart from and return to the same city in Europe: circle trips give you flights between your different destinations within the region or Latin America en route, while with surface sectors you make your own way between your entry and exit points in Latin America. Some bargain fares are only open to students, teachers or people under 26. Fares can also vary considerably between high and low seasons.

United Kingdom For cheap tickets from London, pick up a copy of *City Limits, Time Out, TNT* or any of the other magazines which advertise discount (bucket shop) flights, and check out a few of the advertisers. The magazine *Business Traveller* also has a great deal of good advice on air fare bargains. Most bucket shops are trustworthy and reliable but the occasional sharp operator appears – *Time Out* and *Business Traveller* give some useful advice on precautions to take.

Agents which offer cheap fares to Mexico include Journey Latin America (☎ (081) 747-3108) at 16 Devonshire Rd, Chiswick, London W4 2HD (this company also has an information service for its customers and runs some small-group tours to Mexico); STA Travel (☎ (071) 581-1022) at 74 Old Brompton Rd, London W1 and 117 Euston

Rd, London NW1; and London Student Travel (☎ (071) 730-3402) at 52 Grosvenor Gardens, London SW1.

An unusual and potentially interesting route to Mexico is via Paris and Havana with the Cuban airline Cubana. Journey Latin America quotes around US$650 one-way, US$1050 return for this.

Elsewhere in Europe Discount tickets are available at prices similar to London's in several European cities. Amsterdam, Paris and Frankfurt are among the main cheap flight centres. Air France, KLM, Iberia and the Colombian airline Avianca are some of the airlines whose tickets are handled by discount agents. KLM, Air France and Iberia all offer surface sector fares between Europe and numerous places in Latin America (Iberia's are particularly good value), and Avianca has some interesting round-trip options.

Here are some typical fixed-date return (excursion) fares to Cancún valid at the time of writing:

Amsterdam	US$715
Frankfurt	US$929
London	US$915
Paris	US$880

To/From Australasia
There are no direct flights from Australia to the region. The cheapest way of getting there is via the USA – often Los Angeles. Discount returns from Sydney to Los Angeles cost from A$1200. Cheap flights from the USA to the region are hard to find in Australia. The cheapest Los Angeles/Cancún fares are US$350 return. There are also numerous flights between North American cities and several other destinations within the region (see To/From North America).

If you want to combine a visit to the Mayan region with South America, the cheapest return tickets from Sydney to Lima or Rio de Janeiro are about A$2100. Santiago and Buenos Aires are a little cheaper at about A$1800. If you want to fly into South America and out of the USA, or vice-versa, the best option is to get a return ticket to South America on an airline such as United, which flies to South America via the USA, and simply don't use one of the legs you have paid for. Fortunately, at the time of writing, United's fares for this route were much the same as those of airlines which go directly to South America – discount returns via the USA from Sydney to Buenos Aires, Lima, Santiago or Rio de Janeiro were all available at around A$2130.

Round-the-world tickets with a Mexico/Guatemala option are sometimes available in Australia. STA Travel, with 40 offices around the country, is one of the most popular discount travel agents in Australia. It also has sales offices or agents all over the world.

Fixed-date return (excursion) fares to Cancún from Sydney, via Los Angeles, valid at the time of writing, are around A$2100. To Cancún via Los Angeles one way is A$1100.

A fixed date return (excursion) fare from Auckland, New Zealand, to South America stopping in Los Angeles, Mexico, Buenos Aires, Lima and Santiago, are around NZ$4516.

Departure Tax

A departure tax equivalent to approximately US$10 or US$12 is levied in each of these countries for travellers departing by air for foreign destinations. Exit tax at Belizean land border crossing points is BZ$1 (US$0.50).

LAND
Bus & Train

For details of buses and trains, see the Getting There & Away chapter for each country.

Car

For US and Canadian visitors, taking your own vehicle across the US-Mexico border is a practical and convenient option. The most apparent difficulty in driving your own vehicle is that most North American cars now have catalytic converters which require unleaded fuel. Unleaded fuel is available in many parts of Mexico, but not reliably so. In Guatemala and Belize it is not yet available. You can arrange to have your catalytic converter disconnected, and replaced with a straight piece of exhaust pipe soon after you cross into Mexico (it's illegal to have it done in the USA). Save the converter, and have it replaced before re-crossing the border into the USA.

Coming from overseas, you may want to buy a used car or van in the USA, where they're relatively cheap, drive through the USA to Mexico, and travel the entire Mayan region. One used to be able to sell a car at a profit in Belize, but now the procedures are more complicated and the duties much higher.

Importing Motor Vehicles To take a motor vehicle (car, motorcycle, boat, etc) into Mexico, Guatemala or Belize you will need: the car's current valid registration; proof that you own it (if the registration is in a different name) or, if you don't own it, a notarised affidavit of authorisation from the car's owner stating that you are allowed to take the car out of the USA; your current valid driving licence; and a temporary import permit from the local authorities.

Temporary import permits are normally issued for free at the border when you enter, but the issuance of a permit may require prior purchase of liability insurance. (See Motor Vehicle Insurance in each country's section for details.) In Mexico the permits are normally valid for 90 days; in Guatemala it's 30 days, in Belize the same.

You must have a permit for each vehicle that you bring into Mexico. For example, if you have a motorcycle attached to your car, you must also have a permit for the motorcycle, but there is a catch: one person cannot have more than one permit even if that person owns both vehicles. Consequently, another person travelling with you must obtain the second permit. As with all rules of this sort, though, they are not written in stone.

Another rule for drivers intending to travel

in Mexico: you cannot leave the country without your vehicle even if it breaks down, unless you obtain permission from either the Registro Federal de Vehículos (Federal Registry of Vehicles) in Mexico City or a Hacienda (Treasury Department) office in another city or town. Similar rules apply for Guatemala and Belize.

Don't drive someone else's car across the border. The car will be registered on your tourist card or in your passport, and you will not be permitted to leave the country without taking the car or paying a huge customs import duty. If you drive into Mexico, officials will take your tourist card and issue you a single document which serves as both motor vehicle permit and tourist card; both you and the car must leave Mexico at the same time, surrendering the document as you leave.

Motor Vehicle Insurance US, Canadian or any other 'foreign' motor vehicle liability insurance policies are not recognised as valid by the governments of Mexico, Guatemala or Belize – at least not until the North American Free Trade Agreement (NAFTA) comes into force. In each of these countries you must buy local insurance; thus if you drive your vehicle into all three countries, you will have to buy three separate policies. See each country's section for details.

CROSSING BORDERS
Most of the time and at most entry points, this is a breeze. If you fly into any of these countries you should have few, if any, hassles. If you cross at border points, you may run into other situations. There are a few things that you ought to know.

For more details on land border crossings, see the Getting There & Away sections for each country.

La Mordida
Border officials in Latin American countries sometimes request small 'tips' or unofficial 'fees' from travellers at the border. Usually the *mordida*, the 'bite', is put on you in an official tone of voice: the officer will scribble something on your tourist card, or in a ledger, or stamp your passport, or do some other little action, then say, 'Too dallah'. When crossing from one Latin American country to another, the officials on both sides of the border may play this little game, causing you to part with a quantity of cash before you're finally through the formalities. There are several things you can do to avoid paying.

The first is to look very important by dressing in a suit and tie or other such intimidating clothing. If you are male, wearing dark sunglasses (a favourite expression of machismo, or manliness) can help.

The second is to scowl quietly and act worldly-wise. Scowl all you want, but whatever you do, keep everything formal. Never, *ever* raise your voice, mumble a curse, get angry, or verbally confront a Latin American official. This will get you nowhere – except into deep trouble. Act quietly superior and unruffled at all times.

The third thing is to ask for a receipt, *un recibo*. Some fees are official and legitimate. If the fee is legitimate, you'll be given an official-looking receipt; often the official will show you the receipt booklet when he makes the request, to prove to you that the fee is legitimate. If you don't get a receipt, you've succumbed to the mordida, a tip or bribe.

The fourth thing is to offer some weird currency such as Thai baht or even Norwegian kroner or Dutch guilders or Australian dollars – anything but US dollars or the currency of either of the countries at the border. Border officials are usually used to seeing only US dollars (and some Canadian ones), Mexican pesos, Belizean dollars, Honduran lempiras and Guatemalan quetzals. At the sight of strange money the officer will probably drop the request. If he doesn't, or if the fee turns out to be legitimate, 'search' for several minutes in your belongings and come up with the dollars you need. In the unlikely event that the official will accept the unusual currency, inflate its value, declaring that a nearly worthless note is actually worth big bucks.

TOURS

General and special-interest tours are an increasingly popular way to explore the region. Following are a few of the tour operators which offer these trips.

From the USA

Travel agents at most USA agencies can arrange package deals with a variety of operators.

Pacific Adventures (☎ (714) 684-1227), PO Box 5041, Riverside, California 92517, offers trips oriented to horseback riding, kayaking, scuba diving and sailing.

Mayan Adventure Tours (☎ (206) 523-5309), PO Box 15204 Wedgwood Station, Seattle, Washington 98115-15204, offers unique tours of obscure Mayan sites which are not easily accessible. Small groups of nine to 12 travel in private vehicles and stay in local hotels. Among the trips are Chichén Itzá during the equinox, the Yucatán coast to coast, the indigenous crafts centres of Oaxaca and Guatemala, and hidden beaches of the Yucatán.

Expeditions Inc (☎ (817) 861-9298), PO Box 13594, Arlington, Texas 76094-0594, can take you to about 16 archaeological or colonial destinations in two weeks (send for prices).

From the UK

Journey Latin America (☎ (071) 747-3108), 16 Devonshire Rd, Chiswick, London W4 2HD, runs a few small-group tours using local transport in Mexico. One two-week trip costing around US$1600 from London takes in Mexico City, Teotihuacán, Oaxaca and nearby sites, San Cristóbal de Las Casas, Palenque, Mérida and some Mayan sites in Yucatán.

Explore Worldwide does a 24-night small-group trip with 'expert leaders', which includes Mexico City, Oaxaca, San Cristóbal de Las Casas, Palenque, Tikal, Belize City, Ambergris Cay, Mérida, Uxmal, Chichén Itzá, Sayil and Labná. The company has offices in Aldershot, England (☎ (025) 231 9448); Sydney, Australia (☎ (02) 290 3222); Remuera, Auckland, New Zealand (☎ 545-118); Edmonton, Canada (☎ (403) 439-9118); Oakland, California (☎ (415) 654-1879); and Hong Kong (☎ 5-225-181). From London the trip costs approximately US$2100.

WARNING

The information in this chapter is particularly vulnerable to change – prices for international travel are volatile, routes are introduced and cancelled, schedules change, rules are amended, special deals come and go, borders open and close. Airlines and governments seem to take a perverse pleasure in making price structures and regulations as complicated as possible and you should check directly with the airline or travel agent to make sure you understand how a fare (and ticket you may buy) works. In addition, the travel industry is highly competitive and there are many lurks and perks. The upshot of this is that you should get opinions, quotes and advice from as many airlines and travel agents as possible before you part with your hard-earned cash. The details given in this chapter should be regarded as pointers and are not a substitute for careful, up-to-date research.

Getting Around

In recent years the governments of Mexico, Guatemala and Belize have begun to cooperate in taking measures to facilitate travel throughout the lands of the Maya. Regional air service has improved dramatically, and you can now fly from Cancún directly to Belize City, Chichén Itzá, Tikal or Uxmal and return in a day. You can expect even more flights in years to come.

Bus travel has always been the most dependable means of travel within the region. Numerous private bus companies serve various segments of the region. Usually there are several companies serving the same route, giving you a choice of schedules, prices and comforts.

Unfortunately, car rental companies have yet to join this 'easy access' campaign. Rental cars are expensive in Yucatán, more expensive in Guatemala, and very expensive in Belize. In most cases you may not drive a rental car outside the national territory of the country in which you rented it (that is, you cannot drive it across a border). In those cases where you may drive across borders, you usually need permission in writing from the car rental company. Thus a plan to tour most of the region by rental car often involves different rentals in three countries, and bus or plane in between.

AIR

To really explore the region in detail, most of your travel must be on the ground (by bus or car). But certain parts of the route are best done by air in order to avoid long, hot and fairly boring rides.

For example, Tikal is tedious to reach by road (bus or car), so it makes sense to fly there from Guatemala City, Belize City or Cancún. If you're not particularly interested in spending time on Yucatán's Caribbean coast but you want to see Belize, fly between Cancún and Belize City.

Another long, hot trip to avoid is the one between Campeche and Villahermosa; you may want to return from Campeche and Uxmal to Mérida and fly to Villahermosa (for Palenque).

For details on air travel in the region, see each country's section.

BUS

The prevalent means of transport is bus. You can travel on a bus to 95% of the sites described in this book (the other 5% can be reached by boat or on foot). Bus travel can be fairly comfortable or very uncomfortable, but it is usually cheap.

In general, bus traffic is most intense in the morning (beginning as early as 4 or 5 am), tapering off by mid or late afternoon. In many places within the region there are no buses in the late afternoon or evening.

Routes to remote towns and villages are run for the convenience of villagers going to market in larger market towns. This often means that the only bus departs from the village early in the morning, and returns from the larger market town by mid-afternoon. If you want to visit the village, you may find that you must take this late afternoon bus and stay the night in the village, catching the bus back to the market town the

2nd-class bus travel in La Ruta Maya

next morning. Remote villages rarely have hotels, so you should be prepared to camp.

For details on getting around by bus, see each country's section.

TRAIN

Trains connect Mérida with Campeche, Palenque, Veracruz and other points in Mexico. They also run from Veracruz to Juchitan and along the Soconusco (Pacific coast of Chiapas) to Tapachula. From Ciudad Tecún Umán, across the border from Tapachula in Guatemala, trains run to Guatemala City.

All of these trains are very cheap, all are slow and unreliable, most are quite uncomfortable. Some are unsafe as sneak thieves and robbers work with train crew members to relieve foreign tourists of wallets and cameras. Trains in this region are more a means of high adventure than a means of comfortable, safe transport.

CAR

Private car, camper van or trailer/caravan is perhaps the best way to travel the region. You can go at your own pace and easily reach many areas not served by frequent public transport. The major roads and many of the minor roads are easily passable by any sort of car, and border crossings are fairly easy. But you need private motor vehicle insurance, an import permit and a car which uses leaded fuel or has had its unleaded-fuel catalytic converter removed. See the previous chapter (Getting There & Away) for details on bringing vehicles into the region.

HITCHING

Many people hitch in certain parts of the region. Often it's necessary as bus service is infrequent or nonexistent, particularly to the fairly remote Mayan archaeological sites. However, hitching is not necessarily free transport. In most cases, if you are picked up by a truck, you will be expected to pay a fare similar to that charged on the bus (if there is one). In some areas, pickup and flatbed stake trucks *are* the 'buses' of the region, and every rider pays. Your best bet for free rides is with other foreign tourists who have their own vehicles.

Hitching is never entirely safe in any country in the world, and we don't recommend it. Travellers who decide to hitch should understand that they are taking a small but potentially serious risk. People who do choose to hitch will be safer if they travel in pairs and let someone know where they are planning to go.

BOAT

Though there is no long-distance sea transport within the region, boats are used for public transport in a surprising number of locations.

Motor launches are the favoured means of transport on Guatemala's Lago de Atitlán, and dugout canoes take you up the Río Dulce and El Golfete to Lago de Izabal for a look at the wildlife. Dugouts are also used for excursions on Lago Petén Itzá around Flores (near Tikal).

Belize has the most transport by sea. Fast motor launches connect Belize City, Caye Chapel, Caye Caulker and Ambergris Caye several times daily. Other boats go to the many other cayes several times a week on scheduled services or by charter. There is a twice-weekly boat service connecting Punta Gorda, in southern Belize, with Lívingston and Puerto Barrios in Guatemala. In western Belize, boat, canoe or kayak trips along the rivers of Mountain Pine Ridge are mostly for fun, but also sometimes for transport when the rainy season has turned the unpaved roads to sloughs of mud.

In Mexico, ferryboats and hydrofoils connect the island of Cozumel to the mainland, and ferries run to Isla Mujeres as well. Charter boats and hired fishing boats take you to Isla Holbox and other small uninhabited islands off Yucatán's coast. In Chiapas, you can take a boatride through the stupendous Cañon del Sumidero. Boats also transport adventurous travellers down rivers between Palenque (Mexico) and Flores (Guatemala).

LOCAL TRANSPORT
Bus
Except for Belize City, all major cities and towns have public bus service. Buses are always the US schoolbus type of vehicle, usually rattly and uncomfortable, but always cheap, ranging from US$0.80 in Cancún to US$0.25 in Guatemala City. In most places the buses are insufficient to meet demand, and thus are packed solid at rush hours and perhaps at other times as well.

Jitney
Guatemala City has an extensive jitney cab network which becomes important at night after the city buses have ceased to run.

Taxi
Taxis are quite expensive, charging rates equal to or exceeding those in places like New York City. None have meters, so it's necessary to determine the price of the trip before setting out. Rates are set, but drivers will often try to rip you off by quoting a higher price. This means that you must usually resort to bargaining, or asking several drivers.

Bicycle
Sport bicycling is not yet popular. Roads are often not the smoothest, the sun can be relentless, and one may have to travel long distances between towns. Often there's not much to look at except the walls of jungle which hem in the road. Insects – both those that hit you in the face and those that eat you for lunch – are another disincentive.

This having been said, certain areas are beautiful for biking. The Guatemalan highlands have light traffic, decent roads and manageable distances between towns, but they also present the danger from robbers. Highland Chiapas is similar. Unless you like pedalling in the rain, though, plan your trip for the dry season (from October to May).

Horseback
Horse riding is not so much a means of transport as a means of pleasure, though in the back country of western Belize it is also eminently practical. Treks on horseback are possible in many places, including San Cristóbal de las Casas, Lake Atitlán, Flores, and Mountain Pine Ridge.

Guatemala

Facts about the Country

Guatemala is the heart of the Mayan world, a beautiful, fertile land with a tragic history.

The Maya who live in the highlands amidst breathtaking mountain scenery guard jealously their ancient customs and way of life. Holidays and ceremonies are filled with ancient pageantry, and the weekly markets are ablaze with the vivid colours of traditional handmade costumes.

At the same time, the modern world is penetrating Mayan culture, bringing good things and bad. Money from tourism is helping the Maya to improve their quality of life, education and health, but it is luring the younger generation away from their traditions and toward the raucous, bustling cities.

The distinction between indigenous and 'European' blood, between the traditional and the 'modern', culture and commerce, has been felt strongly here since the days of the

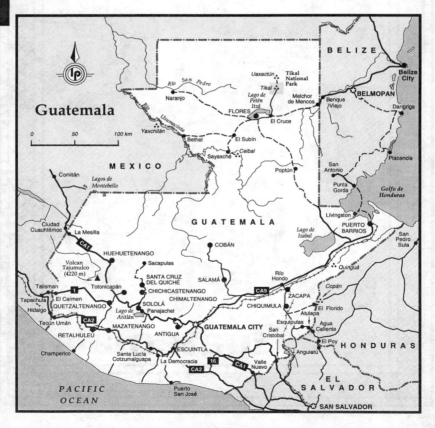

Conquistadors. Today the distinction divides Guatemalan society in two, and has led to oppression and bloody conflict often.

Traditional life and modern values also clash when local farmers and ranchers clear the rainforest to provide for their families. The need is for a livelihood; the method is the traditional one of slash-and-burn; the result is ecological disaster.

The paradoxes of Guatemala are part of its fascination, and part of the reason why you will fall in love with this place.

HISTORY

The history of the country since independence has been one of rivalry and struggle between the forces of left and right. The Liberals have historically wanted to turn backward Guatemala into an enlightened republic of political, social and economic progress. The Conservatives hoped to preserve the traditional verities of colonial rule, with a strong Church and a strong government. Their motto might have been 'power must be held by those with merit, virtue and property'. Historically, both movements have benefited the social and economic elites and disenfranchised the people of the countryside, mostly Maya.

Morazán & the Liberals

The Liberals, the first to advocate independence, opposed the vested interests of the elite Conservatives, who had the Church and the large landowners on their side.

During the short existence of the United Provinces of Central America, Liberal President Francisco Morazán (1830-39) instituted reforms aimed at correcting three persistent problems: the great economic, political and social power of the Church; the division of society into a Hispanic upper class and an Indian lower class; and the region's powerlessness in world markets. This Liberal programme was echoed by Guatemalan Chief of State Mariano Gálvez (1831-38).

But unpopular economic policies, heavy taxes and a cholera epidemic in 1837 led to an Indian uprising which brought a Conservative pig farmer, Rafael Carrera, to power. Carrera held power until 1865, and undid much of what Morazán and Gálvez had achieved. The Carrera government allowed Great Britain to take control of Belize in exchange for construction of a road between Guatemala City and Belize City. The road called for in the treaty was never built, and Guatemala's claims for compensation were never resolved.

Liberal Reforms of Barrios

The Liberals came to power again in the 1870s, first under Miguel García Granados, next under Justo Rufino Barrios, a rich young coffee *finca* (plantation) owner who held the title of president and ruled as a dictator (1873-79). With Barrios at its head the country made great strides toward modernisation with construction of roads, railways, schools, and a modern banking system. In order to boost the economy, everything possible was done to encourage coffee production. Peasants in good coffee-growing areas (up to 1400 metres altitude on the Pacific Slope) were forced off their lands to make way for new coffee fincas, and those living above 1400 metres (mostly Indians), were forced to contribute seasonal labour on the fincas, as on plantations during colonial times. Idealistic Liberal policies, championed by the British and often meant to benefit the common people, ended up oppressing them. Most of the benefits of the Liberal reform movement benefited the finca owners and the traders in the cities.

Succeeding governments generally pursued the same policies. Economic control of the country was by a small group of land-owning and commercial families, foreign companies were given generous concessions, opponents of the government were censored, imprisoned or exiled by the extensive police force, and the government apparatus was subservient to economic interests despite a liberal constitution.

Cabrera & Minerva

Manuel Estrada Cabrera ruled from 1898 to 1920, and his dictatorial style, while bring-

GUATEMALA

ing progress in technical matters, placed a heavy burden on all but the ruling oligarchy. He was, in a way, the Guatemalan version of Mexico's reviled dictator Porfirio Díaz. He fancied himself a bringer of light and culture to a backward land, styling himself the 'Teacher and Protector of Guatemalan Youth'.

He sponsored Fiestas de Minerva (Festivals of Minerva) in the cities, inspired by the Roman goddess of wisdom, invention and technology, and ordered construction of temples to Minerva, some of which still exist (as in Quetzaltenango). Guatemala was to become a 'tropical Athens'. At the same time, however, he looted the treasury, ignored the schools, and spent millions on the armed forces.

Jorge Ubico

When Estrada was overthrown, Guatemala entered a period of instability which ended in 1931 with the election of General Jorge Ubico as president. Ubico ruled as Cabrera had, but more efficiently. Though his word was law, he insisted on honesty in government, and he modernised the country's health and social welfare infrastructure. Debt peonage was outlawed, releasing the Indians from this servitude; but a new servitude of labour contributions to the government road-building programme was established in its place. Other public works projects included the construction of the vast presidential palace on the main plaza in Guatemala City, a fitting symbol of General Ubico's self-esteem.

In the 1940s Ubico dispossessed and exiled the great German coffee finca owners, and otherwise assumed a pro-Allied stance during the war, but at the same time he openly admired Spain's Generalissimo Francisco Franco. In 1944 he was forced to resign and go into exile.

Arévalo & Arbenz

Just when it appeared that Guatemalan politics was doomed to become a succession of well-intentioned but harsh dictators, the elections of 1945 brought a philosopher – Juan José Arévalo – to power. Arévalo, in power from 1945 to 1951, established the nation's social security system, a government bureau to look after Indian concerns, a modern public health system, and liberal labour laws. During his six years as president there were 25 coup attempts by conservative military forces – an average of one coup attempt every three months or less.

Arévalo was succeeded by Colonel Jacobo Arbenz Guzmán in 1951. Arbenz continued the policies of Arévalo, instituting an agrarian reform law that was meant to break up the large estates and foster high productivity on small individually owned farms. He also expropriated vast lands conceded to the United Fruit Company during the Estrada and Ubico years, but now held fallow. Compensation was paid, and the lands were to be distributed to peasants and put into cultivation for food. But the expropriation, supported by the Guatemalan Communist Party, set off alarms in Washington. The CIA organised an invasion from Honduras led by two exiled Guatemalan military officers, and Arbenz was forced to step down. The land reform never took place.

After Arbenz, the country had a succession of military presidents elected with the support of the officers' corps, business leaders, compliant political parties, and the Church. Violence became a staple of political life. Opponents of government power regularly turned up dead, not immediately, and not all at once, but eventually.

Recent Decades

During the 1960s and 1970s, Guatemalan industry developed at a fast pace, and society felt the effects. Most profits from the boom flowed upwards, labour union organisation put more stresses on the political fabric, and migration from the countryside to the cities, especially the capital, produced urban sprawl and slums.

As the pressures in society increased so did the violence of protest and repression, which led to the total politicisation of society. Everyone took sides, usually the poorer classes in the countryside versus the power elite in the cities.

Guatemala Today

In the early 1980s the military suppression of antigovernment elements in the countryside reached a peak. Alarming numbers of people, usually Indian men, were killed in the name of anti-insurgency, stabilisation and anticommunism. The bloodbath led to a cutoff of US military assistance to the Guatemalan government, which led in turn to the election in 1985 of a civilian president, Marco Vinicio Cerezo Arévalo, the candidate of the Christian Democratic Party.

Before turning over power to the civilians, the military ensured that its earlier activities would not be examined or prosecuted, and it established formal mechanisms for the military control of the countryside. There was hope that Cerezo's administration would temper the excesses of the power elite and the military and establish a basis for true democracy. When Cerezo's term ended in 1990, however, many people wondered if any real progress had been made.

President Cerezo was succeeded by Jorge Serrano Elías (1990-1993), an evangelical Christian who ran as the candidate of the conservative Movimiento de Acción Solidaria (Solidarity Action Movement). Serrano opened a dialogue with the URNG, the main guerrilla organisation, with the aim of bringing the decades-long civil war to an end.

When the talks collapsed, the mediator from the Catholic church blamed both sides for intransigence.

As Serrano's popularity declined, he came to depend more on the army for support. On 25 May 1993, after a series of student demonstrations and public protests over price rises and cuts in subsidies, Serrano carried out an *autogolpe* ('auto-coup'). Complaining that the country was sliding into chaos and that the Guatemalan congress was corrupt and infiltrated with narcotics traffickers, he dissolved congress and the Supreme Court of Justice and assumed extraordinary emergency powers.

While Guatemala is indeed a transshipment point for cocaine and heroin from Colombia bound for Mexico and the USA, this is nothing new; and some sources suspect the army of involvement in the drug trade.

The auto-coup was short-lived, however, as popular sentiment was against the move. After a tense few days Serrano was forced to flee into exile. Congress elected Ramiro de León Carpio, the Solicitor for Human Rights and an outspoken critic of the army's strongarm tactics, as the country's new president.

GEOGRAPHY

Guatemala covers an area of 109,000 square km with mountainous forest highlands and jungle plains.

Rigoberta Menchú Tum

Rigoberta Menchu, born in 1959 in Guatemala's southen highlands, lived the life of a typical young Mayan woman until the early 1980's, when the country's internal turmoil affected her tragically. By 1981 she had lost her father, mother and brother to the rampages carried out by the Guatemalan military in the name of 'pacification' of the countryside and the repression of guerilla movements.

Menchú fled to exile in Mexico, where she wrote her story, *I, Rigoberta Menchú*, which was translated and published throughout the world. While in Mexico, and after returning to Guatemala, she worked tirelessly in defence of the rights of indigenous peoples throughout Latin America.

In 1992, Rigoberta Menchú was awarded the Nobel Prize for Peace. The Nobel award provided her and her cause with international stature and support.

All Guatemalans were proud that one of their own had been recognised by the Nobel committee. In the circles of power, however, Menchú's renown was unwelcome, as she is seen as a 'troublemaker'. But among the indigenous people of Guatemala, she is the hero who brought worldwide recognition of their plight. ■

The western highlands linked by the Interamerican Highway are the continuation of Chiapas' Sierra Madre, and include 30 volcanoes reaching heights of 3800 metres in the Cuchumatanes range north-west of Huehuetenango. Land that has not been cleared for Mayan *milpas* (cornfields) is covered in pine forests. Many of the volcanoes are active or dormant, and you should not be surprised to see, some dark night, the red glow of volcanic activity above a distant mountaintop. All this volcanic activity means that this is an earthquake area as well. Major quakes struck in 1773, 1917 and 1976, and there are more to come.

The Pacific Slope of Guatemala is the continuation of Chiapas' Soconusco, with rich coffee, cacao, fruit and sugar plantations along the Pacific Highway (Carretera al Pacifico). Down along the shore the volcanic slope meets the sea, yielding vast beaches of black volcanic sand in a sweltering climate that is difficult to bear, even if you just sit and do nothing. It's great for growing grass, and rich grass is great for fattening cattle, which is what happens here.

South and east along the Interamerican Highway the altitude decreases to about 1500 metres at Guatemala City.

North of Guatemala City the highlands of Alta Verapaz gradually decline to the lowland of El Petén, which is the continuation of southern Yucatán. Petén's climate and topography is like that of Yucatán, hot and humid or hot and dry, depending upon the season. To the south-east of Petén is the valley of the Río Motagua, dry in some areas, moist in others. The Motagua Valley is rich in dinosaur bones, and is wonderful for growing bananas, as you'll see when you visit Quiriguá.

GOVERNMENT

Government in Guatemala has traditionally been one of beautiful theory and brutal reality. Always a constitutional democracy in form, Guatemala has been ruled by a succession of military strongmen ever since Pedro de Alvarado came and conquered the Maya in the 1500s. With a few notable exceptions

such as the administrations of Juan José Arévalo and Jacobo Arbenz Guzmán, Guatemala's government has been controlled for the benefit of the commercial, military, landowning and bureaucratic classes of society, leaving little power to the large number of Indians in the countryside. While the niceties of democracy are observed, real government often takes place by means of intimidation and secret military activities.

With true democracies appearing in Latin America during the 1980s, the election of Vinicio Cerezo Arévalo as president in 1985 was taken as a sign that true democracy might have a chance in Guatemala. However, Cerezo was unable to strengthen civilian government. Abuses of power by military factions continued. Though the presidential elections of 1990 brought a spirited political debate, they also exhibited a wide disparity of views among powerful political factions with high passions and strong ideas. President Jorge Serrano's autocoup of May 1993 was a step backward, a retreat from the democratic ideals which had so recently gained a tenuous footing in Guatemala.

One Guatemalan writer summed up his society this way: a bourgeoisie which doesn't invest in its country, but rather stashes its capital abroad; an incompetent, inept and corrupt political class; a leftleaning intellectual class which keeps to the realm of theory and which refuses to participate in politics because it equates politics with corruption; a political left wing which won't make peace or participate in the mainstream because it knows it has little chance of popular approval; a military class, divided into factions more or less rightist, which sees civil peace and democracy as endangering its claims to impunity, privilege and economic benefits; and a demoralised people who believe in neither their leaders nor the political process as means to make their country prosper.

ECONOMY

The Guatemalan highlands are given over to

agriculture, particularly corn, with some mining and light industry around the larger cities. The Pacific Slope has large coffee, citrus and sugar cane plantations worked by migrant labour from the highlands, and the Pacific coast has cattle ranches and some fishing villages. Coffee is the country's biggest export crop, followed by beef, cotton, cocoa, corn, beans, bananas, sugarcane, vegetables, flowers and fruits.

Guatemala City is the industrial and commercial centre of the country, a copy in miniature of Mexico City, its great sister to the north. Like Mexico City, Guatemala City has problems of immigration, pollution, congestion and street crime arising from its near-monopoly on the commercial life of the country.

Guatemala's Motagua Valley has some mining, but agriculture is most important here, with vast banana plantations. In the lush green hills of Alta Verapaz there are dairy farms, cardamom plantations and forests for timber.

El Petén depends upon tourism and farming for its livelihood, and the two are not happy together. The rapid growth of agriculture and cattle farming is a serious threat to the ecology of Petén, a threat that will have to be controlled if the forests of this vast jungle province are to survive. Tourism, on the other hand, is a positive factor here, providing alternative sources of income in jobs which depend upon the preservation of the ecology for success.

PEOPLE

In Guatemala's population of eight million people, the division between Mayan and Spanish descent is much stricter than in Mexico. Under Spanish rule, most of highland Guatemala was administered by the friars who came to convert the Maya. The friars did a great deal to protect the indigenous people from exploitation by the government authorities, and to preserve traditional Mayan society (though not Mayan religion). But the region around Guatemala City was directly administered by the colonial government without the softening effect of the friars' intervention, and the traditional life of the Maya was largely replaced by a hybrid culture that was neither Mayan nor strictly Hispanic. Interrelations produced a mestizo population known as *ladinos*, who had abandoned their Mayan traditions to adopt the Spanish ways, but who were not accepted into White Spanish society.

Today, Guatemala's Maya are proud of their Mayan heritage, and keep alive the ancient traditions and community practices which give meaning to their lives. Guatemalans of European blood are proud of their ancestry as well; they form the elite of the modern commercial, bureaucratic and military upper classes. Ladinos fill in the middle ground between the Old Guard White Hispanic, European and North American elite and the Mayan farmers and labourers. Ladinos are shopkeepers, merchants, traders, administrators, bureaucrats and especially politicians.

Facts for the Visitor

VISAS & EMBASSIES
Guatemalan Tourist Card

The Guatemalan tourist card is valid for three months from the date of entry to Guatemala. It carries a fee of US$5, payable when you receive the form; anything else is a bribe. You need only a tourist card, not a visa, if you are a citizen of Austria, Belgium, Canada, Denmark, Finland, France, Germany, Holland, Italy, Israel, Japan, Luxembourg, Norway, Spain, Sweden, Switzerland, the UK or the USA. If you are a citizen of Australia, New Zealand, another British Commonwealth or South American country, you should obtain a visa from a Guatemalan consulate before you arrive at the Guatemalan border or airport.

You will be asked to turn in your Guatemalan tourist card when you leave the country by air, or at the border crossing into any other country. If you cross into Honduras on a day pass to visit Copán, the Guatemalan Migración official will usually allow you to return to Guatemala and continue your journey using the same Guatemalan tourist card. For information on this, refer to the section on Copán.

Minors Travelling Alone

If you are under 18 years of age and travelling alone, technically you must have a letter of permission signed by both your parents and witnessed by a Guatemalan consular official in order to enter Guatemala. Call a Guatemalan Consulate if you have questions about this.

Guatemalan Embassies & Consulates

Some of the consulates mentioned here are actually honorary consuls or consular agencies. These posts can issue tourist cards and visas, but they refer more complicated matters to the nearest full consulate, or to the embassy's consular section. All the listings are for embassies unless noted.

Australia
  Guatemala does not maintain an embassy in Australia; contact the Guatemalan Embassy in Tokyo.
Austria
  Kantgasse 3, A-1010 Wien (☎ (222) 715-2970, 713-0713; fax 713-2421)
Belgium
  Blvd General Wahis 53, B-1030 Brussels (☎ (322) 736-0340; fax 736-1889)
Canada
  Embassy, 130 Albert St, Suite 1010, Ottawa, ON K1P 636 5G4 (☎ (613) 224-4322; fax 237-0492)
  Consulate, 615 Boulevard René-Lévesque Ouest, bureau 540, Montréal, QC (☎ (514) 393-9202; fax 874-0319)
  Consulate, 736 Granville St, Suite 1400, Vancouver (☎ (604) 682-4831
Costa Rica
  Avenida Primera, Calles 24 y 28, No 2493, San José (☎ 31-40-74, 31-66-54; fax 31-66-45)
El Salvador
  15 Avenida Norte 135, San Salvador (☎ 22-29-03, 71-22-25; fax 71-30-19)
France
  73 rue de Courcelles, F-75008 Paris (☎ 47-63-90-83, 42-27-78-63; fax 47-54-02-06)
Germany
  Zietenstrasse 16, D-5300 Bonn 2 (☎ (228) 35-86-09; fax 35-49-40)
Honduras
  Embassy, 4ta Calle Arturo López Redezno, Casa 2421, Colonia Las Minitas, Tegucigalpa (☎ 32 50 18, 32-97-04; fax 32-15-80)
  Consulate, 8 Calle TBU 14-15, Avenida Noroeste No 148 TBU, Barrio Los Angeles, San Pedro Sula (☎ 32-50-18, 32-97-04; fax 55-77-48)
Israel
  2 Ben-Eliezer St, 46667 Herzlia-Pituach (☎ (3) 57-45-94, 57-48-12; fax (3) 546-7317)
Italy
  Via Dei Colli Della Farnesina 128, I-00194 Roma (☎ 327-2632; fax 329-1639)
Japan
  KOWA 38 Bldg Room 905, 12-24 Nishi Azabu, 4-Chome, Minato-Ku, Tokyo 105 (☎ (03) 400-1830, 400-1820)
Mexico
  Embassy, Avenida Explanada 1025, Lomas de Chapultepec, 11000 Mexico 4, DF (☎ (5) 540-7520, 520-9249; fax 202-1142)
  Consulate, Calle Héroes de Chapultepec and Cecilio Chi, No 354, Chetumal (☎ (983) 2-85-85; fax 2-85-85)

Consulate, Avenida Central Norte No 12, Ciudad Hidalgo, Chiapas, (☎ 8-01-93, 8-01-84)

Consulate, 2 Avenida Poniente Norte No 28, Comitán, Chiapas (☎ (963) 2-26-69)

Consulate, 2 Calle Oriente No 33, Tapachula, Chiapas (☎ 6-12-52)

Consulate, Paseo de Montejo No 495, Mérida, Yucatán

Nicaragua

Carretera a Masaya Km 11½, Managua (☎ (2) 7-94-78, 7-96-97; fax 7-94-78)

Panama

Calle 55 y Eric Delvalle, Edificio ADIR sixth floor, El Cangrejo (Apdo Postal 2352 Zona 9A) (☎ 69 34 06, 69-34-75; fax 23-19-22)

Spain

Consulate, Calle Rafael Salgado 3, 4o Izquierda, Madrid 16 (☎ 457-7827, 250-4035; fax 458-7894)

Switzerland

Zimmerwaldstrasse 47, 3122 Kehrsatz Berne (☎ (031) 54-36-91)

UK

13 Fawcett St, London SW 10 (☎ (071) 351-3042; fax 376-5708)

USA

Embassy, 2220 R St NW (☎ (202) 745-4952; fax 745-1908

Apart from the embassy in Washington DC there are consular offices in several other cities:

California

2500 Wilshire Blvd, Suite 820, Los Angeles, CA 90057 (☎ (213) 365-9251, 365-9252; fax 365-9245)

10405 San Diego Mission Road, Suite 205, San Diego, CA 92108 (☎ (619) 282-8127; fax 280-5187)

70 Market Street, Suite 660, San Francisco, CA 94102 (☎ (415) 788-5651, 788-5652; fax 788-5653)

Florida

300 Seville Avenue, Suite 210, Coral Gables, FL 33134 (☎ (305) 443-4828, 443-4829; fax 443-4830)

Illinois

180 North Michigan Ave, Suite 1035, Chicago, IL 60601 (☎ (312) 332-1587; fax 332-4256)

Louisiana

1645 World Trade Center, 2 Canal St, New Orleans, LA 70130 (☎ (504) 525-0013; fax 568-0553)

57 Park Avenue, New York, NY 10016 (☎ (212) 686-3837; fax 447-6947)

Texas

508 Elizabeth St, Brownsville, TX 78520 (☎ (512) 541-3131)

10200 Richmond Ave, Suite 270, Houston, TX 77042 (☎ (713) 953-9531; fax 953-9383)

4840 Whirlwind, San Antonio, TX 78217

(☎ (512) 637-0867; fax 634-9348)

Washington State

2001 Sixth Ave, Suite 3300, Seattle, WA 98121 (☎ 728-5920)

MOTOR VEHICLE INSURANCE

The situation in Guatemala is similar to that in Mexico. Liability insurance, available at insurance offices in the border towns, is a good buy because it saves you from a lot of red tape if you injure someone or their property.

Rates are lower here than they are in Mexico.

MONEY
Currency

The Guatemalan quetzal (Q), is named for the country's gorgeous but rare national bird; the quetzal is divided into 100 centavos. There are coins of one, five, 10 and 25 centavos, and bills (notes) of 50 centavos, one, five, 10, 20, 50 and 100 quetzals.

US dollars are the currency to use in Guatemala, because any other currency, even Canadian dollars, is liable to cause delays and problems when being exchanged for quetzals.

Many establishments will accept cash dollars instead of quetzals, usually at the bank exchange rate, or even better, but sometimes worse. Even so, you'll find yourself exchanging your dollars for quetzals at banks because shopkeepers, restaurateurs and hotel desk clerks may not want to deplete their supplies of ready quetzals and take on dollars, which they must then take to the bank.

Banks are generally open from 8.30 or 9 am to 2 pm Monday to Thursday, 8.30 am to 2.30 pm on Friday. A few banks in the major tourist centres may have longer hours, and open on Saturday.

There's a healthy unofficial exchange market for dollars, paying slightly better than the bank rate. The national hotbed of this activity is around the main post office in Guatemala City. At most border crossing points you may find yourself buying quetzals unofficially as there are no banks; at the airport, the bank exchange desks are usually open only during banking hours, and you may find yourself buying your first quetzals (or your last, to pay the US$10-equivalent exit tax) at a shop in the terminal.

Credit & Cash Cards

Major credit cards such as Visa and Master-Card (Eurocard, Access) are accepted at all airline and car rental companies, and at the larger hotels and restaurants; American Express cards are often accepted at the fancier and larger places, and at some smaller ones.

There is a growing number of ATMs (cash machines, called *cajero automático* in the major cities, usually located on bank premises.

Costs

Prices here are among the best in the region: beds in little pensions for US$6 per person in a double, camping places for less, elaborate markets selling fruits and snacks for pennies, cheap eateries called *comedores* offering one-plate meals for US$2 or less, and bus trips at less than US$1 per hour. If you want a bit more comfort, you can readily move up to rooms with private showers and meals in nicer restaurants, and still pay only US$25 per day for room and two – or even three – meals.

Consumer Taxes

Guatemala's IVA is 7%, and there's also a 10% tax on hotel rooms to pay for the activities of the Guatemala Tourist Commission (INGUAT), so a total tax of 17% will be added to your hotel bill. The very cheapest places usually charge no tax.

A departure tax equivalent to about US$10 is levied on travellers departing Guatemala by air.

CLIMATE & WHEN TO GO

In the Guatemalan highlands, temperatures can get down to freezing at night in the mountains, and days can be dank and chill during the rainy season, though warm and delightful in the dry season from October to

May. Guatemala's Pacific coast is tropical, rainy, hot and humid, as is its Caribbean coast, with temperatures often reaching 32°C to 38°C (90°F to 100°F), and almost constant high humidity, abating only a little in the dry season.

The vast jungle lowland of El Petén has a climate and topography like that of Yucatán: hot and humid or hot and dry, depending upon the season.

BUSINESS HOURS

Banks are generally open from 8.30 or 9 am to 2 pm Monday to Thursday, 8.30 am to 2.30 pm on Friday. A few banks in the major tourist centres may have longer hours, and hours on Saturday. Shops open about 9 am and close for lunch around 12.30 or 1 pm, reopening an hour or so later, and remaining open till about 6 pm, Monday to Friday; on Saturday many shops close for the day at 12.30 or 1 pm. Government office hours are officially 7.30 am to 3.30 pm, though there's some absenteeism around lunchtime.

POST & TELECOMMUNICATIONS

Almost every city and town (but not villages) has an Oficina de Correos (post office) where you can buy postage stamps and send or receive mail.

Conexión, a company with offices in Guatemala's larger cities and towns, sends and receives faxes and electronic mail (MCI/Internet) messages from the public at reasonable rates.

Sending Mail

Many Guatemalans rely on private courier services, being distrustful of the national post office. You'll see the offices of these courier services (which often have the word 'express' in their names) in many towns. Some are trustworthy, some are not. The big international express services such as Federal Express, DHL and United Parcel Service have offices in Guatemala City and Antigua.

If you are sending something by air mail from Guatemala, be sure to clearly mark it with the words 'Por Avión'. An air-mail letter sent to Canada or the USA may take anywhere from four to 14 days. Air-mail letters to Europe can take anywhere from one to three weeks.

Receiving Mail
Have mail addressed to you care of Poste Restante, and take your passport when you go to pick it up.

Telephone
Guatel, the local phone company, is separate from the post office.

Local and domestic long-distance calls are very cheap; international calls are extraordinarily expensive. Guatel has offices in all cities and in many large towns such as Panajachel.

Most telephone numbers in Guatemala City have six digits, but some have only five. The shorter numbers work just as well.

International Calls Guatel's international tolls are moderate in quetzal terms, but are figured at a very high rate of exchange (Q1 = US$1), and thus they end up being frightfully expensive. Your best bet, as in Mexico, is to make a short call, inform the other person of a time and telephone number at which you may be reached, then end the call.

At present, collect/reverse-charge calls may be made from Guatemala to the following countries and regions only: Canada, Central America, Mexico, Italy, Spain, Switzerland, USA.

To place an international direct call, dial the international prefix '00' (zero zero), then

To Call	Dial	Cost per Minute US Dollars
Belize City	00 + 501 + local number	$0.40 to $0.60
Los Angeles	00 + 1 + 213 + local number	$1.65 to $2
Montréal	00 + 1 + 514 + local number	$3 to $3.50
Glasgow	00 + 44 + 41 + local number	$6.25 to $7.50
Sydney	00 + 61 + 2 + local number	$6.25 to $7.50

the country code, area or city code, and local number. See the table on this page.

For semi-automatic (operator-assisted) calls, dial 171. The minimum call period is three minutes, and thus the minimum charge to the USA or Canada is about US$6; to countries overseas (ie, outside the western hemisphere), the minimum charge is about US$22.50.

There are also numerous 'direct line' services, such as AT&T's *USADirect*: dial 190 and you will be connected with an AT&T operator in the USA who will complete your collect or credit card call. Here are the direct line numbers:

National Police	120
Intercity Long Distance Calls	121
Fire	123
Directory Assistance	124
Red Cross	125
Correct Time	126
Ambulance	128
International Calls (by Operator)	171
MCI Call USA	189
USADirect (AT&T)	190
España Directo	191
Italia Directo	193
Sprint Express	195
Costa Rica Directo	196
Canada Directo	198

Fax, Telex, Telegraph
See the introductory Facts for the Visitor chapter for details.

MEDIA
With one exception, the national daily newspapers are all in Spanish. The *Guatemala News* is published daily and distributed for free in major hotels and tourist spots in Guatemala City, Antigua and Panajachel Otherwise, your best bet for English-language news is one of the US dailies, which can be found at large newsstands in tourist centres.

DANGERS & ANNOYANCES
See the Facts for the Visitor chapter for general comments on thefts, etc.

The greatest danger is from armed thieves who roam the highlands and the streets of Guatemala City. Don't wander around in Guatemala City late at night. Avoid empty streets in Antigua at night, and don't wander to the outskirts of that town except in a large group. Avoid stopping by the roadside in lonely places in the highlands. In general, ask around for information on where it is safe to go, and where not.

If you are threatened by armed bandits, it's usually best to give up your belongings (and your vehicle) without a struggle as most do not hesitate to use their weapons.

There are incidents of purse-snatching and car-jacking in Guatemala City. If you drive in the city, keep valuables (purses, jewellery, etc) out of sight, and keep the car windows rolled at least half way up at all times. (This discourages thieves from lunging through the window to grab a purse, watch or necklace.) If you are approached by armed car-jackers, embassies suggest that you give up your vehicle without resistance, rather than risk injury or worse.

Guatemala has been the scene of anti-government insurgent activity for a century or so. The guerrillas believe themselves to be fighting for the rights of the common people, and dream of overthrowing the government to establish a populist state. The government sees the guerrillas as a danger to public order and to its own legitimacy, and it attempts to suppress insurgent activity with great severity.

Avoid clashes between government soldiers and guerrillas. Don't go wandering about the countryside at night. Chances are very small that you will have any serious encounter with either group. If you do, don't panic – you should be on your way again in a few minutes with no harm done. In recent years the guerrillas who operate near Tikal have taken to stopping the occasional bus, lecturing its foreign occupants, pilfering stuff from the 'American imperialists' (but not from other nationalities), then sending everyone on their way unharmed.

FOOD

When it comes to cuisine, Guatemala is the poorer cousin to the more elaborate cuisines of Mexico, the USA and Europe. You can find a few Mexican standards such as tortillas topped with beans, meat or cheese; *enchiladas*; *guacamole*, a salad of mashed or chopped avocados, onions and tomatoes; and *tamales*, steamed corn dough rolls, perhaps with a meat or other stuffing.

But mostly you will encounter *bistec*, tough grilled or fried beef, *pollo asado*, grilled chicken, *chuletas de puerco*, pork chops, and lighter fare such as *hamburguesas*, hamburgers, and *salchichas*, sausages like hot dogs. Of the simpler food, *frijoles con arroz*, beans and rice, is cheapest and often best.

One of the unexpected and surprising things about Guatemala, however, is the omnipresence of Chinese restaurants. All the cities and some large towns have at least one Chinese eatery, usually small and not overly authentic, but cheap and good for a change of scene.

GETTING THERE & AROUND

See Getting There & Away in the Guatemala City section, as well as the sections on each border-crossing point.

Guatemala City

Population: 2 million

Guatemala's capital city, the largest urban agglomeration in Central America, sprawls across a range of flattened mountains (altitude 1500 metres), scored by deep ravines.

When you first get to know it, this city of two million people bears resemblances to Mexico City, its great Latin sister to the north. But the superficial resemblances soon give way to purely Guatemalan impressions. There's the huge and chaotic market, typically colourful and disorganised as though Guatemala City was just a gigantic village. There are the ramshackle city buses, without windows, without lights, without paint, sometimes without brakes, which trundle citizens about with surprising efficiency, though hardly in comfort. And there are the thousands of guards in blue clothing carrying very effective-looking firearms. Wherever there's money or status – banks, offices, private clubs, even McDonald's – there are armed guards.

Guatemala City today has few colonial buildings to beautify its aggressive urban sprawl. The colonial buildings are all in nearby Antigua Guatemala, the former capital. What you see here is mostly concrete, but at least the buildings are generally only five or six storeys high, allowing light to flood the narrow streets.

There is probably no reason for you to spend lots of time in Guatemala City. The few interesting sights may be seen in a day or two. But you must know your way around because this is the hub of the country, where all transportation lines meet and where all services are available.

HISTORY

Many cities in this part of the world have seen their histories end with an earthquake. For Guatemala City, it was the terrible *temblor* (earthquake) of 29 July 1773 which began its history. There was no city here at that time. The Spanish capital of Central America was at La Ciudad de Santiago de los Caballeros de Guatemala, known today as Antigua Guatemala, in the Panchoy Valley. The earthquake destroyed much of the colonial capital, and the government decided to move its headquarters to La Ermita Valley, the present site of Guatemala City, hoping to escape any further such terrible destruction. On 27 September 1775 King Carlos III of Spain signed a royal charter for the founding of La Nueva Guatemala de la Asunción, and Guatemala City was officially born.

The fervent hopes for a quakeless future were shaken in 1917, 1918 and 1976 as temblors did major damage to buildings in the capital – as well as in Antigua. The city's comparatively recent founding and its history of earthquakes have left little to see in the way of grand churches, palaces, mansions, or quaint old neighbourhoods.

ORIENTATION
Street Grid System

Guatemala City, like all Guatemalan towns, is laid out according to a street grid system which is logical and easy to use. Avenidas run north-south; Calles run east-west. Streets are usually numbered from north and west (lowest) to south and east (highest); building numbers run in the same directions, with odd numbers on the left-hand side and even on the right as you head south or east. The city is divided into 15 *zonas* (zones); each zona has its own separate version of this grid system.

Addresses are given in this form: '9a Avenida 15-12, Zona 1', which is read '9th Avenue above 15th Street, No 12, in Zone 1'. The building you're looking for (in this case the Hotel Excel), will be on 9th Avenue between 15th and 16th Streets, on the right-hand side as you walk south.

Though some major thoroughfares such as 6a Avenida and 7a Avenida cross through several zones, keeping the same name, most

GUATEMALA

Guatemala
City
(North)

0   250   500 m

GUATEMALA

PLACES TO STAY		9	Pollo Campero	4	Plaza Mayor
		10	Cafetería El Roble	5	Catedral Metropolitana
1	Hotel Centenario	11	Restaurant Bologna	6	Mercado Central
8	Hotel Pan American	16	Restaurant Piccadilly	18	Correos (Main Post
12	Hotel Ritz Continental	17	Los Tilos		Office)
13	Pensión Meza	19	Café Bohemia	20	Guatel (Telephone
14	Hogar del Turista &	21	El Gran Pavo		Company Long-
	Hotel Casa Real	23	Restaurant Altuna		Distance Station)
15	Hotel Lessing House	31	Restaurant Cantón	25	Iglesia Santa Clara
22	Hotel Del Centro	32	Restaurant El Gran	27	Iglesia San Francisco
24	Hotel-Apartamentos		Emperador	28	Policia Nacional
	Guatemala	33	Hotel Colonial	30	Parque Concordia
	Internacional		Restaurant		(Parque Gómez
26	Spring Hotel	34	Delicadezas Hamburgo		Carrillo)
29	Posada Belén	35	Pollo Campero	39	FEGUA Railway
36	Hotel Ajau	38	Cafetín El Rinconcito		Station
37	Hotel Excel			40	Centro Cultural Miguel
		OTHER			Ángel Asturias
PLACES TO EAT				41	Centro Cívico
		2	Palacio Nacional	42	INGUAT Tourist Office
7	Pollo Campero	3	Parque Centenario		

zones have their own unique grid systems. Thus 14 Calle in Zona 10 is a completely different street several miles distant from 14 Calle in Zona 1.

Short streets may be numbered 'A', as in 14 Calle A, a short street running between 14 Calle and 15 Calle.

Guatemala City's street grid has a number of anomalies as well: diagonal streets called *rutas* and *vías*, wandering boulevards called *diagonales*, etc. In smaller Guatemalan cities and towns this street grid system allows you to pinpoint destinations effortlessly.

Landmarks

The ceremonial centre of Guatemala City is the Plaza Mayor (sometimes called the Parque Central) at the heart of Zona 1, surrounded by the Palacio Nacional, the Catedral Metropolitana and the Portal del Comercio. Beside the Plaza Mayor to the west is the large Parque Centenario, the city's central park. Zona 1 is also the retail commercial district, with shops selling clothing, crafts, film, and a myriad of other things. The Mercado Central, a market selling lots of crafts, is behind the cathedral. Most of the city's good cheap and middle-range hotels

are in Zona 1. 6a Avenida running south and 7a Avenida running north are the major thoroughfares which connect Zona 1 with other zonas.

Zona 4, south of Zona 1, holds the modern Centro Cívico (Civic Centre) with various government buildings. In south-western Zona 4 is the city's major market district and chaotic bus terminals.

Zona 9 (west of Avenida La Reforma) and Zona 10 (east of Avenida La Reforma), are south of Zona 4; Avenida La Reforma is the southerly extension of 10a Avenida. These are the fancier residential areas of the city, also boasting several of the most interesting small museums. Zona 10 is the poshest, with the Zona Viva (Lively Zone) arrayed around the deluxe Camino Real Guatemala and Guatemala Fiesta hotels. The Zona Viva holds many of the city's better restaurants and nightclubs. In Zona 9, convenient landmarks are the mini-Eiffel Tower called the Torre del Reformador at 7a Avenida and 2 Calle, and the Plazuela España traffic roundabout at 7a Avenida and 12 Calle.

Zona 13, just south of Zona 9, has the large Parque Aurora, several museums, and the Aeropuerto Internacional La Aurora.

GUATEMALA

PLACES TO STAY

1	Hotel Plaza
4	Hotel Cortijo Reforma
13	Hotel Princess Reforma
17	Hotel Guatemala Fiesta
19	Hotel Camino Real Guatemala
20	Hotel El Dorado

PLACES TO EAT

5	Restaurante El Parador
6	Pastelería Las Américas
7	Puerto Barrios
8	Palacio Royal
9	Hacienda de los Sánchez
10	El Gran Pavo
12	Restaurant Piccadilly
14	Restaurante Excellent
15	Siriaco's
16	La Trattoria
18	Restaurant Bologna

OTHER

2	Market & Terminal de Autobuses
3	Torre del Reformador
6	Museo Popol Vuh
11	Plazuela España
21	Museo Nacional de Arqueología y Etnología
22	Museo Nacional de Arte Moderno
23	Mercado de Artesanía
24	Museo Ixchel del Traje Indígena

INFORMATION
Tourist Office
The tourist office is in the lobby of the INGUAT headquarters (Guatemalan Tourist Commission), (☎ (2) 31-13-33 to 47; fax 31-88-93), 7a Avenida 1-17, Centro Cívico, Zona 5. Look for the blue-and-white sign with the letter 'i' on the east side of the street, next to a flight of stairs a few metres to the south of the railway viaduct which crosses above 7a Avenida. Hours are 8 am to 4.30 pm, on Saturday 8 am to 1 pm, closed Sunday. Staff are friendly and helpful.

Money
Normal banking hours are 8.30 am to 2 pm (2.30 pm on Friday), closed weekends, but several banks have *ventanillas especiales*

(special teller windows) open longer. ATM cash machines are also making their appearance.

Most banks give a maximum of US$100 for an ATM withdrawal, but Banco Credomático, 7a Avenida at 6 Calle, Zona 1, allows US$500 from a MasterCard. Banquetzal has an office, (☎ (2) 51-21-53, 51-20-55), at 10 Calle 6-28, Zona 1, near the Hotel Ritz Continental, that's open from 8.30 am to 8 pm Monday to Friday, and on Saturday from 9 am to 1 pm.

The airport terminal office of Banco de Guatemala is open 7.30 am to 6.30 pm, Monday to Friday.

American Express is represented in Guatemala by Banco del Café SA (☎ (2) 31-13-11, 34-00-40; fax 31-14-18), Avenida La Reforma 9-00, Zona 9.

Post
The city's main post office (☎ (2) 2-61-01/02/03/04/05) is at 7a Avenida 12-11, Zona 1, in the huge pink building. There's no sign, but by the racks of postcards shall ye know it. Hours are 8 am to 7 pm on weekdays, 8 am to 3 pm on Saturday, closed Sunday. Mail service is undependable, especially when sending urgent messages or valuable items, and local citizens and businesses often use private courier companies instead.

Telephone
The national telephone network is operated by Guatel. If you are calling from outside the country, the country code is (502); the city code for Guatemala City is (2); for any other city or town the city code is (9). Most telephone numbers in Guatemala City have six digits, but a few old ones have only five; they still work. If the five-digit number you're dialling doesn't work, try putting a '3' in front of it.

A coin-operated telephone in Guatemala is called a *telefono monedero*.

Embassies & Consulates
Remember that embassies (*embajadas*) and their consular sections (*consulados*) often

have strange, short working hours. Call ahead to be sure the place will be open before you venture out to find it. Unless otherwise noted, the places listed below are embassies.

Austria
6a Avenida 20-25, Zona 10, Edificio Plaza Marítima (4th floor) (☎ (2) 68-11-34, 68-23-24; fax 33-61-80)
Belgium
Embassy & Consulate, Avenida La Reforma 13-70, Zona 9, Edificio Real Reforma (2nd floor) (☎ (2) 31-65-97, 31-56-08; fax 31-47-46)
Canada
Embassy & Consulate, 7a Avenida 11-59, Zona 9, Edificio Galerías España (☎ (2) 32-14-11/12/13; fax 32-14-19)
Costa Rica
Avenida La Reforma 8-60, Zona 9, Edificio Galerías Reforma offices 320 & 902 (☎ & fax (2) 32-05-31)
Denmark
Consulate-General, 7a Avenida 20-36, Zona 1 (☎ (2) 8-10-91, 51-45-47; fax 51-30-87)
El Salvador
12 Calle 5-43, Zona 9 (☎ (2) 32-58-48, 36-24-21; fax 34-39-47)
Finland
Consulate-General, Ruta 2 (24 Calle) 0-70, Zona 4 (☎ (2) 31-31-16/17; fax 31-31-25)
France
Embassy & Consulate, 16 Calle 4-53, Zona 10, Edificio Marbella (☎ (2) 37-40-80, 37-36-39)
Germany
20 Calle 6-20, Zona 10, Edificio Plaza Marítima (☎ (2) 37-00-28/29; fax 37-00-31)
Honduras
16 Calle 8-27, Zona 10 (☎ (2) 37-39-19, 37-19-21; fax 33-46-29)
Israel
13a Avenida 14-07, Zona 10 (☎ (2) 37-13-34, 32-53-05; fax 33-69-50)
Italy
Embassy & Consulate, 5 Avenida 8-59, Zona 14 (☎ (2) 37-45-78, 37-45-88; fax 37-45-38)
Mexico
Embassy, 13 Calle 7-30, Zona 9 (☎ (2) 31-95-73, 32-52-49; fax 34-41-24)
Chancellery, 15 Calle 3-20, Zona 10 (7th floor), Edificio Centro Ejecutivo (☎ (2) 33-72-54/55/56/57/58)
Netherlands
12 Calle 7-56, Zona 9 (4th floor) (☎ (2) 31-35-05; fax 32-48-85)
Nicaragua
10 Avenida 14-72, Zona 10 (☎ (2) 33-64-34, 68-07-85; fax 37-42-64)

Norway
Consulate, 6a Avenida 7-02, Zona 9, office 4 (☎ (2) 31-00-64, 31-67-27; fax 32-00-70)
Panama
Vía 5 No 4-50, Zona 4, Edificio Maya (7th floor) (☎ (2) 32-07-63; fax 34-71-61)
South Africa
Consulate, 10a Avenida 30-57, Zona 5 (CIDEA) (☎ (2) 36-28-90, 34-15-31/35; 36-52-91)
Spain
Consulate, 6 Calle 6-48, Zona 9 (☎ (2) 34-37-87)
Sweden
8a Avenida 15-07, Zona 10 (☎ (2) 37-05-55, 33-65-36)
Switzerland
Embassy & Consulate, 4 Calle 7-73, Zona 9, Edificio Seguros Universales, (5th floor) Apdo Postal 1426 (☎ (2) 36-57-26, 31-37-25; fax 31-85-24)
UK
7a Avenida 5-10, Zona 4, Edificio Centro Financiero Torre II (7th floor) (☎ (2) 32-16-01/02/04; fax 34-19-04)
USA
Embassy & Consulate, Avenida La Reforma 7-01, Zona 10 (☎ (2) 31-15-41; fax 31-88-85).

Immigration Office
If you need to extend your tourist card for a longer stay, contact the Dirección General de Migración (☎ (2) 71-46-82; fax 71-46-78), 41 Calle 17-36, Zona 8, one block off Avenida Castellana.

Bookshops
Try Geminis (☎ (2) 31-67-27, 31-00-64), 6 Avenida 7-24, Zona 9, which carries travel books as well as a good assortment of fiction in several languages.

Medical Services
This city has many private hospitals and clinics. One such is the Centro Médico, (☎ (2) 32 35 55), 6a Avenida 3-47, Zona 10; another is Hospital Herrera Llerandi, (☎ (2) 36-67-71/75, 32-04-44/48), 6a Avenida 8-71, Zona 10. For the names and addresses of others, consult your embassy or consulate, or the yellow pages of the telephone directory under Hospitales.

The Guatemalan Red Cross (☎ (2) 125) is at 3 Calle 8-40, Zona 1. Guatemala City uses a duty-chemist (*farmacia de turno*) system with designated pharmacies remaining open at night and weekends. Ask at your hotel for the nearest farmacia de turno, or consult the farmacia de turno sign in the window of the closest chemist/pharmacy.

ZONA 1

Most of what you'll want to see is in Zona 1 near the Plaza Mayor, bounded by 6 and 8 Calles and 6a and 7a Avenidas.

Plaza Mayor

According to the standard Spanish colonial town-planning scheme, every town in the New World had to have a large plaza for military exercises, reviews and ceremonies. On the north side of the plaza was to be the *palacio de gobierno*, or colonial government headquarters. On another side, preferably the east, there was to be a church (if the town was large enough to merit a bishop then it was a cathedral). On the other sides of the square there could be other civic buildings, or the large and imposing mansions of wealthy citizens. Guatemala's Plaza Mayor is a good example of the classic town plan.

To appreciate the Plaza Mayor, you've got to visit it on a Sunday when it's thronged with thousands of citizens who have come to stroll, lick ice cream cones, play in the fountains, take the air, smooch on a bench, listen to *salsa* music on boom-boxes, and ignore the hundreds of trinket vendors. If you can't make it on a Sunday, try for lunchtime or late afternoon.

Palacio Nacional

On the north side of the Plaza Mayor is the country's Palacio Nacional, built during the dictatorial presidency of General Jorge Ubico (1931-44) at enormous cost. It replaced an earlier palace called El Centenario, which burnt down in 1925. El Centenario had replaced an even earlier palace which was destroyed in the earthquake of 1917.

The palace is where the President of Guatemala has his executive offices. Visit is by free guided tour (Monday to Friday, 8 am to 4.30 pm). The tour takes you through a labyrinth of gleaming brass and polished wood, carved stone and frescoed arches. The frescoes are by Alberto Gálvez Suárez. When you're finished inside, walk around to the rear (north side) of the palace for a look at the bulletproof cars, shrouded in smoked glass and bristling with antennas (and automatic weapons?), of various executive officers.

Catedral Metropolitana

Built between 1782 and 1809 (the towers were finished later, in 1867), the Catedral Metropolitana has survived earthquake and fire much better than the Palacio Nacional, though the quake of 1917 did a lot of damage, and that of 1976 did even more. All has been restored. It's not a particularly beautiful building, inside or out. Heavy proportions and spare ornamentation make it look severe, though it does have a certain feeling of stateliness. Dark old 17th and 18th-century paintings on the walls teach Bible lessons to the recently converted. Little chandeliers and a baldachin over the altar add a formal touch. The cathedral is supposedly open every day from 8 am to 7 pm, though you may find it closed, especially at siesta time.

Mercado Central

Until it was destroyed by the quake of 1976, the central market on 9a Avenida between 6 and 8 Calles behind the cathedral was a place to buy food and other necessities. Reconstructed in the late 1970s, the modern market specialises in tourist-oriented items such as cloth (hand-woven and machine-woven), carved wood, worked leather and metal, basketry and other handicrafts. Necessities have been moved aside to the streets surrounding the market. As you will be visiting the Plaza Mayor, you should take a stroll through here, though there are better places to buy crafts. Market hours are 6 am to 6 pm Monday to Saturday, 9 am to noon Sunday.

The city's true 'central' food market is in Zona 4.

ZONA 2
Parque Minerva

Zona 2 is north of Zona 1. Though mostly a middle-class residential district, its most northern extent holds the large Parque Minerva, itself surrounded by golf courses, the rod-and-gun club, sports grounds and the buildings of the Universidad Mariano Gálvez.

Minerva, goddess of wisdom, technical skill and invention, was a favourite of President Manuel Estrada Cabrera (1898-1920), who fancied himself the country's 'Great Educator'. He accomplished little in the way of educating Guatemala's youth, but he built lots of sylvan parks named for the goddess and quaint little temples in her honour. Otherwise, his presidency is notable for the amount of Guatemalan territory he turned over to the gigantic United Fruit Company for the cultivation of bananas.

For all that, the Parque Minerva is a pretty place, good for just relaxing, strolling among the eucalyptus trees and sipping a soft drink. Be on the alert for pickpockets, purse-snatchers and other such types, who look especially for tourists.

Mapa En Relieve

The prime sight to see in Zona 2 is the Relief Map of Guatemala, called simply the Mapa En Relieve, in the Parque Minerva. Constructed in 1904 under the direction of Francisco Vela, the map shows the country at a scale of 1:10,000, but the height of the mountainous terrain has been exaggerated to 1:2000 for dramatic effect. Little signs indicate major towns and topographical features. Viewing towers afford a panoramic view. This place is odd but fun, and costs only a few centavos for admission (free on Sunday); hours are 8 am to 5 pm every day.

Getting There & Away The Mapa En Relieve and Parque Minerva are two km north of the Plaza Mayor along 6a Avenida, but that street is one-way heading south. You can catch a northbound bus (No 1, 45 or 46) on 5a Avenida in Zona 1.

ZONA 4

Pride of Zona 4 is the Centro Cívico, constructed in the 1950s and '60s. (The complex of buildings actually stretches into Zona 1 and Zona 5 as well.) Here you'll find the Palace of Justice, the headquarters buildings of the Guatemalan Institute of Social Security (IGSS), the Banco de Guatemala, the city hall, and the headquarters of INGUAT. The Banco de Guatemala building bears high-relief murals by Dagoberto Vásquez depicting the history of his homeland; in the city hall is a huge mosaic by Carlos Mérida completed in 1959.

Behind INGUAT is the Ciudad Olímpica sports grounds, and across the street from the Centro Cívico on a hilltop are the Centro Cultural Miguel Ángel Asturias (the national theatre, chamber theatre, open-air theatre and a small museum of old armaments). The Centro Cívico is hardly a tourist attraction, though the useful INGUAT tourist office is here.

Zona 4 is known mostly for its markets and its bus stations, all thrown together in the chaotic south-western corner of the zona near the railway.

ZONA 9
Museo Popol Vuh

If you're at all interested in Mayan and Spanish colonial art you must make a visit to this museum (☎ (2) 34-71-21), named for the famous mythic chronicle of the Quiché Maya. Well-chosen polychrome pottery, figurines, incense burners, burial urns, carved wooden masks and traditional textiles fill several exhibit rooms. Others hold colonial paintings, gilded wood and silver objects. A faithful copy of the Dresden Codex, one of the precious 'painted books' of the Maya, is among the most interesting pieces.

The collection, assembled by Jorge and Ella Castillo, was donated to the Universidad Francisco Marroquín in 1977. It's housed on the 6th level of the Edificio Galerías Reforma, Torre 2, 6th floor, Avenida La Reforma 8-60, Zona 9. Hours are 9 am to 4.30 pm, Monday to Friday; 9 am to 1 pm Saturday (closed Sunday); admission costs US$1 for

GUATEMALA

A tortoise, symbol of the summer solstice, from the Dresden Codex

adults, US$0.25 for students, US$0.10 for children.

ZONA 10

Lying east of Avenida La Reforma, Zona 10 is the upscale district of posh villas, luxury hotels, embassies, and several important museums.

Museo Ixchel (Indian Costumes)

The Museo Ixchel del Traje Indígena (☎(2) 68 07 13) is named for Ixchel, wife of Mayan sky god Itzamná and goddess of the moon and of women in childbirth, among other things. As you approach the museum at 4a Avenida 16-27, Zona 10, you'll see groups of village women in their wonderful traditional dress with their woven artwork spread out around them for sale. Within the museum, photographs and exhibits of textiles and other village crafts show the incredible richness of traditional arts in Guatemala's highland towns. If you enjoy seeing Guatemalan textiles at all, you must make a visit to the Museo Ixchel.

The museum is open Monday to Friday 8.30 am to 5 pm, Saturday 9 am to 1 pm, closed Sunday. Admission costs US$1 for adults, US$0.25 students, and US$0.10 for children.

A new, larger building is presently being built to house the museum on the campus of the Universidad Francisco Marroquín, at the end of 6 Calle, Zona 10. For now, though, you can walk to the Museo Ixchel from the Museo Popol Vuh. Walk south along Avenida La Reforma for seven blocks; you'll pass the Hotel Camino Real on the left. At 16 Calle turn left and walk a few blocks to 4a Avenida, turn right (south) and the museum is only a few metres farther along.

ZONA 13

The major attraction in the southern reaches of the city is the Parque Aurora with its zoo, children's playground, fairgrounds, and several museums offering free admission.

The Moorish-looking Museo Nacional de Arqueología y Etnología (☎ (2) 72-04-89) has a collection of Mayan sculptures, ceramics and jade, plus some displays of traditional handicrafts. Facing the Museo Nacional de Arqueología y Etnología is the Museo Nacional de Arte Moderno (☎ (2) 72-04-67), with a collection of 20th-century Guatemalan art, especially painting and sculpture. Hours at both museums are Monday to Friday from 9 am to 4 pm, Saturday and Sunday from 9 to noon and 2 to 4 pm.

Several hundred metres east of the museums is the city's official handicrafts market, the Mercado de Artesanía (☎ (2) 72-02-08), on 11a Avenida, just off the access road to the airport. Like most official handicrafts markets it's a sleepy place in which shopkeepers display the same sorts of things which you find for sale in hotel gift shops. The place livens up when a tour bus rolls in, but commits itself to slumber again when the bus pulls out. Hours are officially 9 am to 6 pm Monday to Saturday, 9 am to 1 pm Sunday.

KAMINALJUYÚ

Several km west of the centre lie the extensive ruins of Kaminaljuyú (☎ 51 62 24), a Late Preclassic/Early Classic Mayan site which has provided archaeologists with tantalising insights into the early centuries of Mayan florescence. Kaminaljuyú was conquered by the armies of Teotihuacán (near Mexico City), and the resulting culture shows both Mexican and Mayan influences.

Unfortunately, much of Kaminaljuyú, located in Colonia Kaminaljuyú, Zona 7, has been covered by urban sprawl. What has not been covered is presently being excavated. Though you are allowed to visit from 9 am to 4 pm daily, your time would be better spent looking at the artefacts recovered here which are on display in the city's museums.

PLACES TO STAY

Guatemala City has a good range of lodgings in all price ranges. Those at the very bottom end of the price scale, as well as those at the very top, often fill up, but there are usually plenty of rooms to be had at prices in-between. Taxes totalling 17% are added to hotel bills in Guatemala. I've already included those taxes in the prices quoted here.

PLACES TO STAY – BOTTOM END

Perhaps the greatest concentration of low-budget hotels in the city is about eight blocks south of the Plaza Mayor near the Policia Nacional (National Police Headquarters) and the Correos (Post Office), in the area bounded by 6a Avenida 'A' and 9a Avenida, and 14 and 16 Calles. There are at least a dozen decent hotels to choose from, and several handy little restaurants as well. It's very important to keep street noise in mind as you search for a budget room. All the places listed below are in Zona 1.

Hotel Chalet Suizo (☎ (2) 51-37-86), 14 Calle 6-82, has been popular with adventurous travellers for decades. The 25 rooms around a plant-filled courtyard are clean, though some are dark and claustrophobic. The Cafe Suizo provides meals. Rates are US$12/15 a single/double with shared bath, or US$20/25 a single/double with private bath. Book in advance, as the hotel is usually full.

Hotel Lessing House (☎ (2) 51-38-91), 12 Calle 4-35, is run by an efficient señora who offers seven tidy rooms for rent. Rooms can accommodate one (US$7.50), two (US$12), three (US$14.50) or four (US$19); the larger rooms have private showers.

Spring Hotel (☎ (2) 51-42-07, 51-48-76), 8a Avenida 12-65, is often *completo* (full up) because the location is good, the 28 rooms presentable, the courtyard sunny, and the price right: US$12/16/23 a single/double/triple with private shower. Bathless rooms are 25% to 30% cheaper.

Hogar del Turista (☎ (2) 2-55-22), 11 Calle 10-43, has two narrow courtyards which allow in some sun, and two hard-working señoras. Most of the 14 rooms have windows opening onto the courtyards to provide light, but a few are windowless. Prices are high: US$16 a single, US$20 a double with shower. Breakfast is too expensive, but there's free parking.

Right next door is the *Hotel Casa Real* (☎ (2) 2-11-42), 11 Calle 10-57. None of the eight rooms has any plumbing, but some are quite large, with skylights. There's a tidy garden courtyard. Rate is US$6.50 per person.

Hotel Excel (☎ (2) 53-27-09), 9a Avenida 15-12, is a bright, modern place with 17 rooms on three levels around an L-shaped court used as a car park. Rooms with bath go for US$15/18/22 a single/double/triple. Most rooms have colour TV.

Hotel Ajau (☎ (2) 2-04-88), 8a Avenida 15-62, is fairly clean, somewhat cheaper, and a lot quieter than many 9a Avenida hotels. You pay US$7 a double without private shower, US$9 with.

Pensión Meza (☎ (2) 2-31-77), 10 Calle 10-17, is drab and beat-up but busy with international budget travellers who like the sunny courtyard, the camaraderie, the helpful proprietor, and the low price of US$6 per person. Shared baths only. The restaurant serves cheap meals.

PLACES TO STAY – MIDDLE

Guatemala City's middle-range lodging-places offer good value for money. All are comfortable, some quite charming. All these places are in Zona 1, except for the Hotel Plaza.

Posada Belén (☎ (2) 2-92-26, 53-45-30), 13 Calle 'A' 10-30, is on a quiet side street. A charming hostelry, the Belén consists of three neighbouring houses, each with a sunny courtyard. The price is US$28/36 a single/double, with bath. Children under five are not accepted.

Hotel Pan American (☎ (2) 51-04-32, 2-68-07/8/9; fax 2-64-02), 9 Calle 5-63, was this city's luxury hotel before WW II. It still attracts many faithful return visitors who like its faded charm. The 60 rooms are all Art Deco and Biedermeyer, but surprisingly plain. Avoid rooms facing the noisy street. Rates are US$56/65/73 a single/double/triple.

Hotel Plaza (☎ (2) 36-31-73, 31-63-37; fax 2-27-05), Vía 7, 6-16, Zona 4, a Spanish Bauhaus motel with colonial appointments, is one km south of the Centro Cívico and a 15-minute walk east of the market and bus station area. The 57 rooms cost US$42/52 a single/double.

Hotel Del Centro (☎ (2) 2-55-47, 2-59-80; fax 2-27-05), 13 Calle 4-55, is a good, solid hotel, dependable for decades. The 60 large rooms come with shiny baths, colour TV, and often with two double beds; there's a bit of street noise in some. The price is US$55 a double.

Hotel Colonial (☎ (2) 2-67-22, 2-29-55; fax 2-86-71), 7a Avenida 14-19, is a large old city house converted to a hotel with heavy colonial decor. The covered interior court is pleasant, the 47 rooms clean, all with bath. Rates are US$22/28 a single/double.

Hotel-Apartamentos Guatemala Internacional (☎ (2) 8-44-41/42/43/44/45), 6a Avenida 12-21, offers 18 furnished apartments with bedroom (one double bed and one single), small living room with a day bed, tiled bathroom, a kitchen with refrigerator, four-burner cooker, sink and kitchen utensils. The location is convenient, and the price is good: US$36 to US$42 a single, US$42 to US$50 a double.

Hotel Centenario (☎ (2) 8-03-81/82/83), 6 Calle 5-33, on the north side of the Parque Centenario, has 43 comfortable rooms, many with a double and a single bed, plus well-worn but clean showers. There's also a sauna. Prices for this central location are US$20 a single, US$28 a double.

PLACES TO STAY – TOP END

Most luxurious of this city's hotels is the *Hotel Camino Real Guatemala* (☎ (2) 33-46-33; fax 37-43-13; in the USA (800) 228 3000), Avenida La Reforma at 14 Calle, Zona 10, in the midst of the Zona Viva. This is the capital's international-class hotel, with all of the comforts, including swimming pools and lush gardens. Double rooms cost US$165 to US$235.

The other top lodging is the modern *Hotel El Dorado* (☎ (2) 32-28-88, 31-77-77; fax 32-18-77), 7a Avenida 15-45, Zona 9, 01009, which has similar services at nearly identical prices.

Hotel Ritz Continental (☎ (2) 8-08-89, 2-10-85; fax 2-46-59), 6a Avenida 'A' 10-13, Zona 1, 01001, has recently been completely renovated. The 202 rooms are of a four-star standard, and cost US$75/85 a single/double; there's a swimming pool. The location, three blocks south of the Plaza Mayor, is quiet and convenient.

Best value for money near the Zona Viva is the *Hotel Princess Reforma* (☎ (2) 34-45-45; fax 34-45-46), 13 Calle 7-65, Zona 9, 01009, just across Reforma from the Zona Viva on a quiet street. Opened in 1993, the 90-room Reforma is an excellent European-style business hotel without the extensive grounds, but with lower prices: US$105/120 a single/double.

Also in the Zona Viva is the 230-room *Hotel Guatemala Fiesta* (☎ (2) 32-25-55 to 66; fax 68-23-66), 1a Avenida 13-22, Zona 10, almost as posh as the Camino Real, with all the services (including a heated swimming pool), but lower prices: US$112/123/135 a single/double/triple.

Several hundred metres north of the Zona Viva stands the *Hotel Cortijo Reforma* (☎ (2) 36-67-12 to 16), Avenida La Reforma 2-18, Zona 9. This all-suite building offers suites with bedroom, living room, minibar, tiled bathroom with tub and shower, space for a kitchenette, and a tiny balcony. Price for two is US$105.

Newest of the city's luxury hotels is the *Hotel Las Américas* (☎ (2) 33-46-33; fax 37-43-13), Avenida Las Américas at 9 Calle,

Zona 14, operated by Biltmore International, with 189 rooms priced a bit below those at the Camino Real.

PLACES TO EAT – BOTTOM END

It is not difficult to find cheap eats in this city. Fast-food and snack shops abound. But to really save money, head for Parque Concordia, bound by 4a and 5a Avenidas and 14 and 15 Calles in Zona 1. The west side of the park is lined with little open-air food stalls serving sandwiches and snacks at rockbottom prices from early morning to late evening. A meal for US$2 is the rule here.

Delicadezas Hamburgo (☎ 8-16-27), 15 Calle 5-34, Zona 1, on the south side of Parque Concordia, provides a long list of sandwiches at lunch and dinner, as well as German, Guatemalan and American platters at moderate prices. Full meals cost US$4 to US$10. Hours are from 7 am to 10 pm every day.

Restaurant Cantón (☎ 51-63-31), 6a Avenida 14-20, Zona 1, facing the park on its east side, is the place to go for cheap Chinese food. Prices seem high at US$5 to US$8 per platter, but platters are meant to be shared by two or more. The Cantón is open from 9 am to 5 pm and from 5.30 pm to midnight every day of the week.

There are numerous other Chinese restaurants near the corner of 6a Avenida and 14 Calle, Zona 1. The city's other rich concentration of Chinese restaurants is in the blocks west of the Parque Centenario along 6 Calle, where you'll find the *Restaurant Long Wah* (☎ 2-66-11), 6 Calle 3-70, Zona 1, along with several other places such as *Felicidades, Palacio Real* and *China Hilton*.

Restaurante El Gran Emperador, 14 Calle 6-74, Zona 1, next door to the Chalet Suizo, serves both meat-based and vegetarian meals. The set-price meals go for US$1.50 and US$3.

Los Tilos, 11 Calle 6-54, Zona 1, is the place to go for Central European pastries and baked goods. It's appropriately Tirolean with dark wood and a menu of pastries, wholegrain breads and light meals. A cup of coffee and a pastry need cost only US$1 or so. *Café*

Bohemia (☎ 8-24-74), 11 Calle 8-48, Zona 1, is a nearby alternative.

6a Avenida between 10 and 15 Calles has dozens of restaurants and fast-food shops of all types: hamburgers, pizzas, pasta, Chinese, fried chicken. You'll have no trouble eating well for US$3 to US$4.

9a Avenida between 15 and 16 Calles, in the midst of the cheap hotel area, has several good little restaurants. There's the *Cafetín El Rinconcito*, 9a Avenida 15-74, facing the Hotel Capri, which is good for tacos, and the restaurant in the Hotel Capri itself, 9a Avenida 15-63, Zona 1, for more substantial meals. The *Hotel Colonial*, 7a Avenida 14-19, Zona 1, has a slightly better and pricier restaurant.

You might also want to try the *Cafetería El Roble*, 9 Calle 5-46, Zona 1, facing the entrance to the Hotel Pan American. This clean little café is very popular with local office workers who come for breakfast (US$1.75), lunch and dinner (US$3.50).

Pollo Campero (Country Chicken) is the name of Guatemala's Kentucky Fried Chicken clone. You can find branches of the chain on the corner of 9 Calle and 5a Avenida, at 6a Avenida and 15 Calle, and at 8 Calle 9-29, all in Zona 1. Cheerful chicken colours of orange and yellow predominate in these bright, clean places. Two pieces of chicken, french fries (chips), and a soft drink or coffee costs US$3.

PLACES TO EAT – MIDDLE

Most middle-range hotels in Zona 1 offer excellent set-price lunches for US$6 to US$10. Try the *Hotel Del Centro, Hotel Pan American*, and *Hotel Ritz Continental*. My favourite for ambience is definitely the Pan American, 9 Calle 5-63, Zona 1.

Restaurant Altuna (☎ 2-06-69, 51-71-85), 5a Avenida 12-31, Zona 1, is a large restaurant with the atmosphere of a private club, located just a few steps north of the Hotel Del Centro. Specialities are seafood and Spanish dishes. Full cost for a meal is about US$12 per person; it's open for lunch and dinner every day except Monday.

Restaurant Bologna (☎ 51-11-67), 10

Calle 6-20, Zona 1, just around the corner from the Hotel Ritz Continental, is very small but attractive, serving tasty pizzas, spaghetti, ravioli and lasagna for US$3 to US$4 per plate. Hours are 10 am to 10 pm Tuesday to Sunday, closed Monday. The Zona Viva branch, at Plaza Rosa No 2, 13 Calle 1-62, Zona 10, is much fancier.

Several other good restaurants have their main establishments in Zona 1, and branches in Zona 9 or 10.

El Gran Pavo (The Big Turkey, ☎ 2-99-12, 51-09-33), 13 Calle 4-41, Zona 1, is a big place just to the left (west) of the Hotel Del Centro's entrance. The menu seems to include every Mexican dish imaginable. The birria, a spicy-hot soup of meat, onions, peppers and cilantro (coriander leaf), served with tortillas, is a meal in itself at US$2.75. The Big Turkey is open seven days a week from 11.30 am to 1 am. There's another branch (☎ 32-56-93) at 12 Calle 5-54, Zona 9.

Restaurant Piccadilly (☎ 51-42-68, 53-92-23), 6a Avenida 11-01, Zona 1, is among the capital's most popular eateries, with a multinational menu that might have come from the United Nations cafeteria. Most main courses cost US$3 or less. There's another branch of the Piccadilly on the Plazuela España, 7a Avenida 12-00, Zona 9.

PLACES TO EAT – TOP END

The most elegant dining in the city is to be found in the Zona Viva, the several blocks near the Camino Real Guatemala Hotel.

La Trattoria (☎ 31-06-12), 13 Calle 155, Zona 10, is the place to go for good Italian specialities. The façade is lined with potted geraniums, the pleasant dining room with old prints. Service is attentive. You can expect to spend about US$12 or US$15 per person for dinner with wine.

Restaurante El Parador (☎ 32-00-62), Avenida La Reforma 6-70, Zona 9, a block from the Museo Popol Vuh, is an attractive Guatemalan steakhouse. At dinner, meats are priced from US$5 to US$9, fish at US$5 (shrimp costs more), but luncheon is cheaper.

Hacienda de los Sánchez (☎ 36-52-40), 12 Calle 2-25, Zona 10, is where Guatemalan meat-eaters come to pig out. The ambience is aggressively *ranchero*, with a huge tent-pavilion framed by royal palms. Steaks and ribs are priced about US$7 to US$10. The parking lot is full of shiny American pickup trucks. This is where the Marlboro Man eats. It's open every day from noon to midnight.

Puerto Barrios (☎ 34-13-02, 36-56-46), 7a Avenida 10-65, Zona 9, is aggressively nautical the way Hacienda de los Sánchez is aggressively ranchero. This ship-shaped restaurant comes complete with waiters in knee-breeches and frogged coats, oil paintings of buccaneers, portholes for windows, and a big compass by the door. The manager is not even the manager, he's El Capitán. You can easily spend US$16 to US$30 per person here. Come aboard any day from noon to 10 pm.

Siriaco's (☎ 34-63-16), 1a Avenida 1212, Zona 10, very near the Hotel Guatemala Fiesta, is flashy but informal with a sunken dining room and bar, a skylighted patio courtyard, and a menu of the favourite continental specialities. Expect to spend US$15 or so per person for dinner.

Palacio Royal (☎ 31-42-73, 32-38-57), 7a Avenida 11-00, Zona 9, just off the Plazuela España, has a lavish layout encompassing several buildings around the obligatory Chinese garden. You can dine frugally (US$6) or lavishly (US$18).

For equally good Chinese food in more modest surroundings, try the *Restaurante Excellent* (☎ 36-42-78), 2a Avenida 12-74, Zona 10, in the Zona Viva. Prices are similar to those at the Palacio Royal. Hours are noon to 10 pm every day.

ENTERTAINMENT

Wining and dining the night away in the Zona Viva is what many visitors do. If that's beyond your budget, take in a movie at one of the cinemas along 6a Avenida between the Plaza Mayor and Parque Concordia. Walk along the street to see what's playing. Tickets sell for about US$1.50.

GETTING THERE & AWAY

Air

International air routes to Guatemala usually go through Dallas/Fort Worth, Houston, Los Angeles, Miami, Mexico City or San Salvador. If you begin your trip in any other city, you will probably find yourself stopping in one of these 'hub' cities. There are a few exceptions, which are mostly flights from cities in the region operated by smaller local airlines. The following list indicates the cities with direct and nonstop flights to and from Guatemala City, and the airlines which fly them:

Belize City – Aerovías flies on Tuesday, Saturday and Sunday via Flores; Aviateca has two flights daily via Flores.

Cancún – Aerocaribe (Mexicana), Aeroquetzal and Aviateca have daily flights.

Chetumal (Mexico) – Aerovías has a nonstop morning flight on Monday, and flights via Belize City on Wednesday and Friday.

Flores, Petén (for Tikal) – Aerocaribe, Aeroquetzal, Aerovías, Aviateca and several smaller airlines (Aviones Comerciales, TAPSA, Tikal Jets) operate daily (some twice-daily) flights. Fares range from US$75 to US$95 one way.

Houston – Continental has direct flights daily, and Aviateca three flights per week via Mérida.

Los Angeles – daily flights are by American, Aviateca, Mexicana and TACA; most of these flights make at least one stop along the way

Mexico City – Mexicana and Aviateca have daily nonstop flights. Aviacsa has flights on Tuesday, Thursday and Saturday.

Mérida – Aviateca has a morning flight three days per week.

Miami – lots of daily flights by American, Aviateca and TACA; many European airlines connect through Miami.

New York – all flights connect through Miami, Houston or Dallas/Fort Worth.

Oaxaca (Mexico) – Aviacsa has flights on Tuesday, Thursday and Saturday.

San José (Costa Rica) – daily nonstops by American, Continental and Medellín, and a direct flight with one stop by LACSA three times per week.

San Salvador (El Salvador) – daily nonstops by Aviateca, COPA and TACA.

Tapachula (Mexico) – Aviacsa has flights on Sunday, Tuesday, Thursday and Saturday.

Tuxtla Gutierrez (Mexico) – Aviacsa has flights Tuesday, Thursday and Saturday.

Here is how to contact the airlines:

Aeronica (☎ (2) 32-55-41, 31-67-59; fax 32-56-49), 10 Calle 6-20, Zona 9, Nicaragua's national airline

Aeroquetzal (☎ (2) 37-34-67/68/69, 33-71-31; fax 34-76-89), 5 Avenida 15-45, Zona 10, Centro Empresarial, Torre 1, office 1007, a Guatemalan regional carrier

Aerovías (☎ (2) 34-79-35, 31-96-63; fax 32-56-86), Avenida Hincapié at 18 Calle, Zona 13, a Guatemalan regional carrier

Air France (☎ (2) 36-73-71, 36-76-67), Avenida La Reforma 9-00, Zona 9, Edificio Plaza Panamericana, 8th floor, Guatemala City

Aviacsa (☎ (2) 31 97 08, 32-53-81; fax 31-25-16), 12 Calle 7-42, Zona 9, Local A, a Mexican regional airline

Aviateca (☎ (2) 31-82-22, 31-82-27; fax 34-74-01), Avenida Hincapié 12-22, Zona 13, Guatemala's national airline

British Airways (☎ (2) 31-25-55), Avenida La Reforma 8-60, Zona 9, Edificio Galerías Reforma, Torre II, Guatemala City

Continental (☎ (2) 31-20-51 to 55), La Aurora International Airport

COPA (Compañía Panameña de Aviación)(☎ (2) 31-33-76, 31-84-43; fax 31-83-14), 7 Avenida 6-53, Zona 4, Edificio El Triángulo, the Panamanian national carrier

Iberia (☎ (2) 37-39-14/15, 53-65-55), Avenida La Reforma 8-60, Zona 9, Edificio Galerías Reforma

Japan Air Lines (☎ (2) 31-85-97; fax 31-85-31), 7a Avenida 15-45, Zona 9, Guatemala City

KLM Royal Dutch Airlines (☎ (2) 37-02-22), 6a Avenida 20-25, Zona 10, Edificio Plaza Marítima, Guatemala City

LACSA (Líneas Aereas Costariquenses)(☎ (2)-32-39 07, 31-09-06; fax 31-22-84), 7 Avenida 14-44, Zona 9, Edificio La Galería, Oficina 3, the Costa Rican national airline

Lufthansa German Airlines (☎ (2) 37-01-13 to 16), 6a Avenida 20-25, Zona 10, Edificio Plaza Marítima, Guatemala City

Mexicana (☎ (2) 33-60-01, 31-26-97; fax 33-60-96), 13 Calle 8-44, Zona 10, Plaza Edyma, Oficina 104, a Mexican international airline.

SAHSA (☎ (2) 35-29-58, 35-26-71; fax 35-32-57), 12 Calle 1-25, Zona 10, Edificio Géminis 10, Office 208, the Honduran national airline.

TACA International Airlines (☎ (2) 32-23-60, 31-91-72; fax 34 27 75), 7 Avenida 14-35, Zona 9, El Salvador's national airline.

Bus

Among Guatemala's many bus companies, by far the most popular sort of bus is the second-hand American school bus, often with the original seats which allow room enough for school children but are very cramped for adults of European or North American stature. Fares are very cheap and buses plentiful, but most bus activity dies down by late afternoon.

In addition to the school buses, several Guatemalan lines run more comfortable passenger buses on long-distance routes between Guatemala City and the Mexican and Salvadoran borders, and to Puerto Barrios on the Gulf of Honduras.

Guatemala City has no central bus terminal, even though many Guatemalans talk about the Terminal de Autobuses. Ticket offices and departure points are different for each company. Many are near the huge and chaotic market in Zona 4. If the bus you want is one of these, go to the market and ask until you find the bus.

Here is bus route information for most of Guatemala:

Antigua – 45 km, one hour; Transportes Unidos (☎ (2) 2-49-49), 15 Calle 3-65, Zona 1, makes the trip every half-hour for US$0.50 from 7 am to 7 pm stopping in San Lucas Sacatepéquez. See also TURANSA below.

Chichicastenango – 146 km, 3½ hours; Veloz Quichelense, Terminal de Buses, Zona 4, runs buses every half-hour from 5 am to 6 pm, stopping in San Lucas, Chimaltenango and Los Encuentros for a fare of US$2.25.

Chiquimula – 169 km, three hours; Rutas Orientales (☎ (2) 53-72-82, 51-21-60), 19 Calle 8-18, Zona 1, runs buses via El Rancho, Río Hondo and Zacapa to Chiquimula every 30 minutes from 4 am to 6 pm, for US$2.50 to US$3, depending on the bus. If you're heading for Copán, Honduras, change to a Vilma bus at Chiquimula; see El Florido for details.

Cobán – 219 km, four hours; Escobar Monja Blanca (☎ (2) 51-18-78), 8a Avenida 15-16, Zona 1, has buses at 4, 5, 7, 8, 9, 10 am, noon, 2, 2.30, 4, 4.30 and 5 pm stopping at the Biotopo del Quetzal, Purulhá, Tactic and San Cristóbal for US$2 to US$3.

Copán (Honduras) – see El Florido

El Carmen/Talisman (Mexico) – 278 km, five hours; Transportes Galgos (☎ (2) 53-48-68, 2-36-61), 7a Avenida 19-44, Zona 1, runs buses along the Pacific Slope road to this border-crossing point, stopping at Escuintla (change for Santa Lucía Cotzumalguapa), Mazatenango, Retalhuleu and Coatepeque, at 5.45 and 10 am, noon, 3.30 and 5.30 pm, for US$4.50.

El Florido/Copán (Honduras) – 280 km, seven hours; Rutas Orientales (☎ (2) 53-72-82, 51-21-60), 19 Calle 8-18, Zona 1, runs buses via El Rancho, Río Hondo and Zacapa to Chiquimula every 30 minutes from 4 am to 6 pm for US$3. In Chiquimula you transfer to a Vilma bus for the remaining 58-km, 2½-hour trip via Jocotán and Camotán to this border-crossing point. From the border you take a minibus to Copán village and the ruins. Refer to the Copán section for more details.

Esquipulas – 222 km, four hours; Rutas Orientales (☎ (2) 53-72-82, 51-21-60), 19 Calle 8-18, Zona 1, has buses departing every half-hour from 4 am to 6 pm, with stops at El Rancho, Río Hondo, Zacapa and Chiquimula. The trip costs US$3.

Flores (Petén) – 506 km, 14 or 15 hours, US$12; Petenero, at 17a Avenida 10-25, is the favoured company at the moment, with newish buses making the run three times daily (4, 6 and 8 pm from Guatemala City). Others operating this route are Maya Express (☎ (2) 53-9325), 17a Avenida 9-36, Zona 1), and Fuentes del Norte (☎ (2) 8-6094, 51-3817), 17 Calle 8-46, Zona 1, runs buses departing from the capital at 1, 2, 3 and 7 am, and 11 pm, with stops at Morales, Río Dulce, San Luis and Poptún. Buses usually leave Guatemala City and Santa Elena full, anyone getting on midway stands, or rides on the roof.

Huehuetenango – 270 km, five hours; Los Halcones (☎ (2) 8-19-79), 7a Avenida 15-27, Zona 1, runs two buses a day (7 am and 2 pm) up the Interamerican Highway to Huehue, stopping at Chimaltenango, Patzicía, Tecpán, Los Encuentros, and San Cristóbal Totonicapán. The fare is US$3.50.

La Democracia – 92 km, two hours; Chatia Gomerana, Muelle Central, Terminal de Buses, Zona 4, has buses every half-hour from 6 am to 4.30 pm, stopping at Escuintla, Siquinalá (change for Santa Lucía Cotzumalguapa), La Democracia, La Gomera and Sipacate. The fare is US$1.50.

La Mesilla/Ciudad Cuauhtémoc (Mexico) – 380 km, seven hours; El Condor (☎ (2) 2-85-04), 19 Calle 2-01, Zona 1, goes to La Mesilla, on the Interamerican Highway at the border with Mexico, at 4, 9, 10 and 11 am, and 1 and 5 pm daily for US$4.

Panajachel – 147 km, three hours; Rebulli (☎ (2) 51-35-21), 21 Calle 1-34, Zona 1, departs for Lake Atitlán and Panajachel every hour from 7 am to 4 pm, stopping at Chimaltenango, Patzicía, Tecpán Guatemala (for the ruins at Iximché), Los Encuentros, and Sololá, for US$1.75.

Puerto Barrios – 307 km, six hours; Litegua (☎ (2) 2-75-78, 53-81-69), 15 Calle 10-42, Zona 1, has regular buses and also more comfortable Pullman buses every hour from 6 am to 5 pm. Stops are at El Rancho, Teculután, Río Hondo and Los Amates (Quiriguá); fare is US$4.50 or US$6.

Puerto San José – 110 km, 1½ hours; Transportes Unidos, 4 Avenida and 1 Calle, Zona 9, runs buses every 30 minutes from 5.30 am to 6 pm, for US$1.50.

Quetzaltenango – 203 km, four hours; Transportes Galgos, (☎ (2) 2-36-61), 7a Avenida 19-44, Zona 1, makes this run at 5.30, 8.30 and 11 am, and 2.30, 5, 7 and 9 pm, stopping at Chimaltenango, Los Encuentros and Totonicapán, for US$3.

Quiriguá – see Puerto Barrios.

Retalhuleu – see El Carmen and Tecún Umán.

Río Dulce – see Flores.

Río Hondo – see Chiquimula, Esquipulas and Puerto Barrios.

San Salvador (El Salvador) – 268 km, five hours; Melva Internacional (☎ (2) 31-08-74), 3 Avenida 1-38, Zona 9, runs buses from Guatemala City via Cuilapa, Oratorio and Jalpatagua to the Salvadoran border at Valle Nuevo and onward to San Salvador every hour from 5.30 am to 4.30 pm, for US$6.

San Vicente Pacaya – 46 km, two hours; Cuquita, Muelle Central, Terminal de Buses, Zona 4, heads off to this volcano village south-west of the capital at 7 am and 4 pm daily, stopping at Amatitlán, for US$1.

Santa Lucía Cotzumalguapa – see El Carmen, La Democracia and Tecún Umán.

Tecún Umán/Ciudad Hidalgo (Mexico) – 253 km, five hours; Fortaleza (☎ (2) 51-79-94), 19 Calle 8-70, Zona 1, has hourly buses from 1 am to 7 pm, stopping at Escuintla (change for Santa Lucía Cotzumalguapa), Mazatenango, Retalhuleu and Coatepeque.

Tikal – see Flores.

Tourist Minibus

Realising that normal bus transport poses challenges to foreigners, various companies offer tourist minibus services on the main tourist routes (Guatemala City-Aeropuerto La Aurora-Antigua-Panajachel-Chichicastenango). Ask at your hotel about current services and how to book seats.

TURANSA (Servicios Turísticos Antigua S A; ☎ (2) 95-35-74/75/78/82; fax 95-35-83; Supercentro Molino, Local 58-59, Carretera Roosevelt Km 15, Zona 11) operates minibus shuttle and tour services to various touristic sites in the highlands. These services are expensive by Guatemalan standards, but clean, secure and reliable.

TURANSA minibuses make trips in early morning and late afternoon, stopping to pick up passengers at major hotels in Guatemala City (Ritz, Pan American, del Centro and Zona Viva) and at the airport (7.15 am and 6.15 pm) before heading up to Antigua (US$10). Similarly, a minibus circulates among Antigua hotels (4.30 to 5 am and 2.50 to 3.20 pm) before heading for La Aurora airport, arriving at 5.40 am and 4 pm. Fare is US$10 one way.

Other services go from Antigua (depart 8.30 to 9 am) to Panajachel (arriving 11 am, US$12) on Wednesday, Friday and Sunday. The return trip from Panajachel (12 to 12.20 pm) arrives in Antigua at 2.40 pm.

Services to Chichicastenango and other locations are planned for the future. You should reserve your seat in advance. Tickets and current schedules are available at the hotels mentioned in Guatemala City; in Antigua, buy tickets at the Hotel Ramada, Hotel Villa Española, opposite the Posada de Don Rodrigo, and in many other hotels.

A similar service between Antigua and Guatemala City and La Aurora airport is offered by Econo Shuttle (☎(2) 32-34-34). Tickets are on sale in Antigua at Un Poco de Todo and Viajes Tivoli on the main plaza, and at various hotels: Asjemenou, Aurora, Landívar, La Merced, San Jorge.

GETTING AROUND
To/From the Airport

La Aurora International Airport is in Zona 13, the southern part of the city, 10 or 15 minutes from Zona 1 by taxi, half an hour by bus. Car rental offices and taxi ranks are outside, down the stairs from the arrivals level. For the city bus stop you must go up to the departures level and make your way to the small park in front of the terminal. The No 5-Aeropuerto bus comes by every now and then, and will take you through Zonas 9 and 4 to Zona 1.

Taxi fares to various points in the centre are supposedly set rates, but are actually negotiable, and are quite high: from the airport to Zona 9 or 10, US$6; to Zona 4, US$8; to Zona 1, US$12. A tip is expected.

Be sure to establish the destination and price before getting into the taxi.

If you are going directly from the airport to Antigua, see TURANSA, above.

Bus & Jitney

Guatemala City buses often lack windows, paint and seats, but they work, they're cheap, they're frequent, and though often very crowded, they're useful. They are not always safe, however. Theft and robbery are not unusual; there have even been incidents of rape. *Preferencial* buses are newer, safer, not as crowded, and more expensive at about US$0.20 per ride.

6a Avenida (southbound) and 7a Avenida (northbound) in Zona 9 are loaded with buses traversing the city; in Zona 1 these buses tend to swing away from the commercial district and travel along 4a, 5a, 9a and 10a Avenidas. The most useful north-south bus routes are Nos 2, 5 and 14. Note that modified numbers (2A, 5-Bolívar, etc) follow different routes, and may not get you where you expect to go. Any bus with 'Terminal' in the front window stops at the intercity bus 'terminal' near the market in Zona 4.

City buses stop running about 10.30 pm, and jitneys *(ruleteros)* begin to run up and down the main avenues. The jitneys run all night, until the buses resume their rattling rides at 4 am; hold up your hand as the signal to stop a jitney.

Taxi

Taxis are quite expensive, US$4 or US$6 for a normal ride – even a short one – within the city. Be sure to agree on the fare before entering the cab; there are no meters.

Car

Major international rental companies have offices both at La Aurora Airport and in the city centre. The cost is high, about US$60 to US$95 per day total (including rental charges, insurance, charges per km and fuel) for even the cheapest car. Insurance does not protect you from all losses by collision or theft. You will usually be liable for $600 to $1500 or more of damage, after which the insurance covers any loss. Drive safely and park in a secure area at night.

You must show your passport and driving licence when you rent, and you must normally be 25 years or older. If you do not have a valid credit card for the rental, a very large cash deposit may be required; check in advance to avoid disappointment.

As Guatemala grows in popularity as a tourist destination, rental cars become scarcer during the busiest times of year. Reserve a car ahead of time if possible. Sometimes you'll get a better deal if you reserve from your home country.

Note that if you wish to drive a Guatemalan rental car to Copán in Honduras, you must obtain an official letter of permission from the car rental agency to give to the Guatemalan customs official at the border. Without such a letter, you must leave the car at the border and proceed by public transport.

Ahorrent (☎ (2) 32-05-44, 32-75-15; fax 32-05-48), Boulevard Liberación 4-83, Zona 9, and in the Hotel Cortijo Reforma

Avis de Guatemala (☎ (2) 31-27-34, 31-27-47; fax 32-12-63), 12 Calle 2-73, Zona 9

Budget (☎ (2) 32-25-91, 31-65-46; fax 31-28-07), Avenida La Reforma 15-00, Zona 9

Dollar Rent a Car (☎ (2) 34-82-85 to 87, 34-15-38; fax 32-67-45), Avenida La Reforma 6-14, Zona 9 and in the lobby of the Hotel Ritz Continental

Hertz (☎ (2) 32-22-42, 31-53-74; fax 31-79-24), 7a Avenida 14-76, Zona 9, and in the hotels Camino Real and Conquistador Ramada

National (Interrent-Europcar-Tilden) (☎ (2) 68-01-75, 68-30-57; fax 37-02-21), 14 Calle 1-42, Zona 10

Tabarini Renta Autos (☎ (2) 31-61-08, 31-98-14), 2 Calle 'A' 7-30, Zona 10

Tally Renta Autos (☎ (2) 51-41-13, 2-33-27; fax 34-59-25), 7a Avenida 14-60, Zona 1

Tikal (☎ (2) 32-47-21), 2 Calle 6-56, Zona 10

Driving Though traffic in Guatemala City is always heavy and fairly chaotic, major roads in the highlands are free of heavy traffic. The Atlantic Highway has a moderate amount of heavy vehicle traffic. Avoid driving at night. See Dangers & Annoyances at the beginning of this book for safety tips while driving.

Guatemala's Highlands

The highlands, stretching from Antigua to the Mexican border north-west of Huehuetenango, are Guatemala's most beautiful region. The verdant hills are clad in carpets of emerald-green grass, fields of tawny corn and towering stands of pine. All of this lushness comes from the abundant rain which falls between May and October. If you visit during the rainy season, be prepared for some dreary, chilly, damp days. But when the sun comes out, this land is glorious.

Highlights of the region include: Antigua, Guatemala's most beautiful colonial city; Lago de Atitlán, a perfect mirror of blue surrounded by Fuji-like volcanoes; Chichicastenango, where traditional Mayan religious rites blend with the Catholicism introduced by the Spanish; Quetzaltenango,

the commercial and market centre of the south-west; and Huehuetenango, jumping-off place for the cross-border journey to Comitán and San Cristóbal de las Casas in Chiapas, Mexico.

Every town and village in the highlands has a story to tell, usually beginning more than a thousand years ago. Most towns here were already populated by the Maya when the Spanish arrived. The traditional values and ways of life of Guatemala's indigenous peoples are strongest in the highlands. Mayan is the first language, Spanish a distant second.

The age-old culture based on maize is still alive; a sturdy cottage set in the midst of a thriving *milpa* (field of maize) is a common sight, and one as old as Mayan culture itself. Wood smoke wafts through the red roof tiles and beneath the eaves of these chimneyless cottages, and on every road one sees men and women carrying loads of *leña* (firewood) to be used for heating and cooking.

Each highland town has its own market and festival days. Life in a highland town can be *muy triste* (sad, boring) when there's not a market or festival going on, so you should try to visit on those special days.

If you have only three or four days to spend in the highlands, spend them in Antigua, Panajachel and Chichicastenango. With more time you can make your way to Quetzaltenango and the sights in its vicinity such as Zunil, Fuentes Georginas, San Francisco El Alto, Momostenango and Totonicapán.

Huehuetenango and the ruins nearby at Zaculeu are worth a visit only if you're passing through or if you have lots of time; the towns and villages high in the Cuchumatanes mountains north of Huehuetenango offer wonderful scenery and adventures for intrepid travellers.

Warning

Though most visitors never experience any trouble, there have been some incidents of robbery, rape and murder of tourists in the highlands. These have occurred on trails up the volcanoes, on the outskirts of Antigua and Chichicastenango, and at lonely spots

along country roads. They happen at random and are not predictable. If you use caution and common sense, and don't do much roaming or driving at night, you should have a fine time in this beautiful region.

Before you travel in the highlands, contact your embassy or consulate in Guatemala City for information on the current situation and advice on how and where to travel in the highlands. Don't rely on local authorities for safety advice, as they may downplay the dangers. For embassy phone numbers, see the chapter on Guatemala City.

Getting Around

Guatemala City and the Guatemalan/Mexican border station at La Mesilla are connected by the Interamerican Highway, known also as the Carretera Interamericana or as Centroamérica 1 (CA-1). It is a curvy mountain road that must be travelled slowly in many places. Driving the 266 km between Guatemala City and Huehuetenango can take five hours, but the time passes pleasantly amidst the beautiful scenery. (The Pacific Slope Highway (CA-2) via Escuintla and Retalhuleu is straighter and faster, and is the better route to take if your goal is to reach Mexico as quickly as possible.)

Many buses of different companies rumble up and down the highway; for an idea of the service, refer to Getting There & Away in the Guatemala City chapter. As most of the places you'll want to reach are some distance off the Interamerican Highway, you may find yourself waiting at major highway junctions such as Los Encuentros and Cuatro Caminos in order to connect with the right bus. Travel is easiest on market days and in the morning. By mid or late afternoon, buses may be difficult to find, and all short-distance local traffic stops by dinner time. You should too.

Antigua Guatemala

Antigua Guatemala (altitude 1530 metres, population 28,000), or La muy Noble y muy Leal Ciudad de Santiago de los Caballeros

GUATEMALA

Antigua Guatemala

0   100   200 m

de Goathemala, as it was first known, is among the oldest and most beautiful cities in the Americas. Its setting is superb, amidst three magnificent volcanoes named Agua, Fuego and Acatenango. Fuego (Fire) is easily recognisable by its plume of smoke and – at night – by the red glow it projects against the sky. Experienced Guatemala travellers spend as little time in Guatemala City as possible, preferring to make Antigua their base.

Founded in 1542, Antigua Guatemala has weathered 16 damaging earthquakes, floods and fires. The handsome, sturdy colonial buildings which remain have proved their worth over and over again, and Antigua today might be said to be the result of Darwinian architecture: survival of the fittest buildings, nowadays strengthened with steel beams and reinforced concrete; the rubble of the weakest has long since been swept away.

Antigua is a wonderful place to live in or to visit, and lots of people do both. On weekends a long stream of cars and buses brings the citizens of Guatemala City up the serpentine route into the mountains for a day of strolling, shopping and sipping in the former capital. On Sunday evening, traffic jams

GUATEMALA

PLACES TO STAY

2 Pensión Ruiz 1
3 Pensión El Arco
4 Hotel Convento Santa Catalina
5 Posada Asjemenou
9 Pensión Ruiz 2
11 Posada de Don Rodrigo
13 Hotel Casa Santo Domingo
17 Posada Refugio
21 Hotel El Descanso & Cenicienta
24 Hotel El Carmen
26 Hotel Aurora
27 Posada San Francisco
33 Posada Doña Angelina
34 Hotel Posada Don Valentino
41 Hotel El Confort de Antigua
42 La Quinta
43 Casa de Santa Lucía
44 Hotel El Pasaje
58 Hotel Santa Clara
61 Hotel Antigua
62 Hotel San Jorge
63 Ramada Hotel Antigua
64 Mesón Panza Verde

PLACES TO EAT

19 Capri Antigua Cafetería
20 Pizzería Martedino & Pollo Campesino
22 Asados de la Calle del Arco, El Fondo
    de la Calle Real & Sueños del
    Quetzal
25 Restaurant Doña Luisa Xicotencatl
36 Restaurant Italiano El Capuchino
39 Doña María Gordillo Dulces Típicos
40 Mistral
45 El Sereno & Rainbow Reading Room

OTHER

1 La Merced
6 Arco de Santa Catarina
7 Convento de Santa Teresa
8 Convento de las Capucinas
10 TURANSA-Avis Rent a Car Office
12 El Carmen
14 Casa Kójom
15 Terminal de Buses
16 Mercado (Market)
18 Convento de la Compañía de Jesús &
    Handicrafts Market
23 Museo de Santiago & Palacio del
    Ayuntamiento
28 Chevron Fuel Station
29 Cementerio General
30 Mercado (Market)
31 Monumento a Landívar
32 Correos (Main Post Office)
35 Iglesia de San Agustín
37 Parque Central
38 Catedral de Santiago
46 Conexion Telecommunications
47 Guatel (Telephone Office)
48 Cinema
49 Palacio de los Capitanes
50 INGUAT Tourist Office
51 Museo de Arte Colonial & Uni-
    versidad de San Carlos
52 Casa Popenoe
53 Iglesia del Espiritu Santo
54 Iglesia de Santa Lucía
55 Hospital de San Pedro
56 Park & Handicrafts Market
57 Iglesia y Convento de Santa Clara
59 Iglesia de San Francisco
60 Iglesia de San José
65 Escuela de Cristo

Antigua's cobbled streets as the day trippers head home. If you have the opportunity to be in Antigua during Holy Week – especially on Good Friday – seize it; but make your hotel reservations months in advance, as all hotels will be full.

ORIENTATION

Volcán Agua is south-east of the city and visible from most points within it; Volcán Fuego is south-west, and Volcán Acatenango is to the west. The three volcanoes which appear on the city's coat of arms provide easy reference points.

Antigua's street grid uses a modified version of the Guatemala City numbering system. (For details on that system, see Orientation in the Guatemala City chapter.) In Antigua, compass points are added to the avenidas and calles. (Points of the compass in Spanish are norte (north), sur (south), oriente (east) and poniente (west). Calles run east-west, and so 4 Calle west of the Parque Central is 4 Calle Poniente; avenidas run north-south, and 3a Avenida north of the Parque Central is 3a Avenida Norte. The central point is the north-east corner of the city's main plaza, the Parque Central. The city is thus divided into quadrants by 4a Avenida and 4 Calle.

The old headquarters of the Spanish colonial government, called the Palacio de los Capitanes, is on the south side of the parque; you'll know it by its double (two-storey) arcade. On the east side is the cathedral, on the north side is the Palacio del Ayuntamiento (Town Hall) and on the west side are banks and shops.

The Arco de Santa Catarina (Arch of St Catharine), spanning 5a Avenida Norte between 1 Calle and 2 Calle, is another famous Antigua landmark.

Intercity buses arrive at the Terminal de Buses, a large open lot just north of the market, four blocks west of the Parque Central along 4 Calle Poniente. Buses serving towns and villages in the vicinity leave from the terminal as well, or from other points around the market.

INFORMATION
Tourist Office

Antigua's INGUAT tourist office (☎ (9) 32-07-63) is in the Palacio de los Capitanes, at the intersection of 4a Avenida Sur and 5 Calle Oriente. It's open from 8 am to 5 pm, seven days a week. You can pick up a schedule of Semana Santa (Holy Week) events here.

Other useful sources of information are the bulletin boards at Doña Luisa Xicotencatl restaurant and Casa Andinista, described below. Check them for info on renting houses and rooms, bikes or horses; for Spanish lessons, rides to the airport, or tours to Tikal and other sites; and video-bar film schedules.

For places for rent, see also *The Classifieds*, a free weekly booklet distributed in hotels and at the tourist office.

Money

Banks in Antigua, as elsewhere in Guatemala, tend to be open from 9 am to 2 pm Monday to Friday (till 2.30 pm on Friday), but the Banco del Agro, on the north side of the Parque Central, has a *ventanilla especial* (special teller window) which is open longer

hours and on Saturday. Lloyd's Bank is at the north-east corner of the Parque Central, on the corner of 4a Avenida and 4 Calle.

Post & Telecommunications

The post office is at 4 Calle Poniente and Alameda de Santa Lucía, west of the Parque Central near the market. It's open Monday to Saturday from 8 am to noon and 2 to 8 pm (closed on Sunday).

The Guatel telephone office is just off the south-west corner of the Parque Central, at the intersection of 5 Calle Poniente and 5a Avenida Sur. Hours are 7 am to midnight daily. See Post & Telecommunications at the beginning of the Guatemala section for information on using AT&T's USADirect, MCI's Call USA, and Sprint Express services.

Conexión (☎ (9) 32-33-16, fax 32-06-02, Internet 5385706@MCImail.com), 5 Calle Poniente 11-B, will send and/or receive phone, fax, electronic mail and telex messages for you. Prices for sending are fairly high; receiving is cheap. They're open every day. Slightly lower rates are charged at Guisela Fax (☎/fax 32-30-91), 2 Calle Poniente 19.

Bookshops

Rainbow Reading Room, 7a Avenida Sur No 1, at 6 Calle Poniente, has thousands of used books in English and Spanish. They serve cheap food, and sponsor musical programmes in the evenings. Hours are 8 am to 10 pm (till 11 pm on Friday and Saturday).

Un Poco de Todo, at the north-west corner of the Parque Central, has English and Spanish books. It's open Monday to Friday from 9.30 am to 1 pm and 3 to 6 pm.

Casa Andinista, 4 Calle Oriente No 5, just a few steps off the Parque Central, sells Spanish books, postcards and maps.

Librería del Pensativo (☎ 32-07-29), 5a Avenida Norte 29 (between 1 and 2 Calles), just north of the arch on the right-hand side, has some English books among the Spanish ones.

Medical Services

The local hospital is named for Pedro de Betancourt, Antigua's great healer; Hospital de San Pedro (☎ (9) 32-03-01) is at 3a Avenida Sur and 6 Calle Oriente.

Laundry

Wash & Wear Antigua, Alameda de Santa Lucía 52, is a few steps south of the Hotel El Pasaje near 6 Calle Poniente; it's open from 7 am to 7 pm (from 8 am to noon on Sunday). Another laundry is to the left of the Posada Refugio, 4 Calle Poniente No 30.

Toilets

Public toilets are at 4a Avenida and 4 Calle, at the north-east corner of the Parque Central.

PARQUE CENTRAL

After the great earthquake of 1773, the archbishop slept in his carriage in the parque, afraid that an aftershock would bring down the roof of his house on him. Likewise, when I visited several months after the terrible earthquake of February 1976, many *antigüeños* were still encamped in the parque in makeshift tents and shelters of plastic sheeting because their homes had been destroyed.

Today the parque is the gathering place for citizens and foreign visitors alike. On most days the periphery is lined with villagers who have brought their handicrafts – cloth, dolls, blankets, pottery – to sell to tourists; on Sunday the parque is mobbed with marketeers, and the streets on the east and west sides of the parque are closed to traffic in order to give them room. The best prices are to be had late on Sunday afternoon, when the market is winding down.

Palacio de los Capitanes

The Palacio de los Capitanes, built in 1543 as the Palace of the Royal Audiencia & Captaincy-General of Guatemala, has a stately double arcade on its façade which marches proudly across the southern extent of the parque. The façade is original, but most of the rest of the building was reconstructed a century ago. From 1543 to 1773, this building was the governmental centre of all Central America, in command of Chiapas, Guatemala, Honduras and Nicaragua.

Catedral de Santiago

The Catedral de Santiago, on the east side of the parque, was founded in 1542, damaged by earthquakes many times, badly ruined in 1773, and only partially rebuilt between 1780 and 1820. In the 16th and early 17th centuries, Antigua's churches had lavish baroque interiors, but most lost this richness when they were rebuilt after the earthquakes. The present cathedral, stripped of its expensive decoration, occupies what was the narthex of the original edifice. In the crypt lie the bones of Bernal Díaz del Castillo, historian of the Spanish conquest, who died in 1581. Restoration work is being carried out on other parts of the cathedral, but it will never regain its former grandeur.

Palacio del Ayuntamiento

On the north side of the parque stands the Palacio del Ayuntamiento, Antigua's Town Hall, which dates mostly from 1743. In addition to town offices, it houses the Museo de Santiago, which exhibits a collection of colonial furnishings, artefacts and weapons. Hours are 9 am to 4 pm Tuesday to Friday, and 9 am to noon and 2 to 4 pm on Saturday and Sunday (closed on Monday); admission costs US$0.20.

Next door (and with the same hours) is the Museo del Libro Antiguo (Old Book Museum), which has exhibits of colonial printing and binding.

Universidad de San Carlos

The Universidad de San Carlos was founded in 1676, but its main building (built in 1763) at 5 Calle Oriente No 5, half a block east of the parque, now houses the Museo de Arte Colonial (same hours as the Museo de Santiago).

CASA K'OJOM

Guatemala's rich traditional Mayan culture is changing, giving way before the onslaught of modernity as portrayed by tourists and the mass media. In 1984, Samuel Franco Arce began photographing Maya ceremonies and festivals, and recording their music on audio tape. By 1987 he had enough to found Casa K'ojom ('House of Music'), a museum of Mayan music and the ceremonies in which it was used.

Some visitors to Guatemalan towns and villages are lucky enough to witness a parade of the *cofradías*, or some other age-old ceremony. But lucky or not, you can experience some of the fascination of the culture in a visit to Casa K'ojom, Calle de Recoletos, a block west of the bus station. It's open from 9.30 am to 12.30 pm and 2 to 5 pm (till 4 pm on Saturday), and is closed on Sunday. Admission costs US$0.40 (US$1 including the audiovisual show).

Don't miss this museum. Besides the fine collection of photographs of ceremonies, musicians and festivals, Señor Franco has amassed a wealth of objects: musical instruments, tools, masks and figures. These have been arranged to show scenes of traditional Maya life; recordings of the music play softly in the background. Be sure to see the exhibit featuring Maximón, the evil folk-god venerated by the people of several highland towns.

CHURCHES
Once glorious in their gilded baroque finery, Antigua's churches have suffered indignities from both nature and humankind. Rebuilding after earthquakes gave the churches thicker walls, lower towers and belfries, and unembellished interiors; and moving the capital to Guatemala City deprived Antigua of the population needed to maintain the churches in their traditional richness. Still, they are impressive.

La Merced
From the parque, walk three long blocks up 5a Avenida Norte, passing beneath the arch of Santa Catalina (built in 1694 and rebuilt in the 19th century). At the northern end of 5a Avenida is the Iglesia y Convento de Nuestra Señora de La Merced (Church &

Convent of Our Lady of Mercy), known simply as La Merced – Antigua's most striking colonial church. Its baroque façade dates from the mid-19th century.

San Francisco
The next most notable church is the Iglesia de San Francisco, 7 Calle Oriente and 2a Avenida Sur. It dates from the mid-1500s, but little of the original building remains. Rebuilding and restoration over the centuries has produced a handsome structure; reinforced concrete added in 1961 protected the church from serious damage in the 1976 earthquake. All that remains of the original church is the Chapel of Hermano Pedro, resting place of Fray Pedro de Betancourt, a Franciscan monk. Hermano Pedro (Brother Peter) arrived in Antigua in the mid-1600s, promptly founded a hospital for the poor, and earned the gratitude of generations. His intercession is still sought by the ill, who pray fervently by his casket.

Capuchinas
The Convento de las Capuchinas, 2a Avenida Norte and 2 Calle Oriente, was a convent founded in 1736 by nuns from Madrid. Destroyed repeatedly by earthquakes, it is now a museum, with exhibits of the religious life in colonial times.

Other Churches
The Convento de Santa Teresa, ruined in 1773, is at 4a Avenida Norte between 1 and 2 Calles Oriente; the Iglesia y Convento de Santa Clara, 2a Avenida Sur No 27, corner of 6 Calle Oriente, was founded in 1700, rebuilt in 1734 and destroyed in 1773; and the Iglesia y Convento de Santo Domingo, corner of 1a Avenida Norte and Calle de Santo Domingo, was founded in 1664 and ruined – guess when? – in 1773.

The same fate befell the Convento de Nuestra Señora de la Concepción, at the corner of 4 Calle Oriente and Calle del Hermano Pedro, which was founded in 1577, ruined in 1773 and ruined somewhat more in 1976. You might also want to see the Escuela de Cristo, Calle de Fray Rodrigo de la Cruz and Calle del Hermano Pedro, in the south-eastern part of town; it was built as a church, and restored in the mid-1800s.

CASA POPENOE
At the corner of 5 Calle Oriente and 1a Avenida Sur stands this beautiful mansion built in 1636 by Don Luis de las Infantas Mendoza y Venegas. Ruined by the earthquake of 1773, the house stood desolate for 1½ centuries until it was bought in 1931 by Dr and Mrs Popenoe. The Popenoes' painstaking and authentic restoration yields a fascinating glimpse of how the family of an important royal official (Don Luis) lived in the Antigua of the 1600s. The house is open Monday to Saturday from 2 to 4 pm; the guided tour costs US$0.50.

MERCADO & MONUMENTO A LANDÍVAR
At the western end of 5 Calle Poniente is the Monumento a Landívar, a structure of five colonial-style arches set in a little park. Rafael Landívar, an 18th-century Jesuit priest and poet, lived and wrote in Antigua for some time. Landívar's poetry is esteemed as the best of the colonial period, even though much of it was written in Italy after the Jesuits were expelled from Guatemala. Landívar's Antigua house was nearby on 5a Calle Poniente.

Around the Monumento a Landívar on the west side of Alameda de Santa Lucía sprawls the market – chaotic, colourful and always busy. Morning, when all the village people from the vicinity are actively buying and selling, is the best time to come.

CEMETERY
If you have never visited a Mexican or Guatemalan cemetery, you can take the opportunity to stroll through Antigua's large Cementerio General, west of the market and bus terminal. Hints of ancient Mayan beliefs are revealed in the lavishly decorated tombs, many of which also have homey touches, and often fresh flowers or other evidence of frequent visits.

SEMANA SANTA
By far the most interesting time to be in Antigua is during Semana Santa (Holy Week) celebrations, when hundreds of people dress up as pseudo-Israelites, in deep purple robes, to accompany daily religious processions in remembrance of the Crucifixion. Streets are covered in breathtakingly elaborate and colourful *alfombras* (carpets) of coloured sawdust and flower petals. These beautiful but fragile works of art are destroyed as the processions shuffle through them, but are recreated the next morning for another day.

Traditionally, the most interesting days are Palm Sunday, when a procession departs from La Merced (see Churches) in mid-afternoon; Holy Thursday, when a late afternoon procession departs from the Iglesia de San Francisco; and Good Friday, when an early morning procession departs from La Merced, and a late afternoon one from the Escuela de Cristo.

In 1995, Semana Santa begins on 9 April, (Palm Sunday, the Sunday before Easter), and runs until 16 April (Easter Sunday); the dates are 31 March and 7 April in 1996 and 23 March and 30 March in 1997. Have ironclad hotel reservations well in advance of these dates, or plan to stay in another town or in Guatemala City and commute to the festivities.

Warning
On a secular note, beware of pickpockets. It seems that Guatemala City's entire population of pickpockets (numbering perhaps in the hundreds) decamps to Antigua for Semana Santa. In the press of the emotion-filled crowds lining the processional routes, they home in on foreign tourists especially. Razor blades silently slice pocket and bag, and deft hands remove contents seemingly without sound or movement.

LANGUAGE COURSES
Antigua is the nicest place in the country to study Spanish, and there are many schools to choose from – around 70 at last count.

Reports from readers of this book indicate

that price, quality of teaching and satisfaction of students varies greatly from one school to another. Often the quality of the class depends upon the particular instructor, and thus may vary even within a single school. Instructors also tend to move around from one school to another to improve their own incomes and teaching conditions. I've had good reports about the Academia Cervantes and the Centro Lingüístico, but it is difficult to say which schools are recommendable at any given time. If possible, ask for references and talk to someone who has studied at your chosen school recently.

Many of Antigua's Spanish schools are organised into two loose groupings: the Asociación de Academias de Español (Apdo Postal 76, Antigua Guatemala) and the Escuelas Unidas de Español. Both claim to be approved by the Guatemalan Ministry of Education and by INGUAT (Institute of Tourism).

Asociación de Academias de Español

Academia Centroamérica, Abel Alfredo Aquino Cuellar, 1 Calle del Chajón No 19-A (☎ 32-32-97)

Academia Cervantes, Carlos René Aguilar López, 5 Calle Poniente No 42-A (☎ 32-06-35)

Academia de Español Cristiana, Franklin Romeo Contreras, 6a Avenida Norte No 15 (☎ 32-03-67)

Academia Landívar, Héctor Haroldo Pérez Estrada, 2 Calle Oriente No 4

Academia Pedro de Alvarado, Catalina Galindo de Le-cunff, 1 Calle Poniente No 24 (☎ 32-22-66)

Centro Dinámico, Marta Elisa Gaytán, 6a Avenida Norte No 63 (☎ 32-24-40)

Centro Lingüístico Maya, Angel Arturo Miranda Baeza, 5a Calle Poniente No 20 (☎ 32-06-56)

Instituto Antigüeño, José Mario Valle García, 1 Calle Poniente No 33 (☎ 32-26-82)

Proyecto Lingüístico Francisco Marroquín, 4a Avenida Sur No 4 (☎ /fax 32-04-06)

Escuelas Unidas de Español

Arcoiris, 7 Calle Oriente No 19 (☎ 32-29-33)

Cabaguil, 7 Calle Oriente No 3

Colonial, Calzada Santa Lucía Sur y Pasaje Matheu No 7

Donquijote, 9 Calle Poniente No 7 (☎ 32-06-51)

Tecún Umán, 6 Calle Poniente No 34 (☎ 32-27-92)

Independent

Quiché College Level Spanish, 8a Avenida No 15-A (☎ /fax 32-05-75)

PLACES TO STAY – BOTTOM END

Visitors who come to Antigua to attend one of the many Spanish-language schools usually stay in family pensions at low prices – about US$40 per week. The tourist office has information on how to get in touch with willing families. When checking a pension or small hotel, look at several rooms, as some are much better than others.

Some of the best cheap lodgings in town are on the east side of the Alameda de Santa Lucía, across from the market and the bus terminal. The exceptionally attractive and well-kept *Casa de Santa Lucía*, at No 9, between 5 and 6 Calles Poniente, has pseudo-colonial atmosphere and charges US$8/10 a single/double with shower; ring the bell to the left of the door. There's a car park. The friendly *Hotel El Pasaje*, Alameda de Santa Lucía Sur 3, charges US$6/8 a double without/with bath.

The *Posada Doña Angelina*, nearby at 4 Calle Poniente 33, is actually two hotels in one. The older section, on 4 Calle a few steps off the Alameda de Santa Lucía, charges US$5/9/11 a single/double/triple in waterless rooms arranged around a bare courtyard. The newer section of the hotel, also around a courtyard, charges US$10/14/18 for a room with shower.

La Quinta, 5 Calle Poniente 19, is clean, friendly, and near the bus station. Rooms are OK, at US$5/7/9 a single/double/triple without running water.

Posada San Francisco, 3 Calle Oriente 19-A, is good, simple, quiet and family-run, with double rooms for US$6/8 without/with private bath.

Despite its popularity with budget travellers, only parts of the *Posada Refugio*, 4 Calle Poniente 30, are comfortable or clean. The price is US$6/8 a double without/with bath.

Hotel El Descanso (☎ (9) 32-01-42), 5a Avenida Norte 9, '50 steps from the central parque', has 14 small rooms in the building facing the restaurant called Café Café. It's clean and convenient at US$12 to US$16 a double with bath.

Pensión El Arco, 5a Avenida Norte 32, just

north of the Santa Catalina arch, is in part of an old colonial building. The smiling señora makes you feel safe and welcome. Plain and sometimes claustrophobic but nevertheless tidy rooms without bath cost US$3.50 per person. Look at the room before you say yes.

Pensión Ruiz 2, 2 Calle Poniente 25, is slightly cleaner, pleasanter and more expensive (at US$3.50 per person) than its sister establishment, the *Pensión Ruiz 1*, Alameda de Santa Lucía north of 2 Calle Poniente.

Hotel El Confort de Antigua (☎ (9) 32-05-66), 1a Avenida Norte No 2, is clean and beautifully kept. The five rooms share two baths, and cost US$15/20 a single/double.

Hotel Posada Don Valentino (☎ (9) 32-03-84), 5 Calle Poniente No 28, has tiny rooms that are bright and clean, and a nice patio and garden, for US$9/14 a single/double without bath, US$11/16 with. They have a car park one block away.

Hotel Santa Clara (☎ (9) 32-03-42), 2 Avenida Sur No 20, is quiet, proper and clean, with a small garden and some large rooms with two double beds. Rooms with bath are US$10 to US$15 a single, US$13 to US$18 a double.

PLACES TO STAY – MIDDLE
Antigua's mid-range hotels allow you to wallow in the city's colonial charms for a very moderate outlay of cash.

Posada Asjemenou (☎ (9) 32-26-70), 5a Avenida Norte No 31, just north of the arch, is a beautifully renovated house built around a grassy courtyard with a fountain. At this writing, its prices of US$12/18 a double without/with bath make it the best value for money in town. Prices will no doubt rise, though. There's a pay car park nearby.

Hotel Convento Santa Catalina (☎ /fax (9) 32-30-80), 5a Avenida Norte No 28, just south of the arch, is a nicely renovated convent around a courtyard. Large rooms with bath are very reasonably priced at US$22 to US$28 a single, US$28 to US$34 a double.

Recently renovated *Hotel El Carmen* (☎ /fax (9) 32-32-75), 3a Avenida Norte No 9, 03001, is very tidy, and quiet despite its

location only 1½ blocks from the square. Rooms with shower, cable TV and breakfast cost US$33/39 a single/double.

Mesón Panza Verde (☎ /fax (9) 32-29-25), 5a Avenida Sur No 19, four blocks south of the parque, is an elegant American-owned guesthouse and restaurant with comfy, quiet rooms for US$30 to US$40 and suites with fireplace for US$50 to US$60. The restaurant is excellent.

Hotel Aurora (☎ (9) 32-02-17), 4 Calle Oriente 16, is beautiful, with its grassy courtyard graced by a fountain, but the 17 old-fashioned rooms with bath are dark and certainly not fancy. At US$30/35/40 a single/double/triple, it's a bit expensive compared to others in this class. There's a private car park.

Hotel San Jorge (☎ (9) 32-31-32), 4a Avenida Sur No 13, is in a modern building with cable TV, fireplace and bath. Guests here (mostly older couples from the USA) may use the swimming pool and room service facilities of the posh Hotel Antigua nearby. Rooms cost US$25/30/35 a single/double/triple.

PLACES TO STAY – TOP END
Hotel Casa Santo Domingo (☎ (9) 32-01-40, fax 32-01-02), 3 Calle Oriente No 28, is a wonderful luxury hotel set in the partially restored Convent of Santo Domingo (1642) which takes up an entire city block. Rooms are of an international five-star standard, but the public spaces are wonderfully colonial and include a swimming pool. The Dominican friars never had it so good. Rates are US$135/147/164 a single/double/triple, tax included.

Hotel Antigua (☎(9) 32-03-31, 32-02-88, fax 32-08-07; in the USA (800) 223-67-64), 8 Calle Poniente No 1, is a Spanish colonial country club which takes up an entire city block. The 60 rooms have private baths and fireplaces, and many have two double beds. Room rates are US$110/130/150 a single/double/triple, tax included.

Ramada Hotel Antigua (☎ (9) 32-00-11 to 15, fax 32-02-37), 9 Calle Poniente and Carretera a Ciudad Vieja, is the largest and most modern hotel in town, with 155 rooms and suites. Rooms have balconies, fireplaces, modern baths, and colour TV with English-language stations. Rates are US$100 to US$158 per room, tax included.

Posada de Don Rodrigo (☎ (9) 32-02-91, 32-03-87), 5a Avenida Norte 17, is a maze of rooms and restaurants around colonial courtyards. The forecourt is the scene of free marimba concerts each afternoon. Some of the 33 rooms are charming if old-fashioned; others are just drab. Rooms with bath cost US$70/80/90 a single/double/triple, which is too much for what you get. The hotel's restaurants and public areas are much better than its rooms.

PLACES TO EAT – BOTTOM END
Eating cheaply is easy, even in touristy Antigua.

The first place everyone tries is *Restaurant Doña Luisa Xicotencatl*, 4 Calle Oriente No 12, 1½ blocks east of the parque. A small central courtyard is set with dining tables, with more dining rooms on the upper level. The menu lists a dozen sandwiches made with Doña Luisa's own bread baked on the premises, as well as yoghurt, chilli, cakes and pies, and heartier meat dishes, all priced from about US$2.50 to US$5. Alcoholic beverages are served, as is excellent Antigua coffee. The restaurant is open every day for all three meals, and it is usually busy. Doña Luisa, by the way, was Pedro de Alvarado's faithful companion in Antigua, and is buried with him beneath the cathedral.

Mistral, 4 Calle Oriente 7, across the street from Doña Luisa, serves freshly squeezed fruit and vegetable juices, good coffee and sandwiches, with most items priced at US$2 or so. Behind the streetside juice bar is the courtyard dining area, where you can order meat loaf, rabbit stew, steaks, Breton crepes, and other dishes not often found on Guatemalan menus. Most cost US$1.75 to US$2.50. In the evening, return for American video movies in the bar.

Rainbow Reading Room, at 7a Avenida Sur and 6 Calle Poniente, is a lending library, bookstore, travellers' club and restaurant all

in one. Healthy vegetarian dishes are a speciality, as is close camaraderie.

The richest concentration of restaurants is on 5a Avenida north of the parque. *Asados de la Calle del Arco*, just off the parque on the right, serves grilled meats and Tex-Mex food. Try the burritos for US$3.

Right next door to the red-meat place is *Sueños del Quetzal* (☎ (9) 32-26-76), 5a Avenida Norte No 3, a full-service vegetarian restaurant open from 7 am to 10 pm every day. Most of the tables are upstairs.

Half a block north of the parque is *Cenicienta*, 5a Avenida Norte 9. It serves mostly cakes, pastries, pies and coffee, but the blackboard menu often features quiche lorraine and quiche chapín (Guatemalan-style), yoghurt and fruit as well. A slice of something and a hot beverage cost less than US$2.

El Fondo de la Calle Real, 5a Avenida Norte 5, appears to have no room for diners, but that's because all the tables are upstairs. The menu is good and varied for any taste or appetite. The speciality caldo real (hearty chicken soup) for US$2.50 makes a good lunch. Roast chicken, sandwiches, tacos and fondues are priced from US$2.50 to US$5.

Pollo Campesino, 4 Calle Poniente 18, a half-block west of the parque, provides cheap roast chicken in modern surroundings.

Restaurant Pizzería Martedino, also at 4 Calle Poniente 18, sells good pizzas for US$2 to US$5 (depending upon size and ingredients); pasta dishes cost less. The *almuerzo del día* (daily set-price lunch) is a bargain at US$2.50. *Restaurant Gran Muralla*, next door, serves a Guatemalan highland version of Chinese food.

Capri Antigua Cafetería, 4 Calle Poniente 24, near the corner with 6a Avenida Norte, is a simple, modern place that's very popular with younger diners and budget travellers. They usually fill its little wooden benches and tables, ordering soup for less than US$1, sandwiches for only slightly more, or *platos fuertes* (substantial platters) for US$2.20 to US$3.25.

Perhaps the best bargain is the *Restaurant Italiano El Capuchino* (☎ 32-06-13), 6a Avenida Norte 10, between 4 and 5 Calles

Poniente. The daily four-course set-price lunch costs about US$4 or US$5. There's a well-stocked bar.

Not far from the market and bus terminal on 4 Calle Poniente between the Alameda de Santa Lucía and 7a Avenida Sur are several comedores, family-run cookshops specialising in simple food at rock-bottom prices. Look for the *Comedor Antigua* at No 21 and the *Cafetería y Comedor San José* at No 30.

PLACES TO EAT – MIDDLE
The dining room in the *Posada de Don Rodrigo*, 5a Avenida Norte 17, is one of the city's most pleasant and popular places for lunch or dinner. Order a platter of Guatemalan specialities for US$11, or even lomito (beef tenderloin). A marimba band plays most afternoons and every Sunday.

Mesón Panza Verde, 5a Avenida Sur No 19, provides excellent Continental cuisine in an appealing Antiguan atmosphere. The Italian chef is from Bergamo, the food is very good and the prices are moderate - about US$15 per person for a full dinner.

Doña María Gordillo Dulces Típicos, 4 Calle Oriente 11, across the street from the Hotel Aurora, is filled with traditional Guatemalan sweets, desserts and confections to take away, and there's often a crowd of antigüeños lined up to do just that. Delicacies made from milk, fruit, eggs, marzipan, chocolate and sugar compete for customers' affections. Local handicrafts are for sale here as well.

PLACES TO EAT – TOP END
El Sereno (☎(9) 32-00-73), 6 Calle Poniente 30, between the Alameda de Santa Lucía and 7a Avenida Sur, next door to the Tecún Umán School of Spanish, is Antigua's most exclusive restaurant. A colonial house has been nicely restored and modernised somewhat to provide a traditional wooden bar, plant-filled court and several small dining rooms hung with oil paintings. Cuisine is international, leaning heavily on French dishes; the menu changes every week. The short wine list is good but expensive. Expect to pay US$15 to US$22 per person for dinner. Make reservations for lunch (noon to 4 pm) or dinner (6.30 to 9.30 pm) Wednesday to Sunday; it's closed on Monday and Tuesday.

ENTERTAINMENT
Dinner, drinks with friends, or a video movie in the bar at *Mistral* (4 Calle Oriente No 7) are the pleasures of the evening here. Bars for music and dancing open and close frequently. Current trendy favourite is the *Macondo Pub*, 5a Avenida at 2 Calle Poniente, just south of the arch. The *Rainbow Reading Room*, 7a Avenida Sur No 1, at 6 Calle Poniente, has singalongs and similar informal entertainment most evenings.

The *cinema* half a block south of the Parque Central on 5a Avenida Sur mostly has movies in Spanish, but occasionally screens something with subtitles.

THINGS TO BUY
Lots of tourists come to Antigua, and almost as many handicrafts sellers come to cater to their needs for colourful Guatemalan woven goods. Wherever there is an open space to spread their wares, you'll find villagers selling. Look especially for the markets at the corner of 6 Calle Oriente and 2 Avenida Sur; 4 Calle Poniente at 7 Avenida Norte; and in the Parque Central.

In 1958 an ancient Mayan jade quarry near Nebaj, Guatemala, was rediscovered. When it was shown to yield true jadeite (with a hardness of 6.5 to seven) equal in quality to Chinese stone, the mine was reopened. Today it produces jade both for gemstone use and for carving.

When buying jade you must have a fat wad of money, as beautiful well-carved stones can cost US$100 or much more. Look for translucency, purity and intensity of colour, and absence of flaws. Ask the merchant if you can scratch the stone with a pocket knife; if it scratches, it's not true jadeite but an inferior stone.

Antigua has two shops specialising in jade: La Casa de Jade (jade is pronounced HAH-deh), 4 Calle Oriente 3, and Jades (HAH-dess), 4 Calle Oriente 34.

Galería El Sitio (☎ (9) 32-30-37), 5 Calle

Poniente 13/15, specialises in paintings by modern Guatemalan artists. Hours are 10 am to 1 pm and 3 to 7 pm Tuesday to Friday and 11 am to 7 pm on weekends (closed on Monday). Ring the bell on the gate for admission.

GETTING THERE & AWAY

Bus connections with Guatemala City are frequent, and there are direct buses several times daily to Panajachel on Lago de Atitlán. To go directly to other highland towns such as Chichicastenango, Quetzaltenango and Huehuetenango, you may have to take one of the frequent minibuses to Chimaltenango (US$0.40), on the Interamerican Highway, and catch an onward bus from there.

Besides the bus services listed below, there are numerous minibus shuttles for tourists (TURANSA, Econo Shuttle, etc) from Antigua to Guatemala City and La Aurora airport, to Panajachel and Chichicastenango. See Getting There & Away in the Guatemala City section, and ask at your hotel for current services.

Guatemala City (45 km, one hour) – Transportes Unidos (☎ in Guatemala City (2) 2-49-49); 15 Calle 3-65, Zona 1) makes the trip every half-hour from 7 am to 7 pm, stopping in San Lucas Sacatepéquez, for US$0.80.

Izabal, Río Dulce (352 km, eight hours) – Río Dulce Shuttle (☎ in Guatemala City (2) 34-03-23/4, fax 34-03-41; 7 Avenida 14-44, Zona 9) operates tourist minibuses between Antigua and Izabal, on the Río Dulce, on Wednesday, Friday and Sunday (US$32 one way). The trip includes a 45-minute stop at Quiriguá to see its famous stelae.

Panajachel, on Lago de Atitlán (80 km, two hours) – there are several buses daily from Antigua's Terminal de Buses, even more from Chimaltenango.

GETTING AROUND

Buses to outlying villages such as Santa María de Jesús (half an hour, US$0.25) and San Antonio Aguas Calientes (25 minutes, US$0.20) depart from the Terminal de Buses west of the market. It's best to make your outward trip early in the morning and your return trip by mid-afternoon, as services drop off dramatically as late afternoon approaches.

Bicycles and motorbikes are available for hire at a number of places in Antigua for US$25 per day. Try the Hotel Los Capitanes, next to the Los Capitanes cinema, 9a Avenida Sur. Read the safety warning above before venturing out of town on a motorbike.

AROUND ANTIGUA GUATEMALA
Horse Riding

Several stables in Antigua rent horses and arrange for day or overnight tours into the countryside. Ask at the tourist office, or contact R Rolando Pérez (☎ (9) 32-28-09), San Pedro El Panorama No 28.

Ciudad Vieja & San Antonio Aguas Calientes

Six and a half km south-west of Antigua along the Escuintla road (the one which passes the Ramada Antigua Hotel) is Ciudad Vieja (Old City), site of the first capital of the Captaincy General of Guatemala. Founded in 1527, it was destroyed in 1541 when the aptly named Volcán Agua loosed a flood of water pent up in its crater. Cascading down the steep volcano's side, the water carried tonnes of rock and mud over the city, leaving only a few ruins of the Church of La Concepción. There is little to see today.

Past Ciudad Vieja, turn right at a large cemetery on the right-hand side; the unmarked road takes you through San Miguel Dueñas to San Antonio Aguas Calientes. (In San Miguel Dueñas, take the first street on the right – between two houses – after coming to the concrete-block paving; this, too, is unmarked. If you come to the Texaco station in the centre of San Miguel, you've missed the road.)

The road winds through coffee fincas, little fields of vegetables and corn, and hamlets of farmers to San Antonio Aguas Calientes, 14 km from Antigua. As you enter San Antonio's plaza, you will see that the village is noted for its weaving. Market stalls in the plaza sell local woven and embroidered goods, as do shops on side streets (walk to the left of the church to find them). Bargaining is expected.

Volcanoes

Climbing the volcanoes which loom above Antigua is exciting in more ways than one. In recent years robbers have intercepted groups of foreigners from time to time, relieving them of all their goods (including clothing). There have been incidents of rape and murder as well. Still, many visitors take their chances in return for the exhilaration and the beauty of the view.

Check with your embassy in Guatemala City regarding safety before you climb. If you decide to go, it's easy to find a guide. Ask at the tourist office in Antigua, or at your hotel.

Take sensible precautions. Have warm clothing and, in the rainy season, some sort of rain gear. Carry a flashlight in case the weather changes - it can get as dark as night when it rains on the mountain. Take some snacks and water as well.

Volcán Pacaya Various agencies operate tours up Pacaya for about US$25 per person, including a 1½-hour bus ride to the trailhead followed by a two-hour trek to the summit.

Santa María de Jesús & Volcán Agua
Follow 2a Avenida Sur or Calle de los Pasos south toward El Calvario (two km), then continue onward via San Juan del Obispo (another three km) to Santa María de Jesús, nine km south of Antigua. This is the jumping-off point for treks up the slopes of Volcán Agua (3766 metres), which rises dramatically right behind the village.

Santa María (altitude 2080 metres, population 11,000) is a village of unpaved streets and bamboo fences. It has a church and Municipalidad on the main plaza, which is also the bus terminal. Down the street from the church towards the white church in the distance is the *Comedor & Hospedaje El Oasis*, a tidy little pension where you can get a meal or a bed for the night.

Various outfitters in Antigua can furnish details about the Volcán Agua climb. Start very early in the morning, as it can take five hours to reach the summit. If you are not an experienced hiker in good physical condition, don't plan to go all the way. You'll need good lungs, as the air gets mighty thin at 3766 metres.

Chimaltenango

The road westward from Antigua makes its way 17 km up to the ridge of the Continental Divide, where it meets the Interamerican Highway at Chimaltenango, capital of the department (province) of Chimaltenango. This was an old town to the Cakchiquel Maya when the conquistadors arrived in 1526, but today is mostly just a place to change buses, with little to detain you.

Lago de Atitlán

Westward 32 km along the highway from Chimaltenango takes you past the turning for the back road to Lago de Atitlán via Patzicía and Patzún. The area around these two towns has been notable for high levels of guerrilla activity in recent years, and the road is in poor condition in any case, so it's advisable to stay on the Interamerican Highway to Tecpán Guatemala, the starting point for a visit to the ruined Cakchiquel capital city of Iximché.

TECPÁN GUATEMALA

Founded as the Spanish military headquarters during the conquest, Tecpán Guatemala today is a small, somewhat dusty town with numerous handicrafts shops, two small hotels and, nearby, the ruins of the Cakchiquel Maya capital of Iximché.

Tecpan's market day is Thursday. The annual festival in honor of the town's patron saint, Francis of Assisi, is held in the first week of October.

IXIMCHÉ

Set on a flat promontory surrounded by steep cliffs, Iximché (founded in the late 1400s) was well sited to be the capital city of the Cakchiquel Maya. The Cakchiquels were at war with the Quiché Maya, and the city's natural defences served them well.

Lago de Atitlán

0   5   10 km

When the conquistadors arrived in 1524, the Cakchiquels formed an alliance with them against their enemies the Quichés and the Tzutuhils. The Spaniards set up their headquarters right next door to the Cakchiquel capital at Tecpán Guatemala. But Spanish demands for gold and other loot soon put an end to the alliance, and in the ensuing battles, the Cakchiquels were defeated.

As you enter Tecpán you will see signs pointing to the unpaved road leading through fields and pine forests to Iximché, less than six km to the south. You can walk the distance in about an hour, see the ruins and rest (another hour), then walk back to Tecpán – a total of three hours. If you're going to walk, it's best to do it in the morning so that you can get back to the highway by early afternoon, as bus traffic dwindles by late afternoon.

Enter the archaeological site (open from 9 am to 4 pm daily), pass the small museo (museum) on the right, and you come to four ceremonial plazas surrounded by grass-covered temple structures and ball courts. Some of the structures have been cleaned and maintained; on a few the original plaster coating is still in place, and there are even some traces of the original paint.

Places to Stay & Eat
Should you need to stay the night in Tecpán, *Hotel Iximché*, 1 Avenida 1-38, Zona 2, will put you up in basic rooms for US$3 per person, as will *Pensión Doña Ester*, 2 Calle 1-09, Zona 3. Various small eateries provide sustenance.

Getting There & Away
Transportes Poaquileña runs buses to Guatemala City (87 km, 1½ hours) every hal- hour from 3 am to 5 pm. From Guatemala City to Tecpán, buses run just as frequently, from 5 am to 7.30 pm.

LOS ENCUENTROS
Another 40 km westward along the Interamerican Highway from Tecpán brings you to the highway junction of Los Encuentros. There is a nascent town here, based on the presence of a lot of people waiting to catch buses. The road to the right heads north to Chichicastenango and Santa Cruz del Quiché. From this intersection, the Interamerican Highway continues three km north to where a road to the left descends 12 km to Sololá, capital of the department of the same name, and then six km more to Panajachel, on the shores of Lago de Atitlán.

If you are not on a direct bus to Panajachel, you can usually catch a bus or minibus, or even hitch a ride, from Los Encuentros down to Panajachel.

SOLOLÁ
Though the Spaniards founded Sololá (altitude 2110 metres, population 9000) in 1547, there was a Cakchiquel town (called Tzoloyá) here before they came. Sololá's importance comes from its geographic position on trade routes between the Tierra Caliente (hot lands of the Pacific Slope) and Tierra Fría (the chilly highlands). All the traders meet here, and Sololá's Friday market is one of the best in the highlands.

On market days, the plaza next to the cathedral is ablaze with the colours of cos-

A na, a Mayan thatched-roofed hut

tumes from a dozen surrounding villages and towns. Displays of meat, vegetables and fruit, housewares and clothing are neatly arranged in every available space, with tides of buyers ebbing and flowing along the spaces in between. Boys grind coffee in an old-fashioned mill, girls mix up fruit drinks to refresh thirsty marketers, and shoppers haggle over the prices of bright new potatoes, tiny tomatoes, all sorts of greens, spices, oranges and fresh garlic. Several elaborate stands are well stocked with brightly coloured yarn and sewing notions to aid in making the traditional costumes you see all around you.

Every Sunday morning the officers of the traditional religious brotherhoods *(cofradías)* parade ceremoniously to the cathedral for their devotions. On other days, Sololá sleeps.

Places to Stay
Virtually everyone stays in Panajachel, but if you need a bed in Sololá, try the six-room *Posada del Viajero*, 7 Avenida 10-45, Zona 2, or the *Hotel Tzolojya* (☎ (9) 62-12-66), 11 Calle 7-70, Zona 2. *Hotel Santa Ana*, 150 metres uphill from the church tower on the road which comes into town from Los Encuentros, is even simpler.

SOLOLÁ TO PANAJACHEL

The road from Sololá descends more than 500 metres through pine forests in its eight-km course to Panajachel. All the sights and views are on your right, so try to get a seat on the right-hand side of the bus.

Along the way the road passes Sololá's colourful cemetery, and a Guatemalan army base. The fantastic guardpost by the main gate is in the shape of a huge helmet resting upon a pair of soldier's boots. Soon the road turns to snake its way down the mountainside to the lakeshore, offering breathtaking views of the lake and its surrounding volcanoes.

PANAJACHEL

Nicknamed Gringotenango (Place of the Foreigners) by locals and foreigners alike, Pana has long been known to tourists. In the hippy heyday of the 1960s and '70s it was crowded with laid-back travellers in semipermanent exile. When the civil war of the late 1970s and early '80s made Panajachel a dangerous – or at least unpleasant – place to be, many moved on. But in recent years the town's tourist industry has boomed again.

There is no notable colonial architecture in this town, and no colourful indigenous market. It is a small and not particularly attractive place which has developed haphazardly according to the demands of the tourist trade. Compared to the geometric layout and architectural harmony of colonial highland towns, it has nothing. The lake, however, is absolutely gorgeous, and one wants nothing better than to sit for hours watching the play of colours and shadows on the lake's surface and on the slopes of the proud volcanoes as the sun runs its daily course and the clouds provide their evanescent entertainment. At moments like this you can ignore the village lad strolling along the lakeshore with an armful of newspapers shouting *'Miami Herald! Miami Herald!'*

Lago de Atitlán is often still and beautiful early in the day. By noon the Xocomil, a south-easterly wind, may have risen to ruffle the lake's surface. The best time for swimming, then, is in the morning. Note that the lake is a caldera (collapsed volcanic cone) and is more than 320 metres deep. The land drops off sharply very near the shore. Surrounding the lake are three volcanoes: Volcán Tolimán (3158 metres), due south of Panajachel; Volcán Atitlán (3537 metres), also to the south; and Volcán San Pedro (2995 metres) to the south-west.

Six different cultures mingle on the dusty streets of Panajachel. First there are the ladino citizens of the town who operate the levers of its tourist industry; then the Cakchiquel and Tzutuhil Maya from surrounding villages who come to sell their handicrafts to tourists; next are the lakeside villa owners who drive up at weekends from Guatemala City; there are also group tourists who whiz in and out in buses for a few hours, a day, or an overnight; finally, there are the 'traditional' hippies with long hair, beards, bare feet, local dress and Volkswagen minibuses.

Panajachel is the starting point for excursions to the smaller, more traditional indigenous villages on the western and southern shores of the lake. These, too, have been touched by tourism, but retain their charm nonetheless.

Orientation

As you near the bottom of the long hill descending from Sololá, there is a road on the right leading to the Hotel Visión Azul, Hotel Atitlán and those obtrusive white highrise buildings which form a blot on the otherwise perfect landscape. The main road then bears left and becomes the Calle Real (also called Calle Principal), Panajachel's main street.

The geographic centre of town, and the closest thing it has to a bus station, is the intersection of Calle Real and Calle Santander, where you will see the Banco Agricola Mercantil, the INGUAT tourist office and the Mayan Palace Hotel. Calle Santander, lined with stands selling handicrafts, is the main road to the beach. Along it are many of the town's bottom-end lodgings.

North-east along Calle Real are more hotels, restaurants and shops; finally, at the

Top: The commercial centre of Guatemala City, Guatemala (TB)
Bottom: Antigua Guatemala, Guatemala (PW)

Top: Palacio Nacional, Guatemala City, Guatemala (TB)
Middle: A hotel courtyard, Antigua Guatemala, Guatemala (TB)
Bottom: Lake Atitlán and Tolimán Volcano, Guatemala (TB)

GUATEMALA

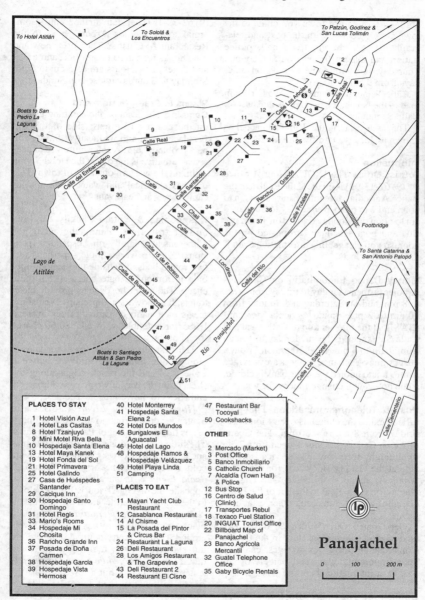

To Hotel Atitlán

To Sololá & Los Encuentros

To Patzún, Godínez & San Lucas Tolimán

Boats to San Pedro La Laguna

Calle Los Árboles

Calle Real

Calle del Embarcadero

Calle Real

Calle Santander

Calle Rancho Grande

Calle Frutales

Ford

Footbridge

To Santa Catarina & San Antonio Palopó

El Chalí

Calle de Londres

Calle 15 de Febrero

Calle de Buenas Nuevas

Calle Panajachel

Calle del Río

Río Panajachel

Calle Los Salpores

Calle Cementerio

Lago de Atitlán

Boats to Santiago Atitlán & San Pedro La Laguna

PLACES TO STAY

1 Hotel Visión Azul
4 Hotel Las Casitas
8 Hotel Tzanjuyú
9 Mini Motel Riva Bella
10 Hospedaje Santa Elena
13 Hotel Maya Kanek
19 Hotel Fonda del Sol
21 Hotel Primavera
25 Hotel Galindo
27 Casa de Huéspedes Santander
29 Cacique Inn
30 Hospedaje Santo Domingo
31 Hotel Regis
33 Mario's Rooms
34 Hospedaje Mi Chosita
36 Rancho Grande Inn
37 Posada de Doña Carmen
38 Hospedaje Garcia
39 Hospedaje Vista Hermosa

40 Hotel Monterrey
41 Hospedaje Santa Elena 2
42 Hotel Dos Mundos
45 Bungalows El Aguacatal
46 Hotel del Lago
48 Hospedaje Ramos & Hospedaje Velázquez
49 Hotel Playa Linda
51 Camping

PLACES TO EAT

11 Mayan Yacht Club Restaurant
12 Casablanca Restaurant
14 Al Chisme
15 La Posada del Pintor & Circus Bar
24 Restaurant La Laguna
26 Deli Restaurant
28 Los Amigos Restaurant & The Grapevine
43 Deli Restaurant 2
44 Restaurant El Cisne

47 Restaurant Bar Tocoyal
50 Cookshacks

OTHER

2 Mercado (Market)
3 Post Office
5 Banco Inmobiliario
6 Catholic Church
7 Alcaldía (Town Hall) & Police
12 Bus Stop
16 Centro de Salud (Clinic)
17 Transportes Rebul
18 Texaco Fuel Station
20 INGUAT Tourist Office
22 Billboard Map of Panajachel
23 Banco Agrícola Mercantil
32 Guatel Telephone Office
35 Gaby Bicycle Rentals

Panajachel

0   100   200 m

north-eastern end of town you come to the town's civic centre, with the post and telegraph offices, church, town hall, police station and market (busiest on Sunday and Thursday, but with some activity on other days from 9 am to noon).

Calle Rancho Grande is the other main road to the beach; it's parallel to, and east of, Calle Santander.

The area east of the Río Panajachel is known as Jucanyá (Across the River).

Information

Tourist Office The INGUAT tourist office (☎ (9) 62-13-92) is on the Calle Real near the Banco Agrícola Mercantil. Hours are 8 am to noon and 2 to 6 pm Wednesday to Sunday, 8 am to noon on Monday (closed on Tuesday). Bus and boat schedules are posted on the door, so you can get this information even if the office is closed.

Money Banco Inmobiliario on Calle los Arboles is open Monday to Friday from 9 am to 8 pm, and on Saturday and Sunday from 10 am to 2 pm. Banco Agrícola Mercantil (BAM), at the intersection of Calle Real and Calle Santander, is open Monday to Friday from 9 am to 3 pm (till 3.30 pm on Friday), but currency-exchange services are provided from 9 am to noon only. If the bank is closed, some hotels will change money for you.

Post & Telecommunications The post office next to the church is open Monday to Friday from 8 am to 4.30 pm. The Guatel office on Calle Santander is open from 7 am to midnight every day. Fax service is available at the Gallery Bookstore (on Calle los Arboles), at the shop called Que Hay de Nuevo (on Calle Real to the left of the Hotel Galindo) and at numerous other establishments.

Get Guated Out (☎ /fax (9) 62-20-15), next to the Gallery Bookstore in the Centro Comercial on Calle los Arboles, can ship your important letters and parcels by air freight or international courier service.

Bookshops The Gallery Bookstore (☎ /fax

(9) 62-20-15) is upstairs in the Centro Comercial, on Calle los Arboles next to the Restaurant Al Chisme. They offer new and used books for sale, a fax service, and travel and ticket sales. Hours are 8.45 am to 6 pm Monday to Saturday (closed on Sunday).

Places to Stay – bottom end

Camping There's a public camping ground on the beach on the east side of the Río Panajachel's mouth in Jucanyá. Safety can be a problem here. A safer but more expensive alternative is the one at the Hotel Visión Azul, on the western outskirts of town. This one has electrical and water hook-ups for campervans and caravans.

Hospedajes & Hotels Luckily for low-budget travellers, Panajachel also has numerous little family-run hospedajes (pensions). They're very simple – perhaps just two rough beds, a bedside table and a light bulb in a room of bare boards – but quite cheap. The better hospedajes provide clean toilets, hot showers and perhaps even some meals at a patio comedor. Prices average US$5 for a double, with a US$0.60 charge for a hot shower.

The first place to look for hospedajes is along Calle Santander midway between Calle Real and the beach. Signs along the street point the way down narrow side streets and alleys to the various hospedajes.

Hospedaje Santa Elena 2, off Calle Santander on the road to the Hotel Monterrey, is tidy and typical of Pana's hospedajes. The little courtyard is planted with bananas and noisy with macaws; the showers provide cold water only. The original *Hospedaje Santa Elena* is in an alley off Calle Real opposite the INGUAT tourist office, closer to the centre but farther from the beach.

Hospedaje Vista Hermosa is a friendly place, with simple rooms on two levels around a small, pretty courtyard. There are hot showers (in the morning only) for a quetzal or so. *Hospedaje Santo Domingo* is a step up in quality but a few steps off the street; follow the road toward the Hotel Monterrey, then follow signs along a shady path. This backpackers' motel has rough timber rooms built around a nice yard. It's quiet, being well away from the noise on Calle Santander. Cold showers, laundry sinks and toilets are available; the price, as usual, is US$5 a double.

The family-run *Posada de Doña Carmen* (☎ (9) 62-20-85), Calle Rancho Grande, is very simple, but tidy and quiet, with a big garden. Stark rooms without running water cost US$4 a double.

Casa de Huéspedes Santander, in an alley off Calle Santander, has clean beds in tidy, bare rooms around a verdant garden for US$3/5/6 a single/double/triple.

Mario's Rooms (☎ (9) 62-13-13), just south of the Guatel office on Calle Santander, is popular with young, adventurous travellers, and is among the best of the hospedajes. Rates for each of the 20 rooms are US$3.25/5 a single/double, and there's a tiny little restaurant-bar. *Hospedaje Mi Chosita*, on Calle El Chali (turn at Mario's Rooms), is tidy, quiet and costs US$5 a double. *Hospedaje Garcia* (☎ (9) 62-21-87), 4 Calle 2-24, Zona 2, farther east along the same street toward Calle Rancho Grande, charges US$3/4 a single/double.

Overlooking the beach near the Hotel Playa Linda are two more places: *Hospedaje Ramos* and *Hospedaje Velázquez*. Both rent rooms for US$5 a double, and both have cold showers only, some beach views and little comedores.

Moving up in both price and comfort, *Hotel Las Casitas* (☎ (9) 62 12 24), across from the market near the church and town hall, rents little brick bungalows with tile roofs. Señora Dalma Gutiérrez is always smiling, cleaning or cooking (all three meals) to keep her guests happy. Rooms cost US$6.50/10/13.50 a single/double/triple with private (hot) shower.

Hotel Fonda del Sol (☎ (9) 62-11-62), Calle Real 2-47, Zona 2, is a two-storey building on the main street across from the Asamblea de Dios church, west of the intersection with Calle Santander. The 15 simple rooms on the upper floor are well used but fairly decently kept, and cost US$8/16 a double without/with private shower. Downstairs is a restaurant.

Hotel Maya Kanek (☎ (9) 62-11-04), Calle Real just down from the church, is a motel-style hostelry. Rooms face a cobbled court with a small garden; the court doubles as a secure car park. The 20 rooms, though simple, are a bit more comfortable than at a hospedaje, and cost US$8.50/12 a single/double. It's quiet here.

Hotel Galindo (☎ (9) 62-11-68), Calle Real north-east of the Banco Agricola Mercantil, has a surprisingly lush garden surrounded by modest rooms which rent for US$14 with private shower. Look at the room before you rent.

Places to Stay – middle

Mid-range lodgings are busiest at weekends. From Sunday to Thursday you may get a discount. All of these lodgings provide private hot showers in their rooms.

Rancho Grande Inn (☎ (9) 62-15-54, 62-22-55, fax 62-22-47), Calle Rancho Grande, has seven perfectly maintained German country-style villas in a tropical Guatemalan setting amidst emerald-green lawns. Some bungalows sleep up to five persons. Marlita Hannstein, the congenial owner, charges a very reasonable US$30 a single, US$40 to US$60 a double, including tax and a full delicious breakfast. In my opinion, this is Pana's best place to stay. Reserve in advance, or be disappointed.

Bungalows El Aguacatal (☎ (9) 62-14-82), Calle de Buenas Nuevas, is aimed at weekenders from the capital. Each modern bungalow has two bedrooms, equipped kitchen, bath and salon, and costs US$25 a double Sunday to Thursday, US$30 on Friday and Saturday.

Mini Motel Riva Bella (☎ (9) 62-13-48, 62-11-77, fax 62-13-53), Calle Real, is a collection of neat two-room bungalows, each with its own parking place. Señora María Gertraude E de Benini oversees maintenance and management. The location is convenient and the price is US$26 a double.

Hotel Dos Mundos (☎ /fax (9) 62-20-78), Calle Santander 4-72, Zona 2, has new bungalows in a walled compound of tropical gardens for US$33 a double.

Hotel Regis (☎ (9) 62-11-49, fax 62-11-52), Calle Santander across from Guatel, is a group of villas in colonial style set back from the street across a lush lawn shaded by palms. The 14 guestrooms are in bungalows facing the lawn, which has a small swimming pool and playground for children. The Swiss family which owns the Regis charges US$33/38/44 a single/double/triple.

Hotel Monterrey (☎ (9) 62-11-26), Calle 15 de Febrero, down an unpaved road going west from Calle Santander (look for the sign), is a blue-and-white, two-storey motel-style building facing the lake across lawns which extend down to the beach. The Monterrey offers you clean and cheerful accommodation with satellite TV and private bath for US$30/40 a single/double.

Hotel Playa Linda ·(☎ (9) 62-11-59), facing the beach at the end of Calle Rancho Grande, has an assortment of rooms, a few with nice views of the lake. Rooms 1 to 5 have views, rooms 6 to 14 do not; most have private baths with hot water, and some have TV with satellite programmes. The rate for a double is US$30 to US$38, the higher price being for rooms with views.

Cacique Inn (☎ /fax (9) 62-12-05), Calle del Embarcadero, off Calle Real at the western edge of town, is an assemblage of pseudo-rustic red tile-roofed buildings arranged around verdant gardens and a swimming pool. The 33 large, comfortable rooms have double beds, fireplaces and locally made blankets. Rates are US$50/57/65 a single/double/triple, tax included.

Hotel Visión Azul (☎ (9) 62-14-26, fax 62-14-19), on the Hotel Atitlán road, is built into a hillside in a quiet location looking toward the lake through a grove of trees. The big, bright rooms in the main building have spacious terraces festooned with bougainvillea and ivy. Modern bungalows a few steps away provide more privacy for families. There's a swimming pool. Prices are US$45/55/65 a single/double/triple.

Places to Stay – top end

The nicest hotel in town is the *Hotel Atitlán* (☎ (9) 62-14-16/29/41), on the lakeshore two km west of the centre. Spacious gardens surround this rambling three-storey colonial-style hotel. Inside are gleaming tile floors, antique wood carvings and exquisite handicraft decorations. The patio has views across the heated swimming pools to the lake. The 42 rooms with private bath have twin beds, and cost US$65/72/90 a single/double/triple.

Hotel del Lago (☎ (9) 62-15-55 to 60, fax 62-15-62; in Guatemala City ☎ (2) 31-69-41, 31-74-61, fax 34-80-16), at the beach end of Calle Rancho Grande, is a modern six-storey building which seems out of place in low-rise, laid-back Panajachel. Besides the beach, the hotel has two swimming pools (one for children) set in nice gardens. Each of its 100 rooms has two double beds and costs US$75 to US$90 a double.

Places to Eat

Panajachel is one of the few places in Guatemala which has some restaurants catering specifically to foreigners.

The cheapest places to eat are down by the beach at the mouth of the Río Panajachel. Right by the river's mouth are crude cookshacks with very low prices. The food stands around the car park cost only a bit more. Then there are the little restaurants just inland from the car park, with names such as *El Xocomil, El Pescador, Los Pumpos, Brisas de Lago* and *Los Alpes*. Not only is the food cheap (US$3 for a fill-up), but the view of the lake is a priceless bonus.

The Grapevine, on Calle Santander, is among the most popular places to eat and drink. The ground floor is the restaurant, serving plates of fish and beef for US$3 to US$5. Upstairs is the video bar, which serves up popcorn, beer, drinks and a good selection of American and European films.

On Calle los Arboles is *Al Chisme* (The Gossip), a favourite with regular Pana foreign visitors and residents, with its shady streetside patio. Breakfasts of English muffins, Belgian waffles and omelettes cost US$2 to US$3. For lunch and dinner, Al

Chisme offers lots of sandwiches, soups, salads, crêpes and chicken pot pie for US$2.75 to US$5. Alcoholic beverages are served.

Next door in the Centro Comercial complex on Los Arboles is *Sevananda Vegetarian Restaurant*, offering sandwiches and vegetable plates for US$2 to US$4. It's open Monday to Saturday from 11 am to 10 pm (closed on Sunday).

Deli Restaurant, on Calle Real next to the Hotel Galindo, has nice gardens with lots of roses, simple tables and chairs, and breakfasts of whole-wheat pancakes and other good things for US$1.50 to US$2.50. For lunch and dinner there are many tofu dishes, sandwiches and big salads for US$2 to US$5. Hours are 8 am to 6.45 pm (closed on Wednesday). The *Deli Restaurant 2*, in a quiet garden at the lake end of Calle Santander, sells sandwiches, cakes and the like to the sounds of soft classical music.

At the *Mayan Yacht Club*, near the intersection of Calle Real and Calle Santander, the pizzas (US$3.50 to US$8) have a good reputation. Hours are 1 to 10 pm daily.

Los Amigos Restaurant, on Calle Santander, is open only for dinner, from 6 to 9.30 pm (closed on Monday) but usually fills up for that meal. One low, darkish room is lit by candles and the glow of good conversation. Soup, a huge burrito and a beer cost about US$6; a 10% service charge is added to the bill.

Restaurant Bar Tocoyal, just across the street from the big Hotel del Lago, at the beach end of Calle Rancho Grande, is a tidy, modern thatch-roofed place serving good moderately priced meals (including fish) for about US$8.

Calle los Arboles, on the north-west side of Calle Real, also has a number of good restaurants. *La Posada del Pintor* and its *Circus Bar* have walls hung with old circus posters, and quiet jazz and rock as background music. Pizzas, boeuf bourguignon, potato salads, steaks, pastas and desserts are all on the menu. You can expect to spend US$6 to US$12 for a full dinner. Portions tend to be small.

Restaurant La Laguna, Calle Real at the intersection of Calle los Arboles, has a pretty front patio and garden with umbrella-covered tables. Bought by the management of the Circus Bar and Posada del Pintor, it was under renovation at my last visit.

Casablanca Restaurant (☎ (9) 62-10-15), at the intersection of Calle Santander and Calle Real, is quite nice but fairly expensive, with a plate of lasagna costing US$6.

Getting There & Away

The town's main bus stop is where Calle Santander meets Calle Real, across from the Mayan Palace Hotel and the Banco Agricola Mercantil, but buses leave from other parts of the town as well, depending upon the company.

Antigua (80 km, two hours) – there are several direct buses daily, or take any bus stopping at Chimaltenango, and change to an Antigua-bound minibus there. TURANSA shuttle minibuses operate as well. See Getting There & Away in the Guatemala City chapter for details.

Chichicastenango (29 km, one hour) – buses (US$1) depart from Panajachel at 6.45, 7.45, 8.45 and 9.45 am. Panajachel Tourist services (see the Guatemala City listing) runs minibuses from Pana to Chichi each Thursday and Sunday at 8 am, returning at 1 pm (US$20 round trip).

Guatemala City (147 km, three hours – Rebuli (☎ (2) 51-65-05), 3a Avenida 2-36, Zona 9, departs for Lago de Atitlán and Panajachel every hour from 7 am to 4 pm, stopping at Chimaltenango, Patzicía, Tecpán Guatemala (for the ruins at Iximché), Los Encuentros and Sololá (US$1.75). Departures from Panajachel are at 5, 5.30, 7, 8, 9.30 and 11.30 am and 1 and 2.30 pm; on Saturday there's also an 11 am bus. Panajachel Tourist Services (☎ /fax 62-14-74), on Calle los Arboles in the Centro Comercial, next to Al Chisme, run tourist minibuses between Pana and Guatemala City several times per week (US$20).

Huehuetenango (159 km, 3½ hours) – catch a bus or minibus to Los Encuentros and wait there for a Huehue-bound bus (see the Guatemala City chapter under Getting There & Away for a schedule of Huehue-bound buses). Alternatively, catch a Morales bus from Panajachel to Quetzaltenango, get out at Cuatro Caminos, and wait for a Huehue bus.

La Mesilla, Mexican border (241 km, five hours) – see Huehuetenango.

Quetzaltenango (99 km, two hours) – buses run by Morales or Rojo y Blanco depart at 5.30, 5.45 and 11.30 am and 2.30 pm (US$1.75).

Getting Around

You can rent bicycles from Alquiler de Bicicletas Gaby, on Calle 14 de Febrero between Calle Santander and Calle Rancho Grande. Otherwise, most people get around Pana on foot. For information on buses and boats to other lakeside villages, see Around Lago de Atitlán.

AROUND LAGO DE ATITLÁN

Various lakeside villages, which can be reached on foot, or by bus or motor launch, are interesting to visit. The most popular destination for day trips is Santiago Atitlán, directly across the lake south of Panajachel, but there are others. Some villages even have places for you to stay overnight. As the southern shore of the lake often has guerrilla and bandit activity, it's best to follow well-travelled routes and to go in a group.

Santa Catarina Palopó to San Lucas Tolimán

Four km east of Panajachel along a winding, unpaved road lies the village of Santa Catarina Palopó. Narrow streets paved in stone blocks, and adobe houses with roofs of thatch or corrugated tin huddled around a gleaming white church: that's Santa Catarina. Chickens cackle, dogs bark and the villagers go about their business dressed in their beautiful traditional costumes. Except for exploring village life and enjoying views of the lake and the volcanoes, there's little in the way of sightseeing. For refreshments, there are several little comedores on the main plaza, one of which advertises 'Cold beer sold here'.

If your budget allows, a drink or a meal at the village's best hotel is pleasant. The *Villa Santa Catarina* (☎ (9) 62-12-91; in Guatemala City (2) 31-98-76, fax 34-62-37) has 30 comfortable rooms with bath and views of the lake. Rooms 24, 25, 26 and 27 (partly) face west and have fine views of Volcán San Pedro; all overlook the pretty swimming pool and grounds right on the shore. The dining room provides moderately priced table d'hôte meals. Rooms cost US$60/66/70 a single/double/triple.

The road continues past Santa Catarina five km to San Antonio Palopó, a larger but similar village. Three km along the way you pass the 31-room *Hotel Bella Vista* (☎ (9) 62-15-66; in Guatemala City (2) 2-68-07/8/9, fax 2-64-02), 8.5 km from Panajachel. Little bungalows, each with private bath, share gardens with a swimming pool, restaurant, private beach and boat dock. In San Antonio there's also the *Hotel Terrazas del Mar*.

Beyond San Antonio and Godínez lies San Lucas Tolimán, busier and more commercial than most lakeside villages. Set at the foot of the dramatic Volcán Tolimán, San Lucas is a coffee-growing town and a transport point on the route between the Interamerican Highway and the Pacific Slope Highway. Market days are Monday, Tuesday, Thursday and Friday. From San Lucas, a rough, badly maintained road goes west around Volcán Tolimán to Santiago Atitlán, then around Volcán San Pedro to San Pedro La Laguna.

Getting There & Away A bus leaves daily (except Saturday) for Guatemala City via Santa Catarina (four km) and San Antonio (11 km) at 9 am, but returns by another route. Buses leave Panajachel daily for San Lucas Tolimán via Santa Catarina and San Antonio at 6.30 am and 4 pm.

Santiago Atitlán

South across the lake from Panajachel, on the shore of a lagoon squeezed between the towering volcanoes of Tolimán and San Pedro, lies the small town of Santiago Atitlán. Though it is the most visited village outside Panajachel, it clings to the traditional lifestyle of the Tzutuhil Maya. The women of the town still weave and wear huipiles with brilliantly coloured flocks of birds and bouquets of flowers embroidered on them. The best day to visit is market day (Friday, with a lesser market on Tuesday), but in fact any day will do.

Santiago is also a curiosity because of its reverence for Maximón (MAH-shee-MOHN), a local deity who is probably a blend of ancient Mayan gods, Pedro de Alvarado (the fierce conquistador of Guatemala) and the biblical Judas. Despised in other highland towns, Maximón is revered in Santiago Atitlán, and his effigy with wooden mask and huge cigar is paraded triumphantly during Holy Week processions (see Holidays & Festivals in the Facts for the Visitor chapter for the dates of Holy Week).

Children from Santiago greet you as you disembark at the dock, selling clay whistles and little embroidered strips of cloth. They'll be right behind, alongside and in front of you during much of your stay here.

Walk to the left from the dock along the shore to reach the street into town. This is the main commercial street. Every tourist walks up and down it between the dock and the town, so it's lined with shops selling woven cloth, other handicrafts and souvenirs.

At the top of the slope is the main square, with the town office and huge church, which dates from the time, several centuries ago, when Santiago was an important commercial town. Within the stark, echoing church are some surprising sights. Along the walls are wooden statues of the saints, each of whom gets a new shawl embroidered by local women every year. On the carved wooden pulpit, note the figures of corn (from which humans were formed, according to Mayan religion), of a quetzal bird reading a book, and of Yum-Kax, the Mayan god of corn. There is similar carving on the back of the priest's chair.

The walls of the church bear paintings, now covered by a thin layer of plaster. A memorial plaque at the back of the church commemorates Father Stanley Francis Rother, a missionary priest from Oklahoma, who was beloved by the local people but despised by ultra-rightist 'death squads', who murdered him right here in the church during the troubled year of 1981.

Places to Stay & Eat Best in town is *Hotel Chi-Nim-Yá*, a simple, basic place with several advantages. The nicest room in the place is No 106, large and airy, with lots of windows and excellent lake views, for US$8 a double. Smaller, less desirable rooms cost only half that much.

Pensión Rosita, to the right of the school and behind the basketball court off the main plaza, has very stark, bare rooms for US$3 per person. The plumbing is primitive.

Restaurant Santa Rita, a few steps from the north-east corner of the plaza past Distribuidor El Buen Precio, boasts 'deliciosos pays' (delicious pies).

The most comfortable and charming place is the *Posada de Santiago* (☎ /fax (9) 62-71-67), one km from the village centre, with six stone bungalows and an excellent dining room on grounds sloping down to the lake. Rates are US$23/30/36/45 a single/double/triple/quad.

Getting There & Away An unpaved road in bad repair connects Santiago and San Lucas Tolimán (16 km), but most visitors reach Santiago by motor launch from Panajachel, which is the safer method. Motor launches depart from the public beach at the foot of Calle Rancho Grande, near the Hotel del Lago. The voyage takes 1¼ to 1½ hours each way, depending upon the winds, and costs US$3.50 return. A tour to three villages, with an hour spent in each, costs US$7.

The *Naviera Santiago* departs from Panajachel at 8.45 and 10 am and 4 pm, returning from Santiago at 11.45 am and 1 pm. *Naviera Santa Fe* leaves Panajachel at 9 and 9.30 am, returning from Santiago at 12.30 and 1 pm.

San Pedro La Laguna

Perhaps the next most popular lakeside town to visit, after Santiago, is San Pedro La Laguna. Its number-two ranking means that fewer flocks of *muchachos* will swirl around you as you stroll the narrow cobblestone streets and wander to the outskirts for a dip in the lake.

Places to Stay & Eat Right near the boat

dock is *Hospedaje Chuasinahu*, the best place in town, with beds for US$2 per night. The *Ti-Kaaj* next door is not quite as good, but takes the overflow if the Chuasinahu is full. *Villa San Pedro*, next door, is an even better choice at US$3 per person. The *Pensión Johanna*, on the other side of the village near another dock, charges similar rates.

Getting There & Away The rough road from San Lucas Tolimán to Santiago Atitlán continues 18 km to San Pedro, making its way around the lagoon and Volcán San Pedro. Coming from Panajachel, you should take a motor launch, of which there are two. *Naviera Pato Poc* departs from the public beach in Panajachel, at the foot of Calle Rancho Grande near the Hotel del Lago, at 10 am and 1 and 5 pm, returning from San Pedro at 11.30 am and 3 pm. *Naviera Santa María* departs from a dock near the Hotel Tzanjuyú, at the western edge of Panajachel, each day at 9.30 am and 2.30 pm, returning

from San Pedro at 1 pm only. The voyage costs US$4 return.

Quiché

The Departamento del Quiché is famous mostly for the town of Chichicastenango, known for its bustling markets on Thursdays and Sundays. Beyond Chichi to the north is Santa Cruz del Quiché, the capital of the department. On its outskirts lie the ruins of K'umarcaaj (or Gumarcaah), also called Utatlán, the last capital city of the Quiché Maya.

The road to Quiché leaves the Interamerican Highway at Los Encuentros, winding its way through pine forests and cornfields, down into a steep valley and up the other side. Women sit in front of their little roadside cottages weaving yet another gorgeous piece of cloth on their simple backstrap looms. Half an hour after leaving Los

---

Traditional Clothing

Anyone visiting the Highlands can delight in the beautiful traditional clothing *(traje indígena)* of the local people. The styles, patterns and colours used by each village are unique, and each garment is the creation of its weaver, with subtle differences from the others.

The basic elements are the *tocoyal* (head-covering), *huipil* (blouse), *córte* or *refago* (skirt), *calzones* (trousers), *tzut* or *kaperraj* (cloth), *paz* or *faja* (sash) and *caîtes* or *xajáp* (sandals).

Women's head-coverings are beautiful and elaborate bands of cloth up to several metres in length, wound about the head and decorated with tassels, pompoms and silver ornaments. In recent years they have been worn only on ceremonial occasions and for tourist photos.

Women's huipiles, however, are worn proudly every day. Though some machine-made fabrics are now being used, most huipiles are made completely by hand. the white blouse is woven on a backstrap loom, then decorated with appliqué and embroidery designs and motifs which are common to the weaver's village. Many of the motifs are traditional symbols. No doubt all had religious or historical significance at one time, though today that meaning may be lost to memory.

Córtes (refajos) are pieces of cloth seven to 10 yards long which are wrapped around the body. Traditionally, girls wear theirs above the knee, married women at the knee and old women below the knee, though the style can differ markedly from region to region.

Both men and women wear fajas, long strips of backcloth-woven cloth wrapped around the midriff as belts. Wrapped with folds upward like a cummerbund, the folds serve as pockets.

Tzutes (male) or kaperraj (female) are the all-purpose cloths carried by local people and used as head-coverings, baby-slings, produce sacks, basket covers and shawls. There are also shawls for women called *perraj*, probably a contraction of kaperraj.

Before the coming of the Spaniards, it was most common for simple leather thong sandals (caîtes, xajáp) to be worn only by men. Even today, many women and children go barefoot, while others have thongs, more elaborate huarache-style sandals, or modern shoes.■

Encuentros, you've travelled the 17 km north to Chichicastenango.

CHICHICASTENANGO

Surrounded by valleys, with nearby mountains looming overhead, Chichicastenango (altitude 2030 metres, population 8000) seems isolated from the rest of Guatemala. It can also seem magical when its narrow cobbled streets and red-tiled roofs are enveloped in mists, as they often are. Chichi is a beautiful, interesting place; not the many shiny tour buses parked near the market nor even the gaggles of camera-toting 'It's Thursday this must be Chichi' tour groups can change that. If you have a choice of days, come for the Sunday market rather than the Thursday one, as the cofradías (religious brotherhoods) often hold processions on Sundays. It's best to arrive in town the day before market day to pin down a room and a bed, and to be up early for the market.

Though isolated, Chichi has always been an important market town. Villagers from throughout the region would walk for many hours carrying their wares to participate in the commerce here – and that was in the days before good roads.

Today, though many traders come by bus, others still arrive on foot. When they reach Chichi's main square, they lay down their loads, spread out a blanket and go to sleep in one of the arcades which surround the square. At dawn on Thursday and Sunday they spread out their vegetables, fruits, chunks of chalk (ground to a powder, mixed with water and used to soften dried maize), balls of wax, handmade harnesses, etc and wait for customers.

Many ladino business types also set up fairly touristy stalls in the Sunday and Thursday markets. Somehow they end up adding to the colour and fascination, not detracting from it.

Besides the famous market, Masheños (citizens of Chichicastenango) are famous for their adherence to pre-Christian religious beliefs and ceremonies. You can readily see versions of these old rites in and around the church of Santo Tomás, and at the shrine of Pascual Abaj on the outskirts of town.

History

Once called Chaviar, this was an important Cakchiquel trading town long before the Spanish conquest. Not long before the conquistadors arrived, the Cakchiquels and the Quichés (based at K'umarcaaj near present-day Santa Cruz del Quiché, 20 km north) went to war. The Cakchiquels abandoned Chaviar and moved their headquarters to Iximché, which was easier to defend. The conquistadors came and conquered K'umarcaaj, and many of its residents fled to Chaviar, which they renamed Chuguilá (Above the Nettles) and Tziguan Tinamit (Surrounded by Canyons). These are the names still used by the Quiché Maya, although everyone else calls the place Chichicastenango, a foreign name given by the conquistadors' Mexican allies.

Government

Chichi has two religious and governmental establishments. The Catholic Church and the Republic of Guatemala appoint priests and town officials to manage their interests, but the local people elect their own religious and civil officers to deal with local matters.

The Indian town government has its own council, mayor and deputy mayor, and a court which decides cases involving local Indians exclusively. Chichi's religious life is centred in traditional religious brotherhoods called cofradías. Membership in the brotherhood is an honourable civic duty; leadership is the greatest honour. Leaders are elected periodically, and the man who receives the honour of being elected must provide banquets and pay for festivities for the cofradía throughout his term. Though it is very expensive, a *cofrade* (member of the brotherhood) happily accepts the burden, even going into debt if necessary.

Each of Chichi's 14 cofradías has a patron saint. Most notable is the cofradía of Santo Tomás, Chichicastenango's patron saint. The cofradías march in procession to church every Sunday morning and during religious

GUATEMALA

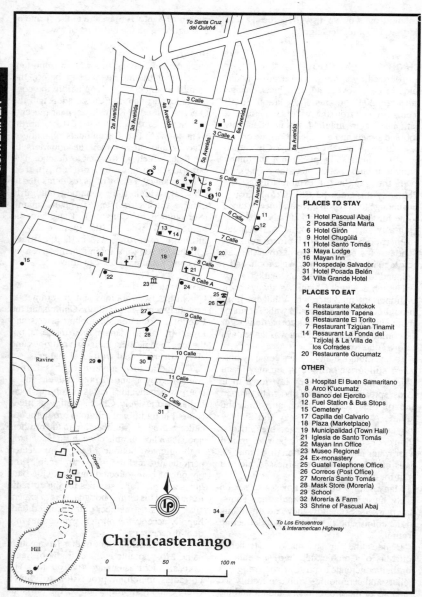

PLACES TO STAY

1 Hotel Pascual Abaj
2 Posada Santa Marta
6 Hotel Girón
9 Hotel Chugüilá
11 Hotel Santo Tomás
13 Maya Lodge
16 Mayan Inn
30 Hospedaje Salvador
31 Hotel Posada Belén
34 Villa Grande Hotel

PLACES TO EAT

4 Restaurante Katokok
5 Restaurante Tapena
6 Restaurante El Torito
7 Restaurant Tziguan Tinamit
14 Resaurant La Fonda del Tzijolaj & La Villa de los Cofrades
20 Restaurante Gucumatz

OTHER

3 Hospital El Buen Samaritano
8 Arco K'ucumatz
10 Banco del Ejercito
12 Fuel Station & Bus Stops
15 Cemetery
17 Capilla del Calvario
18 Plaza (Marketplace)
19 Municipalidad (Town Hall)
21 Iglesia de Santo Tomás
22 Mayan Inn Office
23 Museo Regional
24 Ex-monastery
25 Guatel Telephone Office
26 Correos (Post Office)
27 Morería Santo Tomás
28 Mask Store (Morería)
29 School
32 Morería & Farm
33 Shrine of Pascual Abaj

Chichicastenango

To Santa Cruz del Quiché

To Los Encuentros & Interamerican Highway

0   50   100 m

festivals, the officers dressed in costumes showing their rank. Before them is carried a ceremonial staff topped by a silver crucifix or sun-badge which signifies the cofradía's patron saint. Indian drum and flute, and perhaps a few more modern instruments such as a trumpet, may accompany the procession, as do fireworks. During major church festivals, effigies of the saints are brought out and carried in grand processions, and richly costumed dancers wearing the traditional carved wooden masks act out legends of the ancient Maya and of the Spanish conquest. For the rest of the year, these masks and costumes are kept in storehouses called *morerías*; you'll see them, marked by signs, around the town.

Orientation
Though supposedly laid out to the Spanish colonial street grid plan, Chichi's hilly topography defeats the logic of the plan, and lack of street signs often keeps you wondering where you are. Use our map, identify some landmarks, and you should have little trouble, as Chichi is fairly small.

Information
Tourist Office There is no official tourist information office in Chichi. Ask your questions at the museum on the main square, or at one of the hotels. The Mayan Inn is perhaps the most helpful and best informed.

Money The Banco del Ejercito, across from Restaurant El Mash on 6 Calle, is open Monday to Friday from 9 am to noon and 2 to 5 pm, on Saturday from 9 am to 3 pm and on Sunday from 9 am to 2 pm.

Post & Telecommunications The post office (Correos) is at 7a Avenida 8-47, two blocks south of the Hotel Santo Tomás on the road into town. Very near it is the Guatel telephone office, at 7a Avenida 8-21, on the corner of 8 Calle A.

Market
Years ago, intrepid travellers made their way to this mountain-bound fastness to witness Chichi's main square packed with Indian traders attending one of Guatemala's largest indigenous markets. Today the market has stalls aimed directly at tourists, as well as those for local people.

On Wednesday and Saturday evenings you'll see men carrying bundles of long poles up the narrow cobbled streets to the square, then stacking them out of the way. In the evening the arcades around the square are alive with families cooking supper and arranging their bedding for a night's sleep out of doors.

Between dawn and about 8 or 9 am on Sunday and Thursday, the stacks of poles are erected into stalls, hung with cloth, furnished with tables and piled with goods for sale. In general, the tourist-oriented stalls selling carved wooden masks, lengths of embroidered cloth and garments are around the outer edges of the market in the most visible areas. Behind them, the centre of the square is devoted to things that the villagers want and need: vegetables and fruit, baked goods, macaroni, soap, clothing, spices, sewing notions and toys. Cheap cookshops provide lunch for buyers and sellers alike.

Most of the stalls are taken down by late afternoon. Prices are best just before the market breaks up, as traders would rather sell than carry goods away with them.

Iglesia de Santo Tomás
Though dedicated to the Catholic rite, this simple church, dating from about 1540, is more often the scene of rituals which are slightly Catholic and highly Mayan. The front steps of the church serve much the same purpose as did the great flights of stairs leading up to Mayan pyramids. For much of the day (especially on Sunday), the steps smoulder with incense of copal resin, while indigenous prayer leaders called *chuchkajaues* (mother-fathers) swing censers (usually tin cans poked with holes) containing *estoraque* incense and chant magic words in honour of the ancient Mayan calendar and of their ancestors.

It's customary for the front steps and door of the church to be used only by important church officials and by the chuchkajaues, so you should go around to the right and enter by the side door.

Inside, the floor of the church may be spread with pine boughs and dotted with offerings of maize kernels, bouquets of flowers, bottles of liquor wrapped in corn husks, and candles – candles everywhere. Many local families can trace their lineages back centuries, some even to the ancient kings of Quiché. The candles and offerings on the floor are in remembrance of the ancestors, many of whom are buried beneath the church floor just as Mayan kings were buried beneath pyramids.

On the west side of the plaza is another little whitewashed church, the Capilla del Calvario, which is similar in form and function to Santo Tomás, but smaller.

Museo Regional

In the arcade facing the south side of the square is the Museo Regional, open from 8 am to noon and 2 to 5 pm (closed on Tuesday). In the two large rooms of the museum you can see ancient clay pots and figurines, arrowheads and spearheads of flint and obsidian, copper axe-heads, and *metates* (grindstones for maize).

The museum also holds the Rossbach jade collection, with several beautiful necklaces, figurines and other objects. Ildefonso Rossbach served as Chichi's Catholic priest for many years until his death in 1944.

Shrine of Pascual Abaj

Before you have been in Chichi very long, some village lad will offer to guide you (for a tip) to a hilltop on the outskirts to have a look at Pascual Abaj (Sacrifice Stone), which is the local shrine to Huyup Tak'ah (Mountain Plain), the Mayan earth god. Said to be hundreds – perhaps thousands – of years old, the stone-faced idol has suffered numerous indignities at the hands of outsiders, but local people still revere it. Chuchkajaues come here regularly to offer incense, food, cigarettes, flowers, liquor and Coca-Cola to the earth god, and perhaps even to sacrifice a chicken. The offerings are in thanks and hope for earth's continuing fertility.

Sacrifices do not take place at regular hours. If you're in luck, you can witness one. The worshippers will not mind if you watch, and some (but not all!) won't mind if you take photographs, though they may ask if you want to make an offering (of a few quetzals) yourself. If there is no ceremony, you can still see the idol and enjoy the walk up to the pine-clad hilltop and the views of the town and valley.

There have been some incidents of robbery of tourists walking to visit Pascual Abaj, so the best plan is to join with others and go in a large group.

You don't really need a juvenile guide to find Pascual Abaj. Walk down the hill on 5a Avenida from the Santo Tomás church, turn right onto 9 Calle and continue downhill along this unpaved road, which bends to the left. At the bottom of the hill, when the road turns sharply to the right, bear left and follow a path through the cornfields, keeping the ditch on your left. Signs mark the way. Walk to the buildings just ahead, which include a farmhouse and a morería. Greet the family here. If the children are not in school you may be invited to see them perform a local dance in full costume on your return from Pascual Abaj (a tip is expected).

Walk through the farm buildings to the hill behind, and follow the switchback path to the top and along the ridge of the hill, called Turukaj, to a clearing in which you will see the idol in its rocky shrine. The idol looks like something from Easter Island. The squat stone crosses near it have many levels of significance for the Maya, only one of which pertains to Christ. The area of the shrine is littered with past offerings; the bark of the pines here has been stripped away in places to be used as fuel in the incense fires.

Places to Stay

Chichi does not have a lot of accommodation, and most of what it has is in the higher price range. As rooms are scarce, it's a good idea to arrive early on Wednesday or Saturday to secure a room for the Thursday and

Sunday markets. Safe car parking is available in the courtyard of most hotels.

Places to Stay – bottom end

Hotel Pascual Abaj (☎ (9) 56-10-55), 5 Avenida Arco K'ucumatz 3-38, Zona 1, is a clean little place one long block north downhill from the Arco K'ucumatz. Rooms with shower cost US$8/10 a single/double. The *Posada Santa Marta* across the street is much simpler.

Hotel Girón (☎ (9) 56-11-56), on 6 Calle next to the Restaurant Tziguan Tinamit, is at the rear of the commercial Girón building; walk through to the back. Recently renovated, the 16 rooms are clean, and priced at US$10 a double with shower.

Of the cheap hotels, *Hospedaje Salvador*, two blocks south-west of the Santo Tomás church along 5a Avenida, is the biggest. This maze-like warren of red bricks, tiles and white stucco has 35 rooms on three floors reached by obscure routes. Rooms without bath offer the better value, as the private baths – particularly those on the lower floors – smell quite strongly. Doubles cost US$7 without running water, US$10.50 with private bath.

Hotel Posada Belén (☎ (9) 56-12-44), 12 Calle 5-55, Zona 1, is expensive (US$12/16 a double without/with shower), but will do if all else is full.

Places to Stay – middle

Hotel Chugüilá (☎ /fax (9) 56-11-34), 5a Avenida 5-24, just south of the Arco K'ucumatz, is charming. Most of the 25 colonial-style rooms have private baths, some have fireplaces, and there are even a few two-room suites and a restaurant. For what you get, the price is very reasonable – US$12/16/21 a single/double/triple without bath, US$27/32/36 with private bath.

Maya Lodge (☎ (9) 56-11-67), in the main plaza, has 10 rather dark rooms with clean add-on showers in the very midst of the market. Fairly plain despite some colonial touches, it is comfortable nonetheless, though a bit overpriced. Rates have recently risen to US$25/30 a single/double.

Places to Stay – top end

The best hotel in town is one of the most pleasant in Guatemala. It's the lovely old *Mayan Inn* (☎ (9) 56-11-76, fax 56-12-12), 8 Calle A and 3a Avenida, on a quiet street one long block south-west of the plaza. Founded in 1932 by Alfred S Clark of Clark Tours, it has grown to include several restored colonial houses, their courtyards planted with exuberant tropical gardens, their walls festooned with brilliantly coloured indigenous textiles. The 30 rooms, all with fireplaces, are quite charming, with antique furnishings including carved wooden bedsteads, headboards painted with country scenes, heavily carved armoires and rough-hewn tables. The private bathrooms (many with tubs) may be old-fashioned but they are decently maintained. A staff member in traditional costume is assigned to help you carry your bags, answer any questions you may have and even serve at your table in the dining room, as well as to look after your room – there are no door locks. Rates are US$75/85/101 a single/double/triple.

Hotel Santo Tomás (☎ (9) 56-10-61, 56-13-16, fax 56-13-06), 7a Avenida at 6 Calle, two blocks east of the plaza, is colonial in architecture and decoration but modern in construction and facilities, and thus a favourite with bus tour operators. Each of the 43 rooms has private bath and fireplace; all the rooms are grouped around pretty courtyards with colonial fountains. There's a good bar and dining room as well. Rates are US$70/80/98 a single/double/triple.

Villa Grande Hotel (☎ in Guatemala City (2) 34-81-36/7/8; fax 34-81-34) has 61 modern rooms in low tile-roofed buildings set into a hillside one km south of Chichi's main square along the road into town. There are fine views of the town and mountains, as well as a swimming pool and a restaurant. Rates are US$60 to US$90 a single, US$70 to US$100 a double. The pleasant walk to the centre takes about 10 minutes.

Places to Eat

Finding a meal at a decent price is no

problem. Market days offer the best possibilities for rock-bottom cheap meals.

Places to Eat – bottom end

On Sundays and Thursdays, eat where the marketers do – at the cookshops set up in the centre of the market. These are the cheapest in town. On other days, look for the little comedores near the post office and Guatel office on the road into town (7a Avenida).

Next cheapest places to eat are the *Restaurante Katokok* and *Restaurante Tap ena*, two little *cocinas económicas* on 5a Avenida a block from the Hotel Chugüilá just south of the Arco K'ucumatz.

Restaurant La Fonda del Tzijolaj, upstairs in the Centro Comercial Santo Tomás on the north side of the square, has everything: good views, nice decor, decent food and reasonable prices: US$2 to US$3 for breakfast, twice that for lunch or dinner. It's closed on Tuesday. There are several other restaurants with portico tables in the Centro Comercial. At *La Villa de los Cofrades* you can while away the hours with checkers (draughts) and backgammon. The courtyard of the Centro Comercial is a vegetable market. Similar in feeling and price is *Restaurante El Torito*, upstairs in the Hotel Girón building. Platos fuertes of soup, main course, rice and dessert cost US$3 to US$5. It's open every day for all three meals.

Restaurante Gucumatz, at the corner of 6a Avenida and 8 Calle, is tidy and pleasant, with local foods at low prices. *Restaurant El Mash*, 6 Calle near 5a Avenida, at the back of a little flowered courtyard, has declined since my last visit there but is still serviceable. *Restaurant Tziguan Tinamit*, at the corner of 6 Calle and 5a Avenida, takes its name from the Quiché Mayan name for Chichicastenango. It's popular with locals and foreigners, and is open all day every day.

Pensión Chugüilá is one of the most pleasant places to eat, and there are always a few other travellers to talk with about life on the road. Main-course plates are priced at US$5.

Places to Eat – middle

The two dining rooms at the *Mayan Inn* have pale yellow walls, beamed ceilings, red-tiled floors, stocky colonial-style tables and chairs, and decorations of colourful local cloth. Waiters wear traditional costumes which evolved from the dress of Spanish farmers of the colonial era: colourful headdress, sash, black tunic with coloured embroidery, half-length trousers, and squeaky leather sandals called *caïtes*. The daily set-price meals are the best way to order here; they cost US$5 to US$8 for breakfast and US$13 for lunch or dinner, plus drinks and tip.

The *Hotel Santo Tomás* has a good dining room, but it's often crowded with tour groups. Try to get one of the pleasant courtyard tables, where you can enjoy the sun and the marimba band which plays at lunch time.

Getting There & Away

Chichi has no bus station. The closest thing to a bus stop is the corner of 7a Avenida and 6 Calle, but buses depart from various points around the market, particularly near the Hotel Santo Tomás and the Hotel Chugüilá. Ask any bus driver or police officer by naming your destination, and you'll be directed to the proper spot.

Any bus heading south can drop you at Los Encuentros, where you can catch a bus to your final destination. There are direct buses to Quetzaltenango (94 km, two hours, US$1.25) and to Guatemala City (Veloz Quichelense, 146 km, 3½ hours, US$2.25).

SANTA CRUZ DEL QUICHÉ

The capital of the department of Quiché (altitude 2020 metres, population 13,000) is 19 km north of Chichicastenango. As you leave Chichi heading north along 5a Avenida, you'll pass beneath Arco K'ucumatz, an arched bridge built in 1932 and named for the founder of K'umarcaaj.

Without the bustle of the big market and the big tourism buses, Santa Cruz – which is usually called 'El Quiché' – is quieter and more typical of the Guatemalan countryside than is Chichi. If you visit El Quiché, it is probably because you want to visit the ruins of K'umarcaaj (Utatlán). This is best done early in the morning, as you may have to walk to the ruins and back.

K'umarcaaj

The ruins of the ancient Quiché Mayan capital are three km west of El Quiché along an unpaved road. Start out of town along 10 Calle and ask the way frequently. No signs mark the way and there is no regular transport. Consider yourself very lucky if you succeed in hitching a ride with other travellers who have their own vehicle. Admission to the site costs a few pennies.

The kingdom of Quiché was established in Late Post-Classic times (about the 1300s) from a mixture of indigenous people and Mexican invaders. Around 1400, King K'ucumatz founded his capital at K'umarcaaj and conquered many neighbouring cities. During the long reign of his successor Q'uikab (1425-75), the kingdom of Quiché extended its borders to Huehuetenango, Sacapulas, Rabinal and Cobán, even coming to influence the peoples of the Soconusco region in Mexico.

The Cakchiquels, a vassal people who once fought alongside the Quichés, broke away from their former overlords and established their capital at Iximché during the 1400s.

Pedro de Alvarado led his conquistadors into Guatemala in 1524, and it was the Quichés, under their king, Tecún Umán, who organised the defence of the country. In the decisive battle fought near Quetzaltenango on 12 February 1524, Alvarado and Tecún found one another and locked in mortal combat. Alvarado won, and Tecún was killed. The defeated Quichés invited the victorious Alvarado to visit their capital, where they secretly planned to kill him. Smelling a rat, Alvarado, with the aid of his Mexican auxiliaries and the anti-Quiché Cakchiquels, captured the Quiché leaders instead, burnt them alive, took K'umarcaaj (called Utatlán by his Mexican allies) and destroyed the city.

The history is more interesting than the ruined city, of which little remains but a few grass-covered mounds. Of the 100 or so large

structures identified by archaeologists, only half a dozen are at all recognisable by us mere mortals, and these are uninspiring. The site itself is a beautiful place for a picnic, shaded by tall trees and surrounded by its defensive ravines, which failed to save the city from the conquistadors. Local prayermen keep the fires of ancient Quiché burning, so to speak, by using ruined K'umarcaaj as a ritual site. A long tunnel *(cueva)* beneath the plaza is a favourite spot for prayers and chicken sacrifices.

Places to Stay & Eat

El Quiché has a few little hotels, pensions and restaurants, though if you're looking for comfort rather than price, you may find it more convenient to make Chichicastenango your base.

Hotel San Pascual (☎ (9) 55-11-07), 7 Calle 0-43, 1½ blocks south-east of the plaza, has 40 serviceable rooms for US$5 to US$8 a double; the more expensive rooms have private bath. The newest rooms also have TV, and cost a bit more. The whole place is run by a dynamo señora who also runs a typing school for local children in a room off the lobby.

Near the bus station are even cheaper lodging places, such as *Hospedaje Tropical* and *Hospedaje Hermano Pedro*, charging US$2 per bed; look at the room first and decide if you think it's worth it.

Restaurant 2000 No 2, two blocks west of the square, is simple and cheap. *Restaurant Pic Nic* is next best.

Getting There & Away

Many buses from Guatemala City to Chichicastenango continue to El Quiché (look for 'El Quiché' or just 'Quiché' on the signboard); on market days (Sunday and Thursday) there may be a bus every hour in the morning. The last bus from El Quiché headed south to Chichicastenango and Los Encuentros leaves mid-afternoon, so don't tarry too long here unless you want to spend the night.

El Quiché is the transport point for the sparsely populated and somewhat remote reaches of northern Quiché, which extends all the way to the Mexican border. Ask at the bus station for details. The bus trip over a rough road to Sacapulas, for instance, takes five hours.

NEBAJ

High among the Cuchumatanes lie the Ixil Maya village of Nebaj and its neighbouring villages of Chajul and Cotzal. The scenery is breathtakingly beautiful, and the local people, remote from the cultural influences of TV and modern urbanity, proudly preserve their ancient way of life.

Nebaj's location in this mountain fastness has been both a blessing and a curse. The Spaniards found it difficult to conquer, and wreaked destruction on the inhabitants when they did. In recent years guerrilla forces made the area a base of operations, and the army took strong measures to dislodge them. Many small villages were destroyed, with their surviving inhabitants being herded into 'strategic hamlets', as in the Vietnam War.

Today the area around Nebaj is still troubled, but travellers come here for the scenery, the local culture, the excellent handicrafts, the market (Thursday and Sunday) and, during the second week in August, the annual festival.

Places to Stay & Eat

Pensión Las Tres Hermanas is the best known lodging, charging US$1 for a bed and the same price for a meal. There's hot water in the shower. If the Three Sisters is full, alternatives include the *Pensión Las Gemelitas* and the *Hotel Ixil*.

Getting There & Away

Much of the transport to Nebaj from Sacapulas, Santa Cruz del Quiché and Cobán is by truck, at a fare equivalent to that of the bus. There is a daily market bus departing from Nebaj for Santa Cruz del Quiché about 3 am, returning from El Quiché by mid-morning; it's a five-hour trip.

South-Western Highlands

The departments of Quetzaltenango, Totonicapán and Huehuetenango are more mountainous and less frequented by tourists than regions closer to Guatemala City. The scenery here is just as beautiful and the indigenous culture just as colourful and fascinating. Travellers going to and from the border post at La Mesilla find these towns welcome breaks from long hours of travel, and there are some interesting possibilities for excursions as well.

Highlights of a visit to this area include Quetzaltenango, Guatemala's second-largest city; the pretty nearby town of Zunil, with its Fuentes Georginas hot springs; Totonicapán, a department capital noted for its handicrafts; the Friday market at San Francisco El Alto; the blanket-makers of Momostenango; and the restored Mayan city of Zaculeu near Huehuetenango.

CUATRO CAMINOS

Following the Interamerican Highway westward from Los Encuentros, the road twists and turns ever higher into the mountains, bringing still more dramatic scenery and cooler temperatures. After 58 km you come to another important highway junction known as Cuatro Caminos (Four Roads). The road east leads to Totonicapán (12 km), west to Quetzaltenango (13 km) and north (straight on) to Huehuetenango (77 km). Buses shuttle from Cuatro Caminos to Totonicapán and Quetzaltenango about every half-hour from 6 am to 6 pm.

TOTONICAPÁN

If you want to visit a pleasant, pretty Guatemalan highland town with few other tourists in sight, San Miguel Totonicapán (altitude 2500 metres, population 9000) is the place to go. Buses shuttle into the centre of town from Cuatro Caminos frequently throughout the day.

The ride from Cuatro Caminos is along a beautiful pine-studded valley. As you approach the town you pass a large hospital on the left. Turn around the enormous Minerva fountain and enter town along 17a Avenida.

Totonicapán's main plaza has the requisite large colonial church, and also a municipal theatre, built in 1924 in neoclassical style and recently restored. Buses go directly to the parque (as the plaza is called) and drop you there.

Wander about the town as you like, sitting in the shady parque, listening to the dull clank of the churchbells and shopping for food or a few travel necessities with the local people. This may give you an idea of what it's like to be a Guatemalan in Guatemala.

The Casa de la Cultura Totonicapense (☎ (9) 66-15-75), 8a Avenida 2-17, Zona 1, to the left of the Hospedaje San Miguel on 8a Avenida, has displays of indigenous culture and crafts. The museum administers a wonderful 'Meet the Artisans' programme to introduce tourists to artisans and local families.

Two km from the parque are the Agua Caliente hot springs, a popular bathing place for local people.

Meet the Artisans

In 1991, artisans of the local Quiché community proposed to Señor Carlos Umberto Molino, director of the Casa de la Cultura Totonicapense, a programme to interest tourists in visiting local handicrafts workshops. The programme is now the most interesting activity in town. Starting at 10 am and lasting till about 4 pm, you meet local artisans – toymakers, potters, carvers of wooden masks and musical instruments, weavers, musicians – watch them work, listen to their music, see their dances, experience their living conditions, and eat a homecooked lunch. The programme costs about US$100 for a moderate-sized group, and the money goes directly to the artisans and musicians involved. An extended programme includes a one-night stay in a local home. For information, prices and schedules, contact the museum at the address and telephone number given above.

Festivals

Besides the expected holidays such as Christmas and Holy Week, Totonicapán celebrates the Fiesta de Esquipulas on 15 January in Cantón Chotacaj, three km from the parque.

The festival of the Apparition of the Archangel Michael is on 8 May, with fireworks and traditional dances. More dances follow on the last Sunday in June, with the Festival of Traditional Dance held in the Plaza Central from 9 am to 2 pm.

There's also the Feria Titular de San Miguel Arcángel (Name-Day Festival of the Archangel Saint Michael) from 24 to 30 September, with the principal celebration being on the 29th.

Places to Stay

As you make your way into town, one block before coming to the parque, on the left stands the *Hospedaje San Miguel* (☎ (9) 66-14-52), 3 Calle 7-49, Zona 1. It's a tidy place, not what you'd call Swiss-clean but good for the price – US$4 a double with shared bath, US$5.50 with private shower. The rooms with showers tend to be larger, with three beds. Flash heaters provide the hot water, which is thus fairly dependable.

QUETZALTENANGO

Called Xelajú or simply Xela (SHAY-lah) by its Quiché Mayan citizens, Quetzaltenango (altitude 2335 metres, population 10,000) is the commercial centre of south-western Guatemala. Its good selection of hotels in all price ranges makes it an excellent base for excursions to the nearby towns and villages noted for their handicrafts and hot springs.

History

Quetzaltenango came under the sway of the Quiché Maya of K'umarcaaj when they began their great expansion in the 1300s. Before that it had been a Mam Maya town.

Tecún Umán, the powerful leader of the Quichés, met Pedro de Alvarado on the field of battle near Quetzaltenango on 12 February 1524. The prize was Guatemala, much of which Tecún controlled and all of which the conquistadors wanted. Alvarado struck a mortal blow, Tecún Umán fell dead, and Guatemala was open to the Spaniards.

In the mid-1800s, when the Federation of Central American was founded, Quetzaltenango initially decided on federation with Chiapas and Mexico instead of with Central America. Later changing its mind, the city joined the Central American Federation, and became an integral part of Guatemala in 1840.

With the late 19th-century coffee boom, Quetzaltenango's wealth increased. This is where the finca owners came to buy supplies and where the coffee brokers had their warehouses. Things went along fine, with the city getting richer and richer, until a dual calamity – an earthquake and a volcanic eruption – brought mass destruction and an end to the boom.

The city's position at the intersection of the roads to the Pacific Slope, Mexico and Guatemala City guarantees it some degree of prosperity. Today it's again busy with commerce, both Indian and ladino.

Orientation

The heart of Xela is the Parque Centroamérica, shaded by old trees, graced with neoclassical monuments and surrounded by the town's important buildings: cathedral, banks, tourist office, government headquarters, museum and Guatel telephone office and one of the best hotels. Most of the town's lodging places are found within a couple of blocks of the parque.

Quetzaltenango has several bus stations. The largest and busiest is the 2nd-class Terminal Minerva, on the western outskirts near the Parque Minerva on 6 Calle in Zona 3, next to the market. City buses Nos 2 and 6 run between the terminal and Parque Centroamérica – look for 'Terminal' and 'Parque' signs in the front windows of the buses. First-class bus lines have their own

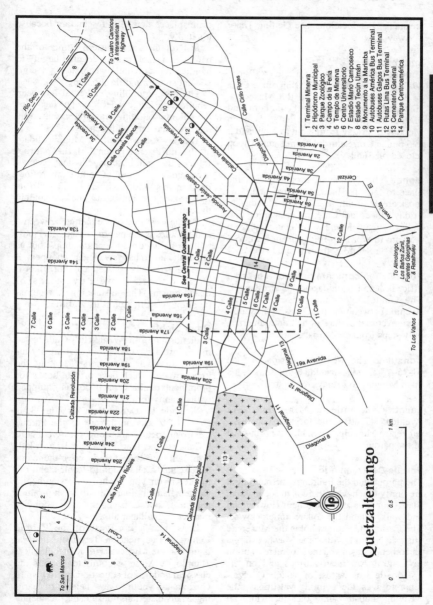

GUATEMALA

Quetzaltenango

1 Terminal Minerva
2 Hipódromo Municipal
3 Parque Zoológico
4 Campo de la Feria
5 Templo de Minerva
6 Centro Universitario
7 Estadio Mario Camposeco
8 Estadio Tecún Umán
9 Monumento a la Marimba
10 Autobuses América Bus Terminal
11 Autobuses Galgos Bus Terminal
12 Rutas Lima Bus Terminal
13 Cementerio General
14 Parque Centroamérica

terminals. For locations, see Getting There & Away.

Information

Tourist Office The tourist office (☎ (9) 61-49-31) is in the right-hand wing of the Casa de la Cultura (also called the Museo de Historia Natural), at the lower (southern) end of the Parque Centroamérica. It's open Monday to Friday from 8 am to 1 pm and 2 to 5 pm, and on Saturday from 8 am to noon (closed on Sunday).

Money The Parque Centroamérica is the place to look for banks. Normal hours for most are 8.30 am to 2.30 pm Monday to Friday. Banco del Café, on the parque at 6 Calle, is open Monday to Thursday from 8.30 am to 8 pm, on Friday from 8 am to 8 pm and on Saturday from 10 am to 2 pm.

Post & Telecommunications The post office is at 15a Avenida and 4 Calle, Zona 1. The Guatel telephone office is on 12a Avenida between 7 and 8 Calles, at the south-western corner of the Parque Centroamérica, only steps from the tourist office.

Consulate The Mexican Consulate (☎ (9) 61-25-47) is at 9a Avenida 6-19, Zona 1. It's open Monday to Friday from 9 to 11 am.

Laundry Lavandería Mini-Max, 14a Avenida C47, at 1 Calle, faces the neoclassical Teatro Municipal, five blocks north-west of the parque.

Parque Centroamérica

The parque and the buildings surrounding it are pretty much what there is to see in Xela. Start your tour at the southern (lower) end and walk around the square anticlockwise. The Casa de la Cultura holds the Museo de Historia Natural, with some Mayan exhibits and others focusing on the Liberal revolution in Central American politics and on the Estado de Los Altos, of which Quetzaltenango was the capital. Marimbas, the weaving industry and other local lore all claim places here. It's fascinating because it's funky.

Just off the south-eastern corner of the parque is a small market devoted largely to handicrafts and daily necessities, a convenient spot for a little shopping.

The once-crumbling cathedral has been rebuilt in the last few decades. The façade of the colonial building was preserved, and a modern sanctuary built behind it.

The city's Town Hall, or Municipalidad, at the north-eastern end of the parque, follows the grandiose neoclassical style so favoured as a symbol of culture and refinement in this wild mountain country. To its right is the Pensión Bonifaz, the best hotel in the centre.

On the west side of the parque between 4 and 5 Calles is the palatial Pasaje Enriquez, built to be lined with elegant shops, but as Quetzaltenango has few elegant shoppers, it has suffered decline. One local tourism brochure defined it well by means of malapropism: 'The outstanding characteristic of the western arch is its grafitti'.

Other Sights

Walk north on 14a Avenida to 1 Calle to see the impressive neoclassical Teatro Municipal. Inside are three tiers of seating, the lower two of which have private boxes for prominent families; each box is equipped with a vanity for the ladies.

Mercado La Democracia, in Zona 3, is about 10 blocks north-west of the Parque Centroamérica. Walk along 14a Avenida to 1 Calle (to the Teatro Municipal), turn left, turn right onto 16a Avenida, cross the major street called Calle Rodolfo Robles, and the market is on your right. It's an authentic Guatemalan city market with fresh produce and meat, foodstuffs and necessities for city dweller and villager alike.

Less than a km west of the Parque Centroamérica, near the Terminal Minerva, is the Parque Minerva with its neoclassical Templo de Minerva, built to honour the classical goddess of education and to inspire Guatemalan youth to new heights of learning. Many historians note that the presidency of Manuel Estrada Cabrera (1898-1920) saw the building of lots of Minerva temples but few schools.

Language Courses

Quetzaltenango has several schools where you can study Spanish with native speakers. I have not attended classes at any of these, and would be grateful for reports on quality of programmes.

Academia Latinoamericana Mayanse, 15a Avenida 6-75 (PO Box 375), Zona 1 (☎ (9) 61-27-07); for information in the USA, c/o Max Kintner and Mary Pliska, 3314 Sherwood Lane, Wichita Falls, TX 76308 (☎ (817) 696-3319)

Guatemalensis Spanish School, 19a Avenida 2-14, Zona 1; for information in the USA, c/o Elizabeth Oudens, 644 33rd Ave, San Francisco, CA 94121 (☎ (415) 221-8965)

Instituto Central America, 1 Calle 16-93, Zona 1 (☎ (9) 61-18-71); for information in the USA, c/o RR 2, Box 101, Stanton, NE 68779 (☎ (402) 439-2943)

Kie-Balam Spanish School, 9a Avenida 0-55, Zona 1 (☎ (9) 61-46-40); for information in the USA, c/o Martha Mora, 1816 N Wells, Chicago, IL 60614 (☎ (708) 888-2514, (312) 642-8019); this school uses income from its classes to support community projects.

Places to Stay – bottom end

Cheap hostelries are concentrated at the northern end of the Parque Centroamérica along 12a Avenida, and south of the parque more or less behind the Casa de la Cultura.

Walk up 12a Avenida from the parque with the Municipalidad on your right and the Cantel textile shop on your left to find the *Pensión San Nicolás*, on the left between 4 and 3 Calles. No one would call it beautiful, but it has a courtyard, a car park, and decent rooms for US$1 to US$1.50 a single, US$2 to US$3 a double, US$3.50 a triple. Look at the room before you pay.

At 2 Calle there are nicer places. Turn right for the *Hotel Horiani*, officially at 12a Avenida 2-23, though you enter on 2 Calle. This place charges US$2 a single, US$4 a double.

Turn left (west) at 2 Calle to find the *Hotel Río Azul* (☎ (9) 63 06 54), 2 Calle 12-15, Zona 1, which offers luxury compared to its neighbours. All rooms here have private shower with hot water, and some even have colour TV. Prices are excellent for what you get: US$8.50/12/16 a single/double/triple. There's even a car park.

Two more places are on 13a Avenida. Follow 2 Calle westward half a block from the Hotel Río Azul and turn left to find the *Casa Kaehler* (☎ (9) 61-20-91), 13a Avenida 3-33, Zona 1, an old-fashioned European-style family pension with seven rooms of various shapes and sizes. Room 7 is the most comfortable. Prices here are US$7/11/14/17 a single/double/triple/quad for rooms with private bath. Rooms without bath are a bit cheaper. This is an excellent, safe place for women travellers; ring the bell to gain entry. The *Hotel Radar 99*, next door, is for dire emergencies only.

Two streets west of Casa Kaehler is *Casa Suiza* (☎ (9) 61-43-50), 14a Avenida 'A' 2-36, Zona 1, with 18 basic rooms grouped around a big courtyard in a fairly convenient location. There's a cheap comedor, and a dozen rooms priced at US$5.50 to US$7 a single, US$10 to US$12 a double, US$14 to US$17 a triple. Bathless rooms have sinks for your morning splash; the more expensive rooms have private showers. Some readers have complained of noise and brusque management here.

South-west of the parque is the huge old *Hotel Kiktem-Ja* (☎ (9) 61-43-04), in the Edificio Fuentes, a colonial-style building at 13a Avenida 7-18, Zona 1. The 20 rooms are on two levels around the courtyard, which also serves as a car park. Fireplaces are available in each room, for a comforting blaze. Rooms cost US$9/11/13 a single/double/triple with private hot shower.

Hotel Capri (☎ (9) 61-41-11), 8 Calle 11-39, Zona 1, a block from the Parque Centroamérica and behind the Casa de la Cultura, offers rooms in a convenient location for US$3 per person with shared bath. Many are filled with foreign students attending local Spanish-language courses.

Places to Stay – middle

If you want to spend a little more for a lot

GUATEMALA

Central Quetzaltenango

0   100   200 m

more comfort, head straight for the family-run *Hotel Modelo* (☎ (9) 63-02-16, 61-25-29; fax 63-13-76), 14a Avenida 'A' 2-31, Zona 1. Pleasant small rooms with tiled showers rent for US$25/30 a single/double in the main hotel, US$14/18 in the simpler annexe. The hotel's good dining room serves breakfast (7.15 to 9.30 am), lunch (noon to 2 pm) and dinner (6 to 9 pm) daily.

Hotel Casa Florencia (☎ (9) 61-23-26), 12a Avenida 3-61, Zona 1, is a relatively new place. Good big rooms with double beds cost US$18/25 a single/double.

Hotel Villa Real Plaza (☎ (9) 61-40-45,

61-62-70; fax 61-67-80), 4 Calle 12-22, Zona 1, a half-block west of the parque, was recently remodelled and is now quite comfortable. The 34 large, airy rooms come with TV, fireplace and private bath and cost US$45/50 a single/double.

The *Pensión Bonifaz* (☎ (9) 61-22-79, 61-42-41), 4 Calle 10-50, Zona 1, near the north-east corner of the Parque Centroamérica, is the city's social centre – a longstanding favourite accommodation for Guatemalans and foreigners alike. The 62 rooms with private bath (some with tubs) are not what you'd call fancy, but they're com-

PLACES TO STAY

4	Casa Suiza
5	Hotel Modelo
8	Hotel Río Azul
9	Hotel Horiani
10	Hotel Quetzalteco
11	Casa Kaehler
12	Pensión San Nicolás
13	Hotel Radar 99
14	Hotel Casa Florencia
19	Hotel Villa Real Plaza
21	Pensión Bonifaz
31	Hotel Kiktem-Ja
36	Hotel Capri

PLACES TO EAT

5	Restaurant Modelo
6	Pizza-Pastelería Bombonier
7	Pizza Ricca
16	El Rincón de los Antojitos
17	Restaurant El Kopetin
18	Restaurant Shanghai
21	Restaurant Bonifaz

36	Restaurant Capri

OTHER

1	Cine Teatro Roma
2	Teatro Municipal
3	Lavandería Mini-Max
15	Post Office
20	Banco de Occidente
22	Pasaje Enriquez
23	Taxis
24	Banco de Guatemala
25	Banco Nacional de Desarrollo Agricola
26	Banco del Café
27	Parque Centroamérica
28	Municipalidad & Banco Industrial
29	Guatel Telephone Office
30	Construbanco
32	Cathedral
33	Casa de la Cultura (Museo de Historia Natural)
34	Tourist Office
35	Small Market

fortably old-fashioned, and some have two double beds. They're divided between the original colonial-style building (the one you enter) and the adjoining modernised building (with wood panelling and modern Danish-style furniture). Rooms in the original building are preferable. The hotel has a good dining room, a cheery bar and pastry shop patronised by Quetzaltenango's gilded youth, and a car park. Rates are US$48/60 a single/double.

The *Hotel del Campo* (☎ (9) 61-20-64, 61-80-82), Km 224, Camino a Cantel, is Quetzaltenango's largest and most modern hotel. Its 104 rooms have showers and TV and are decorated in natural wood and red brick. There's an all-weather swimming pool. Rooms on the lowest floor can be dark, so get a room numbered in the 50s (51, 52, etc). Prices are reasonable: US$30/42 a single/double. The hotel is 4.5 km east of the Parque Centroamérica, a short distance off the main road between Quetzaltenango and Cuatro Caminos; watch for signs for the hotel and for the road to Cantel.

Places to Eat - bottom end

As with hotels, Quetzaltenango has a good selection in all price ranges. Cheapest are the food stalls in and around the small market to the left of the Casa de la Cultura, where snacks and substantial main-course plates are sold for US$1 or less.

A very popular place with good food at good prices is *El Rincón de los Antojitos*, 15a Avenida at 5 Calle, Zona 1. The menu is mostly Guatemalan, with a few concessions to international tastes. All three meals, and vegetarian dishes, are served for US$3 to US$6.

Try also *La Góndola* (☎ 61-21-48), at 10a Avenida beneath the Palacio Municipal, for pizza and Italian specialities.

For sit-down eateries serving everything from tacos to pizza, go to the corner of 14a Avenida and 3 Calle, then walk north (uphill) along 14a Avenida to find the following places.

Restaurant El Kopetin (☎ 61-24-01), 14a Avenida 3-31, is pleasant and modernish, with red tablecloths, natural wood and a family atmosphere. The long and varied menu ranges from hamburgers to Cuban-style sandwiches to filet mignon. Full meals need cost no more than US$1.50 but may go as high as US$4. Alcoholic drinks are served. El Kopetin is open every day.

Pizza Ricca (☎ 61-81-62), 14a Avenida 2-52, has a busy white-coated staff baking pizzas in a wood-fired oven and serving them to hungry customers waiting patiently in comfy booths. Pizzas come in various sizes and prices from US$1.75 to US$6; hamburgers and plates of spaghetti cost US$1.50 to US$2. Beer is served. Pizza Ricca is open all day, every day.

Pizza-Pastelería Bombonier (☎ 61-62-25), 14a Avenida 2-20, serves more pizzas and hamburgers than bonbons, despite its name; many customers order to take away, as there are only a few tables. Both the burgers and pizzas here are cheaper than at Pizza Ricca.

Restaurant Shanghai (☎ 61-41-54), 4 Calle 12-22, Zona 1, is the most convenient Chinese place to the parque. The cuisine is Guatemalan Oriental: pato (duck), camarones (shrimp) and other Chinese specialities for about US$2.50 to US$3.50 per plate. The Shanghai is open daily from 8 am to 9.30 pm.

The dining room of the *Hotel Modelo*, 14a Avenida 'A' 2-31, has good set-price lunches and dinners (US$5).

Places to Eat – middle

The dining room of the *Pensión Bonifaz*, at the north-east corner of the parque, is the best in town. This is where the local social set comes to dine and be seen. Food is good, and prices, though high by Guatemalan standards, are low when compared to those even in Mexico. Soup, main course, dessert and drink can run to US$8 to US$12, but you can spend about half that much if you order only a sandwich and a beer.

Entertainment

Evening entertainment possibilities are limited, as you might expect. It gets chilly when the sun goes down, so you won't want to sit out in the Parque Centroamérica enjoying the balmy breezes – there aren't any.

The *Teatro Roma* (on 14a Avenida 'A', facing the Teatro Municipal) might be playing an interesting movie – perhaps even one in English with Spanish subtitles.

The bars at the *Pensión Bonifaz* and *Hotel Modelo* are good for a drink, a chat and a snack. The Bonifaz features delicious cakes and pastries to go with your coffee or drink.

Getting There & Away

For 2nd-class buses, head out to the Terminal Minerva, on the western outskirts near the Parque Minerva, on 6 Calle in Zona 3, next to the market. City bus Nos 2 and 6 run between the terminal and Parque Centroamérica (look for 'Terminal' and 'Parque' signs in the front window of the bus). You can catch the city bus (US$0.10) to the terminal from 8 Calle at 12a Avenida or 14a Avenida in the centre. The busy Terminal Minerva has almost hourly buses to many highland destinations.

Rutas Lima, Autobuses América and Autobuses Galgos, three 1st-class lines, have their own terminals on Calzada Independencia, the wide boulevard which is the north-easterly continuation of Diagonal 3 (Zona 1) leading out of town to the Cuatro Caminos road; in Zona 2 it is called 7a Avenida.

Autobuses Galgos (☎ (9) 61-22-48) also has an office at Calle Rodolfo Robles 17-43, Zona 1, about a dozen blocks north-west of the parque.

Chichicastenango (94 km, two hours) – direct buses on market days cost US$1.25. If you don't get one of these, change at Los Encuentros.

Guatemala City (203 km, four hours) – lots of companies have plenty of buses departing frequently from Terminal Minerva. Transportes Galgos has seven 1st-class buses daily (US$2.50) stopping at Totonicapán, Los Encuentros (change for Chichicastenango or Panajachel) and Chimaltenango (change for Antigua).

Huehuetenango (90 km, two hours, US$2.50) – hourly buses depart from Terminal Minerva; for 1st-class buses, see La Mesilla.

La Mesilla, Mexican border (170 km, four hours) – Rutas Lima has two 1st-class buses daily to Huehuetenango (US$2.75) and La Mesilla (US$4), departing from Quetzaltenango at 5 am and 6.30 pm, or get a 2nd-class bus from Terminal Minerva to Huehuetenango and change there.

Panajachel (99 km, two hours) – direct buses run by Morales or Rojo y Blanco depart four times daily (US$1.25), or you can take any bus bound for Guatemala City and change at Los Encuentros. Transportes Higueros has Guatemala City-bound buses which stop at Panajachel as well.

Retalhuleu (67 km, two hours) – hourly buses depart from Terminal Minerva (US$1). The daily Rutas Lima bus to the border station at Talisman will also drop you in Retalhuleu.

AROUND QUETZALTENANGO

The beautiful volcanic countryside around Quetzaltenango has numerous possibilities for outings. The natural steam baths at Los Vahos are very primitive, but the outing into the hills surrounding the city can be fascinating whether you take a steam bath or not. The hot springs at Almolonga are basic but also cheap and accessible. Those at Fuentes Georginas are idyllic, still pretty cheap, but not easily accessible unless you have your own transport.

Take note of the market days: Sunday in Momostenango, Monday in Zunil, Tuesday in Totonicapán, Friday in San Francisco El Alto, and Saturday in Totonicapán.

Buses from Quetzaltenango to Almolonga, Los Baños and Zunil depart several times per hour from Terminal Minerva; some buses stop at the corner of 10a Avenida and 10 Calle, Zona 1, to take on more passengers.

Los Vahos

If you're a hiker, and if the weather is good, you might enjoy a trip to the rough-and-ready steam baths at Los Vahos (The Vapours), 3.5 km from Parque Centroamérica. Take a bus headed for Almolonga and ask to get out at the road to Los Vahos. If you're driving, follow 12a Avenida south from the parque to its end, turn left, go two blocks and turn right up the hill; this turn is 1.2 km from the parque. The remaining 2.3 km of unpaved road is steep and rutted - a

GUATEMALA

Indians from Guatemala's highlands playing traditional music

thick carpet of dust in the dry season, mud in the rainy season (when you may want a 4WD vehicle). The first turn along the dirt road is a sharp right (unmarked); at the second you bear left (this is badly marked).

Views of the city on a clear day are remarkable. The road ends at Los Vahos, where you can have a steam bath for only a few quetzals, and (if you've brought food with you) a picnic.

Zunil

Zunil is a pretty market town in a lush valley framed by steep hills and dominated by a towering volcano. As you approach it along the road from Quetzaltenango, you will see it framed as if in a picture, with its white colonial church gleaming above the red-tiled and rusted tin roofs of the low houses.

On the way to Zunil the road passes Almolonga, a vegetable-growing town four km from Quetzaltenango. Just over a km beyond Almolonga, on the left side of the road, is Los Baños, with natural hot springs. The bath installations are quite decrepit, but if a hot bath at low cost is your desire, you may want to stop. Tomb-like enclosed concrete tubs rent for a few quetzals per hour.

Winding down the hill from Los Baños, the road skirts Zunil and its fertile gardens on the right side before intersecting the Cantel to El Zarco road. A bridge crosses a stream to lead into the town; it's one km from the bridge to the plaza.

Zunil is a perfectly typical Guatemalan country town with a particularly pretty church. The church's ornate façade, with eight pairs of serpentine columns, is echoed inside by a richly worked altar of silver. On market day (Monday) the plaza in front of the church is bright with the predominantly red traditional garb of local people buying and selling.

From Zunil, which is 10 km from Quetzaltenango, you can continue to Fuentes Georginas (nine km), return to Quetzaltenango via the Cantel road (16 km), or alternatively, take the jungle-bound toll road down the mountainside to El Zarco junction and the Pacific Slope Highway. Buses depart about every half-hour for the return trip to Quetzaltenango.

Fuentes Georginas

Imagine a steep, high wall of tropical verdure – huge green leaves, ganglions of vines, giant ferns, spongy moss and profusions of tropical flowers – at the upper end of a lush mountain valley. At the base of this wall of greenery is a limpid pool of naturally warm mineral water. A pure white statue of a Greek goddess gazes benevolently across the misty water as families happily splash and play, then clamber out for a drink or a snack at a rustic restaurant right at the pool's edge. This is Fuentes Georginas, the prettiest spa in Guatemala. Though the setting is intensely tropical, the mountain air currents keep it deliciously cool all day.

The pools were built during the presidency of General Jorge Ubico (1931-44) and named in his honour; the present installations date from 1964, when they were restored by INGUAT.

Unfortunately, a major construction project nearby has in recent years robbed Fuentes Georginas of much of its naturally warm water. Enquire about the current condition of the pools before making the trek out here.

Besides the restaurant, there are three sheltered picnic tables with cooking grills (bring your own fuel). Down the valley a few dozen metres are seven cottages for rent at US$12 per night. Each cottage has a hot shower and a fireplace to ward off the mountain chill at night. Admission to the site costs US$0.50, the same again to park a car. Bring a bathing suit, which is required.

Getting There & Away A half-day tour to Fuentes Georginas using one of the taxis parked in the Parque Centroamérica in Quetzaltenango costs US$15 per carload (US$3 to US$5 per person), and includes a visit to Zunil as well as two hours' swimming time at the spa. This is not a bad price, but it doesn't give you much time there. You might want to take the taxi to the baths, bring a picnic, and walk back to Zunil to catch a late afternoon bus. Hitchhiking is not good on the Fuentes Georginas access road, as there are few cars and they are often filled to capacity with large Guatemalan families. The best days to try for a ride are Saturday and Sunday, when the baths are busiest.

If you're driving or hitching, go uphill from Zunil's plaza to the Cantel road (about 60 metres), turn right and go downhill 100 metres to a Pepsi sign ('Baños Georginas'). On the left, an unpaved road heads off into the mountains; the baths are nine km from Zunil's plaza. Walking takes two hours uphill, 1½ hours on the way back down. You'll know you're approaching the baths when you smell the sulphur in the air.

San Francisco El Alto

High on a hilltop (2610 metres) overlooking Quetzaltenango (17 km away) stands the market town of San Francisco El Alto. Six days a week it's a sleepy sort of place, but on Friday it explodes with activity as thousands of country people pour into the sloping plaza for the huge market. Soon the large plaza, surrounded by the requisite church and Municipalidad and centred on a cupola-like mirador (lookout), is covered in country goods. Stalls spill into neighbouring streets, and the press of traffic is so great that a special system of one-way roads is established to avoid monumental traffic jams. Vehicles entering the town on market day must pay a small fee.

San Francisco's market is not heavy with handicrafts as are those in Chichicastenango and Antigua, though you will find some nice crafts here, such as Momostenango blankets. Rather, this is a real people's market at which you'll find anything and everything needed by a Guatemalan highland villager. If you're not particularly excited by markets and you've seen one of the others, you can give this one a miss. If you love markets, come.

Places to Stay & Eat The lodging and eating situation here is dire. If you're in need of a bed you'll have to suffer the *Hotel y Cafetería Vista Hermosa* (☎ (9) 66-10-30), 3a Avenida 2-22, Zona 1. The 25 rooms here

are ill-kept (though a few on the front enjoy good views), service is nonexistent and the cafeteria rarely has any food to serve. Other than that, it's disappointing. Doubles cost US$4 with shared bath, US$5.50 to US$7.50 with private shower.

As for eating, the *Comedor San Cristóbal*, near the Hospedaje San Francisco de Assis, may be your best bet, but that's not saying much.

Momostenango

Beyond San Francisco El Alto, 22 km from Cuatro Caminos (35 km from Quetzaltenango) along a fairly rough unpaved country road, this village in a pretty mountain valley is Guatemala's famous centre for the making of *chamarras*, the thick, heavy woollen blankets which you have no doubt already used to protect yourself from the chill of a highland night. The villagers also make ponchos and other woollen garments. As you enter the village square after an hour of bashing over the bad road, you will see signs inviting you to watch the blankets being made, and to purchase the finished products. The best time to do this is on Sunday, which is market day; haggle like mad. You might also want to hike three km north to the hot springs of Pala Chiquito, where the blankets are washed and the dyes fixed.

Momostenango is also noted for its adherence to the ancient Mayan calendar, and for observance of traditional rites. Hills about two km west of the plaza are the scene of these ceremonies, coordinated with the important dates of the calendar round (see Facts about the Region for details on the Mayan calendar). Unfortunately, it's not as easy to witness these rites as it is to visit the Shrine of Pascual Abaj at Chichicastenango.

Places to Stay & Eat For comfort and price, it's best to catch the mid-afternoon bus back to Quetzaltenango. If you miss it, *Casa de Huéspedes Paclom* charges US$6 for a bare double room; water to the toilets is shut off at night, there is no shower in the hotel and the food is no treat. *Hospedaje Roxana*, on the plaza, is marginally better. There are several basic comedores on the plaza.

Getting There & Away Catch an early bus from Quetzaltenango's Terminal Minerva, or at Cuatro Caminos, or at San Francisco El Alto. There are five or six buses daily, the last one returning from Momostenango by about 3 pm.

HUEHUETENANGO

Separated from the capital by mountains and a twisting road, Huehuetenango (altitude 1902 metres, population 40,000) has that self-sufficient air exuded by many mountain towns: we may be small but we're the centre of everything here. Coffee growing, mining, sheep raising, light manufacturing and agriculture are the main activities in this region. The lively Indian market is filled daily with traders who come down from the Sierra de los Cuchumatanes, the mountain range (highest in Central America), which dominates the department of Huehuetenango. Surprisingly, the market area is about the only place you'll see colourful traditional costumes in this town, as most of its citizens are ladinos who wear modern clothes.

For travellers, Huehuetenango is usually a stage on the journey to or from Mexico. After leaving San Cristóbal de las Casas or Comitán, taking an hour or so at the border, Huehuetenango is the logical place to spend your first night in Guatemala. It's a good introduction to Guatemalan highland life: a pleasant town with a selection of hotels, an interesting market, and the ruins of ancient Zaculeu on the outskirts.

History

Huehuetenango was a Mam Maya region until the 1400s when the Quichés, expanding from their capital at K'umarcaaj near present-day Santa Cruz del Quiché, pushed them out. Many Mam fled into neighbouring Chiapas, which still has a large Mam-speaking population near its border with Guatemala. In the late 1400s, the weakness of Quiché rule brought about civil war which engulfed the highlands and provided a chance for Mam independence. The troubles lasted for decades, coming to an end in the summer of 1525 after the arrival of Gonzalo de Alvarado, brother of Pedro, who conquered the Mam capital of Zaculeu for the king of Spain.

Orientation

The town centre is five km north of the Interamerican Highway. The new bus station and new market are three km from the highway along the road to the centre (6 Calle), on the east side. The bus station is underused, and most buses continue right into the centre.

Almost every service of interest to tourists is in Zona 1 within a few blocks of the plaza. The old market, bordered by 1a and 2a Avenidas and 3 and 4 Calles in Zona 1, is still the busy one, especially on Wednesday, which is market day. Four blocks west of the market on 5a Avenida between 2 and 3 Calles is the main plaza, called the parque, the very centre of town and reference point for finding any other address. Hotels and restaurants are mostly near the parque, except for one or two small hotels near the new bus station and one motel out on the Interamerican Highway.

Information

The post office is at 2 Calle 3-54, right next to the Guatel telephone office across the street from the Hotel Mary, half a block east of the plaza. There is a Mexican consulate in the Farmacia Del Río, at the corner of 5a Avenida and 4 Calle.

Town-operated *servicios sanitarios* (toilets) are on 3 Calle between 5a and 6a Avenidas, only a few steps west of the plaza. Farmacias (chemists) and banks are dotted around the centre.

Parque Central

Huehuetenango's main plaza is shaded by nice old trees and surrounded by the town's imposing buildings: the Municipalidad (with its band shell on the upper floor) and the huge colonial church. The plaza has its own little

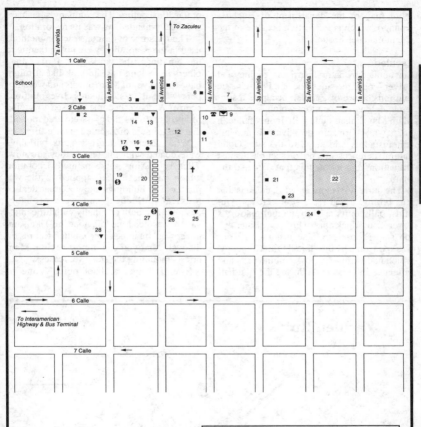

Huehuetenango

0   100   200 m

PLACES TO STAY

2   Auto Hotel Vásquez
3   Hospedaje El Viajero
4   Hotel Zaculeu
5   Hotel Central
6   Pensión Astoria
7   Hotel Mary
8   Mansión El Paraíso
14 Hotel Roberto's
21 Hotel Maya

PLACES TO EAT

1   Doña Estercita Cafetería
7   Panadería Pan Delis
    & Restaurant Regis
13 Maxi Pizza
16 Los Pollos
21 Rico Mac Pollo

25 Panadería del Trigo
28 Pizza Hogareña

OTHER

9   Post Office
10 Guatel Telephone Office
11 Municipalidad (Town Hall)
12 Parque Central
15 Servicios Sanitarios (Toilets)
17 Bancafé (Banco del Café)
18 Farmacia Berlín
19 Banco del Ejercito
20 Taxis
22 Market
23 Farmacia Ruiz
24 Servicios Santiarios (Toilets)
26 Mexican Consulate
27 Banco de Guatemala

relief map of the department of Huehue-tenango, which is interesting because of the Cuchumatanes Mountains.

Zaculeu

Surrounded by natural barriers – ravines and a river – on three sides, the late Post-Classic religious centre of Zaculeu occupies a strategic defensive location which served its Mam Maya inhabitants well. It only failed in 1525 when Gonzalo de Alvarado and his conquistadors laid siege to the site. Good natural defences are no protection against starvation, and it was this that defeated the Mam.

The current wisdom about Zaculeu is that it is boring; a bad restoration left its pyramids, ball courts and ceremonial platforms covered in a thick coat of greying plaster. It's too stark, too clean. The restoration work was sponsored by the United Fruit Company, which had extremely powerful interests and influence in Guatemala during the first half

of the 20th century. The company's business was heavy-handed, as was its restoration.

Though some of the construction methods used in the restoration were not authentic to the buildings, the work goes farther than others in making the site look like it might have to the eyes of Mam priests and worshippers when it was still an active religious centre. We have become so used to seeing ruddy bare stones and grass-covered mounds that the tidiness of Zaculeu is unsettling.

When Zaculeu flourished, its buildings were coated with plaster, as they are now. What is missing is the painted decoration which must have been applied to the wet plaster. The buildings show a great deal of Mexican influence, and were probably designed and built originally with little innovation. Zaculeu is no Palenque, no Tikal, and never was. Imagine some painted figures on the walls and you can almost see the Mam priests mounting the steep staircases.

The park-like archaeological zone of

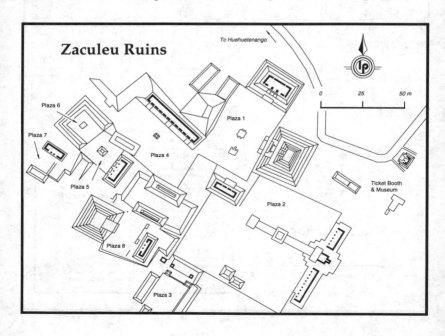

Zaculeu Ruins

Zaculeu is four km north of Huehuetenango's main plaza. It's open daily from 8 am to 6 pm; admission is US$0.20 after you sign the register. Cold soft drinks are available. The small, modern museum has drawings of scenes from the Spanish conquest, a Mam burial urn and potsherds. You're allowed to climb on the restored structures as much as you want, but it's forbidden to climb the grassy mounds which await excavation.

Getting There & Away There are several routes by which to reach Zaculeu from the Parque Central. Jitney trucks and vans depart from the corner of 3a Avenida and 4 Calle (between the church and the market) near Rico Mac Pollo and head north along 5a Avenida toward Zaculeu. 'Esperanza' buses travel this route as well. Some go fairly close to the ruins, others do not; ask. Another route goes west via 3 Calle and out past the Campo de la Feria (fairgrounds). To walk all the way from the main plaza takes about 45 minutes.

Places to Stay
Huehuetenango has a useful selection of low-budget places to stay, but nothing fancy. Your first explorations should be along 2 Calle between 3a and 7a Avenidas, just off the plaza; there are four little hotels and six eating places in this three-block stretch, and two more hotels half a block off 2 Calle.

Hotel Central (☎ (9) 64-12-02, 64-14-67), 5a Avenida 1-33, facing the Hotel Zaculeu half a block north-west of the plaza, has 17 largish, simple and well-used rooms. Showers are shared, but the water is usually hot. Two people pay US$5 in a double room; some rooms have three and four beds. At least one reader had valuables stolen from his padlocked room here, though. The hotel's comedor provides cheap meals; you might want to come and enjoy them even if you don't stay here. It opens for breakfast at 7 am, which is earlier than most other places in town.

Hotel Roberto's (☎ (9) 64-15-26), 2 Calle 5-49, half a block west of the plaza, is another tidy place in a convenient location,

with 21 rooms around a courtyard. Rates are a low US$2 per person in rooms without running water. The courtyard comedor serves good food cheap. *Hospedaje El Viajero*, across the street, is not as good.

Hotel Mary (☎ (9) 64-15-69), 2 Calle 3-52, is a block east of the plaza facing Guatel. It's a cut above the other places: the 25 small rooms have bedspreads and other nice touches. The ground-floor Restaurant Regis is handy, as is the Panadería Pan Delis bakery-café next door. Room rates at the Mary are US$4 to US$5 a single, US$6 to US$8 a double and US$9 to US$11 a triple; the higher-priced rooms have private bath.

Auto Hotel Vásquez (☎ (9) 64-13-38), 2 Calle 6-67, has a car park in the front, and 20 small, fairly cheerless but usable rooms at the back (US$2.50 per person, with private bath).

Hotel Maya, 3a Avenida 3-55, behind the church and just to the left of Rico Mac Pollo, resembles a barracks in its cinder-blockiness, but manages to be a bit more cheerful than lower-priced places. The location is convenient. Rates are US$2 per person in rooms without bath, US$3 per person in rooms with bath.

Even lower in price are places such as the family-operated *Mansión El Paraíso*, 3a Avenida 2-41, in the block behind the Municipalidad. This vision of paradise is fairly gloomy, very barracks-like, but very cheap at less than US$1.75 per person (cold-water communal showers only). *Pensión Astoria* (☎ (9) 64-11-97), 4a Avenida 1-45, is similar.

The best place in town is the *Hotel Zaculeu* (☎ (9) 64-10-86), 5a Avenida 1-14, facing the Hotel Central half a block north-west of the plaza. This colonial-style place has a lovely garden courtyard, and a good dining room that was under renovation the last time I looked in. Rooms near the hotel entrance open onto the courtyard and are preferable to those at the back of the hotel; all 20 rooms have private showers and rent for US$20 to US$45 a double.

On the Interamerican Highway, two km north-west of the turn-off to Huehuetenango is the *Hotel Pino Montano* (☎ in Guatemala City (2) 31 07 61), Carretera Panamericana Km 259 (Apdo Postal 20), Huehue's interpretation of an American roadside motel. Boxy bungalows housing 18 rooms are arranged behind a glass-enclosed restaurant and office. Though modern, it manages to be dreary, the only cheer coming from the gospel singing at revival meetings held in a nearby field on some evenings. Double rooms with bath and lots of hot water cost US$16.

Places to Eat

Especialidades Doña Estercita Cafetería y Pastelería is on 2 Calle, across the street from the Auto Hotel Vásquez. A tidy, cheerful place, it serves pastries as well as more standard dishes.

The *Restaurant Regis* and *Panadería Pan Delis* are next to the Hotel Mary, at 2 Calle 3-52. Another good bakery is the *Panadería del Trigo*, at the corner of 4a Avenida and 4 Calle.

Los Pollos, 3 Calle between 5a and 6a Avenidas, half a block west of the plaza, advertises that it is open 24 hours a day. Two pieces of chicken with salad, chips and a soft drink cost US$2.50. Burgers and smaller chicken meals are even cheaper. *Rico Mac Pollo*, 3a Avenida between 3 and 4 Calles, next to the Hotel Maya, is a similar chicken place.

Just a bit farther from the plaza are the *Pizza Hogareña*, 6a Avenida 4-45, and the *Restaurante Rincón*, 6a Avenida 'A' 7-21, serving fairly good pizza as well as churrasco (Guatemalan-style beef), cheap sandwiches and delicious fruit licuados. Getting a meal for under US$3 is easy; it's possible to eat for US$2.

Probably the best restaurant in town is the *Steak House*, at the intersection of 4a Avenida and 2 Calle, where a full meal of Chinese food or steak should cost no more than US$5 or so.

Getting There & Away

The new bus terminal is in Zona 4, two km south-east of the plaza along 6 Calle, but most buses still depart from 1a Avenida between 2 and 3 Calles. Second-class buses run between the terminal and the Guatemalan border post at La Mesilla (84 km, 2½ hours, US$1.25) about every hour between 5 am and 4 pm. There are also a few 1st-class buses (with slightly higher fares).

Hourly buses head down the Interamerican Highway to Cuatro Caminos (74 km, 1¾ hours, US$2) and Quetzaltenango's Terminal Minerva (90 km, two hours, US$2.50). Los Halcones (☎ in Guatemala City (2) 8-19-79; 7a Avenida 15-27, Zona 1) runs two buses a day down the Interamerican Highway to Guatemala City (270 km, five hours, US$3.50).

LA MESILLA

There is a distance of four km between the Mexican and Guatemalan immigration posts at La Mesilla/Ciudad Cuauhtémoc, and you must take a collective taxi (US$1). There is no bank on either the Guatemalan or Mexican side, but moneychangers will do the deal – at a worse rate.

When you're done with border formalities, take the next bus out. If it's going directly to your chosen destination, so much the better. If not, go as far as Huehuetenango or Comitán and change buses. There is more onward bus traffic from these cities than from the border; any later bus leaving the border and heading past these cities will no doubt stop in town to pick up passengers anyway.

TODOS SANTOS CUCHUMATÁN

If you're up for a trek into the Cuchumatanes, two buses per day depart at 4 am and 11 am from the corner of 1a Avenida and 4 Calle, near the Pensión San Jorge in Huehuetenango, on the 40-km ride to Todos Santos Cuchumatán. The road is rough, the mountain air chilly and the journey slow, but the scenery is spectacular. Return buses leave Todos Santos at 5.30 and 11.30 am and 1 pm for Huehue.

The picturesque town of Todos Santos Cuchumatán (altitude 2450 metres, population 2000) is one of the few in which the

Top: 'Mayan Relics' shop, Panajachel, Guatemala (TB)
Bottom: Chichicastenango, Guatemala (PW)

Masks on sale at the market, Chichicastenango, Guatemala (TB)

traditional Mayan tzolkin calendar is still remembered and (partially) observed. Saturday is market day. It's possible to take some vigorous treks from the town into the mountains, and to rejuvenate in the traditional Mam sauna.

Accommodation consists of two primitive, cheap hospedajes: *Tres Olguitas* and *La Paz*. There are also rooms in private homes. People with rooms to rent will probably solicit your business as you descend from your bus, and charge US$1 per person. Try the house attached to the café and shop *Ruinas de Tecumanchun*.

A few small comedores provide food; *Comedor Katy* is perhaps the best. You'll need these places because the buses – which are run to take villagers into Huehue for shopping, and then home again – don't return there until early the next morning.

GUATEMALA

Guatemala's Pacific Slope

A lush, humid region of tropical verdure, Guatemala's Pacific Slope is the south-easterly extension of Mexico's Soconusco. The volcanic soil is rich, and is good for growing coffee at the higher elevations, palm oil seeds and sugar cane at the lower. Vast fincas (plantations) exploit the land's economic potential, drawing seasonal workers from the highland towns and villages, where work is scarce. Along the Pacific shore are endless stretches of beaches of dark volcanic sand. The temperature and humidity along the shore are always uncomfortably high, day and night, rainy season and dry. The few small resorts attract mostly local – not foreign – beach-goers.

To travellers, the Pacific Slope is mostly the fast highway called the Carretera al Pacífico (CA-2), which runs from the border crossings at Ciudad Hidalgo/Tecún Umán and Talismán/El Carmen to Guatemala City. The 275 km between the Mexican border at Tecún Umán and Guatemala City can be covered in about four hours by car, five by bus – much less than the 342 km of the Interamerican Highway through the south-western highlands between La Mesilla and Guatemala City, which takes seven hours. If speed is your goal, the Pacific Slope is your route.

Most of the towns along the Carretera al Pacífico are muggy, somewhat chaotic and hold little of interest for travellers. The beach villages are worse – unpleasantly hot, muggy and dilapidated. There are exceptions, though. Retalhuleu, a logical stopping place if you're coming from the Mexican border, is pleasant and fun to visit. Nearby is the active archaeological dig at Abaj Takalik. The pre-Olmec stone carvings at Santa Lucía Cotzumalguapa, eight km west of Siquinalá, and those at La Democracia, nine km south of Siquinalá, are unique, and if you travel the Carretera al Pacífico you must stop to see them. The port town of Iztapa and its beach resort of Likín can fill the need if you simply must get to the beach. Near Guatemala City, Lago de Amatitlán is the citified version of the more beautiful Lago de Atitlán.

The Carretera al Pacífico is good and very fast, which is exactly how the 1st-class buses drive it.

CIUDAD TECÚN UMÁN

This is the preferable and busier of the two Pacific Slope border-crossing points, with a bridge linking Ciudad Tecún Umán (Guatemala) with Ciudad Hidalgo (Mexico). The border posts are open 24 hours a day. Basic hotels and restaurants are available, but you'll want to get through the border and on your way as soon as possible.

Minibuses and buses run frequently between Ciudad Hidalgo and Tapachula, 38 km to the north (see the Soconusco section in the Highland & Pacific Chiapas chapter for details). From Ciudad Tecún Umán there are frequent buses heading east along the Carretera al Pacífico, stopping at Coatepeque, Retalhuleu, Mazatenango and Escuintla before climbing into the mountains to Guatemala City. If you don't find a bus to your destination, take any bus to Coatepeque or, preferably, Retalhuleu, and change buses there.

EL CARMEN

Though you can cross at El Carmen, you will encounter much less hassle and expense if you cross at Tecún Umán, described above.

A toll bridge across the Río Suchiate connects Talismán (Mexico) and El Carmen (Guatemala). The border-crossing posts are open 24 hours every day. Minibuses and trucks run frequently between Talismán and Tapachula, half an hour (20 km) away.

There are few services at El Carmen, and those there are are very basic. There is good bus service from El Carmen to Malacatán, on the San Marcos-Quetzaltenango road, and to Ciudad Tecún Umán, 39 km to the south. There are also fairly frequent 1st-class buses

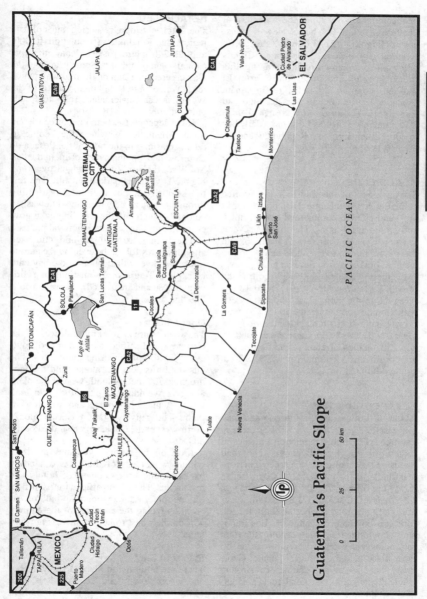

Guatemala's Pacific Slope

to Guatemala City along the Carretera al Pacífico (278 km, five hours, US$4). Transportes Galgos (☎ (2) 53-48-68, 2-36-61), 7a Avenida 19-44, Zona 1, Guatemala City, is only one company operating along this route. It runs five buses daily from El Carmen, stopping at Ciudad Tecún Umán, Coatepeque, Retalhuleu, Mazatenango and Escuintla (change for Santa Lucía Cotzumalguapa). Rutas Lima has a daily bus to Quetzaltenango via Retalhuleu and El Zarco junction.

COATEPEQUE

Set on a hill in the midst of lush coffee plantations, Coatepeque is a brash, fairly ugly and chaotic commercial centre, noisy and humid at all times. The town is several km north of the Carretera al Pacífico, and there is no reason to stop here unless you're a coffee broker or you have an emergency.

Of the town's hotels, the 39-room *Hotel Mansión Residencial* (☎ (9) 75-20-18), 0 Avenida 11-49, Zona 2, is about the best, with double rooms priced at US$24 with private bath. It has a restaurant. *Hotel Virginia* (☎ (9) 75-18-01), Carretera al Pacífico Km 220, on the Carretera al Pacífico, has 15 air-conditioned rooms for US$15/20 a single/double.

EL ZARCO JUNCTION

About 40 km east of Coatepeque and nine km east of Retalhuleu on the Carretera al Pacífico is El Zarco, the junction with the toll road north to Quetzaltenango. The road winds up the Pacific Slope, carpeted in tropical jungle, rising more than 2000 metres in the 47 km from El Zarco to Quetzaltenango. The toll is less than US$1. Just after the upper toll booth, the road divides at Zunil: the left fork goes to Quetzaltenango via Los Baños and Almolonga (the shorter route); the right fork goes via Cantel. For information on these places and the beautiful Fuentes Georginas hot springs near Zunil, see Around Quetzaltenango in the Guatemala's Highlands chapter.

RETALHULEU

The Pacific Slope is a rich agricultural region, and Retalhuleu (population 40,000, altitude 240 metres) is its clean, attractive capital – and proud of it. Some years ago the citizens erected a sign on the highway which read 'Welcome to Retalhuleu, Capital of the World'. Most Guatemalans refer to Retalhuleu simply as Reu (RAY-oo).

If Coatepeque is where the coffee traders trade, Retalhuleu is where they come to relax, splashing in the pool at the Posada de Don José and sipping a cool drink in the bar. You'll see their expensive Range Rovers and big 4WD vehicles parked outside. The rest of the citizens get their kicks strolling through the plaza between the whitewashed colonial church and the wedding-cake government buildings, shaded by royal palms.

The balmy tropical air and laid-back attitude are restful. In the evening the parque (plaza) is alive with strollers and noisy with blackbirds. Tourists are something of a curiosity in Reu and are treated very well. You'll like this place.

Orientation

The town centre is four km south-west of the Carretera al Pacífico along a grand boulevard lined with towering palm trees. The bus station is near the market and the fairgrounds, 700 metres south-west of the plaza along 5a Avenida 'A'. To find the plaza, look for the twin church towers and walk toward them. The railway station is two blocks north-west of the plaza, very near the Posada de Don José.

Most of the services you may need are within two blocks of the plaza, including banks, public toilets, cinemas, hotels and restaurants. There is no official tourist office, but people in the Municipalidad, on 6a Avenida facing the east side of the church, will do their best to help with vexing problems.

Places to Stay

There are bottom-end places to stay in Reu and several low-priced, central hotels. Two of the most convenient are just half a block

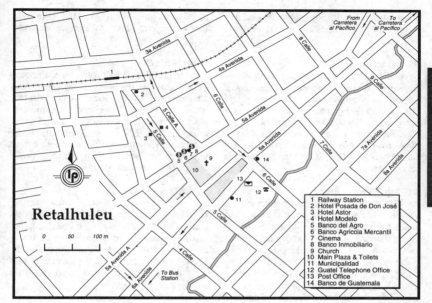

Retalhuleu

0   50   100 m

1   Railway Station
2   Hotel Posada de Don José
3   Hotel Astor
4   Hotel Modelo
5   Banco del Agro
6   Banco Agricola Mercantil
7   Cinema
8   Banco Inmobiliario
9   Church
10 Main Plaza & Toilets
11 Municipalidad
12 Guatel Telephone Office
13 Post Office
14 Banco de Guatemala

west of the plaza. The better of the two is the *Hotel Astor* (☎ (9) 71-04-75), 5 Calle 4-60, Zona 1, with a pretty courtyard, nine well-kept if simple rooms with showers, and its own parking lot. Rates are US$7/12/15 a single/double/triple with private shower, US$4.75 per person in rooms without bath.

Hotel Modelo (☎ (9) 71-02-56), 5 Calle 4-53, Zona 1, just across from the Hotel Astor, is a similar big old place with seven rooms on two floors around a cavernous central court. The rooms are of different sizes, with ceiling fans and small add-on showers. Prices are the same as at the Astor.

For even cheaper rooms, look at the *Hospedaje San Francisco*, 250 metres along 6a Avenida from the church on the right-hand side, at 8 Calle.

The nicest place in town is the *Hotel Posada de Don José* (☎ (9) 71-01-80, 71-08-41), 5 Calle 3-67, Zona 1, across the street from the railway station and two blocks north-west of the plaza. On weekends the Don José is often filled with finca owners in town for relaxation; at other times you can get an air-conditioned room with private bath for US$18/28/36 a single/double/triple; sometimes reductions are offered. The 35 rooms are on two levels overlooking the swimming pool, and the café and restaurant tables beneath an arcade surrounding the pool.

Out on the Carretera al Pacífico are several other hotels. These tend to be 'tropical motels' by design, with bungalows, swimming pool and restaurant. *Hotel Siboney* (☎ (9) 71-03-72, 71-01-49), Cuatro Caminos, San Sebastian, is at the eastern end of town where Calzada Las Palmas meets the Carretera al Pacífico. The 24 air-conditioned, bath-equipped rooms here are priced about the same as at the Posada de Don José. *Hotel La Colonia* (☎ (9) 71-00-54/38), Carretera al Pacífico Km 178, is one km east of the Siboney. It has a fairly luxurious layout, with 45 rooms with private baths (but no air-conditioning) in bungalows around the swimming pool. Prices are as at the Posada de Don José.

Places to Eat

Several little restaurants facing the plaza – *Cafetería Nuevos Horizones, Restaurant El Patio*, etc – provide meals at low prices (under US$3). For the best meal in town, head for the *Posada de Don José*, where the pleasant restaurant offers beef and chicken plates for US$4 to US$6 and a big, full meal can be had for US$7 to US$10. Breakfast is served here as well.

Getting There & Away

As Reu is the most important town on the Carretera al Pacífico, transport is easy. Most buses travelling along the highway stop at the city's bus station, so you can catch a bus to Guatemala City (186 km, four hours, US$3 to US$4), Quetzaltenango (67 km, two hours, US$2) or the Mexican border at Ciudad Tecún Umán (78 km, 1½ hours, US$1.75) almost every hour from about 7 am to 5 pm.

AROUND RETALHULEU
Abaj Takalik

There's nothing to see in Retalhuleu proper, but about 30 km to the west is the active archaeological dig at Abaj Takalik (ah-BAH tah-kah-LEEK), where exciting finds have already been made. Large 'Olmecoid' stone heads have been discovered, along with many other objects, which date the site as one of the earliest in all of the Mayan realm. The site has yet to be restored and prettified for tourists, so don't expect a Chichén Itzá or Tikal. But if you're truly fascinated with archaeology and want to see it as it's done, make a visit.

It's difficult to reach Abaj Takalik without your own vehicle; you may have to hire a taxi from Retalhuleu (US$20 to US$30). To do it by bus, early in the morning take any bus heading west towards Coatepeque, go about 15 km west along the Carretera al Pacífico and get out at the road, on the right, to El Asintal. It's five km to El Asintal (you may

have some luck hitching); Abaj Takalik is four km beyond El Asintal along an unpaved road.

CHAMPERICO

Built to serve as an exit route for shipments of coffee during the boom of the late 1800s, Champerico, 38 km south-west of Retalhuleu, is a tawdry, sweltering, dilapidated place that sees few tourists – and with good reason. Though there are several cheap hotels and restaurants, you would do better to reserve your seaside time for more attractive parts of La Ruta Maya.

MAZATENANGO

East of Retalhuleu, about 26 km along the Carretera al Pacífico, is Mazatenango (population 38,000, altitude 370 metres), capital of the department of Suchitepéquez. It's a centre for farmers, traders and shippers of the Pacific Slope's agricultural produce. There are a few serviceable hotels if you need to stop in an emergency.

SANTA LUCÍA COTZUMALGUAPA

Another 71 km eastward from Mazatenango brings you to Santa Lucía Cotzumalguapa (population 20,000, altitude 356 metres), an important stop for anyone interested in Mayan art and culture. In the sugar-cane fields and fincas near the town stand great stone heads carved with grotesque faces, and fine relief scenes in stone. The mystery is, who carved these ritual objects, and why?

The town itself, though pleasant, is unexciting, with little to keep you. The people in town and in the surrounding countryside are descended from the Pipils, an Indian culture known to have historic, linguistic and cultural links with the Nahuatl-speaking peoples of central Mexico. In Early Classic times, the Pipils who lived here grew cacao, the 'money' of the time. They were obsessed with the Mayan/Aztec ball game and with the rites and mysteries of death. Pipil art, unlike the flowery and almost romantic style of the true Maya, is cold, grotesque and severe, but still very finely done. What were these 'Mexicans' doing in the midst of

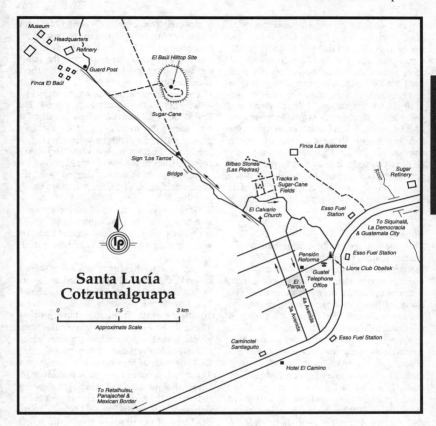

Santa Lucía
Cotzumalguapa

0   1.5   3 km

Approximate Scale

Mayan territory? How did they get here and where did they come from? Archaeologists do not have many answers. There are other concentrations of Pipils, notably in the Motagua Valley of south-eastern Guatemala, and in western El Salvador. Today these people share a common lifestyle with Guatemala's other indigenous groups, except for their mysterious history.

A visit to Santa Lucía Cotzumalguapa allows you to examine this unique 'lost culture' by visiting a number of its carved stones. Though the sites are accessible to travellers without their own transport, a car

certainly simplifies matters. In your explorations you may get to see a Guatemalan sugar-cane finca in full operation.

Orientation

Santa Lucía Cotzumalguapa is north-west of the Carretera al Pacífico. In its main square (El Parque), several blocks from the highway, are copies of some of the famous carved stones to be found in the region.

There are three main archaeological sites to visit: Bilbao, a finca right on the outskirts of Santa Lucía; Finca El Baúl, a large plantation farther from the town, at which there are two sites (a hilltop site and the finca headquarters); and Finca Las Ilusiones, which has collected most of its findings into a museum near the finca headquarters. Of these sites, Bilbao and the hilltop site at El Baúl are by far the most interesting. If time and energy are short, make for these.

If you have a car, good. If you don't and you want to see the sites in a day, haggle with a taxi driver in Santa Lucía's main square for a visit to the sites. It's hot and muggy and the sites are several km apart, so you will really be glad you rode at least part of the way. If you do it all on foot and by bus, pack a lunch so you won't have to return to town. The perfect place to have a picnic is the hilltop site at El Baúl.

Bilbao

This site was no doubt a large ceremonial centre which flourished about 600 AD. Ploughs have unearthed (and damaged) hundreds of stones during the last few centuries; thieves have carted off many others. In 1880 many of the best stones were removed to museums abroad, including nine stones to the Dahlem Museum in Berlin.

Known locally as simply *las piedras* (the stones), this site actually consists of several separate sites deep within tall stands of sugar cane. The fields come right to the edge of the town. From Santa Lucía's main square, go north uphill on 3a Avenida to the outskirts of town. Pass El Calvario church on your right, and shortly thereafter turn sharp right. A hundred metres along, the road veers to the right but an unpaved road continues straight on; follow the unpaved road. The canefields are on your left, and you will soon see a path cut into the high cane.

At times when the cane is high, finding your way around would be very difficult if it weren't for the swarms of local boys that coalesce and follow you as you make your way along the edge of the canefields. At the first sign of bewilderment or indecision they'll strike: *'Las piedras? Las piedras?'* You answer *'Si!'* and they'll lead you without hesitation into the sea of waving cane along a maze of paths to each site. A tip

is expected, of course, but it needn't be large and it needn't be given to every one of the multitude of guides. The boys are in school many days but are dependably at the ready on weekends, holidays and during school vacation time.

The boys may lead you to the sites in a different order from that which follows. The first stone is flat with three figures carved in low relief; the middle figure's ribs show prominently, as though he were starving. A predatory bird is in the upper left-hand corner. Holes in the middle-right part of the stone show that thieves attempted to cut the stone apart in order to make it more easily portable.

Next is an elaborate relief showing players in a ball game (an obsession of the Pipils), fruit, birds, animals and cacao bean pods, for which this area was famous and which made it rich.

Farther into the fields are more stones, several of them badly weathered and worn so that the figures are difficult to make out. The last stones the boys show you are a 10-minute walk from the starting-point. These bear Mexican-style circular date glyphs and other mysterious patterns which resemble closely those used by people along the Gulf coast of Mexico near Villahermosa. These two peoples must have had close relations, but just how they did so is a mystery.

Finally, the boys lead you along a broad unpaved track in the canefields back to the dead end of the unpaved road from which you began. If you go south from this point you can join 4a Avenida and continue to the main square.

To go on to El Baúl, however, you can save time by backtracking to the point where you turned sharp right just beyond El Calvario church. Buses heading out to El Baúl pass this point every few hours, or you can hitchhike. If you're driving, you'll have to return to the centre along 4a Avenida and come back out on 3a Avenida, as these roads are one way.

Finca El Baúl

Just as interesting as las piedras is the hilltop

site at El Baúl, which has the additional fascination of being an active place of pagan worship for local people. This is an excellent place for a picnic. Some distance from the hilltop site on another road, next to the finca headquarters, is the finca's private museum of stones uncovered on the property.

The hilltop site at El Baúl is 4.2 km northwest of El Calvario church. From the church (or the intersection just beyond it), go 2.7 km to a fork in the road just beyond a bridge; the fork is marked by a sign reading Los Tarros. Take the right-hand fork, an unpaved road. From the Los Tarros sign it's 1.5 km to the point where a dirt track crosses the road; on your right is a tree-covered 'hill' in the midst of otherwise flat fields. The 'hill' is actually a great ruined temple platform which has not been restored. Make your way across the field and around the south side of the hill, following the track to the top. If you have a car, you can drive to within 50 metres of the top.

If you visit on a weekend, you may find several worshippers paying their respects to the idols here. They will not mind if you visit as well, and are usually happy to pose with the idols for photographs, in exchange for a small 'contribution'.

Of the two stones here, the great grotesque half-buried head is the most striking. The elaborate headdress, 'blind' eyes with big bags beneath them, beak-like nose and idiotic 'have a nice day' grin seem at odds with the blackened face and its position, half-buried in the ancient soil. The head is stained with wax from candles, with liquor and other drinks, and with the smoke and ashes of incense fires built before it, all part of worship. The idol may have reason to be happy - people have been coming here to pay homage for over 1400 years.

The other stone is a relief carving of a figure surrounded by circular motifs which may be date glyphs. A copy of this stone may be seen in the main square of Santa Lucía Cotzumalguapa.

From the hilltop site, retrace your steps 1.5 km to the fork with the Los Tarros sign. Take the other fork this time (what would be the left fork as you come from Santa Lucía), and follow the paved road three km to the headquarters of Finca El Baúl. (If you're on foot, you can walk from the hilltop site back to the unpaved road and straight across it, continuing on the dirt track. This will eventually bring you to the asphalt road which leads to the finca headquarters. When you reach the road, turn right.) Buses trundle along this road every few hours, shuttling workers between the refinery and the town centre.

Approaching the finca headquarters (six km from Santa Lucía's main square), you cross a narrow bridge at a curve; continue uphill and you will see the entrance on the left, marked by a machine-gun pillbox. Beyond this daunting entrance you pass workers' houses, and a sugar refinery on the right, and finally come to the headquarters building, guarded by several men with rifles. The smell of molasses is everywhere. Ask permission to visit the museum and a guard will unlock the gate just past the headquarters building.

Within the gates, sheltered by a palapa, are numerous sculpted figures and reliefs found on the plantation, some of which are very fine. Unfortunately, nothing is labelled.

Behind the palapa are several pieces of machinery once used on the finca but now retired. One of these is a small Orenstein & Kopdel steam locomotive manufactured in Berlin in 1927; there is an even smaller, older, more primitive locomotive as well.

Finca Las Ilusiones

The third site is very close to Bilbao – indeed, this is the finca which controls the Bilbao canefields – but, paradoxically, access is more difficult. Your reward is the chance to view hundreds of objects, large and small, which have been collected from the finca's fields over the centuries.

Leave the town centre by heading east along Calzada 15 de Septiembre, the boulevard which joins the highway at an Esso fuel station. Go north-east for a short distance, and just past another Esso station on the left is an unpaved road which leads, after a little more than one km, to Finca Las Ilusiones and its museum. If the person who holds the museum key is to be found, you can have a look inside. If not, you must be satisfied with the many stones collected around the outside of the museum.

Places to Stay & Eat

Pensión Reforma, Calzada 15 de Septiembre at 4a Avenida, is certainly not beautiful, but will do for a night. Rooms cost US$3/5 a single/double.

Out on the highway, just a few hundred metres west of the town, is the *Caminotel Santiaguito* (☎ (9) 84-54-35/6/7), Km 90.4, Carretera al Pacífico. 'Famous since 1956', it's a fairly lavish layout (for Guatemala's Pacific Slope) with spacious tree-shaded grounds, a nice swimming pool and a decent restaurant. The pool is open to nonguests upon payment of a small fee. Motel-style air-conditioned rooms with private bath cost US$16/22 a single/double. They're liable to be full on weekends, as the hotel is something of a resort for local people. In the spacious restaurant cooled by ceiling fans, you can order a cheeseburger, fruit salad and soft drink for US$4, or an even bigger meal for US$6.50 to US$8.

Across the highway from the Caminotel is the *Hotel El Camino*, with rooms that are hot and somewhat noisy because of highway traffic. Prices are similar to those at the Pensión Reforma, but you get less for your money here.

Getting There & Away

Esmeralda 2nd-class buses shuttle between Santa Lucía Cotzumalguapa and Guatemala City (4a Avenida and 2 Calle, Zona 9) every half-hour or so between 6 am and 5 pm, charging US$1.50 for the 90-km, two-hour ride. You can also catch any bus travelling along the Carretera al Pacífico between Guatemala City and such points as Mazatenango, Retalhuleu or the Mexican border.

To travel between La Democracia and Santa Lucía, catch a bus running along the Carretera al Pacífico between Santa Lucía

and Siquinalá (eight km); change in Siquinalá for a bus to La Democracia.

Between Santa Lucía and Lago de Atitlán you will probably have to change buses at Cocales junction, 23 km west of Santa Lucía and 58 km south of Panajachel.

LA DEMOCRACIA

South of Siquinalá 9.5 km along the road to Puerto San José is La Democracia (population 4200, altitude 165 metres), a nondescript Pacific Slope town that's hot both day and night, rainy season and dry. Like Santa Lucía Cotzumalguapa, La Democracia is in the midst of a region populated from early times with – according to some archaeologists – mysterious cultural connections to Mexico's Gulf coast.

At the archaeological site called Monte Alto, on the outskirts of the town, huge basalt heads have been found. Though cruder, the heads resemble those carved by the Olmecs near Veracruz several thousand years ago. The Monte Alto heads could be older than, as old as or more recent than the Olmec heads. We just don't know.

Today these great 'Olmecoid' heads are arranged around La Democracia's main plaza. As you come into town from the highway, follow signs to the museo, which will cause you to bear left, then turn left, then turn left again. Stroll around the plaza admiring these interesting, mysterious objects. After seeing the heads, you might like to enjoy the shade of the huge tree in the plaza's centre.

Facing the plaza, along with the church and the modest Palacio Municipal, is the small, modern Museo Rubén Chevez Van Dorne, with other fascinating archaeological finds. The star of the show is an exquisite jade mask. Smaller figures, 'yokes' used in the ball game, relief carvings and other objects make up the rest of this important small collection. On the walls are overly dramatic paintings of Olmecoid scenes; there's more drama than meaning or accuracy. A rear room has more of the dramatic paintings, and lots of potsherds only an archaeologist could love. The museum is open from 8 am to noon and 2 to 5 pm; admission costs US$0.50.

Places to Stay & Eat
La Democracia has no places to stay and few places to eat. The eateries are very basic and ill-supplied, and it's best for you to bring your own food and buy drinks at a place facing the plaza. *Café Maritza*, right next to the museum, is a picture-perfect hot-tropics hangout with a *rockola* (jukebox) blasting music, and a small crew of semisomnolent locals sipping and sweltering.

Getting There & Away
Chatia Gomerana, Muelle Central, Terminal de Buses, Zona 4, Guatemala City, has buses every half-hour from 6 am to 4.30 pm on the 92-km, two-hour ride between the capital and La Democracia. Buses stop at Escuintla, Siquinalá (change for Santa Lucía Cotzumalguapa), La Democracia, La Gomera and Sipacate. The fare is US$1.50.

AROUND LA DEMOCRACIA
The road south from La Democracia continues 42 km to Sipacate, a small and very basic beach town. The beach is on the other side of the Canal de Chiquimulilla, an intracoastal waterway. Though there are a few scruffy, very basic places to stay, you'd be better off saving your beach time for Puerto San José, 35 km to the east, reached via the road from Escuintla.

ESCUINTLA
Set amidst lush tropical verdure, Escuintla should be an idyllic place where people swing languidly in hammocks and concoct pungent meals of readily available exotic fruit and vegetables. But it's not.

Escuintla is a hot, dingy, dilapidated commercial and industrial city that's very important to the Pacific Slope's economy, but not at all important to you. It is an old town, inhabited by Pipils before the conquest but now solidly ladino. Though it does have some fairly dingy hotels and restaurants, it provides no reason why you should use them.

You might have to changes buses in Escuintla. The main bus station is in the southern part of town; this is where you catch buses to Puerto San José. For Guatemala City, you can catch very frequent buses in the main plaza.

PUERTO SAN JOSÉ, LIKÍN & IZTAPA
Guatemala's most important seaside resort leaves a lot to be desired, even when compared to Mexico's smaller, seedier places. But if you're eager to get into the Pacific surf, head south from Escuintla 50 km to Puerto San José and neighbouring settlements.

Puerto San José (population 14,000) was Guatemala's most important Pacific port in the latter half of the 19th century and well into the 20th. Now superseded by the more modern Puerto Quetzal to the east, Puerto San José languishes and slumbers; its inhabitants languish, slumber, play loud music and drink. The beach, inconveniently located across the Canal de Chiquimulilla, is reached by boat.

A smarter thing to do is head west along the coast five km (by taxi or private car) to Balneario Chulamar, which has a nicer beach and also a suitable hotel or two.

About five km to the east of Puerto San José is Balneario Likín, Guatemala's only up-market Pacific resort. Likín is much beloved by well-to-do families from Guatemala City who have seaside houses on the tidy streets and canals of this planned development.

About 12 km east of Puerto San José is Iztapa, Guatemala's first Pacific port, first used by none other than Pedro de Alvarado in the 1500s. When Puerto San José was built in 1853, Iztapa's reign as the port of the capital city came to an end, and it relaxed into a tropical torpor from which it has yet to emerge. Having lain fallow for almost a century and a half, it has not suffered the degradation of Puerto San José. Iztapa is comparatively pleasant, with several small, easily affordable hotels and restaurants on the beach. The bonus here is that you can catch a Transportes Pacifico bus from the market in Zona 4 in Guatemala City all the way to Iztapa (four hours), or pick it up at Escuintla or Puerto San José to take you to Iztapa.

MONTERRICO

Similar in many ways to the rest of Guatemala's Pacific coast, Monterrico has three things to attract you.

The first attraction is the Biotopo Monterrico-Hawaii, a 20-km-long nature reserve comprising coastal mangrove swamps filled with bird and aquatic life. Its most famous denizens are perhaps the endangered leatherback and Ridley turtles, who lay their eggs on the beach in many places along the coast. Boat tours of the reserve can be had for only a few dollars.

The second attraction is the beach, the dramatic black volcanic sand crashing with surf.

The third is the *Hotel El Baule Beach*, a cosy 10-room hotel run by former Peace Corps Volunteer Nancy Garver. Rooms are right on the beach, and cost US$5 to US$10 per person with private bath and shower. Meals are reasonably priced as well. As there is little other accommodation, make advance reservations by sending a telegram to the Hotel Baule Beach, Monterrico, Taxisco,

Santa Rosa 06024. The hotel is reached by a half-hour ferry ride from the village of La Avellana. Buses reach La Avellana via Taxisco and Escuintla from Guatemala City.

LAGO DE AMATITLÁN

A placid lake backed by a looming volcano, situated a mere 25 km south of Guatemala City – that's Amatitlán. It should be a pretty and peaceful resort, but unfortunately it's not. The hourglass-shaped lake is divided by a railway line, and the lakeshore is lined with industry at some points. On weekends people from Guatemala City come to row boats on the lake (its waters are too polluted for swimming), or to rent a private hot tub for a dip. Many people from the capital own second homes here.

There's little reason for you to spend time here. If you really want to have a look, head for the town of Amatitlán, just off the main Escuintla-Guatemala City highway. Amatitlán has a scruffy public beach area where you can confirm your suspicions. If you have a car and some spare time, a drive around the lake offers some pretty scenery. Perhaps the lake will one day be restored to its naturally beautiful state.

Central & Eastern Guatemala

North and east of Guatemala City is a land of varied topography, from the misty, pine-covered mountains of Alta Verapaz to the hot, dry-tropic climate of the Río Motagua Valley. The Carretera al Atlantico (Highway to the Atlantic, CA-9) heads north-east from the capital and soon descends from the relative cool of the mountains to the dry heat of a valley where dinosaurs once roamed.

Along its course to the Atlantic are many interesting destinations, including the beautiful highland scenery around Cobán; the palaeontology museum at Estanzuela; the great pilgrimage church at Esquipulas, famous throughout Central America; the first-rate Mayan ruins at Copán, just across the border in Honduras; the marvellous Mayan stelae and zoomorphs at Quiriguá; and the tropical lake of Izabal and jungle waterway of Río Dulce. The Carretera al Atlantico ends at Puerto Barrios, Guatemala's Caribbean port, from which you can take a boat to Lívingston, a laid-back hideaway peopled by Black Afro-Guatemalans.

The departments of Baja Verapaz and Alta Verapaz were once known for their bad hospitality. In the time before the Spanish conquest, this mountainous highland region was peopled by the Rabinal Maya, noted for their warlike habits and merciless victories. They battled the powerful Quiché Maya for a century but were never conquered by that imperial nation.

When the conquistadors arrived, they too had trouble defeating the Rabinals. It was Fray Bartolomé de las Casas who convinced the Spanish authorities to try peace where war had failed. Armed with an edict which forbade Spanish soldiers from entering the region for five years, the friar and his brethren pursued their religious mission, and succeeded in pacifying and converting the Rabinals. From a land of constant battle, these highlands became a region of peace. It was renamed Verapaz (True Peace), and is now divided into Baja Verapaz, with its

capital at Salamá, and Alta Verapaz, centred on Cobán.

The two departmental capitals are easily accessible along a smooth, fast, asphalted road which winds up from the hot, dry valley through wonderful scenery into the mountains, through long stretches of coffee-growing country. Along the way to Cobán is one of Guatemala's premier nature reserves, the Biotopo del Quetzal. Beyond Cobán, along rough unpaved roads, are the country's most famous caverns.

SALAMÁ

Highway 17, also marked CA-14, leaves the Carretera al Atlantico at El Rancho, forks again at San Jerónimo and heads west up into the forested hills. Descending the other side of the ridge, it winds down into the broad valley of the Río Salamá, and enters the capital of the department of Baja Verapaz, 20 km from the Carretera.

Salamá (population 11,000, altitude 940 metres) is an attractive town with some reminders of colonial rule. The main plaza boasts an ornate colonial church. A colonial bridge on the outskirts once carried all the traffic to this rich agricultural region but is today used only by pedestrians. If you find reason to stop in Salamá, try to do so on a Sunday, when the market is active.

Places to Stay & Eat

Should you want to stay the night, the *Hotel Tezulutlán*, just off the main square behind the Texaco fuel station, is simple and cheap. Fifteen rooms with private showers, arranged around a pleasant courtyard, rent for US$6 a single, US$10 a double. The *Hotel Juárez*, 10a Avenida 5-55, Zona 1, is larger, with 26 rooms, and somewhat cheaper as well.

For food, try *Restaurant El Ganadero*, a half-block off the main square on the road into town. A lunch of chicken or beef might cost US$4 to US$6, a sandwich much less.

GUATEMALA

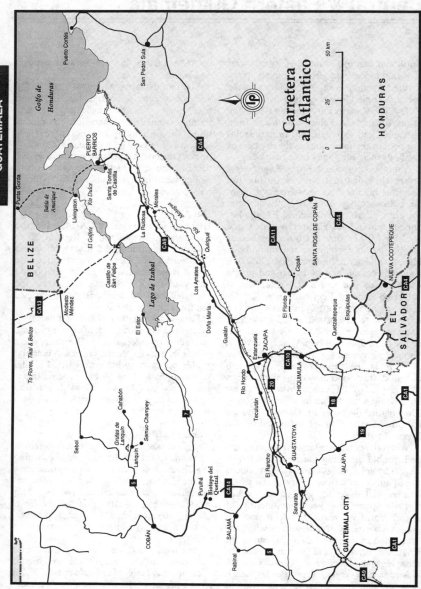

Getting There & Away

As this is a departmental capital, there are frequent buses to and from Guatemala City. Salamateca (☎ (2) 8 17 16), 9a Avenida 19-00, Zona 1 in Guatemala City, has buses running about every two hours from 5.45 am to 4.45 pm on the 151-km, three-hour trip. The fare is US$2.

AROUND SALAMÁ

Nine km west of Salamá along Highway 5 is the village of San Miguel Chicaj, known for its weaving.

Continue along the same road for another 18 km to reach the colonial town of Rabinal, founded in 1537 by Fray Bartolomé de las Casas as a base for his proselytising. Rabinal has gained fame as a pottery-making centre (look especially at the handpainted chocolate cups), and for its citrus fruit harvest (November and December). Market day here is Sunday.

Two small hotels, the *Pensión Motagua* and the *Hospedaje Caballeros*, can put you up, though you might decide to return to Salamá instead.

BIOTOPO DEL QUETZAL

Stay on the main highway (CA-14) instead of turning left for Salamá, and another 34 km brings you to the Mario Dary Rivera Nature Reserve, commonly called the Biotopo del Quetzal, Guatemala's quetzal reserve at Km 161, just east of the village of Purulhá.

If you stop here intent on seeing a quetzal, Guatemala's national bird, you may be disappointed, because the birds are rare and elusive. Stop instead to explore and enjoy the lush high rainforest ecosystem which is preserved here, and which is the natural habitat of the quetzal. The reserve, founded in 1977, is open daily from 6 am to 4 pm (you must leave the grounds by 5 pm). Drinks (but no food) are available at the site. Guides may be hired to explain the rainforest to you.

Two nature trails wind through the reserve: the 1800-metre Sendero los Helechos (Fern Trail) and the Sendero los Musgos (Moss Trail), which is twice as long. As you wander through the dense growth,

A quetzal, the national bird of Guatemala

treading on the rich, dense, spongy humus and leaf-mould, you'll see many varieties of epiphytes (air plants) which thrive in the humid jungle atmosphere: lichens, ferns, liverworts, bromeliads, mosses and orchids. The Río Colorado cascades through the forest along a geological fault. Deep in the forest is Xiu Ua Li Che (Grandfather Tree), some 450 years old, which was alive when the conquistadors fought the Rabinals in these mountains.

Places to Stay

The reserve has its own camping places, so if you have the equipment, this is the best place to stay. Officially, you are supposed to obtain permission to camp from CECON, the Center for Conservation Studies of the University of San Carlos (☎ (2) 31-09-04), Avenida La Reforma 0-63, Zona 10, Guatemala City.

There are two lodging places within a short distance of the Biotopo. Just beyond the Biotopo, another 200 metres up the hill toward Purulhá and Cobán, is the *Pensión y Comedor Ranchito del Quetzal*, a rustic hospedaje. Being the only lodging right by the Biotopo keeps the Ranchito's rates high for what you get: US$12 for a double with shower. In fact, you must pay US$0.40 just to set foot on the Ranchito's grounds. Meals are equally pricey, but convenient.

Should you be looking for more comfort, the *Posada Montaña del Quetzal* (☎ (2) 35-18-05 in Guatemala City during business hours), Carretera a Cobán Km 156, Purulhá, Baja Verapaz, is five km back along the road toward the Carretera al Atlantico. This attractive hostelry has 18 little white stucco tile-roofed bungalow-cabins, each with a sitting room and fireplace, a bedroom with three beds and a private bathroom, for US$25/35 a single/double. You can usually catch a bus to shuttle you between the Biotopo and the posada, or hitch a ride.

The village of Purulhá, slightly less than five km west of the Biotopo, has a very basic medical clinic and a small market, but no other services.

COBÁN

The asphalt road from the Biotopo to Cobán is good, smooth and fast, though curvy, with light traffic. As you ascend into the evergreen forests, tropical flowers are still visible here and there. Signs by the roadside advertise the services of brokers willing to buy farmers' harvests of cardamom and coffee and dairy cattle. As you enter Cobán, a sign says 'Bienvenidos a Cobán, Ciudad Imperial', referring to the charter granted in 1538 by Emperor Charles V. About 126 km from the Carretera al Atlantico, you reach Cobán's main plaza.

The town now called Cobán (population 20,000, altitude 1320 metres) was once the centre of Tezulutlán (Tierra de Guerra in Spanish, the Land of War). Alvarado's conquistadors overran western Guatemala in short order, but the Rabinal Maya of Verapaz fought them off until Fray Bartolomé and his brethren came and conquered them with religion.

A later conquest came in the 19th century when German immigrants moved in and founded vast coffee fincas. Cobán took on the aspect of a German mountain town as the finca owners built town residences with steeply pitched roofs, elaborate gingerbread bargeboards and other decoration, and gathered to exchange the morning's news in Central European-style cafés. The era of German cultural and economic domination ended during WW II, when the USA prevailed upon the Guatemalan government to deport the powerful finca owners, many of whom actively supported the Nazis.

Today Cobán can be a pleasant town to visit, though much depends upon the season. For most of the year it is often overcast, dank, chill and cheerless; in the midst of the dry season (January to March) it can be misty, or bright and sunny with marvellous clear mountain air. The departmental festival is held in Cobán during the first week of August.

There is not a lot to do in Cobán except enjoy the local colour and the mountain scenery, and use the town as a base for visits to the Grutas de Lanquín and Cuevas Semuc-Champey nearby.

Orientation

The main plaza (el parque) features a disconcertingly modern concrete bandstand. Most of the services you'll need – banks, hotels, restaurants, bus stations – are within a few blocks of the plaza and the cathedral. The shopping district is around and behind the cathedral.

Places to Stay

Near the main plaza, the *Pensión Familiar*

GUATEMALA

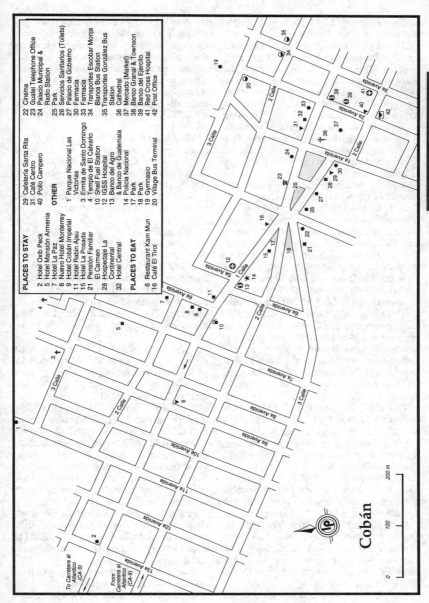

PLACES TO STAY
2 Hotel Oxib Peck
5 Hotel Mansión Armenia
7 Hotel La Paz
8 Nuevo Hotel Monterrey
9 Hotel Cobán Imperial
11 Hotel Rabin Ajau
15 Hotel La Posada
21 Pensión Familiar El Carmen
28 Hospedaje La Continental
32 Hotel Central

PLACES TO EAT
6 Restaurant Kam Mun
16 Café El Tirol
29 Cafetería Santa Rita
31 Café Centro
40 Pollo Campero

OTHER
1 Parque Nacional Las Victorias
3 Ermita de Santo Domingo
4 Templo de El Calvario
10 Shell Fuel Station
12 IGSS Hospital
13 Banco del Agro & Banco de Guatemala
14 Policía Nacional
17 Park
18 Park
19 Gymnasio
20 Village Bus Terminal
22 Cinema
23 Guatel Telephone Office
24 Palacio Municipal & Radio Station
25 Park
26 Servicios Sanitarios (Toilets)
27 Palacio de Gobierno
30 Farmacia
33 Farmacia
34 Transportes Escobar Monja Blanca Bus Station
35 Transportes González Bus Station
36 Cathedral
37 Mercado (Market)
38 Banco Granai & Townson
39 Banco del Ejército
41 Red Cross Hospital
42 Post Office

Cobán

To Carretera al Atlántico (CA-9)

From Carretera al Atlántico (CA-9)

0   100   200 m

El Carmen (☎ (9) 51-17-50) is very simple and fairly beat-up, but the price is good – US$6 a double with shared bath. There's a small, cheap café attached. *Hotel La Paz*, 6a Avenida, Zona 1, 1½ blocks north of the plaza, charges US$3 per person, which is too expensive. To get a room, ask at the shop to the right of the hotel. At this writing, the *Hospedaje La Continental*, on the main plaza, is the most basic lodging of them all. When the tourist boom hits Cobán with a vengeance, however, it will no doubt be fixed up and become an expensive hotel with colonial charm.

A step up in quality and price is the *Hotel Oxib Peck* (☎ (9) 51-10-39), 1 Calle 12-11, Zona 1, six blocks (750 metres) west of the plaza on the road out of town. By Guatemalan standards it's clean and bright, with a nice little garden in front, plus a dining room. The 11 rooms are tidy, with clean tiled showers, but are plain and have no windows to the outside. Rates are US$6.50 per person.

Hotel Cobán Imperial (☎ (9) 51-11-31), 6a Avenida 1-12, Zona 1, 250 metres from the plaza, is actually administered along with the adjoining *Nuevo Hotel Monterrey*. Most rooms have add-on tiled baths, and also TVs, which are necessary for a 'view', as few rooms have windows to the outside. It's popular with Guatemalan families. Rates are US$6 to US$8 a single, US$8 to US$12 a double.

The old-fashioned *Hotel Rabin Ajau* (☎ (9) 51-22-96), 1 Calle 5-37, Zona 1, is well located and fairly well kept, but its disco is noisy. There's a restaurant and parking. Rooms with private shower cost US$8/10/12 a single/double/triple.

The *Hotel Central* (☎ (9) 51-14-42), 1 Calle 1-79, Zona 4, is tidy, run by women, arranged around a flowered courtyard, and decently priced at US$10 a double.

Hotel Mansión Armenia (☎ (9) 51-22-84), 7a Avenida 2-18, Zona 1, one block from Templo de El Calvario, is clean, fairly new and quiet. Rooms are cell-like, as usual, but equipped with private bath and cable TV for US$17/22 a single/double.

Best in town is the *Hotel La Posada* (☎ (9) 51-14-95), 1 Calle 4-12, Zona 2, just off the plaza in the very centre of town. Colonial in style, its colonnaded porches are festooned with tropical flowers and furnished with easy chairs and hammocks from which to enjoy the mountain views. The rooms have nice old furniture, fireplaces, and wall hangings of local weaving, and rent for US$28/34/42 a single/double/triple with private bath.

The *Park Hotel* (☎ /fax (9) 51-45-39), in Santa Cruz Verapaz at Km 196.5, 16 km south-east of Cobán, has modern little bungalows and a restaurant, all set amidst tropical forest in park-like grounds. The price of US$15/20/28 a single/double/triple affords excellent value for money.

Places to Eat

Virtually all of Cobán's hotels have their own restaurants.

Café El Tirol, near the Hotel La Posada, advertises 'the best coffee' in four languages. Facing a bust of Fray Bartolomé de las Casas is a cosy room in which to enjoy pastries and coffee for US$1 to US$2. Breakfast and light meals are served as well. It's closed on Monday.

Cafetería Santa Rita, facing the main square, is small, modern, tidy and popular with locals. The reason is no secret: good breakfasts for US$1 to US$2, lunches and dinners for US$2.50 to US$4.

The *Café Centro* (☎ 51-21-92), 1 Calle between 1a and 2a Avenidas, near the cathedral, in the building called the Centro Comercial El Gallo, has a varied lunch and supper menu (no breakfast), and a dining room with views through large windows. Substantial plates of chicken (US$2.75) and beef (US$4) are offered, along with a variety of sandwiches (US$1 to US$2).

Pollo Campero, the Guatemalan fried-chicken franchise, has an outlet across from the post office on 2a Avenida at 2 Calle. The gilded youth of Cobán gather here for three meals a day.

You have to walk almost 500 metres from the plaza to reach the *Restaurant Kam Mun*, 1 Calle at 9a Avenida, on the road out of town. When you get there you can sample Chinese food in a pleasant, clean little place and pay US$5 to US$8 for a full meal.

Hotel La Posada, the charming mountain inn, has a pleasant dining room with simple food. Tough beef in tomato sauce, rice, spinach, avocado, bread, salad and a soft drink are yours for US$7.

Getting There & Away

Transportes Escobar Monja Blanca (☎ (2) 51-18-78), 8a Avenida 15-16, Zona 1 in Guatemala City, runs about 10 buses a day from 4 am to 4 pm on the 219-km, four-hour trip to Guatemala City, stopping at the Biotopo del Quetzal, Purulhá and Tactic, for US$2 to US$3. You can catch these buses at El Rancho, the intersection of the Carretera al Atlantico and the highway to Cobán.

Getting Around

Because it is a good base for exploring the surrounding mountains, Cobán now has several places where cars may be rented. Budget Rent-a-Car (☎ (9) 51-20-59) is in the same building complex as the Café Tirol. For details on car rentals, see Getting Around in the Guatemala City section.

AROUND COBÁN

Like San Ignacio in the Maya Mountains of Belize, Cobán is becoming an established base for organised excursions to sites in the surrounding mountains. Several small companies have been founded just for this purpose. For example, Marcio and Ashley Acuña (☎ (9) 51-12-68) run ecotours from Cobán to Semuc-Champey and also to many Mayan jungle sites such as La Candelaria, Seibal, Aguateca, Dos Pilas, Yaxchilán, Yaxhá, Nakun, Tikal, Uaxactún and Río Azul. No doubt other operators will start up by the time you visit Cobán.

San Juan Chamelco

About 16 km south-east of Cobán is the village of San Juan Chamelco, with swimming at the Balneario Chio. In Aldea (district) Chajaneb, Jerry Makransky rents comfortable, simple bungalows for US$10 per person per day, with vegetarian meals included. If you need to get away from it all, this may be just the place.

San Pedro Carchá

Six km east of Cobán on the way to Lanquín, San Pedro Carchá offers swimming at the Balneario Las Islas, as well as transport by bus farther along to Lanquín.

Grutas de Lanquín

If you don't mind bumping over bad and/or busy roads, the best excursion to make from Cobán is to the caves near Lanquín, a pretty village 61 km to the east.

The Grutas de Lanquín are a short distance north-west of the town, and extend for several km into the earth. Have a powerful torch (flashlight) or two, pay the US$2 admission fee at the Municipalidad (Town Hall) in Lanquín, and make sure that the attendant is on duty at the caves to turn on the lights for you.

Though the first few hundred metres of cavern has been equipped with a walkway and is lit by diesel-powered electric lights, most of this subterranean system is untouched. If you are not an experienced spelunker, you should think twice about wandering too far into the caves.

The Río Lanquín runs through the caves before coming above ground to run down to Lanquín, offering swimming possibilities at several points. If you have camping equipment you can spend the night near the cave entrance. Otherwise, there are a few very simple hostelries in Lanquín.

Semuc-Champey

Ten km south of Lanquín along a rough, bumpy, slow road is Semuc-Champey, famed for a natural wonder: a great limestone bridge 300 metres long, on top of which is a series of pools of cool, flowing river water good for swimming. The water is from the Río Cahabón, and most of it passes beneath the bridge underground. Though this bit of paradise is difficult to reach, the beauty of its setting and the perfection of the water make it all worth it.

GUATEMALA

Getting There & Away From Cobán, take a bus to San Pedro Carchá, six km to the east along the Lanquín-Cahabón road; buses leave very frequently from the village bus terminal down the hill behind the Town Hall in Cobán. From San Pedro Carchá, buses leave three times daily (starting at 5.30 am) on the three-hour ride to Lanquín. The last of three return buses departs from Lanquín for San Pedro Carchá in the early afternoon, so you should probably plan to stay the night, either camping at Grutas de Lanquín or Semuc-Champey or staying in a small hospedaje in Lanquín.

There are occasional buses and trucks to Semuc-Champey. Otherwise, it's a longish, hot walk unless you have your own vehicle, in which case it's a slow, bumpy drive.

RÍO HONDO

Continuing north-eastwards along CA-9, 47 km from El Rancho junction (133 km from Guatemala City) is Río Hondo junction, 10 km west of where CA-10 heads south to Chiquimula and Nuevo Ocotepeque (Honduras), with turn-offs to Esquipulas and the ruins at Copán, just across the border in Honduras.

The town of Río Hondo is north-east of the junction, but lodging places hereabouts list their address as Río Hondo, Santa Cruz Río Hondo or Santa Cruz Teculután – it's all the same place. Just a few km west of the junction are several motels right on CA-9, which provide a good base for explorations of this region if you have your own vehicle.

Those travelling by bus on a low budget can find suitable cheap accommodation at Copán and Esquipulas, though the situation at Quiriguá is more difficult.

Places to Stay & Eat

Note that the Río Hondo motels are looked upon as weekend resorts by local people and even residents of Guatemala City, so they may be heavily booked on weekends.

Cheapest here is the *Hotel Santa Cruz* (☎ (9) 41-71-12), where double rooms with fan and bath go for US$15. The restaurant is popular as well.

Motel Longarone (☎ /fax (9) 41-71-26), Carretera al Atlantico Km 126, Santa Cruz Río Hondo, right across the highway, is the old standard in this area, a comfortable place with a fuel station and spacious, airy dining room at the front. The 54 air-conditioned rooms, all with private showers, are in cement-block bungalow buildings behind the restaurant, arranged around the beautiful swimming pool beneath lofty palm trees amidst tropical gardens. Rates are a reasonable US$18 to US$22 a single, US$27 to US$33 a double and US$45 for a room that sleeps four. Expect to spend about US$6 to

---

Cardamom

The world's coffee-drinkers know that high-quality coffee is important to Guatemala's export trade, but few know that Guatemala is the world's largest exporter of cardamom. In Alta Verapaz, cardamom is more important to the local economy than coffee, providing livelihoods for some 200,000 people.

Cardamom, *(Elettaria cardamomum)*, a herbaceous perennial of the ginger family, is native to the Malabar Coast of India, but was brought to Alta Verapaz by German coffee-finca owners. The plants grow to a height between 1½ and six metres, with coarse leaves up to 75 cm long, hairy on the underside. The flowers are white. The fruit is a green, three-sided oval capsule holding 15 to 20 dark, hard, reddish-brown to brownish-black seeds.

Though the cardamom plants grow readily, it is difficult to cultivate, pick and sort the best grades, so fragrant cardamom commands a high price. That does not matter to the people of Saudi Arabia and the Arabian Gulf states, who purchase over 80% of the world supply. They pulverise the seeds and add the powder to the thick, syrupy, pungent coffee which is a social and personal necessity in that part of the world. ■

US$8.50 for a full meal here, less for a sandwich or a plate of spaghetti.

Hotel El Atlantico (☎ (9) 41-71-60), Carretera al Atlantico Km 126, just to the west of the Motel Longarone, is a clone of the Longarone, being precisely the same in layout and much the same in decor, though slightly higher in price: US$28/33/38 a single/double/triple.

Across the highway from these two, on the north side, is the *Hotel Nuevo Pasabién* (☎ (9) 41-72-01), Carretera al Atlantico Km 126. It's slightly more rustic than the other two, with some guestrooms in an older two-storey wooden building and other rooms in the familiar bungalow units. A passable restaurant faces the highway and a swimming pool is there to refresh you. All rooms have private bathroom; the more expensive ones are more modern and comfortable, and have fans and TVs. Rates are US$18 to US$22 a double.

Nine km east of these places, right at the junction with CA-10, the road heading south, is the *Motel Río* (☎ (9) 41-12-67), Carretera al Atlantico Km 136. It's fairly beat-up but is certainly convenient, especially if you don't have your own wheels. Double rooms with private shower go for US$6.

ESTANZUELA

Travelling south from Río Hondo along CA-10 you are in the midst of the Río Motagua Valley, a hot expanse of what is known as 'dry tropic', which once supported a great number and variety of dinosaurs. Three km south of the Carretera al Atlantico you'll see a small monument on the right-hand (west) side of the road. The monument commemorates the terrible earthquake of 4 February 1976, which killed or injured many Guatemalans and destroyed dozens of villages in this area. The Motagua Valley lies along a geological fault line, and the monument makes this graphically evident. On the roadway, one can actually see how the earth shifted during the earthquake: the white centre line has shifted noticeably to one side.

Less than two km south of the earthquake monument is the small town of Estanzuela,

with its Museo de Paleontología filled with dinosaur bones. American palaeontologist Bryan Patterson did research in the Motagua Valley for many years; much of what he found has been gathered together in this private museum now managed by Roberto Woolfolk Saravia. Though Señor Woolfolk is often absent, the museum is open from 9 am to 5 pm every day except Monday; admission is free. To find the museum, go west from the highway directly through the town for one km, asking along the way for 'el museo'. Next door to the museum is a small shop selling cold drinks and snacks.

Within the museum are most of the bones of three big dinosaurs, including those of a giant ground sloth some 30,000 years old, and a prehistoric whale. Other exhibits include early Mayan artefacts and other objects which Patterson came across during his research.

ZACAPA

Capital of the department of the same name, Zacapa (population 18,000, altitude 230 metres) is several km east of the highway. It offers little to travellers, though the locals do make cheese, cigars and superb old rum. The few hotels in town are basic but will do in an emergency; better accommodation is to be had in Río Hondo and Esquipulas.

CHIQUIMULA

Another departmental capital set in a mining and tobacco-growing region, Chiquimula (population 24,000, altitude 370 metres) is a major market town for all of eastern Guatemala, with lots of buying and selling activity every day. It's also a transportation point and overnight stop for those making their way to Copán in Honduras.

Orientation & Information

Chiquimula is easy to get around on foot. Banco del Café, on the main plaza (called the Parque Ismael Cerna), has long hours: 8.30 am to 8 pm Monday to Thursday, 8 am to 8 pm on Friday and 10 am to 2 pm on Saturday. Banco del Agro's hours are 9 am to 3 pm

Chiquimula

0   50   100 m

PLACES TO STAY

4 Hotel Victoria
9 Hotel Chiquimulja
11 Hotel Hernández
12 Pensión España
14 Hospedaje Río Jordan
15 Hotel Posada Perla de
   Oriente
21 Hotel Posada de Don
   Adán

PLACES TO EAT

5 Restaurant El Dorado
10 Restaurant El Tesoro
18 Pupucería Guanachapi
20 Restaurant Las Vegas

OTHER

1 Transportes Vilma
   Bus Station
2 Bus Terminal
3 Correos y
   Telegraphos (Post &
   Telegraph Office)
6 Banco de Guatemala
7 Banco del Café
8 Banco del Agro
13 Chevron Fuel Station
16 Palacio de Gobierno
17 Guatel Telephone
   Office
19 Market

Monday to Friday and 9 am to 1 pm on Saturday.

Places to Stay

Hotel Chiquimulja (☎ (9) 42-03-87), 3 Calle 6-51, is on the north side of the plaza between two Chinese restaurants. Rooms come with private showers, with fan or air-conditioning, and range in price from US$5 to US$8 a single, US$8 to US$12 a double.

Hotel Victoria (☎ (9) 42-22-38), 2 Calle at 10a Avenida, is convenient to the bus station, offering small rooms with fan, TV and add-on showers for US$9 a double. The restaurant is good and cheap, with big breakfasts for US$2.

A block east of the Chiquimulja, downhill on the same street (3 Calle), are several even cheaper places. *Hotel Hernández* is clean, simple and quietish, renting rooms without running water for US$3 per person, or US$4 per person for a room with private shower. The neighbouring *Pensión España* is even more basic, with closet-like rooms, but it has gardens and it's cheaper. *Hospedaje Río Jordan* (☎ (9) 42-08-87), 3 Calle 8-91, a block further east, charges US$2 to US$3.50 a single, US$4

to US$6 a double, the higher price being for rooms with fans. You can park your vehicle in the courtyard.

Hotel Posada de Don Adán (☎ (9) 42-05-49), 8a Avenida 4-30, Zona 1, is new, clean and proper. It's run by an efficient señora, who charges US$17 for a double with fan, shower and TV.

The best in town is the *Hotel Posada Perla de Oriente* (☎ (9) 42-00-14, 42-01-52), 12a Avenida 2-30, with extensive grounds and a small swimming pool. Rooms are simple, with fan, shower and TV, and cost US$12. This place may soon be upgraded – and the prices raised substantially.

Places to Eat

Eating in Chiqui is easy, as there are lots of cheap little places. Try the *Pupucería Guanachapi*, across the street from the Pensión España. Sit at the long counter, watch the cooks at work and fill up for only a few quetzales.

Restaurant El Tesoro, on the main square, serves Chinese food at reasonable prices.

For a step up in quality, try the *Restaurant El Dorado*, 3 Calle between 5a and 6a Avenidas, where you can dine on the shady terrace around the rear courtyard. Full meals cost US$5 to US$8.

Another good choice is the *Restaurant Las Vegas*, on 8a Avenida off 4 Calle, perhaps Chiquimula's best, with fancy plants, jazzy music, a well-stocked bar, and full meals for US$6 to US$10. Appropriate for its name, the Las Vegas claims to be open 24 hours a day.

Getting There & Away

Chiquimula is not a destination but a transit point. Your goal is no doubt the fabulous Mayan ruins at Copán in Honduras, just across the border from El Florido, Guatemala.

Rutas Orientales (☎ (2) 53-72-82, 51-21-60), 19 Calle 8-18, Zona 1 in Guatemala City, runs buses via El Rancho, Río Hondo and Zacapa to Chiquimula every half-hour from 4 am to 6 pm (169 km, three hours, US$3 to US$4).

If you're heading for Copán, change to a Transportes Vilma bus (pronounced BEEL-mah) at Chiquimula for the trip via Jocotán and Camotán to El Florido, the village on the Guatemalan side of the border. For more details, see the Copán section.

It's easy to get back to Río Hondo junction (35 km) from Chiquimula; just hop on any bus heading north. From Río Hondo you can catch buses eastward to Quiriguá and Puerto Barrios.

You can also easily catch a bus from Chiquimula's busy bus terminal southward to Esquipulas (55 km, one hour, US$1.25).

ESQUIPULAS

From Chiquimula, CA-10 goes south into the mountains, where it's cooler and a bit more comfortable. After an hour's ride through pretty country, the highway descends into a valley ringed by mountains. Halfway down the slope there is a mirador (lookout) from which to get a good view. The reason for a trip to Esquipulas is evident as soon as you catch sight of the place: the great Basílica de Esquipulas which towers above the town, its whiteness shining in the sun.

The view has changed little in more than a century and a half:

Descending, the clouds were lifted, and I looked down upon an almost boundless plain, running from the foot of the Sierra, and afar off saw, standing alone in the wilderness, the great church of Esquipulas, like the Church of the Holy Sepulchre in Jerusalem, and the Caaba in Mecca, the holiest of temples...I had a long and magnificent descent to the foot of the Sierra.
John L Stephens (1841)

History

This town may have been a place of pilgrimage even before the Spaniards' conquest. Legend has it that the town takes its name from a noble Mayan lord who ruled this region when the Spanish arrived, and who received them in peace rather than going to war.

With the arrival of the friars, a church was built, and in 1595 an image of Christ carved from black wood was installed in it. The steady flow of pilgrims to Esquipulas became a flood after 1737, when Pedro Pardo de Figueroa, Archbishop of Guatemala, came here on pilgrimage and went away cured of a chronic ailment. Delighted with this development, the prelate commissioned a huge new church to be built on the site. It was finished in 1758, and the pilgrimage trade has been the town's livelihood ever since. As in Chaucer's day, no one goes on a pilgrimage without spending some money.

Orientation & Information

The church is your lodestone and landmark in Esquipulas; it's the centre of everything. Most of the good cheap hotels are within a block of it, as are numerous small restaurants. The town's only luxury hotel is on the outskirts, along the road back to Chiquimula. There's a Honduran consulate in the Hotel Payaquí, facing the park.

Basilica

A massive pile of stone which has resisted the power of earthquakes for almost 2½ centuries, the basilica is approached through

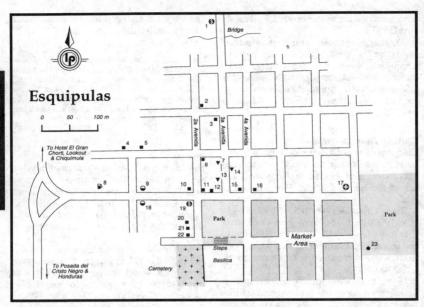

Esquipulas

0   50   100 m

To Hotel El Gran
Chorti, Lookout
& Chiquimula

To Posada del
Cristo Negro &
Honduras

Bridge

2a Avenida
3a Avenida
4a Avenida

Park

Park

Steps

Basilica

Cemetery

Market
Area

GUATEMALA

PLACES TO STAY

2   Hotel Legendario
3   Hotel Monte Cristo
4   Hotel Internacional
5   Pensión Santa Rosa
6   Pensión La Favorita
10 Hotel Lucam
11 Hotel El Ángel
12 Pensión Victoria
15 Hotel San Pablo
16 Hotel San José

20 Hotel Payaquí
21 Hotel El Peregrino
22 Hotel Los Angeles

PLACES TO EAT

7   Restaurant y Cafetería
    Victoria
13 Comedor y Cafetería
    Beato Hermano
    Pedro
14 Comedor Rosy

OTHER

1   Banco del Café
8   Shell Fuel Station
9   Transportes Guatesqui
    Bus Station
17 Centro de Salud
18 Rutas Orientales Bus
    Station
19 Banco del Ejercito
23 Cinema

---

a pretty park and up a flight of steps. The impressive façade and towers are floodlit at night.

Inside, the devout approach El Cristo Negro with great reverence, many on their knees. Incense, the murmur of prayers and the shuffle of sandalled feet fills the air. To get a close view of the famous Black Christ you must enter the church from the side.

Shuffling along quickly, you may get a good glimpse or two before being shoved onwards by the press of the crowd behind you. On Sundays, religious holidays and (especially) during the festival around 15 January, the press of devotees is intense.

When you leave the church and descend the steps through the park, notice the vendors selling straw hats that are decorated with artificial flowers and stitched with the name 'Esquipulas'. Just as the devout Muslim grows a beard or takes on the title of Hajji after making the pilgrimage to Mecca, so Central Americans who have seen the Black Christ at Esquipulas buy a flowered hat to let their neighbours know of their pilgrimage.

Places to Stay
Many hotels have religious names: Los Angeles (the angels), San José (St Joseph), Posada del Cristo Negro, etc. On holidays and during the annual festival, every hotel in town is filled, whatever the price; weekends are fairly busy as well, with prices substantially higher. On weekdays when there is no festival, ask for a *descuento* (discount) and you'll probably get it.

Places to Stay – bottom end
The best place to search for a cheap room is in the streets to the north of the basilica.

The family-run *Pensión Santa Rosa* is typical of the small back-street places, charging US$7 a double in a waterless room. Nearby *Pension La Favorita* is similar, and there are several others on this street.

Hotel Los Angeles (☎ (9) 43-12-54), 2a Avenida 11-94, at the south-west corner of the park, has 39 rooms arranged around a bright inner courtyard. Doubles with shower cost US$11 on weekdays, US$15 on weekends.

Hotel San José, at the north-east corner of the park, is typical, renting tiny waterless rooms for US$2.75 per person on weekdays, US$3.50 on weekends, or rooms with showers for US$4/5. *Hotel San Pablo*, on the north side of the park, is similar, as are *Hotel El Ángel* and the *Hotel Lucam*.

Hotel Monte Cristo (☎ (9) 43-14-53), 3a Avenida 9-12, has 34 quite good rooms with bath for US$18 a double – good value for money.

Hotel El Peregrino (☎ (9) 43-10-54) has two kinds of rooms, all with private bath. Older rooms cost US$13 a double and newer ones with TV are US$25.

Places to Stay – middle
Hotel Legendario (☎ (9) 43-10-22, 43-14-78), is new, nice and quite comfortable, with a swimming pool. It's also reasonably priced, at US$35 for a double room with air-conditioning, private bath and TV.

Hotel Internacional (☎ /fax (9) 43-11-31) is new, clean and pleasant, with small, dark bath-equipped guestrooms priced at US$30 a double with fan and TV (US$44 with air-conditioning).

Hotel Payaquí (☎ (9) 43-11-43, fax 43-13-71), 2a Avenida 11-56, facing the park, has a swimming pool, a car park and a restaurant with a view of the park. Its 40 rooms (with bath) are priced high for what you get, at US$29 a double.

Hotel Posada del Cristo Negro (☎ (9) 43-14-82), Carretera Internacional a Honduras Km 224, is two km from the church, out of town on the way to Honduras. Broad green lawns, a pretty swimming pool, a large dining room and other services make it elaborate. In the 1960s, this might have been Guatemala's best country-club resort. Comfortable rooms with private bath and TV cost US$28 a double.

Places to Stay – top end
Hotel El Gran Chortí (☎ (9) 43-11-48/57, fax 43-15-51), Km 222, is one km west of the church on the road to Chiquimula. The lobby floor is a hectare of black marble; behind it is a serpentine swimming pool set amidst umbrella-shaded café tables, lawns and gardens. There's a games room for the children, and of course a good restaurant, bar and cafeteria. The rooms have all the comforts: air-conditioning, cable TV, fridge, telephone and terrace. Rates reflect the comforts: US$45/60 a single/double, US$80 for a junior suite (sleeps four) and US$110 for a master suite (sleeps six).

Places to Eat
As with hotels, so with restaurants: all are more expensive here than in other parts of Guatemala. Low-budget restaurants are clustered at the north end of the park where hungry pilgrims can find them readily. It is

very important to ask in advance the price of each food item you order, and to add up your bill carefully.

The street running north opposite the church has many small eateries. I predict that at some point, it will be closed to all but pedestrian traffic and the restaurants will be able to have sidewalk dining areas.

Comedor Rosy, on the street opposite the park, is tidy and cheerful, with big bottles of pickles on the tables. Sandwiches go for US$2 or so. *Restaurante y Cafetería Victoria* across the street is a bit fancier, with table-cloths and plants, but prices are about the same.

Comedor y Cafetería Beato Hermano Pedro realises what the dining situation is in this town, and advertises *'Coma bien y pague menos!'* ('Eat well and pay less!') - set prices for full meals are around US$2. 'Come on in and convince yourself!'

All of the mid-range and top-end hotels have their own dining rooms, where you can find somewhat fancier fare.

Getting There & Away
Minibuses shuttle between Esquipulas and Chiquimula frequently from early morning until late afternoon. Look for them hawking for passengers along Esquipulas' main street.

Rutas Orientales (☎ (2) 53-72-82, 51-21-60), 19 Calle 8-18, Zona 1 in Guatemala City, has buses departing every half-hour from 4 am to 6 pm, with stops at El Rancho, Río Hondo, Zacapa and Chiquimula (222 km, four hours, US$3). If you're going to Copán, take any bus as far as Chiquimula and switch to a Transportes Vilma bus there. See the Chiquimula and Copán sections for details.

COPÁN (Honduras)
The ancient city of Copán, 12 km from the Guatemalan border in Honduras, is one of the most outstanding Mayan achievements, ranking with Tikal, Chichén Itzá and Uxmal in splendour. To fully appreciate Mayan art and culture, you must visit Copán for at least a few hours and preferably overnight. This can be done on a long day trip by private car,

public bus or organised tour, but it's better to take two days, staying the night in the town of Copán Ruinas. If you must see Copán in a day, make your base at Río Hondo, Chiquimula or Esquipulas.

History
Early Times Farmers moved into the Copán valley about 1000 BC, enticed by the fertile riverbed land and the reliable supply of fresh water from the Río Copán. Located near important trade routes, Copán must have had significant commercial activity since early times, though little archaeological evidence of this has been found.

In fact, excavations at Copán have yielded surprisingly few clues to the life of these Copanecs between the time when the earliest farmers arrived and the beginning of the Classic period (around 450 or 500 AD). There are a few artefacts which suggest that the Copanecs had some trading relationship with the Olmecs of Mexico and/or the Olmecoid peoples of Guatemala's Pacific Slope. But it's surprising to find so little evidence from the Late Pre-Classic period, when the Mayan ceremonial centres at El Mirador, Tikal and Uaxactún were already important and growing.

Classic Period There may have been several princely families sharing dominion at Copán prior to 435 AD, but around that date all power was gathered into the hands of one family ruled by a mysterious king named Mah K'ina Yax K'uk' Mo' (Great Sun Lord Quetzal Macaw). Thus was founded a dynasty which was to rule throughout Copán's florescence during the Classic period (250 to 900 AD).

Of the early kings who ruled from about 435 to 628 AD, we know little. Only a few names have yet been deciphered: Cu Ix, the fourth king, Waterlily Jaguar (the seventh), Moon Jaguar (the 10th) and Butz' Chan (the 11th).

Among the greatest of Copán's kings was Smoke Imix (Smoke Jaguar), the 12th king, who ruled from 628 to 695. Smoke Imix was wise, forceful and rich, and he built Copán into a major military and commercial power in the region. He may have taken over the nearby princedom of Quiriguá, as one of the famous stelae there bears his name and image. By the time he died, in 695, Copán's population had grown significantly.

Smoke Imix was succeeded by 18 Rabbit (695-738), the 13th king, who willingly took over the reigns of power and pursued further military conquest. In a war with his neighbour, King Cauac Sky, 18 Rabbit was captured and beheaded, to be succeeded by Smoke Monkey (738-49), the 14th king. Smoke Monkey's short reign left little mark on Copán.

In 749, Smoke Monkey was succeeded by his son Smoke Shell (749-63), one of Copán's greatest builders. Smoke Shell, the 15th king, who may have been Copán's Justinian, commissioned the construction of the city's most famous and important monument, the great Hieroglyphic Stairway which climbs the side of Temple 26. The grandeur of his works may have been meant to resurrect the glory – and thus the power – of the reign of Smoke Imix. The stairway immortalises the achievements of the dynasty from its establishment until 755, when the stairway was dedicated. It is the longest such inscription ever discovered in the Maya lands.

Yax Pac (Rising Sun), Smoke Shell's successor and the 16th king of Copán, ruled from 763 to 820. He continued the beautification of Copán, even though the dynasty's power seems to have been declining and its subjects had fallen on hard times. During Yax Pac's reign the population of Copán reached a peak of about 20,000, and the Main Group of buildings, which includes the Hieroglyphic Stairway, was 'finished' – or at least not changed significantly between that time and today. Copán's power base crumbled, perhaps because of trade difficulties and probably because its population had grown beyond its ability to feed itself.

Yax Pac died in 820 and was succeeded by U Cit Tok, of whom archaeologists have been able to learn nothing. It seems this last king of the Copán dynasty may have stayed on the throne for only a few years. The last carved date found at Copán is 822. After that, though Copán was still inhabited and farmed, its rulers – whoever they may have been – left none of the splendid stone records so artfully crafted by their predecessors. By the year 1200 or thereabouts, even the farmers had departed, and the royal city of Copán was reclaimed by the jungle.

Rediscovery It was John L Stephens who brought Copán to the world's attention after his visit in the winter of 1841. Stephens relates a story of the Spaniards' conquest: the ruler of this region, named Copán Calel, was the same one who had received the Spaniards peacefully at Esquipulas, which was then under his control. When the Spaniards let him know that he was about to be out of a job, Copán Calel reconsidered his earlier benevolence and retreated to Copán (probably close to, but not in, the ruins) to defend his rule. The Spaniards attacked, and after a long, fierce battle, they were victorious.

After the conquest, though the ruins at Copán were known, they were ignored. Few good Catholics wanted anything to do with the *ídolos* (idols) that stood in the dense jungle. When Stephens and his colleague Frederick Catherwood arrived to see the idols, they knew that Copán was one of the most significant archaeological sites in all of the Americas.

The jungle growth was thick and the work difficult. 'We could not see ten yards before us, and never knew what we should stumble upon next.' They saw a bit of sculpture buried in the earth.

I leaned over with breathless anxiety while the Indians worked, and an eye, an ear, a foot, or a hand was disentombed; and when the machete rang against the chiselled stone, I pushed the Indians away, and cleared out the loose earth with my hands. The beauty of the sculpture, the solemn stillness of the woods, disturbed only by the scrambling of monkeys and the chattering of parrots, the desolation of the city, and the mystery that hung over it, all created an interest higher, if possible, than I had ever felt among the ruins of the Old World.

After carefully studying and drawing as many stelae, 'altars' and glyphs as possible, Stephens approached the lessor of the land, Don José Maria, with an offer to buy the three years remaining on the lease. Stephens knew that as soon as he wrote about Copán, European explorers would come, buy the ruins and ship them to the great Continental museums. In the three years left of the lease, he proposed to explore the ruins fully, ship them to New York and establish a 'great national museum of American antiquities'.

The reader is perhaps curious to know how old cities sell in Central America. Like other articles of trade, they are regulated by the quantity in market, and the demand; but, not being staple articles, like cotton and indigo, they were held at fancy prices, and at that time were dull of sale. I paid fifty dollars for Copán. There was never any difficulty about price. I offered that sum, for which Don Jose Maria thought me only a fool; if I had offered more, he would probably have considered me something worse.

Stephens never prosecuted his claim to Copán, and the city was unclaimed when the English archaeologist Alfred P Maudslay came to do the first scientific investigation of it in 1885. Later research and preservation work was carried out by the Peabody Museum of Harvard University, the Carnegie Institution of Washington and the Instituto Hondureño de Antropología y Historia.

Orientation
There are two Copáns - the town and the ruins; the town is about 12 km east of the Guatemala-Honduras border. Confusingly, the town is named Copán Ruinas, though the actual ruins are just over one km east of the town. Minibuses from the border will usually take you on to the ruins after a stop in the town. If not, there is a footpath *(sendero peatonal)* alongside the road; the walk is a pretty one, past several stelae and unexcavated mounds.

In the town, young lads approach you offering to arrange horse rides and hikes to a nearby waterfall. Most hotels can arrange these activities as well.

Information
Visiting the Ruins The archaeological site is open daily from 8 am to 4 pm; admission costs about US$5. In the Visitors' Centre

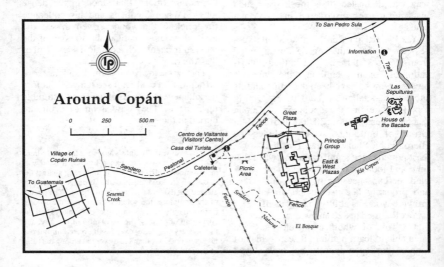

(Centro de Visitantes) building at the entrance to the ruins, you'll find the ticket seller, a theatre featuring free English-language audiovisual shows and a bookshop. Nearby are a patio restaurant *(La Cafetería)*, with a counter at which you can buy snacks and cold drinks, and souvenir and handicrafts shops in *La Casa del Turista*. Cheaper food is available across the road at the *Comedor Mayapán*. There's a picnic area along the path to the Principal Group of ruins. A nature trail *(sendero natural)* enters the forest several hundred metres from the Visitors' Centre.

You can camp at the ruins, outside the fence; water and toilets are available.

There are at least 4500 mounds containing ruins in the Copán Valley, 3500 of them in the 24 sq km immediately surrounding the Principal Group. Besides the Principal Group, there are two other important concentrations of ruins: El Bosque Residential Zone to the south-west and Las Sepulturas Residential Zone to the east; only Las Sepulturas is open to visitors.

Principal Group

The Principal Group of ruins is about 400 metres beyond the Visitors' Centre across well-kept lawns, through a gate in a strong fence and down shady avenues of trees.

Stelae of the Great Plaza The path leads to the Great Plaza and what archaeologist and art historian Linda Schele has termed 'a forest of kings' – a 'grove' of huge, intricately carved stelae portraying the rulers of Copán. To the Maya, a stela was reminiscent of a tree, and trees had special religious and political significance as symbols of power and greatness. Only Quiriguá has a comparable collection of great stelae, and even those did not approach the delicate and sensitive high-relief renderings of the works at Copán. Most of Copán's best stelae date from 613 to 738, during the reigns of Smoke Imix (628-95) and 18 Rabbit (695-738). All seem to have originally been painted; a few traces of red paint survive on Stela C. Many stelae had vaults beneath or beside them in which sacrifices and offerings could be placed.

Many of the stelae on the Great Plaza portray King 18 Rabbit, including Stelae A, B and 4. Perhaps the most beautiful stela in the Great Plaza is Stela A (731 AD), now in danger of crumbling because of centuries of exposure to the elements. Nearby and almost equal in beauty are Stela 4 (731), Stela B (731), depicting 18 Rabbit upon his accession to the throne, and Stela C (782) with a turtle-shaped altar in front; this last stela has figures on both sides. Stela E (614), erected on top of Structure 1 on the west side of the Great Plaza, is among the oldest stelae.

Stela D (736), at the northern end of the Great Plaza at the base of Structure 2, also portrays King 18 Rabbit. On its back are two columns of hieroglyphs; at its base is an altar with fearsome representations of Chac, the rain god. In front of the altar is the burial place of Dr John Owen, an archaeologist with the expedition from Harvard's Peabody Museum who died during the work in 1893.

On the east side of the plaza is Stela F (721), which has a more lyrical design, with the robes of the main figure flowing around to the other side of the stone, where there are glyphs. Altar G (800), showing twin serpent heads, is among the last monuments carved at Copán. Stela H (730) may depict a queen or princess rather than a king. Stela 1 (692), on the structure which runs along the east side of the plaza, is of a person wearing a mask. Stela J, farther off to the east, resembles the stelae of Quiriguá in that it is covered in glyphs, not human figures.

Ball Court & Hieroglyphic Stairway South of the Great Plaza, across what is known as the Central Plaza, is the ball court *(Juego de Pelota)*, dating from 731. It's the second largest in Central America. The one you see is the third on this site; the other two smaller ones were buried by this construction. Note the macaw heads carved at the top of the sloping walls. The central marker in the court was the work of King 18 Rabbit.

South of the ball court is perhaps Copán's most famous monument, the Hieroglyphic

GUATEMALA

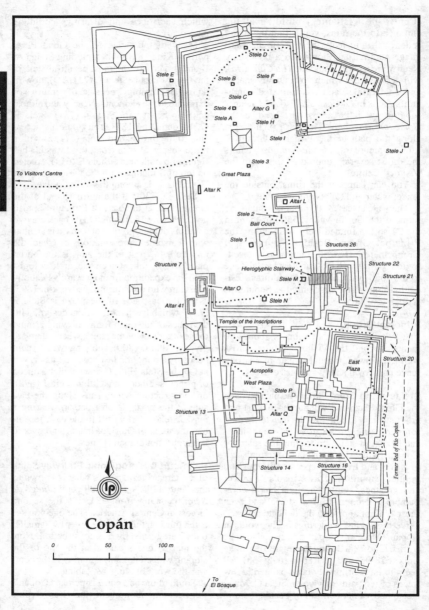

Stele D

Stele E
Stele B   Stele F
Stele C
Stele 4   Alter G
Stele A   Stele H
Stele I
Stele J

To Visitors' Centre
Stele 3
Great Plaza
Altar K
Altar L
Stele 2
Ball Court
Stele 1
Structure 26
Structure 7
Hieroglyphic Stairway
Structure 22
Structure 21
Stele M
Altar O
Stele N
Altar 41
Temple of the Inscriptions
Structure 20
East Plaza
Acropolis
West Plaza
Stele P
Structure 13
Altar Q
Former Bed of Río Copán
Structure 14   Structure 16

Copán

0   50   100 m

To El Bosque

Stairway (743), the work of King Smoke Shell. Today it's protected from the elements by a roof, which lessens the impact of its beauty, but you can still get an idea of how it looked. The flight of 63 steps bears a history – in several thousand glyphs – of the royal house of Copán; the steps are bordered by ramps inscribed with more reliefs and glyphs. The story inscribed on the steps is still not understood because the stairway was partially ruined and the stones jumbled. At the base of the Hieroglyphic Stairway is Stela M (756), bearing a figure (probably King Smoke Shell) in a feathered cloak; glyphs tell of the solar eclipse in that year. The altar in front shows a plumed serpent with a human head emerging from its jaws.

Beside the stairway, a doorway leads in to a system of tunnels dug by archaeologists to explore the structures beneath the Hieroglyphic Stairway. Discovered during these explorations was the tomb of a nobleman, a royal scribe who may have been the son of King Smoke Imix. The tomb, discovered in June 1989, held a treasure trove of painted pottery and beautiful carved jade objects, which are now in Honduran museums. More recently, a royal tomb thought to be that of Yax Kuk Mo, founder of the dynasty (about 400 AD), was discovered. It may have been fully explored by the time you visit, but the system of tunnels is not open to the public.

Acropolis The lofty flight of steps to the south of the Hieroglyphic Stairway is called the Temple of the Inscriptions. On top of the stairway, the walls are carved with groups of hieroglyphs. On the south side of the Temple of the Inscriptions are the East Plaza and West Plaza. In the West Plaza, be sure to see Altar Q (776), among the most famous sculptures here. Around its sides, carved in superb relief, are the 16 great kings of Copán, ending with the altar's creator, Yax Pac. Behind the altar was a sacrificial vault in which archaeologists discovered the bones of 15 jaguars and several macaws, probably sacrificed to the glory of Yax Pac and his ancestors.

The East Plaza also contains evidence of

Yax Pac – his tomb, beneath Structure 18. Unfortunately, the tomb was discovered and looted long before archaeologists arrived. Both the East and West Plazas hold a variety of fascinating stelae and sculptured heads of humans and animals. For the most elaborate relief carving, climb Structure 22 on the northern side of the East Plaza. Excavation and restoration is still under way.

El Bosque & Las Sepulturas
Excavations at El Bosque and Las Sepulturas have shed light on the daily life of the Maya of Copán during its golden age.

Las Sepulturas, once connected to the Great Plaza by a causeway, may have been the residential area where rich and powerful nobles lived. One huge, luxurious residential compound seems to have housed some 250 people in 40 or 50 buildings arranged around 11 courtyards. The principal structure, called the House of the Bacabs ('Officials'), had outer walls carved with the full-sized figures of 10 males in fancy feathered headdresses; inside was a huge hieroglyphic bench.

To get to Las Sepulturas, leave the main site at Copán and go 1½ km north-east along the main road to a separate entrance.

Archaeological Museum
The small, well-organised and well-designed Museo Regional de Arqueología Maya, on the plaza in the town, is worthwhile if only to see Stela B, portraying King 18 Rabbit, up close and away from the blazing sun. This great builder-king was the one who unfortunately lost his head to the king of Quiriguá. Other exhibits, including painted pottery, carved jade, Mayan glyphs and the calendar round, are also interesting and informative. The museum is open daily from 8 am to 4 pm; admission is on the same ticket as to the archaeological site.

Places to Stay
The town of Copán Ruinas is a small, sleepy, orderly place of white stucco buildings gathered around a pleasant main square. Several inexpensive hotels can provide lodging.

Hotel Paty is closest to the ruins, right on

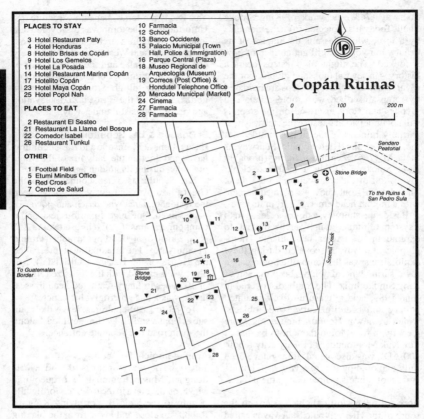

PLACES TO STAY

3 Hotel Restaurant Paty
4 Hotel Honduras
8 Hotelito Brisas de Copán
9 Hotel Los Gemelos
11 Hotel La Posada
14 Hotel Restaurant Marina Copán
17 Hotelito Copán
23 Hotel Maya Copán
25 Hotel Popol Nah

PLACES TO EAT

2 Restaurant El Sesteo
21 Restaurant La Llama del Bosque
22 Comedor Isabel
26 Restaurant Tunkul

OTHER

1 Footbal Field
5 Etumi Minibus Office
6 Red Cross
7 Centro de Salud
10 Farmacia
12 School
13 Banco Occidente
15 Palacio Municipal (Town Hall, Police & Immigration)
16 Parque Central (Plaza)
18 Museo Regional de Arqueología (Museum)
19 Correos (Post Office) & Hondutel Telephone Office
20 Mercado Municipal (Market)
24 Cinema
27 Farmacia
28 Farmacia

Copán Ruinas

the town side of the stone bridge. Rooms are being upgraded at this writing, and will probably be priced at US$11 a double with private shower.

Just up the street from the Paty is *Hotelito Brisas de Copán*, a bit tidier and more cheerful. It's managed by a friendly señora and room prices are the same as at the Paty.

Hotel Los Gemelos, half a block south of the Paty on the way to the plaza, is the third place to look, offering clean waterless rooms for US$8 a double. *Hotel Honduras*, diagonally across the street from the Paty, has a courtyard with a mango tree, and rooms with

shower for only slightly more than its neighbours charge for waterless rooms.

Hotelito Copán has very basic rooms opening onto a narrow car park, but it's neatly kept and charges just US$6 for a double room.

Hotel La Posada, across from the fancy Hotel Marina Copán, will do if all else is full. Rooms are bare but cheap, at US$3.50/6 a single/double.

Hotel Popol Nah is a modern house renting waterless rooms at the standard prices of US$8 per double.

The *Hotel Marina Copán* (☎ (5-04-98)

3070/1, fax 0957), just off the plaza, is the best in town. The flower-filled interior court leads the way to a swimming pool and to 40 air-conditioned, bath and TV-equipped rooms costing US$33 a double. The dining room is good as well.

If the Marina is full, try the *Hotel Maya Copán* (☎ (5-04-98) 3436), an old-fashioned and slightly overpriced place. Usable rooms with shower are US$14/18 a single/double.

Construction of a five-star hotel was begun some years ago by the Honduran government. As often happens with government projects, progress was slow and costs high. Recently the project was privatised, so there may be a five-star hotel in operation by the time you arrive.

Also, a hotel of rustic cabañas designed for ecotourism groups is to be opened northeast of Las Sepulturas along the main road.

Places to Eat

The *Restaurant Tunkul* is the main gathering spot in town. It has good food, good music, good company and a book exchange. The Tunkul is open every day from around 9 am to midnight; happy hour is from 6 to 7 pm.

Many hotels have their own little eateries which fill the need for food. There are also other similar places around. *Comedor Isabel* is small, cheap and family-run. *Restaurant El Sesteo* is dark, and the food cheap and local. *La Llama del Bosque* serves more interesting food than most Copán places at only slightly higher prices. With tourist traffic to Copán increasing rapidly, there will no doubt be fancier places opening soon.

Getting There & Away

Bus It's 280 km (seven hours by bus) from Guatemala City to El Florido, the Guatemalan village on the Honduran border. If you travel by organised tour or private car, it's faster and you can make the trip in one day, but it's exhausting and far too rushed. Starting from Río Hondo, Chiquimula or Esquipulas, it still takes a full day to get to Copán, tour the ruins and return, but it's more easily possible.

Rutas Orientales (☎ (2) 53-72-82, 51-21-60), 19 Calle 8-18, Zona 1 in Guatemala City, runs buses from the capital via El Rancho, Río Hondo and Zacapa to Chiquimula every half-hour from 4 am to 6 pm (169 km, three hours, US$3).

At Chiquimula, change to a Transportes Vilma bus for the remaining 58-km, 2½-hour trip (US$2) via Jocotán and Camotán to El Florido. Vilma buses leave Chiquimula for El Florido at 6, 9, 10.30 and 11.30 am and 12.30, 1.30, 3.30 and 4.30 pm (but this last bus reaches the border too late to cross); return buses depart from El Florido for Chiquimula at 5.30, 6.30, 7.30, 8.30, 9.30 and 10 am, noon, and 1 and 3 pm.

TURANSA, the company which runs minibus shuttles between Antigua and Guatemala City, also has weekend shuttle service between Antigua, Esquipulas and Copán. The minibus departs from Antigua at 6 am on Saturday, returning by 7 pm on Sunday, having visited Copán and stayed the night in Esquipulas. The US$80 round-trip fare does not include meals, hotel or border-crossing fees. See the Antigua and Guatemala City Getting There & Away sections for details on contacting TURANSA.

If you need a Honduran visa in advance, you can obtain it at the Honduran Consulate in Esquipulas.

If you're coming from Esquipulas, you can get off the bus at Vado Hondo, the junction of CA-10 and the road to El Florido, and wait for a bus there; but as the bus may fill up before departure, it may be just as well to go the extra eight km into Chiquimula and secure your seat before the bus pulls out.

Car Drive south from Chiquimula 10 km, north from Esquipulas 48 km, and turn eastward at Vado Hondo (Km 178.5 on CA-10). There's a small motel just opposite the turning, which will do if you need a bed. A sign reading 'Vado Hondo Ruinas de Copán' marks the way on the two-hour, 50-km drive from this junction to El Florido.

The road is unpaved but is usually in good condition and fairly fast (an average of 40 km/h). Twenty km north-east of Vado Hondo are the Chorti Maya villages of Jocotán and

Camotán, set amidst mountainous tropical countryside dotted with thatched huts in lush green valleys. Jocotán has a small Centro de Salud (medical clinic) and the *Hotel/Pension Ramirez*, a half-block north of the hilltop church and main square. You can stay in a room with shower for US$3.50 per person; a bathless room costs less. There's a small restaurant as well.

Along the road you may have to ford several small streams. This causes no problem unless there has been an unusual amount of rain during previous days.

Crossing the Border The village of El Florido, which has no services beyond a few soft-drink stands, is 1.2 km west of the border. At the border crossing are a few snack stands and the very basic *Hospedaje Las Rosas*, which can put you up in an emergency.

Allow at least 45 minutes (one to 1½ hours with a car) for border formalities; the border is open from 7 am to 6 pm.

Moneychangers will approach you on both sides of the border willing to change Guatemalan quetzals for Honduran lempiras or either for US dollars. The lempira is worth about US$0.17 (US$1 = HL6). Though quetzals and US dollars may be accepted at some establishments in the town of Copán Ruinas, the clerks at the ruins and the museum feel more comfortable accepting only Honduran currency. You will also have an easier time paying for your minibus ride from the border to the town if you have lempiras. You might want to change at least US$20 into lempiras to pay for customs fees, the minibus ride to the town and return, lunch, and entry to the ruins and the museum. If you plan to stay the night, change more.

You must present your passport and tourist card to the Guatemalan immigration and customs authorities, pay fees (some of which are unauthorised) of US$6, then cross the border and do the same thing with the Honduran authorities. If you just want a short-term permit to enter Honduras and plan to go only as far as Copán, tell this to the Honduran immigration officer and he will

charge you a fee of US$3. With such a permit you cannot go farther than the ruins and you must leave Honduras by the same route. If you want to travel farther in Honduras, ask for a standard visa, which costs US$10 and may take a bit more time.

When you return through this border point, you must again pass through both sets of immigration and customs and pay fees (lower this time). The Guatemalan immigration officer should give you your old tourist card back without charging the full fee for a new one.

If you are driving a rented car, you will have to present the Guatemalan customs authorities at the border with a special letter of permission to enter Honduras, written on the rental company's letterhead and signed and sealed by the appropriate company official. If you do not have such a letter, you'll have to leave your rental car at El Florido and continue to Copán by minibus.

On the Honduran side of the border are several little cookshacks where you can get simple food and cool drinks while waiting for a minibus to leave. Etumi minibuses depart from the border every 40 minutes throughout the day, charging US$1 for the 12-km, half-hour ride.

To return to the border from the town of Copán Ruinas (a half-hour trip), go to the Etumi Minibus office next to the Hotel Honduras to find out when the next minibus will depart.

QUIRIGUÁ

From Copán it is only some 50 km to Quiriguá as the crow flies, but the lay of the land, the international border and the condition of the roads makes it a journey of 175 km. Like Copán, Quiriguá is famed for its intricately carved stelae. Unlike Copán, the gigantic brown sandstone stelae at Quiriguá rise as high as 10.5 metres. Standing like sentinels in a quiet tropical park, the stelae of Quiriguá inspire thoughts and questions about the ancient Maya – who they were, how they lived and what made them erect these tremendous monuments.

A visit to Quiriguá is easy if you have your

GUATEMALA

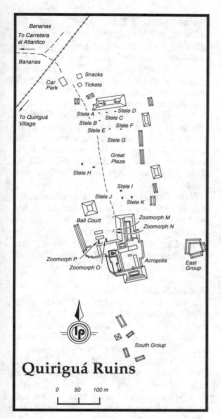

Quiriguá Ruins

0   50   100 m

which it was a dependency during much of the Classic period. Of the three sites in this area, only the present archaeological park is of interest.

The location lent itself to the carving of giant stelae. Beds of brown sandstone in the nearby Río Motagua had cleavage planes suitable for cutting large pieces. Though soft when first cut, the sandstone dried hard in the air. With Copán's expert artisans nearby for guidance, Quiriguá's stonecarvers were ready for greatness. All they needed was a great leader to inspire them – and to pay for the carving of the huge stelae.

That leader was Cauac Sky (725-84), who decided that Quiriguá should no longer be under the control of Copán. In a war with his former suzerain, Cauac Sky took King 18 Rabbit of Copán prisoner in 737 and later had him beheaded. Independent at last, Cauac Sky commissioned his stonecutters to go to work, and for the next 38 years they turned out giant stelae and zoomorphs dedicated to the glory of King Cauac Sky.

Cauac Sky was followed by his son Sky Xul (784-800), who lost his throne to a usurper, Jade Sky. This last great king of Quiriguá continued the building boom initiated by Cauac Sky, reconstructing Quiriguá's Acropolis on a grander scale.

Quiriguá remained unknown until John L Stephens arrived in 1840. Impressed by its great monuments, he lamented the world's lack of interest in them:

Of one thing there is no doubt: a large city once stood there; its name is lost, its history unknown; and...no account of its existence has ever before been published. For centuries it has lain as completely buried as if covered with the lava of Vesuvius. Every traveller from Yzabal to Guatimala has passed within three hours of it; we ourselves had done the same; and yet there it lay, like the rock-built city of Edom, unvisited, unsought, and utterly unknown.

Stephens tried to buy the ruined city in order to have its stelae shipped to New York, but the owner, Señor Payes, assumed that Stephens, being a diplomat, was negotiating on behalf of the US government and that the government would pay. Payes quoted an

own transport; it's more difficult but certainly not impossible if you're travelling by bus. From Río Hondo junction it's 67 km along the Carretera al Atlantico to the village of Los Amates, where there is a hotel and restaurant. The village of Quiriguá is 1.5 km east of Los Amates, and the turn-off to the ruins is another 1.5 km to the east. Following the access road south from the Carretera al Atlantico, it's 3.4 km through banana groves to the archaeological site.

History

Quiriguá's history parallels that of Copán, of

extravagant price, and the deal was never made.

Between 1881 and 1894, excavations were carried out by Alfred P Maudslay. In the early 1900s all the land around Quiriguá was sold to the United Fruit Company and turned into banana groves. The mighty and (some would say) malignant company is gone, but the bananas and Quiriguá remain. Restoration of the site was carried out by the University of Pennsylvania in the 1930s.

Ruins
The beautiful park-like archaeological zone is open from 7 am to 5 pm daily; admission costs US$1. A small stand near the entrance sells cold drinks and snacks, but you'd do better to bring your own picnic.

Despite the sticky heat and (sometimes) the bothersome mosquitos, Quiriguá is a wonderful place. The giant stelae on the Great Plaza are all much more worn than those at Copán. To impede their further deterioration, each has been covered by a thatched roof. The roofs cast shadows which make it difficult to examine the carving closely and almost impossible to get a good photograph. But somehow this does little to inhibit one's sense of awe.

Seven of the stelae, designated A, C, D, E, F, H and J, were built during the reign of Cauac Sky and carved with his image. Stela E is the largest Mayan stela known, standing some eight metres above ground, with another three metres or so buried in the earth. It weighs almost 60,000 kg. Note the exuberant, elaborate headdresses, the beards on some of the figures (an oddity in Mayan art), the staffs of office held in the kings' hands, and the glyphs on the stelae's sides.

At the far end of the plaza is the Acropolis, far less impressive than the one at Copán. At its base are several zoomorphs, blocks of stone carved to resemble real and mythic creatures. Frogs, tortoises, jaguars and serpents were favourite subjects. The low zoomorphs can't compete with the towering stelae in impressiveness, but as works of art, imagination and mythic significance, the zoomorphs are superb.

Places to Stay & Eat
In the village of Quiriguá, 700 metres south of the highway, is the *Hotel Royal*, a Caribbean-style wooden structure with large rooms holding four or five beds, a cold-water washbasin and shower, and a toilet, perhaps with a seat. Beds cost US$4 each; doubles with private shower cost US$14.

At Los Amates, three km west of Quiriguá village, is a Texaco fuel station. About 100 metres east of the Texaco station is the *Ranchón Chileño*, the best restaurant in the area. Here you can get good, filling meals for about US$6 and light meals for half that much.

Hotel Doña María, Carretera al Atlantico Km 181, at Doña María Bridge, is 24 km west of Los Amates. Behind the sad façade is an airy dining room with a view of the river. The rooms (US$4 per person) are musty, dark and claustrophobic, but there are few alternatives.

Getting There & Away
The turn-off to Quiriguá is 205 km (four hours) north-east of Guatemala City, 70 km north-east of the Río Hondo junction, 43 km south-west of the road to Flores in El Petén, and 90 km south-west of Puerto Barrios.

Transportes Litegua (☎ (2) 2 75 78), 15 Calle 10-42, Zona 1 in Guatemala City, has regular buses from the capital to Puerto Barrios every hour from 6 am to 5 pm, and several Pullman express buses (faster and more comfortable) as well. Stops are at El Rancho, Teculután, Río Hondo and Los Amates (Quiriguá). The fare is US$4.50 or US$6 if you go all the way to Puerto Barrios. The driver will usually oblige if you ask to be dropped off at the access road to the archaeological site rather than three km west at Los Amates.

The transport centre in this area is Morales, about 40 km north-east of Quiriguá. This is where it's easiest to catch a bus for Río Dulce.

Getting Around
Waiting at the junction of the Carretera al Atlantico and the Quiriguá access road are

men on motorbikes. They run a primitive shuttle service from the highway to the archaeological site and the banana company headquarters, charging a few quetzals for the 3.4-km ride. You cannot depend on them to take you back from the archaeological site to the highway unless you establish a time in advance.

If you're staying in the village of Quiriguá or Los Amates and walking to and from the archaeological site, you can take a short cut along the railway branch line which goes from the village through the banana fields, crossing the access road very near the entrance to the archaeological site.

LAGO DE IZABAL

The large lake to the north-west of the Carretera al Atlantico has hardly been developed for tourism at all. Head north-west from Morales and La Ruidosa junction (Carretera al Atlantico Km 245) along the road to Flores in El Petén, and after 34 km you reach the village of Río Dulce, also known as El Relleno.

From beneath the bridge you can hire a motorboat (you must bargain for a price) to take you to the Castillo de San Felipe, the region's major tourist attraction, though the fortress is reachable on foot. Boat owners can also take you downriver to El Golfete, Chocón-Machacas Nature Reserve and Lívingston, but prices for the hire of the boat will be higher than if you do the trip from Lívingston. For details of the trip, see the Lívingston section.

Castillo de San Felipe

The fortress of San Felipe de Lara, about one km west of the bridge, was built in 1652 to keep pirates from looting the villages and commercial caravans of Izabal. Though it deterred the buccaneers a bit, a pirate force captured and burnt the fortress in 1686. By the end of the next century, pirates had disappeared from the Caribbean and the fort's sturdy walls served as a prison. It later became a tourist attraction.

El Estor

The major settlement on the north-western shore is El Estor, once a nickel-mining town but now growing in popularity as a way-station for intrepid travellers on the Cobán-Lago de Izabal route through the Panzós Valley. Three buses make the seven-hour, US$3 run each day, leaving Cobán at 5, 8 and 11 am and El Estor at 5, 7 and 8.30 am.

The link from El Estor to the Carretera al Atlantico is completed by the El Estor-Mariscos ferry, which leaves El Estor at 5 am and departs from Mariscos for the return journey at 1 pm. Buses run from Mariscos down to the highway.

There's nothing to do in El Estor, but there are a few small lodging places, including the *Hotel Vista del Lago*, with rooms for US$3/6 a single/double. There are even cheaper places as well.

Places to Stay & Eat

In Río Dulce near the bridge are several cheap hotels. *Café El Sol* is typical, charging US$4 per person in rooms with private bath. More expensive and comfortable resort hotels are just a few km east on the shores of the river.

Touricentro Marimonte (☎ (9) 47-85-85; in Guatemala City (2) 34-49-64/5; fax (2) 32-23-52), on the south bank of the river by the road to Tikal, has a country-club layout with expansive lawns, a wooden main lodge and little two to four-bed cabañas. You can rent a room in the lodge or in a cabaña for US$40/58 a single/double. Meals are served in the dining room. On weekends the Marimonte is liable to be quite full.

Near the Castillo, the *Hotel Don Humberto* can put you up for US$4 per person if you don't have your own camping equipment.

THE ROAD TO FLORES

North across the bridge is the road into El Petén, Guatemala's vast jungle province. It's 208 km to Santa Elena and Flores, and another 65 km to Tikal.

The road from the Carretera al Atlantico to Modesto Méndez is not bad, but from

Méndez to Santa Elena it's in terrible condition. It's a bone-jangling ride of at least six hours to Flores.

Some years ago the German government gave the Guatemalan government a grant to improve the road. Once they reached Guatemala City, those millions of Deutschmarks are said to have disappeared without trace – and without a new road being built.

A new grant with stricter controls was approved, but at the last minute the Germans withheld the money, fearing that an improved road would encourage the migration of farmers into El Petén.

The forest here is disappearing at an alarming rate, falling to the machetes of subsistence farmers using the ancient slash-and-burn method of cultivation. Sections of forest are felled and burnt off, crops are grown for a few seasons until the fragile jungle soil is exhausted, and then the farmer moves deeper into the forest to slash and burn new fields. Cattle ranchers, slashing and burning the forest to make pasture, have also contributed to the damage.

Reportedly, the grant for a new road will be approved and the money forthcoming after the Guatemalan government has put controls in place to prevent the destruction of the forest. The people of El Petén are being informed of the threat to their land. Within a decade the forest may either be badly compromised or safely preserved for future generations – more likely, it will remain an ecological battleground for years to come. Until the forest is safe, the road will probably remain terrible – unpaved, cratered and rutted, with crude ferries of logs to ford rivers – with few services.

Places to Stay & Eat

Along the way to Flores there are only small jungle hamlets at which simple meals are sometimes available.

The best facilities are at Carole DeVine's Finca Ixobel (☎ (9) 50-73-63) in Poptún. For several decades Carole has offered travellers tent sites, palapas for hanging hammocks, beds and good homemade meals, with or without meat. Camping (with cold-water showers) costs US$2 to US$3 per person. Beds are US$4 in dormitories, or pay US$8/10/12 for a single/double/triple with hot shower. Bread, granola, yoghurt and pastries are made fresh daily. Meals offer excellent value, right up to the eat-all-you-like buffet dinner for US$6.

Getting There & Away

See the sections on Flores or Guatemala City for bus details. The buses reach Río Dulce about five hours after leaving Guatemala City, and are usually packed full by the time they reach Río Dulce. You'll have a better chance if you board at Morales.

If you're driving, fill your fuel tank before leaving Río Dulce, take some food and drink, and start early in the morning.

PUERTO BARRIOS

Heading eastward from La Ruidosa junction, the country becomes even more lush, tropical and humid until you arrive at Puerto Barrios (population 35,000).

The powerful United Fruit Company, which moved into Guatemala at the beginning of the 20th century, owned vast plantations in the Río Motagua Valley and many other parts of the country. The company built railways to ship its produce to the coast, and it built Puerto Barrios to put that produce onto ships sailing for New Orleans and New York. Laid out as a company town, Puerto Barrios has wide streets arranged neatly on a grid plan, and lots of Caribbean-style wood-frame houses, many on stilts.

When United Fruit's power and influence declined in the 1960s, the Del Monte company became successor to its interests. But the heyday of the imperial foreign firms was past, as was that of Puerto Barrios. A new, modern, efficient port was built a few km to the south-west, at Santo Tomás de Castilla, and Puerto Barrios settled into tropical torpor.

Early in the morning, before the sun is high and the humid heat overpowering, Puerto Barrios can be a pleasant place. Children in fresh clothes scamper along the

United Fruit Company

As late as 1870, the first year that bananas were imported to the USA, few Americans had ever seen a banana, let alone tasted one. By 1898 they were eating 16 million bunches annually.

In 1899 the Boston Fruit Company merged with the interests of the Brooklyn-born Central American railroad baron Minor C Keith to form the United Fruit Company. The aim was to own and cultivate large areas of Central American land by well-organised modern methods, providing predictable harvests of bananas which Keith, who controlled virtually all of the railroads in Central America, would then carry to the coast for shipment to the USA.

Central American governments readily granted United Fruit rights, at low prices, to large tracts of undeveloped jungle, for which they had no other use. The company provided access to the land by road and/or rail, cleared and cultivated it, built extensive port facilities for the export of fruit, and offered employment to large numbers of local workers.

By 1930, United Fruit was capitalised at US$215 million, and was the largest employer in Central America. The company's Great White Fleet of transport ships was one of the largest private navies in the world. By controlling Puerto Barrios and railroads serving it, all of which it had built, United Fruit effectively controlled all of Guatemala's international commerce, banana or otherwise.

The company soon came to be referred to as *El Pulpo*, The Octopus, by local journalists, who accused it of corrupting government officials, exploiting workers and, in general, of exercising influence far beyond its role as a foreign company in Guatemala.

United Fruit's treatment of its workers was paternalistic. Though they worked long and hard for low wages, the workers' wages were higher than for other farmwork, and they received housing, medical care and in some cases schooling for their children. Still, indigenous Guatemalans were required to 'give right of way to Whites and remove their hats when talking to them'. And the company took out of the country far more in profits than it put in: between 1942 and 1952 the company paid stockholders almost 62 cents in dividends for every dollar invested.

The US government, responding to its rich and powerful constituents, saw its role as one of support for United Fruit and defence of its interests.

On 20 October 1944, a liberal military coup paved the way for Guatemala's first free elections ever. The winner and new president was Dr Juan José Arévalo Bermejo, a professor who, inspired by the New Deal policies of Franklin Roosevelt, sought to remake Guatemala into a democratic, liberal nation guided by 'spiritual socialism'. His successor, Jacobo Arbenz, was even more vigorous in pressing the reform programme. Among Arbenz's many supporters was Guatemala's small Communist party.

Free at last from the repressions of past military dictators, labour unions clamoured for better conditions, with almost constant actions against *la Frutera* (United Fruit). The Guatemalan government, no longer willing to be bought off, demanded more equitable tax payments from the company, and divestiture of large tracts of its unused land.

Alarm bells sounded in the company's Boston headquarters and in Washington, where powerful members of Congress and the Eisenhower administration – including Secretary of State John Foster Dulles – were convinced that Arbenz was intent on turning Guatemala Communist. Several high-ranking US officials had close ties to United Fruit, and others were persuaded by the company's effective and expensive public relations and lobbying campaign that Arbenz was a threat.

During the summer of 1954, the CIA planned and carried out an invasion from Honduras by 'anti-communist' Guatemalan exiles which resulted in Arbenz's resignation and exile. The CIA's hand-picked 'liberator' was Carlos Castillo Armas, a military man of the old caste, who returned Guatemala to rightist military dictatorship. The tremendous power of the United Fruit Company had set back democratic development in Guatemala by at least half a century.

A few years after the coup, the US Justice Department brought suit against United Fruit for operating monopolistically in restraint of trade. In 1958 the company signed a consent decree, and in the years following it surrendered some of its trade in Guatemala to local companies, and some of its land to local owners. It yielded its monopoly on the railroads as well.

Caught up in the 'merger mania' of the 1960s, United Fruit merged with United Brands, which collapsed as the financial climate worsened in the early 1970s. In 1972, the company sold all of its remaining land in Guatemala to the Del Monte corporation. ∎

GUATEMALA

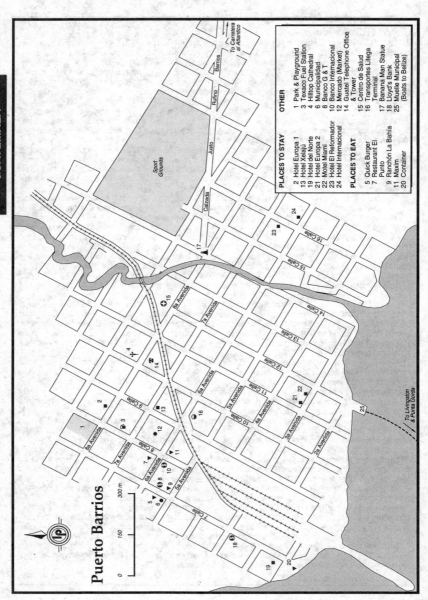

Puerto Barrios

0   150   300 m

PLACES TO STAY

2   Hotel Europa 1
13 Hotel Xelajú
19 Hotel del Norte
21 Hotel Europa 2
22 Motel Miami
23 Hotel El Reformador
24 Hotel Internacional

PLACES TO EAT

5   Quick Burger
7   Restaurant El Punto
9   Ranchón La Bahía
11 Maxim
20 Container

OTHER

1   Park & Playground
3   Texaco Fuel Station
4   Hilltop Cathedral
6   Municipalidad
8   Banco G & T
10 Banco Internacional
12 Mercado (Market)
14 Guatel Telephone Office & Tower
15 Centro de Salud
16 Transportes Litega Terminal
17 Banana Man Statue
18 Lloyd's Bank
25 Muelle Municipal (Boats to Belize)

streets to school and men and women off to work greet one another with smiles and chatter. By midday the heat has settled in. In the evening, when the noisy bars and brothels along 9 Calle get going, Puerto Barrios takes on an entirely different feeling.

For foreign visitors, Puerto Barrios is little more than the jumping-off point for a visit to Lívingston, the fascinating Black Guatemalan enclave on the north-western shore of the Río Dulce. As the boats for Lívingston leave at odd hours, you may find yourself staying the night in Puerto Barrios.

Orientation

Because of its spacious layout, you must walk or ride farther in Puerto Barrios to get from place to place. For instance, it's 800 metres from the bus terminal by the market to the Muelle Municipal (Municipal Boat Dock) at the foot of 12 Calle, from which boats depart for Lívingston. You are liable to be in town just to take a boat, so you may want to select a hotel near the dock.

Places to Stay

Motel Miami (☎(9) 48-05-37), 3a Avenida at 12 Calle, is a relatively new place one block from the dock. Rooms are arranged around a central courtyard used as a safe car park. Rates are US$10 a double with private bath, US$14 a double if you want air-conditioning (which you might). If you're driving and need a safe place to leave your car while you visit Lívingston, Señora Lidia Maribel Monjarás, proprietor of the Miami, will allow you to park it in her courtyard for US$2 per day.

Hotel Europa 2 (☎ (9) 48-12-92) is next to the Miami and is similar in accommodation and price. The original *Hotel Europa 1* (☎ (9) 48-01-27), on 8a Avenida between 8 and 9 Calles, is 1½ blocks from the cathedral and Guatel telephone office (look for the openwork cross on top of the steeple, and the Guatel signal tower). Fairly clean, pleasant and quiet, it charges US$8 for one of the 28 double rooms with shower. *Hotel Xelajú*, nearby at 7a Avenida and 9 Calle, charges a

bit less for bathless rooms and provides safe parking in its courtyard.

In a class by itself is the old *Hotel del Norte* (☎ (9) 48-00-87), 7 Calle at 1a Avenida, at the waterfront end of 7 Calle, 1.2 km from the dock (you must walk around the railway yard). In its airy dining room overlooking the Bahía de Amatique, you can almost hear the echoing conversation of turn-of-the-century banana moguls and smell their pungent cigars. Spare, simple and agreeably dilapidated, this is a real museum piece, with 31 rooms renting for US$12/18 a double with shared/private bath. Meals are served in the dining room. Service is refined, careful and elegantly old-fashioned, but the food can be otherwise.

For fancier lodgings you must head out of town. East of the stream bed and south of the main road, Calzada Justo Rufino Barrios, are two more comfortable hotels. The 36-room *Hotel El Reformador* (☎ (9) 48-05-33), 16 Calle and 7a Avenida No 159, is a modern building offering rooms with private bath for US$11 a double. *Hotel Internacional*, around the corner, is similar.

Puerto Barrios's fanciest is the *Hotel Puerto Libre* (☎ (9) 48-30-66, fax 76-27-24), at the junction of the Carretera al Atlantico, the road into Puerto Barrios, and the road to Santo Tomás de Castilla, five km from the boat dock. Rebuilt after a fire in 1992, its 34 rooms come with private bath and air-conditioning. There's a swimming pool and a restaurant which overlooks it. Rates are US$44/55 a single/double.

Places to Eat

Though this is hardly a gourmet's mecca, you will not starve in Puerto Barrios.

Quick Burger, on 7 Calle next to the Municipalidad, is modern, clean, cheap and not far from the centre of the town. Full meals can be had for US$3 or less.

Ranchón La Bahía, across the street from the Municipalidad on 7 Calle, is a Caribbean-style thatch-and-bamboo cottage with Latin music playing. Come here for beans and rice, fried bananas and other regional specialities for US$5 or less.

Maxim (☎ 48-22-58) is a funky Chinese place at the corner of 6a Avenida and 8 Calle. Chop suey and beer at US$6 is typical.

Among the tidier modern places is *Restaurant El Punto*, beneath the arches at the corner of 6a Avenida and 8 Calle, where full meals cost US$6 or so.

Perhaps the oddest eatery in town is *Container*, a café and drinks stand at the foot of 7 Calle, near the Hotel del Norte. It's made of two steel shipping containers, and the chairs and tables set out in the street afford a fine view of the bay.

Getting There & Away
Bus Transportes Litegua on 6A Avenue at 9 Calle (☎ in Guatemala City (2) 2-75-78; 15 Calle 10-42, Zona 1) has regular buses along the Carretera al Atlantico to Puerto Barrios every hour from 6 am to 5 pm, and Pullman express buses (faster and more comfortable) at 10 am and 5 pm. The 307-km journey takes 6 hours, with stops at El Rancho, Teculután, Río Hondo and Los Amates (Quiriguá); the fare is US$4.50 or US$6.

You can store your luggage at the terminal for about US$0.20 per day.

Boat Boats to Lívingston depart from the Muelle Municipal at the foot of 12 Calle at 10.30 am and 5 pm daily, arriving in Lívingston 1½ hours later; on busy days there may be a 3 pm boat as well. Return trips from Lívingston depart at 5 am and 2 pm, with a 7 am boat on some busy days. The one-way fare is US$1. Get to the dock at least 30 minutes prior to departure (45 minutes is better) for a decent seat; otherwise you could end up standing the whole way.

Twice-weekly boats from Puerto Barrios to Punta Gorda (in southern Belize) depart at 7.30 am on Tuesday and Friday. They used to stop in Lívingston, but no longer do so. Ask at the dock at the foot of 12 Calle for details. If you take this boat, you must pass through Guatemalan customs (aduana) and immigration (migración) before boarding the boat. Allow some time, and have your passport and tourist card handy.

LÍVINGSTON
The Garifuna (Garinagu, or Black Carib) people of Lívingston and southern Belize are the descendants of Africans brought to the New World as slaves who escaped or were shipwrecked in the Caribbean. Intermarrying with shipwrecked sailors of other races and with the indigenous Maya, they developed a distinctive culture and language incorporating African, Mayan and European elements. They trace their roots through legend to the Honduran island of Roatan, where they were settled by the British after the Garifuna revolt of 1795.

As you come ashore in Lívingston, you will be surprised to meet Black Guatemalans who speak Spanish as well as their traditional language; some also speak the musical English of Belize and the islands. The town – really a village – of Lívingston is an interesting anomaly, with a laid-back, very Belizean way of life, groves of coconut palms, gaily painted wooden buildings, and an economy based on fishing and tourism.

Orientation
After being in Lívingston for half an hour, you'll know where everything is. Walk up the hill from the dock along the village's main street. The fancy Hotel Tucán Dugú is on your right, with several small restaurants on your left. The street off to the left at the base of the hill goes to the Casa Rosada and several other hotels. At the top of the hill another street goes left to several hotels and restaurants. There is no bank in Lívingston, and the dollar exchange rate offered in the shops and hotels is not particularly good, so you should come with enough quetzals to cover your stay.

Río Dulce Cruises
Lívingston is the starting point for boat rides on the Río Dulce to enjoy the tropical jungle scenery, have a swim and a picnic, and explore the Chocón-Machacas Nature Reserve, 12 km west along the river. The 7200-hectare reserve was established to protect the beautiful river landscape, the

valuable mangrove swamps and, especially, the manatees (sea cows) which inhabit the waters (both salt and fresh) of the Río Dulce and El Golfete.

There are several ways to make the voyage up the Río Dulce. A mail launch departs from Lívingston for the trip upriver every Tuesday and Friday at about 11 am, charging US$5 per passenger. Motorised dugout canoes called *cayucos* act as tour boats, taking groups of travellers upriver for about US$10 per person. If you hire a native canoe for the trip, the cost could be higher. Almost anyone in Lívingston – your hotel clerk, a shopkeeper, a restaurant waiter – can tell you who's currently organising trips up the river.

Shortly after you leave Lívingston, the river enters a steep-walled gorge, its walls hung with great tangles of jungle foliage and bromeliads and the humid air noisy with the cries of tropical birds. A hot spring forces sulphurous water out at the base of the cliff, providing a delightful place for a swim.

Emerging from the gorge, the river eventually widens into El Golfete, a lake-like body of water that presages the even vaster expanse of Lago de Izabal. On the northern shore of El Golfete is the Biotopo Chocón-Machacas. The nature reserve's boat dock is good for swimming. A network of 'water trails' (boat routes around several jungle lagoons) provide ways to see the bird, animal and plant life of the reserve. A nature trail begins at the Visitors' Centre and winds its way through forests of mahogany, palms and rich tropical foliage. Jaguars and tapirs live in the reserve, though your chances of seeing one are slight. The walrus-like manatees are even more elusive. These huge, shapeless, fairly ugly mammals can weigh up to a tonne, yet they glide effortlessly beneath the calm surface of the river. Even though they are aquatic beasts with flippers rather than arms, they suckle their young.

From El Golfete and the nature reserve, some boats will continue upriver to the village of Río Dulce, where the road into El Petén crosses the river (see the Lago de Izabal section). If you didn't stop to visit the Castillo de San Felipe before, now's your chance.

Las Siete Altares

Beaches in Lívingston are mostly disappointing, as the jungle comes right down to the water's edge in most places. Those beaches which do exist are often clogged with vegetation as well. The Seven Altars is a series of freshwater falls and pools about five km (1½ hours' walk) north-west of Lívingston along the shore of the Bahía de Amatique. It's a pleasant goal for a walk along the beach and a good place for a picnic and a swim. Follow the shore northwards to the mouth of a river. Ford the river, and a path into the woods leads to the falls. If you'd rather not do the ford, boats at the mouth of the river will ferry you across for a few quetzals.

Places to Stay – bottom end

Hotel Caribe, a minute's walk along the shore to the left as you come off the boat dock, is a simple, family-run place right on the water offering double rooms for US$5 a double (shared bath).

Casa Rosada (☎ (9) 17-11-21) is another 700 metres (a five-minute walk) along the shore, just past the auxiliary electric generating plant. Nice little bungalows in a private compound right on the water go for US$20 a double and all three meals are served. It's a good idea to reserve in advance by phone, mail or telegram, as there are only five rooms and they're often full.

Up the hill from the boat dock, on the left side of the main street, is the *Hotel Río Dulce*, an authentic two-storey wood-frame Caribbean place painted blue. Bare rooms without running water cost US$6. A bit farther along, turn left down the side street to reach the *Hotel Marina*, which is also cheap. *Hotel Garifuna* is good, at US$11 a double with private bath.

Turn right at the Catholic church for the *Parador Flamingo*, on the shore of the Bahía de Amatique. It has eight tidy rooms in a walled compound for US$10 a double. The *African Place*, a restaurant with several rooms to rent, will put you up for US$9 a double with shared bath.

Places to Stay – middle
Amongst all this laid-back and low-priced Caribbean lodging, the 45-room *Hotel Tucán Dugú* (☎ (9) 48-15-72 to 88; in Guatemala City (2) 31-52-13, fax (2) 34-52-42), just up from the boat dock on the right, is a luxurious anomaly. Modern but still definitely Caribbean in style, with lots of dark mahogany, bamboo and red tile, it has many conveniences and comforts, including lush tropical gardens, a pretty swimming pool, and a jungle bar where you might expect to see Hemingway or Bogart. Rooms are fairly large with modern bathrooms, ceiling fans and little balconies overlooking the pool and the gardens. For this you pay US$55/65 a single/double, tax included.

Places to Eat
Food in Lívingston is a bit more expensive than in the rest of Guatemala because most of it (except fish and coconuts) must be brought across from Puerto Barrios.

The main street is lined with little comedores, *tiendas* (shops) and *almacenes* (stores). Your best plan may be to choose the place which is currently the most popular. *Restaurant El Malecón*, just up the hill from the boat dock, on the left, is airy and rustic, with a loyal local clientele and good views of the water. A full meal of Caribbean-inspired fare can be had for US$6.

A bit farther up the hill, the *Tropic*, on the right-hand side, is half restaurant and half shop; it's favoured by the thriftiest crowd. Turn left just beyond the ice plant (Fábrica de Hielo) to find the *Restaurant Saby*, on the left, a typical Caribbean bamboo eatery with local music playing. Meals of rice and beans and similar cost US$3 to US$4. The fancier *Restaurant Margoth*, beyond it, was empty at my last visit.

The very funky *African Place*, on the way to the Hotel Flamingo, looks like a miniature Moorish palace and serves a variety of exotic and local dishes; full meals are available for US$5 or less.

For the best (and most expensive) dining in town, head for the dining room of the *Hotel Tucán Dugú*. A good, complete dinner with drinks goes for US$10 to US$15.

Entertainment
Some nights of the week, the busiest place in town, with the loudest music, is the Templo Evangélico Iglesia del Nazareno (Evangelical Church of the Nazarene), opposite the Restaurant Margoth. If Caribbean Christianity is not your idea of nightlife, check out any of the numerous bars with loud reggae and cheap drinks.

Getting There & Away
The only way to get to Lívingston is by boat. For details, see the Puerto Barrios section.

El Petén

In the dense jungle cover of Guatemala's vast north-eastern department of El Petén, you may hear the squawk of parrots, the chatter of monkeys and the rustlings of strange animals moving through the bush. The landscape here is utterly different from that of Guatemala's cool mountainous highlands or its steamy Pacific Slope.

The monumental Mayan ceremonial centre at Tikal is a major stop on La Ruta Maya. The ruins of Uaxactún and Ceibal, though not so easily accessible, are perhaps more exciting to visit for that reason. Several dozen other great cities lie hidden in El Petén's jungles, accessible only to archaeologists with aircraft or to artefact poachers with stonecutting tools.

The battle for El Petén is raging even as you read this. Will it be left alone and preserved as one vast natural and archaeological

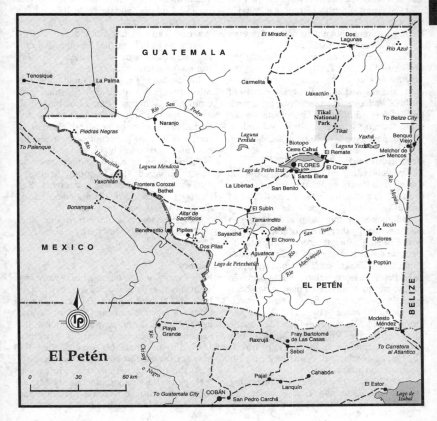

zone? Will its forests be cut and cut by farmers and cattle ranchers until the lush green carpet of trees and vines all but disappears, as has happened just across the border in Mexico? Or will the idea of La Ruta Maya – careful environmental and archaeological preservation through managed development with economic benefits for all – triumph? The consciousness of the Petenecos is being raised, and there is some hope that the idea of La Ruta Maya may succeed. In 1990 the Guatemalan government established the one-million-hectare Maya Biosphere Reserve, including most of northern El Petén. The Guatemalan reserve adjoins the vast Calakmul Biosphere Reserve in Mexico and the Río Bravo Conservation Area in Belize, forming a huge multinational reserve of over two million hectares.

There are three reasons to penetrate the forests of El Petén: firstly to visit Tikal, the greatest Mayan religious centre yet discovered; secondly to enjoy the great variety of birdlife, including the rare, shy quetzal; and thirdly to see a different Guatemala, one of small farming villages and jungle hamlets, without paved roads or colonial architecture.

Getting Around

The roads leading into El Petén – from the Carretera al Pacifico and from Belize – have been left in a state of disrepair, partly due to lack of funds and partly because better roads would encourage migration of farmers and ranchers from other areas of the country. With El Petén's forests already falling to the machete at an alarming rate, good new roads might prove disastrous. Thus road transport in El Petén is slow, bumpy, uncomfortable and sometimes unsafe. There have been several incidents of robbery of buses travelling along the roads between Río Dulce and Flores and the Belizean border at Melchor de Mencos/Benque Viejo del Carmen. For current information on the safety of travelling these roads, call your embassy or consulate in Guatemala City.

The only exception is the road connecting Flores/Santa Elena and Tikal, a good, fast asphalt road built so that tourists arriving by air in Santa Elena can proceed quickly and comfortably to Tikal, 71 km to the northeast. The Guatemalan government long ago decided to develop the adjoining towns of Flores (El Petén's departmental capital), Santa Elena and San Benito, on the shores of Lago de Petén Itzá, into the tourism centre of the region. The airport, hotels and other services are here, and it is from this base that visitors can tour the region. Though there are a few small hotels at Tikal, other services are limited, and no more can be built.

FLORES & SANTA ELENA

The town of Flores (population 2000) is built on an island on Lago de Petén Itzá. A 500-metre causeway connects Flores to her sister town of Santa Elena (altitude 110 metres, population 17,000) on the lakeshore. Adjoining Santa Elena to the west is the town of San Benito (population 22,000).

Flores, being the departmental capital, is more dignified, with its church, small government building and municipal basketball court arranged around the main plaza atop the hill in the centre of the island. The narrow streets of Flores, paved in cement blocks, hold numerous small hotels and restaurants.

Santa Elena is a disorganised town of dusty unpaved streets, open drainage ditches, small hotels and restaurants. San Benito is even more disorganised but is lively, with its honky-tonk bars.

The three towns actually form one large settlement, usually referred to simply as Flores.

History

Flores was founded on an island (petén) by the Itzaes after their expulsion from Chichén Itzá, and it was named Tayasal. Though Cortés dropped in on King Canek of Tayasal in 1524 while on his way to Honduras, the meeting was peaceable. Only in March of 1697 did the Spaniards finally bring the Maya of Tayasal forcibly under their control.

At the time of its conquest, Flores was perhaps the last major functioning Mayan ceremonial centre, covered in pyramids and temples, with idols in evidence everywhere.

GUATEMALA

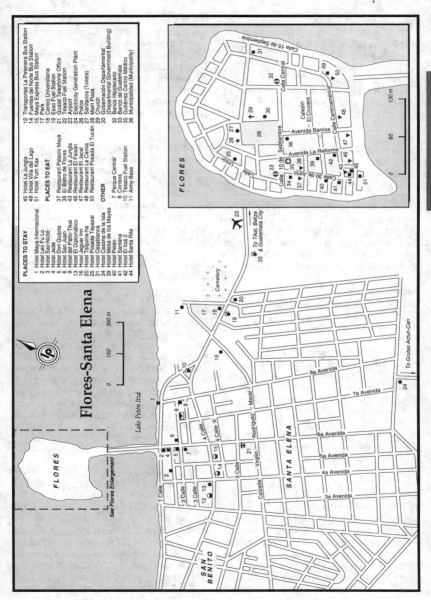

Flores–Santa Elena

PLACES TO STAY

1 Hotel Maya Internacional
2 Hotel Leo Fu Lu
3 Hotel Sac-Nicté
4 Hotel Jade
5 Hotel Don Quijote
6 Hotel San Juan
9 Hotel del Patio-Tikal
13 Hotel Diplomático
16 Hotel Jaguar Inn
20 Hotel Tzíquina-ha
25 Hotel Posada Tayazal
31 Hotel Casablanca
34 Hotel Casona de la Isla
39 Hotel Mesa de los Mayas
40 Hotel Petén
41 Hotel Santana
42 Hotel El Itzá 2
44 Hotel Santa Rita
45 Hotel La Jungla
49 Hotel Villa del Lago
51 Hotel Yum Kax

PLACES TO EAT

37 Restaurant Palacio Maya
38 El Bistro de Flores
43 Restaurant La Jungla
46 Restaurant El Faisán
47 Restaurant El Tucán
48 Restaurant La Canoa
50 Restaurant Posada El Tucán

OTHER

7 Parque Central
8 Correos
10 Texaco Fuel Station
11 Army Base
12 Transportes La Petenera Bus Station
14 Fuentes del Norte Bus Station
15 Maya Express Bus Station
17 Park
18 Centro Universitaria
19 Esso Fuel Station
21 Guatel Telephone Office
22 Texaco Fuel Station
23 Airport
24 Electricity Generation Plant
26 Police
27 Sanitarios (Toilets)
28 Main Plaza
29 Church
30 Gobernación Departamental (Departmental Government Building)
32 Banco Hipotecario
33 Banco de Guatemala
35 Gutiérrez Centro Médico
36 Municipalidad (Municipality)

The God-fearing Spanish soldiers destroyed these 'pagan' buildings. Today when you visit Flores you will see not a trace of them, although the modern town is doubtless built on the ruins and foundations of Mayan Tayasal.

When Tayasal was conquered, its Mayan citizens fled into the jungle, giving rise to the myth of a 'lost' Mayan city.

Orientation

The airport is on the eastern outskirts of Santa Elena, two km from the causeway connecting Santa Elena and Flores. Each bus company has its own terminal (see the Flores map).

Hotels in Flores and Santa Elena are in the bottom-end and middle price ranges. The top-end hotels are on the north-west shore of the lake near El Remate, about 35 km from Santa Elena. El Remate also has some cheaper hotels; see that section for details.

Information

Tourist Office There is an INGUAT tourist information desk at the airport, open generally from 8 am to 5 pm.

Money Banco Hipotecario in Flores is open from 8.30 am to 2.30 pm Monday to Friday (till 3.30 pm on Friday). Banco de Guatemala in Flores is open during the same hours. You may also be able to change dollars to quetzals at your hotel.

Post & Telecommunications The Post & Telegraph office (Correos y Telégrafos) is just west of the Hotel del Patio-Tikal in Santa Elena.

Grutas Actun-Can

The caves of Actun-Can, also called La Cueva de la Serpiente (The Cave of the Serpent), are of the standard limestone variety. No serpents are in evidence, but the cave-keeper will turn on the lights for you after you've paid the US$1.75 admission fee (8 am to 5 pm daily), and may give you the rundown on the cave formations, which

suggest animals, humans and various scenes. Bring a torch (flashlight) if you have one.

At the cave entrance is a shady picnic area. Actun-Can makes a good goal for a walk from Santa Elena. To find it, walk south on 6a Avenida past the Guatel office. About one km from the centre of Santa Elena, turn left, go 300 metres and turn right at the electricity generating plant. Go another one km to the site.

Lago de Petén Itzá

As you stroll around town, particularly in Flores, locals will present themselves and offer boat rides around the lake. Many are freelance agents who get a commission; it's better to talk with the boat owner directly. You should bargain over the price, and inspect the boat. Stops on a tour might include the lagoons at La Guitarra and Petencito, the settlements of San Andrés and San José, and of course the Biotopo Cerro Cahuí.

Places to Stay – bottom end

Santa Elena The bottom-end hotels in Santa Elena are cheaper than those in Flores.

Hotel Don Quijote, not far from the causeway to Flores, is cheap, though the rooms are nothing special. Rates are US$2.50 to US$4 a single, US$4.50 to US$7.50 a double; more expensive rooms have running water.

Hotel Jade, even nearer to the causeway, has long been a favourite with backpackers because of its handy location, washbasin and clothesline for laundry, and its low prices: US$2/6 a single/double. Renovation and expansion is raising the comfort level – and the prices – here, though.

Hotel Leo Fu Lo, next door, was still being built at my last visit but should be similar to the Jade.

Hotel San Juan (☎ (9) 81-15-62) is the starting place for many bus trips. The fan-equipped rooms are musty, dilapidated and a bit overpriced (US$7 for a waterless double), but convenient to the buses. Doubles with private bath cost US$14 (US$25 with air-conditioning). Some rooms have little TVs.

Hotel El Diplomático, a biggish three-storey building in the southern part of town, near the market, is fairly beat-up by the marketeers who use it regularly, but it is certainly cheap at US$2 to US$2.50 per person.

Flores The very plain *Hotel Casablanca* (☎ (9) 50-14-67) charges US$11 a double with shower, US$9 without. Some rooms have lake views.

Hotel Santa Rita (☎ (9) 50-12-66) is clean, family-run, and excellent value at US$10/13 a single/double with private shower. *Hotel Mesa de los Mayas* (☎ /fax (9) 50-12-40) has a few quite comfortable rooms above the restaurant for US$10/14/26 a single/double/triple with private shower and fan.

The cheerful, family-run *Hotel Villa del Lago* (☎ (9) 50-14-46) is very tidy as Petén hotels go, with clean shared showers, some lake views, and waterless rooms priced at US$9/11/13 a single/double/triple.

Posada El Túcan, next door, has forgettable rooms at US$8 a double without running water.

Hotel Yum Kax (☎ (9) 81-13-86/68), to the left as you arrive on the island along the causeway, is named for the Mayan god of maize (pronounced yoom-KASH). It's often flooded by a rise in the lake's water level, but when it's not it offers 43 plainish rooms with private bath and either fan or air-conditioning for US$18 to US$24 a double. *Hotel La Jungla*, across the street, is a bit cheaper.

Hotel El Itzá 2 (☎ (9) 50-06-86) is dumpy but may improve with time. Rooms cost US$9 with private shower.

Hotel Petén (☎ /fax (9) 50-06-62) has a small courtyard with tropical plants, and a pleasant roof terrace. The 14 comfy if plain double rooms rent for US$22 with private shower, electric hot-water showerhead and fan. Try to get a room on the top floor (Nos 33, 34, etc) with a view of the lake; these cost US$26 a double. The adjoining *Hotel Santana* is similar, though less attractive.

Places to Stay – middle
Santa Elena The *Hotel Jaguar Inn* (☎ (9)

50-00-02; fax 50-06-62), Calzada Rodríguez Macal 8-79, Zona 1, is comfortable without being fancy, but slightly inconveniently located 150 metres off the main road near the airport. It's good if you have a vehicle. Rooms cost US$22 a double with private bath and fan.

Flores *Hotel Casona de la Isla* (☎ /fax (9) 50-16-63) was constructing a small swimming pool at my last visit, so prices may rise. Currently they are US$20/30/40 a single/double/triple with shower and fan, somewhat more with air-conditioning.

Places to Stay – top end
Santa Elena *Hotel Tziquina-ha* (☎ (9) 50-13-59; fax 50-01-74), on the south side of the highway near the airport, has modern concrete-and-stucco buildings arranged on landscaped lawns, with a restaurant and pool. The 36 high-ceilinged rooms are gloomy and a bit musty, but each has a minibar, TV, tiled bath (shower) and air-conditioning. You can get a room for US$45/60 a single/double.

Hotel del Patio-Tikal (☎ in Guatemala City (2) 50-33-65, fax 50-43-13) looks severe from the outside but is actually a nice colonial-style hotel with a pretty central courtyard. The 21 rooms have ceiling fan, cable TV and private bath, and rent for US$65 a double.

Hotel Villa Maya (☎ Guatemala City (2) 34-81-36, fax (2) 34-81-34), on Petenchel Lagoon about 10 km east of Santa Elena, has 84 double rooms with private bath, ceiling fan, hot water, beautiful views of the lake and blissful quiet. The modern architecture of the four-unit lakeside bungalows uses traditional local elements in a harmonious way. There's a patio restaurant, three tennis courts and two swimming pools. Prices are US$90/100/110 a single/double/triple.

Places to Eat
As with hotels, the restaurants in Santa Elena tend to be cheaper than those in Flores. All are fairly simple, and open all the time. Beer, drinks and sometimes even wine are served.

Each hotel in the middle and top-end categories has its own restaurant.

Santa Elena *Comedor El Caracolito*, in the Hotel San Juan, is handy for bus passengers. A fruit plate costs US$2.25, fried chicken US$3.50.

For a change of cuisine, *Hotel Leo Fu Lo* has a small Chinese restaurant.

Flores Besides the familiar Guatemalan items, the *Restaurant La Mesa de los Maya* lists tepezcuintle (a rabbit-sized jungle rodent) on its menu, as well as armadillo and wild turkey (pavo silvestre). A mixed plate of these exotic meats goes for US$9, a vegetarian plate is US$5 and chicken costs even less.

The *Restaurant Palacio Maya* is open long hours (7 am to 11 pm every day), charges low to moderate prices (US$3 for spaghetti, US$6 for tepezcuintle) and has a varied menu.

Restaurant Posada El Túcan, next to the Villa del Lago, has a thatched roof, and a fine lakeside terrace which catches any breeze. Set breakfasts cost US$2 to US$3, lunches and dinners US$5 to US$8. Have the lake fish for about US$6.

Restaurant La Canoa is cheaper and plainer, but its dark, high-ceilinged dining room appeals to adventurous travellers, as does the decent food at low prices. *Restaurant El Faisan* is also cheap.

Restaurant La Jungla has a tiny streetside terrace where you can dine from the now-familiar burgers-spaghetti-tepezcuintle menu. Prices are similar to those at the Palacio Maya.

El Bistro de Flores (Chez Michel) is the poshest eatery on the island, with a smooth European-style decor, creative dishes such as game fondue, continental favourites like chicken Kiev, and the inevitable tepezcuintle (no doubt milk-fed). Prices are higher, but not by much. Main courses cost about US$6. It's open every day from 10 am to 4 pm and 6 to 10 pm.

Getting There & Away

Air Though it is possible to visit Tikal on a one-day excursion by plane from Guatemala City, I encourage you to stay over at least one night in Flores – there is a great deal to see and experience, and a day trip simply cannot do it justice.

The airport at Santa Elena (usually called 'the airport at Flores') is quite busy these days with flights from Guatemala City, Belize City and Cancún. For information on flights to and from these places, see those sections. Aerovías, TAPSA and Aeroquetzal all charge about US$55 one way for the flight between Flores and Guatemala City.

Four days a week, Aerovías flies between Flores and Belize City (US$50 one way).

Aeroquetzal flies from Flores to Guatemala City, then on to Cancún on Tuesday and Saturday (US$175 one way).

More regional airlines will be opening up routes to and from Flores in the near future. Ask at travel agencies in Cancún, Mérida, Belize City, Guatemala City and other major cities of the region for details. Your travel agent at home may not be able to get up-to-date information on some of these small regional carriers.

When you arrive at the airport in Flores you may be subjected to a cursory customs and immigration check, as this is a special customs and immigration district. If you are arriving from Belize or Mexico, you will, of course, pass through the normal customs and immigration procedures.

Bus Travel by bus to or from Flores is slow and uncomfortable, with the exception of the road to Tikal. Each bus company has its own bus station (see the Flores map).

Belize City (222 km, seven hours) – Transportes Pinita 2nd-class buses (US$8) depart from the market daily at 5, 8 and 10 am, connecting with a Novelo bus (US$3) at the Belizean border.

Ceibal – see Sayaxché, below.

Chetumal, Mexico (350 km, nine hours) – a special direct 1st-class bus (US$35) departs from the Hotel San Juan each morning, bypasses Belize City and goes straight to Chetumal. At Chetumal it connects with an ADO bus heading north along the coast to Cancún at 2 pm. To go 2nd class you must take the Transportes Pinita and Novelo buses to Belize City (see Belize City), then a Batty bus (US$5) to Chetumal. It's somewhat slower and less convenient but less than half the price of the special 1st-class bus.

El Naranjo – see From El Petén to Chiapas, below.

El Remate/Puente Ixlu (35 km, 45 minutes) – Tikal-bound buses and minibuses (see Tikal) will drop you here; buses running to and from Melchor de Mencos will drop you at Puente Ixlu/El Cruce, less than two km south of El Remate.

Guatemala City (506 km, 14 or 15 hours, US$12) – Transportes La Petenera, at 17a Avenida 10-25 in Guatemala City, is the favoured company at the moment, with newish buses making the run three times daily (4, 6 and 8 pm from Guatemala City). Others operating this route are Maya Express (☎ (2) 53-93-25; 17a Avenida 9-36, Zona 1 in Guatemala City) and Fuentes del Norte (☎ (2) 8-60-94, 51-38-17; 17 Calle 8-46, Zona 1 in Guatemala City). Buses depart from the capital at 1, 2, 3 and 7 am and 11 pm, with stops at Morales, Río Dulce, San Luis and Poptún. They usually leave Guatemala City and Santa Elena full, so passengers getting on midway must stand.

Melchor de Mencos (101 km, three or four hours) – 2nd-class Transportes Pinita buses (US$2.50) depart from the market at 5, 8 and 10 am for this town on the Belizean border. Buses (US$0.50) and share-taxis (US$2) take you to Benque Viejo and San Ignacio every hour or so.

Palenque (Mexico) – see From El Petén to Chiapas, below.

Sayaxché (61 km, two hours) – 2nd-class buses (US$2) run by Transportes Pinita depart at 6 am and 1 pm, with other buses returning from Sayaxché at these same times. There are also tours from Santa Elena via Sayaxché to the Mayan ruins at Ceibal (about US$30 per person round trip).

Tikal (71 km, two hours or more by bus, one to 1½ hours by minibus) – buses (US$2.50) depart from the market daily at 7 am and noon; return trips from Tikal are at similar times, making it necessary to stay overnight or find other means of returning to Flores. Minibuses depart each morning from various hotels (6, 8 and 10 am), the Flores airport (meeting all flights) and various mid-range hotels in Flores and Santa Elena for the ride to Tikal. The round-trip fare is US$9. Return trips are made at 2, 4 and 5 pm for the same fare. Your driver will anticipate that you'll want to return to Flores that same afternoon; if you know which return trip you plan to be on, they'll hold a seat for you on the same minibus or arrange a seat in a colleague's minibus. If you stay overnight in Tikal and want to take a minibus to Flores, it's a good idea to reserve a seat with

one of the minibus drivers when they arrive in the morning. Don't wait until departure time and expect to find a seat – you might not. A taxi (for up to four people) from the town or the airport to Tikal costs US$40 round trip.

Uaxactún (25 km, one hour, US$2) – a bus departs from Flores at 8 am, returning from Uaxactún at 11.30 am or noon, allowing enough time for a quick visit to the ruins.

Getting Around

Bus For destinations such as the small villages around the lake and in the immediate vicinity, there are sometimes seats available in the minibuses which depart from the market area in Santa Elena.

Car Several hotels, car-rental companies and travel agencies in Flores/Santa Elena offer vehicles for rent, including cars, 4WD Suzukis, pick-up trucks and minibuses. The place to find car-rental companies is in the arrivals hall at Flores airport – two there are Koka (☎ (9) 50-12-33, 50-15-26) and Los Jades (☎ (9) 50-17-41/34). Basic rates for a car are about US$30 per day, plus US$0.30 per km (the km charge will far exceed the daily rental charge). You should haggle for an all-inclusive, unlimited-km fee, which may be US$50 to US$70 per day.

Boat It is often possible to hire a *cayuco* (local boat) for cruises and tours on Lago de Petén Itzá. Any hotel clerk can help you with this.

EL REMATE

Once little more than a few thatched huts 35 km north-east of Santa Elena on the Tikal road, the village of El Remate has recently grown into a small town, thanks to the tourist trade. From El Remate an unpaved road snakes its way around the north-east shore of the lake to the Biotopo Cerro Cahuí and the luxury Camino Real hotel.

El Remate is less than two km north of Puente Ixlu, also called El Cruce, the settlement right at the junction of the Flores-Tikal-Melchor de Mencos roads.

With their newfound prosperity, Rematecos have built a Balneario Municipal

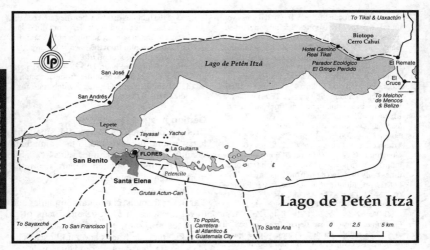

Lago de Petén Itzá

(Municipal Beach) just off the highway and have opened several cheap pensions and small hotels.

Biotopo Cerro Cahuí

At the north-east end of Lago de Petén Itzá, about 43 km from Santa Elena (1½ km west of El Remate), the Biotopo Cerro Cahuí covers 651 hectares of hot, humid, subtropical forest. Within the reserve are mahogany, cedar, ramón, broom, sapodilla and cohune palm trees, as well as many species of lianas (climbing plants), bromeliads (air plants), ferns and orchids. The ramón trees yielded fodder to the ancient Maya, and the hard wood of the sapodilla was used in temple door lintels which have survived from the Classic period to our own time.

Animals in the reserve include spider monkeys, howler monkeys, ocelots, bears, white-tailed deer, raccoons, armadillos and some 21 other beasts. In the water are 24 species of fish, turtles and snakes, and the *Crocodylus moreletti*, the Petén crocodile. The birdlife, of course, is rich and varied. Depending upon the season and migration patterns, you might see kingfishers, ducks, herons, hawks, parrots, toucans, woodpeck-

ers and the famous ocellated (or Petén) turkey, a beautiful big bird which reminds one very much of a peacock.

The reserve is open daily from 7 am to 5 pm for walking along its nature trails.

Places to Stay & Eat

Several small hotels and pensions are being built right in El Remate, and more are opening all the time.

The traditional lodging place in the area is the *Parador Ecológico El Gringo Perdido* (The Lost Gringo Ecological Inn; ☎ in Guatemala City (2) 36-36-83), situated on the north-eastern shore of the lake three km west of El Remate. Shady, rustic hillside gardens hold a little restaurant, a bucolic camping area, and simple but pleasant bungalows and dormitories. Rates range from US$3 for a camping place through US$14 for a dormitory bunk to US$20/24 a single/double. Meals cost US$6 for breakfast, US$10 for lunch or dinner. As there are no other eating places nearby, a bed and three meals starts at US$40 per person per day.

At my last visit, a new luxury hotel was under construction in El Remate, but for now the *Hotel Camino Real Tikal* (☎ Guatemala

City (2) 33-46-33) is the fanciest hotel in El Petén. Located within the Biotopo Cerro Cahuí five km west of El Remate, the Camino Real has 120 air-conditioned rooms with all the comforts: private bath, remote-controlled cable TV and mahogany decoration. Two restaurants and two bars keep guests happy, as do tennis courts, swimming pools, water sports on the lake, and all the other top-class services. Rates are US$165/176 a single/double, tax included.

Getting There & Away
Any bus or minibus going north from Santa Elena to Tikal can drop you at El Remate. Taxis from Santa Elena or the airport will take you to the reserve for US$20.

TIKAL
There is nothing like Tikal. Towering pyramids rise above the jungle's green canopy to catch the sun. Howler monkeys swing noisily through the branches of ancient trees as brightly coloured parrots dart, squawking, from perch to perch. When the complex warbling song of some mysterious jungle bird is not filling the air, the buzz of tree frogs provides background noise.

Certainly the most striking feature of Tikal is its steep-sided temples, rising to heights of more than 44 metres. But Tikal is different from Chichén Itzá, Uxmal, Copán and most other great Mayan sites because it is deep in the jungle. Its many plazas have been cleared of trees and vines, its temples uncovered and partially restored, but as you walk from one building to another you pass beneath the dense canopy of the rainforest. Rich smells of earth and vegetation, peacefulness and animal noises all contribute to an experience not offered by any other major Mayan site.

If you visit from December to February, expect some cool nights and mornings. March and April are the hottest months, and water is scarcest then. The rains begin in May or June, and with them come the mosquitos – have repellent and, for camping, a mosquito net. July to September is muggy and buggy. October and November see the end of the occasional rains and a return to cooler temperatures.

Day trips by air from Guatemala City to Tikal are popular, and they do allow you to get a glimpse of this spectacular site in the shortest possible time. But Tikal is so big that you need at least two days to see even the major parts thoroughly.

History
Tikal is set on a low hill, a fact which is difficult to confirm if you fly over but which is evident as you walk up to the Great Plaza from the entry road. The hill, affording relief from the surrounding low-lying swampy ground, may be why the Maya settled here around 700 BC. Another reason was the abundance of flint, the valuable stone used by the ancients to make clubs, spearpoints, arrowheads and knives. The wealth of flint meant good tools could be made, and flint could be exported in exchange for other goods. Within 200 years the Maya of Tikal had begun to build stone ceremonial structures, and by 200 BC there was a complex of buildings on the site of the North Acropolis.

Classic Period By the time of Christ, the Great Plaza was beginning to assume its present shape and extent. With the dawn of the Early Classic period about 250 AD, Tikal was an important religious, cultural and commercial city with a large population. King Yax Moch Xoc, who ruled about 230 AD, is looked upon as the founder of the dynasty which ruled Tikal thereafter.

Under Yax Moch Xoc's successor, King Great Jaguar Paw, who ruled in the mid-300s, Tikal adopted a new and brutal method of warfare used by the rulers of Teotihuacán in central Mexico. Rather than meeting their adversaries honourably on the plain of battle in hand-to-hand combat, the army of Tikal used auxiliary units to encircle the enemy and, by throwing spears, to kill them at a distance. This first use of 'air power' among the Maya of Petén enabled Smoking Frog, the Tikal general, to conquer the army of Uaxactún; thus Tikal became the dominant kingdom in Petén.

GUATEMALA

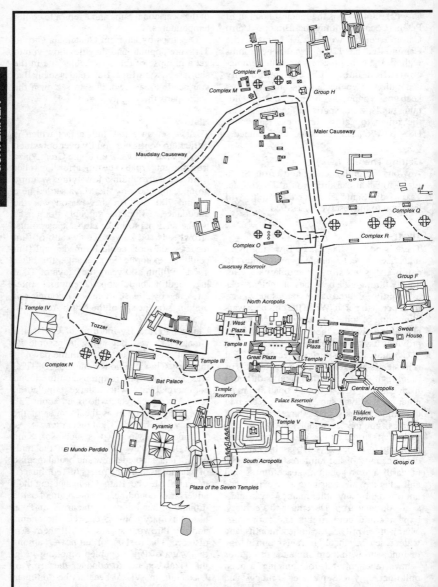

Complex P
Complex M
Group H
Maler Causeway
Maudslay Causeway
Complex Q
Complex R
Complex O
Causeway Reservoir
Group F
Temple IV
North Acropolis
Tozzer
West Plaza
Sweat House
Causeway
Temple II
East Plaza
Complex N
Temple III
Great Plaza
Temple I
Bat Palace
Temple Reservoir
Central Acropolis
Palace Reservoir
Hidden Reservoir
Pyramid
Temple V
El Mundo Perdido
South Acropolis
Group G
Plaza of the Seven Temples

GUATEMALA

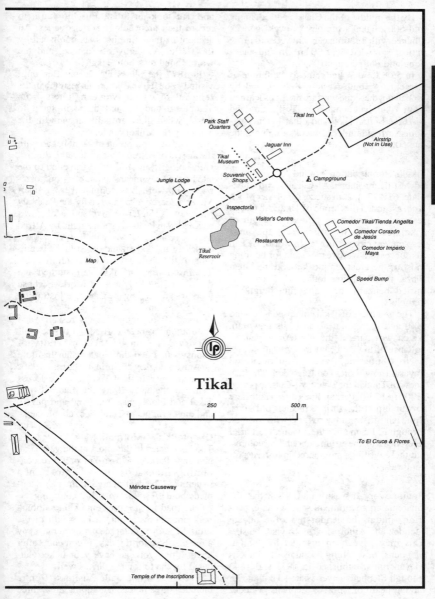

Park Staff Quarters

Tikal Inn

Airstrip (Not in Use)

Tikal Museum

Jaguar Inn

Souvenir Shops

Jungle Lodge

Campground

Inspectoría

Visitor's Centre

Comedor Tikal/Tienda Angelita

Comedor Corazón de Jesús

Restaurant

Comedor Imperio Maya

Tikal Reservoir

Map

Speed Bump

Tikal

0   250   500 m

To El Cruce & Flores

Méndez Causeway

Temple of the Inscriptions

By the middle of the Classic period, in the mid-500s, Tikal's military prowess and its alliance with Teotihuacán allowed it to grow until it sprawled over 30 sq km and had a population of perhaps 100,000.

In 553, Lord Water came to the throne of Caracol (in south-western Belize), and by 562, using the same warfare methods learned from Tikal, had conquered Tikal's king and sacrificed him. Tikal and other Petén kingdoms suffered under Caracol's rule until the late 600s.

Tikal's Renaissance Around 700 a new and powerful king named Ah Cacau (Lord Chocolate, 682-734), 26th successor of Yax Moch Xoc, ascended the throne of Tikal. Ah Cacau restored not only the military strength of Tikal, but also its primacy as the most resplendent city in the Mayan world. He and his successors were responsible for building most of the great temples around the Great Plaza, which survive today. Ah Cacau was buried beneath the staggering height of Temple 1.

The greatness of Tikal collapsed in around 900, and it was not alone in its downfall, which was part of the mysterious general collapse of lowland Mayan civilisation.

No doubt the Itzaes, who occupied Tayasal (now Flores) on Lago de Petén Itzá, knew of Tikal in the Late Post-Classic period (1200 to 1530). Perhaps they even came here to worship at the shrines of their old gods. Spanish missionary friars who moved through El Petén after the conquest left brief references to these junglebound structures, but these writings mouldered in libraries for centuries.

Rediscovery It wasn't until 1848 that the Guatemalan government sent out an expedition, under the leadership of Modesto Méndez and Ambrosio Tut, to visit the site. This may have been inspired by John L Stephens' best-selling accounts of fabulous Mayan ruins, published in 1841 and 1843 (though Stephens never visited Tikal, never having heard of it). Like Stephens, Méndez

and Tut took an artist, Eusebio Lara, to record their archaeological discoveries. An account of their findings was published by the Berlin Academy of Science, and the world found out about Tikal.

In 1877 the Swiss Dr Gustav Bernoulli visited Tikal. His explorations resulted in the removal of carved wooden lintels from Temples I and IV and their shipment to Basel, where they are still on view in the Museum für Völkerkunde.

Scientific exploration of Tikal began with the arrival of Alfred P Maudslay, the English archaeologist, in 1881, who travelled to the site by the only means available – on horseback. His work was continued by Teobert Maler, a German sponsored by the Peabody Museum at Harvard University. Maler was succeeded in Peabody sponsorship by Alfred M Tozzer and R E Merwin. Tozzer worked tirelessly at Tikal on and off from the beginning of the century until his death in 1954. The inscriptions at Tikal were studied and deciphered by Sylvanus G Morley, whose work was funded by the Carnegie Institution of Washington.

Since 1956, archaeological research and restoration has been carried out by the University Museum of the University of Pennsylvania and the Guatemalan Instituto de Antropología y Historia. In the mid-1950s an airstrip was built at Tikal to make access easier. In the early 1980s the road between Tikal and Flores was improved and paved, and direct flights to Tikal were abandoned.

Orientation & Information

Tikal is located in the midst of the vast Tikal National Park, a 575-sq-km preserve containing thousands of separate ruined structures. The central area of the city occupied about 16 sq km with 3000 buildings.

The road from Flores enters the national park boundaries about 15 km south of the ruins. When you enter the park you must pay a fee of US$6 for the day; if you enter after about 3 pm, you can have your ticket validated for the following day as well.

The area around the Visitors' Centre includes three hotels, a camping area, three small comedores, a tiny post office, a police post, an excellent little museum and a rarely used airstrip. From the Visitors' Centre it's a 20 to 30-minute walk south-west to the Great Plaza.

The walk from the Great Plaza to the Temple of the Inscriptions is over one km; from the Great Plaza to Complex P, it's one km in the opposite direction. To visit all of the major building complexes you must walk at least 10 km, probably more.

For complete information on the monuments at Tikal, pick up a copy of *Tikal – A Handbook of the Ancient Maya Ruins*, by William R Coe (University Museum of the University of Pennsylvania, Philadelphia, 1967 and later editions). The guide is on sale in Flores and at Tikal, but it may be cheaper if you buy it in your own country; it is cheaper in the USA, for instance.

The ruins are open from 6 am to 5 pm; you may be able to get permission to visit the Great Plaza until 8 pm on moonlit evenings by applying to the Inspectorería to the west of the Visitors' Centre. Carry a flashlight if you stay after sunset–there are no street lights in the jungle!

Great Plaza

Follow the signs to reach the Great Plaza. The path comes into the Great Plaza around Temple I, the Temple of the Grand Jaguar. This was built to honour – and to bury – King Ah Cacau; the king may have worked out the plans for the building himself, but it was erected above his tomb by his son, who succeeded to the throne in 734. Ah Cacau's rich burial goods included 180 beautiful jade objects, 90 pieces of bone carved with hieroglyphs, pearls, and stingray spines which were used for ritual bloodletting. At the top of the 44-metre-high temple is a small enclosure of three rooms covered by a corbelled arch. The zapote-wood lintels over the doors were richly carved; one of them is now in a Basel museum. The lofty roofcomb which crowned the temple was originally adorned with reliefs and bright paint. It may have symbolised the 13 realms of the Mayan heaven.

The climb up is dangerous (at least two people have tumbled to their deaths so far) but the view from the top is magnificent.

Temple II, directly across the plaza from Temple I, was once almost as high, but now measures 38 metres without its roofcomb. This one seems a bit easier to climb and the view is just as stupendous.

The North Acropolis, while not as immediately impressive as the twin temples, is of great significance. Archaeologists have uncovered about 100 different structures, the oldest of which dates from before the time of Christ, with evidence of occupation as far back as 400 BC. The Maya built and rebuilt on top of older structures, and the many layers, combined with the elaborate burials, added sanctity and power to their temples. Look for the two huge wall masks, uncovered in an earlier structure and now protected by roofs. The final version of the Acropolis, as it stood around 800 AD, had more than 12 temples atop a vast platform, many of them the work of King Ah Cacau.

On the plaza side of the North Acropolis are two rows of stelae. Though hardly as impressive as the magnificent stelae at Copán or Quiriguá, these served the same purpose: to record the great deeds of the kings of Tikal, to sanctify their memory and to add 'power' to the temples and plazas which surrounded them.

Central Acropolis

On the south side of the Great Plaza, this maze of courtyards, little rooms and small temples is thought by many to have been a palace where Tikal's nobles lived. Others think the tiny rooms may have been used for sacred rites and ceremonies, as graffiti found within them suggest. Over the centuries the configuration of the rooms was repeatedly changed, suggesting perhaps that this 'palace' was in fact a noble or royal family's residence changed to accommodate different groups of relatives. A hundred years ago, one part of the acropolis, called Maler's Palace, provided lodgings for archaeologist Teobert Maler when he worked at Tikal.

West Plaza

The West Plaza is north of Temple II. On its north side is a large Late Classic temple. To the south, across the Tozzer Causeway, is Temple III, 55 metres high. Yet to be uncovered, it allows you to see a temple the way the last Tikal Maya and first White explorers saw them. The causeway leading to Temple IV was one of several sacred ways built among the temple complexes of Tikal, no doubt for astronomical as well as aesthetic reasons.

South Acropolis & Temple V

Due south of the Great Plaza is the South Acropolis. Excavation has hardly even begun on this huge mass of masonry covering two hectares. The palaces on top are no doubt from Late Classic times (the time of King Ah Cacau), but earlier constructions probably go back 1000 years.

Temple V, just east of the South Acropolis, is 58 metres high and was built around 700 AD (again, in the reign of Ah Cacau). Unlike the other great temples, this one has rounded corners, and one very tiny room at the top. The room is less than a metre deep, but its walls are up to 4½ metres thick. The view (as usual) is wonderful, giving you a 'profile' look at the temples on the Great Plaza.

Plaza of the Seven Temples

On the other side of the South Acropolis is the Plaza of the Seven Temples. The little temples, all quite close together, were built in Late Classic times, though the structures beneath must go back at least a millenium. Note the skull and crossed bones on the central temple (the one with the stela and altar in front). On the north side of the plaza is an unusual triple ball court; another, larger version in the same design stands just south of Temple I.

El Mundo Perdido

About 400 metres south-west of the Great Plaza is El Mundo Perdido (the Lost World), a large complex of 38 structures with a huge pyramid in its midst. Unlike the rest of Tikal, where Late Classic construction overlays

work of earlier periods, El Mundo Perdido exhibits buildings of many different periods: the large pyramid is thought to be essentially Preclassic (with some later repairs and renovations); the Talud-Tablero Temple (or Temple of the Three Rooms), Early Classic; and the Temple of the Skulls, Late Classic.

The pyramid, 32 metres high and 80 metres along the base, has a stairway on each side, and had huge masks flanking each stairway, but no temple structure at its top. Each side of the pyramid displays a slightly different architectural style. Tunnels dug into the pyramid by archaeologists reveal four similar pyramids beneath the outer face; the earliest (Structure 5C-54 Sub 2B) dates from 700 BC, making the pyramid the oldest Mayan structure at Tikal.

Temple IV & Complex N

Complex N, near Temple IV, is an example of the 'twin-temple' complexes popular among Tikal's rulers during the Late Classic period. These complexes are thought to have commemorated the completion of a katun, or 20-year cycle in the Mayan calendar. This one was built in 711 by King Ah Cacau – that great builder – to mark the 14th katun of Baktun 9. The king himself is portrayed on Stela 16, one of the finest stelae found at Tikal.

Temple IV, at 64 metres in height, is the highest building at Tikal and the highest Indian building known in the western hemisphere. It was completed about 741, in the reign of Ah Cacau's son. From the base it looks like a steep little hill. Clamber up the path, holding onto trees and roots, to reach the metal ladder which will take you to the top. Another metal ladder, around to the side, lets you climb to the base of the roofcomb. The view is almost as good as from a helicopter - a panorama across the jungle canopy. If you stay up here for the sunset, climb down immediately thereafter, as it gets dark on the path very quickly.

Temple of the Inscriptions

Compared to Copán or Quiriguá, there are relatively few inscriptions on buildings at

Jade Mask

building materials for a causeway now named after Alfred Maudslay, which runs south-west to Temple IV. Group H had some interesting graffiti within its temples.

Complexes Q and R, about 300 metres due north of the Great Plaza, are very Late Classic twin-pyramid complexes with stelae and altars standing before the temples. Complex Q is perhaps the best example of the twin-temple type, as it has been mostly restored. Stela 22 and Altar 10 are excellent examples of Late Classic Tikal relief carving, dated 771.

Complex O, due west of these complexes on the western side of the Maler Causeway, has an uncarved stela and altar in its north enclosure. An uncarved stela? The whole point of stelae was to record great happenings. Why did this one remain uncarved?

Tikal Museum

The museum, in the Visitors' Centre, is small but has some fascinating exhibits, including the burial goods of King Ah Cacau, carved jade, inscribed bones, shells, stelae and other items recovered from the excavations. There is no extra charge for admission.

Places to Stay

Some intrepid visitors sleep atop Temple IV, convincing the guards to overlook this illegal activity for a consideration of US$6 per person, but this is not to be recommended. Safety is a major concern.

Otherwise, there are only four places to stay at Tikal, and in the interests of the environment no more lodgings will be built – water is scarce here, and the land cannot support many more humans.

Most of the places are booked in advance by tour groups, even though most groups (and individuals as well) stay near Lago de Petén Itzá and shuttle up to Tikal for the day. In recent years I have heard numerous complaints of price gouging, unacceptable accommodation and 'lost' reservations at these hotels. It is probably best to stay in Flores or El Remate and visit Tikal on day trips.

Cheapest of Tikal's lodgings is the official

Tikal. The exception is this temple, 1.2 km south-east of the Great Plaza. On the rear of the 12-metre-high roofcomb is a long inscription; the sides and cornice of the roofcomb bear glyphs as well. The inscriptions give us the date 766 AD. Stela 21 and Altar 9, standing before the temple, date from 736. The stela had been badly damaged (part of it was converted into a *metate* for grinding corn!) but has now been repaired.

Warning Note that the Temple of the Inscriptions is remote from the other complexes, and there have been incidents of robbery and rape of single travellers and couples. Ask a guard before you make the trek out here, or come in a group.

Northern Complexes

About one km north of the Great Plaza is Complex P. Like Complex N, it's a Late Classic twin-temple complex which probably commemorated the end of a katun. Complex M, next to it, was partially torn down by the Late Classic Maya to provide camping area by the entrance road and the disused airstrip. Set in a nice lawn of green grass with some trees for shade, it should be an idyllic camping ground, but it's not. Often the toilets and showers do not work, and the charge for tent space is US$6 per person.

Largest and most modern of the hotels is the 32-room *Jungle Lodge* (☎ in Guatemala City (2) 76-02-94; 29 Calle 18-01, Zona 12), built originally to house the archaeologists excavating and restoring Tikal. Accommodation is in thatched or tin-roofed bungalows, or in the half-timbered main building, which also houses the dining room, bar and reception desk. Rooms without bath cost US$18 a double; with bath (no hot water), the cost is US$40. The bungalows with bath are newer than those without, and they must be reserved in advance.

The *Jaguar Inn*, to the right of the museum as you approach on the access road, has only two rooms. The price is US$32. Four tents rent for US$12 a double.

Tikal Inn, past the Jaguar Inn as you walk away from the small museum down towards the old airstrip, has 17 rooms in the main building, as well as bungalows (which are slightly nicer). The swimming pool, dry for years, was fixed up and filled on my last visit. The rooms are quite simple and clean, with walls that extend only partway up to the roof and thus afford little conversational privacy. Rooms cost US$40 a double in the main building, US$50 in the bungalows. At 9 pm the electricity goes off.

Places to Eat

As you arrive in Tikal, look on the right-hand side of the road to find the three little comedores: *Comedor Imperio Maya, Comedor Corazón de Jesús, Comedor Tikal* and *Tienda Angelita*. The Comedor Imperio Maya, first on the way into the site, seems to be the favoured one. You can buy cold drinks and snacks in the adjoining tienda (shop). All three comedores are similar in comforts and style (there are none), all are rustic and pleasant, all are run by local people and all serve huge plates of fairly tasty food at low prices. The meal of the day is almost always a piece of roast chicken, rice, salad, fruit and a soft drink for US$4.

Picnic tables beneath shelters are located just off Tikal's Great Plaza, with itinerant soft-drink pedlars standing by, but no food is sold. If you want to spend all day at the ruins without having to make the 20 to 30-minute walk back to the comedores, carry food with you.

The restaurant in the *Visitors' Centre*, across the street from the comedores, serves fancier food at fancier prices. Tenderloin of beef (lomito) is featured, as are other steaks, at US$10 a portion. Plates of fruit cost less.

Meals at the *Jungle Lodge* are not overly expensive. Breakfast is served from 7 to 9 am, lunch from 12.30 to 2 pm and dinner from 7.30 to 8.30 pm.

Getting There & Away

For details of transport to and from Flores/Santa Elena, see that section. Coming from Belize, you can get off the bus at El Cruce/Puente Ixlu. Wait for a northbound bus or minibus – or hitch a ride with an obliging tourist – to take you the remaining 35 km to Tikal. Note that there is very little northbound traffic after lunch. If you come to Puente Ixlu in the afternoon, it's probably best to continue to Flores or El Remate for the night rather than risk being stranded at El Cruce.

You don't need a car to get to Tikal, but a vehicle of your own can be useful for visiting Uaxactún.

Warning Occasionally, armed guerrillas or robbers stop a bus or minibus on the Tikal-Flores road, take passengers' valuables, then allow the bus to go on its way. The few incidents so far have not resulted in physical harm.

The US Department of State's Citizens' Emergency Service (☎ (202) 647-52-25) in Washington, DC can provide up-to-date reports through its automatic telephone information service. In Guatemala, ask at your embassy in Guatemala City, or simply ask the locals in Flores for news on the current situation.

UAXACTÚN

Uaxactún (pronounced wah-shahk-TOON), 25 km north of Tikal along a poor, unpaved road through the jungle, was Tikal's political and military rival in Late Preclassic times. It was conquered by Tikal's King Great Jaguar Paw in the mid-300s, and was subservient to its great sister to the south for centuries thereafter.

During the rainy season (from May to October), you may find it difficult to get to Uaxactún. At other times of the year, ask in Flores or Tikal about the condition of the road. You may be advised to make the hour-long drive only in a vehicle with 4WD, whether bus, pick-up truck or rented car. A bus leaves Tikal daily for Uaxactún at around 8 am if road conditions allow, returning from Uaxactún around noon, for US$2.

If you're driving, fill your fuel tank in Flores; there is no fuel available at Tikal or Uaxactún. You might also want to pack some food and drink, though drinks and a few snacks are on sale in the village at Uaxactún.

The road (a jeep track really) winds through the jungle, up and down hills, through sloughs of mud where you'll need that 4WD. You may encounter one or two other vehicles on this road, in which case you must do some fancy manoeuvring to get by.

When you arrive at Uaxactún, sign your name in the register at the guard's hut (at the edge of the disused airstrip, which now serves as pasture for cattle). About halfway down the airstrip, roads go off to the left and to the right to the ruins. If you have your own equipment, there's plenty of places to camp.

Ruins

The pyramids at Uaxactún were uncovered and put in a stabilised condition so that no further deterioration would result; they were not restored. White mortar is the mark of the repair crews, who had patched cracks in the stone to prevent water and roots from entering. Much of the work on the famous Temple E-VII-Sub was done by Earthwatch volunteers in 1974; among them was Jane A Fisher,

a Uaxactún-lover who later married the author of this guidebook.

Turn right from the airstrip to reach Group E and Group H, a 10 to 15-minute walk. Perhaps the most significant temple here is E-VII-Sub, among the earliest intact temples excavated, with foundations going back perhaps to 2000 BC. It lay beneath much larger structures, which have been stripped away. On its flat top are holes, or sockets, for the poles which would have supported a wood-and-thatch temple.

About a 20-minute walk to the north-west of the runway are Group A and Group B. At Group A, early excavators sponsored by Andrew Carnegie simply cut into the sides of the temples indiscriminately, looking for graves. Sometimes they used dynamite. This unfortunate work destroyed many of the temples, which are now in the process of being reconstructed.

EASTWARDS TO BELIZE

It's 101 km from Flores eastwards to Melchor de Mencos, the Guatemalan town on the border with Belize.

Transportes Pinita buses depart for Melchor at 5 am. The road from Flores to El Cruce/Puente Ixlu is good, fast asphalt. If you're coming from Tikal, start early in the morning and get off at El Cruce to catch a bus or hitch a ride westward. For the fastest, most reliable service, however, it's best to be on that 5 am bus.

East of El Cruce the road reverts to what's usual in El Petén – unpaved mud in bad repair. The trip to Melchor takes three or four hours. There is guerrilla and bandit activity along this road, and a remote chance that your bus will be stopped and its passengers relieved of their valuables.

At the border you must hand in your Guatemalan tourist card before proceeding to Benque Viejo in Belize, about three km from the border. See the section on Benque Viejo for transport information to Benque Viejo, San Ignacio, Belmopan and Belize City. If you arrive in Benque early enough in the day, you may have sufficient time to visit

GUATEMALA

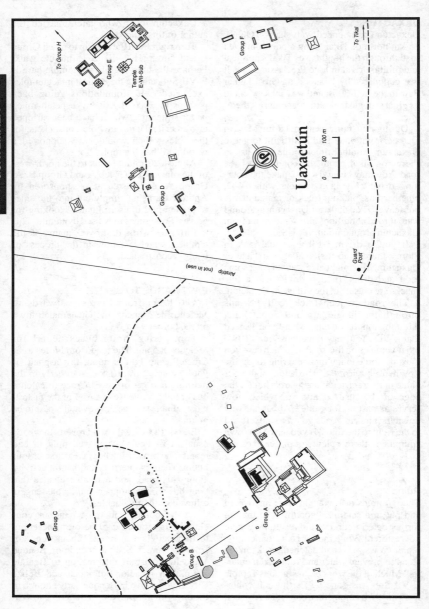

Uaxactún

To Group H
Group E
Temple E-VII-Sub
Group F
Group D
Group C
Group B
Group A
Airstrip (not in use)
Guard Post
To Tikal

0   50   100 m

the Mayan ruins of Xunantunich on your way to San Ignacio.

FROM EL PETÉN TO CHIAPAS (MEXICO)

There are currently three routes through the jungle from Flores (Guatemala) to Palenque (Mexico).

Via El Naranjo

The traditional route is via bus to El Naranjo, then by boat down the Río San Pedro to La Palma, then by bus to Tenosique and Palenque.

Buses to El Naranjo (on the Río San Pedro) depart from the market daily at 5 am and 12.30 pm on the rough, bumpy, 125-km, six-hour, US$4.50 ride. El Naranjo is a hamlet with a few thatched huts, large military barracks, an immigration post and a few basic lodging places. From El Naranjo you must catch a boat on the river for the four-hour cruise to the border town of La Palma. From La Palma you can go by bus to Tenosique (1½ hours), then by bus or combi to Emiliano Zapata (40 km, one hour), and from there by bus or combi to Palenque.

Going in the reverse direction, travel agencies in Palenque offer to get you from Palenque to La Palma by minibus in time to catch a special 9 am boat to El Naranjo, and then the bus to Flores, arriving there around 7 pm the same day. The cost is about US$55 per person. Though somewhat more expensive than doing it yourself, it is faster, surer and more convenient, and avoids a dreary overnight in El Naranjo.

Via Bethel & Frontera Corozal

The newer route is by bus from Flores via El Subín crossroads to the hamlet of Bethel (four hours, US$3), on the Río Usumacinta. Frequent cargo boats make the two-hour trip downriver to Frontera Corozal in Mexico, charging a few dollars for the voyage. A hired boat might cost US$15. There are no services in Bethel except a small shop.

At Frontera Corozal (also called Frontera Echeverría), there is a restaurant but no lodging. From Frontera, a chartered boat to Yaxchilán might cost US$60, but sometimes you can hitch a ride with a group for US$10 or so. The one bus per day takes six hours to reach Palenque; the fare is US$5.

Coming from Palenque, you can visit Yaxchilán and Bonampak ruins en route to Flores. Take Autobus Lagos de Montebello (behind Hotel Maya Tulipanes) from Palenque to Bonampak (six hours, US$5); buses leave at 3 and 9 am and 6 and 8 pm. Jump out at the turnoff for Bonampak; there is no accommodation here, but with camping gear or a hammock you'll do OK. After the hike to Bonampak, return to the road and catch a passing bus to Frontera Corozal (1½ hours, US$2); they go by around 4 and 8 pm. You will need to camp at Frontera.

The next day, make your excursion to Yaxchilán, then catch (or hire) a boat to Bethel in Guatemala. Clear customs in Bethel, change money and catch a bus to Flores. Buses leave at 4 and 11.30 am and 2 pm.

Via Pipiles & Benemerito

From Sayaxché, you can negotiate a ride on one of the cargo boats for the eight-hour trip (US$8) down the Río de la Pasión via Pipiles (the Guatemalan border post) to Benemerito, in the Mexican state of Chiapas. From Benemerito, proceed by bus or boat to the ruins at Yaxchilán and Bonampak, and then onward to Palenque. Buses run directly between Benemerito and Palenque (10 hours, US$12) as well.

SAYAXCHÉ & CEIBAL

The town of Sayaxché, 61 km south of Flores through the jungle, is the closest settlement to a half-dozen Mayan archaeological sites, including Aguateca, Altar de Sacrificios, Ceibal, Dos Pilas, El Caribe, Itzán, La Amelia and Tamarindito. Of these, Ceibal is currently the best restored and most interesting, partly because of its Mayan monuments and partly because of the river voyage and jungle walk necessary to reach it.

Sayaxché itself is of little interest, but its few basic services allow you to eat and to stay overnight in this region.

Orientation

The bus from Santa Elena drops you on the north bank of the Río de la Pasión. The main part of the town is on the south bank. Frequent ferries carry you over the river for a minimal fare.

Ceibal

Unimportant during the Classic Period, Ceibal grew rapidly thereafter, attaining a population of perhaps 10,000 by 900 AD. Much of the population growth may have been due to immigration from what is now Chiapas, in Mexico, because the art and culture of Ceibal seems to have changed markedly during the same period. The Post-Classic Period saw the decline of Ceibal, after which its low ruined temples were quickly covered by a thick carpet of jungle.

Today Ceibal is not one of the most impressive of Mayan sites, but the journey to Ceibal is among the most memorable. A two-hour voyage on the jungle-bound Río de la Pasión brings you to a primitive dock. After landing, you clamber up a narrow, rocky path beneath gigantic ceiba trees and ganglions of jungle vines to reach the archaeological zone.

Smallish temples, many of them still (or again) covered with jungle, surround two principal plazas. In front of a few temples, and standing seemingly alone on paths deeply shaded by the jungle canopy, are magnificent stelae, their intricate carvings still in excellent condition.

Getting There & Away Day trips to Ceibal are organised by various agencies and drivers in Santa Elena and Flores for about US$30 to US$50 per person round trip. It can be done cheaper on your own, but this is significantly less convenient.

Buses depart from Santa Elena at 6 am and 1 pm for Sayaxché (two hours, US$2.50), where you must strike a deal with a boat owner to ferry you up the river – a two-hour voyage – and back. The boat may cost anywhere from US$30 to US$60, depending upon its size and capacity. From the river, it's less than 30 minutes' walk to the site. You should hire a guide to see the site, as some of the finest stelae are off the plazas in the jungle.

Other Ruins

Of the other Mayan sites near Sayaxché, none is currently as interesting or as well restored as Ceibal. Dos Pilas is presently under excavation, but not equipped to receive visitors without their own camping gear. From Dos Pilas, the minor sites of Tamarindito and Aguateca may be reached on foot and by boat, but they are unrestored, covered in jungle and of interest only to the very intrepid.

Places to Stay & Eat

Hotel Guayacan, just up from the dock on the south side of the river in Sayaxché, is basic and serviceable. A double costs US$8 without water, US$11 with cold shower. The *Hotel Mayapan*, up the street to the left, has cell-like rooms for US$5 a double.

Restaurant Yaxkin is typical of the few eateries in town: basic, family-run and cheap.

Top: Main plaza in La Democracia, with Olmecoid basalt heads, Guatemala (TB)
Bottom: Bas-relief from the Cotzumalguapa culture, Santa Lucía Cotzulmalguapa, Guatemala (TB)

Top: The basilica of Esquipulas, Guatemala (TB)
Left: Workers building a protective palapa above a stela at Quiriguá (TB)
Right: Ceibal Ruins, El Petén, Guatemala (TB)

Belize

Facts about the Country

This English-speaking tropical country with its highly unlikely mixture of peoples and cultures is being 'discovered', and it is changing fast.

Belize is tiny: the population of the entire country is les than 200,000 (the size of a small city in Mexico, Europe or the USA), and its 23,300 sq km area is only slightly more than that of Massachusetts or Wales.

Those who say the political scene here is turbulent are referring to the purple rhetoric and high emotions of politics. Belize is a democracy, and has never had a military coup; indeed, it does not have an army, only the tiny Belize Defence Force. The prime minister's official car is a 4WD vehicle; some prime ministers have been known to give rides to hitchhikers.

Belize is friendly, laid-back, beautiful, proud, poor, and hopeful for the future. It's difficult not to love the place, but it happens. If a visitor is disappointed, usually it is because of unrealistic expectations. A few points must be kept in mind:

Belize is not yet fully prepared to receive lots of visitors. Services in some areas are few, far between, basic and somewhat expensive. The country has a small number of hotels, most simple, but these may be full when you arrive, leaving you little choice of accommodation. There are only two paved roads in the whole country, so transport can be slow. Public transport is either by small aeroplane or used schoolbus, so many hotels and lodges operate their own tour minibuses to allow guests to take excursions with some level of convenience.

Over half of the tourists who visit Belize go straight to the cayes. Some spend their whole time in the islands; others use island hotels as bases for excursions to other parts of the country. Likewise, many visitors to the mountains of western Belize go straight from the airport to their reserved room at a small forest lodge or resort. When they want to make an excursion, they sign up for a guided tour operated by the lodge. These tours, like the lodges, are small, convenient and personal, and often priced higher than mass-market excursions.

If you expect convenience, comfort and ultra-cheapness while travelling independently, you may not think the best of Belize. But if you are adaptable and adventurous, you'll love it.

HISTORY
Colonial Times

In the opinion of its Spanish conquerors, Belize was a backwater good only for cutting logwood to be used for dye. It had no obvious riches to exploit, and no great population to convert for the glory of God and the profit of the conquerors. Far from being profitable, it was dangerous, because the barrier reef tended to tear the keels from Spanish ships which attempted to approach the shore.

Though Spain 'owned' Belize, it did little to rule it, as there was little to rule. The lack of effective government and the safety afforded by the barrier reef attracted English and Scottish pirates to Belizean waters during the 1600s. They operated mostly without serious hindrance, capturing Spanish galleons heavily laden with the gold and other riches taken from Spain's American empire. In 1670, however, Spain convinced the British government to clamp down on the pirates' activities. The pirates, now unemployed, mostly went into the logwood business, becoming lumberjacks instead of buccaneers.

By today's standards, the erstwhile pirates made bad timber managers, cutting logwood indiscriminately and doing damage to the jungle ecosystem.

During the 1700s the Spanish wanted the British loggers out of Belize, but with little control over the country and more important things to attend to in other parts of its empire, Spain mostly ignored Belize. The British did not. As British interests in the Caribbean

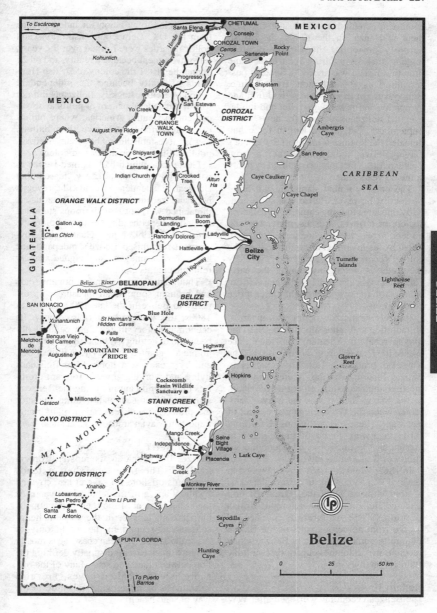

Belize

BELIZE

countries increased, so did British involvement in Belize. In the 1780s, the British actively protected the former pirates' logging interests, assuring Spain at the same time that Belize was indeed a Spanish possession. This was a fiction. By this time, Belize was already British by tradition and sympathy, and it was with relief and jubilation that Belizeans received the news, on 10 September 1798, that a British force had defeated the Spanish armada off St George's Caye. Belize had been delivered from Spanish rule, a fact that was ratified by treaty some 60 years later.

The country's new status did not bring prosperity, however. Belize was still essentially one large logging camp, not a balanced society of farmers, artisans, merchants and traders. When the logwood trade collapsed, killed by the invention of synthetic dyes, the colony's economy crashed. It was revived by the trade in mahogany during the early 1800s, but this also collapsed when African sources of the wood brought fierce price competition.

Belize's next trade boom was in arms, ammunition and other supplies to sell to the Mayan rebels in Yucatán, who fought the War of the Castes during the mid-1800s. The war also brought a flood of refugees to Belize. First it was the Whites and their mestizo lieutenants driven out by the wrath of the Maya; then it was the Maya themselves when the Whites regained control of Yucatán. These people brought farming skills that were to be of great value in expanding the horizons and economic viability of Belizean society.

In 1862, while the USA was embroiled in its Civil War and unable to enforce the terms of the Monroe Doctrine, Great Britain declared Belize to be the colony of British Honduras. The declaration encouraged people from numerous parts of the British Empire to come and settle in Belize, which accounts in part for the country's present-day ethnic diversity.

Modern Times

The Belizean economy worsened after WW II, which led to agitation for independence from the UK. Democratic institutions and political parties were formed over the years, self-government became a reality, and on 21 September 1981 the colony of British Honduras officially became the independent nation of Belize. Luckily, Belizeans did not follow the general pattern of political development in Central America, where bullets often have more influence than ballots. Despite its establishment by pirates, Belize's political life is surprisingly nonviolent.

Guatemala, which had claimed Belize as part of its national territory, feared that Belizean independence would kill forever its hopes of reclaiming it. The Guatemalans threatened war, but British troops stationed in Belize kept the dispute to a diplomatic squabble. In 1992 a new Guatemalan government recognised Belize's independence and territorial integrity, and signed a treaty relinquishing its claim.

Though the logwood and mahogany trade had brought some small measure of prosperity to Belize in the late 1700s and early 1800s, this was never a rich country. Its economic history in the 20th century has been one of getting by, benefiting from economic aid granted by the UK and the USA, and by money sent home from Belizeans living and working abroad. Tourism promises to be significant in raising the Belizean standard of living and in providing funds for the protection and restoration of its many important Mayan archaeological sites.

GEOGRAPHY

Belize, like Yucatán, is mostly tropical lowland. The limestone shelf extends eastwards offshore for several km, covered by about a five-metre depth of seawater. At the eastern extent of the shelf is the famous barrier reef, longest in the western hemisphere and second in the world only to Australia's. The Belizean coastline is mostly swampy mangrove, indistinctly defining the line between land and sea. Many of the offshore islands, called cayes, are also surrounded by mangrove, with little in the way of sand beach.

Northern Belize is low tropical country, very swampy along the shore. Rainfall is lightest in the north, heaviest in the south.

In the western and southern parts of the country, the Maya Mountains rise to almost 1000 metres. Even here the forest is lush and well watered, humid even in the dry season but more pleasant than the lowlands.

GOVERNMENT

British colonial rule left Belize with a tradition of representative democracy which continued after independence. The British monarch is Belize's head of state, represented on Belizean soil by the governor-general, who is appointed by the monarch with the advice of the Belizean prime minister. The Belizean legislature is bicameral, with a popularly elected House of Representatives, and a nominated Senate similar in function to the British House of Lords.

The prime minister is the actual political head of Belize, and since independence the prime minister has usually been George Price, a founder of the People's United Party (PUP). The PUP was born in the 1950s during the early movement for independence from the UK. For the first decade of its existence, the PUP was seen as anti-British, and its leaders were harassed by the colonial authorities. But by 1961 the British government saw that Belizean independence was the wave of the future. Price went from being a thorn in the British side to being the prospective leader of a fledgling nation.

In 1964 Belize got a new constitution for self-government, and the PUP, led by Price, won the elections in 1965, 1969, 1974 and 1979. The PUP was the leading force for full independence, achieved in 1981. Despite this success, the party did not fulfil the dreams of Belizeans for a more prosperous economy, a failure due in part to world market conditions beyond its control. The party was also seen as having been in power too long; there were charges of complacency and corruption.

The PUP's main opposition, the multi-party coalition later named the United Democratic Party (UDP), won the elections of 1984 under the slogan 'It's time for a change', and Manuel Esquivel replaced George Price as prime minister. Priding itself on its handling of the economy, the UDP gained more ground in municipal elections held at the end of the decade. But the early national election of September 1989 held a surprise: PUP took 15 seats in the House of Representatives while the UDP took only 13. The venerable George Price changed places with Manuel Esquivel, taking the prime minister's seat while Esquivel resumed his at the head of the opposition.

In 1993, the PUP called early elections, secure in its popularity and intent on extending its mandate for an additional three years. To most Belizeans, a PUP victory was a foregone conclusion. Many PUP adherents didn't bother to vote, but UDP supporters did, and the UDP squeaked to victory by the slimmest of margins – a single vote in some districts. Manuel Esquivel became prime minister again, while PUP supporters looked on in disbelief.

ECONOMY

Farming of fruits, vegetables and maize, and cattle ranching are important in the lands west and south of Belize City, as is forestry in the Maya Mountains. In the north are large sugar-cane plantations and processing plants. The cayes (islands) offshore depend on tourism and fishing for their income, but these two pursuits are sometimes in conflict. The spiny lobster and some types of fish have been seriously overexploited.

With many small, remote airstrips, a weak naval force and a sufficient number of compliant persons in official positions, Belize has also become a transshipment point for illicit drugs. Marijuana is said to be grown in industrial quantities near Orange Walk Town, and a certain amount of it obviously makes its way onto the streets of Belize City, along with some crack cocaine.

POPULATION & PEOPLE

The peoples of Mexico and Guatemala,

however diverse and interesting, are easily outdone by the fabulous, improbable ethnic diversity of little Belize, with a population of less than 200,000.

The Maya of Belize are of three linguistic groups. In the north, bordering Yucatán, they speak Yucatec and also probably Spanish. Use of the Mayan language is decreasing, that of Spanish is increasing, and English – the official language of Belize – is making inroads on both. The Mopan Maya live in Cayo district in western Belize, near the border town of Benque Viejo; the Kekchi live in far southern Belize in and around Punta Gorda. Pure-blooded Maya make up only about 10% of Belize's population, while fully one-third of Belize's people are mestizos, some of whom immigrated from Yucatán during the 19th century. In recent years, political refugees from Guatemala have been added to Belize's Mayan population.

The largest segment of Belizeans is Creole, descendants of the African slaves and British pirates who first settled here to exploit the country's forest riches. Racially mixed and proud of it, Creoles speak a fascinating, unique dialect of English which, though it sounds familiar at first, is utterly unintelligible to a speaker of standard English. Most of the people you meet and deal with in Belize City and Belmopan are Creole.

Southern Belize is the home of the Garinagus (or Garifunas, also called Black Caribs), who account for less than 10% of the population. The Garinagus are of South American Indian and African descent. They look more African than Indian, but they speak a language that's much more Indian than African, and their unique culture combines aspects of both peoples.

Besides the Maya, the mestizos, the Creoles and the Garinagus, Belize has small populations of Chinese restaurateurs and merchants, Lebanese traders, German-Swiss Mennonite farmers, Indians from the subcontinent, Europeans and North Americans.

LANGUAGE

Belize is English-speaking, officially. But the Black Creoles, its largest ethnic group (over half of the population) speak their own colourful creole dialect as well as standard English, and when they speak standard English it is with the musical lilt of the Caribbean. Spanish is the first language in the north and in some towns in the west. You may also hear Mayan, Chinese, Mennonite German, Lebanese Arabic, Hindi and Garifuna, the language of the Garinagu people of Stann Creek district.

Facts for the Visitor

VISAS & EMBASSIES
Belizean Embassies & Consulates
Some of the consulates mentioned here are actually honorary consuls or consular agencies. These posts can usually issue visas, but they refer more complicated matters to the nearest full consulate, or to the embassy's consular section.

Because Belize is a small country and far from rich, its diplomatic affairs overseas are usually handled by the British embassies and consulates. Here are the diplomatic posts in Canada, Germany and the USA:

Canada
> Belize High Commission to Canada, 112 Kent St, Suite 2005, Place de Ville, Tower B, Ottawa, Ontario K1P 5P2 (☎ (613) 232-73-89, 232-74-53, fax 232-58-04)

Germany
> Honorary Consul, Wolf Kahles, Lindenstrasse 46-48, 7120 Beitigheim, Bissingen (☎ (71) 42-39-25, fax 42-32-25)

USA
> Embassy, 2535 Massachusetts Ave NW, Washington DC 20008 (☎ (202) 332-96-36, fax (202) 332-67-41)
>
> *California*
> Honorary Consul, Mr Ernesto Castillo, 1650 South Wilton Place, Los Angeles, CA 90019 (☎ (213) 385-64-99)
>
> *Florida*
> Honorary Consul, Mr Theodore Gonzalez Fr, 8244 NW 68th St, Miami, FL 33166 (☎ (305) 477-36-36)
>
> *Louisiana*
> Honorary Consul, Mr Salvador A Figueroa, 837 Gravier St, Suite 310, New Orleans, LA 70112 (☎ (504) 523-77-50)
>
> *Michigan*
> Honorary Consul, Dr Lennox Pike, 27166 Selkirk, Southfield, MI 48706 (☎ (313) 559-74-07)
>
> *New York*
> Belize Mission to the United Nations, 820 Second Ave, New York, NY 10017 (☎ (212) 599-02-33, fax 599-33-91)
>
> *Texas*
> Belizean Honorary Consul, Mr Al Dugan, 1415 Louisiana, Suite 3100, Houston, TX 77002 (☎ (713) 658-02-07)

Belizean Visitor's Permit
British subjects and citizens of Commonwealth countries, citizens of the USA, and citizens of Belgium, Denmark, Finland, Greece, Holland, Mexico, Norway, Panama, Sweden, Switzerland, Tunisia, Turkey and Uruguay who have a valid passport and an onward or return airline ticket from Belize do not need to obtain a Belizean visa in advance. The rubber stamp made in your passport by the Belizean immigration official at the border or at the airport is your visitor's permit. If you look young and grotty or poverty-stricken, the immigration officer may demand to see your airline ticket out, and/or a sizable quantity of money or travellers' cheques before you're admitted.

Foreign Embassies & Consulates
A few countries have ambassadors resident in Belize. Many others appoint nonresident ambassadors who handle Belizean affairs from their home countries.

Belgium
> Consular Representative, Marelco Ltd, Queen St, Belize City (☎ (2) 4-57-69/73)

Canada
> Consulate, 83 North Front St, Belize City (☎ (2) 3-10-60)

Denmark
> Consulate, 13 Southern Foreshore, Belize City (☎ (2) 7-21-72)

European Union
> Commission of the European Union, corner Eyre and Hutson Sts, Belize City (☎ (2) 7-27-85, 3-20-70)

France
> Honorary Consul, 9 Barracks Rd, Belize City (☎ (2) 3-27-08)

Germany
> Honorary Consul, 123 Albert St, Belize City (☎ (2) 7-33-43)

Guatemala
> Embassy, Mile 6, Northern Highway, Ladyville (☎ (25) 26-34, 26-12)

Honduras
> Consulate, 91 North Front St, Belize City (☎ (2) 4-58-89)

Israel
Honorary Consul, 4 Albert St, Belize City (☎ (2) 7-39-91, 7-31-50)
Italy
Consular Representative, 18 Albert St, Belize City (☎ (2) 7-30-86)
Mexico
Embassy, 20 North Park St, Belize City (☎ (2) 3-01-93/4); note that the new Mexican Embassy is under construction in Belmopan
Netherlands
Honorary Consul, 14 Central American Blvd, Belize City (☎ (2) 7-36-12, 3-27-48)
Nicaragua
Honorary Consul, Mile 2½, Northern Highway, Belize City (☎ (2) 4-42-32)
Norway
Consulate General, 1 King St, Belize City (☎ (2) 7-70-31)
Panama
Consulate, 5481 Princess Margaret Drive, Belize City (☎ (2) 4-49-41)
Sweden
Honorary Consul, 11 Princess Margaret Drive, Belize City (☎ (2) 4-41-17)
UK
British High Commission, 34-36 Half Moon Ave, Roseapple St, Belmopan (☎ (8) 2-21-46/7)
USA
Embassy, 29 Gabourel Lane, Belize City (☎ (2) 7-71-61)

MONEY
Currency
The Belizean dollar (BZ$) bears the portrait of Queen Elizabeth II, and is divided into 100 cents. Coins are of one, five, 10, 25 and 50 cents, and one dollar; bills (notes) are all of the same size but differ in colour, and come in denominations of one, two, five, 10, 20, 50 and 100 dollars.

The Belizean dollar's value has been fixed for many years at US$1 = BZ$2, but recently there has been talk about devaluation.

You can exchange US and Canadian dollars and pounds sterling at any bank; other currencies are more difficult to exchange. Cash US dollars are accepted in many establishments, and some also accept US dollar travellers' cheques.

Because US dollars are so widely accepted, there's a problem with quoting prices. People quote prices in dollars, and you must make sure that you know whether the dollars are US or Belizean, otherwise you might end up being surprised with a bill twice as high as you had anticipated. You may find yourself asking 'US or Belize?' dozens of times each day. Often people will quote prices as '20 dollars Belize, 10 dollars US' just to make it clear.

Credit & ATM Cards
Major credit cards such as Visa and MasterCard (Eurocard, Access) are accepted at all airline and car-rental companies, and at the larger hotels and restaurants everywhere; American Express cards are often accepted at the fancier and larger places, and at some smaller ones. Smaller establishments which accept credit cards may add a surcharge (usually 5%) to your bill when doing so.

Cash cards, used to obtain cash from automated teller machines (ATMs), are just coming into use in Belize. There are few cash machines, and so far these work only with cards issued in Belize by the bank providing the machine.

Costs
Though a poor country, Belize is more expensive than you might anticipate. A small domestic economy and a large proportion of imports keep prices high. That fried-chicken dinner which cost US$3 in Guatemala costs US$5 in Belize, and is no better. That very basic waterless pension room, cheap in Guatemala and Mexico, costs US$7 to US$9 per person on Caye Caulker. You will find it difficult to live for less than US$15 per day for room and three meals in Belize; US$20 is a more realistic bottom-end figure, and US$25 makes life a lot easier.

Consumer Taxes
In Belize, a tax of 6% is added to your bill for hotel room, meals and drinks, but there is no value-added tax.

CLIMATE & WHEN TO GO
It is comfortably warm during the day in the Maya Mountains, cooling off a bit at night. The rest of the country is hot and humid day and night for most of the year. In the

rainforests of southern Belize, the humidity is very high because of the large amount of rainfall (almost four metres per year). Out on the cayes, tropical breezes waft constantly through the shady palm trees, providing natural air-conditioning; on the mainland, you swelter.

The busy winter season is from mid-December to April. As with the rest of the area, the dry season (November to May) is the better time to travel, but prices are lower and lodgings on the cayes easier to find in summer. If you do visit in summer (July to November), be aware that this is hurricane season. Belize City was badly damaged by hurricanes, with heavy loss of life, in 1931, 1961 and 1978.

TOURIST OFFICES

Belize has two tourist offices in Yucatán, Mexico (see the addresses below). For information in other countries, contact a Belizean diplomatic representative, or contact the Belize Tourist Board or Belize Tourism Industry Association in Belize City directly. For addresses, see Information in the Belize City section.

Cancún
Belize Tourist Board, Hotel Parador Lobby, Avenida Tulum 26, Supermanzana 5
Mérida
Belize Tourist Board, Calle 58 No 488-B at Calle 43, Mérida 97000

BUSINESS HOURS

Banking hours depend upon the individual bank, but most are open Monday to Friday from 8 am to noon or 1 pm; some are also open from 1 to 3 pm, and many have extra hours on Friday from 3 to 6 pm. Most banks and many businesses and shops are closed on Wednesday afternoon. Shops are usually open from 8 am to noon Monday to Saturday, and from 1 to 4 pm on Monday, Tuesday, Thursday and Friday. Some shops have evening hours from 7 to 9 pm on those days as well. Most businesses and offices are closed on Sunday.

POST & TELECOMMUNICATIONS
Post

Belize has the traditional red pillar letter boxes familiar to the British. An airmail letter sent to Canada or the USA may take anywhere from four to 14 days. Airmail letters to Europe take one to three weeks.

To claim Poste Restante mail, present your passport or other identification; there's no charge.

Telephone

The telephone system is operated by Belize Telecommunications Ltd, with offices (open from 8 am to noon and 1 to 4 pm Monday to Friday, and from 8 am to noon on Saturday) in major towns.

Local calls cost BZ$0.25 (about US$0.13). To call from one part of Belize to another, dial 0 (zero), then the one or two-digit area code, then the four or five-digit local number.

Here are Belize's area codes:

Ambergris Caye	26
Belize City	2
Belmopan/Spanish Lookout	8
Benque Viejo	93
Burrell Boom	28
Caye Caulker	22
Corozal	4
Dangriga	5
Independence/Placencia	6
Ladyville	25
Orange Walk	3
Punta Gorda	7
San Ignacio	92

Calls dialled direct (no operator) from Belize to other western hemisphere countries cost BZ$3.20 (US$1.60) per minute; to Europe, BZ$6 (US$3) per minute; to all other countries, BZ$8 (US$4) per minute. The best plan for calling internationally from Belize is to dial your call direct from a telephone office; or you can call collect from your hotel. Be sure to ask before you call what the charges (and any hotel surcharges) may be. Here are some useful numbers:

BELIZE

Directory assistance	113
Local & regional operator	114
Long-distance (trunk) operator	110
International operator	115
Fire & Ambulance	90
Police	911

To place a collect call, dial the international operator (115), give the number you want to call and the number you're calling from, and the operator will place the call and ring you back when it goes through. Rates for operator-assisted calls are the same as for direct-dial calls, but the minimum initial calling period is three minutes.

The large American long-distance companies provide international service as well. Rates for these services may be higher than calling directly via BTL lines, however. To reach AT&T's USADirect service, dial 555; this service is not available from coin-operated telephones. For Sprint Express, dial 556; from coin-operated telephones, dial *4 (that's asterisk-4). MCI Call USA service is not yet available from Belize.

Fax

Fax service is available from many hotels and businesses.

MEDIA

Belizean newspapers are small in size, circulation and interest. Most are supported by one political party or another, so much space is devoted to political diatribe.

Foreign newspapers such as the *Miami Herald* are difficult to find. Few newsstands – even those in the luxury hotels and resorts – carry current foreign periodicals.

Belize Review is the local effort at a monthly ecotourism magazine, priced at US$3 for about 40 pages. The magazine is published by Belize Review Ltd (☎ (2) 7-48-92, fax 7-77-86), 7 Church St, Belize City.

Radio Belize provides local news and rap music on the AM (middle wave) band.

There are two local television stations. Programming consists mainly of rebroadcast US satellite feeds, with a few hours of local content such as ceremonies and special sports events.

FOOD

Cooking in Belize is mostly borrowed – from the UK, from the Caribbean, from Mexico, from the USA. Being a young, small, somewhat isolated and relatively poor country, Belize never developed its own elaborate native cuisine. Local dishes such as *boil-up* rarely appear on restaurant menus. Even so, there is some good food to be had.

The traditional staple of the Belizean diet is rice and beans. As a Belizean wag described it to me on my first visit years ago, 'We eat a lot of rice and beans in Belize, and when we get tired of that, we eat beans and rice'. The mixed rice and red beans usually come with other ingredients – chicken, pork, beef, fish, vegetables, even lobster – plus some spices and condiments like coconut milk. 'Stew beans with rice' is stewed beans on one side of the plate, boiled rice on the other side, and chicken, beef or pork on top. For garnish, sometimes you'll get slices of fried plantain (cooking banana).

More exotic traditional foods include armadillo, venison, and *gibnut* or *paca*, a small brown-spotted rodent similar to a guinea pig. These are served more as a curiosity than as staples of the diet.

Getting There & Around

Getting There & Away

You can get to Belize by air, road or boat.

AIR

International air routes to Belize City tend to go through Miami, Houston or Los Angeles. The most convenient flight from many points is Continental's nonstop from Houston to Belize City. American Airlines flies from Miami, and TACA from Los Angeles.

American Airlines (☎ (2) 3-25-22/3/4/5/6; fax 3-17-30), corner of New Rd and Queen St (PO Box 1680), Belize City

Continental (☎ (2) 7-83-09, 7-84-63; fax 7-81-14), 32 Albert St, in a little Hindu-esque 'temple'

SAHSA (☎ (2) 7-70-80, 7-20-57; fax 3-07-95), the Honduran airline, corner of New Rd and Queen St, Belize City

TACA (☎ (2) 7-73-63; 7-71-85, fax 7-52-13), the Costa Rican airline, is at 41 Albert St (Belize Global Travel)

In the past there has been service by small regional airlines between Cancún and Belize City, and though there is currently no service operating on this route, it may be revived in future as traffic increases.

Several small airlines fly between Flores and Belize City, with connections to and from Guatemala City. Tropic Air has tours by air Monday to Friday from San Pedro (US$200) at 8 am and 2 pm, departing from Belize City's Goldson International Airport (US$155 return) at 8.30 am and 2.30 pm, returning from Flores Monday to Friday at 9.30 am and 3.30 pm. The tour price includes air fare, ground transport to Tikal, lunch, and a guided tour of the archaeological site; departure taxes are extra.

A departure tax of BZ$20 (US$10) and an airport security fee of BZ$2.50 (US$1.25) are levied on travellers departing by air to foreign destinations.

BUS

Several companies operate direct buses from Chetumal (Mexico) to Belize City. Other companies run between Belize City and Benque Viejo del Carmen on the Guatemalan border, connecting with Guatemalan buses headed for Flores (near Tikal). Some of these lines arrange connections so that you can travel between Flores and Chetumal directly, with only brief stops in Belize to change buses. For details see under Chetumal in the Yucatán section and under Flores in the Guatemala section.

Exit tax at Belizean land border-crossing points is BZ$1 (US$0.50).

BOAT

Scheduled small passenger boats ply the waters between Punta Gorda, in southern Belize, and Puerto Barrios, in eastern Guatemala. Boats can be hired for special trips, and if there are enough passengers to split the cost, it can be reasonable. See the Punta Gorda and Puerto Barrios sections for details.

Getting Around

Belize is a small country with a few basic transportation routes. Here is information for travelling to most destinations in the country.

AIR

With few paved roads, Belize depends greatly on small aeroplanes (de Havilland Twin Otter, Cessna, etc) for fast, reliable transport within the country.

Belize City has two airports. Philip S W Goldson International Airport (BZE), at Ladyville, 16 km north-west of the centre, handles all international flights. The Municipal Airport (TZA) is 2.5 km north of the city centre, on the shore. Most local flights will stop and pick you up at either airport, but fares are almost always lower from Municipal, so if you have a choice use that one.

There are two main domestic air routes which the small aeroplanes follow from Belize City: Belize City-Caye Chapel-Caye Caulker-San Pedro-Corozal and return along the reverse route; and Belize City-Dangriga-Placencia/Big Creek-Punta Gorda and return along the reverse route. Often the planes do not stop if they have no passengers to put down, or reservations for passengers to pick up, so be sure to reserve your seat in advance whenever possible.

Airline Companies

Here are the main Belizean airline companies:

Tropic Air (☎ (26) 20-12, 21-17, 20-29, fax (26) 23-38), PO Box 20, San Pedro, Ambergris Caye, is the largest and most active of Belize's small airlines. Their telephone number in Belize City is (2) 4-56-71. For information in the USA contact Tropic Air (☎ (800) 422-3435, (713) 440-1867), PO Box 42808-236, Houston, TX 77242.

Maya Airways (☎ (2) 7-72-15, 7-23-13, fax 3-05-85), 6 Fort St (PO Box 458), Belize City, has a similar schedule of flights to points in Belize. For information in the USA call ☎ (800) 552-3419.

Island Air (☎ (2) 3-11-40 in Belize City, (26) 24-35 in San Pedro, Ambergris Caye) flies between Belize City and San Pedro via Caye Chapel and Caye Caulker.

Skybird Air Services (☎ (2) 3-25-96, 3-37-44 in Belize City, (26) 2200 in San Pedro) also flies the route between Belize City and San Pedro via Caye Chapel and Caye Caulker.

Aerovías (☎ (2) 7-54-45; in the USA ☎ (305) 883-1345), the Guatemalan regional airline, operates several flights per week between Belize City's Goldson International Airport and Flores (near Tikal) in Guatemala (US$50 one way), with onward connections to Guatemala City. For details, see Flores in the El Petén chapter of the Guatemala section.

Domestic Flights

Here is information on flights from Belize City to various points. Fares are one way from Municipal/International:

Big Creek; BGK – see Placencia.

Caye Caulker; CLK/CKR (10 minutes, US$20/35) – flights to San Pedro stop at Caye Caulker on request; see San Pedro.

Caye Chapel; CYC (10 minutes, US$20/35) – flights to San Pedro stop at Caye Chapel on request; see San Pedro.

Corozal; CZH (one to 1½ hours, US$50/65) – Tropic Air's 8.30 am and 2.30 pm flights from Belize City to Caye Chapel, Caye Caulker and San Pedro continue to Corozal, then turn around and return from Corozal at 10.15 am and 3.30 pm via San Pedro, Caye Caulker and Caye Chapel to Belize City.

Dangriga; DGA (20 minutes, US$25/38) – Maya Airways flies from Belize City's Municipal Airport at 6.30, 7 and 9 am, noon and 2 and 3.45 pm; Tropic Air has one daily flight, at 7.30 am.

Placencia; PLA (25 to 35 minutes, US$47/55) – flights designated as to Placencia or Big Creek may in fact land at any of three airstrips: Placencia (PLA), on the Placencia peninsula two km north of Placencia village; Big Creek, on the west side of the Placencia lagoon just south of Independence; or Savannah, five km inland west of Big Creek. Transport from Savannah and Big Creek to Placencia can be expensive and difficult, even impossible, especially in the afternoon and evening. Make sure your flight lands right at Placencia, on the peninsula just south of the Rum Point Inn. Maya Airways operates five flights daily (only one on Sunday) from Belize City via Dangriga; Tropic Air has flights from Belize City at 8.30 am and 1.30 and 4.30 pm, returning to Belize City at 7.20 and 9.50 am and 2.50 pm.

Punta Gorda; PND (55 minutes, US$60/70) – departures from Belize City are the same as for Placencia. Tropic Air has three flights per day and Maya Airways has four (two on Sunday). Tropic Air flights depart from Punta Gorda for Belize City at 9.25 am and 2.25 and 5.25 pm; Maya Airways flights leave Punta Gorda at 8 and 10.25 am and 1.25 and 3.25 pm.

San Pedro, Ambergris Caye; SPR (20 minutes, US$20/35) – Tropic Air flies every hour on the half-hour from 7.30 am to 5 pm, stopping at Caye Chapel and Caye Caulker on request. The 8.30 am and 2.30 pm flights continue from San Pedro to Corozal. Island Air has nine, Maya Airways five and Skybird Air Services six flights daily between Belize City and San Pedro.

BUS

Most Belizean buses are used American schoolbuses. The larger companies operate frequent buses along the country's three major roads. Smaller village lines tend to be run on marketeers' schedules: from the smaller town to the larger town in the morning, returning in the afternoon. Trucks willing to take on passengers go to some remote sites, travelling on rough roads which are sometimes impassable after heavy rains.

Each major bus company has its own terminals. Belize City's bus terminals are near the Pound Yard Bridge, along or near the Collett Canal on West Collett Canal St, East Collett Canal St, or neighbouring streets. This is a rundown area not good for walking at night; take a taxi.

Batty Brothers Bus Service (☎ (2) 7-71-46), 54 East Collett Canal St, operates buses along the Northern Highway to Orange Walk, Corozal and Chetumal (Mexico), and Venus Bus Lines (☎ (2) 7-33-54, 7-73-90), Magazine Rd, operates buses along similar routes. Both Urbina's Bus Service and Escalante's Bus Service run between Belize City and Chetumal via Orange Walk and Corozal.

Novelo's Bus Service (☎ (2) 7-73-72), 19 West Collett Canal St, is the line to take to Belmopan, San Ignacio, Xunantunich, Benque Viejo and the Guatemalan border at Melchor de Mencos.

Z-Line Bus Service (☎ (2) 7-39-37) runs buses south to Dangriga, Big Creek (for Placencia) and Punta Gorda, operating from the Venus Bus Lines terminal on Magazine Rd in Belize City.

Pilferage of luggage is a problem, particularly on the Punta Gorda route. Give your luggage only to the bus driver or conductor, and watch as it is stored. Be there when the bus is unloaded to retrieve your luggage at once.

Here are the details on buses from Belize City to major destinations:

Belmopan (84 km, 1½ hours, US$2) – see Benque Viejo.

Benque Viejo (131 km, four hours, US$3) – Novelo's operates buses from Belize City to Belmopan, San Ignacio and Benque Viejo every hour on the hour daily from 11 am to 7 pm (noon to 5 pm on Sunday). Batty Brothers operates six morning buses westward between 5 and 10.15 am. Several of these go all the way to Melchor de Mencos in Guatemala. Returning from Benque/Melchor,

buses to San Ignacio, Belmopan and Belize City start at 6 am; the last bus leaves at 3.30 pm.

Chetumal, Mexico (160 km, four hours, express 3¼ hours, US$5) – Venus Bus Lines has buses departing from Belize City every hour on the hour from noon to 7 pm; departures from Chetumal are hourly from 4 to 10 am. Batty's has buses every two hours on the hour for the same price. Urbina's and Escalante's also have frequent services.

Corozal (155 km, 3½ hours, US$4) – virtually all Batty's and Venus buses to and from Chetumal stop in Corozal, and there are also several additional buses. There are frequent southbound buses in the morning but few in the afternoon; almost all northbound buses depart from Belize City in the afternoon.

Dangriga (170 km, five hours, US$5.50) – Z-Line has five buses daily (four on Sunday).

Flores, Guatemala (235 km, five hours, US$20) – a minibus departs from the Texaco station on North Front St, near the north-east end of the Swing Bridge, at 10 am for Flores. Some boats from the cayes can get you back to Belize City in time to catch it. Otherwise, take a bus to Melchor de Mencos (see Benque Viejo), and transfer to a Guatemalan bus.

Independence (242 km, seven hours, US$7) – buses bound for Punta Gorda stop at Independencia, from whence you may be able to find a boat over to Placencia. The boats can be expensive or difficult to find; the shuttle bus from Dangriga direct to Placencia along the peninsula is cheaper and more dependable.

Placencia (260 km, eight hours, US$9) – take a Z-Line bus to Dangriga, then the shuttle bus from The Hub guesthouse (Monday, Wednesday, Friday and Saturday at 2 pm) to Placencia.

Melchor de Mencos, Guatemala (135 km, 4¼ hours, US$3) – see Benque Viejo.

Orange Walk (94 km, two hours, US$3) – same schedule as for Chetumal.

Punta Gorda (339 km, eight hours, US$8) – Z-Line has two buses daily, at 8 am and 3 pm. Return buses from Punta Gorda via Independencia to Belize City depart at 5 and 11 am.

San Ignacio (116 km, three hours, US$2.75) – see Benque Viejo.

CAR

Belize has two good asphalt-paved two-lane roads: the Northern Highway between the Mexican border near Corozal Town and Belize City, and the Western Highway between Belize City and the Guatemalan border at Benque Viejo del Carmen. Most other roads are narrow one or two-lane dirt roads; many are impassable after heavy rains.

Anyone who must drive a lot in Belize has a 4WD vehicle: Jeep, Land Rover, Trooper or high-clearance pick-up truck. If you bring your own vehicle or rent one in Belize, keep in mind that sites off the main roads may be accessible only by 4WD, especially between May and November.

Fuel stations are found in the larger towns and along the major roads. Gasoline/petrol is usually sold by the US gallon (3.79 litres) for about US$2.50; that's US$0.66 per litre. Unleaded fuel is currently unavailable in Belize.

Rental

The cost of renting a car in Belize has come down substantially in recent years. Especially if you are travelling with two to four people, the cost is now reasonable. Generally, renters must be at least 25 years of age, have a valid driving licence, and pay by credit card or leave a large cash deposit. Cars may not normally be driven out of Belize.

Note that there is no need to rent a car for travel on any of the cayes. Bicycles, motorbikes and electric golf carts are for rent in San Pedro (Ambergris Caye) and Caye Caulker, and these are sufficient if your feet get tired.

Your rental car will probably have a speedometer and odometer marked in km, though distances and speed limits are traditionally expressed in miles and miles per hour here.

On the mainland, most car-rental companies have representatives at the Goldson International Airport; many will also deliver or take return of cars at Municipal Airport.

The best rental rates are currently at Budget Rent-a-Car (☎ (2) 3-24-35, 3-39-86, fax 3-02-37), 771 Bella Vista (PO Box 863), Belize City, opposite the Belize Biltmore Plaza Hotel on the Northern Highway, 4.5 km north of central Belize City. Most of its Suzuki and Vitara cars have 4WD, AM-FM cassette radios and air-conditioning, and are priced from US$50 to US$90 per day (US$300 to US$540 per week) with unlimited kilometrage. The Collision Damage Waiver costs an additional US$12 per day. Budget's service is said to be excellent.

Other companies include Avis (☎ (2) 3-19-87, fax 3-02-25), 50 Vernon St near the New Bridge, and at the Radisson Fort George Hotel; Hertz (☎ (2) 3-27-10, fax 3-20-53), PO Box 445, Belize City, four km north of the centre along the Northern Highway; and National (☎ (2) 3-15-87, 3-37-93, fax 3-15-86), 126 Freetown Rd, Belize City, with offices at the Belize Biltmore Plaza Hotel.

Motor Vehicle Insurance

Liability insurance is required in Belize, and you must have it for the customs officer to approve the temporary importation of your car. It can usually be bought at booths just across the border in Belize for about US$1 per day. Note that the booths are generally closed on Sunday, meaning no insurance is sold that day and no temporary import permits are issued. If you're crossing with a car, try to do it in the morning on a weekday.

Driving in Belize

Except in Cayo district, there are few mileage or directional signs to point the way to towns or villages. One-way streets are often unmarked.

MOTORBIKE & BICYCLE
Rental

Bike Belize (☎ (2) 3-38-55, fax 3-19-63), 74 Cleghorn St, Belize City, at the Bakadeer Inn, rents motorised trailbikes (US$45 a day, US$240 a week), minibikes and motor scooters (US$30 a day, US$76 for three days), as well as bicycles (US$8 a day, US$20 for three days), and can offer advice on trekking routes and camping places.

BOAT

Fast motor launches zoom between Belize City, Caye Chapel, Caye Caulker and Ambergris Caye frequently every day.

Preparations

This boat trip is usually fast, windy and

bumpy; it is not particularly comfortable. You will be in an open boat with no shade for at least 45 minutes, so provide yourself with sunscreen, a hat and/or clothing to protect you from the sun and the spray. If you sit in the bow there's less spray, but you bang down harder when you come over a wave. Sitting in the stern gives a smoother ride, but you may get dampened by spray.

Choosing a Boat

Launches tie up by the A & R Texaco fuel station on North Front St, two blocks northwest of the Swing Bridge. Most boats leave Belize City between 8 and 10 am, and stop at Caye Chapel on the way to Caye Caulker; a few go on to San Pedro (on Ambergris Caye). After 10 am, outbound boats are more difficult to find. It is preferable to take a morning boat, as these are the ones in better condition. The few boats which wait around for passengers in the afternoon are usually in worse condition. I have heard from several readers who have left on afternoon boats and have been stranded on sand bars or in open water as night fell, after inexperienced captains lost their way or unseaworthy boats lost power.

As you walk toward the boats by the Texaco station, hawkers will approach to lead you to this or that boat, swearing that it is leaving right away and that it's the fastest. Don't listen to them. Look the boats over and choose only a strong, seaworthy boat in good condition with a big motor (preferably two). I always look for one with a two-way radio as well. This may be important, as these boats carry neither emergency equipment nor life jackets. The best boats may charge a bit more, but it's worth it for the peace of mind. Above all, refuse to sail in an overloaded craft.

The fare for the voyage to Caye Caulker is usually US$8 to US$10 one way, but may be a bit higher depending upon the craft, the season, the number of people, or any of a dozen other factors. The trip against the wind takes 40 minutes to one hour, depending upon the speed of the boat. Ask the price before you board the boat, and don't pay until you're safely off the boat at your destination; legitimate boat owners won't ask you to pay before then.

Across Haulover Creek from the Texaco station, just west of the Swing Bridge on Regent St West, is the dock for the Thunderbolt Express and Libra Express boats (☎ in San Pedro (026) 22-17, 21-59) which make the run between San Pedro on Ambergris Caye and Belize City, stopping at Caye Caulker and Caye Chapel along the way. *Thunderbolt* leaves San Pedro each morning at 7 am, reaches Belize City by 9 am, and departs from Belize City for the voyage back to San Pedro at 4 pm (1 pm on Saturday). *Libra* leaves San Pedro at 7.30 am and returns from Belize City at 1 pm. Fares are US$9.50 from Belize City to Caye Caulker, US$14 to San Pedro. In San Pedro, the Express ticket office is on Almond St.

Triple J ties up right at the north-eastern end of the Swing Bridge. It leaves Belize City at 9 am for the trip to San Pedro (Ambergris), and leaves Pedro for Belize City at 3 pm.

Andrea I and *Andrea II* (☎ (2) 7-49-88) leave Belize City from Southern Foreshore (by the Bellevue Hotel) for San Pedro, Ambergris Caye (☎ (26) 25-78) at 4 pm Monday to Friday (1 pm on Saturday, no boat on Sunday); the return trip to Belize City leaves San Pedro at 7 am. The fare is US$14/20 one way/return, and the voyage takes 1¼ to 1½ hours.

Belize City

Ramshackle, colourful, fascinating, daunting, homely – these are only a few of the words that can be used to describe the country's biggest city (population 80,000) and former capital. The tropical storms which periodically razed the town in the 19th and early 20th centuries still arrive to do damage to its ageing wooden buildings, but they also flush out the open drainage canals, redolent with pollution, which crisscross the town. When there's no storm, Belize City bustles and swelters.

Few people come to Belize City for a holiday; most people pass through while changing buses or planes. If you need a hospital, a spare part for a car or a new sleeping bag, you'll come to Belize City to get it.

ORIENTATION

Haulover Creek, a branch of the Belize River, runs through the middle of the city, separating the commercial centre (Albert, Regent, King and Orange Sts) from the slightly more genteel residential and hotel district of Fort George to the north-east. Hotels and guesthouses are found on both sides of the Swing Bridge.

Albert St (in the centre) and Queen St (in the Fort George and King's Park neighbourhoods) are joined by the Swing Bridge across Haulover Creek. It seems as though everything and everybody in Belize City crosses the Swing Bridge at least once a day. The bridge, a product of Liverpool's ironworks (1923), is swung open daily at 5.30 am and 5.30 pm to let tall-masted boats through. When the Swing Bridge is open, virtually all vehicular traffic in the centre of the city grinds to a halt in hopeless gridlock.

Each of Belize's bus companies has its own terminal. Most are on the west side of West Collett Canal St near Cemetery Rd. See Getting There & Away at the end of this chapter for details.

INFORMATION
Tourist Offices

The Belize Tourist Board (☎ (2) 7-72-13, 7-32-55; fax 7-74-90), 83 North Front St (PO Box 325), just a few steps south of the post office, is open from 8 am to noon and 1 to 5 pm Monday to Thursday and until 4.30 pm on Friday; it's closed on weekends.

The Belize Tourism Industry Association (☎ (2) 7-57-17, 7-87-09, fax 7-87-10), 99 Albert St (PO Box 62), can provide information about its members, which include most of the country's hotels, restaurants, tour operators and other travel-related businesses. Hours are Monday to Friday from 8.30 am to noon and 1 to 4.30 pm (till 4 pm on Friday).

Money

The Bank of Nova Scotia (☎ (2) 7-70-27/8/9), on Albert St, is open Monday to Friday from 8 am to 1 pm, and on Friday afternoon from 3 to 6 pm.

The Atlantic Bank Limited (☎ (2) 7-71-24), 6 Albert St, is open Monday, Tuesday and Thursday from 8 am to noon and 1 to 3 pm, on Wednesday from 8 am to 1 pm and on Friday from 8 am to 1 pm and 3 to 6 pm.

Also on Albert St is the prominent Belize Bank (☎ (2) 7-71-32/3/4/5), 60 Market Square (facing the Swing Bridge), and Barclay's Bank (☎ (2) 7-72-11), 21 Albert St.

Post & Telecommunications

The main post office is at the northern end of the Swing Bridge, at the intersection of Queen and North Front Sts. Hours are 8 am to noon and 1 to 5 pm daily. If you want to pick up mail at the American Express office, it's at Belize Global Travel Service (☎ (2) 7-73-63/4), 41 Albert St (PO Box 244).

Belize Telecommunications Limited, or BTL (☎ (2) 7-70-85), 1 Church St, runs all of Belize's telephones, and does it pretty

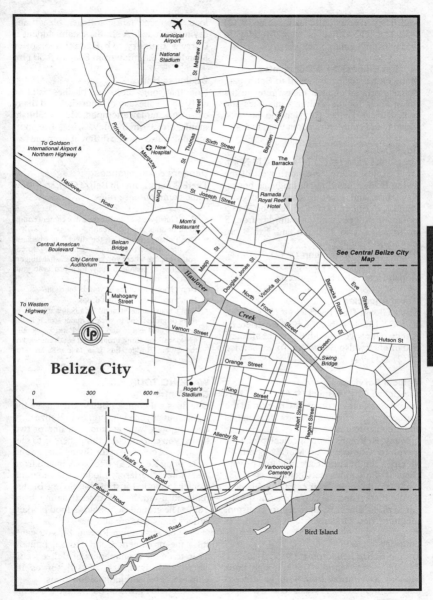

Belize City

BELIZE

well. They have a public fax machine (☎ (2) 4-52-11). The office is open Monday to Friday from 8 am to 5 pm.

Foreign Embassies & Consulates
Many embassies have moved to Belmopan, Belize's official capital. Please refer to the list in Facts for the Visitor. Embassies and consulates in Belize City tend to be open Monday to Friday from about 9 am to noon.

Bookshops
The Book Center (☎ (2) 7-74-57), 114 North Front St, just a few steps north-west of the Swing Bridge, has English-language books, magazines and greeting cards. Hours are Monday to Friday from 8 am to noon, 1 to 5 pm and 7 to 9 pm, and on Saturday from 8 am to noon, 1 to 4.30 pm and 7 to 9 pm (closed on Sunday).

The Belize Book Shop (☎ (2) 7-20-54), Regent St and Rectory Lane, across from the Mopan Hotel, also has a selection of books.

Travel Agencies
Belize Global Travel Service (☎ (2) 7-73-64, fax 7-52-13), 41 Albert St, is an experienced agency which works with the major airlines. You might try also Belize Air Travel Service (☎ (2) 7-31-74), 28 Regent St.

Medical Services
The Belize City Hospital (☎ (2) 7-72-51) is on Eve St near the corner of Craig St, in the northern part of town. A new hospital is under construction.

Many Belizeans with medical problems travel to Chetumal or Mérida (both in Mexico) for treatment. A modern, private clinic is the Clinica de Chetumal (☎ (983) 2-65-08), Avenida Juárez, Chetumal, near the old market and the city's other hospitals. For serious illnesses, they fly to Houston, Miami or New Orleans.

Laundry
Try the Belize Laundromat (☎ (2) 3-11-17), 7 Craig St near Marin's Travel Lodge, open Monday to Saturday from 8 am to 5.15 pm (closed on Sunday). A wash costs US$5 per load, detergent, fabric softener, bleach and drying included. A similar establishment is Carry's Laundry, 41 Hyde Lane, open Monday to Saturday from 8 am to 5.30 pm.

Business Hours
Note that some shops and businesses close early on Wednesday or Thursday, and many close on Saturday afternoon. Most establishments close on Sunday, when transport schedules also may be different from the rest of the week.

Dangers & Annoyances
There is petty crime in Belize City, so follow some commonsense rules:

- Don't flash wads of cash, expensive camera equipment or other signs of wealth.
- Don't change money on the street – not because it's illegal, but because changing money forces you to expose where you keep your cash. Muggers will offer to change money, then just grab your cash and run off.
- Don't leave valuables in your hotel room.
- Don't use or deal in illicit drugs.
- Don't walk alone at night. It's better to walk in pairs or groups and to stick to major streets in the centre, Fort George and King's Park. Especially avoid walking along Front Street south and east of the Swing Bridge; this is a favourite area for muggers.

WALKING TOUR
City Centre
One does not come to Belize City to see the sights, but anyone who comes to Belize City does enjoy a walk around – in one or two hours, you can see everything there is to see.

Start – of course – at the Swing Bridge and walk along Regent St, one block inland from the shore. The large, modern Commercial Center to the left just off the Swing Bridge replaced a ramshackle market dating from 1820. The ground floor holds a food market; offices and shops are above.

As you start down Regent St, you can't miss the prominent Court House, built in 1926 to be the headquarters of Belize's colonial administrators. It still serves its administrative and judicial functions.

Battlefield Park is on the right just past the

Court House. Always busy with vendors, loungers, con men and other slice-of-life segments of Belize City society, the park offers welcome shade in the sweltering midday heat.

Turn left just past the Court House and walk one long block to the waterfront street, called Southern Foreshore, to find the Bliss Institute. Baron Bliss was an Englishman with a happy name and a Portuguese title who came to Belize on his yacht to fish. He seems to have fallen in love with Belize without ever having set foot on shore. When he died – not too long after his arrival – he left the bulk of his wealth in trust to the people of Belize. Income from the trust has paid for roads, market buildings, schools, cultural centres and many other worthwhile projects over the years.

The Bliss Institute (☎ (2) 7-72-67) is open Monday to Friday from 8.30 am to noon and 2 to 8 pm, and on Saturday from 8 am to noon (closed on Sunday). Belize City's prime cultural institution, it is home to the National Arts Council, which stages periodic exhibits, concerts and theatrical works. There's a small display of artefacts from the Mayan archaeological site at Caracol and, upstairs, the National Library.

Continue walking south to the end of Southern Foreshore, then south on Regent St to reach Government House (1814), the residence of the governor-general. Belize attained independence within the British Commonwealth in 1981, and since that time the job has been purely ceremonial. Down beyond Government House is Bird Island, a recreation area accessible only on foot. A sign above the gateway declares that it offers 'entertainment for all except troublemakers'.

Inland from Government House, at the corner of Albert and Regent Sts, is St John's Cathedral, the oldest and most important Anglican church in Central America, dating from 1847.

A block south-west of the cathedral is Yarborough Cemetery, whose gravestones outline the turbulent history of Belize back to 1781.

Walk back to the Swing Bridge northward along Albert St. You'll pass the offices of the Belize Tourism Industry Association and Continental Airlines (in an unlikely little Hindu fantasy 'temple'). Busy Albert St is the city's main commercial thoroughfare.

Northern Neighbourhoods

Cross the Swing Bridge heading north and you'll come face-to-face with the wood-frame Paslow Building, which houses the city's main post office. Go straight along Queen St to see the city's quaint wooden police station and, eventually, the US Embassy, in the Fort George neighbourhood among some pretty Victorian houses.

Make your way to the southern tip of the peninsula. You pass through the luxury hotel district and emerge at the Baron Bliss Memorial, next to the Fort George lighthouse. There's a small park here and a good view of the water and the city.

Walk north around the point, pass the Radisson Fort George Hotel on your left and walk up Marine Parade to Memorial Park, next to the Chateau Caribbean hotel and the Mexican Embassy. The park's patch of green lawn is a welcome sight.

PLACES TO STAY – BOTTOM END

The cheapest hotels in Belize City are often not safe because of break-ins and drug dealing. I've chosen the places below for relative safety as well as price. If one should prove unsafe, or if you find a good, safe, cheap place, please let me know. The 6% lodging tax has been included in the prices given below.

Best all round, and often full, is the six-room *Sea Side Guest House* (☎ (2) 7-83-39), 3 Prince St, on the upper floor, between Southern Foreshore and Regent St. Sea Side has the friendly atmosphere and low prices of a youth hostel, a quiet location in one of the city's better districts, and clean, decent rooms. Bunks in shared rooms cost US$9, or pay US$14/19 for a single/double. Meals are good; book in advance. Arrive early in the

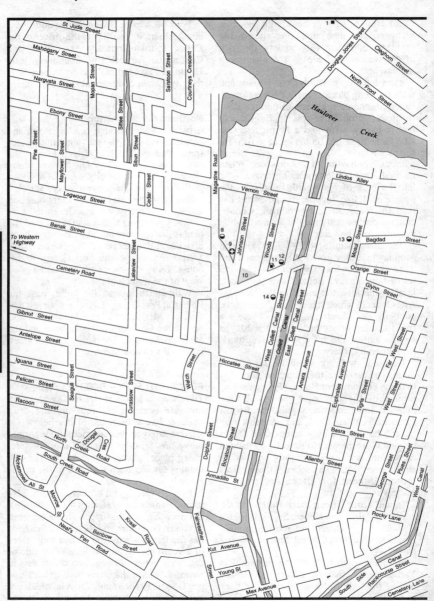

Central Belize City

BELIZE

0   250   500 m

PLACES TO STAY

1 Bakadeer Inn
4 Freddie's Guest House
6 Marin's Travelodge
7 Royal Orchid Hotel
15 North Front Street Guest House
16 Bon Aventure Hotel
17 Mira Rio Hotel
18 Riverside Hotel
19 Glenthorne Manor
25 Belize Guest House
35 Eyre Street Guest House
39 Chateau Caribbean Hotel
40 Radisson Fort George Hotel
42 Colton House
43 Bliss Hotel
44 Isabel Guest House
56 Hotel El Centro
64 Sea Side Guest House
65 Bellevue Hotel
72 Hotel Mopan

PLACES TO EAT

21 Kee's Bakery
22 Golden Dragon Restaurant
23 Pete's Pastries
26 Pearl's Pizzería
28 Celebrations
47 Holiday Ice Cream Parlour

57 Macy's
58 Bluebird Ice Cream Parlour
60 Dit's Restaurant
63 GG's Café & Patio
68 Pete's Pastries
69 New Horizon Restaurant

OTHER

1 Bike Belize
2 Clock Tower
3 Methodist Church
5 Old Belize City Hospital
8 Venus & Z-Line Bus Station
9 Matron Roberts Health Centre
10 Constitution Park
11 Esso Fuel Station
12 Urbina's Bus Stop
13 Batty Brothers Bus Station
14 Novelo's Bus Station
20 American Airlines & TAN-SAHSA
24 US Embassy
27 Police Headquarters
29 Upstairs Café
30 Catholic Church
31 Boats to Caye Caulker & Ambergris Caye
32 Thunderbolt & Libra Express (Boats to Caye Caulker & Ambergris Caye)

33 Triple J Boat Dock
34 Main Post Office (Paslow Building)
36 Mexican Embassy
37 Belize Tourist Board & Canadian Consulate
38 Memorial Park
41 Baron Bliss Memorial
45 Commercial Centre
46 Market Square
48 Belize Bank
49 Barclays Bank
50 Taxi Stand
51 Battlefield Park
52 Court House
53 Belize Telecommunications Ltd
54 Bliss Institute
55 Bank of Nova Scotia
59 Atlantic Bank
61 Belize Global Travel Service
62 Italian Consular Agency
66 Andrea Boats to Ambergris Caye
67 Belize Air Travel Service
70 Methodist Church
71 Continental Airlines
73 Belize Tourism Industry Association
74 St John's Cathedral
75 Playground
76 Government House
77 German Consulate

morning for the best chance of getting a bed here.

Isabel Guest House (☎ (2) 7-31-39), PO Box 362, is above Matus Store overlooking Market Square, but is entered by a rear stairway – walk around the Central Drug Store to the back and follow the signs. Clean and family-run, it offers double rooms with shower for US$22.

Eyre Street Guest House (☎ (2) 7-77-24), 7 Eyre St, is a nice quiet old Fort George house, restored but simple and homey, with waterless rooms priced at US$14/22 a single/double (US$32 with private shower).

Freddie's Guest House (☎ (2) 4-43-96), 86 Eve St, is the tidiest guesthouse in Belize. Freddie and Tona Griffith keep their three small guestrooms spotless; the showers gleam and shine. Two rooms share one bath and cost US$19 a double; the room with private bath costs US$22.

North Front Street Guest House (☎ (2) 7-75-95), 124 North Front St, just east of Pickstock St, has seen better days, but is still a favourite of low-budget travellers, despite the noisy street and nightclub nearby. Bathrooms are shared, and bunks in the eight rooms cost US$6 to US$7.50. Double rooms cost US$13. Breakfast and dinner are served if you order ahead. Check out the bulletin board.

There are other cheap hotels in this area, including the *Riverside Hotel*, and the *Mira Rio Hotel* (☎ (2) 4-49-70), 59 North Front St. The seven rooms here are slightly more expensive but come with sink and toilet. The bar overlooks Haulover Creek. *Bon Aventure Hotel* (☎ (2) 4-42-48, 4-41-34; fax 3-11-34), 122 North Front St, right next to the North Front St Guest House, has nine rooms at US$12 a double (shared bath) and US$22 a double (private bath).

Marin's Travelodge (☎ (2) 4-51-66), 6 Craig St, is on the upper floor of a fairly well-kept yellow wooden Caribbean house with a comfy swing on the verandah and seven rooms for rent. Shared showers are clean, and the price for the basic, plain, clean rooms is right – US$6/8 a single/double.

PLACES TO STAY – MIDDLE

Belize City's prettiest guesthouse is undoubtedly *Colton House* (☎ (2) 4-46-66), 9 Cork St, near the Radisson Fort George Hotel. The gracious 60-year-old wooden colonial house has been beautifully restored. Large, airy, cheerful rooms cost US$32/37 a single/double with shared bath, US$37/42 with private bath; add US$5 for air-conditioning. Morning coffee is served, but no meals.

Glenthorne Manor (☎ (2) 4-42-12), 27 Barracks Rd (PO Box 1278), is a nice Victorian house with a small garden, high ceilings and eclectic furnishings. There are only four rooms, all with breakfast included: US$32/42/47 for a single/double/triple. Get the suite with its own verandah if it's available.

The *Bakadeer Inn* (☎ (2) 3-14-00; fax 3-19-63), 74 Cleghorn St, is quiet and clean, offering air-conditioned rooms with bath, fridge, fan and cable TV for US$40/45 a single/double. Breakfast is available for US$4. The hotel is right next to Bike Belize, the place to visit to rent motorbikes and bicycles.

Hotel El Centro (☎ (2) 7-50-77, 7-77-39; fax 7-45-53), 4 Bishop St (PO Box 2267), has a marble façade and 12 small, tidy, modern guestrooms with cable TV, phone and air-conditioning for US$35 to US$40 a double.

Hotel Mopan (☎ (2) 7-33-56, 7-73-51; fax 7-53-83), 55 Regent St, is a big old Caribbean-style wood-frame place. The very basic rooms are quite expensive for what you get (US$27/37/43 a single/double/triple with fan, US$37/48/51 with air-conditioning), but the ambience is pure Belize. Meals are served, and there's a congenial bar.

Bliss Hotel (☎ (2) 7-25-52, 7-33-10), 1 Water Lane, doesn't look like much from the outside, but the inside is better. It has 20 rooms, all with private bath, which can be dark and musty, but are clean and usable. There's also a little kidney-shaped swimming pool, and the family management is good. Rates are US$27.50 a double with fan, US$40 with air-conditioning.

Royal Orchid Hotel (☎ (2) 3-27-83; fax 3-27-89), at the corner of New Rd and Victoria St, is a modern hotel without the homey feel of the city's guesthouses, but with 22 air-conditioned rooms equipped with private bath, cable TV and fans. There's a restaurant and bar. Rooms cost US$48/59 a single/double.

Chateau Caribbean Hotel (☎ (2) 3-08-00; fax 3-09-00), 6 Marine Parade (PO Box 947), by Memorial Park, was once a gracious old Belizean mansion, then a hospital; it's now a comfortable if simple hotel with 25 air-conditioned guestrooms and a dining room. Rates are a bit too high at US$73/84 a single/double, but are discounted somewhat in the off season (May to October). Rooms in the 'annexe' behind the main building are not quite so pretty, but larger and a bit cheaper.

The 35-room *Bellevue Hotel* (☎ (2) 7-70-51/2, fax 7-32-53), 5 Southern Foreshore (PO Box 428), near King St, is in the city centre not far from the Bliss Institute. The hotel's unimpressive façade hides a tidy modern interior with 35 comfortable, air-conditioned, TV-equipped rooms (US$83/86 a single/double). There's a restaurant and bar.

BELIZE

PLACES TO STAY – TOP END

The city's long-time favourite is the *Radisson Fort George Hotel* (☎ (2) 7-74-00; fax 7-38-20), 2 Marine Parade (P O Box 321). Its 76 air-conditioned rooms have all the comforts; those in the Club Section are larger. Besides a swimming pool, a good restaurant and a bar, the Fort George has its own boat dock for cruise and fishing craft. Rooms cost US$95 to US$138 a single, US$118 to US$155 a double. For reservations in the USA ☎ (800) 333-33-33.

The city's newest luxury hotel is the 120-room *Ramada Royal Reef Hotel* (☎ (2) 3-26-70, fax 3-26-60), Kings Park. Opened in 1991, it has all the luxury facilities, including a swimming pool and a marina, and rates of US$105/130 a single/double. For reservations in the USA ☎ (800) 228-98-98.

Belize Biltmore Plaza (☎ (2) 3-23-02, fax 3-23-01), Mile 3, Northern Highway, is in the Bella Vista section, 4.5 km north of the centre on the way to Ladyville and Goldson International Airport. The 90 air-conditioned rooms offer excellent value for money at US$88 a single or double. The Victorian Room's cuisine is among the tastiest in the city, and the bar is often lively with karaoke or live music.

PLACES TO EAT

Belize City is not noted for its cuisine, but there is some decent food.

GG's Café & Patio (☎ 7-43-78), 2-B King St, may be the tidiest little eatery in the city. Arched windows and a tiled floor give it a modern feel, and the pretty patio to the left of the café is the place to eat in good weather. 'The best hamburgers in town' cost less than US$3 to US$4; big plates of rice and beans with beef, chicken or pork are just US$3.50. Lily's is open from 11.30 am to 2.30 pm and 5.30 to 9 pm (until 10 pm on Friday and Saturday). It's closed on Sunday.

Pearl's Pizzeria, 13 Handyside St, serves quite good pizza and cold Belikin beer for US$6 or so. They'll pack pizza to take away.

Macy's (☎ 34-19), 18 Bishop St, has consistently good Caribbean Creole cooking, friendly service and decent prices. Fish fillet with rice and beans costs about US$4, armadillo or wild boar a bit more. Hours are 11.30 am to 10 pm (closed on Sunday).

Dit's Restaurant (☎ 33-33-0), 50 King St, is a homey place with powerful fans and a loyal local clientele who come for huge portions and low prices. Rice and beans with beef, pork or chicken costs US$3, and burgers are a mere US$1.50. Cakes and pies make a good dessert at US$1 per slice. Dit's is open from 8 am to 9 pm every day.

Ice-cream parlours serving sandwiches and hamburgers are also good places for cheap meals. The menu may be limited, but the prices are usually good and the surroundings pleasant.

Bluebird Ice Cream Parlour (☎ 7-39-18), 35 Albert St, facing the Atlantic Bank, is a very popular place in the commercial centre of town. Besides ice cream, there are sandwiches and burgers (US$1 to US$2), and fried chicken for twice as much.

Celebrations (☎ 4-57-89), 16 Queen St, not far beyond the post office on the opposite side of the street, is a clean, cheerful and convenient ice-cream parlour serving rice and beans for US$2, sandwiches for US$1 and ice-cream sundaes for just slightly more.

Pete's Pastries (☎ 4-49-74), 41 Queen St (near Handyside St), serves good cakes, tarts, and pies of fruit or meat. A slice and a soft drink costs US$1; my favourite is the raisin pie. You might try Pete's famous cowfoot soup, served on Saturday only (US$1.50) or a ham and cheese sandwich (US$1). Pete's is open from 8.30 am to 7 pm (8 am to 6 pm on Sunday). There's another store at 71 Albert St, near Dean St, in the centre of town.

Kee's Bakery, 53 Queen St at Barracks Rd, is where all Belize City buys its fresh bread and rolls.

Golden Dragon Chinese Restaurant (☎ 7-28-17), in a cul-de-sac off Queen St, is one of the city's several Chinese restaurants, with a long menu heavy on chow mein and chop suey, wonton soup and sweet-and-sour dishes. Full meals cost US$6 to US$14.

The dining room at the *Radisson Fort George Hotel* (☎ 7-74-00) has perhaps the most genteel service in the city, and good food at moderate prices. For a hearty burger and a beer (US$10), try the adjoining Paddles lounge.

Mom's Restaurant, a Belize City institution for many years, has moved to a new location: 7145 Slaughter House Rd, near the Technical College.

ENTERTAINMENT
There's lots of interesting action at night in Belize City. The problem is that much of it is illegal or dangerous.

Be judicious in your choice of nightspots. Clubs and bars that look like dives probably are. If drugs are in evidence, there's lots of room for trouble, and as a foreigner you'll have a hard time blending into the background.

The lounges at the upmarket hotels – Radisson Fort George, Ramada Royal Reef – are sedate, respectable and safe. The Belize Biltmore Plaza Hotel, 4.5 km from the centre on the Northern Highway, has karaoke many nights, live music on others.

The *Upstairs Café*, on Queen St a half-block north-east of the Swing Bridge, has cheap beer and is often fun, though on some evenings it gets rowdy. The club called *The Big Apple*, across from the North Front Street Guest House two blocks north-west of the Swing Bridge, has been here for years. The action depends upon the crowd, of course.

GETTING THERE & AWAY
Belize City is the country's transport nexus. Buses, boats and planes take you from here to any other part of Belize. For information on air travel, see Getting Around in the Belize Getting There & Around chapter.

GETTING AROUND
Belize City is not large, and most people get around on foot.

To/From the Airports
An airport shuttle service (☎ (2) 3-43-67, 7-39-77) operates between Goldson International Airport and Belize City daily, departing from the airport at 6 and 8 am, noon and 4 and 6 pm, and stopping at Pallotti High School, the corner of Central American Blvd and Vernon St, the corner of Central American Blvd and Cemetery Rd, and Pound Yard Bridge near all the city's bus terminals. The one-way fare is US$2.50.

Shuttles run from Belize City to the airport at 5.30, 7.15 and 11.15 am and 3.30 and 5.30 pm.

The taxi fare to or from the international airport is US$15.

It takes about half an hour to walk from the air terminal three km out the access road to the Northern Highway; from here it's easy to catch a bus going either north or south.

Going to Municipal Airport, normal city taxi fares apply: US$2.50 for one person.

Taxi
Trips by taxi within Belize City cost US$2.50 for one person, plus US$0.50 for each extra person. For reliable taxi service, use an organised group such as Seven Candles Cab service (☎ (2) 3-19-79), which can also organise excursions to points of interest throughout Belize.

Car & Motorbike
See Getting Around in the preceding chapter for rental details.

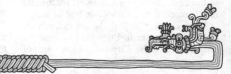

The Cayes

Belize's 290-km-long barrier reef, the longest in the western hemisphere, is the eastern edge of the limestone shelf which underlies most of La Ruta Maya. To the west of the reef the sea is very shallow – usually not much more than four or five metres deep – which allows numerous islands called cayes (pronounced 'keys') to bask in warm waters.

Of the dozens of cayes, large and small, which dot the blue waters of the Caribbean off the Belizean coast, the two most popular with travellers are Caye Caulker and Ambergris Caye. Caulker is commonly thought of as the low-budget island, where hotels and restaurants are considerably less expensive than on resort-conscious Ambergris.

Both islands have an appealing, laid-back Belizean atmosphere. No one's in a hurry here. Stress doesn't figure in the lives of many islanders. Pedestrian traffic on the sandy unpaved streets moves at an easy tropical pace. The fastest vehicle is a kid on a bicycle. Motor vehicles are few and mostly parked.

Island residents include Creoles, mestizos, and a few transplanted North Americans and Europeans. They run lobster and conch-fishing boats, hotels and pensions, little eateries, and island businesses which supply the few things necessary in a benevolent tropical climate.

CAYE CAULKER

Approaching Caye Caulker (population 800) on the boat from Belize City, you glide along the eastern shore, which is overhung with palm trees. Dozens of wooden docks jut out from the shore to give moorings to boats. Off to the east, about two km away, the barrier reef is marked by a thin white line of surf.

Caye Caulker (called Hicaco in Spanish, sometimes Corker in English) lies some 33 km north of Belize City and 24 km south of Ambergris Caye. The island is about seven km long from north to south, and only about 600 metres wide at its widest point. Mangroves cover much of the shore and coconut palms provide shade. The village is on the southern portion of the island. Actually Caulker is now two islands, ever since Hurricane Hattie cut the island in two just north of the village. The cut is called, simply, The Cut. It has a tiny beach, with swift currents running through it, and it marks the northern limits of the settlement.

You disembark and wander ashore to find a place of sandy unpaved 'streets' which are actually more like paths. The government has carefully placed 'Go Slow' and 'Stop' signs at the appropriate places, even though there are no vehicles in sight and everyone on Caulker naturally goes slow and stops frequently. The stops are often to get a beer – most right hands spend much of the day wrapped around a cold one. Virtually constant sea breezes keep the island comfortable even in Belize's sultry heat. If the wind dies, the heat immediately becomes noticeable, as do the sandflies and mosquitoes.

Many gardens and paths on the island have borders of conch shells, and every house has its 'catchment', or large cistern, to catch rainwater for drinking.

Orientation & Information

The village has two principal streets: Front St to the east and Back St to the west. The distance from The Cut in the north to Shirley's Guest House at the southern edge of the village is a little more than one km.

The Belize Telecommunications telephone office is open from 8 am to noon and 1 to 4 pm Monday to Friday, and from 8 am to noon on Saturday (closed on Sunday).

Water Sports

The surf breaks on the barrier reef, easily visible from the eastern shore of Caye Caulker. Don't attempt to swim out to it, however – the local boaters speed their powerful craft through these waters and are

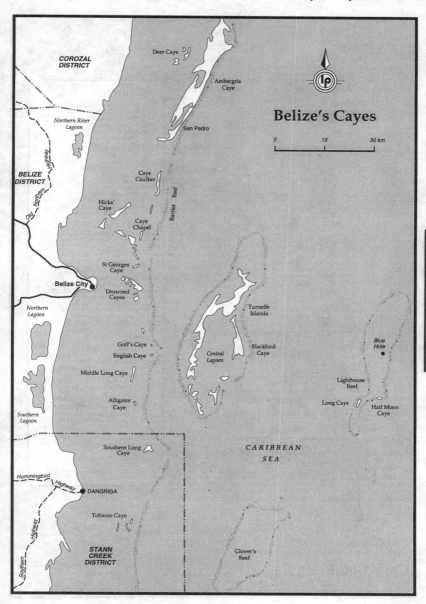

Belize's Cayes

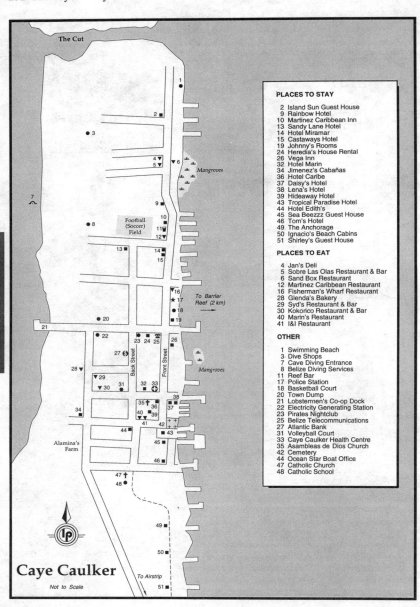

PLACES TO STAY

2 Island Sun Guest House
9 Rainbow Hotel
10 Martinez Caribbean Inn
13 Sandy Lane Hotel
14 Hotel Miramar
15 Castaways Hotel
19 Johnny's Rooms
24 Heredia's House Rental
26 Vega Inn
32 Hotel Marin
34 Jimenez's Cabañas
36 Hotel Caribe
37 Daisy's Hotel
38 Lena's Hotel
39 Hideaway Hotel
43 Tropical Paradise Hotel
44 Hotel Edith's
45 Sea Beezzz Guest House
46 Tom's Hotel
49 The Anchorage
50 Ignacio's Beach Cabins
51 Shirley's Guest House

PLACES TO EAT

4 Jan's Deli
5 Sobre Las Olas Restaurant & Bar
6 Sand Box Restaurant
12 Martinez Caribbean Restaurant
16 Fisherman's Wharf Restaurant
28 Glenda's Bakery
29 Syd's Restaurant & Bar
30 Kokorico Restaurant & Bar
40 Marin's Restaurant
41 I&I Restaurant

OTHER

1 Swimming Beach
3 Dive Shops
7 Cave Diving Entrance
8 Belize Diving Services
11 Reef Bar
17 Police Station
18 Basketball Court
20 Town Dump
21 Lobstermen's Co-op Dock
22 Electricity Generating Station
23 Pirates Nightclub
25 Belize Telecommunications
27 Atlantic Bank
31 Volleyball Court
33 Caye Caulker Health Centre
35 Asambleas de Dios Church
42 Cemetery
44 Ocean Star Boat Office
47 Catholic Church
48 Catholic School

The Cut

Mangroves

Football
(Soccer)
Field

To Barrier
Reef (2 km)

Mangroves

BELIZE

Back Street

Front Street

Alamina's
Farm

To Airstrip

Caye Caulker

Not to Scale

completely heedless of swimmers. Several foreign visitors have died from boat-propeller injuries. Swim only in protected areas.

A short boat ride takes you out to the reef to enjoy some of the world's most exciting snorkelling, diving and fishing. Boat trips are big business on the island, so you have many to choose from. Ask other visitors to the island about their boating experiences, and use this information to choose a boat. Virtually all of the island residents are trustworthy boaters, but it's still good to discuss price, duration, areas to be visited and the seaworthiness of the boat. Boat and motor should be in good condition. Even sailboats should have motors in case of emergency (the weather can change quickly here). The cost is usually around US$10 to US$13 per person; lunch is sometimes included.

Underwater visibility is up to 60 metres. The variety of underwater plants, coral and tropical fish is wonderful. Be careful not to touch the coral, to prevent damage both to it and to yourself; coral is sharp, and some species sting or burn their assailants.

Among the more interesting places to dive is in the underwater caves off the western shore of the island. The cave system here is elaborate and fascinating, but cave diving is a special art. You should not go down without an experienced guide and the proper equipment (strong lights, etc). The dive shops on the island can tell you what – and what not – to do.

Dive trips to the Blue Hole can be arranged through any of several dive shops or travel agencies, including Dolphin Bay Travel and Belize Diving Service (☎ (22) 21-43; fax 22-17). A one-day trip including three dives costs US$150 to US$168 per person, gear included. A three-day trip with meals and accommodation costs US$290 to US$308. For more information on dive sites, see the section on Ambergris Caye.

Beach-goers will find the water warm, clear and blue, but not much in the way of beach. Though there's lots of sand, it doesn't seem to arrange itself in nice, long, wide stretches along the shore. Most of your sunbathing will be on docks or in deck chairs at your hotel. Caulker's public beach, at The Cut to the north of the village, is nothing special – it's tiny and crowded.

Places to Stay – bottom end

Among the comforts you pay for on Caulker are shade and pretty grounds. *Lena's Hotel* (☎ (22) 21-06) has 11 rooms in an old building right on the water, with no grounds to speak of. Rates are fairly good for what you get: US$12 a double in the busy winter season.

Daisy's Hotel (☎ (22) 21-23) has 11 rooms in several blue-and-white buildings which get full sun most of the day. Rooms with table or floor fans, and shared bath, cost US$11 a double; with private shower the rate is US$18.

Hideaway Hotel (☎ (22) 21-03), behind the Asambleas de Dios Church, is a hot two-storey cement-block building with six bare rooms on the ground floor; all have table fans (ceiling fans are preferable). There's no beach, no shade and no grounds, and the church rocks with up-tempo hymns some nights, but prices are fairly good – US$11 a double in summer, US$13 in winter.

Hotel Edith's is tidy and proper, with tiny rooms, each with a private shower; they're priced at US$15 a single, US$18 a double (one bed) or US$22 a double (two beds).

Hotel Miramar (☎ (22) 21-57) has rooms on two floors in a building facing the sea. Rooms with private bath cost US$22.50.

Castaways (☎ (22) 22-94) has six rooms. They're quite clean, and cost a reasonable US$13 a double. There's a restaurant and bar as well.

Johnny's Rooms (☎ (22) 21-49) has clean hotel rooms for US$14 a double, and cabañas for US$26 with private bath.

Places to Stay – middle

Martinez Caribbean Inn (☎ (22) 21-13) has taken over the old Reef Hotel at the centre of the village. The two-storey wood-and-masonry building has a porch for sitting, a bar nearby (it can be noisy, but doesn't go late at night), and rooms with private

Diving for lobsters

showers. You pay US$20/25 a single/double for a good location.

Hotel Marin is not on the shore but it has some trees and gardens, and porches off the bungalows for hanging hammocks. Prices are good: a double with shared bath costs US$12 in summer, US$18 in winter; with private shower, prices are US$22 in summer, US$28 in winter.

Sylvano and Kathy Canto's *Island Sun Guest House* (☎ (22) 22-15) has only two rooms, but both have fans and private baths. The cost is US$30 or US$40 a double. It's neat, quiet and near the beach.

Tom's Hotel (☎ (22) 21-02) has nice, tidy, white buildings. There are 20 rooms, priced at US$10/12 a single/double with shared bathrooms.

Places to Stay – top end
Jimenez's Cabañas (☎ (22) 21-75) has little thatched huts with walls of sticks, each with a private shower. The place is quaint, quiet, relaxing, atmospheric and family-run, and constitutes very good value at US$18 to

US$25 a double, US$28 a triple and US$33 for four.

Tropical Paradise Hotel (☎ (22) 21-24, fax 22-25) pretty much lives up to its name. Choose from six tidy panelled rooms in a long wooden building (US$25/28 a single/double with private shower and ceiling fans), or an equal number of individual yellow cabins with ceiling fans and private baths (some with tubs) for US$33/38. There's a nice modern restaurant and bar, and a big dock for boats or sunning. Owner Ramón Reyes keeps everything in good shape.

Shirley's Guest House (☎ (22) 21-45, fax 22-64), along the south-eastern shore, has nice bungalows with four rooms (two upstairs, two down) boasting mahogany floors, good ventilation and fans. Each pair of rooms shares a bath. Rates are US$33 a single, US$36 to US$44 a double.

The Anchorage rents its four thatched, whitewashed bungalows for US$33 a double in winter, about half that in summer. Each bungalow has a cold-water shower – but how cold is the water here? Its location, at the southern end of town, is quiet.

Ignacio's Beach Cabins, just south of The Anchorage, is a collection of thatched cottages shaded by dozens of gently swaying palm trees. The cottages are quite simple (why would you need more on Caulker?), but rates are satisfying: US$12 to US$20 per hut, with private shower, depending upon the hut and the season.

Sea Beezzz Guest House (☎ (22) 21-76) is a solid, two-storey house on the shore with a nice patio garden in front. Safe, secure and comfortable, with hot water in the private showers and a dining-room service for all three meals, its only disadvantage is that it closes down for the summer. Rates are US$35 to US$50 per room.

Rainbow Hotel (☎ (22) 21-23, fax 21-72), just north of the boat docks on the way to The Cut, is a two-storey concrete building. Plain but clean rooms go for US$32 (ground floor) or US$36 (upper floor) a double with tiled private shower, fan, and a window facing eastwards out to sea.

Vega Inn (☎ (22) 21-42; fax in Belize City (2) 3-15-80), owned by the congenial Vega family – Antonio ('Tony'), Lydia and Maria – has several tidy waterless rooms upstairs in a wooden house, with clean showers down the hall; these go for US$20/24 a single/double. Other, much bigger rooms with private showers are in a concrete building and cost US$45/55. All rooms have wall fans; there's some shady space in front of the house for sitting. An adjoining shady camping area is just the place to pitch your tent, for US$6 per person. The Vegas rent snorkelling equipment, and little sailboats (Sunfish), and can sign you up for snorkelling or sport-fishing trips. For reservations, write to them at PO Box 701, Belize City.

Heredia's House Rental (☎ (22) 21-32) can arrange room or house rentals for two days or more. Call, or write to PO Box 1018, Belize City.

Places to Eat

Though they serve such 'luxury' items as lobster and conch, there are no fancy restaurants on Caulker. Even so, prices are not dirt cheap because much must be brought from the mainland. The island's simple eateries are supplemented by little shops selling sandwiches, snacks and baked goods.

Sobre las Olas, north of the centre, on the water, is a simple, tidy open-air place with a wooden dock, a bar and umbrella-topped tables, as well as an indoor dining room across the road. Standard Belizean fare is served from 7 am to 10 pm every day but Monday. Expect to pay US$5 to US$8 for a full meal. Just to the north, the *Sand Box* is similar, with tasty food and decent prices.

Fisherman's Wharf Restaurant also has shady tables out by the water, and a 'breakfast nook' upstairs. Prices are low: burgers (including a fishburger) for US$2, Belikin beer for US$1.50. This is a popular place.

The *Martinez Caribbean Inn* restaurant features lots of sandwiches, burgers and antojitos (garnaches, tacos, panuchos, etc), as well as rice and beans with chicken or lobster. For breakfast, a coffee and a fruit plate costs less than US$4. Lunch or dinner can cost US$3.50 to US$8. They concoct a tasty rum punch here, sold by the bottle or the glass.

Marin's Restaurant, a block west of the Tropical Paradise, serves up fresh seafood in its outdoor garden and mosquito-proof screened dining room. Try the whole grilled catch of the day (about US$5).

Nearby is the *I & I Restaurant*, upstairs in a frame building with a dining deck overlooking the street. The reggae, playing constantly, sets the proper island mood. The food is a bit fancier than normal, and moderate in price.

The restaurant at the *Tropical Paradise Hotel* is busy all day because it serves the island's most consistently good food in big portions at decent prices. In the light, cheerful dining room, breakfast is served from 8 am to noon, lunch from 11.30 am to 2 pm and dinner from 6 to 10 pm. You can order curried shrimp or lobster for US$10, many other things for less.

Entertainment

After one evening on the island, you'll know what there is to do in the evening. The *Reef Bar*, by the Reef Hotel, has a sand floor and tables holding clusters of bottles (mostly beer) as semipermanent centrepieces. This is the gathering, sipping and talking place for the locals.

Getting There & Away

Details on transport to and from Caye Caulker are included in Getting Around in the introductory Belize chapter.

Getting Around

Caulker is so small that most people walk everywhere. There are a few bicycles, and locals with things to carry use electric golf carts. Besides, this is an island – all serious transport is done by boat.

AMBERGRIS CAYE & SAN PEDRO

The largest of Belize's cayes, Ambergris (pronounced am-BER-griss) lies 58 km north of Belize City. It's over 40 km long,

BELIZE

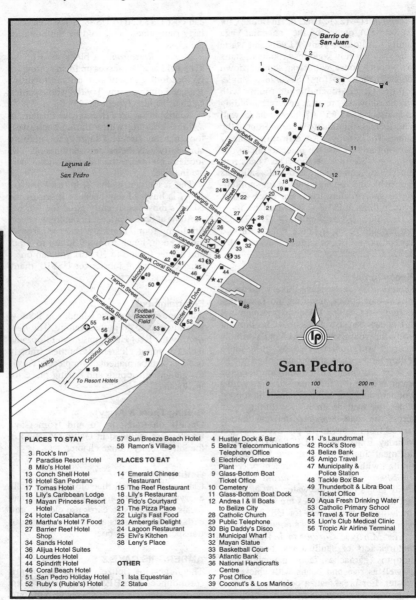

San Pedro

0   100   200 m

Laguna de San Pedro

Barrio de San Juan

Caribeña Street

Pelican Street

Coral Street

Ambergris Street

Angel Street

Pescador

Bucaneer Street

Black Coral Street

Almond Street

Tarpon Street

Esmeralda Street

Coconut Drive

Barrier Reef Drive

Football (Soccer) Field

Airstrip

To Resort Hotels

BELIZE

PLACES TO STAY		OTHER	

PLACES TO STAY

- 3 Rock's Inn
- 7 Paradise Resort Hotel
- 8 Milo's Hotel
- 13 Conch Shell Hotel
- 16 Hotel San Pedrano
- 17 Tomas Hotel
- 18 Lily's Caribbean Lodge
- 19 Mayan Princess Resort Hotel
- 24 Hotel Casablanca
- 26 Martha's Hotel 7 Food
- 27 Barrier Reef Hotel Shop
- 34 Sands Hotel
- 36 Alijua Hotel Suites
- 40 Lourdes Hotel
- 44 Spindrift Hotel
- 46 Coral Beach Hotel
- 51 San Pedro Holiday Hotel
- 52 Ruby's (Rubie's) Hotel

- 57 Sun Breeze Beach Hotel
- 58 Ramon's Village

PLACES TO EAT

- 14 Emerald Chinese Restaurant
- 15 The Reef Restaurant
- 18 Lily's Restaurant
- 20 Fido's Courtyard
- 21 The Pizza Place
- 22 Luigi's Fast Food
- 23 Ambergris Delight
- 24 Lagoon Restaurant
- 25 Elvi's Kitchen
- 38 Leny's Place

OTHER

- 1 Isla Equestrian
- 2 Statue

- 4 Hustler Dock & Bar
- 5 Belize Telecommunications Telephone Office
- 6 Electricity Generating Plant
- 9 Glass-Bottom Boat Ticket Office
- 10 Cemetery
- 11 Glass-Bottom Boat Dock
- 12 Andrea I & II Boats to Belize City
- 28 Catholic Church
- 29 Public Telephone
- 30 Big Daddy's Disco
- 31 Municipal Wharf
- 32 Mayan Statue
- 33 Basketball Court
- 35 Atlantic Bank
- 36 National Handicrafts Centre
- 37 Post Office
- 39 Coconut's & Los Marinos

- 41 J's Laundromat
- 42 Rock's Store
- 43 Belize Bank
- 45 Amigo Travel
- 47 Municipality & Police Station
- 48 Tackle Box Bar
- 49 Thunderbolt & Libra Boat Ticket Office
- 50 Aqua Fresh Drinking Water
- 53 Catholic Primary School
- 54 Travel & Tour Belize
- 55 Lion's Club Medical Clinic
- 56 Tropic Air Airline Terminal

Top: Belize City from the roof of Fort George Hotel, Belize (TB)
Bottom: Beach and jetty, Caye Caulker, Belize (TB)

Top: Tropical Paradise Hotel, Caye Caulkler, Belize (TB)
Bottom: Small hotel, Placencia, Belize (TB)

and on its northern side almost adjoins Mexican territory.

Most of the island's population of 2000 lives in the town of San Pedro, near the southern tip. The barrier reef is only one km east of San Pedro. In the morning, before the workday noises begin, stand on one of the docks on the town's eastern side – you can hear the low bass roar of the surf breaking over the reef.

San Pedro started life as a fishing town but is now Belize's prime tourist destination. Over half of the tourists who visit Belize fly straight to San Pedro, and use it as their base for excursions elsewhere. Even so, San Pedro is certainly no Cancún, though there has been some small-scale development in recent years.

Like Caye Caulker, Ambergris has an engaging, laid-back atmosphere. A sign in a local restaurant has it right: 'No shirt, no shoes – *no problem!*'. San Pedro is sandy streets with little traffic, lots of Caribbean-style wooden buildings (some on stilts), and few people who bother to wear shoes. Everyone is friendly, and everyone is looked upon as a person – not a tourist, not a source of dollars, but a person.

Orientation

It's about one km from the Paradise Hotel (in the northern part of town) to the airport (in the south), so everything is within easy walking distance unless you're burdened with lots of luggage. You'll want a taxi only to reach the few resort hotels which lie several km south of the airport.

San Pedro has three main north-south streets, which used to be called Front St (to the east), Middle St and Back St (to the west). Now these streets have tourist-class names: Barrier Reef Drive, Pescador St and Angel Coral St, but some islanders might still use the old names.

Information

Money You can change money easily in San Pedro, but keep in mind that US dollars are accepted in many establishments.

Both the Atlantic Bank and the Belize Bank are near the Spindrift Hotel. The Atlantic Bank (☎ (26) 21-95) is open on Monday, Tuesday and Thursday from 8 am to noon and 1 to 3 pm, on Wednesday from 8 am to 1 pm, on Friday from 8 am to 1 pm and 3 to 6 pm, and on Saturday from 8.30 am to noon. Belize Bank is open Monday to Thursday from 8 am to 3 pm, on Friday from 8 am to 1 pm and 3 to 6 pm, and on Saturday from 8.30 am to noon.

Post San Pedro's post office is on Bucaneer St between Barrier Reef Drive and Pescador St. Hours are 8 am to noon and 1 to 5 pm (until 4.30 pm on Friday) on weekdays. It's closed on Saturday and Sunday.

Telephone The Belize Telecommunications telephone office, up north on Pescador St, is open Monday to Friday from 8 am to noon and 1 to 4 pm, and on Saturday from 8 am to noon (closed on Sunday).

Travel & Dive Agencies Most hotels, travel agencies and dive shops in San Pedro can arrange for a day's snorkelling or scuba diving, or for excursions to the mainland lasting one to several days. Here are some of the leading agencies:

Amigo Travel, Barrier Reef Drive near the Hotel Sands (☎ (26) 21-80; fax 21-92)
Fantasea Watersports, at the Victoria House (☎ /fax (26) 25-76)
Island Adventures, on the beach at Fido's Courtyard (☎ /fax (26) 26-97)
Out Island Divers, PO Box 7, San Pedro (☎ (26) 21-51; in the USA ☎ (800) 258-3465)
Travel & Tour Belize, PO Box 42, corner Barrier Reef Drive and Bucaneer St, in the Alijua Suites building (☎ (26) 25-35; fax 21-85); another office is on Esmeralda St

Water Sports

Ambergris is good for all water sports: scuba diving, snorkelling, sailboarding, boating, swimming, deep-sea fishing and sunbathing. Many island hotels have their own dive shops which rent equipment, provide instruction and organise diving excursions. In fact, just about any local can put you in

BELIZE

touch with someone organising water-sports trips.

Hire a fishing boat for US$135 a day (deep-sea fishing for US$350 a day), or a boat and guide for a two-tank dive (US$45, plus equipment rental costs of about US$36). Take a full diving certification course (US$350) or just sign up for a full-day barbecue beach picnic on a remote beach (US$40, lunch included). Rent a canoe (US$30 a day) or a snorkel, mask and fins (US$8). You could also take a bird-watching cruise (US$20) or go sailing and snorkelling for the day (US$35, drinks included).

Among the favourite seafaring destinations near and far are:

- Blue Hole, a deep sinkhole of vivid blue water where you can dive to 40 metres, observing the cave with diving lights
- Caye Caulker North Island, the relatively uninhabited northern part of Caulker, with good snorkelling, swimming and places for a beach barbecue
- Glover's Reef, about 50 km east of Dangriga, one of only three coral atolls in the western hemisphere (the other two, Lighthouse Reef and the Turneffe Islands, are also in Belize)
- Half Moon Caye, a small island on Lighthouse Reef, 113 km east of Belize City, with a lighthouse, excellent beaches, and spectacular submerged walls teeming with marine flora & fauna (underwater visibility can extend over 60 metres); the caye is a bird sanctuary, and home to the rare Pink-Footed Booby
- Hol Chan Marine Reserve, with submerged canyons 30 metres deep busy with large fish; the canyon walls are covered with colourful sponges
- Lighthouse Reef (which includes Half Moon Caye), one of three coral atolls in the western hemisphere, lying 100 km east of Belize City
- Mexico Cave, filled with colourful sponges, lobsters and shrimp
- Palmetto Reef, with lots of canyons, surge channels, and many varieties of coral (hard and soft), sponges and fish
- Punta Arena, an area of underwater canyons and sea caves teeming with fish, rays, turtles, sponges and coral
- San Pedro Cut, the large break in the barrier reef used by the larger fishing and pleasure boats
- Tres Cocos Cut, a natural break in the barrier reef which attracts a variety of marine life
- Turneffe Islands, a large atoll 30 km east of Belize City teeming with coral and alive with fish and large rays.

For those who don't fancy diving or snorkelling but who still want to see some of the marvellous marine life, tours in glass-bottom boats are run by several companies. About the cheapest is the two-hour tour (9 to 11 am or 2 to 4 pm) for US$10. Buy your tickets in the house to the left of Milo's Hotel, at the northern end of Barrier Reef Drive, and board the boat at the dock due east of there.

Swimming is best off the pier at the Paradise Hotel. All beaches are public, and you can probably use their lounge chairs if it's a slow day. At Ramon's Village there is a very nice thatched cabaña for sunset-watching at the end of the pier.

Horse Riding
Isla Equestrian (☎ (26) 28-95), off Pescador St, can arrange for riding about the island.

Mainland Excursions
Many visitors to Belize fly to Ambergris and make it their base for excursions by plane or boat to other parts of this small country. Tours are available to the Mayan ruins at Altun Ha and Xunantunich, to the Belize Zoo, Crooked Tree Bird Sanctuary, the Baboon Sanctuary and Mountain Pine Ridge, and even to Tikal (in Guatemala). Any hotel or travel agency can fill you in on tours.

Places to Stay – bottom end
Though there are some cheap places to stay here, they are small, few in number and rarely offer particularly good value for money. Wherever you stay, you'll never be more than a minute's walk from the water.

Milo's Hotel (☎ (26) 20-33), PO Box 21, on Barrier Reef Drive, has nine small, dark, fairly dismal rooms above a shop in a blue-and-white Caribbean-style building. It's quiet and cheap, and often full for these reasons. Rooms with shared showers go for US$8/11/14 a single/double/triple. Newer rooms with private shower and air-conditioning are much more expensive.

Tomas Hotel (☎ (26) 20-61), Barrier Reef Drive, offers very good value for money. This family-run place charges US$21 (summer) or US$28 (winter) for eight light, airy double rooms with private baths (some with tubs). Two rooms have double beds; the others have a double and a single, making them good for families or threesomes.

Martha's Hotel (☎ (26) 20-53), corner of Ambergris and Pescador Sts, has 16 rooms. All have private bath, and sometimes the sink is in the room because the bathroom is so small. Rooms 11 and 12 are lighter and airier than the rest. Rates are US$20/32/42 a single/double/triple in summer (US$28/38/48 in winter), or US$55 for four.

Hotel San Pedrano (☎ (26) 20-54, fax 20-93), corner of Barrier Reef Drive and Caribeña St, has one apartment and seven rooms, all with private bath. Though most rooms don't have ocean views, they do have nice wooden floors and well-maintained patio furniture. The apartment rents for US$150 per week and has a double bed and two single beds, while the rooms rent for US$27/33/38 a single/double/triple in winter; summer prices are a few dollars lower. Add US$5 per room for air-conditioning.

Ruby's (or *Rubie's*) *Hotel* (☎ (26) 20-63; fax 24-34), PO Box 56, at the south end of Barrier Reef Drive, is close to the airport and right on the water. Five of the nine rooms here have private showers; not all of the rooms overlook the sea. Rates are US$11/14 a single/double with shared bath, US$29 to US$38 a double with private bath.

Lily's Caribbean Lodge (☎ (26) 20-59), off the east end of Caribeña St and facing the sea, has 10 clean, pleasant rooms; several (especially those on the top floor) have good sea views. Doubles cost US$27 in summer, US$38 in winter. There's a tidy restaurant on the ground floor. The *Conch Shell Hotel* (☎ (26) 20-62), north of Lily's, was under renovation at my last visit.

Lourdes Hotel (☎ (26) 20-66), on Pescador St, is very plain and well used. No one would call it beautiful, few would call it pleasant – but it is cheap at US$12/20 a single/double with private shower.

Places to Stay – middle

Many of these hotels cater to divers, who are often willing to pay more for a room – any room – if the diving's good. Note that some of these hotels charge 10% or 15% for service in addition to the 6% government room tax. I've included both of these extra charges in the rates quoted below. Most places listed here accept major credit cards.

The *Barrier Reef Hotel* (☎ (26) 20-75, fax 27-19), on Barrier Reef Drive in the centre of town, is a landmark, its attractive Caribbean wood-frame construction captured by countless tourist cameras daily. Most of the 10 rooms are not in this structure, however, but in a newer and less charming concrete-block addition at the back. The bonus here is air-conditioning – good on sticky hot days. The rates during the winter season are US$52/70/80 a single/double/triple.

Spindrift Hotel (☎ (26) 20-18, 21-74; fax 22-51; in the USA ☎ (800) 327-19-39), corner of Bucaneer St and Barrier Reef Drive, has a good location right in the centre of town on the beach. It's a modern, fairly attractive building, and the 30 comfortable rooms range from a smaller room with one double bed, ceiling fan and a view of the street (US$53 a double) to a room with two double beds, air-conditioning and a view of the sea (US$90 a double). There are also several apartments (US$120 to US$180).

Hotel Casablanca (☎ (26) 23-27; fax 29-92), on Pescador St between Pelican and Ambergris Sts, opened its doors late in 1993 with only five rooms, but those are quite comfortable. Rates are US$85 to US$120 a double, depending upon the room and the season.

San Pedro Holiday Hotel (☎ (26) 20-14, fax 22-95), PO Box 1140, Belize City, is on Barrier Reef Drive in the southern part of town. It's a comfortable modern building on the beach, with a full list of services. Rates are US$90 to US$130 for rooms, bungalows and apartments.

Places to Stay – top end

Ambergris has many resort hotels, but none are huge, Cancún-style high-rises. On Ambergris, a resort is often a collection of thatched bungalows which can house

BELIZE

upwards of two dozen people. All rooms mentioned below have private baths; most have air-conditioning as well.

Victoria House (☎ (26) 20-67, fax 24-29; in the USA ☎ (800) 247-51-59, (713) 662-80-00), PO Box 22, is an idyllic small resort hotel three km south of the airport, on the beach. The beach, the lawns and the 31 rooms are beautifully kept; there's a good dining room, a bar and a dive shop. Here you're away from it all, but San Pedro town is a quick 10-minute (free) bike ride, shuttle van or (rentable) golf cart away. You pay US$130 to US$210 a double from mid-December to mid-April, lower rates at other times.

Ramon's Village (☎ (26) 20-71; fax 22-14; in the USA ☎ (601) 649-1990; fax 649-1996), on Coconut Drive south of the Tropic Air terminal, has 60 rooms in two-storey cabañas, thatched Tahitian-style, facing a good beach. Dive shop, boats for excursions, jet-skis, sailboards, lounge chairs for sunbathing, a swimming pool with bar surrounded by coconut palms...it's got everything, and it's very well kept. Some cabañas have sea views, many have porches for sitting, and all come with at least a king-size bed or two double beds. Rates range from US$125 to US$185 a double.

Paradise Resort Hotel (☎ (26) 20-83; fax 22-32; in the USA ☎ (800) 451-8017), at the northern end of Barrier Reef Drive, is a favourite amongst Ambergris cognoscenti and has a superb location. Its 25 rooms, cabañas and villas are large, airy and attractive. The hotel has its own dock and dive shop. Winter rates range from US$60 to US$125 a double.

The *Belize Yacht Club* (☎ (26) 27-77; fax 27-68; in the USA ☎ (800) 448-8355) has several Spanish-style two-storey buildings arranged around a swimming pool amidst lawns stretching to the beach. Accommodation is in air-conditioned suites with full kitchens, and costs US$160 in the winter. This is San Pedro's classy spot, less than one km south of the airport.

Sun Breeze Beach Hotel (☎ (26) 21-91; fax 23-46), PO Box 14, at the southern end of Barrier Reef Drive not far from the airport, is a nice, fairly new, Mexican-style two-storey concrete building with a sandy inner court opening towards the beach and the sea. Shady tiled porticos set with easy chairs are great for lounging and watching nothing happen. The 34 air-conditioned rooms are attractive and comfortable, and priced at US$100 to US$135 a single, US$115 to US$150 a double, US$125 to US$160 a triple in winter.

Rock's Inn (☎ (26) 23-26; fax 23-58; in the USA ☎ (800) 735-9520), PO Box 50, is a new three-storey all-suite hotel on the beach at the northern end of town. Suites include fully furnished kitchens and cost US$100 to US$130 a double. A similar place is *Alijua Hotel Suites* (☎ (26) 27-91, fax 23-62), in the centre on Barrier Reef Drive.

Mayan Princess Resort Hotel (☎ (26) 27-78; fax 27-84), PO Box 1, is an up-to-date condominium building right in the town centre, on the beach. When suites (with kitchenette) are not occupied by their owners, they are rented to travellers for US$120/140 a single/double.

Places to Eat

Perhaps the first place you'll wander into is *Fido's Courtyard*, on Barrier Reef Drive. Walk past The Pizza Place (see below) and you'll find several eating places, an art gallery and a travel agency around a shady deck area overlooking the sea. The Bar serves drinks such as rum and Coke or beer for US$1.75. The Island Grill, open from 6 am to 6 pm (closed on Wednesday), serves sandwiches, burgers, steaks and fish at prices ranging between US$5 and US$14.

The Pizza Place (☎ 24-44) serves breakfast, as well as pizzas (US$10 to US$17), sandwiches and ice-cream concoctions. They'll deliver pizzas within San Pedro town.

Elvi's Kitchen (☎ 21-76), on Pescador St near Ambergris St, is the old reliable here, typically Belizean, offering substantial servings, prices for every budget, and food cooked to order. A big plate of fish & chips is yours for US$7; rice and beans with fish costs US$5. You can spend as little as US$1.75 for a ham and cheese sandwich. Try their licuados of banana, melon, papaya, pineapple, soursap or watermelon.

Ambergris Delight, on Pescador St near Pelican St (inland, not on the beach), serves fried chicken, burgers and pies, as well as the inevitable rice and beans, at low prices. It's closed on Wednesday. This is also the ticket office for the *Andrea I* and *Andrea II* boats, which ply the waves to Belize City.

Estel's Dine by the Sea, on the beach near the Alijua Hotel, is not particularly cheap, but has an eclectic menu and a great location. Rice and beans goes for US$6, a Mexican plate for US$12; Belikin is only US$1.25, however. It's closed on Tuesday.

Emerald Restaurant, on Barrier Reef Drive, is one of San Pedro's several Chinese restaurants, with a long menu and low prices. Filling Chinese platters cost US$4 to US$9; burgers are even cheaper (US$3). Food can be packed to take away. It's open every day. The other good Chinese restaurant is the *Jade Garden*, a five-minute walk south of Ramon's Village.

Lily's (☎ 20-59), in Lily's Hotel, off the eastern end of Caribeña St, is a family-run place specialising in seafood. A seafood lunch or dinner might cost US$10 to US$15; breakfasts are served for about US$5.

Luigi's Fast Food, across from the Hotel Casablanca on Pescador St, has cheap lunch-eon specials of rice and beans with chicken, fish or meat.

The *Barrier Reef Hotel*, on Barrier Reef Drive, has a small restaurant on its ground floor, specialising in pizza: nine, 12 and 16-inch pizzas priced from US$7.50 to US$17, depending upon ingredients. They also serve shrimp cocktails, a few sandwiches and nachos.

Mary Ellen's Little Italy Restaurant (☎ 28-66), in the Spindrift Hotel, is a step up in comfort and quality, with indoor, patio and beachside dining. Spaghetti plates and Italian main courses cost US$5 to US$15; sandwiches are less. It's closed from 2 to 5.30 pm.

A new place with lots of promise is the *Lagoon Restaurant*, on Pescador St in the Hotel Casablanca building. The experienced chef can cook anything from Thai pork satay, to coq au vin and chayote Maya, to black bean lasagna. For the quality and variety offered, it's very reasonable – about US$15 to US$20 for a full dinner (the only meal served).

Entertainment

Sipping, sitting, talking and dancing are part of everyday life on Ambergris. Many hotels have comfortable bars, often with appropriate sand floors, thatched roofs and reggae music.

The *Tackle Box Bar*, on a wharf at the eastern end of Black Coral Drive, is a San Pedro institution. Very popular with divers and boat owners, it's a good place to get the latest information on diving trips and conditions, boat rentals and excursions.

Fido's, on Barrier Reef Drive near Pelican St, always has a lively crowd in the evenings, sometimes playing bingo.

Big Daddy's, located right next to San Pedro's church, is the town's hot nightspot, often featuring live reggae, especially during the winter.

To drink with the locals in a real cantina at lower prices, head for *Los Marinos*, on Pescador St at Bucaneer St. Don't expect a beautiful place; this is a real Mexican-style cantina, and women may not find the atmosphere very welcoming or comfortable.

Getting There & Away

For details on getting to and from Ambergris Caye, see Getting Around in the introductory Belize chapter.

Getting Around

It's no more than a 10-minute walk to any place in town from the airport, less from the boat docks. A taxi from the airport to any place in town costs US$3; to hotels south of town, the fare is US$6.

San Pedranos get around on foot, or by bicycle, dune buggy, golf cart and pick-up truck. A few huge slab-sided Ford station wagons act as taxis. You can rent bicycles,

BELIZE

motor bikes and golf carts at several locations. See Travel & Dive Agencies, above.

OTHER CAYES

Though Ambergris and Caulker are the most easily accessible and popular cayes, it is possible to arrange visits to others. Serious divers are the usual customers at camps and resorts on the smaller cayes. Often a special flight or boat charter is necessary to reach the cayes, and this can be arranged when you book your lodgings. Most booking offices are in Belize City, as the smaller cayes have infrequent mail service and no telephones (only radios).

Caye Chapel

Just south of Caye Caulker, Caye Chapel holds the *Pyramid Island Resort* (☎ (2) 4-44-09, fax 3-24-05), PO Box 192, Belize City.

St George's Caye

Fourteen km east of Belize City, St George's Caye was the first capital of the Belize settlement, between 1650 and 1784, and saw the decisive battle of 1798 between the British settlers and a Spanish invasion force.

Today it holds *St George's Lodge* (☎ (2) 4-41-90; fax 3-04-61), PO Box 625, Belize City, a 16-room, moderately priced resort. For reservations in the USA ☎ (800) 678-6871. There is also the *Cottage Colony Resort* (☎ (2) 7-70-51/2; fax 7-32-53), PO Box 428, Belize City.

Spanish Lookout Caye

Spanish Bay Resort (☎ (2) 7-72-88, 7-27-25; fax 7-27-97, 71 North Front St (PO Box 35), Belize City), is on Spanish Lookout Caye, between Belize City and the Turneffe

Islands. It's a five-cabaña, family-run place where you can really get away from it all.

Turneffe Islands

A coral atoll about 30 km east of Belize City, the Turneffe Islands hold numerous lodgings, from low-budget camps like the six-room *Turneffe Flats* (☎ (2) 4-56-34; 56 Eve St, Belize City) to the luxury *Turneffe Islands Lodge* (fax (03) 02-76; in the USA ☎ (800) 338-8149; fax (904) 641-5285), PO Box 480, Belize City. The lodge itself has only a radio hook-up.

Half Moon Caye

This caye is in Lighthouse Reef, and has been protected as the Half Moon Caye Natural Monument. Standing less than three metres above sea level, the caye's 18 hectares hold two distinct ecosystems. To the west is lush vegetation fertilised by the droppings of thousands of seabirds, including some 4000 Red-footed Boobys, the wonderfully named Magnificent Frigatebird, and some 98 other species of birds; to the east, there is less vegetation but more coconut palms. Loggerhead and hawksbill turtles, both endangered, lay their eggs on the southern beaches. There is no accommodation, but camping is allowed in designated areas. Organised boat trips stop at Half Moon Caye and the Blue Hole, nearby.

Gallows Point Caye

Just off Belize City, Gallows Point Caye has the six-room guesthouse called *The Wave* (☎ (2) 7-30-54), 9 Regent St, Belize City.

Southern Cayes

For details of cayes off the southern Belizean coast, see the Southern Belize chapter.

Northern Belize

Low-lying, often swampy, and cut by rivers and lagoons, northern Belize has a varied topography of broadleaf forest, pine forest and savanna, and tropical riparian forests filled with vines and epiphytes. The shoreline in the north is often vague – a wide band of marshy land edged with dense mangrove.

This is also farming country. Sugar cane is a major crop, but many farmers are branching out to different crops rather than be held hostage to the fluctuations of the commodities markets.

The north has several significant biosphere reserves. Largest and most significant is the Río Bravo Conservation Area, over 1000 sq km of tropical forests, rivers, ponds and Mayan archaeological sites in the western part of Orange Walk District. Spread along the Mexican and Guatemalan borders, the Río Bravo reserve joins the Maya Biosphere Reserve in Guatemala and the Calakmul Reserve in Mexico to form a vast multinational reserve.

Other reserves include the Shipstern Wildlife Reserve, south of Sarteneja on the large peninsula to the south-east of Corozal Town. Shipstern is an excellent place for birdwatching, as is the Crooked Tree Wildlife Sanctuary, midway between Orange Walk and Belize City. The Bermudian Landing Community Baboon Sanctuary, west of Belize City, protects the black howler monkey.

The ancient Maya prospered in northern Belize, scooping up the rich soil and piling it onto raised fields, and at the same time creating drainage canals. These *chinampas* (raised growing-beds surrounded by water) supported many rich coastal trading towns.

At Cerros, across the bay from Corozal Town, a small Mayan fishing settlement became a powerful kingdom in Late Pre-Classic times. At least a dozen other powerful Mayan cities flourished here, but like Cerros they are somewhat difficult to reach, and their largely unrestored temples do not seem particularly impressive to eyes that have seen Tikal, Chichén Itzá or even Tulum. Not so Lamanai, which is one of the best sites to visit in Belize.

BERMUDIAN LANDING COMMUNITY BABOON SANCTUARY

There are no real baboons in Belize, but locally the black howler monkey is given that name. Though there are howler monkeys throughout the Mayan areas, the black howler, an endangered species, exists only in Belize, and like so much wildlife in the rapidly developing Mayan lands, its existence is threatened.

In 1985 a group of local farmers were organised to help preserve the black howler and to protect its habitat by harmonising its needs with their own. Care is taken to leave the forests along the banks of the Belize River where the black howler feeds, sleeps and – at dawn and dusk – howls (loudly and unmistakably). You can learn all about the black howler, and the other 200 kinds of animals and birds to be found in the Reserve, at the Visitors' Centre (☎ (2) 4-44-05) in the village of Bermudian Landing.

Black howlers are vegetarians, and spend most of the daylight hours cruising the treetops in groups of four to eight, led by a dominant male. Various fruits, flowers, leaves and other tidbits keep them happy, and they don't seem to mind visitors lurking below.

You must tour the sanctuary with a guide (US$3 per hour, US$11 per half-day). For further information about the sanctuary, check with the Belize Audubon Society (☎ (2) 7-73-69), 49 Southern Foreshore, Belize City. For full ecological information, buy a copy of the field guide to the sanctuary (US$15).

Places to Stay & Eat

Camping is allowed at the Visitors' Centre

for US$2. There are also simple rooms (US$12 a double), and simple, inexpensive meals.

Getting There & Away
Private buses leave Orange St in Belize City (one from the corner of Mussel St, the other from the corner of George St) after lunch, Monday to Saturday, for the hour-long ride to Bermudian Landing. Departures from Bermudian Landing for Belize City are at 5.30 am, meaning that if you take the bus, you must plan to stay the night. The return fare is US$3.50.

ALTUN HA & MARUBA
Northern Belize's most famous Mayan ruin is at Altun Ha, 55 km north of Belize City along the Old Northern Highway, near the village of Rockstone Pond, 16 km south of Maskall.

The northern highway divides at the town of Sand Hill, with the new highway going north-west and the old one heading north-east. The road is narrow, potholed and broken in places, passing through jungle and the occasional hamlet.

Altun Ha (Mayan for 'Rockstone Pond') was undoubtedly a small (population about 3000) but rich and important Mayan trading town, with agriculture also playing an important role in its economy. Altun Ha had formed as a community by at least 600 BC, perhaps several centuries earlier, and the town flourished until the mysterious collapse of Classic Mayan civilisation in around 900 AD. Most of the temples you will see in Altun Ha date from Late Classic times, though burials indicate that Altun Ha's merchants were trading with Teotihuacán in Pre-Classic times.

Altun Ha is open daily from 9 am to 5 pm; admission costs US$1.50. There are modern toilets and a drinks shop at the site, but no accommodation.

Of the grass-covered temples arranged around the two plazas here, the largest and most important is the Temple of the Masonry Altars (Structure B-4), in Plaza B. The restored structure you see dates from the first

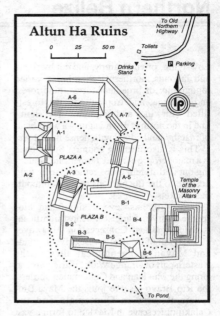

half of the 7th century AD, and takes its name from altars on which copal resin was burnt and beautifully carved jade pieces were smashed in sacrifice. Excavation of the structure in 1968 revealed many burials of important officials. Most sites had been looted or desecrated, but two were intact. Among the jade objects found in one of these was a unique mask sculpture portraying Kinich Ahau, the Mayan sun god, the largest known well-carved jade object from the Mayan area.

In Plaza A, Structure A-1 is sometimes called the Temple of the Green Tomb. Deep within it was discovered the tomb of a priest/king dating from around 600 AD. Tropical humidity had destroyed the king's garments and the paper of the Mayan 'painted book' which was buried with him, but many riches were intact: shell necklaces, pottery, pearls, stingray spines used in blood-letting rites, jade beads and pendants, and ceremonial flints.

Places to Stay

Camping, though not strictly legal, is sometimes permitted; ask at the site.

Three km north of Maskall is the luxury Maruba Resort (☎ (3) 2-21-99; in the USA ☎ (713) 799-2031; fax 795-8573), Mile 40.5, Old Northern Highway. This 'jungle spa' is decorated with an artist's fine eye; the grounds are perfectly kept and the staff is exceedingly welcoming. If you want to escape to an oasis in a tropical jungle, this is it. Tours of the country's sights are available for when you want to get out for a day. Rooms cost US$210 a double, breakfast and dinner included. If your budget allows, you can stop here for lunch (about US$20) when you visit Altun Ha.

Getting There & Away

The 'New Alignment' of the Northern Highway passes well inland of Altun Ha, and so does most of its traffic, leaving little activity on the Old Northern Highway. The easiest way to visit the site is on a tour. Many travel agencies run tours daily from Belize City and San Pedro (Ambergris Caye). Hitching is usually disappointing, but you might ask about trucks and buses leaving Belize City's Farmers' Market (on Central American Blvd just north of Haulover Creek) for the town of Maskall, north of Altun Ha.

CROOKED TREE WILDLIFE SANCTUARY

Midway between Belize City and Orange Walk Town, three km west of the Northern Highway, lies the fishing and farming village of Crooked Tree. In 1984 the Belize Audubon Society succeeded in having 12 sq km around the village declared a wildlife sanctuary, principally because of the wealth of birdlife. Migrating birds flock to the rivers, swamps and lagoons here each year during the dry season (November to May, which is winter up north). Varieties include various species of herons, ducks, kites, egrets, ospreys, kingfishers and hawks.

Among Crooked Tree's most famous winter visitors is a large group of jabiru storks which come here to nest. With a wing-span of 2½ metres, the jabiru is the largest flying bird in the western hemisphere. Black howler monkeys, Morelet's crocodiles, coatimundis, iguanas and turtles also have habitats at Crooked Tree.

For details about the sanctuary, check with the Belize Audubon Society (☎ (2) 7-73-69), 49 Southern Foreshore (PO Box 1001), Belize City.

Places to Stay & Eat

Bird's Eye View Lodge (☎ (2) 4-41-01, PO Box 1976, Belize City), is located in Crooked Tree Village near the lagoon. Four of the five rooms in the concrete building have two double beds; the other one has one double bed. All have private baths. Rooms cost US$60/75 a single/double. Meals are available, as are sites for camping.

Also in the village is the *Paradise Inn* (☎ (25) 25-35; fax 25-34), renting simple cabañas for US$38/50 a single/double. They have a restaurant as well.

Getting There & Away

Two buses run from Belize City to Crooked Tree daily; for current times, ask at the Belize Audubon Society or at the Batty Brothers or Venus Bus Lines bus stations. If you start early from Belize City, Corozal Town or Orange Walk Town, you can bus to Crooked Tree Junction, walk to the village, learn about the reserve's flora & fauna at the Visitors' Centre, spend some time bird-watching, and head out again.

A faster, more comfortable but more expensive alternative is to take a day-long tour from Belize City. Several travel agencies organise these for about US$75 per person.

CHAN CHICH LODGE

Chan Chich Lodge (☎ in Belize City (02) 7-56-34; fax 7-69-61), 1 King St (PO Box 37), Belize City, is among the most luxurious of Belize's jungle lodges. Its location is incredible: thatched cabañas fill the central plaza of a Mayan archaeological site! Resident ornithologists have identified more than 260 species of birds here. Each of the 12

BELIZE

cabañas has private bath, fan, two queen-sized beds, and a verandah. Rooms cost US$90/115 a single/double; meals cost US$30 per person per day. For information and reservations in the USA, ☎ (800) 343-8009.

Chan Chich is located in Orange Walk District between the settlement of Gallon Jug and the Guatemalan border, and is best reached by chartered plane from Belize City, though there is an all-weather road (210 km, 3½ hours from Belize City).

LAMANAI

By far the most impressive site in this part of the country is Lamanai, in its own archaeology reserve on the New River Lagoon, near the settlement of Indian Church. Though much of the site remains unexcavated and unrestored, the trip to Lamanai, by motorboat up the New River, is an adventure in itself.

Figuring 1½ hours' boat travel each way, and somewhat over two hours at the site, the excursion to Lamanai takes most of a day.

As with most sites in northern Belize, Lamanai ('Submerged Crocodile', the original Mayan name of the place) was occupied as early as 1500 BC, with the first stone buildings appearing between 800 and 600 BC. Lamanai flourished in Late Pre-Classic times, growing to be a major ceremonial centre with immense temples long before most other Mayan sites.

Unlike many other sites, Maya lived here until the coming of the Spanish in the 1500s. The ruined Indian church (actually two of them) to be found nearby attests to the fact that there were Maya here for the Spanish friars to convert. Convert them they did, but by 1640 the Maya had reverted to their ancient forms of worship. British interests later built a sugar mill, now in ruins, at Indian Church. The archaeological site was excavated by David Pendergast in the 1970s and '80s.

You motor for 1½ hours up the New River from the Tower Hill toll bridge south of Orange Walk, between river banks crowded with dense jungle vegetation. Along the way,

your boatman/guide points out the many local birds and will almost certainly spot a crocodile or two. Along the way you pass the Mennonite community at Shipyard. Finally the river opens out into the New River Lagoon, a broad and very long expanse of water which can be choppy during the frequent rainshowers.

Landing at Lamanai settlement (open from 9 am to 5 pm daily), sign the visitors' book, pay the admission fee (US$1.50) and wander into the dense jungle, past gigantic guanacaste, ceiba and *ramón* (breadnut) trees, strangler figs, allspice, epiphytes and black orchids, Belize's national flower. In the canopy overhead one can sometimes see one of the five groups of howler monkeys resident in the archaeological zone.

A tour of the ruins takes at least 1½ hours (two or three hours is more comfortable).

Of the 60 significant structures identified here, the grandest is Structure N10-43, a huge Late Pre-Classic building rising more than 34 metres above the jungle canopy. Other buildings along La Ruta Maya are taller, but this one was built well before the others. It's been partially uncovered and restored.

Not far from N10-43 is Lamanai's ball court, a smallish one, partially uncovered.

To the north along a path in the jungle is Structure P9-56, built several centuries later, with a huge stylised mask of a man in a crocodile-mouth headdress four metres high emblazoned on its south-west face. Archaeologists have dug deep into this structure (from the platform level high on the east side) to explore for burials and to document the several earlier structures which lie beneath.

Near this structure is a small temple and a very fine ruined stela. The tall stela of fine limestone once stood on the front face of the temple. Apparently some worshippers built a fire at the base of the stela, and later doused it with water. The hot stone stela, cooled too quickly by the water, broke and toppled. The low-relief carving of a majestic figure is extremely fine.

There is a small museum near the boat

landing, with quite interesting figurative pottery and some large flint tools.

Places to Stay & Eat
Lamanai Outpost Lodge (no phone), Lamanai, Orange Walk District, is a five-minute boat ride (a 15-minute walk) south of the archaeological zone. Situated on a hillside sloping down to the lagoon, the well-kept, new lodge buildings enjoy panoramic views. Guests stay in modern bungalows with fans and private baths. Meals are available at moderate prices in the cheerful dining room (lunch costs US$8), and there's a bar. Rooms cost US$77/101 a single/double. Two, three and four-night tour packages, including transfers to and from Belize City or the international airport, river excursions, wildlife walks and tours of Lamanai, are available.

Getting There & Away
Lamanai can be reached by road (58 km) from Orange Walk via San Felipe except when heavy rains mire the road, but there is no regular bus service, and the bumpy road trip is just as long but not nearly so enjoyable as the river trip.

Take a sun hat, sunblock cream, insect repellent, shoes (rather than sandals), lunch and a beverage (unless you plan to take a tour which includes lunch). From May to October, a raincoat or parka is useful to ward off an afternoon shower.

The main base for river departures is the Tower Hill toll bridge, seven km south of Orange Walk on the Northern Highway. The Novelo brothers (Antonio and Herminio) run Jungle River Tours (☎ (3) 2-22-93; fax 2-37-49), 20 Lovers' Lane (PO Box 95), Orange Walk Town, and have excellent reputations as guides and naturalists. Contact them at the bridge or at the Lovers' Cafe (near the south-east corner of the central park in Orange Walk Town), or make a reservation by phone or fax. Be at their boat dock, on the north-west side of the Tower Hill toll bridge, by 9 am for the day-long trip (back by 4 pm), which includes lunch, beverages

and the guided tour along the river and at Lamanai (US$50 per person, with a minimum of four persons).

The *Lamanai Lady* motorboat departs from Jim's Cool Pool, just north of the toll bridge (by Novelo's), at 9 am daily (be there by 8.30 am) for the river tour to Lamanai. The boat ride and guided tour costs US$28 per person; a boxed lunch is another US$7. You can book your tour at the Batty Brothers bus terminal in Belize City (☎ (2) 7-20-25; fax 7-89-91).

It's possible to take the 6 am Batty's bus from Belize City to Orange Walk, get out at the Tower Hill toll bridge, and be in time for the 9 am departure of the boats for Lamanai. Boats return to the bridge before 4 pm, allowing you to catch the 4 pm Batty's bus southward back to Belize City. An entire tour from Belize City to Lamanai via the *Lamanai Lady*, and then return to Belize City, costs US$52. Book at Batty's in Belize City.

ORANGE WALK
The agricultural and social centre of northern Belize is this town of some 10,000 people, 94 km north of Belize City. It's important to the farmers (including many Mennonites) who till the soil of the region, raising sugar cane and citrus fruits. Another important crop is said to be marijuana. Orange Walk is not very important to visitors unless you're bound for one of the archaeological sites or wildlife reserves nearby, in which case its modest hotels and many Chinese restaurants are useful.

The centre of town is the shady central park on the east side of the main road, called Queen Victoria Ave. The town hospital is in the northern outskirts, readily visible on the west side of the road.

Cuello & Nohmul Archaeological Sites
Near Orange Walk is Cuello, a Mayan site with a 3000-year history but little to show for it. Archaeologists have found plenty here, but you will find only a few grassy mounds. The site is on private property, that of the

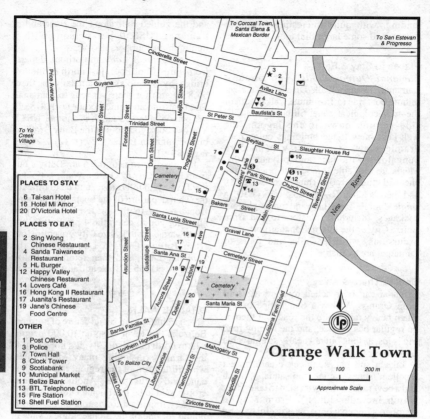

PLACES TO STAY

6 Tai-san Hotel
16 Hotel Mi Amor
20 D'Victoria Hotel

PLACES TO EAT

2 Sing Wong
   Chinese Restaurant
4 Sanda Taiwanese
   Restaurant
5 HL Burger
12 Happy Valley
   Chinese Restaurant
14 Lovers Café
16 Hong Kong II Restaurant
17 Juanita's Restaurant
19 Jane's Chinese
   Food Centre

OTHER

1 Post Office
7 Police
7 Town Hall
8 Clock Tower
9 Scotiabank
10 Municipal Market
11 Belize Bank
13 BTL Telephone Office
15 Fire Station
18 Shell Fuel Station

Orange Walk Town

0   100   200 m

Approximate Scale

Cuello Brothers Distillery (☎ (3) 2-21-41), four km west of Orange Walk along Yo Creek Rd. Call and ask for permission before you tramp around the site. The distillery, on the left-hand (south) side of the road, is unmarked; the site is through and beyond it.

Nohmul, near the village of San Pablo (12 km north of Orange Walk), was a much more important site, with a lofty acropolis looming over the surrounding countryside. Though a vast site, most of it is now covered in grass and sugar cane. To take a look at what there is, walk two km west of San Pablo; you may need a guide to find it.

Places to Stay

Orange Walk Town has several hotels, none of them very grand. *Hotel Mi Amor* (☎ (3) 2-20-31; fax 2-34-62), 19 Queen Victoria Ave (PO Box 117), is perhaps the best choice: simple and clean. Its rooms cost US$22 with one bed, US$30 with two, US$38 with air-conditioning.

Tai-san Hotel (☎ (3) 2-27-52), 30 Queen Victoria Ave, north of the plaza, has seven bathless rooms above a fairly noisy Chinese restaurant. Rates are US$11/15 a single/ double.

Best in town is the *D'Victoria Hotel* (☎ (3)

2-25-18; fax 2-28-47), 40 Queen Victoria Ave (PO Box 74), which boasts a swimming pool and disco. Guestrooms are priced at US$22 to US$25 with private bath, US$38 to US$55 with air-conditioning.

Places to Eat

Locals favour *Juanita's*, on Santa Ana St near the Shell fuel station, a simple place with local fare at low prices.

HL Burger, three blocks north of the park on the main road, has good cheap burgers (US$2), rice and bean plates, and ice cream.

When it comes to Chinese restaurants, Orange Walk has them. *Happy Valley*, at Church and Main Sts, and *Sing Wong*, at Main St and Avilez Lane, are about the nicest, along with the *Sanda Taiwanese Restaurant*, near HL Burger. The *Hong Kong II* restaurant, right next to the Hotel Mi Amor, is favoured by locals. *Jane's Chinese Food Centre* is about three blocks down the main street from it.

The Diner is also a favourite local place, located on the northern outskirts to the west of the hospital (follow the signs).

Getting There & Away

Southbound buses pass through town at least every hour (usually on the hour, and sometimes on the half-hour as well) from 4.30 am to about 12.30 pm, with a few later buses. Northbound buses pass through at 15 minutes before the hour from 1.45 pm to 8.45 pm. It's 61 km to Corozal Town (1½ hours, US$2) and 94 km to Belize City (two hours, US$2.50).

COROZAL TOWN

Corozal is a farming town of some 9000 people. Several decades ago the countryside was given over completely to sugar cane (there's a refinery south of the town). Today, though sugar is still important, crops are now diversified. The land is fertile, the climate is good for agriculture and the town is prosperous. Many of those who do not farm commute to Orange Walk or Belize City to work.

Corozaleños, most of whom speak Spanish as their first language, are pleasant folks, and you may find that people greet you on the street or at least offer a smile. The North American expatriate community here is considerable. Retirement developments in Consejo Shores have turned into comfortable gringo ghettos. If you spend any time at all in Corozal, you're sure to hear many stories from Yanks and Canadians who left it all behind to pursue the good life in quiet Belize.

History

Corozal's Mayan history is long and important. On the northern outskirts of the town are the ruins of a Mayan ceremonial centre once called Chetumal, now called Santa Rita. Across the bay at Cerros is one of the most important Late Pre-Classic sites yet discovered.

Maya have been living around Corozal since 1500 BC. Modern Corozal Town dates from only 1849, however. In that year, refugees from the War of the Castes in Yucatán fled across the border to safe haven in British-controlled Belize. They founded a town, and named it after the cohune palm, a symbol of fertility. For years it had the look of a typical Caribbean town, until Hurricane Janet roared through in 1955 and blew away many of the old wooden buildings on stilts. Much of Corozal's cinder-block architecture dates from the late 1950s.

As late as the 1970s, when Belize's Northern Highway was a potholed moonscape negotiated only by trucks, Corozal Town enjoyed a prosperous if small tourist trade. Travellers would cross the border from Mexico and relax on the shores of Corozal before taking the punishing trip southward in the back of a truck. Now that the highway is improved and is served regularly by buses, most travellers go straight through Corozal to Belize City or beyond.

Orientation & Information

Though founded by the Maya, Corozal now resembles a Mexican town, with its plaza, its Palacio Municipal and its large church. The chimes of the clock tower keep everyone on

BELIZE

BELIZE

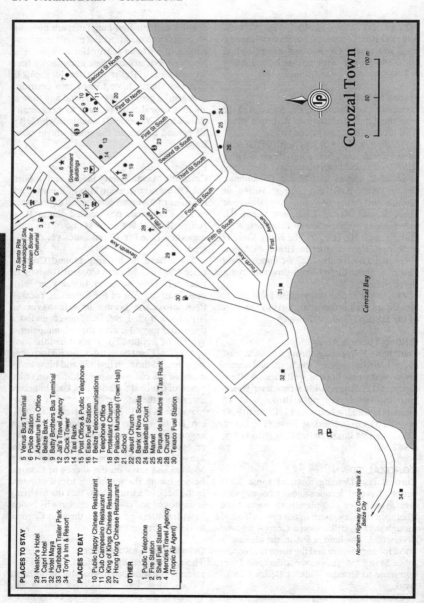

Corozal Town

Corozal Bay

To Santa Rita
Archaeological Site,
Mexican Border &
Chetumal

Northern Highway to Orange Walk &
Belize City

PLACES TO STAY

29 Nestor's Hotel
31 Capri Hotel
32 Hotel Maya
33 Caribbean Trailer Park
34 Tony's Inn & Resort

PLACES TO EAT

10 Public Happy Chinese Restaurant
11 Club Campesino Restaurant
20 King of Kings Chinese Restaurant
27 Hong Kong Chinese Restaurant

OTHER

1 Public Telephone
2 Fire Station
3 Shell Fuel Station
4 Menzies Travel Agency
  (Tropic Air Agent)

5 Venus Bus Terminal
6 Police Station
7 Adventure Inn Office
8 Belize Bank
9 Batty Brothers Bus Terminal
12 Jal's Travel Agency
13 Clock Tower
14 Taxi Rank
15 Post Office & Public Telephone
16 Esso Fuel Station
17 Belize Telecommunications
   Telephone Office
18 Protestant Church
19 Palacio Municipal (Town Hall)
21 School
22 Jesuit Church
23 Bank of Nova Scotia
24 Basketball Court
25 Market
26 Parque de la Madre & Taxi Rank
28 Church
30 Texaco Fuel Station

schedule. You can walk easily to any place in town. Even Tony's Inn & Resort, on the south-western outskirts, is only a 20-minute walk from the plaza.

The Belize Bank on the north side of the plaza is open for currency exchange Monday to Friday from 8 am to 1 pm, and also on Friday afternoon from 3 to 6 pm.

Santa Rita Archaeological Site

Santa Rita is a small, nicely kept park with one small restored Mayan temple, located just over one km north-west of the Venus bus terminal in Corozal. Go north on the main highway; after 700 metres bear right, just before the statue. After another 100 metres turn left at the Restaurant Hennessy and go straight on for 300 metres to the site. The 'hill' on the right is actually a temple. The site is open (for free) during daylight hours.

The Santa Rita site was discovered almost a century ago by amateur archaeologist Thomas Gann, Corozal's town physician. Called Chetumal by the Maya, this city sat astride important riverine trade routes, and had its share of wealth. The jade and pottery artefacts found here have been dispersed to museums, and the important frescoes destroyed.

Cerros Archaeological Site

There is more to see at Cerros (also called Cerro Maya) than at Santa Rita: namely a temple more than 20 metres high, but the site is mostly a mass of grass-covered mounds. Cerros flourished in Late Pre-Classic times, and has yielded important artefacts.

Negotiate with a boat owner to ferry you across Corozal Bay and back from Corozal.

Places to Stay – bottom end

Camping *Caribbean Trailer Park* (☎ (4) 2-20-45), PO Box 55, about 500 metres south of the plaza, has large swaths of lush grass shaded by coconut palms. Amenities include usable toilets, mouldy showers and all hook-ups. Rates are US$3.50 per person for a tent, US$7 in a camper van (RV). Talk to Jim or Donna, who live at the north end of the park.

The park is marked only by a sign reading 'Caribbean Restaurant'.

Hotels *Hotel Maya* (☎ (4) 2-20-82), PO Box 112, on Seventh Ave (the main road) about 400 metres south of the plaza, is somewhat dilapidated, but run by nice people. The 17 aged (but clean) rooms are often all occupied. Cheap meals are served in the adjoining eatery. Rates are a bit high: US$19 for a room with one double bed, US$24 with two beds. All rooms have private showers. As for meals, sandwiches cost about US$2, burgers a bit more and a full fried-chicken dinner US$6.

Nestor's Hotel (☎ (4) 2-23-54), 125 Fifth Ave South, used to be the budget travellers' favourite, but the bar downstairs is now patronised mostly by Corozal's cool youth, who come to drink beer by the pitcher. Rooms are cheap at US$11 a single, US$14 to US$19 a double. Hot water is solar heated.

Capri Hotel (☎ (4) 2-20-42), at the southern end of Fourth Ave, has 30 small, fairly dingy rooms, some with private bath, priced a bit lower than Nestor's. Upkeep is not the best, however, and the noise from the bar can be deafening, so look upon the Capri as a last resort.

Places to Stay – middle

About one km south of the plaza on the shore road is *Tony's Inn & Resort* (☎ (4) 2-20-55; fax 2-28-29), PO Box 12, an attractive holiday enclave with landscaped grounds and lawn chairs set to enjoy the view of the bay. It has its own swimming lagoon, satellite TV, and an air-conditioned restaurant and bar. The 26 rooms on two floors come with fan or air-conditioner, and cost US$60 to US$84 a double in winter (about 20% cheaper in summer).

Adventure Inn (☎ (4) 2-21-87; fax 2-22-43), PO Box 35, is 12 km north-east of the centre, overlooking the bay in Consejo Shores. The atmospheric bungalows hold 20 rooms with private showers, and are priced at US$65 a double. For more information and reservations, apply to the hotel's office

BELIZE

in Corozal, on Fourth Avenue 1½ blocks north of the plaza.

Places to Eat

The *Hotel Maya* and *Tony's Inn* have decent restaurants. Otherwise, there are many small Chinese restaurants, such as the *Public Happy Restaurant* on Fourth Ave at Second St North. Chow mein, chop suey, lobster or fish with rice, and many other items are listed on the menu. Portions cost US$1.75 to US$5, depending upon the ingredients and the size of the portion.

The *Club Campesino* has grilled meats, chicken etc, but opens only at 6.30 pm for dinner, drinks and late-night socialising.

Getting There & Away

Air Corozal Town has its own little airstrip (code CZL) several km south of the centre, reached by taxi (US$4 – you can share the cost with other passengers). It is only an airstrip – there's no shelter and not even so much as a vendor selling soft drinks, so there's no point in arriving too early for your flight. If it's raining, you'll wait in the rain. Taxis meet all incoming flights.

Tropic Air (☎ in San Pedro, Ambergris Caye (026) 25-42, 20-12) has two flights daily between Corozal Town and San Pedro, Ambergris Caye (20 minutes, US$30 one way). You can connect at San Pedro with flights to Belize City, and from Belize City to other parts of the country. For information and tickets, apply to Menzies Travel Agency, across the road from the Venus bus terminal.

Bus Venus Bus Lines (☎ (4) 2-21-32) and Batty Brothers Bus Service operate frequent buses between Chetumal (Mexico) and Belize City, stopping at Corozal Town. For details, see Chetumal (in the Yucatán section of this book) and also Getting Around in the introductory Belize chapter.

Buses leave Corozal Town and head south via Orange Walk for Belize City at least every hour from 3.30 am to 11.30 am, with extra buses on the half-hour during busy times. From Belize City to Corozal, departures are on the hour between noon and 7 pm.

Belize City (155 km, 3½ hours) – many Venus and Batty Brothers buses daily (US$4)

Chetumal (30 km, one hour with border formalities) – many Venus and Batty Brothers buses daily (US$1)

Orange Walk (61 km, 1½ hours) – many Venus and Batty Brothers buses daily (US$2)

NORTH TO MEXICO

Corozal Town is 13 km south of the border-crossing point at Santa Elena/Subteniente López. Most of the Venus and Batty Brothers buses travelling between Chetumal and Belize City stop at Corozal Town. Otherwise, hitch a ride or hire a taxi (expensive at US$12) to get you to Santa Elena. From Subteniente López, minibuses shuttle the 12 km to Chetumal (Combi Corner) frequently all day.

Santa Elena border station has nothing more than the requisite government offices and one or two very basic restaurants.

Southern Belize

Southern Belize is perhaps the most remote stretch of La Ruta Maya. The roads are long and usually in bad condition, the towns are small, and access to sites requires time, energy and – sometimes – money. But if you want to explore off the tourist track, southern Belize is the place to do it.

Among the places to visit are Dangriga, main town of Stann Creek District, centre of the Black Carib Garinagu (or Garifuna) culture; the Cockscomb Basin Jaguar Preserve; Placencia, where life is similar to that on the cayes; and Punta Gorda, near several unrestored Mayan sites. From Punta Gorda there are boats across the bay to Puerto Barrios (in Guatemala).

HUMMINGBIRD HIGHWAY

Heading south from Belmopan, the Hummingbird Highway is well paved as far as the Caves Branch River (19 km), but then degenerates as it bumps and grinds its way south and east to Dangriga.

Blue Hole National Park

Just under 20 km south of Belmopan is Blue Hole National Park, where underground tributaries of the Sibun River bubble to the surface and fill a deep limestone sinkhole about 33 metres deep and 100 metres in diameter. After running out of the sinkhole and down a short distance, the stream cascades into a domed cavern. Deliciously cool on the hottest days, the cavern makes an excellent swimming hole. The park is open daily from 8 am to 4 pm.

A rugged nature trail leads 2.5 km from the Blue Hole to St Herman's Cave. For an easier walk, follow the Hummingbird Highway north to a separate path to St Herman's, 400 metres off the highway. The cave is entered from the bottom of a large limestone sinkhole. Mayan artefacts dating from the Classic Period have been found in the cave. As there is no electric lighting, you must bring a flashlight to penetrate the cave to any distance.

Onward to Dangriga, the road crosses several rivers emptying out of the Maya Mountains to the south, and passes through plantations of cacao, bananas and citrus, before coming to the junction of the Southern Highway and the road into Dangriga.

DANGRIGA

Once called Stann Creek Town, Dangriga (population 10,000) is the largest town in southern Belize. It's much smaller than Belize City, but friendlier and quieter. B Nicholas, Belize's most famous painter, lives and works in Dangriga near the Bonefish Hotel. His paintings are displayed in banks, hotel lobbies and public buildings throughout the country. Stop in at his studio and have a look.

There's not much to do here except spend the night and head onwards – unless it's 19 November. Read on.

History

Dangriga's citizens are descendants of the Black Caribs, people of mixed South American Indian and African blood, who inhabited the island of St Vincent as a free people in the 1600s. By the end of the 1700s, British colonisers had brought the independent-minded Caribs under their control and transported them from one island to another in an effort to subdue them. In the early 1800s, oppression and wandering finally brought many of the Black Caribs to southern Belize. The most memorable migration took place late in 1832, when on 19 November a large number of Caribs reached Belize from Honduras in dugout canoes. The event is celebrated annually in Belize as Garifuna Settlement Day. Dangriga is the place to be on 19 November, when the town explodes in a frenzy of dancing, drinking and celebration of the Garifuna heritage.

BELIZE

PLACES TO STAY

2	Pelican Beach Resort
17	Cameleon Central Hotel
21	Riverside Hotel
24	The Hub
27	Soffie's Hotel
28	Río Mar Hotel
31	Bonefish Hotel
33	Pal's Guest House

PLACES TO EAT

1	Airport Café
6	Silver Garden
9	Relis Chinese Restaurant
16	Sunrise
18	Starlight
20	Burger King
24	The Hub Restaurant
27	Soffie's Restaurant
28	Río Mar Restaurant

OTHER

3	BTL Telephone Towers
4	Water Tower ('Reservoir')
5	Ice Factory
7	Affordable Corner Store & Laundromat
8	Treasure House Travel Agency
10	Police
11	BTL Telephone Office
12	Public Health Center
13	Hospital
14	Courthouse
15	Barclay's Bank
19	Chemist's/Pharmacy
22	Scotiabank
23	Fish Market
25	BTIA Tourist Information (PJ's Gift Shop)
26	Belize Bank
29	Baptist Church
30	Post Office
32	B Nicholas, Artist
34	Shell Fuel Station
35	Texaco Fuel Station

BELIZE

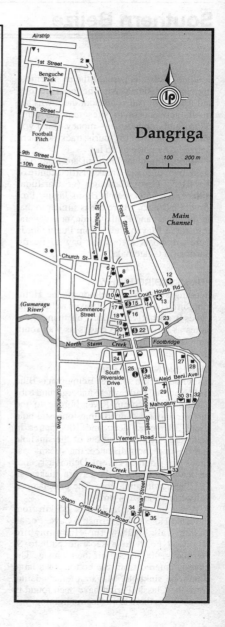

Dangriga

Orientation & Information

North Stann Creek (also called the Gumaragu River) empties into the Gulf of Honduras at the centre of the town. Dangriga's main street is called St Vincent

St south of the creek and Commerce St to the north. The bus station is on St Vincent St at the southern end of the bridge over the creek. The airstrip, two km north of the centre, near the Pelican Beach Resort, has a café and a small airline building.

Though there is no government tourist office, the Belize Tourism Industry Association has an office of sorts at PJ's Gift Shop (☎ (5) 2-22-66) just south of the bridge, at 21 St Vincent St.

Treasure House Travel Agency (☎ (5) 2-25-78), 64 Commerce St, can handle questions about airline tickets and the like.

The Affordable Corner Store & Laundromat is open from 9 am to noon and 2 to 8 pm (the last wash is at 5 pm). It's closed on Thursday afternoon and on Sunday.

Places to Stay

Among the cheapest places is the *Cameleon Central Hotel* (☎ (5) 2-20-08), 119 Commerce St, which advertises itself as 'safe, clean and economical'. Rates are US$6.50 per person in waterless rooms.

The Hub (☎ (5) 2-30-64; fax 2-28-13), 573 South Riverside Drive (PO Box 56), is a congenial place with a shady front terrace, and six rooms (some with private showers) going for US$7/12 a single/double with shared bath, US$12/17 with private bath.

On the south bank of North Stann Creek, at the creek's mouth, are two good choices. The *Río Mar Hotel* (☎ (5) 2-22-01), 977 Southern Foreshore, at the corner of Waight's St, has nine tidy, clean rooms, all with bath and most with TV, at US$18 to US$28, single or double. The upstairs rooms are preferable. The restaurant and bar serve good cheap meals and drinks.

Nearby is *Soffie's Hotel* (☎ (5) 2-27-89), 970 Chatye St, with 10 serviceable rooms ranging in price from US$22 to US$33, the most expensive having air-conditioning; all have private bath. There's a restaurant on the ground floor, and good views of the water from upstairs.

Riverside Hotel (☎ (5) 2-21-68; fax 2-22-96), 5 Commerce St, at the north end of the bridge, has 12 rooms with clean shared showers for US$11 per person.

Pal's Guest House (☎ (5) 2-20-95), 868-A Magoon St, is spartan but clean, with a sea breeze and the sound of the surf. You pay US$17 a double in a room with shared bath, US$23 with private bath and TV.

Bonefish Hotel (☎ (5) 2-21-65; fax 2-22-96), 15 Mahogany Rd (PO Box 21), is comfortable – the 10 big, clean rooms have fans, air-conditioning, TV and private bath for US$64 a double. There's a dining room as well.

Pelican Beach Resort (☎ (5) 2-20-44, fax 2-25-70), PO Box 14, is Dangriga's upmarket lodging place. It's at the north end of town, on the beach, and boasts a restaurant, bar, sand beach, boat dock, and a full programme of tours to sites in the area. Simple rooms with bath cost US$50 to US$69 a single, US$65 to US$87 a double. The Pelican also has cottages on South Water Caye (US$105 per day for up to four persons).

Places to Eat

The Hub, *Río Mar Hotel* and *Soffie's Hotel* have good, cheap restaurants. The *Bonefish* and *Pelican* are the upmarket places.

Otherwise, the locals favour *Burger King*, a tidy lunchroom on Commerce St with a long and varied menu, from burgers to fish fillet and chicken. Their breakfast special of eggs, refried beans, toast and coffee is good at US$2.75.

Most of the other restaurants along Commerce St are Chinese: the *Sunrise*, *Starlight*, *Silver Garden* and *Relis*, serving full meals for about US$6.

Getting There & Away

Air Maya Airways serves Dangriga. For details, see under Getting Around in the Getting There & Around chapter for Belize.

Bus Z-Line has five buses daily from Belize City (170 km, five hours, US$5.50) via Belmopan. Return buses leave Dangriga at 5, 6 and 9 am for Belize City; on Sunday, departures are at 10 am and 3 pm.

BELIZE

Two of the buses from Belize City continue southward to Independence (for Placencia, 85 km, 2½ hours, US$3) and Punta Gorda (169 km, six hours, US$5.50), departing from Dangriga at noon and 7 pm (on Sunday, at 2 pm only).

A faster, better way to Placencia is via the shuttle van (☎ (5) 2-27-02; in Belize City ☎ (2) 7-39-77, 7-78-11) which departs from The Hub hotel in Dangriga at noon on Monday, Wednesday, Friday and Saturday, stopping at Hopkins village, and arriving in Placencia at 2 pm (US$4).

Jaguar

SOUTHERN CAYES
Several cayes are customarily accessed from Dangriga.

Tobacco Caye's lodging possibilities include *Island Camps* (☎ (2) 7-21-09, (05) 2-22-01), 51 Regent St, Belize City; *Reef End Lodge*, PO Box 10, Dangriga; and *Fairweather & Friends,* PO Box 240, Belize City.

Dangriga's Pelican Beach Resort (see above) has cottages on South Water Caye.

Glover's Atoll Resort (☎ (8) 2-21-49, 2-31-80; fax 2-35-05, 2-32-35), PO Box 563, Belize City, has simple beachfront cabañas – candles for light, rainwater to drink, outhouse, etc – on one of the outer cayes, a five-km, six-hour boat trip from Sittee River Village near Hopkins (south of Dangriga). You must take some supplies, including food and towels, as this is a very simple place, but there's lots of water-sports equipment for rent, excellent diving and very few other people to disturb the tranquillity. The basic cost is US$55 per person per week for lodging (US$30 if you camp), plus US$40 per person return for transport by boat. The boat departs from Sittee River every Sunday morning at 8 am.

SOUTHERN HIGHWAY
The Southern Highway, south of Dangriga, is unpaved and can be rough, especially in the rainy months, but along the way are some good opportunities for experiencing untouristy Belize.

Hopkins
The farming and fishing village of Hopkins (population 1100) is seven km east of the Southern Highway, on the coast. Most of its people are Garinagus, living as the coastal inhabitants of Belize have lived for centuries.

If you're interested in simple living and Garinagu culture, visit Hopkins and stay at the *Sandy Beach Lodge*, at the southern end of the village. The lodge has six simple thatched rooms renting for US$13/20 a single/double with shared bath, US$20/27 with private bath. Meals cost US$5 for breakfast or dinner, US$7 for lunch. For reservations in Dangriga, contact Gasper Martin at The Hub or Janice Lambert at PJ's Gift Shop, or call the Hopkins community telephone: ☎ (5) 2-20-33.

Sittee River
Another small coastal village where you can get away from it all is Sittee River. *Prospect Cool Spot Guest House & Camp Site* (☎ (5) 2-20-06, 2-23-89; ask for Isaac Kelly, Senior) will put you up in adequate simplicity for US$10/15 a single/double (US$2.50 in a tent). Simple, inexpensive meals are served.

Cockscomb Basin Wildlife Sanctuary
Almost halfway between Dangriga and Independence is the village of Maya Centre, where a track goes 10 km west to the Cockscomb Basin Wildlife Sanctuary, sometimes called the Jaguar Reserve.

BELIZE

Created in 1984, the sanctuary now covers over 40,000 hectares (100,000 acres). The varied topography and lush tropical forest make this an excellent place to observe Belizean wildlife. Within the reserve are found wild cats including jaguars, pumas, ocelots, margays and jaguarundis. Other animals, many the prey of the cats, include agouti, anteater, armadillo, Baird's tapir, brocket deer, coati, kinkajou, otter, paca, peccary and the weasel-like tayra. Reptiles, some of which are deadly poisonous, include the Boa constrictor and the fer-de-lance. There are birds galore.

There's no public transport to the reserve, but the walk through the lush forest is a pretty one. At the reserve is a camp site (US$2 per person), several simple shared rental cabins (US$10 per person), a visitors' centre, and numerous hiking trails. Though you cannot be assured of seeing a jaguar (though this is their preferred habitat), you will certainly enjoy seeing many of the hundreds of other species of birds, plants and animals in this rich environment.

For information, contact the Belize Audubon Society (☎ (2) 7-73-69), 29 Regent St (PO Box 1001), Belize City, or the Cockscomb Basin Wildlife Sanctuary, PO Box 90, Dangriga.

PLACENCIA

Perched at the southern tip of a long, narrow sandy peninsula, Placencia (population 600) is 'the caye you can drive to'. Not too long ago, the only practical way to get here was by boat from the mainland at Independence/Big Creek. Now there is a road all the way down the peninsula, and an airstrip just north of the town. But Placencia still has the wonderful laid-back ambience of the cayes, along with beaches, varied accommodation, and friendly local people. Activities here are the same as on the cayes: swimming, sunbathing, lazing, water sports, and excursions to cayes and to points inland.

Orientation

The village of Placencia is at the southern tip of the narrow peninsula. The town owes its layout to years gone by, when all commerce and activity was carried out by boat and there was little use for streets. Thus, the village's main north-south 'street' is actually a narrow concrete footpath less than a metre wide which threads its way among simple wood-frame houses (some on stilts) and beachfront lodges.

An easy walk takes you anywhere. From the camping ground at the northern end of the village, it's only 1½ km to the southern tip of the peninsula. Various resorts are scattered along the coast north of Placencia from Rum Point to Seine Bight Village.

An unpaved road skirts the town to the west, ending at the peninsula's southern tip, which is the bus stop.

There is no central landmark in the village and no town square. At the southern end you'll find the wharf, the fuel station, the bus stop and the ice house. Midway to the north, the Flamboyant Restaurant gives about as much civic focus as one gets (or wants) in Placencia.

On the mainland to the west are the towns of Mango Creek (to the north), Independence (in the middle) and Big Creek (to the south). Though they started out as villages with different names, they have coalesced into one larger settled area. Many Belizeans use the names interchangeably.

Information

Heidi Ribary at Placencia Visitor Services (☎ (6) 2-31-53; fax 2-32-63) can answer many questions about Placencia, and book rooms and excursions. In fact, almost any Placencian knows of a good, cheap room for you, and has a relative or friend who runs boat trips to the reef and cayes.

Beaches & Excursions

Daily life in Placencia is much like that at any other Belizean holiday destination: water sports, camaraderie, and excursions to cayes and inland attractions.

Unlike most of the cayes, Placencia has good palm-lined beaches on its east side.

BELIZE

BELIZE

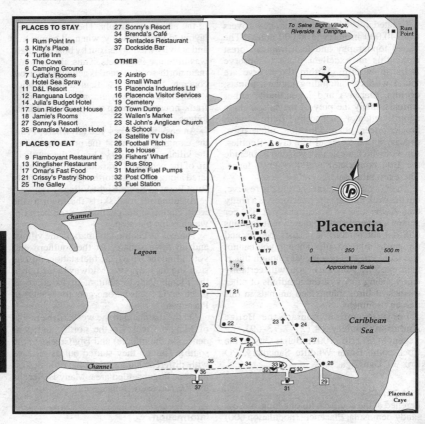

PLACES TO STAY
1 Rum Point Inn
3 Kitty's Place
4 Turtle Inn
5 The Cove
6 Camping Ground
7 Lydia's Rooms
8 Hotel Sea Spray
11 D&L Resort
12 Ranguana Lodge
14 Julia's Budget Hotel
17 Sun Rider Guest House
18 Jamie's Rooms
27 Sonny's Resort
35 Paradise Vacation Hotel

PLACES TO EAT
9 Flamboyant Restaurant
13 Kingfisher Restaurant
17 Omar's Fast Food
21 Crissy's Pastry Shop
25 The Galley
27 Sonny's Resort
34 Brenda's Café
36 Tentacles Restaurant
37 Dockside Bar

OTHER
2 Airstrip
10 Small Wharf
15 Placencia Industries Ltd
16 Placencia Visitor Services
19 Cemetery
20 Town Dump
22 Wallen's Market
23 St John's Anglican Church & School
24 Satellite TV Dish
26 Football Pitch
28 Ice House
29 Fishers' Wharf
30 Bus Stop
31 Marine Fuel Pumps
32 Post Office
33 Fuel Station

To Seine Bight Village, Riverside & Dangriga

Rum Point

Placencia

0   250   500 m

Approximate Scale

Channel

Lagoon

Channel

Caribbean Sea

Placencia Caye

When you're tired of the beach, contact a member of the Placencia Tourist Guide Association (there are 16) and arrange for some sailing, snorkelling, scuba diving, fly and sport fishing, bird and manatee watching, overnight camping on remote cayes, and excursions to jungle rivers and the Cockscomb Basin Reserve.

Places to Stay

Placencia has lodgings in all price ranges. Bottom-end and mid-range accommodation is in the village; top-end places are several

km to the north along the beach. Most houses in the village rent rooms, whether they call themselves a 'hotel' or not. Ask at one, and if it's full, they'll give you a suggestion for another to try. Good places for lodging references are the Kingfisher Restaurant, Ranguana Lodge, D & L Resort and Lydia's Rooms.

Placencia's camping area is at the northern edge of the village, on the beach. Pitch your tent or hang your hammock among the coconut palms for US$2 per person. Services are primitive.

Lydia's Rooms (☎ (6) 2-31-17), sometimes called Conrad & Lydia's Rooms, has simple rooms (shared baths) for US$8/12 a single/double. They also have a house for rent.

Paradise Vacation Hotel is a tidy white board structure with bathless rooms renting for US$13 to US$22 a double. *Jamie's* is similar.

Sun Rider Guest House (☎ (6) 2-32-36) has good, clean rooms fronting on a beach with shady palms (US$23 a double). One room has two beds and a kitchenette (US$39).

Julia's Budget Hotel is central, clean enough, and certainly cheap at US$8/11/17 a single/double/triple without bath.

The *Hotel Sea Spray*, right in the centre of the village, has a variety of rooms, from those which share baths (US$15) to rooms with bath (US$20 to US$38).

Sonny's Resort (☎ (6) 2-31-03; fax (2) 3-28-19), to the south, has clean white rooms (US$44) and cabañas (US$58) with shower. There's a good restaurant and bar as well.

Ranguana Lodge (☎/fax (6) 2-31-12) has tidy and attractive, if simple, mahogany cabins right on the beach for US$50 to US$60 a double, with private shower. Each room has a fan, refrigerator, coffee-maker and balcony. They knock US$10 off the price if you do your own daily cleaning.

Rum Point Inn (☎ (6) 2-32-39; fax 2-32-40) is Placencia's long-time favourite. George, Corol and Wade Bevier's place has spacious free-form concrete cabins, a dining room with sea view, and a good library on Mayan and ecological subjects. Rates are US$187/228 a single/double, tax, service and all meals included. Tours to the reef, cayes and throughout Belize are available.

Kitty's Place (☎ (6) 2-32-27; fax 2-32-26), north of the centre, is a Caribbean Victorian lodge with cabañas on the beach. Rooms cost US$35 to US$58 a single, US$46 to US$69 a double, the cheaper being without private bath. Apartments (which sleep up to six) cost US$81 to US$110 a double.

Nautical Inn (☎/fax (6) 2-23-10) is a new, attractive establishment in Seine Bight

Village, an unspoiled Belizean fishing village north of Placencia. Ben and Janie Ruoti are equipped for all adventures, renting motor bikes, running diving and coastal tours, etc. Comfortable modern rooms cost US$125/170 a single/double, tax, service and three meals included.

Places to Eat

A social centre of the village is the *Flamboyant Restaurant* (formerly Jene's), with indoor and outdoor tables and the usual list of sandwiches, rice and beans, and fish dishes for US$3 to US$6.

Kingfisher Restaurant, in the centre, has a fine view of the sea, and a menu stretching from the lowly cheese sandwich (US$1.50) to a shrimp or lobster dinner (US$12). This is another of Placencia's social centres. Neighbouring *Sonny's Resort* also has a good restaurant and bar.

Omar's Fast Food, in the Sun Rider Guest House, has homemade food and low prices, with views of the beach.

Brenda's Café is a cosy thatched eatery down on the southern shore, with cheap, delicious daily specials for about US$3 or US$4.

The Galley, west of the main part of the village, is a favourite for long dinners with good conversation. A full meal with drinks costs about US$9 to US$12.

Tentacles Restaurant is another evening favourite – a breezy, atmospheric place with its popular Dockside Bar built on a wharf out in the water.

Getting There & Away

Air Maya Airways and Tropic Air serve Placencia with daily flights. For details, see Getting Around in the introductory Belize chapter. Be sure that your plane lands at Placencia airstrip on the peninsula, several km north of Placencia village. The airstrip, by the way, has no services whatsoever, not even a place to shelter, but the Rum Point Inn is a 10-minute walk to the north.

Bus Shuttle buses run between Dangriga and Placencia on Monday, Wednesday,

BELIZE

Friday and Saturday, departing from Placencia at 6 am, Dangriga at noon on the two-hour, US$4 trip. For more information, see Getting There & Away in the Dangriga section.

The Z-Line buses running south from Dangriga to Independence can drop you there, whence it is possible in principle to find a boat going across the bay to Placencia. However, this may not be all that simple (or cheap), so if you travel this way, do so as early as possible in the day. To return northward, Z-Line buses leave Independence for Dangriga (2½ hours) and Belize City at 5 and 7.30 am, and 1.30 pm.

PUNTA GORDA

At the southern end of the Southern Highway is Punta Gorda (population 3000), the southernmost town of any size in Belize. Rainfall and humidity are at their highest, and the jungle at its lushest, in the Toledo District which surrounds Punta Gorda. Punta Gordians endure over four metres of rain per year – prepare yourself for at least a short downpour almost every day.

Known throughout Belize simply as 'PG', this sleepy town was founded for the Garinagus who emigrated from Honduras in 1823. In 1866, after the American Civil War, some Confederate veterans received land grants from the British government and founded a settlement here, but it didn't endure.

Though still predominantly Black Carib, it is also home to the usual bewildering variety of Belizean citizenry: Americans, British, Canadians, Chinese, Creole, East Indian, Garinagu, Lebanese and Kekchi Maya.

Fishing was the major livelihood for almost two centuries, but now farming is important as well. There is also an increasing tourist trade, as PG is the base for excursions inland to the Mayan archaeological sites at Lubaantun and Nim Li Punit, the Mayan villages of San Pedro Colombia and San Antonio, and the Blue Creek Cave.

Late in February each year, Punta Gorda celebrates the International Rainforest Festival, which pursues an ecological theme.

Orientation & Information

The town centre is the triangular park with a bandstand and the distinctive blue-and-white clock tower. The airstrip is 350 metres to the north-west, and the dock for boats to and from Guatemala is even closer.

Near the boat dock is the Toledo Visitors' Information Centre (☎ (7) 2-24-70), PO Box 73, also known as the Belize Tourism Industry Association, supervised by Antonio and Yvonne Villoria of Dem Dats Doin (see Around Punta Gorda, below). It's open daily (except Thursday and Sunday) from 9 am to 1 pm.

The Garinagus

Southern Belize is the home of the Garinagus (or Garifunas, also called Black Caribs), people of mixed South American Indian and African blood, who inhabited the island of St Vincent as a free people in the 1600s. By the end of the 1700s, British colonisers had brought the independent-minded Caribs under their control and transported them from one island to another in an effort to subdue them.

In the early 1800s, oppression and wandering finally brought many of the Black Caribs to southern Belize. The most memorable migration took place late in 1832, when on 19 November a large number of Caribs reached Belize from Honduras in dugout canoes. The event is celebrated annually in Belize as Garifuna Settlement Day.

The Garinagus, who account for less than 10% of Belize's population, look more African than Indian, but they speak a language that's much more Indian than African, and their unique culture combines aspects of both peoples.

Most of the citizens of Dangriga, chief town of the Stann Creek District, are Garinagus. Dangriga is the place to be on Garifuna Settlement Day as the town explodes in a frenzy of dancing, drinking and celebration of the Garifuna/Garinagu heritage. ■

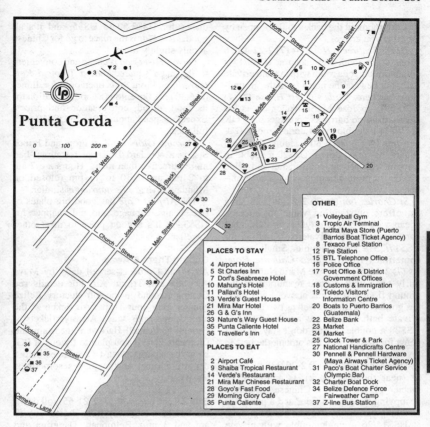

Punta Gorda

0   100   200 m

PLACES TO STAY

4 Airport Hotel
5 St Charles Inn
7 Dorl's Seabreeze Hotel
10 Mahung's Hotel
11 Pallavi's Hotel
13 Verde's Guest House
21 Mira Mar Hotel
26 G & G's Inn
33 Nature's Way Guest House
35 Punta Caliente Hotel
36 Traveller's Inn

PLACES TO EAT

2 Airport Café
9 Shaiba Tropical Restaurant
14 Verde's Restaurant
21 Mira Mar Chinese Restaurant
28 Goyo's Fast Food
29 Morning Glory Café
35 Punta Caliente

OTHER

1 Volleyball Gym
3 Tropic Air Terminal
6 Indita Maya Store (Puerto
    Barrios Boat Ticket Agency)
8 Texaco Fuel Station
12 Fire Station
15 BTL Telephone Office
16 Police Office
17 Post Office & District
    Government Offices
18 Customs & Immigration
19 Toledo Visitors'
    Information Centre
20 Boats to Puerto Barrios
    (Guatemala)
22 Belize Bank
23 Market
24 Market
25 Clock Tower & Park
27 National Handicrafts Centre
30 Pennell & Pennell Hardware
    (Maya Airways Ticket Agency)
31 Paco's Boat Charter Service
    (Olympic Bar)
32 Charter Boat Dock
34 Belize Defence Force
    Fairweather Camp
37 Z-line Bus Station

BELIZE

Organised Tours

You will have experienced virtually all of the thrills Punta Gorda offers within a few minutes of your arrival. However, PG is an excellent base for excursions to more exciting places. For ideas, see Around Punta Gorda, below.

Places to Stay

Punta Gorda's lodging is resolutely budget class, with only a few more expensive places. As PG is becoming more popular, I predict that there will be many more good lodgings opening soon.

Nature's Way Guest House (☎ (7) 2-21-19) is the intrepid travellers' gathering place. This converted house charges US$9/14 a single/double in waterless rooms with clean shared showers. Trips by minibus and boat can be arranged to all points of interest around PG.

Mahung's Hotel (☎ (7) 2-20-44), 11 North Main St, has an older section at the front with waterless rooms (shared bath) at US$8/13 a single/double. At the back are more modern rooms with private bath for US$14/20 a single/double. *Pallavi's Hotel*, also on North Main St, is similar. A new section of more modern rooms at the back should be open by the time you arrive.

Dorl's Seabreeze Hotel (☎ (7) 2-22-43), 6 Front St, is good, and cheap at US$9/14 a single/double for a room with fan and private bath, but beware the noise from the ground-floor bar here. *Verde's Guest House* (☎ (7) 2-20-69), on José Maria Nuñez St, is the standard-frame barracks construction – OK at US$11 a double in a waterless room. *G & G's Inn* (☎ (7) 2-26-80), facing the main square, has good prices: US$20 a double in a room with private shower, fan and cable TV. On the ground floor is a small restaurant-bar.

St Charles Inn (☎ (7) 2-21-49), 23 King St, offers outstanding value for money. Clean, well-kept (even stylish, for PG), it has comfy rooms with private bath and fan for US$17/23 a single/double. Small groups sometimes fill it. *Punta Caliente Hotel* (☎ (7) 2-25-61), 108 José Maria Nuñez St, is fairly new, with a good restaurant on the ground floor and rooms above. Each room has good ventilation as well as two fans, and private bath. Prices are good: US$22 to US$28 a double. If you don't stay, at least come for dinner, which is among the best in town.

Mira Mar Hotel (☎ (7) 2-20-33), 95 Front St (near the boat dock), is among PG's fancier places, with a Chinese restaurant occupying the ground floor and a porch for watching passers-by. Rooms can be simple, at US$14/26 a single/double with private bath, or more elaborate (US$59 with bath, TV and air-conditioning).

The sleepy *Airport Hotel*, near the airport, is useful if all else is full.

The *Traveller's Inn* (☎ (7) 2-21-65, 2-25-68), at the southern end of José Maria Nuñez St, next to the Z-Line bus station, is PG's status address. For US$33/57 a single/double you get a modern air-condi-tioned room with private bath, breakfast included.

Places to Eat
Punta Caliente serves stew pork, fish fillet, beans and rice with chicken, and similar dishes for US$3.50 to US$5, and it's all good. *Mira Mar* is the place to go for Chinese at only slightly more.

Goyo's Fast Food is cheap and convenient to the main square. *Shaiba Tropical Res-taurant*, on Front St, is open only for dinner (at 6.30 pm), but enjoys a good reputation for its food, mood, conversation and prices. Expect to spend about US$6 to US$10 for a full meal.

Morning Glory Café, at Front and Prince Sts, is a standard Belizean restaurant-bar, more attractive than many. Hours are 7 am to 2 pm and 6.30 to 11 pm (closed on Monday). *Sylvia's Restaurant* is similar.

The *Airport Café* has good big plates of rice, beans, cabbage and red snapper for US$3.75. It's a good place to meet other travellers.

Getting There & Away
Air Punta Gorda is served daily by Maya Airways and Tropic Air. For details see Getting Around in the introductory Belize chapter. Buy your Tropic Air tickets at the airport, and your Maya Airways tickets at Pennell & Pennell Hardware (at Main and Clements Sts). If you plan to fly out of PG, be at the airstrip at least 15 minutes before departure time, as the planes sometimes leave early.

Bus Z-Line buses (☎ (7) 2-21-65) roll down the Southern Highway from Belize City (8 am and 3 pm), Belmopan, Dangriga and Independence, returning northward at 5 and 11 am, for US$8.

Boat The boat to Puerto Barrios (Guatemala) departs from Punta Gorda at 2 pm on Tuesday and Friday (US$10). In the other direction, the boat departs on the same days at 7.30 am. Boat tickets are sold at the Indita Maya store (☎ 2-20-65), 24 Middle St, after 9.30 am on sailing days. Buy your tickets as early as possible, and pack provisions for the voyage as nothing is for sale on board.

Passenger traffic between PG and Puerto Barrios is increasing, and you may find other boat services operating. If not, you can charter a 10-person boat to take you to Lívingston (US$150) or Puerto Barrios (US$200) in Guatemala, or even to the Bay Islands in Honduras.

AROUND PUNTA GORDA

Punta Gorda is a good base for numerous excursions into the countryside of Toledo district.

San Pedro Columbia

There are several reasons to visit San Pedro Columbia, a Kekchi Maya village 41 km north-west of Punta Gorda. One reason is to observe the Guatemalan lifestyle of the inhabitants, whose ancestors fled the tedious life of the coffee fincas in Alta Verapaz to find freedom in Belize. Their Guatemalan highland customs, traditions and dress have been preserved to a remarkable degree, and differ markedly from those of the lowland Mopan or 'Belizean' Maya. The other reasons are Dem Dats Doin and the Mayan ruins at Lubaantun.

Dem Dats Doin Dem Dats Doin is an innovative ecological farm founded by Antonio and Yvonne Villoria. Photovoltaic cells for electricity, biogas methane for light and refrigeration, natural insect repellents and fertilisers in place of chemicals – the farm is a showcase of what a determined, sensitive and knowledgeable couple can do to promote appropriate technology and sustainable farming.

A tour of the farm costs US$5 and takes between one and two hours. Bed and breakfast is sometimes available; check in advance.

The Indigenous Experience The Villorias also supervise a programme for home stays with Mayan families, called The Indigenous Experience. They will put you in touch with a village family who will welcome you into their home, provide you with a hammock and meals, and also let you share in their traditional way of life. No special allowances are made for you, so you should be fully prepared for very simple living conditions.

In return for roughing it, you'll learn a lot, and will provide valuable cash income to help the family get by.

Hammock rent is US$4 per night; meals cost US$1.50 each. The Villorias ask a US$5 fee for putting you in touch with a family. You should enquire in advance by mail if possible, and enclose US$2 to pay for postage and printing.

Lubaantun The Mayan ruins at Lubaantun, just over a km north-west of the village, are aptly named. Lubaantun ('Fallen Stones') has been excavated to some extent, but not restored. The temples are still mostly covered with jungle, so you will have to use your imagination to envisage the great city which once stood here.

The archaeologists have found evidence that Lubaantun flourished until the late 700s, after which little was built. In its heyday, the merchants of Lubaantun traded with people on the cayes, in Mexico and Guatemala, and perhaps beyond.

The principal temple at Lubaantun, built like its neighbours along a ridge of hills, is 12 metres high and 30 metres long. The precision stonework of this city seems to have been erected without benefit of mortar.

Getting There & Away San Pedro Columbia is 41 km north-west of Punta Gorda off the Southern Highway. A bus can drop you at the fuel station on the highway; from here it's a walk of almost six km to the village. If you catch a San Antonio bus from the main plaza in Punta Gorda, it will get you 2½ km closer to San Pedro.

More expensive, but also quicker and more dependable, are the minibus tours. Nature's Way Guest House will take up to six persons on a tour to San Pedro and Lubaantun for US$88, or about US$15 per person. This tour can be combined with a visit to Blue Creek Cave (see below) at a total cost of US$113, or US$19 per person.

Nim Li Punit

About 36 km north-west of Punta Gorda, just north of Big Falls and less than a km west of

BELIZE

the Southern Highway, stand the ruins of Nim Li Punit, a less impressive site than Lubaantun. Nim Li Punit ('Big Hat') may in fact have been a tributary city to larger, more powerful Lubaantun.

Today, Nim Li Punit's distinction lies in its stelae, some of which are very large. Discovered by oil prospectors in 1974, it was soon looted by antiquities thieves. Later, archaeologists did some excavation and preliminary studies but little restoration or stabilisation. Nim Li Punit, named for the headgear to be seen on one of its prominent stelae, is still mostly covered by jungle.

San Antonio & Blue Creek

The Mopan Maya of San Antonio are descended from former inhabitants of the Guatemalan village of San Luis Petén, just across the border. As have unfortunate Guatemalans for centuries, the San Antonians fled oppression in their home country to find freedom in Belize. They brought their ancient customs with them, however, and you can observe a traditional lowland Mayan village on a short visit here. If you are here during a festival, your visit will be much more memorable.

About six km west of San Antonio, near the village of Santa Cruz, is the archaeological site of Uxbenka, which has numerous carved stelae.

South of San Antonio about 20 km lies the village of Blue Creek, and beyond it the nature reserve of Blue Creek Cave. Hike into the site (less than a km) along the marked trail and enjoy the rainforest around you, and the pools, channels, caves and refreshingly cool waters of the creek system. Nature's Way Guest House also runs minibus excursions to Blue Creek Cave: it's US$100 for up to six persons, or about US$17 per person.

Places to Stay There is one small hotel in San Antonio: *Bol's Hilltop Hotel*, with beds for US$5. If you'd prefer not to stay the night, arrange a day excursion from Punta Gorda.

Getting There & Away The San Antonio bus runs for the convenience of San Antonio villagers going into the big city, departing from the village each morning at 5 am for Punta Gorda and returning from Punta Gorda at 4 pm.

Western Belize

Western Belize is the country's highlands, with peaks rising above 300 metres. The land is beautiful. What has been cleared is cultivated by diligent farmers who produce most of Belize's fresh fruits and vegetables.

Some travellers pass through Cayo District, stopping for a few days in San Ignacio in order to take a short excursion into the forests of Mountain Pine Ridge. Others come for a week or so, staying at one of the dozen forest lodges which provide simple accommodation, meals, and the opportunity to explore the area by canoe, mountain bike or a 4WD vehicle, on horseback or on foot.

Most lodges are well away from the towns (which is the point), but this means you will probably eat most of your meals at the lodges. Figure in this cost when you plan your budget.

The road west leaves Belize City along Cemetery Rd (right through Lords Ridge Cemetery), which continues westward as the Western Highway. Along the way you pass Hattieville, founded in 1961 after Hurricane Hattie wreaked destruction on Belize City. Many residents sought refuge from the storm's violence in this inland spot. Some decided to stay, and Hattieville was born.

BELIZE ZOO

The Belize Zoo & Tropical Education Centre (☎ (92) 33-10), PO Box 474, Belize City, is home to a variety of indigenous Belizean cats and other animals kept in natural surroundings. The zoo's terrain, 46 km west of Belize City (Mile 29), hasn't been cleared; it's as if cages just appeared from nowhere and then paths were cleared for tourists. A sign marks the turning for the zoo, on the north side of the road; the entrance is less than one km off the highway. Hours are 9.30 am to 4 pm daily; admission costs US$5, and it goes to a worthy cause. The zoo is closed on major Belizean holidays.

The Belize Zoo had an odd beginning. In 1983, Ms Sharon Matola was in charge of 17

Keel-billed Toucan

BELIZE

Belizean animals during the shooting of a wildlife film entitled *Path of the Raingods*. By the time filming was over, her animals were partly tame, and thus might not have survived well in the wild. With the movie budget exhausted, there were no funds to support the animals, so Ms Matola founded the Belize Zoo. In 1991 the zoo was substantially enhanced with spacious natural enclosures for the inhabitants and a modern visitors' centre.

Take a map leaflet and follow the marked trails through the zoo, a microcosm of Belize's ecological wealth. The self-guided tour takes 45 minutes to an hour. You'll see Baird's tapir (Belize's national animal), and the gibnut or paca *(tepezcuintle)*, a sort of rodent which appears on some Belizean dinner tables. Jaguar, ocelot, howler monkey, peccary, vulture, stork and even a crocodile appear during the fascinating tour. People spend a lot of money at Disneyland to see hokey mechanical replicas of such wild creatures; here they're all real, and right at home.

Getting There & Away

See Getting Around in the introductory Belize chapter for details on buses running along the Western Highway between Belize City and San Ignacio. Just ask to get out at the Belize Zoo. Look at your watch when you get out; the next bus will come by in about an hour.

BANANA BANK LODGE

A short distance east of Belmopan, at Mile 47 (Km 76) on the Western Highway, a dirt track heads north two km to Banana Bank Lodge (☎ (8) 2-31-80; fax (08) 2-23-66), PO Box 48, Belmopan. This is the Belizean version of a dude ranch, operated by John and Carolyn Carr. They'll take you on horseback trips into the bush, show you where to swim or paddle a canoe, and introduce you to their pets. Rates for one of the nine rooms and all three meals work out to US$65 to US$95 a single, US$105 to US$122 a double per day. An excursion on horseback costs US$45 per person, lunch included.

GUANACASTE PARK

Almost four km east of Belmopan, and a few metres north of the junction of the Western and Hummingbird Highways, is Guanacaste National Park. This small (21-hectare) nature reserve at the confluence of Roaring Creek and the Belize River holds a giant guanacaste tree which survived the axes of canoe makers and still rises majestically in its jungle habitat. The great tree supports a whole ecosystem of its own, festooned with bromeliads, epiphytes, ferns and dozens of other varieties of plants. Wild orchids flourish in the spongy soil among the ferns and mosses, and several species of 'exotic' animals pass through. Birdlife is abundant and colourful.

Admission is free (donations are accepted). The reserve is open every day from 8 am to 4.30 pm. Stop at the information booth to learn about the short nature trails in the park. If you're in Belize City when you read this, you can get more information from the

Belize Audubon Society (☎ (2) 7-73-69), 49 Southern Foreshore, Belize City.

Just west of the highway junction, across the bridge, is the village of Roaring Creek, with several small restaurants.

BELMOPAN

In 1961, Hurricane Hattie all but destroyed Belize City. Many people were sceptical when, in 1970, the government of Belize declared its intention to build a model capital city in the geographic centre of the country, but certain that killer hurricanes would come again, and that Belize City could never be properly defended from them, the government decided to move.

During its first decade Belmopan was a lonely place. Weeds grew through cracks in the streets, a few bureaucrats dozed in new offices and insects provided most of the city's traffic. But a quarter of a century after its founding, Belmopan has begun to come to life. Its population (now over 4000) is growing slowly, some embassies have moved here, and when, inevitably, the next killer hurricane arrives, the new capital will no doubt get a population boost.

Orientation & Information

Belmopan, just under four km south of the Western Highway, is a small place easily negotiated on foot. The bus stops are near the post office, police station, market and telephone office. Unless you need to visit the British High Commission (☎ (8) 2-21-46/7), 34/36 Half Moon Ave, or the US Embassy's Belmopan office (☎ (8) 2-26-17), you'll probably only stay long enough to have a snack or a meal at one of the restaurants near the bus stops. Most of the town's few hotels, unfortunately, are a 10-minute walk from the bus stops.

Archaeology Department

If you're excited about Mayan ruins, examine the archaeological treasures preserved in the vault at the Archaeology Department (☎ (8) 2-21-06). There is no museum yet, but if you call and make an

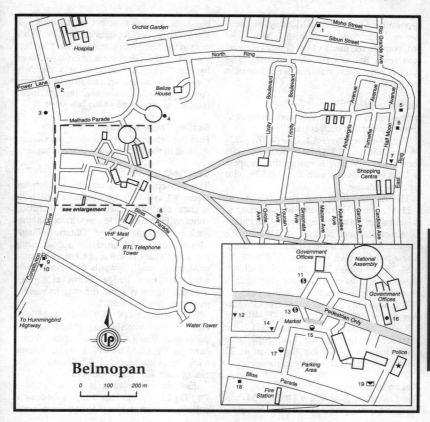

Belmopan

0   100   200 m

BELIZE

PLACES TO STAY

- 1 Hotel El Rey
- 5 Bull Frog Inn
- 6 Circle A Hotel
- 18 Belmopan Convention Hotel

PLACES TO EAT

- 7 New Capital Restaurant
- 10 Yoli's Restaurant & Bar
- 12 China Restaurant & Bar
- 14 Caladium Restaurant

OTHER

- 2 New Mexican Embassy
- 3 Ministries of Home Affairs & Defense
- 4 Ministries of Finance & Foreign Affairs
- 8 Social Security Clock Tower
- 9 Shell Fuel Station
- 11 Barclays Bank
- 13 Belize Bank
- 15 Batty Brothers Bus Stop
- 16 Department of Archaeology & Archaeological Vault
- 17 Novelo's Bus Stop
- 19 Post Office

appointment for a visit on Monday, Wednesday or Friday afternoon from 1.30 to 4.30 pm, you can see many of the artefacts recovered from Belize's rich Mayan sites. The vault is only a few minutes' walk from the bus stops.

Places to Stay

Belmopan is a bureaucrats' and diplomats' town, not one for budget travellers.

The 14-room *Circle A Lodge* (☎ (8) 2-22-96; fax 2-36-16), 35-37 Half Moon Ave, has seen better days, but is among the cheapest at US$34 a double with fan, US$39 with air-conditioning.

The neighbouring *Bull Frog Inn* (☎ (8) 2-21-11; fax 2-31-55), also with 14 rooms, is Belmopan's nicest place to stay. Its cheerful air-conditioned rooms cost US$50/67 a single/double, and there's a good restaurant. A few blocks away, the *Hotel El Rey* (☎ (8) 2-34-38), 23 Moho St, is cheapest of all, but cheerless and basic. Rates are US$20/25 a single/double with bath and ceiling fan.

The hopefully named *Belmopan Convention Hotel* (☎ (8) 2-21-30, 2-23-40; fax 2-30-66), 2 Bliss Parade (PO Box 237), is the most convenient to the bus stops. Pay US$53/64 a single/double for one of its 20 air-conditioned, bath-equipped rooms.

Places to Eat

The *Caladium Restaurant* (☎ 2-27-54), on Market Square just opposite the Novelo's bus stop, is your best bet in the centre of town. Daily special plates cost US$4. *Yoli's*, next to the Shell fuel station on the road into town, is a less convenient alternative. Over by the Circle A Lodge there's the *New Capital Restaurant*, specialising in Chinese cuisine. *China Restaurant*, though much simpler, is very close to the bus stops.

Getting There & Away

Bus For details on bus transport, see Getting Around in the introductory Belize chapter.

CENTRAL FARM

The Western Highway continues westward through Cayo District, climbing slowly to higher altitudes through lush farming country. Tidy country towns with odd names such as Teakettle Village, Ontario Village, Mount Hope and Unitedville appear along the way. Near the town of Central Farm, a road heads south towards San Antonio in Mountain Pine Ridge. Signs along the Western Highway point the way to various guest ranches and lodges.

Riverwalk B&B (☎ (92) 30-26), at Mile 62 (Km 100), is a ranch house high on a hill with panoramic views. Two comfortable rooms here go for US$55/66/77 a single/double/triple, breakfast included. A half-day's horse riding costs US$25 per person.

Just across the road is *Caesar's Place* (☎ (92) 23-41), PO Box 48, San Ignacio. It offers guestrooms, camping and camper-van

---

Chicle & Chewing Gum

Chicle is the pinkish to reddish-brown gum, actually the coagulated milky sap, or latex, of the sapodilla tree *(Achras Zapota)*, a tropical evergreen native to the Yucatán Peninsula and Central America. *Chicleros* (chicle-workers) enter the forests and cut large gashes in the sapodillas' trunks, making a patter of V-shaped cuts as high as 10 metres. The sap runs from the wounds and down the trunk to be collected in a container at the base. After being boiled, it ise shaped into blocks for shipping. The cuts often kill the tree, and chicle harvesting has often resulted in the serious depletion of sapodilla forests.

First used as a substitute for natural rubber (to which the sapodilla is related), by about 1890 chicle was best known as the main ingredient in chewing gum.

As a result of war research for a rubber substitute during the 1940s, synthetic substitutes were developed for chicle. Now chewing gum is made mostly from these synthetic substitutes. Flavourings such as sugar, mint, fruit essences, licorice or pine gum are added, according to local preference. ■

(RV) sites with hook-ups, as well as horse riding and tours. For details, contact Eva's Restaurant in San Ignacio.

Mountain Equestrian Trails (☎ (8) 2-31-80, 2-21-49; fax 2-32-35), Mile 8 (Km 13), Mountain Pine Ridge Rd, Central Farm PO, Cayo District, is a jungle lodge specialising in horse riding. Over 100 km of forest trails have been laid out since the lodge opened in 1986, and the personnel are experts at matching riders (with or without horseback experience) to their well-behaved mounts. Accommodation in cabañas with private bath and paraffin (kerosene) lighting costs US$64/75/86 a single/double/triple; meals cost US$5/10/12 per person for breakfast/lunch/dinner.

SAN IGNACIO (CAYO)

San Ignacio, also called Cayo, is a prosperous farming and holiday centre in the lovely tropical Macal River valley. In general it's a quiet place of about 8000 people (counting the population of neighbouring Santa Elena, on the east side of the river). At night the quiet disappears and the jungle rocks to music from the town's bars, and restaurants which sometimes serve as bars.

Market day is Saturday, with the marketeers setting up behind the Hotel Belmoral, at the bus station. The small market building beneath Hawkesworth Bridge, built through the largesse of Baron Bliss, has some vegetables and fruits on sale every day.

There's nothing much to do in town, but San Ignacio is a good base from which to explore the natural beauties of Mountain Pine Ridge. Horseback treks, canoe trips on the rivers and creeks, spelunking in the caves, bird-watching, touring the Mayan ruins of Xunantunich and Cahal Pech, and hiking in the tropical forests are all popular ways to spend time. This is the district of macaws, mahogany, mangoes, jaguars and orchids.

San Ignacio, with its selection of hotels and restaurants, is also the logical place to spend the night before or after you cross the Guatemalan border. The Belizean town on the border, Benque Viejo, has only limited facilities.

Orientation

San Ignacio is west of the river; Santa Elena is to the east. The two are joined by the one-lane Hawkesworth Bridge, San Ignacio's landmark suspension bridge. As you come off the western end of the bridge, turn right and you'll be on Burns Ave, the town's main street. Almost everything in town is accessible on foot.

Information

Tourist Office By the time you arrive, the Belize Tourism Industry Association (BTIA) should have opened its information office on Burns Ave. The town's traditional information exchange is Eva's Restaurant & Bar (see below).

Money Belize Bank, on Burns Ave, is open Monday to Friday from 8 am to 1 pm (also on Friday afternoon from 3 to 6 pm) for money exchange.

Post & Telecommunications San Ignacio's post office is on the upper floor of Government House. It's open Monday to Friday from 8 am to noon and 1 to 5 pm, and on Saturday from 8 am to 1 pm.

Belize Telecommunications has an office on Burns Ave north of Eva's, in the Cano's Gift Shop building. Hours are Monday to Friday from 8 am to noon and 1 to 4 pm, and on Saturday from 8 am to noon (closed on Sunday).

Medical Services The very simple, basic San Ignacio Hospital (☎ (92) 20-66) is up the hill off Waight's Ave, to the west of the centre.

Cahal Pech

The best way to visit the hilltop Mayan site of Cahal Pech is to take a picnic. It's less than two km uphill from Hawkesworth Bridge.

BELIZE

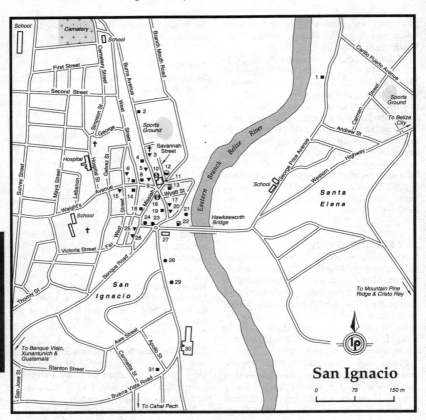

San Ignacio

0   75   150 m

Follow the Buena Vista Rd for one km, uphill and past the San Ignacio Hotel, until you see a large thatched structure (a nightclub) and a radio antenna atop a hill. Turn left and follow the signs uphill to Cahal Pech.

From the site headquarters building, follow the path down, then up, for 150 metres to the small collection of temples arranged around a plaza. These have been partially restored, and in some places stuccoed, as they would have been in Classic Mayan times.

The site is open from 9 am to 4.30 pm; admission costs US$1.50.

Organised Tours

Lodges in Mountain Pine Ridge (for more information see later in this section) operate their own tours and excursions on foot, by canoe and on horseback. But you can also take similar excursions using a cheap hotel in San Ignacio as your base. Every hotel and most restaurants in town will want to sign you up. Compare offerings, shop around and talk to other travellers before making your choice. Most of the trips offered give good value for money.

Many guides and excursion operators advertise their services at Eva's Restaurant

PLACES TO STAY

1 Snooty Fox Guest House
2 Venus Hotel
4 Central Hotel & Farmers' Emporium
7 Hi-Et Hotel
8 24A West Street Guest House
11 New Belmoral Hotel
14 Martha's Guest House
18 Maxima Hotel
19 Hotel Plaza
30 Hotel San Ignacio
31 Hotel Piache

PLACES TO EAT

3 Serendib Restaurant
5 Eva's Restaurant & Bar
6 Red Rooster Restaurant
9 Ice Cream Paradise
11 Tai San Chinese Restaurant

15 Maxim's Chinese Restaurant
17 New Lucky Restaurant
20 Oriental Restaurant & Bar
25 Rosy's Nice Food
26 Roots Restaurant

OTHER

10 Atlantic Bank
12 Bus Station
13 Esso Fuel Station
16 Belize Bank
21 Market Building
22 Shell Fuel Station
23 Taxi Rank
24 Town Hall, Library & Toilets
27 Government House, Police Station & Post Office
28 Fire Station
29 Electricity Generating Plant

BELIZE

($\mathbf{\varpi}$/fax (92) 22-67). Drop by and see what's available.

Among the favourite trips are:

- Voyages by boat or canoe along the Macal, Mopan and Belize rivers; a favourite goal on the Macal River is the Pantí Medicine Trail at Ix Chel Farm
- A visit to a Mennonite community, usually combined with a tour of the Hershey chocolate company's cacao plantation
- An overland excursion to the caves at Río Frio
- A picnic and swim in the pools at Río On
- A walk to the 300-metre waterfall at Hidden Valley (which is less than spectacular at dry times of the year)
- An overland trip to the Mayan ruins at Caracol
- A stop at the Tanah Maya Art Museum and Mayan slate-carving workshop of the Garcia sisters, just north of San Antonio
- A trip to Chechem Ha's Mayan ceremonial cave and a picnic at Vaca Falls
- Tubing through caves along the Chiquibul River
- An excursion to Tikal (Guatemala), either for the day or overnight.

Easy Rider ($\mathbf{\varpi}$ (92) 33-10), a stable on the outskirts, will pick you up in San Ignacio and take you on a horseback excursion into the jungle for US$30 per person, lunch included. Shorter rides can be had for US$20.

Bob Jones at Eva's Restaurant can arrange a day trip to Tikal (Guatemala) for less than US$60 per person, lunch included.

Places to Stay – bottom end

The very tidy *Snooty Fox Guest House* ($\mathbf{\varpi}$ (92) 35-56), 64 George Price Ave, Santa Elena, in a residential neighbourhood, has clean, attractive rooms with bath for US$33 a double. There's an apartment with two bedrooms and a kitchen (US$45). All rooms have private bath, TV and stereo. The view of the town is excellent. A long stairway leads down to the river, where you can rent a canoe. To find the Snooty Fox, walk east over Hawkesworth Bridge and follow the main road to the left. At a fork, continue left (the main road is to the right); the guesthouse is 500 metres along on the left-hand side.

Martha's Guest House ($\mathbf{\varpi}$ (92) 22-76), 10 West St, above the August Meat Market, is a modern home offering two spare rooms (which share a bath) for US$14 and US$16 a double. If you like family atmosphere, you'll love it here.

Central Hotel ($\mathbf{\varpi}$ (92) 22-53), 24 Burns Ave, is among the town's cheapest hotels, and a bargain at US$10/14 a single/double in rooms without running water. *Jaguar Hotel*, across the street at 19 Burns Ave, is plain, basic and well used, though not as well kept as its neighbour. Prices are US$6 per person with shared bath.

Hi-Et Hotel (☎ (92) 28-28), 12 West St, at the corner of Waight's Ave, is a family-run place, and when you stay here you have the feeling that you're part of that family. Two people pay US$11 for a room with shared bathroom. Across the street at 24-A West St, José Espat rents rooms for the same price.

New Belmoral Hotel (☎ (92) 20-24), 17 Burns Ave, at the corner of Waight's Ave, has 15 good rooms with bath and cable TV for US$18/23 a single/double.

Venus Hotel (☎ (92) 32-03), 29 Burns Ave, is newish, clean and bright. Of its 25 rooms, most are without private shower and cost US$11/14 a single/double; the shared showers are new and clean, if cramped. Rooms with private shower cost US$18/23. All rooms have ceiling fans, and some (especially rooms 10 and 16) have views of the football fields and the river.

Maxima Hotel (☎ (92) 39-93), on Missiah St, is new, clean and good. It's also reasonably priced: US$25 a double with private bath and fan, US$5 more with air-conditioning. *Hotel Plaza* (☎ (92) 33-32), 4-A Burns Ave, is similarly nice and new, at identical prices. Many rooms here have TV sets.

Places to Stay – middle

Hotel San Ignacio (☎ (92) 20-34, 21-25, fax 21-34), PO Box 33, on Buena Vista Rd about one km uphill from the police station, enjoys magnificent views of the jungle and river from its swimming pool and balconies. It's a great place to stay, but its 25 rooms are often full, especially on weekends. Rooms cost US$46/53/64 a single/double/triple. A few double rooms without balconies are cheaper – ask for them if you want to save money. The hotel has a restaurant, bar and disco.

Mida's Resort (☎ (92) 21-01; fax 31-72), on Branch Mouth Rd, 700 metres from the bus station, has thatched bungalows with shared bath for US$27/35/54 a single/double/triple (US$40/47 a single/double with private bath). Camping is available at US$5 per adult.

For other ranches near San Ignacio, see the section on Mountain Pine Ridge.

Places to Eat

Eva's Restaurant & Bar (☎/fax (92) 22-67) is the information and social centre of the expatriate set – temporary and permanent – in San Ignacio. Daily special plates at US$3 to US$5 are the best value, but there's also chilmoles (black bean soup), chicken curry, beef soup, sandwiches, burgers and many other dishes. A beer garden out the back is for those who want to drink more than to eat. Note that Eva's has fax service (sending and receiving).

Maxim's Chinese Restaurant, at the corner of Far West St and Bullet Tree Rd, serves fried rice, sweet-and-sour dishes, and vegetarian plates which range in price from US$2 to US$4. The restaurant is small and dark, and open from 11.30 am to 2.30 pm and 5 pm until midnight.

Other choices for Chinese food are *Tai San* (at the back of the Hotel Belmoral, by the bus station), and the *New Lucky* and *Oriental* (on Burns Ave across from the Belize Bank).

Across Burns Ave and north a few metres from Eva's is the *Serendib Restaurant*, serving – of all things – Sri Lankan dishes, here in the Belizean jungle. Service is friendly, the food is good, and prices are not bad, ranging from US$3.50 for the simpler dishes, up to US$10 for steak or lobster. Lunch is served from 9.30 am to 3 pm, dinner from 6.30 to 11 pm.

Ice Cream Paradise, on Burns Ave across from the Belmoral Hotel, serves sandwiches and light meals as well as ice cream in clean, attractive surroundings.

Red Rooster Restaurant, on Far West St, is noted for its good, cheap pizza.

Getting There & Away

Buses operate to and from Belize City (116 km, three hours, US$2.75), Belmopan (32 km, 45 minutes, US$1.50) and Benque Viejo (15 km, 20 minutes, US$0.50). For details, see Getting Around in the introductory Belize chapter.

Taxis congregate near the traffic circle at the west end of Hawkesworth Bridge, and charge surprisingly high rates for short trips out of town. A trip of a few km can easily cost US$5 to US$10.

MOUNTAIN PINE RIDGE

Western Belize has lots of beautiful, unspoiled mountain country dotted with waterfalls and teeming with wild orchids, parrots, keel-billed toucans and other exotic flora & fauna. Almost 800 sq km to

the south and east of San Ignacio has been set aside as the Mountain Pine Ridge Forest Reserve.

The rough forest roads in the reserve are often impassable in the wet season, and not easily passable even when it's dry. Inaccessibility is one of Mountain Pine Ridge's assets, for it keeps this beautiful land in its natural state for visitors willing to see it by 4WD vehicle, on horseback, on foot or along its rivers in canoes.

Access roads into the Mountain Pine Ridge Reserve go south off the Western Highway in Santa Elena (across the river

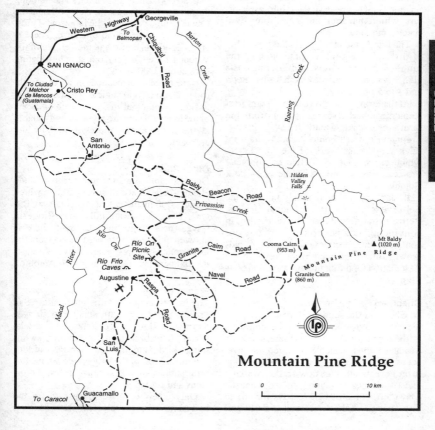

Mountain Pine Ridge

from San Ignacio) and near Georgeville (about nine km east of San Ignacio).

Pantí Medicine Trail

Among the most fascinating excursions is the one to the Pantí Medicine Trail at Ix Chel Farm (fax (92) 22-67), located right next to Chaa Creek Cottages, 13 km south-west of San Ignacio. Named for Dr Eligio Pantí, a healer in San Antonio village who uses traditional Mayan herb cures, the Trail was established by Dr Rosita Arvigo. Dr Arvigo, an American, studied medicinal plants with Dr Pantí, then began several projects to spread the wisdom of traditional healing methods and to preserve the rainforest habitats which harbour an incredible 4000 species of plants.

The Pantí Medicine Trail is the first of her efforts, a self-guiding path among the jungle's natural cures. Admission costs US$5; it's open every day from 8 am to noon and 1 to 5 pm.

At the farm's shop you can buy Rainforest Remedies, herbal cures drawn from the farm's resources and marketed by the Ix Chel Tropical Research Foundation. Profits from sales support the work of the foundation, which carries out the Belize Ethnobotany Project in association with the New York Botanical Garden.

In January 1993, working through the Belize Association of Traditional Healers, Belize's traditional healers succeeded in convincing the government to transfer control of 2500 hectares (6000 acres) of old-growth forest, renamed Terra Nova, to the Association for the careful preservation of its flora.

Chechem Ha Mayan Cave

At Chechem Ha, south of Benque Viejo, is a recently discovered Mayan cave complete with ceremonial pots. Members of the Morales family, which discovered the cave, act as guides, leading you up the steep slope to the cave mouth, then down inside, walking and sometimes crouching, to see what the Maya left. A fee of US$25 pays for one to three people. Take water and a flashlight.

You can also camp at Chechem Ha, or sleep in one of the recently built cabañas. For further details, ask at your lodge, or contact Bob at Eva's Restaurant.

Caracol

In the southern reaches of the reserve lies Caracol, a vast Mayan city engulfed in jungle. The archaeologists are still at work here, and nothing has been restored, but Caracol is obviously of major importance to studies of Mayan archaeology, culture and history.

The vast site encompasses some 88 sq km, with 36,000 structures marked so far. Among the most impressive are the Acropolis and the Canaa temple complex, the largest and most massive yet to be found in Belize. There is also a good ball court, and the Temple of the Wooden Lintel, a very old structure dating back some 2000 years.

Caracol can be reached on an overnight trip in a good 4WD vehicle. The best way is to sign up for a tour in San Ignacio or at one of the lodges. There are no services available at the site, beyond those offered by the archaeologists.

Other Sites

Other suitable goals for forest trips include Hidden Valley Falls (a silver cascade which plunges 300 metres into a misty valley), Río On's pools and waterfalls, and Río Frio Caves (near Augustine). Camping here is allowed only with prior permission from the Department of Forestry, and only at Augustine and near the settlement of San Antonio.

Places to Stay

The forests and mountains surrounding San Ignacio are dotted with small inns, lodges and ranches offering accommodation, meals, hiking, horseback trips, spelunking, swimming, bird-watching and similar outdoor activities. Most of the lodges below have full programmes of hikes, horse rides, excursions and activities.

Only a few of these lodges are for the budget traveller; the rest are more expensive, though they offer good value for money. I've given simple room rates here, but at the more expensive lodges you can take advantage of package arrangements which include lodging, meals and tours; these can save you money.

Though you can sometimes show up unannounced and find a room, these are small, popular places, so it's best to write or call ahead for reservations as far in advance as possible. When you do, ask for information on activities as well.

Among the inexpensive places is *Rancho Los Amigos* (☎ (93) 24-83 and leave a message), almost two km south of the highway from San José Succotz over an atrocious road. It's a good place to get away from it all on a budget. Ed and Virginia Jenkins did just that when they moved here 16 years ago from Los Angeles, California. They've built four cool, thatch-roofed stone cabins for guests, and charge US$25 per person for bed and all three meals. Lighting is by paraffin (kerosene) lamps; bath and toilet facilities are shared. Vegetarian meals are available.

Parrot's Nest (☎ (92) 37-02), at the edge of the wilderness in Bullet Tree Falls northwest of San Ignacio, is aptly named: guests stay in treehouse-like thatched cabins built high on stilts. The lodge is the brainchild of Fred Prost, who founded the Sea Side Guest House in Belize City in 1988. Baths are shared, but there's electricity all the time, and a beautiful site surrounded by the river on three sides. Prices are as beautiful as the lodge: US$20 a double. Three meals cost US$13 per person. Besides hiking and canoeing, there's horse riding for only US$18 per day. You can reach Bullet Tree Falls by taxi (US$15) or bus from San Ignacio. This is the best of the budget places.

Maya Mountain Lodge (☎ (92) 21-64, fax 20-29), 9 Cristo Rey Rd (PO Box 46, San Ignacio) is the closest lodge to San Ignacio, being just over two km from the centre. (Follow the signs from near the Esso fuel station in Santa Elena.) The thatched cottages have fans and private showers with hot water. Meals are served in the verandah res-

taurant. Tours to most destinations in Mountain Pine Ridge and beyond can be arranged; mountain bikes and canoes are available for rent. Bart and Suzi Mickler, the owners, are walking encyclopaedias of Belizean jungle lore, and educate others though their Educational Field Station and Rainforest Institute. The 14 rooms and cottages are priced at US$47 to US$82, single or double. Homestyle meals cost US$7/6/15 for breakfast/lunch/dinner.

Several other lodges (Chaa Creek, duPlooy's, Black Rock, Ek' Tun) are reached by a common, rough road which goes south from the Western Highway at a point eight km west of San Ignacio, three km east of Benque Viejo.

Chaa Creek Cottages (☎ (92) 20-37, fax 25-01), PO Box 53, San Ignacio, Cayo, is right on the banks of the Macal River right next to Ix Chel Farm and the Pantí Medicine Trail. The 16 thatch-roofed cottages set in tropical gardens are beautifully kept and richly decorated with Mayan textiles and local crafts; all have fans and private baths. Rates are US$90/115/135/155 a single/double/triple/quad, breakfast included. Lunch costs US$6 to US$9 and dinner is US$16.50. This is the most pristine of the Maya Mountain lodges. Chaa Creek is five km south of the Western Highway over a very rough, slow road.

There are three levels of accommodation at *duPlooys' Riverside Cottages & Hotel* (☎ (92) 33-01; in the USA ☎ (803) 722-1513), Big Eddy, San Ignacio, Cayo: rooms in the Pink House have fans and shared baths and cost US$42/53/64 a single/double/triple, breakfast included. Bungalows and rooms in the Jungle Lodge have fans and private baths and cost US$115 to US$143 a single, US$156 to US$210 a double and US$210 to US$255 a triple, three meals included. Besides the normal array of Mountain Pine Ridge activities, duPlooys' offers you a white sandy beach for sunbathing, and swimming in the Macal River. To find duPlooys', follow the directions given for Chaa Creek Cottages; after four km, follow the duPlooys' sign and turn right. The lodge is just under three km farther along this rough road.

Also take the Chaa Creek/duPlooys' turning from the Western Highway to reach *Black Rock River Lodge* (☎ (92) 23-41), PO Box 48, San Ignacio, Cayo, a simpler place with thatch-topped tent cottages, solar electricity generation and solar-heated hot water. Black Rock is over 11 km off the highway, a drive of about 35 minutes. For details, ask at Caesar's Place, described above under Central Farm.

Ek' Tun (☎ (93) 25-36, fax 24-46; in the USA ☎/fax (303) 442-6150), General Delivery, Benque Viejo, Cayo, is a low-impact environmental resort 16 km into the jungle in the midst of an area littered with Mayan ruins. Follow the Black Rock road, which may be impassable; you might have to continue by river, on horseback or on foot. Ken and Phyllis Dart are still building their resort, but have the dining room, bar and several cabañas completed. A full programme of activities and tours is offered. Accommodation in a thatched bungalow with private bath costs US$117/149/181/212 a single/double/triple/quad; meals cost US$32 per person per day.

Nabitunich (☎/fax (92) 20-96), on San Lorenzo Farm, is another attractive collection of thatched cottages on a hillside sloping down to the river. In this case, the towering ruins of Xunantunich are right on the opposite bank of the river. Theresa Graham and family host you, preparing plentiful four-course meals after a day of swimming or canoeing on the river, horse riding or touring. You pay US$91 a double for a cabaña with bath and fan, breakfast and dinner included. Nabitunich ('stone house' in Mayan) is two km east of Benque Viejo, then one km north downhill toward the river.

Windy Hill Cottages (☎ (92) 20-17; fax 30-80), at Graceland Ranch, San Ignacio, has all the facilities: swimming pool, riding horses, nature trail, canoes ready for a paddle on the Mopan River, and a full programme of optional tours. Accommodation in cabañas with private bath and ceiling fan costs US$48/64/80 a single/double/triple;

meals cost US$5/7/12.50 for breakfast/lunch/dinner. To find it, go west 2½ km from San Ignacio and look for the signs for the road going north.

By the way, the famous *Chan Chich Lodge*, at Gallon Jug, near the Guatemalan border north of Spanish Lookout, is accessible by road from Orange Walk Town. See the Northern Belize chapter for details.

Getting There & Away

Unless you have your own transport, you'll have to depend on taxis or the hospitality of your Mountain Pine Ridge lodge hosts to transport you between San Ignacio and the lodges. Sometimes the lodges will shuttle you at no extra cost; sometimes they'll arrange a taxi for you.

XUNANTUNICH

Xunantunich (pronounced shoo-nahn-too-NEECH) is Belize's best Mayan site. Though other sites such as Caracol and Lamanai promise to be more important, Xunantunich (Stone Maiden) is currently the archaeological pride of Belize.

Set on a levelled hilltop overlooking the Mopan River, Xunantunich controlled the riverside track which led from the hinterlands of Tikal down to the Caribbean. During the Classic period, a ceremonial centre flourished here. Other than that, not too much is known. The kings of Xunantunich erected a few beautiful stelae inscribed with dates, but we have no full history of their reigns as we have at Tikal, Copán and other sites.

Archaeologists have uncovered evidence that an earthquake damaged the city badly about 900 AD, after which the place may have been largely abandoned. Archaeological work is continuing under the guidance of Dr Richard Leventhal from the University of California at Los Angeles.

Though it is an interesting site, and its tallest building – El Castillo – is impressive as it rises some 40 metres above the jungle floor, Xunantunich will perhaps disappoint you after you've seen Tikal, Chichén Itzá, Uxmal or Palenque. It has not been extensively restored, as those sites have, and the

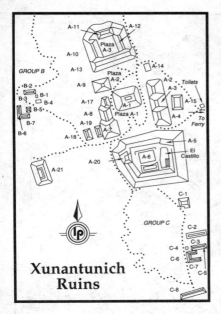

Xunantunich Ruins

approach from the courtyard – goes only as far as the temple building. To climb to the roofcomb you must go around to the south side and use a separate set of steps. On the east side of the temple, a few of the masks which once surrounded this structure have been restored.

Getting There & Away
The ferry to Xunantunich is opposite the village of San José Succotz, 8.5 km west of San Ignacio, 1.5 km east of Benque Viejo. From the ferry it's a walk of two km uphill to the ruins.

Novelo's buses on their way between San Ignacio and Benque Viejo will drop you at the ferry (US$0.35). There are also jitney taxis shuttling between San Ignacio and Benque Viejo, which will take you for US$1. Make your excursion to Xunantunich in the morning to avoid the ferry operator's lunch break. Ferry hours are 8 am to noon and 1 to 5 pm; the ferry crosses on demand. There is no fee for passengers or cars, except on weekends, when cars pay US$0.50 each way.

When you return, cross on the ferry and have a cold drink at the Xunantunich Hotel & Saloon across the road. You can wait for the bus to San Ignacio here. If your goal is Benque Viejo, you can walk there from the ferry in about 15 minutes.

BENQUE VIEJO DEL CARMEN
A foretaste of Guatemala just two km east of the border – that's Benque Viejo del Carmen. The name and lingua franca are Spanish, and the people are Spanish-speaking Maya or ladinos. Some ambitious maps of the town make it look like a prosperous, orderly place, but it's more like a jungle outpost. Hotels and restaurants are very basic. You're better off staying and eating in San Ignacio if you can.

Benque Viejo stirs from its normal tropical somnolence in mid-July, when the Benque Festival brings three days of music and revelry. Then it's back to sleep.

Places to Stay & Eat
Benque's lodging and dining choices are

jungle has grown around and over the excavated temples. But the walk from the ferry beneath arches of palm fronds, the tropical plants and animals, and the lack of crowds at the site are compensations.

Xunantunich is open from 9 am to 5 pm; admission costs US$1.50. In the rainy season (June to October), bugs can be a problem; you may need your repellent. There are no facilities at Xunantunich except picnic tables, pit toilets and a cistern of murky rainwater for drinking, so bring water and perhaps a picnic or snacks.

The path from the guardian's hut leads to Plaza A-2, surrounded by low, bush-covered buildings, and then on to Plaza A-1, dominated by Structure A-6: El Castillo. A thatched pavilion near El Castillo provides shelter from the sun or rain. On the edges of the grassy plazas, hummingbirds hover in the humid air, sucking nectar from brilliantly coloured tropical flowers. The stairway on the north side of El Castillo – the side you

BELIZE

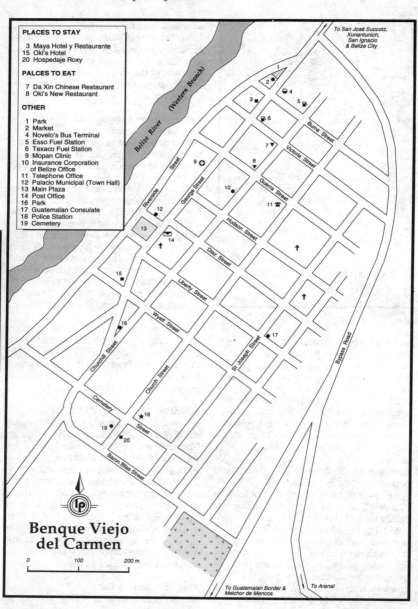

PLACES TO STAY

3 Maya Hotel y Restaurante
15 Oki's Hotel
20 Hospedaje Roxy

PALCES TO EAT

7 Da Xin Chinese Restaurant
8 Oki's New Restaurant

OTHER

1 Park
2 Market
4 Novelo's Bus Terminal
5 Esso Fuel Station
6 Texaco Fuel Station
9 Mopan Clinic
10 Insurance Corporation
    of Belize Office
11 Telephone Office
12 Palacio Municipal (Town Hall)
13 Main Plaza
14 Post Office
16 Park
17 Guatemalan Consulate
18 Police Station
19 Cemetery

Benque Viejo
del Carmen

0   100   200 m

decidedly modest. You can do much better in San Ignacio.

Maya Hotel y Restaurante (☎ (93) 21-16), 11 George St, is a dreary family-run lodging near the bus terminal. The 10 rooms have lots of bunks; most have no running water (communal showers). The restaurant serves all three meals. Rates are US$8/12 a single/double without bath, US$14/19 with private shower.

Next best is the *Hospedaje Roxy*, on Church St at the south-western end of town. It's family-run and charges US$7 per person.

Oki's Hotel (☎ (93) 20-06), 47 George St, has 11 very basic rooms (some very cramped and dark) in a converted village house. The communal showers and toilets are usable. The price is US$6 per person.

Places to Eat

The *Da Xin* Chinese restaurant is currently the town favourite for both eating and drinking. *Oki's New Restaurant* is the fanciest place in town, which isn't saying much.

Getting There & Away

There are frequent jitney taxis (US$2) and hourly buses (US$0.35) between San Ignacio and Benque Viejo. A few buses go all the way to Melchor de Mencos in Guatemala. From Benque Viejo, taxis shuttle back and forth from the border, charging a high US$4 for the three-km ride, so you might want to make the 35-minute walk instead.

WEST TO GUATEMALA

Cross early in the morning to have the best chance of catching buses onward. Get your passport (and, if applicable, your car papers) stamped at the Belizean station, then cross into Guatemala. The border station is supposedly open 24 hours a day, but officers are usually only on duty from 6 am to midnight. If you need a Guatemalan visa (see Visas & Embassies in the Guatemalan Facts for the Visitor chapter), as citizens of most British Commonwealth countries do, you should obtain it before you reach the border. Guatemalan tourist cards (US$5) are obtainable at the border.

There also two banks at the border for changing money. Note that the rates for exchanging Belize dollars to Guatemalan quetzals, and vice versa, are very poor. Use up your local currency before you get to the border, then change hard foreign currency, preferably US dollars.

The Guatemalan town of Melchor de Mencos has several cheap hotels and restaurants.

If you've crossed the border in the morning, you'll be able to catch a Transportes Pinita bus westward to Flores. To go on to Tikal, get off the bus at El Cruce (Puente Ixlu), 36 km east of Flores, and wait for another bus, minibus or obliging car or truck to take you the final 35 km north to Tikal. Note that the flow of traffic from El Cruce to Tikal drops dramatically after lunch.

BELIZE

Yucatán

Facts about Yucatán

The largest, most populous and most developed region of the Mayan world is in Mexico. The south-eastern states of Campeche, Chiapas, Quintana Roo, Tabasco and Yucatán can boast more and bigger Mayan archaeological sites than Guatemala and Belize combined. The ruins of Bonampak, Chichén Itzá, Cobá, Palenque, Uxmal, Yaxchilán and other sites are equalled only by the great cities of Tikal in Guatemala and Copán in Honduras.

Though the 'modern' Maya of Mexico cherish their ancient culture, most of them seem more distant from it than the Maya of highland Guatemala. The exception to this rule is highland Chiapas, where Indian cultures are basically an extension of those found in Guatemala's highlands.

There is much more to Mexico than the Maya, of course. The country's prime international resort – Cancún – is here, and each of the region's colonial cities – Campeche, Mérida, San Cristóbal de las Casas and Valladolid – has its particular charm.

The region that consists of Chiapas, Tabasco and the Yucatán Peninsula is here referred to as Yucatán for short.

HISTORY

Geographically removed from the heart of Mexico, the colonists of the Yucatán Peninsula participated little in Mexico's War of Independence. Even though Yucatán joined liberated Mexico, the peninsula's long isolation gave it a strong sense of independence, and Mexico's Mayan region desired little subsequent interference from Mexico City.

War of the Castes

Not long after independence, the Yucatecan ruling classes were again dreaming of independence, this time from Mexico, and perhaps union with the USA. With these goals in mind, the *hacendados* made the mistake of arming and training their Mayan peons as local militias in anticipation of an invasion from Mexico. Trained to use European weaponry, the Maya envisioned a release from their own misery and boldly rebelled against their Yucatecan masters.

The War of the Castes of 1847 began in Valladolid, a city known for its particularly strict and oppressive laws against the Maya; a Maya was not allowed to enjoy the main plaza or the prominent streets, but had to keep to the back streets and the outskirts. The Mayan rebels quickly gained control of the city in an orgy of killing, looting and vengeance. Supplied with arms and ammunition by the British through Belize, they spread relentlessly across Yucatán.

In little more than a year the Mayan revolutionaries had driven their oppressors from every part of Yucatán except Mérida and the walled city of Campeche. Seeing the Whites' cause as hopeless, Yucatán's governor was about to abandon the city when the rebels saw the annual appearance of the winged ant. In Mayan mythology, corn (the staff of life) must be planted at the first sighting of the winged ant. If the sowing is delayed, Chac, the rain god, will be affronted and respond with a drought. The rebels abandoned the attack and went home to plant the corn. This gave the Whites and mestizos time to regroup and receive aid from their erstwhile enemy, the government in Mexico City.

The Talking Cross

The counter-revolution against the Maya was without quarter and vicious in the extreme. Between 1848 and 1855, the Indian population of Yucatán was halved. Some Mayan combatants sought refuge in the jungles of southern Quintana Roo. There they were inspired to continue fighting by a religious leader working with a ventriloquist who, in 1850 at Chan Santa Cruz, made a sacred cross 'talk' (the cross was an important Mayan religious symbol long before the coming of Christianity). The talking cross convinced the Maya that their gods had made them invincible, and they continued to fight until 1866.

The governments in Mexico City and Mérida largely ignored the Mayan rebels of Chan Santa Cruz until the turn of the century, when Mexican troops with modern arms subdued the region. The shrine of the talking crosses at Chan Santa Cruz was destroyed, the town was renamed Felipe Carrillo Puerto in honour of a progressive Yucatecan governor, and the local Maya were allowed a good deal of autonomy. The region was only declared a Mexican 'territory' in 1936 and did not become a state until 1974. Today, if you visit Felipe Carrillo Puerto, you can visit the restored shrine of the talking cross above a cenote in what is now a city park.

Yucatán Today

Although the post-WW II development of synthetic fibres led to the decline of the henequen (rope) industry, it still employs about a third of the peninsula's workforce. The slack has been more than picked up by the oil boom in Tabasco and Chiapas, the fishing and canning industries of the peninsula and the rapid growth of tourism in the past decade. Though the power elite is still largely of Spanish or mestizo parentage, Yucatán's Maya are better off today than they have been for centuries.

A good number of Maya till the soil as their ancestors have done for centuries, growing staples like corn and beans. Subsistence agriculture is little different from the way it was in the Classic period, with minimal mechanisation.

GEOGRAPHY

The Mexican Mayan lands include cool pine-clad volcanic mountain country, hot and dry tropical forest, dense jungle rainforest, broad grassy savannas and sweltering coastal plains.

Yucatán Peninsula

The Yucatán Peninsula is one vast flat limestone shelf rising only a few metres above sea level. The shelf extends outward from the shoreline for several km under water. If you approach Yucatán or Belize by air, you should have no trouble seeing the barrier reef which marks the limit of the peninsular limestone shelf. On the landward side of the reef the water is shallow, usually no more than five or 10 metres deep; on the seaward side is deep water.

The underwater shelf makes Yucatán's coastline wonderful for aquatic sports, keeping the waters warm and the marine life (fish, crabs, lobsters, tourists) abundant, but it makes life difficult for traders. At Progreso, north of Mérida, the *muelle* (wharf) extends from dry land for several km across the shallow water to reach water deep enough to receive ocean-going vessels.

The only anomaly in the flat terrain of Yucatán is the low range of the Puuc Hills near Uxmal, which attains heights of several hundred metres.

Because of their geology, northern and central Yucatán have no rivers and no lakes. The people on the land have traditionally drawn their fresh water from *cenotes*, limestone caverns with collapsed roofs, which serve as natural cisterns. Rainwater which falls between May and October collects in the cenotes for use during the dry season from October to May. South of the Puuc Hills there are few cenotes, and the inhabitants traditionally have resorted to drawing water from limestone pools deep within the earth. These wells *(chenes)* give the region its name.

Yucatán is covered in a blanket of dry thorny forest, which the Maya have traditionally slashed and burned to make space for planting crops or pasturing cattle. The soil is red and good for crops in some areas, poor in others, and cultivating it is hot, hard work.

Tabasco

West of the peninsula along the Gulf coast is the state of Tabasco, low, well-watered and humid country which is mostly covered in equatorial rainforest. The relative humidity at Palenque (just across the state border in Chiapas) averages 78%. The lush rainforest is endangered by farmers and cattle ranchers

YUCATÁN

who slash and burn it to make way for more crops and cattle which, in this climate, are guaranteed to thrive.

Besides its agricultural wealth, Tabasco is one of Mexico's most important petroleum-producing regions.

Chiapas

Chiapas is a huge state comprising several distinct topographical areas. The northern part of the state is lowland and low hills similar to those of Tabasco, well watered, sparsely populated, and dotted with important Mayan cities such as Palenque, Toniná, Bonampak and Yaxchilán.

The central and south-central area is mountainous and volcanic, rising from several hundred metres in the west to more than 3900 metres in the south-east near the Guatemalan border. Rainfall varies from less than 40 cm at Tuxtla Gutiérrez, the state capital, to more than 200 cm on the mountain slopes facing the Pacific Ocean. The high country around San Cristóbal de las Casas is known locally as the *tierra fría*, or cold country, because of the altitude and many cloudy days. The mountains here are covered in forests of oak and pine. The Continental Divide follows the ridge of the Sierra Madre, towering above the Pacific littoral.

South and west of the Sierra Madre is the Pacific slope of the mountains and the coastal plain, known as the Soconusco. Rainfall here is abundant as the weather arrives from the west and the clouds dump their wet loads as they ascend to vault the high mountains. Cotton is the choice crop on the plain, but on the mountain slopes (up to 1400 metres) it's cacao and coffee.

GOVERNMENT

Theoretically, the United Mexican States (Estados Unidos Mexicanos) is a multiparty democracy with an elected president, a bicameral legislature, and an independent judiciary. The individual states of the union have similar governments, with state legislatures and elected governors.

In fact, Mexican political life has been dominated since the 1930s by one political party, the gigantic Partido Revolucionario Institucional, or PRI ('el PREE'). Presidential candidates are selected by the party's top leadership led by the current president, and they invariably win election as the party has complete control over the powerful government media apparatus and patronage system. A president serves one term of six years, *el sexenio*, and is not eligible for re-election.

During his or her term, Mexico's president is the worthy successor of Moctezuma or Cortés, vested with enormous power and treated as royalty. The president's job is to guide the country with the huge PRI party apparatus, and assure the succession of the chosen PRI candidate at the end of the sexenio.

In recent decades, bad government has led to the rise of a true opposition – not just the tame opposition secretly supported by the PRI – in the form of the Partido de Acción Nacional, or PAN, which has claimed victory in some local contests despite massive fraud on the part of the PRI.

In the elections of 1988, fraud was not quite so massive and the PRI candidate, Carlos Salinas de Gortari, won by the smallest margin in PRI history. He has taken several bold steps to alleviate some of Mexico's most pressing problems and win back the popular support which had been lost to the PRI.

In the Mérida municipal elections of December 1993, the opposition PAN candidate was declared the winner despite the usual accusations that, in some polling districts, there were twice as many votes cast for the PRI as there were eligible voters in the district.

ECONOMY

Yucatán, without plentiful water resources, has minimal agriculture, with some cattle ranches. The important exception is the cultivation of henequen, the plant from which sisal rope is made.

The export economy based on henequen thrived in the latter half of the 19th century. By WW I it was said that Mérida had more millionaires per capita than any other city in the world. The plantation owners were a de facto Yucatecan aristocracy and built opulent mansions along Mérida's Paseo de Montejo, many of which still stand. They decorated their homes with the artistic treasures of the world and sent their children off to the best schools of Europe.

With the invention of synthetic fibres such as nylon, henequen lost much of its importance, but it is still a significant part of Yucatán's agriculture.

Besides henequen, Yucatán has some pig and chicken farms, and light industry around Mérida and Chetumal. Tourism is very important in the states of Yucatán and neighbouring Quintana Roo.

Campeche is an important fishing port for fish, lobsters and shrimp, much of the catch being for export. Towns along the northern coast of the peninsula also depend on fishing.

By far the richest sector of the Mexican economy is petroleum. The deposits beneath Tabasco and Veracruz are among the richest in the world. Campeche has petroleum reserves as well.

Farming, mining, forestry and oil exploration are important in Chiapas, as is tourism. Tuxtla Gutiérrez, the Chiapan capital, is one of Mexico's coffee-production centres. The cattle ranches in Tabasco and Chiapas along the Gulf coast are expanding into the rainforest, threatening the tropical ecosystem and triggering revolts by indigenous peoples who are being swept from their traditional lands.

PEOPLE

Over millennia, the Maya of Yucatán and Chiapas have intermarried with neighbouring peoples, especially those of central Mexico with whom they had diplomatic and commercial relations and the occasional invasion and conquest. During the 20th century they have also intermarried, to some degree, with the descendants of the conquering Spanish. People of mixed Mayan and Spanish blood are called mestizos. Most of Mexico's population is mestizo, but the Yucatán Peninsula has an especially high proportion of pure-blooded Maya. In many areas of Yucatán and Chiapas, Mayan languages prevail over Spanish, or Spanish may not be spoken at all – only Mayan. In remote jungle villages, some modern cultural practices descend directly from those of ancient Mayan civilisation.

Thanks to the continuation of their unique cultural identity, the Maya of Yucatán are proud without being arrogant, confident without the *machismo* seen so frequently elsewhere in Mexico, and kind without being servile. And with the exception of those who have become jaded by the tourist hordes of Cancún, many Maya retain a sense of humour and a pleasant disposition.

YUCATÁN

Facts for the Visitor

VISAS & EMBASSIES
Mexican Tourist Card

The Mexican tourist card (it's actually a multicopy paper form) costs US$5. As you present your card to the immigration official upon entering Mexico, he or she may ask how long you expect to stay in Mexico. Say 'three months' or you're liable to get less time.

Don't lose your tourist card, as obtaining another one from the Migración (Immigration) officials is a long, frustrating, time-consuming process.

When you leave Mexico, you're supposed to turn in your tourist card. You will certainly have to produce it and hand it over if you leave the country by air, or if you cross into Guatemala. You may not be asked for it if you travel to one of the Mexican cities along the US border and then cross over into the USA.

Parent & Child If you are an adult travelling with a child under 18 years of age, the Mexican immigration officer will require you to show a notarised affidavit from the child's other parent permitting you to take the child into Mexico. This is to prevent separated, divorcing or divorced parents from absconding to Mexico with a child against the wishes – or legal actions – of the other parent. If both parents are travelling together with the child or children, there's no problem and no affidavit is needed.

If you have any questions about this procedure, talk them over in advance of your trip with a Mexican diplomatic representative. Don't wait until you're at the border or airport without an affidavit and the immigration officer won't permit you and the child to enter the country!

Mexican Embassies & Consulates

Some of the consulates mentioned here are actually honorary consuls or consular agencies. These posts can issue tourist cards and

visas, but they refer more complicated matters to the nearest full consulate, or to the embassy's consular section.

Australia
 Embassy, 14 Perth Ave, Yarralumla, Canberra ACT 2600 (☎ (06) 73-3905/47/63)
 Consulate, 49 Bay St, Double Bay, Sydney, NSW 2028 (☎ (02) 326-1292/1311)
Austria
 Embassy, Renngasse 4, 1010 Wien (Vienna) (☎ (222) 535-1776/77/78/79)
Belgium
 Embassy, Rue Paul-Emile Jansson 6, 1050 Brussels (☎ (2) 648-2671/2703)
 Consulate, Quellinstraat 42, Bus 2, 2018 Antwerpen (☎ 234-1861, 231-7316/7)
Belize
 Embassy, 20 North Park St, Belize City (☎ 45367, 44301, 78742)
Canada
 Embassy, 206-130 Albert St, Ottawa, ON K1P 5G4 (☎ (613) 233-8988/9272)
 Consulates:
 1000 Sherbrooke West, Suite 2215, Montréal, QC H3A 3G4 (☎ (514) 288-2502/4816)
 60 Bloor St W, Suite 203, Toronto, ON M4W 3B8 (☎ (416) 922-2718/3196)
 310-625 Howe St, Vancouver, BC V6C 2T6 (☎ (604) 684-3547/5725)
Costa Rica
 Embassy, 7a Avenida No 1371, San José (☎ 22-55-28, 22-54-85)
El Salvador
 Embassy, Paseo General Escalon No 3832, San Salvador (☎ 98-10-84, 98-11-76)
France
 Embassy, 9 rue de Longchamps, 75116 Paris (☎ 45.53.99.34, 45.53.76.43)
 Consulate, 4, Rue Notre-Dame des Victoires, 75002 Paris (☎ 40.20.07.32/33, 42.61.51.80)
Germany
 Embassy, Oxfordstrasse 12-16, 5300 Bonn 1 (☎ (228) 63-12-26/28)
 Consulates:
 Neue Mainzer Strasse 57, 6000 Frankfurt 1 (☎ (069) 23-61-34, 23-57-09)
 Hallerstrasse 70-1, 2000 Hamburg 13 (☎ (040) 45-89-50, 44-87-74)
Guatemala
 Embassy, 16 Calle 1-45, Zona 10, Guatemala City (☎ (2) 68-02-02, 68-28-27)

Consulate, 13 Calle 7-30, Zona 9, Guatemala City (☎ (2) 36-65-04, 36-35-73, 31-81-65)

Honduras
Embassy, Calle República del Brasil Suroeste 2028, Colonia Palmira, Tegucigalpa (☎ 32-64-71, 32-40-39)

Israel
Embassy, 14 Hey I'yar , Kikar Ha-Medina, Tel Aviv (☎ (03) 210-266/268)

Italy
Embassy, Via Lazzaro Spallanzani No 16, 00161 Roma (☎ (6) 440-2319/2323)
Consulate, Via Cappuccini 4, Milano (☎ (2) 349-8782)

Japan
Embassy, 2-15-1, Nagata-cho, Chiyoda-Ku, Tokyo 100 (☎ (3) 581-2150, 581-1131/35)

Netherlands
Embassy, Nassauplein 17, 2585 EB The Hague (☎ (70) 60-29-00, 60-68-57)
Consulate, Groothandelsgebow, Stationsplein 45, Rotterdam (☎ (010) 126-084)

Nicaragua
Embassy, Km 45, Carretera a Masaya, Colonia 25 Varas Arriba (Altamira), Managua (☎ (2) 75380, 75275/79)

Panama
Embassy, Calle 50 at Calle San José, Bank of America Bldg, 5th floor, Panama City 7 (☎ 63-50-21)

Spain
Embassy, Avenida Paseo de la Castellana No 93, 7th floor, Madrid 28046 (☎ (1) 456-1349/1496)
Consulate, Avenida Diagonal No 626, 4th floor, Barcelona 08021 (☎ (343) 200-6265, 201-1822)

Sweden
Embassy, Grevgatan 3, 114 53 Stockholm (☎ (8) 661-6175, 660-3970)

Switzerland
Embassy, Bernestrasse 57, 3005 Berne (☎ (31) 43-18-14, 43-18-75)

UK
Embassy, 8 Halkin St, London SW1 (☎ (071) 235-6393/51, 245-9030)

USA
Embassy, 2829 16th St NW, Washington, DC 20009 (☎ (202) 234-6000/1/2/3)
Apart from the embassy in Washington DC there are consular offices in many other cities throughout the USA, particularly in the border states of California and Texas :

Arizona
515 10th St, Douglas, AZ 85607 (☎ (602) 364-2275)
135 Terrace Ave, Nogales, AZ 85621 (☎ (602) 287-2521)
700 East Jefferson, Suite 150, Phoenix, AZ 85034 (☎ (602) 242-7398/9)

California
331 W 2nd St, Calexico, CA 92231 (☎ (619) 357-3863/3880)
2839 Mariposa St, Fresno, CA 93721 (☎ (209) 233-3065/9770)
125 East Paseo de la Plaza, Suite 300, Los Angeles, CA 90012 (☎ (213) 624-9387/8)
1506 South St, Sacramento, CA 95814 (☎ (916) 446-4696/9024)
588 W 6th St, San Bernardino, CA 92401 (☎ (714) 888-2500/4700)
1333 Front St, Suite 200, San Diego, CA 92101 (☎ (619) 231-8414/8427)
870 Market St, Suite 528, San Francisco, CA 94102 (☎ (415) 392-5554)
380 N 1st St, Suite 102, San Jose, CA 95112 (☎ (408) 294-3414/5)

Colorado
707 Washington St, Denver, CO 80203 (☎ (303) 830-0523/0704)

Florida
780 NW LeJeune Rd, Suite 525, Miami, FL 33126 (☎ (305) 441-8780/83)

Georgia
410 South Tower, One CNN Center, Atlanta, GA 30303 2705 (☎ (404) 688-3258/3261)

Illinois
300 N Michigan Ave, 2nd floor, Chicago, IL 60601 (☎ (312) 855-1380/84)

Louisiana
1140 World Trade Center Bldg, 2 Canal St, New Orleans, LA 70130 (☎ (504) 522-3596/7)

Massachusetts
20 Park Plaza, Suite 321, Statler Building, Boston, MA 02116 (☎ (617) 426-4942/8782)

Michigan
1515 Book Building, Washington Blvd at W Grand River, Detroit, MI 48226 (☎ (313) 965-1868/9)

Missouri
823 Walnut St, Kansas City, MO 64106 (☎ (816) 421-5956)
1015 Locust St, Suite 922, St Louis, MO 63101 (☎ (314) 436-3233/3426)

New Mexico
Western Bank Bldg, 401 5th St, NW, Albuquerque, NM 87102 (☎ (505) 247-2139/2147)

New York
8 E 41st St, New York, NY 10017 (☎ (212) 689-0456/60)

Pennsylvania
Independence Mall E, 575 Philadelphia Bourse Bldg, Philadelphia, PA 19106 (☎ (215) 922-4262/3834)

Texas
200 E 6th St, Suite 200, Hannig Row Building, Austin, TX 78701 (☎ (512) 478-2300/2866/9031
Elizabeth & E 7th Sts, Brownsville, TX 78520 (☎ (512) 542-4431/2051)

800 N Shoreline, 1 Shoreline Plaza, 410 North Tower, Corpus Christi, TX 78401 (☎ (512) 882-3375/5964)

1349 Empire Central, No 100, Dallas, TX 75247 (☎ (214) 630-7341/2024)

1010 S Main St, Del Rio, TX 78840 (☎ (512) 775-2352/9451)

140 Adams St, Eagle Pass, TX 78852 (☎ (512) 773-9255/6)

910 E San Antonio St, PO Box 812, El Paso, TX 79901 (☎ (915) 533-3644/5)

4200 Montrose Blvd, Suite 120, Houston, TX 77006 (☎ (713) 524-4861/2300)

1612 Farragut St, Laredo, TX 78040 (☎ (512) 723-6360/1741)

1220 Broadway Ave, Lubbock, TX 79401 (☎ (806) 765-8816)

1418 Beech St, No 102-104, McAllen, TX 78501 (☎ (512) 686-0243/4)

730 O'Riety St, Presidio, TX 79845 (☎ (915) 229-3745)

127 Navarro St, San Antonio, TX 78205 (☎ (512) 227-9145/6)

Utah
182 South 600 East, Suite 202, Salt Lake City, UT 84102 (☎ (801) 521-8502/3)

Washington State
1411 4th Ave, Fourth Avenue Bldg, Suite 410, Seattle, WA 98101 (☎ (206) 343-3047, 682-8996)

MONEY
Currency
The Mexican unit of currency is the New Peso (N$), which is further divided into 100 centavos. Mexican coins come in denominations of one, five, 10, 20 and 50 centavos, and one peso. Notes (bills) are in denominations of one, five, 10, 50, 100 and 500 New Pesos.

Money exchange is supposedly at free market floating rates which may change daily, but government economic policies tend to support the peso and as a result the peso is now seriously overvalued.

In such heavily touristed areas as Cancún and Cozumel you can often spend US dollars as easily as pesos at hotels, restaurants and shops. Most of the time you won't get as good an exchange rate as if you changed your dollars for pesos at a bank; sometimes the rate in hotels, restaurants and shops will be downright outrageous. However, in other establishments, dollars are accepted at an exchange rate as good as or better than that of the banks as an inducement to get you to spend your money there.

Credit Cards
The major credit cards such as Visa and MasterCard (Eurocard, Access) are accepted at all airline and car rental companies, and at the larger hotels and restaurants; American Express cards are often accepted at the fancier and larger places, and at some smaller ones.

Many smaller establishments will readily accept your card, even for charges as little as US$5 or US$10; Cancún, for example, lives on credit cards, and even has some telephones which accept these cards for long-distance (trunk) calls.

Costs
At this writing, the peso is overvalued and things in Mexico cost more than they should, relative to similar goods and services in other countries.

Cancún and Cozumel are the two most expensive places in the country, far more expensive than Mexico City or even Acapulco. Small towns such as Tizimín and Izamal, not being heavily touristed, are much cheaper. Cities like Mérida and San Cristóbal de las Casas offer a good range of prices, with good value for money.

A single budget traveller staying in bottom-end or lower middle-range accommodation and eating two meals a day in restaurants may pay US$15 to US$30 per day, on average, for those basics. Add in the other costs of travel (roughly US$2 per hour on long-distance buses, snacks, purified water and soft drinks, admission to archaeological sites, etc), and you may spend more like US$20 to US$40 per day.

If there are two or more of you sharing accommodation, costs per person come down considerably. Double rooms are often only a few dollars more than singles, and triples or quadruples only a little more expensive than doubles.

Consumer Taxes

Mexico has a value-added tax called the Impuesto de Valor Agregado (IVA), usually referred to as *el IVA* (ehl EE-bah). By law the tax must be *included* in virtually any price quoted to you; it should not be added afterwards. Signs in shops and notices on restaurant menus usually reiterate this fact as *incluye el IVA* or *IVA incluido*. When asking prices, it's still not a bad idea to confirm that the tax will not be added to the price later.

Airport usage taxes are levied on all passengers on each flight. The tax on international flights departing Mexico is equivalent to approximately US$12; domestic departure taxes are less.

Student Discounts

Discounts for foreign students are virtually unknown. A few places offer small discounts on admission fees to students under 26 who hold a card from either the Servicio Educativo de Turismo de los Estudiantes y la Juventud de México (SETEJ) or Consejo Nacional de Recursos para la Atención de la Juventud (CREA). These cards also entitle you to youth hostel membership. CREA cards can be obtained at most youth hostels in Mexico.

CLIMATE & WHEN TO GO
Yucatán

It is always hot in Yucatán, often reaching temperatures around 40°C (100°F) in the heat of the day. From May to October, the rainy season makes it hot and humid. From October to May it is hot and dry. There are occasional showers even in the dry season. The violent but brief storms called *nortes* can roll in any afternoon, their black clouds, high winds and torrents of rain followed within an hour by bright sun and utterly blue sky.

The dry season is generally preferred for travel in Yucatán because you needn't dodge the raindrops, the heat is not as muggy and, most importantly, it's winter in most of North America and Europe! November and early December are perhaps the best times as there are fewer tourists and prices are low.

From mid-December to April is the busy winter tourism season when premium prices prevail, with surcharges around Christmas, New Year and Easter. May, the end of the dry season, and June, when the rains begin, are the hottest and muggiest months. If you have a choice of months, don't choose these. July and August are hot, not too rainy, and busy with the summer travel crowd. September and October are pretty good for travel as the traffic decreases markedly, and so do the rains.

Tabasco & Chiapas

The low-lying state of Tabasco is always hot and muggy, but more pleasant in the dry season (October to May) than the rainy season. As in Yucatán, it's always hot here; unlike Yucatán, this area is not seasonally crowded with tourists.

Mountainous northern Chiapas can get lots of rain in summer, but at least it's cool at the higher altitudes. In winter the air is cool most of the time, warming up considerably on sunny days, though many days are overcast. In the *tierra fría* around San Cristóbal de las Casas, mornings and evenings are usually chilly (a thrill after the sticky heat of Palenque!) and the nights downright cold (though frost is rare), especially if it's raining, which it often is from May to October.

The Soconusco, the Pacific Slope in Chiapas and Guatemala, is hot and humid all the time, and frequently rainy in summer.

TOURIST OFFICES

Government tourist offices (federal, state and local) are a fair source of information. They have the latest information on the most visited areas and on official tourist matters such as tourist card requirements. They can also issue tourist cards and automobile permits. If they cannot issue what you need or answer your query, then they can usually direct you to someone who can.

Tourist Offices Abroad

For information on planning your trip, contact the Mexican Government Tourist

YUCATÁN

Office in your home country, at the address listed below.

Canada
  1 Place Ville Marie, Suite 2409, Montréal, Québec H3B 3M9 (☎ (514) 871-1052)
  181 University Ave, Suite 1112, Toronto, Ontario M5H 3M7 (☎ (416) 364-2455)
France
  34 Ave George V, 75008 Paris (☎ (1) 47.20.69.07)
Germany
  Wiesenhüttenplatz 26, D600 Frankfurt-am-Main 1 (☎ (69) 25-34-13)
Italy
  Via Barberini No 3, 00187 Rome (☎ (6) 474-2986)
Spain
  Calle de Velázquez No 126, Madrid 28006 (☎ (1) 261-1827)
UK
  7 Cork St, London W1X 1PB (☎ (071) 734-1058)
USA
  10100 Santa Monica Blvd, Suite 2204, Los Angeles, CA 90067 (☎ (213) 203-8151)
  Two Illinois Center, 233 Michigan Ave, Suite 1413, Chicago, IL 60601 (☎ (312) 565-2785)
  405 Park Ave, Suite 1002, New York, NY 10022 (☎ (212) 755-7261)
  2707 North Loop West, Suite 450, Houston, TX 77008 (☎ (713) 880-5153)

BUSINESS HOURS

Banks are open from 9 am to 1.30 pm, Monday to Friday. Businesses are generally open from 9 am to 2 pm and 4 to 7 pm, Monday to Friday; various sorts of shops are open on Saturday as well. Shops and offices close for siesta from roughly 1 or 2 to 4 or 5 pm, then open again until 7 or 8 pm.

POST & TELECOMMUNICATIONS

Almost every city and town (but not villages) has an Oficina de Correos (post office) where you can buy postage stamps and send or receive mail.

Sending Mail

If you are sending something by airmail from Mexico, be sure to clearly mark it with the words 'Por Avión'. An airmail letter sent to Canada or the USA may take anywhere from four to 14 days. Airmail letters to Europe can take anywhere from one to three weeks.

Receiving Mail

Receiving mail in Mexico can be tricky. You can send or receive letters and packages care of a post office if they're addressed as follows:

Jane SMITH (surname should be in capitals)
a/c Lista de Correos
Mérida, Yucatán
(numerical postal code if possible) MEXICO

When the letter arrives at the post office, the name of the addressee is placed on an alphabetical list called the Lista de Correos which is updated daily. If you can, check the list yourself because the letter might be listed under your first name instead of your surname.

To claim your mail, present your passport or other identification; there's no charge. The snag is that many post offices only hold Lista mail for 10 days before returning it to the sender. If you think you're going to pick mail up more than 10 days after it has arrived, have it sent to you at Poste Restante, Correo Central, Town/City, State, Mexico. Poste Restante holds mail for up to a month but no list of what has been received is posted. Again, there's no charge for collection.

If you can arrange for a private address to receive mail, do so. There's less chance of your mail getting put aside, lost or returned to the sender if you're late in picking it up.

Telephone

The local company is Teléfonos de México, or TelMex for short. Telephone numbers in Mexico have different numbers of digits for different cities and towns. You must dial seven digits in Mexico City, but only six in Mérida, and only five in Palenque, etc.

Local calls are inexpensive and easy to place from public telephones (call boxes) and *casetas de teléfonos* (telephone call stations in shops).

Long-Distance Calls You may see the

abbreviation *Lada* in connection with long distance calls; it's short for *larga distancia* (long distance). Domestic and international long-distance/trunk calls are exorbitantly taxed. Be warned! A 15-minute operator-assisted call to the USA can easily cost US$60, much more to Europe or Australia.

Tolls for calls placed from the USA or Canada to Mexico are much cheaper than for the same call placed from Mexico to Canada or the USA. Use a short call from Mexico to advise the call's recipient of your hotel telephone number in Mexico, and agree on a time for them to call you back (don't forget time zone differences).

From a *caseta de larga distancia*, or long-distance call station, an operator will connect your number. Calls may cost anywhere from US$1 to US$2 per minute within Mexico, or US$2 to US$5 per minute to the USA or Canada, or even more for countries farther away. Ask before you call.

A collect/reverse charge call *(llamada por cobrar)* is usually much cheaper than a normal operator-assisted call, but you may end up paying one or two dollars for the privilege of discovering that the party you're calling collect is not at home.

It is now possible to use direct foreign telephone services. Dial (95-800) 462-4240 for AT&T, or (95-800) 674-7000) for MCI, to be connected with an operator in the USA. In my experience these services do not work from all Ladatel phones. You may have to keep trying different phones. Those directly in front of TelMex offices seem to work best.

Ladatel Phones Ladatel call stations have blue handsets and small liquid-crystal displays, and are clearly marked with the word Ladatel. Calling instructions are posted on Ladatel phones in Spanish, English, and French. From a Ladatel phone you can dial long-distance calls directly to any place in the world at much lower prices than operator-connected calls.

You must be well supplied with peso coins or Ladatel tokens or debit cards.

To call San Francisco, press 95 + 415 + the local number; for Toronto, 95 + 519 + the

local number; for London press 98 + 44 + 71 + the local number; for Melbourne press 98 + 61 + 3 + the local number. If you don't know the country code of the place you're calling, refer to the list in the Post & Telecommunications section of the introductory Facts for the Visitor chapter.

Fax, Telex, Telegraph
See the introductory Facts for the Visitor chapter for details.

MEDIA
The English-language *Mexico City News* is distributed throughout Mexico wherever tourists gather. Price varies with sales point, but is usually about US$1. Mexico has a thriving local Spanish-language press as well as national newspapers. Even small cities often have two or three newspapers of their own. In Mérida it's *El Diario de Yucatán*. Chiapas has its own excellent independent magazine, *Perfil del Sureste*, which comes out every two months and covers many issues that the authorities would prefer to keep quiet.

For those interested in a nonestablishment view of events, *La Jornada* is a good national daily with a mainly left-wing viewpoint which covers a lot of stories that other papers don't. *Proceso* is a weekly news magazine with a similar approach.

FOOD
It's tantalising to consider that some of the dishes prepared in Yucatán's kitchens today may be very similar to ones served in ancient times to Mayan royalty. Many traditional ingredients such as turkey *(pavo)*, venison *(venado)* and fish *(pescado)* were available in ancient times, as they are today.

Yucatán's resident chilli is the habanero, and my own personal anthropological theory holds that in the old days the victims of human sacrifice were given a choice: munch a habanero or have your heart carved out. Most thought the heart option offered a less painful end. If you go after a habanero chilli, you had better be equipped with a steel tongue.

Despite its reputation as a fissionable material in vegetable form, the habanero is an important ingredient in *achiote*, the popular Yucatecan sauce which also includes chopped onions, the juice of sour Seville oranges, *cilantro* (fresh coriander leaf) and salt. You'll see a bowl of achiote on most restaurant tables in Yucatán. Put it on your food – or ignore it – as you like.

A local hearty breakfast favourite is *huevos motuleños*, or eggs in the style of the town of Motul, east of Mérida. Fresh tortillas are spread with refried beans, then topped with an egg or two, then garnished with chopped ham, green peas and shredded cheese, with a few slices of fried banana on the side. It can be slightly picante or muy picante, depending upon the cook.

An authentic Yucatecan lunch or supper might begin with *sopa de lima* (lime soup), a chicken stock containing shreds of chicken meat, bits of tortilla and lime juice. It's tangy and delicious if made well; made badly, it's greasy.

For a main course you might order *pollo pibil*, chicken marinated in achiote sauce, sour Seville orange juice, garlic, black pepper, cumin and salt, then wrapped in banana leaves and baked. There are no nuclear chillis to blow your head off. A variant is *cochinita pibil*, made with suckling pig instead of chicken.

The restaurant named Los Almendros in Ticul, Yucatán, claims to have created *poc-chuc*, slices of pork marinated in sour orange juice, cooked and served with a tangy sauce and pickled onions. A more traditional pork dish is *frijol con puerco*, the Mayan version of pork-and-beans, with black beans, tomato sauce and rice.

Another hearty dish is *puchero*, a stew made with chicken and pork, carrots, cabbage, squash (marrow) and sweet potato.

The turkey is native to Yucatán, and has been used as food for millenia. *Pavo relleno negro*, or dark stuffed turkey, is slices of turkey over a 'filling' made with pork and beef, all topped by a rich dark sauce.

Venison (venado), also native to Yucatán, is perhaps best as a *pipián de venado*, steamed in banana leaves a la pibil and topped with a sauce made with ground squash (marrow) seeds.

Lighter traditional dishes include *papadzules*, tortillas sprinkled with chopped hard-boiled eggs, rolled up and topped with a sauce made with squash or pumpkin seeds. *Salbutes* are the native tacos: fried corn tortillas topped with shredded turkey meat, avocado and pickled onions. *Panuchos* are similar, but made with refried beans.

As for seafood, the all-time favourite is *pescado frito*, simple fried fish, but there's also *langosta* (lobster), usually just the tail. The most interesting seafood concoctions are the ceviches, cocktails made of raw or parboiled seafood in a marinade of lime juice, tomato sauce, chopped onion and cilantro. Cheapest is the *ceviche de pescado* made with whatever fish is in season and cheap in the markets. More choices available include *ceviche de camarones* (with shrimp) and *ceviche de ostiones* (with oysters).

At the open-air markets and cookshops, you'll need to know some Spanish to read the menus: *higado encebollado* is liver and onions, *longaniza* is a spicy sausage, *pollo asado o frito* is roasted or fried chicken, *bistec de res/puerco* is a beef or pork steak, *puerco empanizado* is a crumbed pork chop, *bistec a la Mexicana* is bits of beef sautéed with chopped tomatoes and hot peppers.

YUCATÁN

Getting There & Around

AIR

Cancún

Cancún's international airport is unquestionably the busiest airport in the region, with the most flights both regional and international.

Aerocaribe (in Cancún ☎ (988) 4-81-03, 4-20-00, 4-12-31, 4-21-33), covers destinations in the Yucatán peninsula and beyond, in small and medium-sized planes.

Mérida

Most international flights to Mérida are connections through Mexico City or Cancún; there is no nonstop international service except for Aeroméxico's two daily flights from Miami.

Domestic service includes half a dozen Mexicana flights daily from Mexico City to Mérida, and one or two by Aeroméxico as well. Aerocaribe are taking over most of the intermediate air traffic between Cancún, Mérida and Mexico City, meaning that if you want to fly to or from Cancún (US$60 one way, US$94 round-trip excursion), Chetumal, Villahermosa, or Tuxtla Gutiérrez (for San Cristóbal de las Casas), you should talk to those airlines.

Villahermosa

Because of its oil wealth, Villahermosa has good air services, with links to Mérida, Cancún, Tuxtla Gutiérrez and Mexico City.

Tuxtla Gutiérrez

Tuxtla has a few flights per week to other major cities, but air transport is mostly by small local airlines which fly small planes around the rugged Chiapan terrain. There are airstrips or airports at Tuxtla Gutiérrez, Ocosingo, Palenque, San Cristóbal de las Casas, Tapachula, and the ruins of Bonampak. The major airport for the region, however, is at the Tabascan capital of Villahermosa.

LAND

Mexico can be entered by land from the USA at 24 points. For details, refer to Lonely Planet's *Mexico – a travel survival kit*.

For notes on entering Mexico from Guatemala and Belize, see the relevant sections under each country in this book.

Bus

In Mexico the buses range from luxury-class air-conditioned cruisers to shabby but serviceable village buses. On most routes there is both 1st and 2nd-class service; 2nd class costs a little less than 1st class. The 1st-class equipment may or may not be more comfortable than 2nd class, but 1st-class routes are often faster than 2nd class because they make fewer stops. Luxury service is available on the busiest long-haul routes.

Car

Insurance Though not strictly required in Mexico, it is foolish to travel without Mexican liability insurance. If there is an accident and you cannot show a valid insurance policy, you will be arrested and not permitted to leave the locale of the accident until all claims are settled, which could be weeks or months. Mexico's legal system follows the Napoleonic model in which all persons involved in an incident are required to prove their innocence; trial is by a court of three judges, not by a jury. Your embassy can do little to help you in such a situation, except to tell you how stupid you were to drive without local insurance.

Mexican insurance is sold in US, Guatemalan and Belizean towns near the Mexican border. Approaching the border from the USA you will see billboards advertising offices selling Mexican policies. At the busiest border-crossing points (Tijuana, Mexicali, Nogales, Agua Prieta, Ciudad Juárez, Nuevo Laredo and Matamoros), there are insurance offices open 24 hours a day.

YUCATÁN

Prices for Mexican policies are set by law in Mexico, so bargain-hunting isn't easy. Instead of discounts (which cannot be offered), insurance offices offer incentives such as free guidebooks and/or maps, connections to automobile clubs and other treats.

Mexican motor vehicle insurance policies are priced so as to penalise the short-term buyer with extremely high rates. You may pay almost as much for a one-month policy (which is approximately US$200 average) as you would for a full year's policy.

Cancún & Isla Mujeres

In the 1970s Mexico's ambitious tourism planners decided to outdo Acapulco with a brand new world-class resort in Yucatán. The place they chose was a deserted sandspit offshore from the little fishing village of Puerto Juárez, on Yucatán's eastern shore. The island sandspit was shaped like a lucky '7'. The name of the place was Cancún.

As Cancún was discovered by the world, so was nearby Isla Mujeres. This tropical island had earlier been a haven for local mariners and adventurous young travellers in search of the simple life at low prices. Though Isla Mujeres retains some of its earlier allure, it is now also a day trip destination for boatloads of Cancúnites.

Cancún

Population: 250,000

The Mexican government built Cancún as an investment in the tourism business. Vast sums were sunk into landscaping and infrastructure, so the roads are straight and well paved, the water potable (so they say) right from the tap. Cancún's *raison d'être* is to shelter planeloads of tourists who fly in (usually on the weekend) to spend one or two weeks in a resort hotel before flying home again (usually on a weekend).

During their stay they can get by with speaking only English, spending only dollars and eating only familiar food. During the day, group tourists enjoy the beaches, hire a car or board a bus for an excursion to Chichén Itzá or Tulum, or browse in an air-con shopping mall straight out of Dallas. At night they dance and drink in clubs and discos to music that's the same all over the world. They have a good time. This is the business of tourism.

In the last two decades, Cancún has grown from a tiny jungle village into one of the world's best known holiday resorts. Dozens of mammoth hotels march along the island's shore as it extends from the mainland nine km eastward, then 14 km southward, into the turquoise waters of the Caribbean. At the north the island is joined to the mainland by a bridge which leads to Ciudad Cancún; at the south a bridge joins a road leading inland to the international airport.

These days Ciudad Cancún is looking a bit bedraggled. Rumor has it that previous municipal governments caused large amounts of public money to disappear, leaving little for civic services.

ORIENTATION

Cancún is actually two places in one. On the mainland lies Ciudad Cancún, a planned community founded as the service centre of the resort. On the 23-km-long sandy island is the Zona Hoteles, or Zona Turística, with its palatial hotels, theme restaurants, shopping malls, water sports centres and so on.

If you want to stay right on the beach, you must stay in the Zona Hoteles, out on the island. With the exception of the youth hostel, there are no budget hotels here. You can choose from among the few older, smaller, moderately priced hotels, or the many new, luxurious, pricey hotels.

Those who are content to trundle out to the beach by bus or taxi can save pots of money by staying on the mainland, in Ciudad Cancún, in one of the smaller, low to medium-priced hotels, many of which have swimming pools. Restaurants in the city centre range from ultra-Mexican taco joints to fairly smooth and expensive places where the Zona Hoteles people come to 'find someplace different for dinner'.

In Ciudad Cancún, the main north-south thoroughfare is called Avenida Tulum; it's a one-km-long tree-shaded boulevard lined with banks, shopping centres, small hotels, restaurants and touts selling time-share condominiums. On the east side of the boulevard

YUCATÁN

PLACES TO STAY

1 Hotel Posada Mariano
2 Hotel Uxmal
3 Hotel María Isabel
5 Hotel El Alux
6 Hotel Plaza Caribe
8 Hotel Cotty
9 Hotel Tankah
10 Hotel Canto
14 Hotel Parador
15 Hotel Novotel
16 Hotel Margarita
17 Hotel Suites
 Caribe Internacional
18 Hotel Hacienda Cancún
24 Hotel Plaza del Sol
31 Hotel Antillano

PLACES TO EAT

4 El Rincón Yucateco
19 Mandarin House
21 Mercado Municipal 28
22 Restaurant-Jazz Club
 100% Natural
23 Perico's
25 La Habichuela

26 Restaurant Pop
29 Restaurant El Pescador
32 Cafeteria San Francisco
33 Rosa Mexicano
34 El Tacolote
36 Pizza Rolandi
42 Los Almendros

OTHER

7 Bus Station
11 Caseta de Larga Distancia Central
12 Monument to the
 History of Mexico
13 Aerocaribe & Aero Cozumel
20 Main Post Office
27 City Hall (Ayuntamiento)
28 Department in Defence of the Tourist
30 Fama Cancún Bookstore
35 Monument to the
 North-South Dialogue
37 Quintana Roo
 State Tourism Office
38 US Consular Agency
39 Aeroméxico
40 Mexicana
41 Aviacsa
43 Plaza de Toros

Ciudad Cancún

0   100   200 m

To Airport &
Tulum

is the City Hall, marked 'Ayuntamiento Benito Juárez'.

Cancún International Airport is about eight km south of Avenida Tulum. Puerto Juárez, the port for passenger ferries to Isla Mujeres, is about three km north of Avenida Tulum. Punta Sam, the dock for the slower car ferries to Isla Mujeres, is about five km north of Avenida Tulum.

Isla Cancún is shaped like a '7'. Coming from Ciudad Cancún, the main road is Blvd Kukulcán (sometimes called Avenida or Paseo Kukulcán), a four-lane divided highway going east along the top of the '7' for nine km before reaching the convention centre near Punta Cancún. The youth hostel and the few moderately priced hotels are located in the first few kms of Blvd Kukulcán. At the convention centre, the boulevard turns south for another 14 km before reaching Punta Nizuc and rejoining the mainland.

INFORMATION
Tourist Office
There are tourist kiosks dispensing maps and answers to questions daily at several points along Avenida Tulum.

The State Tourism Office for Quintana Roo (☎ (98) 84-80-73,) is in a stone-faced building at the corner of Avenida Cobá and Avenida Carlos J Nader, a block off Avenida Tulum on the way to the Zona Hoteles, on the left-hand side of the road.

The 'Department in Defense of the Tourist', 26 Avenida Tulum, is next to the Multibanco Comermex, to the left (north) of the municipality. It's the place to go with problems or complaints.

Money
Banks on Avenida Tulum are open from 9 am to 1.30 pm, but many limit foreign exchange transactions to between 10 am and noon. Casas de cambio usually are open from 8 or 9 am to 1 pm and again from 4 or 5 pm till 7 or 8 pm; some casas are open seven days a week.

Post
The main post office (Oficina de Correos, Cancún, Quintana Roo 77500) is at the western end of Avenida Sunyaxchén. Hours for buying stamps and picking up Lista de Correos (poste restante) mail are from 8 am to 7 pm Monday to Friday, 9 am to 1 pm Saturday and holidays, closed Sunday. For international money orders and registered mail, hours are 8 am to 6 pm Monday to Friday, 9 am to noon Saturday and holidays, closed Sunday.

Telephone
You'll find Ladatel telephones, those easy-to-use long-distance machines, in both the arrival and departure terminals of Cancún's airport, in the bus station off Avenida Tulum and in front of the post office at the western end of Avenida Sunyaxchén. There are also special Ladatel phones in the Plaza Caracol Shopping Centre which accept credit cards (Visa, MasterCard, Access, Eurocard) near the McDonald's restaurant and in the hall near the Gucci shop.

The conveniently located Caseta de Larga Distancia Central, Avenida Uxmal 18 at the corner of Margaritas, across from the bus station, has public phone and fax service.

Foreign Consulates
The US Consular Agent (☎ (98) 84-24-11) is located at the offices of Intercaribe Real Estate, 86 Avenida Cobá, one block east off Avenida Tulum as you go towards the Zona Hoteles. Though the office is open from 9 am to 2 pm and 3 to 6 pm daily except Sunday, the consular agent is only on duty from 10 am to 2 pm Tuesday to Saturday.

If the agent is not available, call the US Consulate General in Mérida (open 7.30 am to 3.30 pm weekdays) at ☎ (99) 25-50-11; in an emergency after hours or on holidays, call ☎ (99) 25-54-09. There is always a duty officer available to help in an emergency.

Other countries have consular agents reachable by telephone. If yours is not listed here, call your consulate in Mérida, or your embassy in Mexico City (see the beginning of this section).

Canada
 (☎ (98) 84-37-16)
Costa Rica
 (☎ (98) 84-48-69)
Germany
 In the Club Lagoon (☎ (98) 83-09-58, 83-28-58)
Italy
 (☎ (98) 83-21-84)
Spain
 (☎ (98) 84-58-39)
Sweden
 In the office of Rentautos Kankun in Ciudad Cancún (☎ (98) 84-72-71, 84-11-75)

Travel Agencies
Any travel agent can book or change a flight for you. Most of the big hotels and many of the smaller, moderately priced hotels have travel agencies of their own.

Bookshops
A store with periodicals and books in several languages is Fama Cancún, Avenida Tulum 105, near the corner with the southern end of Tulipanes.

Medical Services
There are several hospitals and clinics, including the large IMSS (Social Security), Cruz Roja (Red Cross). Contact the American Hospital at (98) 84-64-30 or 84-60-68).

Laundry & Dry Cleaning
There are several shops offering these services. The Lavandería Maria de Lourdes, near the hotel of the same name, is on Calle Orquideas off Avenida Yaxchilán. You might also try the Lavandería y Tintorería Cox-Boh, Avenida Tankah 26, Supermanzana 24. Walk toward the post office along Avenida Sunyaxchén; in front of the post office, bear right onto Avenida Tankah and Cox-Boh is on the right-hand side of the street.

Laundry costs US$3.50 per kg for bulk service. To have a pair of trousers washed and ironed costs US$3.50, or $6.50 for dry cleaning. Washing and ironing a shirt costs US$2.25. Cox-Boh is open every day except Sunday.

MAYAN RUINS
There are Mayan ruins in Cancún and while they are not particularly impressive they are worth a look if you have lots of time. Most extensive are the ruins in the Zona Arqueológica El Rey, south of the Sheraton and Conrad hotels. Heading south along Blvd Kukulcán from Punta Cancún, watch for the marker for Km 17. Just past the marker there's an unpaved road on the right which leads to the ruins, open from 8 am to 5 pm every day; admission costs US$2. El Rey consists of a small temple and several ceremonial platforms.

If you've seen larger ruins, you may want to take just a quick glimpse at El Rey. If so, continue on Blvd Kukulcán 700 metres past the Km 17 marker and up the hill. At the top of the hill, just past the restaurant La Prosperidad de Cancún, you can survey the ruins without hiking in or paying the admission charge.

The tiny Mayan structure and chac-mool statue set in the beautifully kept grounds of the Sheraton Hotel are actually authentic ruins found on the spot.

ARCHAEOLOGICAL MUSEUM
The Museo de Antropología y Historia, next to the Convention Centre in the Zona Hoteles, has a limited collection of Mayan artefacts. Although most of the items are from the Post-Classic period (1200-1500 AD), including jewellery, masks and skull deformers, there is a Classic period hieroglyphic staircase inscribed with dates from the 6th century as well as the stucco head which gave the local archaeological zone its name of El Rey (The King).

BEACHES
The dazzling white sand of Cancún's beaches is light in weight and cool underfoot even in the blazing sun. That's because it is composed not of silica but rather of microscopic plankton fossils called disco-aster (a tiny star-shaped creature). The coolness of the sand has not been lost on Cancún's ingenious promoters, who have dubbed it 'air-conditioned'. Combined with the crystalline azure waters of the Caribbean, it makes for beaches that are pure delight.

All of these delightful beaches are open to you because all Mexican beaches are public property. Several of Cancún's beaches are set aside for easy public access, but you should know that you have the right to walk and swim on any beach at all. In practice it may be difficult to approach certain stretches of beach without going through a hotel's property, but few hotels will notice you walking through to the beach in any case.

Starting at Ciudad Cancún and heading out to Isla Cancún, all the beaches are on the left-hand side of the road as you go; the lagoon is on your right. They are: Playa Las Perlas, Playa Linda, Playa Langosta, Playa Tortugas, Playa Caracol, and then Punta Cancún, the point of the '7'. South from Punta Cancún are the long stretches of Playa Chac-Mool and Playa del Rey, reaching all the way to Punta Nizuc at the base of the '7'.

Beach Safety

As any experienced swimmer knows, a beach fronting on open sea can be deadly dangerous and Cancún's eastern beaches are no exception. Though the surf is usually gentle, undertow is a possibility and sudden storms (called *nortes*) can blacken the sky and sweep in at any time without warning. The local authorities have devised a system of coloured pennants to warn beachgoers of potential dangers. Look for the coloured pennants on the beaches where you swim:

Blue Normal, safe conditions
Yellow Use caution, changeable conditions
Red Unsafe conditions: use a swimming pool instead

Getting There & Away

To reach the beaches, catch any bus marked 'Hoteles', or 'Zona Hoteles' going south along Avenida Tulum or east along Avenida Cobá. The cost of a taxi depends upon how far you travel. For details, see Getting Around at the end of the Cancún section.

SNORKELLING

Most snorkellers who wish to explore reefs pay a visit to nearby Isla Mujeres – see that section for information. If you just want to see the sparser aquatic life off Cancún's beaches, you can rent snorkelling equipment for about US$8 from most luxury hotels.

The bigger hotels and travel agencies can also book you on day-cruise boats which take snorkellers to La Bandera, Los Manchones, Cuevones and Chital reefs.

SCUBA DIVING

This expensive sport is all the pricier in equipment rental and boat transport from Cancún. Veteran divers might prefer nearby Cozumel's justly famous Palancar Reef. Nonetheless, agencies and hotels rent gear and provide passage to some fine reefs in the vicinity. Los Manchones and Cuevones reefs, situated between Cancún and Isla Mujeres, afford diving depths of 10 to 15 metres.

FISHING

Deep-sea fishing excursions can be booked through a travel agent or one of the large hotels.

OTHER WATER SPORTS

Numerous dive shops and water sports marinas offer rentals of waterskis, sailboats, sailboards, jet-skis, scuba and snorkelling gear. Many of the larger hotels have water sports shops with similar rentals.

PLACES TO STAY – BOTTOM END.

Though there are more than 20,000 hotel rooms in Cancún, this resort offers the low-budget traveller the worst selection of cheap accommodation at the highest prices of any place in Mexico.

To make your room search as easy as possible, I've arranged my hotel recommendations on walking itineraries starting from the bus station. If you arrive by air and take a minibus into town (see below under Getting Around), your minibus driver will drop you at your chosen hotel at no extra charge.

In general, bottom-end rooms range from US$25 to US$45 a double, tax included, in

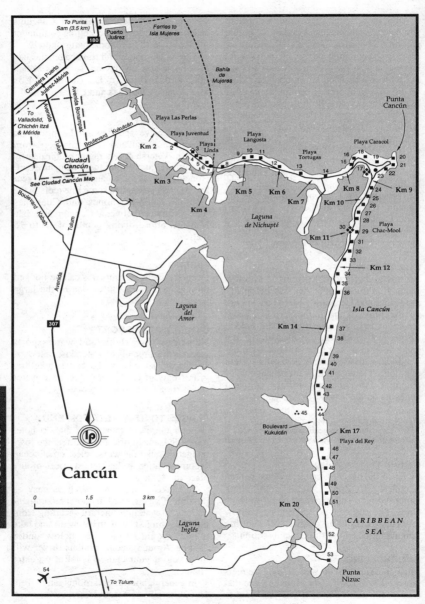

Cancún

PLACES TO STAY

2	Club Verano Beat
3	Villa Deportiva Juvenil (Youth Hostel)
4	Playa Blanca Hotel & Marina
5	Hotel Carrousel
6	Aquamarina Beach Hotel
8	Calinda Cancún Beach
9	Hotel Casa Maya Cancún
10	Hilton International Cancún
11	Villas Tacul
12	Hotel Maya Caribe
13	Hotel Dos Playas
14	Stouffer Presidente
15	Hotel Viva
16	Fiesta Americana Cancún
18	Hotel Camino Real Caribe
19	Fiesta Americana Coral Beach Cancún
20	Camino Real Cancún
21	Hyatt Regency Cancún
22	Krystal Cancún
24	Hotel Aristos Cancún
25	Miramar Misión
26	Hotel Inter-Continental
27	Hyatt Cancún Caribe
28	Fiesta Americana Plaza Cancún
29	Hotel Aston Flamingo
31	Hotel Brisas del Caribe
32	Hotel Baccara
33	Hotel Beach Club Cancún
34	Meliá Turquesa Hotel
35	Sheraton Cancún Resort & Towers
36	Paraíso Radisson Cancún
37	Hotel Tropical Oasis
38	Cancún Palace
39	Marriott's Cancún Resort
40	Meliá Cancún Hotel
41	Fiesta Americana Condesa
42	Hotel Oasis Cancún
43	Omni Cancún Hotel
46	Holiday Inn Crowne Plaza Cancún
47	Cancún Playa Hotel
48	Hotel Solymar
49	Ramada Renaissance Hotel Cancún
50	Aston Solaris Cancún
51	Hotel Casa Maya Caribe
52	Hotel Conrad Cancún
53	Club Méditerranée

OTHER

1	Ferry Service Office
7	Playa Linda Marine Terminal
17	Plaza Caracol Shopping Centre
23	Convention Centre
30	Flamingo Plaza
44	San Miguelito Archaeological Site
45	Zona Arqueológica El Rey
54	International Airport

the busy winter season. Prices drop 15% to 20% in the less busy summer months. For this amount of money you'll get a room with private bathroom, fan and probably air-conditioning and the hotel might even have a small swimming pool.

Youth Hostel

Four km from the bus station, the IYH youth hostel is the only low-budget lodging in the Zona Hoteles. Officially called the *Villa Deportiva Juvenil* (☎ (98) 83-13-37), it's at Blvd Kukulcán Km 3.2, on the left-hand (north) side of the road just past the Km 3 marker as you come from Ciudad Cancún. Look for the sign which reads 'Deportiva Juvenil'.

Single-sex dorm beds (there are over 600 of them) go for US$10. Camping costs US$5; for that price you get a locker and the right to use the hostel's facilities as there are none for the camping area itself. Meals are available in the hostel's cafeteria.

Avenida Uxmal

All of Cancún's cheap hotels are in Ciudad Cancún and many are within a few blocks of the bus station. Go north-west on Avenida Uxmal and you'll come to the following cheap lodgings:

Hotel El Alux (☎ (98) 84-06-62, 84-05-56), Avenida Uxmal 21, is only a block from the bus station. Air-con doubles with shower go for US$38. An *alux*, by the way, is the Mayan version of a leprechaun.

Across Uxmal on the south side is the *Hotel Cotty* (☎ (98) 84-13-19, 84-05-50), Avenida Uxmal 44, a motel-style place that's more or less quiet. Doubles with shower and air-con cost US$38, slightly more with two double beds and TV. There's off-street parking.

A few steps farther along Uxmal is Calle Palmera, one of Cancún's loop streets: you'll cross Palmera and then the next street you come to will be the other end of Palmera. Look down the street at the first junction

YUCATÁN

heading west along Avenida Uxmal and you'll see the *Hotel María Isabel* (☎ (98) 84-90-15), Calle Palmera, a tiny place with a quieter location. Doubles with private shower and air-con cost US$36.

Farther west along Uxmal, on the left-hand side just before the corner with Avenida Chichén Itzá, stands the *Hotel Uxmal* (☎ (98) 84-22-66, 4-23-55), Uxmal 111, a clean, family-run hostelry where US$34 will buy you a double room with fan and/or air-con, TV and off-street parking.

Rock-bottom lodgings are available just a bit farther along at the *Hotel Posada Mariano* (☎ (98) 84-39-73), Avenida Chichén Itzá near Uxmal, SM 62, 100 metres to the right of the big Coca-Cola bottling plant. The lobby door has iron bars and basic double rooms go for US$18 with fan, private shower and hot water.

Avenida Yaxchilán

If you've not found what you want, back-track on Uxmal to Yaxchilán. Near Avenida Sunyaxchén is the *Hotel Canto* (☎ (98) 84-12-67), on Calle Tanchactalpen. Rooms with private shower and air-con cost US$36.

Avenidas Sunyaxchén & Tankah

Staying here puts you close to the post office and Mercado 28 with its good, cheap eateries.

Just off Yaxchilán stands the *Hotel Hacienda Cancún* (☎ (98) 84-12-08, 84-36-72), Sunyaxchén 39-40, on the right-hand (north) side. For US$45 (single or double) you get an air-con room with colour TV and private bath, use of the hotel's pretty swimming pool and patio and a good location.

Continue along Sunyaxchén to the post office and bear right onto Avenida Tankah. Watch on the right-hand side of the street for the *Hotel Tankah* (☎ (98) 84-44-46, 84-48-44), Tankah 69, charging US$25 for a double with fan, US$7 more with air-con.

PLACES TO STAY – MIDDLE

Middle-range hotel rooms cost from US$50 to US$95 in the busy winter season, somewhat less during the summer. During the very slow times (late May to early June, October to mid-December), prices may be only half those quoted here, particularly if you haggle a bit. These hotels offer air-con rooms with private bath and colour cable TV, a swimming pool, restaurant and perhaps some other amenities such as a bar, lifts (elevators) and shuttle vans from the hotel to the beach.

Near the Bus Station

Directly across from the bus station is the *Hotel Plaza Caribe* (☎ (98) 84-13-77; fax 84-63-52; toll-free (91) 800-2-15-15), offering very comfortable air-con rooms and all the amenities for US$75 a double in summer, US$95 in winter.

Avenida Tulum

Hotel Parador (☎ (98) 84-13-10; fax 84-97-12), Avenida Tulum 26, is a modern building with 66 rooms, all with two double beds, charging US$60 a single/double.

Directly across Avenida Tulum from the Parador is the *Hotel Novotel* (☎ (98) 84-29-99; fax 84-31-62), Tulum 75 (Apdo Postal 70). Despite its name, it is not a member of the French hotel chain. With fan, rooms go for US$45 a single/double; with air-con, US$65. They have triples and quad rooms as well.

My favourite hotel is the *Hotel Antillano* (☎ (98) 84-15-32; fax 84-18-78), Calle Claveles. The 48 guestrooms offer good value for money at US$50/65/80 a single/double/triple.

Avenida Yaxchilán

Hotel Plaza del Sol (☎ (98) 84-13-09; fax 84-92-09), Avenida Yaxchilán 31, corner of Jazmines, has 87 nice rooms with two double beds priced at US$75/90 a single/double, as well as all the services.

A block farther along Yaxchilán stands the *Hotel Margarita* (☎ (98) 84-93-33; fax 84-92-09), with management, services and prices similar to the Plaza del Sol.

Across Yaxchilán from the Margarita is the *Hotel Suites Caribe Internacional* (☎ (98) 84-30-87; fax 84-19-93), Avenidas

Yaxchilán con Sunyaxchén 36. The 80 rooms here include normal double rooms, but also junior suites with two beds, sofa, kitchenette with cooker and refrigerator, and a living room. Prices for doubles are similar to the Plaza del Sol, with the suites a bit higher.

Zona Hoteles

A few of the older, smaller or simpler hotels on Isla Cancún charge rates around US$100 for a double room during the high winter season. In summer, many more bargains are to be had. Going along Blvd Kukulcán from Ciudad Cancún, all are on the left-hand (north or east) side of the road, and you will come to them in the order given below. Note that the km markers given in the text and on the map of Isla Cancún are as accurate as we can make them but may not be precise – many of the hotels have very wide frontages.

The *Playa Blanca Hotel & Marina* (☎ (98) 83-03-44; in the USA (800) 221-4726), Apdo Postal 107, is at Km 3.5; it's a 161-room hotel with lush gardens, comfortable air-con rooms, several bars and three restaurants.

The *Aquamarina Beach Hotel* (☎ (98) 83-14-25; fax 83-17-51; in the USA (800) 446-8976), Blvd Kulkulcán Km 3.5 (Apdo Postal 751), was built with tour groups of young adult sunlovers in mind. Some rooms have a kitchenette and refrigerator.

Hotel Maya Caribe (☎ (98) 83-20-00), Blvd Kukulcán Km 6 (Apdo Postal 447), has 64 rooms, each with two double beds, minibar, balcony, hammock and a view of either the ocean or the lagoon. This one is a favourite of Mexican and Mexican-American vacationers.

PLACES TO STAY – TOP END

Cancún's top places range from comfortable but boring to luxurious full-service hosteleries of an international standard. Prices range from US$150 to US$250 and more for a double room in winter. All the top places are located on the beach, many have vast grounds with rolling lawns of manicured grass, tropical gardens, swimming pools

(virtually all with swim-up bars – a Cancún necessity) and facilities for sports such as tennis, handball, waterskiing and sailboarding. Some are constructed in whimsical fantasy styles with turrets, bulbous domes, minarets, dramatic glass canopies and other architectural megalomania. Guestrooms are air-con, equipped with minibar and TV linked to satellite receivers for US programs.

Isla Cancún is now seriously overbuilt, and hoteliers are willing to offer good deals in order to fill their rooms. To get the most advantageous price at any of these luxury hotels, you should sign up for an inclusive tour package which includes lodging. If you have not come with a group, you can find the best value for money at the *Hotel Viva* at Blvd Kukulcán, Km 8 (☎ (98) 83-01-08) or the *Hotel Aristos Cancún* (☎ (98) 83-00-11) at Km 9 (Apdo Postal 450).

Other places to look for good value are these:

Km 4 *Calinda Cancún Beach* (☎ (98) 83-16-00; in the USA (800) 221-2222) facing the Playa Linda Marine Terminal. Decor here is of red tiles, white stucco and modern muted colours, all with a light, airy feel.

Km 8.5 *Fiesta Americana Cancún* (☎ (98) 83-14-00; in the USA (800) 343-7821) is an oddity, resembling nothing so much as an old-city streetscape, an appealing jumble of windows, balconies, roofs and other features.

Camino Real Cancún (☎ (98) 83-01-00; fax 83-17-30; in the USA (800) 228-3000), Apdo Postal 14, was one of Cancún's first luxury hotels and thus had the best pick of locations. Situated at the very tip of Punta Cancún, the Camino Real enjoys panoramic sea views, a lavish country club layout, lots of restaurants and bars and full luxury service.

Hyatt Regency Cancún (☎ (98) 83-09-66; fax 3-13-49; in the USA (800) 228-9000), Apdo Postal 1201, shares Punta Cancún with the Camino Real. It's a gigantic cylinder with a lofty open court at its core and the 300 guestrooms arranged round it.

Km 14 *Cancún Palace* (☎ (98) 85 05 33; fax 5-15-93; in the USA (800) 346-8225), Blvd Kukulcán (Apdo Postal 1730), works extra hard to offer good value to guests. The 421 rooms and suites have all the amenities you'd expect, including balconies with water views and all the services.

PLACES TO EAT

Nowhere in Mexico have I found more mediocre food at higher prices than in Cancún. Don't expect too much from Cancún's restaurants and when you get a memorable meal (and you will have at least a few) you'll be pleasantly surprised.

PLACES TO EAT – BOTTOM END

As usual, market eateries provide the biggest portions at the lowest prices. Ciudad Cancún's market, near the post office, is a building set back from the street and emblazoned with the name Mercado Municipal Artículo 115 Constitucional. Called simply Mercado 28 (that's 'mercado veinte y ocho') by the locals, it has shops selling fresh vegetables, fruits and prepared meals.

In the second courtyard in from the street are the eateries: *Restaurant Margely*, *Cocina Familiar Económica Chulum*, *Cocina La Chaya*, etc. These are pleasant, simple eateries with tables beneath awnings and industrious señoras cooking away behind the counter. Most are open for breakfast, lunch and dinner and all offer full meals (comidas corridas) for as little as US$3.50, and sandwiches for less.

El Rincón Yucateco, Avenida Uxmal 24, across from the Hotel Cotty, serves good Yucatecan food. Service is from 7 am to 10 pm every day. Main courses cost US$3 to US$5.

El Tacolote, on Avenida Cobá across from the big red IMSS hospital, is brightly lit and attractive with dark wood benches. Tacos – a dozen types – are priced from US$1 to US$4. El Tacolote (the name is a pun on taco and *tecolote*, owl) is open from 7 to 11.30 am for breakfast, then till 10 pm for tacos.

Between the Hotel Parador and the Ayuntamiento is the *Restaurant Pop* (☎ 4-19-91), Avenida Tulum 26, a modern place with an air-con dining room and shaded patio tables out the front. The food is not exciting, but there's yogurt, fresh fruit salads, hamburgers and sandwiches, soups, spaghetti, cakes and desserts. Expect to spend about US$6 or $10 for a filling meal, more if you're very hungry or drink several cervezas. Pop (the name is

that of the first month of the 18-month Mayan calendar) is open from 8 am to 10.30 pm (closed Sunday).

The *Cafetería San Francisco*, in the big San Francisco de Assis department store on the east side of Avenida Tulum, has welcome air-conditioning. You can spend as much as US$16 for a full, heavy meal with dessert and drink, but most people keep their bill below US$8. The cafetería is open from 7 am to 11 pm daily.

PLACES TO EAT – MIDDLE

If you're willing to spend between US$15 and US$25 for dinner you can eat fairly well in Cancún.

Most of the moderately priced restaurants are located in the city centre. The *Restaurant El Pescador* (☎ 84-26-73), Tulipanes 28, has been serving dependably good meals since the early days of Cancún. The menu lists lime soup and fish ceviche for starters, then charcoal-grilled fish, red snapper in garlic sauce and beef shish kebab. El Pescador is open for lunch and dinner (closed Monday).

Pizza Rolandi (☎ 84-40-47), Avenida Cobá 12, between Tulum and Nader just off the southern roundabout, is an attractive Italian eatery open every day. It serves elaborate one-person pizzas (US$5 to US$10), spaghetti plates and more substantial dishes of veal and chicken. Watch out for drink prices. Hours are 1 pm to midnight (Sunday, 4 pm to midnight).

Every visitor to Cancún makes the pilgrimage to *Los Almendros* (☎ 84-08-07), Avenida Bonampak at Calle Sayil across from the bullring, the local incarnation of Yucatán's most famous restaurant. Started in Ticul in 1962, Los Almendros set out to serve *platillos campesinos para los dzules* (country food for the bourgeoisie, or townfolk). The chefs at Los Almendros (The Almond Trees) claim to have created pocchuc, a dish of succulent pork cooked with onion and served in a tangy sauce of sour orange or lime. If you don't know what to order, try the *combinado yucateco*, or Yucatecan combination plate. A full meal here costs about US$20 per person. Come any day for lunch or dinner.

Restaurant-Jazz Club 100% Natural (☎ 84-36-17), Avenida Sunyaxchén at Yaxchilán, is an airy café. Though the menu lists several natural food items such as fruit salads and juices, green salads and yogurt, they also serve hamburgers, enchiladas, wine and beer.

Perico's (☎ 4-31-52), Avenida Yaxchilán 71 at Calle Marañón, is quintessential Cancún, a huge thatched structure stuffed with stereotypical Mexican icons: saddles, enormous sombreros, baskets, bullwhips, etc. An army of señors and señoritas dressed in Hollywood-Mexican costumes doesn't serve so much as 'dramatise your dining experience'. Oh, well. But if you're in the mood for dinner à la Disney, Perico's will do. The menu is heavy with the macho fare most popular with group tourists: filet mignon, jumbo shrimp, lobster, barbecued spareribs. After the show, fork over US$20 to US$30 per person to pay your bill. It's supposedly open from noon to 2 am, but may in fact serve only dinner.

You can get Chinese food at *Mandarin House* (☎ 84-71-83), Avenida Sunyaxchén at Avenida Tankah. Classics such as Cantonese chicken and moo goo guy pan are on the menu for lunch and dinner from 1 to 10.30 pm every day but Tuesday (closed). A full meal need cost only US$12, or less.

PLACES TO EAT – TOP END

Traditionally, Mexican restaurants have followed the European scheme of simple decor and elaborate food. Cancún, however, caters mostly to the sort of sun-baked North Americans who seem to prefer simple food served in elaborate surroundings. Half the menus in town are composed of such grill-me items as steak, jumbo shrimp, fish fillet and lobster tail. Thus Cancún's expensive restaurants are elaborate, with rhapsodic menu prose, lots of tropical gardens, mirrors, waterfalls, paraphernalia, even fishtanks and aviaries of exotic birds. The food can be good, forgettable or execrable. If the last, at least you'll

have pleasant music and something to look at as you gnaw and gag.

The exceptional places are listed below.

Ciudad Cancún

A long-standing favourite is *Rosa Mexicano* (☎ 84-63-13), Calle Claveles 4, the place to go for unusual Mexican dishes in a pleasant hacienda decor. There are some concessions to Cancún such as tortilla soup and filete tampiqueña, but also squid sautéed with three chillis, garlic and scallions and shrimp in a *pipían* sauce (ground pumpkin seeds and spices). Dinner, served daily from 5 to 11 pm, goes for US$25 to US$40.

Another dependable favourite (since 1977) is *La Habichuela* (☎ 84-31-58), Margaritas 25, just off Parque Las Palapas in a residential neighbourhood. The menu tends to dishes easily comprehended and easily perceived as elegant: shish kebab flambé, lobster in champagne sauce, jumbo shrimp and beef tampiqueña: US$30 to US$42 per person for dinner. Hours are 1 pm to about 11 pm, every day of the year. La Habichuela (LAH-b'CHWEH-lah) means The Stringbean.

Isla Cancún

Visiting gringos flock to *Carlos 'n' Charlie's* (☎ 83-13-04), Blvd Kukulcán Km 5.5, opposite the Casa Maya, because they enjoy the who-cares atmosphere, jokey waiters, purple menu prose, decent food and they don't mind paying US$30 to US$45 for dinner. Trendy Mexican dishes (guacamole, fajitas, ceviche) join the requisite steaks, shrimp and lobster on the menu.

ENTERTAINMENT

Most of the nightlife is loud and bibulous, as befits a supercharged beach resort. If the theme restaurants don't do it for you, take a dinner cruise on a mock pirate ship.

The local Ballet Folklorico performs some evenings at various halls for about US$40 per person, which includes dinner. The dancers come on at 8.30 pm. Don't expect the finesse and precision of the performances in Mexico City.

Bullfights (four bulls) are held each Wednesday afternoon at 3.30 pm in the Plaza de Toros at the southern end of Avenida Bonampak, across the street from the Restaurant Los Almendros, about one km from the centre of town. Tickets cost about US$15 and can be purchased from any travel agency.

THINGS TO BUY

There are gift shops and touts everywhere in Cancún, with crafts from all over Mexico, often at exorbitant prices. Save your shopping for other Mexican destinations. If you hanker for a hammock, buy it in Mérida. Still, window-shopping in Cancún's air-con and luxurious shopping centres can be good fun.

GETTING THERE & AWAY
Air
Cancún's international airport is busy with scheduled flights and also lots of charter traffic. Be sure to ask your travel agent about charter and group flights, which can be quite cheap, especially in summer.

For fares and departure points from North America, see the introductory Getting There & Away chapter.

Aerocaribe is a regional airline owned by Mexicana Inter; it offers a special fare deal called the Mayapass, good for a series of flights at reduced prices. Aerocaribe has flights to points in Yucatán and beyond, in small and medium-sized planes at these prices (one-way): Chetumal US$100, Cozumel US$50, Mérida US$90, Mexico City US$200, Oaxaca US$250, and Villahermosa US$180. Excursion fares offer better deals than these one-way fares.

Aerocaribe are also presently running flights on an experimental basis between Cancún and Belize City and Cancún and Flores (for Tikal) in Guatemala.

Aviacsa is a regional carrier based in Tuxtla Gutiérrez, Chiapas, with flights from Cancún to Mérida, Mexico City, Oaxaca, Tapachula, Tuxtla Gutiérrez, Villahermosa, and points in Guatemala. Airline contact addresses are:

Aerocancún, Oasis building, Blvd Kukulcán (☎ (98) 83-21-44)
Aerocaribe, Avenida Tulum 29, at the roundabout intersection with Avenida Uxmal (☎ (98) 84-20-00)
Aeroméxico, Avenida Cobá 80, between Tulum and Bonampak (☎ (98) 84-35-71; fax 86-00-79)
American Airlines, at Cancún airport (☎ (98) 86-00-55; toll-free (91-800) 5-02-22)
Aviacsa, Avenida Cobá 55 (☎ (98) 87-42-14; fax 84-65-99; toll-free (91-800) 0-06-22)
Aviateca, Plaza México, Avenida Tulum 200 (☎ (98) 84-39-38)
Continental, at Cancún airport (☎ (98) 86-00-40; toll-free (91-800) 9-00-50)
LACSA, Edificio Atlantis, Avenida Bonampak at Avenida Cobá (☎ (98) 87-31-01)
Mexicana, Avenida Cobá 39 (☎ (98) 87-44-44)
Northwest, at Cancún airport (☎ (98) 86-00-46)
Taesa, Avenida Yaxchilán 31 (☎ (98) 87-43-14)
United, at Cancún airport (☎ (98) 86-01-58; fax 86-00-25)

Bus
Several companies share the traffic to and from Cancún, including Autotransportes de Oriente Mérida-Puerto Juárez SA, Autotransportes del Caribe, and Espresso de Oriente. Services are 2nd, 1st or luxury class.

The bus station on Avenida Uxmal just west of Avenida Tulum serves them all. The station has a cafeteria, snack shops and a newsstand.

Across from the bus station entrance is the ticket office of Interplaya, which runs shuttle buses down the Caribbean coast to Tulum every 20 minutes all day, stopping at major towns and points of interest along the way.

Here are some major routes:

Chetumal – 382 km, seven hours, US$9 to US$13; a dozen buses daily.
Chichén Itzá – 205 km, three to 3½ hours, US$5 to US$8; same as Mérida.
Mexico City – 1772 km, 27 hours, US$45 to US$55; six buses daily.
Mérida – 320 km, 5½ to six hours, US$8 to US$14; buses at least every half hour.
Playa del Carmen – 65 km, one hour, US$2; Interplaya buses every 20 minutes; others 12 times daily.
Puerto Morelos – 36 km, 40 minutes, US$1; Interplaya buses every 20 minutes; others 12 times daily.

Tizimin – 212 km, three hours, US$5; four daily via Valladolid.

Tulum – 132 km, two hours, US$3 to US$4; Interplaya buses every 20 minutes; other buses about every two hours.

Valladolid – 161 km, two hours, US$5 to US$8; same as Mérida

Villahermosa – 915 km, 14 hours, US$30; three daily buses by ADO.

GETTING AROUND
To/From the Airport

Orange-and-beige airport vans (Transporte Terrestre, US$6.50) monopolise the trade, and will often overcharge you for a private taxi-style ride when you should be paying for a shared ride.

The route into town is invariably via Punta Nizuc and north up Isla Cancún along Blvd Kukulcán, passing all of the luxury beach-front hotels before reaching the youth hostel and Ciudad Cancún. If your hotel is in Ciudad Cancún, the ride to your hotel may take as long as 45 minutes. At the end of the ride, many passengers tip the driver.

The alternative to the van is to take a taxi, or hire a van for a private trip, straight to your hotel. This costs US$30.

If you walk out of the airport and follow the access road, you can often flag down a taxi which will take you for less because the driver is no longer subject to the expensive regulated airport fares. Walk the two km to the highway and you can flag a passing bus, which is very cheap.

To return to the airport you must take a taxi, or hop off a southbound bus at the airport junction and walk the two km to the terminal.

Bus

Although it's possible walk everywhere in Ciudad Cancún, to get to the Zona Hoteles, catch a 'Ruta 1, Zona Hoteles' local bus heading southward along Avenida Tulum. The fare depends upon distance travelled, and ranges from US$0.35 to US$1.

To reach Puerto Juárez and the Isla Mujeres ferries, take a Ruta 8 bus ('Pto Juárez' or 'Punta Sam').

Taxi

Cancún's taxis do not have meters so you must haggle over fares. Generally, the fare between Ciudad Cancún and Punta Cancún (Hyatt, Camino Real and Krystal hotels and the Convention Centre) is US$4 or US$5. To the airport costs US$16. To Puerto Juárez you'll pay about US$4.

Ferry

There are frequent passenger ferries to Isla Mujeres. Local buses (Ruta 8, US$0.55) take about 20 minutes from stops on Avenida Tulum to the Puerto Juárez and Punta Sam ferry docks if you're going to Isla Mujeres. Taxis cost about US$4. See that section for details.

Isla Mujeres

Population: 13,500

Isla Mujeres (Island of Women), has a reputation as a 'backpackers' Cancún', a place where one can escape the mega-resort for the laid-back life of a tropical isle – at bargain prices. Though this was true for many years, it is less true today.

The chief attribute of Isla Mujeres is its relaxed social life in a tropical setting with surrounding waters that are turquoise blue and bathtub warm. If you have been doing some hard travelling through Mexico, you will find many travellers you met along the way taking it easy here. Others make it the site of their one to two-week holiday. Many visitors have a hard time tearing themselves away.

The principal beach is rather small, however, and the island as a whole not all that attractive. Most of the palm trees were killed by a blight, the rest swept away by Hurricane Gilbert in 1988 and the part of the island not built up consists of Yucatán scrub bush. The ballyhooed snorkelling at Garrafón National Park is overrated because of crowding. Prices, while not outrageous like Cancún's, are higher than you will find

YUCATÁN

in most of Mexico. And Cancún makes itself felt each morning as boatload after boatload of package tourists arrive on Isla Mujeres for a day's excursion.

HISTORY

Although it is said by some that the Island of Women got its name because Spanish buccaneers kept their lovers here while they plundered galleons and pillaged ports, a less romantic but still intriguing explanation is probably more accurate. In 1519, a chronicler sailing with Hernández de Córdoba's expedition wrote that when the conquistadors' ships were forced by high winds into the island's harbour, the crew reconnoitred. What they found onshore was a Mayan ceremonial site filled with clay figurines of females. Today, some archaeologists believe that the island was a stopover for the Maya en route to worship their goddess of fertility, Ixchel, on the island of Cozumel. The clay idols are thought to represent the goddess.

ORIENTATION

The island is about eight km long and anywhere from 300 to 800 metres wide. The good snorkelling and some of the better swimming beaches are on the southern part of the island along the western shore; the eastern shore is washed by the open sea and the surf is dangerous. The ferry docks, the town and the most popular sand beach (Playa Cocoteros) are at the northern tip of the island.

INFORMATION
Tourist Office

The Delegación Estatal de Turismo (State Tourism Department, ☎ (987) 7 03 16) faces the basketball court in the main plaza.

Money

The island's Banco del Atlantico at Juárez 5 and Banco Serfin, at Juárez 3, are so packed during the two hours a day (10 am to noon, Monday to Friday) when foreign currency may be exchanged that many travellers change money at a lower rate at a grocery store, their hotel or at the tourist office.

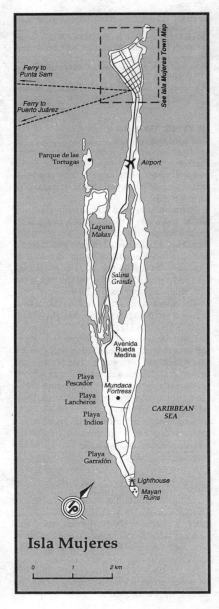

Isla Mujeres

Post

The post office, next to the market, is open Monday to Friday from 8 am to 7 pm, Saturday and Sunday from 9 am to 1 pm.

Laundry

Lavandería Automática Tim Phó, Avenida Juárez at Abasolo, is modern and busy.

GARRAFÓN NATIONAL PARK

Although the waters are translucent and the fish abundant, Garrafón is perhaps a bit over-rated. Hordes of day trippers from Cancún fill the water during the middle of the day, so you are more often ogling fellow snorkellers than aquatic life. Furthermore, the reef is virtually dead, which makes it less likely to inflict cuts but reduces its colour and the intricacy of its formations.

The water can be extremely choppy, sweeping you into jagged areas. When the water is running fast here – not an unusual occurrence – snorkelling is a hassle and can even be dangerous. Those without strong swimming skills should be advised that the bottom falls off steeply quite close to shore; if you are having trouble, you might not be noticed amidst all those bobbing heads.

Garrafón is open daily from 8 am to 5 pm and the earlier you get here (see the Getting Around section at the end of this chapter), the more time you will have free of the milling mobs from Cancún. Admission to the park costs US$3. There are lockers for your valuables – recommended as a safeguard. Snorkelling equipment can be rented for the day at US$6. Garrafón also has a small aquarium and museum.

PLAYA COCOTEROS

Walk west along Calles Hidalgo or Guerrero to reach Playa Cocoteros, sometimes called Playa Los Cocos, the town's principal beach. The slope of the beach is very gradual and the transparent and calm waters are only chest-high far from the shore. However, the beach is relatively small for the number of sunseekers.

PLAYA LANCHEROS

Five km south of the town and 1.5 km north of Garrafón is Playa Lancheros, the south-ernmost point served by local buses. The beach is less attractive than Cocoteros, but there are free festivities on Sundays and you might want to come to enjoy the music.

MAYAN RUINS

Just past Garrafón National Park, at the southern tip of the island, are the badly ruined remains of a temple to Ixchel, Mayan goddess of the moon, fertility and other worthy causes. Observed by Hernández de Córdoba when his ships were forced by high winds into the island's coastal waters in 1519, the temple has been crumbling ever since. Hurricane Gilbert almost finished it off in 1988.

There's really little left to see here other than a fine sea view and, in the distance, Cancún. The clay female figurines were pilfered long ago and a couple of the walls were washed into the Caribbean.

You can walk to the ruins, beyond the lighthouse at the south end of the island, from Garrafón.

MUNDACA FORTRESS

The story behind the ruins of this house and fort are more intriguing than what remains of

Ixchel, old moon goddess and goddess of fertility

them. A slave-trading pirate, Fermín Antonio Mundaca de Marechaja, fell in love with a visiting Spanish beauty. To win her, the rogue built a two-storey mansion complete with gardens and graceful archways as well as a small fortress to defend it. While Mundaca built the house, the object of his affection's ardour cooled and she married another islander. Brokenhearted, Mundaca died and his house, fortress and garden fell into disrepair.

The Mundaca Fortress is east of the main road near Playa Lancheros, about six km south of the town. Watch for signs.

SCUBA DIVING

Diving to see sunken ships and beautiful reefs in the crystalline waters of the Caribbean is a memorable way to pass time on Isla Mujeres. If you're a qualified diver, you'll need a licence, rental equipment and a boat to take you to the good spots. All of these are available from Mexico Divers (Buzos de México, ☎ (987) 7-01-31), Avenida Rueda Medina at Madero. Costs range from US$50 to US$100 depending upon how many tanks you use up.

A regular stop on the dive-boat's route is the Sleeping Shark Caves, about five km north of the island and at 23 metres' depth, where the otherwise dangerous creatures are alleged to be lethargically nonlethal due to the low oxygen content of the caves' waters. Veteran divers say it's foolish to test the theory: you could become shark bait. It's far better to explore the fine reefs off the island like Los Manchones, La Bandera, Cuevones or Chital.

PLACES TO STAY

During the busy seasons (mid-December to March and midsummer), many island hotels are booked solid by midday; at these times prices are also highest (as given here).

Places to Stay – bottom end

Poc-Na (☎ (987) 7-00-90), on Matamoros at Carlos Lazo, is a privately run youth hostel. The fan-cooled dormitories take both men and women together. The charge for bunk

and bedding is US$5; you must put down a deposit on the bedding.

Hotel Caribe Maya (☎ (987) 7-01-90), Madero 9, between Guerrero and Hidalgo, charges US$17 a double with fan, US$24 with air-con – a bargain.

Hotel El Caracol (☎ (987) 7-01-50), Matamoros 5, between Hidalgo and Guerrero, is run by a smiling and efficient señora. The tidy restaurant off the lobby serves meals at decent prices. Rooms have insect screens, ceiling fans, clean tiled bathrooms and many have two double beds. You pay US$28/38 a double with fan/air-con.

Hotel Martínez (☎ (987) 7-01-54), Madero 14, is an older hotel. Some rooms have sea views, all have ceiling fans, private baths and well-used furnishings. Doubles go for US$18.

Almost across the street is the *Hotel Osorio* (☎ (987) 7-00-18), Madero at Juárez, has an older section with huge, clean rooms with fan and bath for US$20 a double; and a newer, tidier section for US$30.

Autel Carmelina (☎ (987) 7-00-06), Guerrero 4, also has OK cheap rooms: US$16/20/30 for one/two/three beds, single or double.

Hotel Las Palmas (☎ (987) 7-04-16), Guerrero 20, across from the Mercado Municipal, offers drear but cheap rooms with fan and bath for US$14/17 a single/double.

Hotel Marcianito (☎ (987) 7-01-11), Abasolo 10, between Juárez and Hidalgo, is a place to try if everything else is full.

Hotel Isleño (☎ (987) 7-03-02), Madero 8 at the corner of Guerrero, has rooms with ceiling fans and good cross-ventilation, without/with bath for US$18/24 a double. There's a shared bathroom for every three guestrooms. Get a room on the upper floor if you can.

Places to Stay – middle

Moderately priced rooms have private baths, and usually (but not always) air-con, perhaps a balcony and/or a nice sea view, restaurant, bar and swimming pool.

The *Hotel Perla del Caribe I* (☎ (987) 7-04-44; fax 7-00-11), Madero just east of

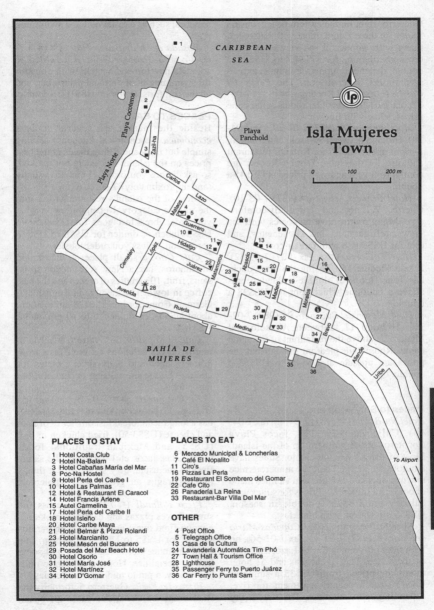

Isla Mujeres Town

CARIBBEAN SEA

Playa Cocoteros

Playa Norte

Playa Panchold

Playa Pancholo

0   100   200 m

CARLOS

LAZO

Mateos

Guerrero

Hidalgo

Juárez

Avenida

Rueda

Medina

López

Cemetery

Matamoros

Abasolo

Madero

Morelos

Bravo

Allende

Uribe

Zazil-ha

BAHÍA DE MUJERES

To Airport

YUCATÁN

PLACES TO STAY

1 Hotel Costa Club
2 Hotel Na-Balam
3 Hotel Cabañas María del Mar
8 Poc-Na Hostel
9 Hotel Perla del Caribe I
10 Hotel Las Palmas
12 Hotel & Restaurant El Caracol
14 Hotel Francis Arlene
15 Autel Carmelina
17 Hotel Perla del Caribe II
18 Hotel Isleño
20 Hotel Caribe Maya
21 Hotel Belmar & Pizza Rolandi
23 Hotel Marcianito
25 Hotel Mesón del Bucanero
29 Posada del Mar Beach Hotel
30 Hotel Osorio
31 Hotel María José
32 Hotel Martínez
34 Hotel D'Gomar

PLACES TO EAT

6 Mercado Municipal & Loncherías
7 Café El Nopalito
11 Ciro's
16 Pizzas La Perla
19 Restaurant El Sombrero del Gomar
22 Cafe Cito
26 Panadería La Reina
33 Restaurant-Bar Villa Del Mar

OTHER

4 Post Office
5 Telegraph Office
13 Casa de la Cultura
24 Lavandería Automática Tim Phó
27 Town Hall & Tourism Office
28 Lighthouse
35 Passenger Ferry to Puerto Juárez
36 Car Ferry to Punta Sam

Guerrero, right on the eastern beach, has 63 rooms on three floors, most with balconies, many with wonderful sea views and good cross-ventilation, for US$45 to US$75 a double, depending upon view; most expensive rooms have air-con. The *Perla del Caribe II* (ex-Hotel Rocamar, ☎ (987) 7-05-87; fax 7-01-01) has older rooms at the same prices, some with fine views.

Hotel Belmar (☎ (987) 7-04-29; fax 7-04-29), Hidalgo between Abasolo and Madero, is right above the Pizza Rolandi restaurant and run by the same family. Rooms are comfy, well kept and well priced at US$45 a double.

Hotel Francis Arlene (☎ (987) 7-03-10), Guerrero 7, is new and particularly comfortable. Many rooms have balconies with sea views, refrigerators and kitchenettes, and rent for US$30/38 with fan/air-con.

Hotel D'Gomar (☎ & fax (987) 7-01-42), Rueda Medina 150, facing the ferry dock, has four floors of double-bedded rooms above a boutique which rent for US$38 a double.

Hotel Mesón del Bucanero (☎ (987) 7-02-36), Hidalgo 11, between Abasolo and Madero, is above the restaurant of the same name. Rooms are pleasant enough but the prices are upscale at US$45 to US$55 a double.

Places to Stay – top end

Hotel Na-Balam (☎ (987) 7-04-46; fax 7-04-46), Calle Zazil-Ha 118, faces Playa Cocoteros at the northern tip of the island. Most of the 12 spacious junior suites have fabulous sea views. There are numerous nice touches, such as the bathroom vanities made of colourful travertine. Prices for suites with balcony are US$75 a double in season, US$55 off season, with breakfast.

Near Na Balam is *Hotel Cabañas María del Mar* (☎ (987) 7-02-13; fax 7-01-56), on both sides of Avenida Carlos Lazo, also right on the beach. The 12 cabañas and 51 hotel rooms are priced from US$35 a single to US$150 for a deluxe apartment for five, depending upon amenities. There are many

services, such as a restaurant and swimming pool.

Posada del Mar Beach Hotel (☎ (87) 7-00-44; fax 7-02-66). Avenida Rueda Medina 15A, is a new top-end hostelry with a beautiful swimming pool, tropical palapa bar, and all the comforts. Rates are US$100 a double.

PLACES TO EAT

Beside the market are several *cocinas económicas* (economical kitchens) serving simple but tasty and filling meals at the best prices on the island. Prices are not marked, so ask before you order. Hours are usually (and approximately) 7 am to 6 pm.

Most of the island's restaurants fall into the middle category. Depending upon what you order, breakfast goes for US$3.50 to US$5, lunch or dinner for US$8 to US$18 per person, unless you order lobster.

Café Cito, a small place at Juárez and Matamoros, has a New Age menu: croissants, fruit, 10 varieties of crepes and the best coffee in town. The menu is in English and German. Come for breakfast (8 am to noon, about US$5), or supper (6 to 10 pm, about US$10).

Café El Nopalito, on Guerrero near Matamoros, serves delicious set breakfasts from 8 am to noon and daily special plates for US$6 to US$8, specialising in healthful but fancy food.

El Bucanero (☎ 7-02-36), Avenida Hidalgo 11 between Abasolo and Madero, has a long menu: breakfast omelettes of ham and cheese (US$3.50), fried chicken or fish (US$5) and Mexican traditional foods (enchiladas, tacos etc) for about the same. Besides the usual, they serve offbeat things like asparagus au gratin with wholemeal bread.

Pizza Rolandi (☎ 7-04-30), across the street, serves pizzas and calzones cooked in a wood-fired oven, and pastas with various sauces, for US$5 to US$9 per person. The menu includes fresh salads, fish and some Italian specialities. Hours are 1 pm to midnight daily, 6 pm to midnight on Sunday.

Pizzas La Perla, Guerrero 5, formerly the Restaurant La Peña, serves soup, pasta, steak, chicken and the like in a glass-walled dining room overlooking the sea. Meals cost about US$10 and are served from 8 am to midnight.

The *Restaurant El Sombrero de Gomar*, Hidalgo at Madero, has movie-Mexican decor on two levels, blasts rock music, and offers an all-you-can-eat luncheon buffet for US$10, or à la carte choices for US$4 to US$14. The menu is eclectic and international.

Facing the ferry docks is the *Restaurant-Bar Villa Del Mar* (☎ 7-00-31), Avenida Rueda Medina 1 Sur, which is fancier in decor and ambience but not much higher in price.

ENTERTAINMENT

The first place to go is the main plaza, where there's always something to watch (a football match, a basketball or volleyball game, an impromptu concert or serenade) and lots of somebodies watching it.

As for discos, there's Buho's (☎ 7-00-86), which is also a restaurant and bar, in the Hotel Cabañas María del Mar, Avenida Carlos Lazo 1, at Playa Cocoteros. It's been here a while and is usually satisfactory. Nearby is the Bad Bones Café, next to the north lighthouse, for a change of pace.

Tequila Video Bar (☎ 7-00-19), at the corner of Matamoros and Hidalgo, is a favourite with locals (who don't feel they must be near the beach), but draws a respectable number of foreigners as well. Hours are 9 pm to 3 am every day except Monday.

GETTING THERE & AWAY
Ferry
There are three points of embarkation from the mainland by ferry to Isla Mujeres, 11 km off the coast.

To/From Puerto Juárez Take a Ruta 8 bus heading north on Avenida Tulum (US$0.30) or a taxi (US$2.50) to Puerto Juárez, about three km north of Ciudad Cancún's Avenida Tulum.

From Puerto Juárez, the official schedule says that passenger ferries depart every hour on the half-hour from 8.30 am to 8.30 pm, with extra boats at 6 and 10 am. In practice, the schedule depends upon demand and if few people show up for a particular voyage, it'll be cancelled. One-way fare is US$2 on the slower boats (30 to 40 minutes), or US$4 on the faster (15 or 20 minute) *Caribbean Express* or *Caribbean Miss*.

To/From Punta Sam Car ferries (which also take passengers) depart from Punta Sam, about five km north of Avenida Tulum and 3.5 km north of Puerto Juárez. The car ferry is more stable but less frequent and slower, taking 45 minutes to an hour to reach the island.

Ferries leave Punta Sam at 7.15 and 9.45 am, noon, 2.30, 5.15 and 8.15 pm. Departures from Isla Mujeres are at 6, 8.30 and 11 am and at 1.15, 4, and 7.15 pm. Passengers pay US$1.50; a car costs US$8. If you're taking a car, be sure to get to the dock an hour or so before departure time. Put your car in line and buy your ticket early.

To/From Playa Linda Terminal Four times daily, *The Shuttle* (☎ (98) 84-63-33, 84-66-56) departs from Playa Linda on Isla Cancún for Isla Mujeres. Voyages are at 9 and 11.15 am, 4 and 7 pm from Playa Linda; return voyages depart Isla Mujeres at 10 am, 12.30, 5 and 8 pm. The round-trip fare is US$14, but this includes free beer and soft drinks on board.

Show up at the Playa Linda Marine Terminal, Blvd Kukulcán Km 5 on Isla Cancún, just west of the bridge, between the Aquamarina Beach and Calinda Cancún hotels, at least 30 minutes before departure so you'll have time to buy your ticket and get a good seat on the boat.

GETTING AROUND
Bus
By local bus from the market or dock, you can get within 1.5 km of Garrafón; the terminus is Playa Lancheros. The personnel at Poc-Na Youth Hostel can give you an idea of the bus's erratic schedule. Locals in league

with taxi drivers may tell you the bus doesn't exist.

If you walk to Garrafón, bring some water – it's a hot, two-hour, six-km walk. By taxi, it costs about US$2 to Garrafón, just over US$1 to Playa Lancheros. Rates are set by the municipal government and are posted at the ferry dock, though the sign is frequently defaced by the taxi drivers.

Bicycle & Moped

Bicycles can be rented from a number of shops on the island including Sport Bike, on the corner of Juárez and Morelos, a block from the ferry docks. Before you rent, compare prices and the condition of the bikes in a few shops, then arrive early in the day to get one of the better bikes. Costs are US$3 to US$5 for four hours, only a bit more for a full day; you'll be asked to plunk down a deposit of US$8 or so.

Everybody and his/her grandmother is prepared to rent you a motorbike on Isla Mujeres. Shop around, compare prices and look for these two things: new or newer machines in good condition, full gas tanks and reasonable deposits. Cost per hour is usually US$5 or US$6 with a two-hour minimum, US$22 all day, or even cheaper by the week. Shops

away from the busiest streets tend to have better prices, but not necessarily better equipment. Many places also rent motorised golf carts, which seat four, at a higher price.

When driving, remember that far more people are seriously injured on motorbikes than in cars. Your enemies are inexperience, speed, sand, wet or oily roads and other people on motorbikes. Don't forget to slather yourself with sunblock before you take off. Be sure to do your hands, feet, face and neck thoroughly.

AROUND ISLA MUJERES
Isla Contoy Bird Sanctuary

You can take an excursion by boat to tiny Isla Contoy, a national bird sanctuary, about 25 km north of Isla Mujeres. It's a treasure trove for birdwatchers, with an abundance of brown pelicans, olive cormorants and red-pouched frigates, as well as frequent visits by flamingoes and herons. There is good snorkelling both en route and just off Contoy.

Getting There & Away For a one-day excursion (about US$30 per person), ask at the Sociedad Cooperativa Transporte Turística 'Isla Mujeres' (☎ (987) 7-02-74) on Avenida Rueda Medina to the north of the ferry docks.

Central & Northern Yucatán

VALLADOLID
Population: 80,000

Small and manageable with an easy pace of life, graced with many handsome colonial buildings and provided with a few hotels and restaurants, Valladolid is a good place to stop, spend the night and get to know the real Yucatán. It can also be your base from which to visit the important Mayan ruins at Chichén Itzá, 40 km farther west.

Heading west from Cancún takes you through the town of Nuevo Xcan, where the road from Cobá and Tulum meets the Cancún-Mérida highway. Nuevo Xcan has a few serviceable little restaurants.

If you're driving, beware the new toll highway (Cuota). Huge signs west of Nuevo Xcan will direct you to bear right onto the highway, which is outrageously expensive – US$24 for about half the trip to Mérida. Continue straight on, ignoring the signs, go beneath a new underpass, and you will be following the old road (*libra*, free). It is not as smooth or fast, but it costs nothing. The highway signs are expressly designed to catch and fool tourists driving rental cars from Cancún to Chichén Itzá and Mérida. Few Mexicans take the Cuota, and all know about the old road.

Valladolid, 160 km (about two hours) west of Cancún and 40 km (half an hour) east of Chichén Itzá, has no sights of stop-the-car immediacy, so few tourists do stop here. Most prefer to hurtle on through to the next major site. It's just as well, for this preserves Valladolid for the rest of us who want to enjoy it.

History
The Mayan ceremonial centre of Zací was here long before the Spanish arrived to lay out a new city on the classic Spanish colonial plan. The initial attempt at conquest in 1543 by the conquistador Francisco de Montejo, nephew of Montejo El Adelantado, was thwarted by fierce Mayan resistance, but El Adelantado's son Montejo El Mozo ultimately conquered the Indians and took the town.

During much of the succeeding colonial era, Valladolid's distance from Mérida, its humidity and surrounding rainforests kept it isolated and thus relatively autonomous of royal rule. With the French and American revolutions as a catalyst, in 1809 local Mayan leaders plotted a rebellion which was discovered and quashed. Nonetheless, the seeds of future unrest were sown and Valladolid would play an important role in the next uprising.

Brutally exploited and banned along with the mestizos from even entering this town of pure-blooded Spanish, the Maya rebelled and in the War of the Castes of 1847 they made Valladolid their first point of attack. Besieged for two months, Valladolid's Spanish defenders were finally overcome; many of the citizens fled to the safety of Mérida and the rest were slaughtered by the Mayan forces.

Today, Valladolid is a marketing centre for agricultural products and crafts, with some light industry as well. Although it may appear sleepy, Valladolid is a prosperous seat of agrarian commerce and is the principal city of the peninsula's midsection.

Orientation & Information
The old highway goes right through the centre of town, though all signs will direct you to the Cuota, north of town. To follow the old highway eastbound, follow Calle 41; westbound, Calle 39 or 35. The bus terminal is on Calle 37 between Calles 54 and 56, eight blocks from the plaza.

Recommended hotels are on the main plaza, called the Parque Francisco Cantón Rosado, or just a block or two away from it.

The post office is on the east side of the main plaza at Calle 40 No 195A. Hours are

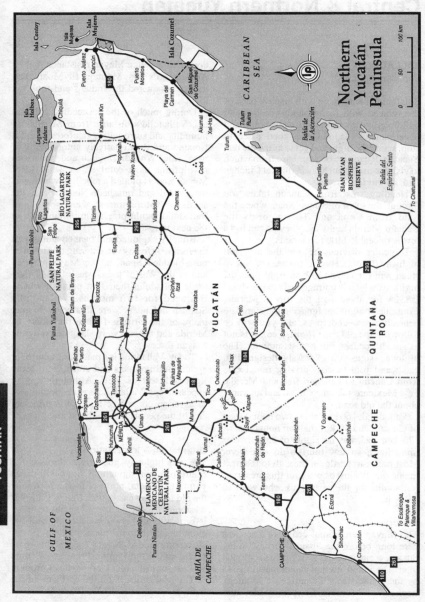

Monday to Friday from 8 am to 6 pm, Saturday 9 am to 1 pm.

Church of San Bernardino de Siena & Convent of Sisal

Although Valladolid has a number of interesting colonial churches, the Church of San Bernardino de Siena and the Convent of Sisal, one km south-west of the plaza along Calle 41A, are said to be the oldest Christian structures in Yucatán. Constructed in 1552, the complex was designed to serve a dual function as fortress and church, given the enmity of the Indians toward the Spaniards.

If you venture inside, apart from the miracle-working Virgin of Guadalupe on the altar, the church is relatively bare of ornamentation. During the uprisings of 1847 and 1910, angry Indians responded to the clergy's links with landowners by stripping the church of its decoration.

Other Churches

Other churches of note are the Cathedral of San Gervasio, facing onto the main plaza; Santa Ana at the corner of Calles 41 and 34, La Candelaria at Calles 44 and 35; San Juan Iglesia at the corner of Calles 49 and 40; and Santa Lucía at the corner of Calles 40 and 27.

Cenote Zací

Cenotes, those vast underground wells formed of limestone, were the Maya's most dependable source of water. The Spaniards depended upon them also and the Spanish town of Valladolid benefited in its early years from several cenotes in the area. The Cenote Zací, Calle 36 between Calles 39 and 37, a three-block walk from the plaza, is perhaps the most famous.

It's set in a pretty park which also holds the town's museum exhibits, an open-air amphitheatre and traditional stone-walled thatched houses. The cenote itself, at the end of a flight of slippery stairs, is vast, dark and formidable. If this is your first cenote, you'll be impressed; if you don't think you'll get the chance to see another, by all means make the short walk to this one. It's open daily from 8 am to 8 pm; admission costs US$2 for adults, half-price for children.

Cenote Dzitnup (Xkakah)

More impressive and beautiful, but less easily accessible, is Cenote Dzitnup, also called Cenote Xkakah, seven km west of Valladolid's main plaza. Follow the old highway west towards Mérida for five km; you'll pass a Coca-Cola bottling plant on the right-hand side. Turn left (south) at the sign for Dzitnup and go two km to the site, on the left. A taxi from Valladolid's main plaza charges US$10 for the excursion there and back, with half an hour's wait.

Another way to reach the cenote is on a bicycle rented from the Refaccionaría de Bicicletas de Paulino Silva on Calle 44 between Calles 39 and 41, facing Hotel María Guadalupe; look for the sign 'Alquiler y Venta de Bicicletas'. Rental costs US$2 per hour. The first five km are not particularly pleasant because of the traffic, but the last two km are on a quiet country road. It should take you only 20 minutes to pedal to the cenote.

Another way to get there is to hop aboard a westbound bus, ask the driver to let you off at the Dzitnup turning, then walk the final two km (20 minutes) to the site.

Cenote Dzitnup is open from 7 am to 5 pm daily. Admission costs US$1.50. There's a restaurant and drinks stand. If you've brought a bathing suit and towel you can go for a swim here.

Places to Stay – bottom end

Hotel María Guadalupe (☎ (985) 6-20-68), Calle 44 No 188, between Calles 39 and 41, is a study in modernity in this colonial town. The simple rooms here go for US$9/11/15 a single/double/triple with private shower and fan.

The *Hotel Zací* (☎ (985) 6 21 67), Calle 44 No 191, between Calles 37 and 39, has rooms built around a quiet, long-and-narrow courtyard with a swimming pool. You may choose from rooms with fan (prices are US$16/25/34 a single/double/triple) or with air-con (US$25/34/44).

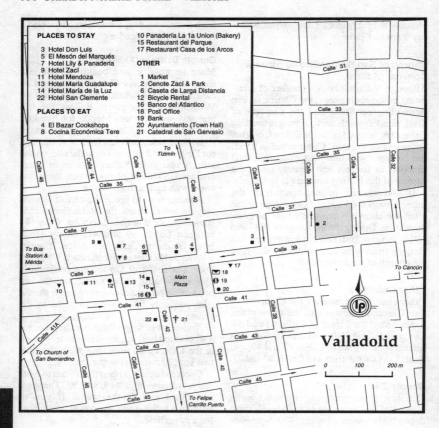

PLACES TO STAY

3 Hotel Don Luis
5 El Mesón del Marqués
7 Hotel Lily & Panadería
9 Hotel Zací
11 Hotel Mendoza
13 Hotel María Guadalupe
14 Hotel María de la Luz
22 Hotel San Clemente

PLACES TO EAT

4 El Bazar Cookshops
8 Cocina Económica Tere

10 Panadería La 1a Union (Bakery)
15 Restaurant del Parque
17 Restaurant Casa de los Arcos

OTHER

1 Market
2 Cenote Zací & Park
6 Caseta de Larga Distancia
12 Bicycle Rental
16 Banco del Atlantico
18 Post Office
19 Bank
20 Ayuntamiento (Town Hall)
21 Catedral de San Gervasio

Valladolid

Across the street and a few doors south is the *Hotel Lily* (☎ (985) 6-21-63), Calle 44 No 190. Rooms are cheaper: US$13 to US$16 a double with bath and fan. The housekeeping could be a lot better.

Places to Stay – middle

If you're willing to spend more money, the rest of the town's hotel choices are open to you. All have swimming pools, restaurants and secure parking facilities.

The best is *El Mesón del Marqués* (☎ (985) 6-20-73; fax 6-22-80), Calle 39 No 203, on the north side of the main plaza. It

has two beautiful colonial courtyards, and modernised guestrooms with air-con. Rates are US$45 to US$58 a single, US$50 to US$70 a double.

Next best is the *Hotel San Clemente* (☎ (985) 6-22-08; fax 6-35-14), Calle 42 No 206 at the corner of Calle 41, at the southwest corner of the main plaza. Colonial decoration abounds, but the 64 rooms have private baths and either air-con or fans costing US$22 to US$30 a single, US$28 to US$33.

Hotel Don Luis (☎ (985) 6-20-08), Calle 39 No 191, at the corner of Calle 38, is a motel-style structure with a palm-shaded patio and swimming pool and acceptable rooms. Singles with fan and bath cost US$25, doubles US$30, slightly more for air-con.

Hotel María de la Luz (☎ (985) 6-20-70; fax 6-20-71) is on Calle 42 near Calle 39, at the north-west corner of the plaza. Boasting one of the more popular restaurants on the square, it also has serviceable air-con rooms for US$30.

Places to Eat – bottom end

El Bazar is a collection of little open-air market-style cookshops at the corner of Calles 39 and 40 (north-east corner of the plaza). This is my favourite place for a big cheap breakfast. At lunch and dinnertime, comidas corridas of soup, main course and drink cost less than US$4. There are a dozen eateries here – Doña Mary, El Amigo Panfilo, Sergio's Pizza, La Rancherita, El Amigo Casiano, etc – open from 6.30 am to 2 pm and from 6 pm to about 9 or 10 pm.

For a bit more you can dine at the breezy tables in the *Hotel María de la Luz*, over-looking the plaza. Substantial sandwiches sell for US$1.50 to US$2.75, main course platters of meat or chicken for about twice as much.

Places to Eat – middle

For those willing to spend a bit more, the *Restaurant Casa de los Arcos* (☎ (985) 6-24-67), on Calle 39 between Calles 38 and 40, half a block east of the plaza, serves Yucatecan cuisine in pleasant dining rooms. Start with sopa de lima, continue with pork loin Valladolid-style (in a tomato sauce), or grilled pork steak with achiote sauce and finish up with guava paste and cheese for US$11 to US$15 per person. The restaurant is open every day from 7 or 8 am to 10 pm.

The other good middle-range restaurant in town is the dining room of *Hotel El Mesón del Marqués*, Calle 39 No 203 on the north side of the main plaza.

Getting There & Away

Bus The bus terminal is on Calle 37 between calles 54 and 56, eight blocks from the plaza. It has a long-distance telephone station with fax service. Main companies are Auto-transportes de Oriente Mérida-Puerto Juárez and Expresso de Oriente. Here are daily departures:

Cancún – 160 km, two hours, US$6; seven *local* (originating here), hourly de paso from 6 am to 9 pm.

Chichén Itzá – 42 km, 30 to 45 minutes, US$1; frequent buses

Chiquilá (for Isla Holbox) – 155 km, 2½ hours, US$5; at least one bus daily.

Cobá – 106 km, two hours, US$4; two buses

Izamal – 115 km, two hours, US$4; Autobuses del Centro del Estado de Yucatán operates five buses

Mérida – 160 km, three hours, US$6; seven *local* (originating here), hourly de paso from 6 am to 9 pm.

Motul – 156 km, three hours, US$6; Autobuses del Noreste runs five buses via Dzitas, Tunkas, Izamal and Tixcocob.

Playa del Carmen – 230 km, 3½ hours, US$8.50; two buses.

Río Lagartos – 103 km, two hours, US$4; the 10 am bus to Tizimin continues to Lagartos; or change buses at Tizimin.

Tizimin – 51 km, one hour, US$2; Autobuses del Noreste en Yucatán operates buses at 10 am and 1.30 pm.

Tulum – 360 km, six hours, US$11; two buses.

Taxi A quicker, more comfortable but more expensive way to Cancún is by taking one of the shared taxis parked outside the bus station, which leave as soon as all seats are filled. The trip costs approximately twice the bus fare.

EKBALAM

Midway from Valladolid to Tizimin, turn right (east) following signs to Santa Rita and Ekbalam to find the Ekbalam archaeological site, 10½ km along butterfly-busy roads through fields of corn and beans.

The site is open during daylight hours for US$3 (plus a tip if you follow the guide).

The temple mounds are still largely covered by jungle, as is the great plaza, but the guide, Sr Anastasio Vaas, will show you cisterns, a subterranean entry, a *sacbé* (ancient ceremonial road, paved with lime-

YUCATÁN

stone), several stelae with high relief carving, and other features. From the top of the main pyramid, the tedious flatness of the landscape is broken only by a few small tree-covered 'hills' on the horizon – other tree-covered pyramids marking other once-great Mayan cities.

Excavation continues from May to July annually under the auspices of the National Geographic Society (USA), the Middle American Research Institute, Tulane University and Davidson College.

TIZIMIN

Many travellers bound for Río Lagartos will change buses in Tizimin (Place of Many Horses), a farming centre of note (cattle ranches, beehives and citrus groves make the wealth here). There is little to warrant an overnight stay, so Tizimin is relatively free of tourists.

The main plaza is pleasant. Two great colonial structures, the Convento de los Tres Reyes Magos (Monastery of the Three Wise Kings) and the Convento de San Francisco de Assis (Monastery of Saint Francis of Assisi) are worth a look. Five lengthy blocks

from the plaza, north-west on Calle 51, is a modest zoo, the Parque Zoológico de la Reina.

The Banco del Atlantico, next to the Hotel San Jorge on the south side of the plaza, will change money for you between 10 am and noon from Monday to Friday. Banco Internacional is open from 9 am to 1.30 pm.

Places to Stay

Hotel San Jorge (☎ (986) 3-20-37), Calle 53 No 411, near Calle 52, on the south side of the plaza, is perhaps the town's best and boasts a swimming pool the size of a hot tub. Basic but serviceable rooms with private bath and fan cost US$23/30 for a double with fan/air-con.

Hotel San Carlos (☎ (986) 3-20-94), Calle 54 No 407, 1½ long blocks from the plaza is built like a motel, and charges identical prices.

Posada María Antonia (☎ (986) 3 23 84), Calle 50 No 408, on the east side of the Parque de la Madre, also has comfy rooms. Those with fan are priced the same; doubles with air-con cost US$28. The reception desk is also a long-distance telephone station.

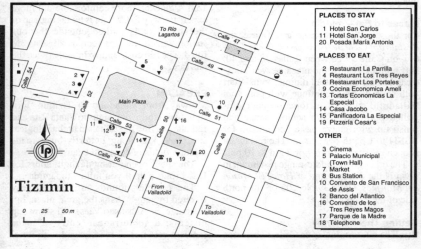

PLACES TO STAY
1   Hotel San Carlos
11 Hotel San Jorge
20 Posada María Antonia

PLACES TO EAT
2   Restaurant La Parrilla
4   Restaurant Los Tres Reyes
6   Restaurant Los Portales
9   Cocina Economica Ameli
13 Tortas Economicas La Especial
14 Casa Jacobo
15 Panificadora La Especial
19 Pizzería Cesar's

OTHER
3   Cinema
5   Palacio Municipal (Town Hall)
7   Market
8   Bus Station
10 Convento de San Francisco de Assis
12 Banco del Atlantico
16 Convento de los Tres Reyes Magos
17 Parque de la Madre
18 Telephone

Tizimin

0   25   50 m

Places to Eat

The market, a block north-west of the bus station, has the usual cheap eateries.

Perhaps the best dining in town is at *Restaurant Los Tres Reyes* (☎ 3-21-06), on the corner of Calles 52 and 53. It opens early for breakfast and is a favourite with town notables who take their second cup of coffee around 9 am. Lunch or dinner costs US$3 to US$5.

Tortas Económicas La Especial, on the main square, has cheap sandwiches and drinks, as does the *Cocina Económica Ameli*.

Otherwise, there's *Pizzería Cesar's*, at the corner of Calles 50 and 53, facing the Parque de la Madre. Pizza and pasta are the attractions here, in the evening (5.30 to 11 pm) only. You can eat in air-conditioned comfort for US$2.50 to US$6 or so.

Restaurant Los Portales is near the august portals of the Palacio Municipal (Town Hall) on the north-east side of the plaza. It's a simple place, good for a quick sandwich or burger and a cold drink. *Restaurant La Parrilla*, on the north-west side of the plaza, is another simple place open for lunch and dinner only.

For snacks, make-your-own breakfasts and bus food, drop by the *Panificadora La Especial* on Calle 55, down a little pedestrian lane from the plaza.

Getting There & Away

Autobuses del Noreste en Yucatán operates daily buses from Valladolid to Tizimin (51 km, one hour, US$2) at 10 am and 1.30 pm. From Cancún and Puerto Juárez, there are several direct buses to Tizimin (215 km, four hours, US$7). There are several daily 1st and 2nd-class buses between Tizimin and Mérida via Valladolid. For Río Lagartos there are three 1st-class departures and five daily 2nd-class buses which continue to San Felipe.

RÍO LAGARTOS

For those interested in the most spectacular flamingo colony in Mexico, it is worth going out of your way to this little fishing village 103 km north of Valladolid and 52 km north of Tizimin. In addition to thousands of flamingos, the estuaries are home to snowy egrets, red egrets, great white herons and snowy white ibis. Although Río Lagartos (Alligator River) was named after the once substantial alligator population, don't expect to see any of the reptiles as hunting has virtually wiped them out.

The town of Río Lagartos itself, with its narrow streets and multihued houses, has little charm, though the panorama of the boats and the bay is pleasant. Were it not for the flamingos, you would have little reason to come here. Although the state government has been making noises about developing the area for tourism, this has not happened yet.

At the centre of town is a small triangular plaza, the Presidencia Municipal (Town Hall) and the Conasupo store.

Flamingos

The sight of a foreigner in Río Lagartos provokes in any local citizen a Pavlovian response: the mouth opens, the larynx tenses, the lungs compress and out come the words 'Los flamingos! A la playa!' The response from the foreigner is equally automatic: 'Sí!'

YUCATÁN

Yucatecan flamingos

Your first encounter with a Lagartan thus highlights your first duty here; to find a reliable boat-owner and a good price for the trip to see the flamingos or to swim at the beach nearby.

The Spanish word *flamenco*, which means 'flaming', makes sense in terms of the bird's name as you approach a horizon of hundreds of brilliantly hued, flaming red-pink birds. When the flock takes flight, the sight of the suddenly fiery horizon makes the long hours on the bus to get here all worthwhile. However, in the interests of the flamingos' well-being, convince your local guide not to frighten the birds into flight. Being frightened away from their habitat several times a day can't be good for them, however good it may be for the guide's business.

Birdwatching by Boat Everybody in town will offer to set you up with a boat. Haggling over price is essential. In general, a short trip (two to three hours) to see a few nearby local flamingos and to have a swim at the beach costs US$20 to US$35 for a five-seat boat. The much longer voyage (four to six hours) to the flamingos' favourite haunts costs US$75 or so for the boat, or about US$15 per person for a full load. If you can't put together a suitable itinerary by yourself, you might inquire at the Hotel María Nefertiti.

Birdwatching on Foot If you walk some of the 14 km along the beach from the lagoon out to Punta Holohit on the sea, you will most likely see colourful bird life. Among the species common here are egrets, herons, flamingos, ibis, cormorants, stilts, pelicans and plovers. Wear some decent footwear that you can get wet as well as clothes that you can go in the water with. You might be able to arrange to have a boat pick you up at Punta Holohit for your return if you walk all the way.

Places to Stay & Eat
The *Hotel María Nefertiti* (☎ 1-4-15), Calle 14 No 123, is the only hostelry in town. Rooms with bath and fan in this hulk of a place cost US$25 a double.

The cavernous palapa-shaded *Restaurant Los Flamingos* at the back is equally empty most of the time. The *Restaurant Familiar Isla Contoy*, just down from the Flamingo on the water, is perhaps a better bet. To find the hotel, walk from the triangular plaza keeping the Presidencia Municipal on your left. Pass Conasupo on your right and at the next corner turn left and walk 100 metres to the hotel.

It is sometimes possible to rent a bed or a pair of hammock hooks in a local house, which brings down considerably the cost of sleeping.

If the hotel's restaurant is empty, you might do better by grabbing a bite at the *Restaurant La Económica* directly across the street from it. There's also the *Restaurant Los Negritos* facing a little park with a statue of Benito Juárez, two blocks inland from the main square.

Getting There & Away
Autobuses del Noreste en Yucatán operates daily buses from Valladolid to Tizimin (51 km, one hour, US$2) at 10 am and 1.30 pm. The 10 am bus goes on to Río Lagartos (103 km, two hours, US$4); if you miss this one, you must change buses in Tizimin. There is also one direct bus daily between Tizimin and Mérida.

SAN FELIPE
Population: 400

This tiny, unspoiled fishing village of traditional brightly painted wooden fishing cabins on narrow streets, 12 km west of Río Lagartos, makes a nice day trip from Río Lagartos. While the waters are not Caribbean turquoise and there's little shade, in spring and summer scores of visitors come here to camp. Other than lying on the beach, birdwatching is the main attraction, as just across the estuary at Punta Holohit there is abundant bird life.

Places to Stay & Eat
There are no hotels in San Felipe, but the proprietor of La Herradura grocery store

near the pier will tell you about inexpensive house rentals. Spartan rooms are sometimes available for rent above the Cinema Marrufo. Campers are ferried across the estuary to islands where they pitch tents or set up hammocks.

A few simple restaurants and tiendas provide food and drink.

Getting There & Away

Some buses from Tizimin to Río Lagartos continue to San Felipe and return. The 12-km ride takes about 20 minutes.

ISLA HOLBOX

Fed up with the tourist hordes of Cancún, Isla Mujeres and Cozumel? Want to find a beach site virtually devoid of gringos? In that case Isla Holbox (pronounced HOHL-bosh) might appeal to you. But before you make haste for the island note that the most basic facilities are in short supply and the beaches are not Cancún-perfect strips of clean, air-conditioned sand. To enjoy Isla Holbox, you must be very willing to rough it.

The 25-km by three-km island has sands that run on and on, as well as tranquil waters where you can wade out quite a distance before the sea reaches shoulder level. Moreover, Isla Holbox is absolutely magic for shell collectors, with a galaxy of shapes and colours. The fishing families of the island are friendly – unjaded by encounters with exotic tourists or the frenetic pace of the urban mainland.

As to drawbacks, the seas are not the translucent turquoise of the Quintana Roo beach sites, because here the Caribbean waters mingle with those of the darker Gulf. Seaweed can create silty waters near shore at some parts of the beach. While there are big plans to develop Isla Holbox one day, at the time of writing there is only one modest hotel, the aptly named *Hotel Flamingo* (with doubles for US$12) and a few snack shops. Most travellers camp or stay in spartan rooms rented from locals.

Getting There & Away

Bus If you are going from Isla Mujeres or Cancún to Isla Holbox, catch a direct bus from Puerto Juárez or Cancún.

Ferry To reach Isla Holbox, you take the ferry from the unappealing port village of Chiquilá. Buses make the 2½-hour trip three times a day from Valladolid to Chiquila and in theory the ferry is supposed to wait for them. However, it may not wait for a delayed bus or may even leave early (!) should the captain feel so inclined.

It is therefore recommended that you reach Chiquilá as early as possible. The ferry is supposed to depart for the island at 8 am and 3 pm and make the trip in about an hour. Ferries return to Chiquila at 2 and 5 pm. The cost is US$2.50.

Try not to get stuck in Chiquila, as it is a tiny hole of a port with no hotels, no decent camping and very disappointing food service.

CHICHÉN ITZÁ

The most famous and best restored of Yucatán's Mayan sites, Chichén Itzá will awe the most jaded of ruins visitors. Many mysteries of the Mayan astronomical calendar are made clear when one understands the design of the 'time temples' here. But one astronomical mystery remains: why do most people come here from Mérida and Cancún on day trips, arriving at 11 am, when the blazing sun is getting to its hottest point and departing around 3 pm when the heat finally begins to abate? Climbing El Castillo at midday in the awful heat and humidity is my idea of torture.

I strongly recommend that you stay the night nearby and do your exploration of the site either early in the morning or late in the afternoon, or both. Should you have the good fortune to visit Chichén Itzá on the vernal equinox (which is 20 to 21 March) or autumnal equinox (21 to 22 September), you can witness the light-and-shadow illusion of the serpent ascending or descending the side of the staircase of El Castillo. The illusion is almost as good in the week preceding and the week following the equinox.

YUCATÁN

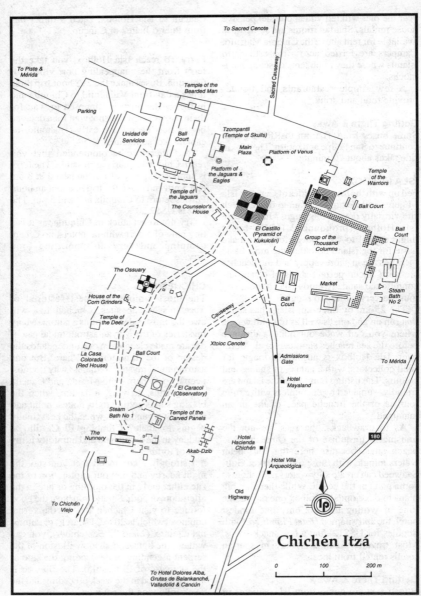

To Sacred Cenote

To Piste & Mérida

Parking

Unidad de Servicios

Ball Court

Temple of the Bearded Man

Tzompantli (Temple of Skulls)

Main Plaza

Platform of Venus

Platform of the Jaguars & Eagles

Temple of the Warriors

Ball Court

Temple of the Jaguars

The Counselor's House

El Castillo (Pyramid of Kukulcán)

Group of the Thousand Columns

Ball Court

The Ossuary

Market

House of the Corn Grinders

Ball Court

Steam Bath No 2

Temple of the Deer

Causeway

Xtoloc Cenote

La Casa Colorada (Red House)

Ball Court

Admissions Gate

To Mérida

Hotel Mayaland

El Caracol (Observatory)

Steam Bath No 1

Temple of the Carved Panels

The Nunnery

Hotel Hacienda Chichén

Akab-Dzib

Hotel Villa Arqueológica

180

Old Highway

To Chichén Viejo

Chichén Itzá

To Hotel Dolores Alba, Grutas de Balankanché, Valladolid & Cancún

0   100   200 m

YUCATÁN

History

Most archaeologists agree that Chichén Itzá (The Mouth of the Well of the Itzaes) was first settled during the Late Classic period between 550 and 900 AD and was pure Mayan. In about the 10th century, the city was largely abandoned for unknown reasons.

The city was resettled about 1100 AD. Shortly thereafter, Chichén was invaded by the Toltecs, who had moved down from their central highlands capital of Tula, north of present-day Mexico City. The Toltecs fused their culture with that of the Maya, incorporating the cult of Quetzalcóatl (Kukulcán in Mayan).

Quetzalcóatl, the plumed serpent, was a blonde king with great powers who was supposedly cast out of his kingdom and exiled from the central highlands to Mexico's south-east. Legend had it that he would reappear and bring a great era with him. This legend would ultimately help pave the way for Cortés in his conquest of Mexico.

In Chichén Itzá you will see images of Chac, the Mayan rain god and Quetzalcóatl, the plumed serpent, throughout the city. However, because there appears to be evidence of Toltec influence long before the supposed Toltec invasion, there is speculation that Tula had once been a colony of Chichén and that Toltec influence filtered back to the Yucatán.

The warlike Toltecs contributed more than their architectural skills. They elevated human sacrifice to a near obsession, for there are numerous carvings of the bloody ritual in Chichén. After a Toltec leader moved his political capital to Mayapán while keeping Chichén as his religious capital, Chichén Itzá fell into decline. Why it was subsequently abandoned in the 14th century is a mystery, but the once-great city remained the site of Mayan pilgrimages for years afterward.

Orientation

Highway 180 skirts the archaeological site to the east and north. Coming from Cancún, you approach Chichen Itzá from the south along an access road formed by the old highway. It's 1.5 km from Highway 180 to the eastern entrance to the ruins. On the way you pass the Villa Arqueológica, Hacienda Chichén and Mayaland luxury hotels. The moderately priced Hotel Dolores Alba is 3.1 km east of the eastern entrance to the ruins, on the highway to Cancún.

Except for these hotels, Chichén's lodgings, restaurants and services are ranged along one km of highway in the village of Piste (PEESS-teh), to the west (Mérida) side of the ruins. It's 1.5 km from the western entrance of the ruins to the first hotel (Piramide Inn) in Piste, or 2.5 km from the ruins to the village square (actually a triangle), shaded by a huge tree. Buses generally stop at the square; you can make the hot walk to or from the ruins in 20 to 30 minutes.

Chichén's little airstrip is north of the ruins, on the north side of the highway.

Information

Money You can change money in the Unidad de Servicios at the western entrance to the ruins, or at your hotel.

Telephone For long-distance calls, go to the Teléfonos de México caseta de larga distancia in Piste. Look for the Restaurant Xaybe, across the highway from the Hotel Misión Chichén; the caseta is in the same group of buildings, open from 8 am to 9 pm.

Archaeological Zone Chichén Itzá is open every day from 8 am to 5 pm; the interior passageway in El Castillo is open only from 11 am to 1 pm and from 4 to 5 pm. Admission to the site costs US$7; US$10 extra for your video camera and US$7 extra if you use a tripod with your camera. Admission is free to children under 12 years of age, and to all on Sunday. Parking costs US$1.25. Explanatory plaques are in Spanish, English and French.

The main entrance to the ruins is the western one, with a large car park and a big, modern entrance building called the Unidad de Servicios, open 8 am to 10 pm. The Unidad has a small but worthwhile museum (open 8 am to 5 pm) with sculptures, reliefs, artefacts and explanations of these in Spanish, English and French. The Chilam Balam Auditorio next to the museum has audio-visual shows about Chichén in English at noon and 4 pm. In the central space of the Unidad stands a scale model of the archaeological site and off towards the toilets is an exhibit on Thompson's excavations of the sacred cenote in 1923. There's also a souvenir and book shop, currency exchange desk (open 9 am to 1 pm) and a *guardarropa* at the main ticket desk where you can leave your belongings (US$0.35) while you explore the site.

Sound-and-light shows are held each evening in Spanish from 7 to 7.35 pm for US$1.50 and in English from 9 to 9.35 pm for US$2.

El Castillo

The first temple here was pre-Toltec, built around 800 AD. But the present 25-metre-high structure, built over the old one, has the plumed serpent sculpted along the stairways and Toltec warriors represented in the doorway carvings of the temple at the top.

The pyramid is actually the Mayan calendar formed in stone. Each of El Castillo's nine levels is divided in two by a staircase, making eighteen separate terraces which commemorate the eighteen 20-day months of the Vague Year. The four stairways have 91 steps each; add the top platform and the total is 365, the number of days in the year. On each façade of the pyramid are 52 flat panels, reminders of the 52 years in the Calendar Round.

Most amazing of all, during the spring and autumn equinoxes (around 21 March and 21 September), light and shadow form a series of triangles on the side of the north staircase which mimic the creep of a serpent (note the serpent's head at the bottom of the staircase). The serpent appears to ascend in March and descend in September. This illusion lasts three hours and 22 minutes and was all arranged by the brilliant Mayan architects and astronomers who designed El Castillo.

There's another, older pyramid *inside* El Castillo with a brilliant red jaguar throne with inlaid eyes and spots of shimmering jade. The inner sanctum also holds a Toltec chac-mool figure.

The inner pyramid is only open from 11 am to 1 pm and 4 to 5 pm. The dank air inside can make climbing the stairs a sweltering, slippery experience.

Principal Ball Court

This is only one of the city's eight courts, but it's the best preserved and largest ball court in all of Mexico. The field is flanked by temples at either end and bounded by towering parallel walls with stone rings cemented up high.

Carvings show players with padding on their elbows and knees. It is thought that they played a soccer-like game with a hard rubber ball, forbidding the use of hands. Other carvings show players wielding bats; it appears that if a player hit the ball through one of the stone hoops, his team was declared the winner. It may be that during the Toltec period the losing captain, and perhaps his teammates as well, were sacrificed.

Along the walls of the ball court are some fine stone reliefs, including scenes of decapitations of players. Acoustically the court is amazing – a conversation at one end can be heard 135 metres away at the other end, and if you clap, you hear a resounding echo.

Temple of the Bearded Man & Temple of the Jaguars

The structure at the northern end of the ball court, called the Temple of the Bearded Man after a carving inside it, has some finely sculpted pillars and reliefs of flowers, birds and trees. The Temple of the Jaguars, to the south-east, has some rattlesnake-carved columns and jaguar-etched tablets. Inside are faded mural fragments depicting a battle.

Tzompantli

The Tzompantli, a Toltec term for Temple of Skulls, is between the Temple of the Jaguars and El Castillo. You can't mistake it because the T-shaped platform is festooned with carved skulls and eagles tearing open the chests of men to eat their hearts. In ancient

Carving of a jaguar eating a human heart, Platform of the Jaguars & Eagles, Chichén Itzá

days this platform held the heads of sacrificial victims.

Platform of the Jaguars & Eagles

Adjacent to the Temple of Skulls, this platform's carvings depict jaguars and eagles gruesomely grabbing human hearts in their claws. It is thought that this platform was part of a temple dedicated to the military legions responsible for capturing sacrificial victims.

Platform of Venus

The Toltec Venus is a feathered serpent bearing a human head between its jaws. The platform is decked with feathered snake figures.

Sacred Cenote

The Sacred Cenote, 300 metres (a five-minute walk) north of the Platform of Venus along a crushed-stone road, is an awesome natural well some 60 metres in diameter and 35 metres deep. There are ruins of a small steam bath next to the cenote, as well as a modern drinks stand with toilets.

Around the turn of the century, Edward Thompson, a Harvard professor and US Consul to the Yucatán, bought a hacienda which included Chichén for US$75. He had the cenote dredged, and artefacts, gold and jade jewellery from all parts of Mexico were recovered along with the skeletons of men, women and – mostly – children. These objects were given to Harvard's Peabody Museum, which later returned many of them.

The artefacts' origins show the far-flung contact the Maya had; there are some items from as far away as Colombia.

Subsequent diving expeditions in 1923 and later in the 1960s, sponsored by the US National Geographic Society, brought up hundreds more artefacts.

Group of the Thousand Columns

Comprising the Temple of the Warriors, Temple of Chac-Mool and Sweat House or Steam Bath, this group takes its name from the forest of pillars in front.

The platformed temple greets you with a statue of the reclining god, Chac, as well as stucco and stone-carved animal deities. The temple's roof, once supported by columns entwined with serpents, disappeared long ago.

Archaeological work in 1926 revealed a Temple of Chac-Mool beneath the Temple of the Warriors. You may enter via a stairway on the north side. The walls inside have badly deteriorated murals of what is thought to be the Toltecs' defeat of the Maya.

Just east of the Temple of the Warriors lies the rubble of a Mayan sweat house, with an underground oven and drains for the water. The sweat houses were regularly used for ritual purification.

Ossuary

The Ossuary, otherwise known as the Bone-house or High Priest's Grave, is a ruined pyramid. As with most of the buildings in this southern section, the architecture is more Puuc than Toltec.

La Casa Colorada

La Casa Colorada, or The Red House, was named by the Spaniards for the red paint of the mural on its doorway. This building has

YUCATÁN

little Toltec influence and its design shows largely a pure Puuc-Mayan style. Referring to the stone latticework at the roof façade, the Maya named this building Chichán-Chob, or House of Small Holes.

El Caracol

Called El Caracol (The Giant Conch Snail) by the Spaniards for its interior spiral staircase, the observatory is one of the most fascinating and important of all of Chichén Itzá's buildings. Its circular design resembles some central highlands structures, although, surprisingly, not those of Toltec Tula. In a fusion of architectural styles and religious imagery, there are Mayan Chac rain god masks over four external doors facing the cardinal directions.

The windows in the observatory's dome are aligned with the appearance of certain stars at specific dates. From the dome the priests decreed the times for rituals, celebrations, corn-planting and harvests.

Nunnery & Annexe

Thought by archaeologists to have been a palace for Mayan royalty, the Nunnery, with its myriad rooms, resembled a European convent to the conquistadors, hence their name for the building. The Nunnery's dimensions are imposing: its base is 60 metres long, 30 metres wide and 20 metres high. The construction is Mayan rather than Toltec, although a Toltec sacrificial stone stands in front. A small building added onto the west side is known as the Annexe. These buildings are in the Puuc-Chenes style, particularly evident in the lower jaw of the Chac mask at the opening of the Annexe.

Akab-Dzib

On the path east of the Nunnery, the Akab-Dzib is thought by some archaeologists to be the most ancient structure excavated here. The central chambers date from the 2nd century. Akab-Dzib means Obscure Writing in Mayan and refers to the south-side Annexe door whose lintel depicts a priest with a vase etched with hieroglyphics. The writing has never been translated, hence the name. Note

the red fingerprints on the ceiling, thought to symbolise the deity Itzamna, the sun god from whom the Maya sought wisdom.

Chichén Viejo

Chichén Viejo, or Old Chichén, comprises largely unrestored, basically Mayan ruins, though some have Toltec additions. Here you'll see a pristine part of Chichén without much archaeological restoration.

Grutas de Balankanché

In 1959 a guide to the Chichén ruins was exploring a cave on his day off. Pushing against a cavern wall, he broke through into a larger subterranean opening. Archaeological exploration revealed a path that runs some 300 metres past carved stalactites and stalagmites, terminating at an underground pool.

The Grutas de Balankanché (Balankanché Caves) are six km east of the ruins of Chichén Itzá, and two km east of the Hotel Dolores Alba on the highway to Cancún. Second-class buses heading east from Piste toward Valladolid and Cancún will drop you at the Balankanché road. You'll find the entrance to the caves 350 metres north of the highway.

As you approach the caves, you enter a pretty botanical garden displaying many of Yucatán's native flora, including many species of cactus. In the entrance building is a little museum, a shop selling cold drinks and souvenirs and a ticket booth. Plan your visit for an hour when the compulsory tour and Light & Colour Show will be given in a language you can understand: the 40-minute show (minimum six persons, maximum 30) is given in the cave at 11 am, 1 and 3 pm in English, at 9 am, noon and 2 and 4 pm in Spanish and at 10 am in French. Tickets are available betwen 9 am to 4 pm (last show) daily. Admission costs US$7, (US$2.50 Sunday).

Places to Stay

Most of the lodgings convenient to Chichén are in the middle and top-end price brackets. No matter what you plan to spend on a bed, be prepared to haggle off-season (May, June, September and October) when prices should be lower at every hotel.

Places to Stay – bottom end

Camping There's camping at the *Piramide Inn & Trailer Park* (☎ (985) 6-26-71 ext 115) on the eastern edge of Piste (closest to the ruins). For US$5 per person you can pitch a tent, enjoy the Piramide Inn's pool and watch satellite TV in the lobby. There are hot showers and clean, shared toilet facilities. Those in vehicles pay US$15 for two for full hook-ups.

Hotels Unfortunately, there's not much. *Posada Chac-Mool*, just east of the Hotel Misión Chichén on the opposite (south) side of the highway in Piste, is now overpriced and dingy at US$22 for a double with shower and fan. *Posada El Paso*, a few dozen metres west of the Stardust Inn, is a much better choice, at the same price. *Posada Poxil* (☎ (985) 6-25-13 ext 116 or 123), at the western end of the town, charges the same for relatively clean, quiet rooms.

Places to Stay – middle

Hotel Dolores Alba (☎ in Mérida (99) 21-37-45), Carretera Km 122, is just over three km east of the eastern entrance to the ruins and two km west of the road to Balankanché, on the highway to Cancún. (Ask the bus driver to stop here.) There are more than a dozen rooms surrounding a small swimming pool. The dining room is good (breakfasts US$3 to US$4, dinner US$10), which is important as there is no other eating facility nearby. They will transport you to the ruins, but you must take a taxi, bus or walk back. Single/double rooms with fan and shower cost US$18/22; with air-con, US$27/33.

Stardust Inn, next to the Pirámide Inn in Piste and less than two km from the ruins, is an attractive place with two tiers of rooms surrounding a palm-shaded swimming pool and restaurant. Air-con rooms with TV cost US$44 single or double.

The *Pirámide Inn* next door has been here for years. Its grounds are very pretty, having had years to mature, and its swimming pool is a blessing on a hot day. There's a selection of different rooms, some older, some newer (look before you buy), all air-conditioned and priced at US$39/48/56/65 a single/double/triple/quad. Here, you're as close as you can get to the archaeological zone's western entrance.

Places to Stay – top end

All of these hotels have beautiful swimming pools, restaurants, bars, well-kept tropical gardens, comfortable guest rooms and tour groups coming and going. Several are very close to the ruins. If you are going to splurge on just one expensive hotel in Mexico, this is a good place to do it.

Hotel Mayaland (☎ in Mérida (99) 25-21-22; fax 25-70-22; toll-free in USA (800) 235-4079), a mere 200 metres from the eastern entrance to the archaeological zone, is the oldest (1923) and most gracious at Chichén. From the lobby you look through the main portal to see El Caracol framed as in a photograph. Rooms are priced at US$112 a double. For reservations, call the Mérida office of Mayaland Tours at ☎ (99) 25-23-42, 25-22-46; fax (99) 25-70-22.

Sister hotel to the Mayaland is the *Hotel Hacienda Chichén*, just a few hundred metres farther from the ruins on the same eastern access road. This was the hacienda where the archaeologists lived when excavating Chichén. Their bungalows have been refurbished and new ones built. It's the choice of the discerning traveller who wants to avoid the crowds of the tour buses yet have some comforts. Rooms in the garden bungalows have ceiling fans and private baths, but no TVs or phones. These are available for US$99 a double. The dining room serves simple meals at moderate prices. The Hacienda Chichén usually closes from May to October. For reservations, call as for the Mayaland.

The *Hotel Villa Arqueológica* (☎ (985) 6-28-30), Apdo Postal 495, Mérida, is a few hundred metres east of the Mayaland and

Hacienda Chichén on the eastern access road to the ruins. Run by Club Med, it's a modern layout with a good restaurant, tennis courts and swimming pool. Rooms are fairly small but comfortable and air-conditioned and priced at US$85/96/104 a single/double/triple.

On the western side of Chichén, in the village of Piste, the *Hotel Misión Chichén* (☎ (985) 6-26-71 ext 104; in USA (800) 648-7818) is two km from the ruins entrance on the north side of the highway. It's comfortable without being distinguished. Singles/doubles cost US$79/90.

Places to Eat

The cafeteria in the *Unidad de Servicios* at the western entrance to the archaeological zone serves mediocre food at high prices in pleasant surroundings.

The highway through Piste is lined with little restaurants, most of them fairly well tarted up in a Mayan villager's conception of what foreign tourists expect to see. Prices are fairly high for what you get and most of these places serve only table d'hôte meals at lunch, which means you must pay one set price for a full-course meal; you can't pick and choose from a menu or just order something light as one might want to do in the heat.

Of the Piste restaurants, the *Restaurant Sayil*, facing the Hotel Misión Chichén, is probably the cheapest; it's a plain little *restaurante económico* serving cochinita or pollo pibil for US$3.25, rice with garnish for US$1.25 and egg dishes for US$2. Another simple little eatery with wooden benches and tables is the *Restaurant Parador*.

Prices are only slightly higher at the attractive, family-run *Restaurant Carrousel*, where you can order a platter of pollo pibil or cochinita pibil for under US$8, eggs and a few antojito choices for even less. The big palapa-covered dining room is pleasant and open from 10.30 am to 6.30 pm.

If you are willing to spend the money, the *Restaurant Xaybe* opposite the Hotel Misión Chichén has good cuisine, usually served buffet style in a surprisingly formal, air-conditioned dining room for the tour bus clientele. Figure on paying US$11.50 for lunch, and just slightly more for dinner, for all you can eat. Customers of the restaurant get to use its swimming pool for free, but even if you don't eat here, you can still swim for about US$2.

Most tarted up of the restaurants in Piste is the fantastical *Restaurant Fiesta*, which is worth a look if not a meal. The luncheon table d'hôte goes for US$11.50, but you can order from the menu in the evening, when substantial portions of meat cost US$7, of tacos US$3.50 to US$6

The luxury hotels all have restaurants, with the Club Med-run *Villa Arqueológica* serving particularly distinguished cuisine. If you try its French-inspired Mexican-Mayan restaurant, it'll cost you about US$25 per person for a table d'hôte lunch or dinner, and almost twice that much if you order à la carte – but the food is good.

Getting There & Away

Air Aerocaribe runs one-day excursions by air from Cancún to Chichén Itzá in little planes, charging US$99 for the flight.

Bus All the considerable bus traffic between Mérida, Valladolid and Cancún, both 1st and 2nd-class (at least two dozen buses daily), passes by Chichén Itzá. Here are some bus routes from Piste:

Cancún – 205 km, 3 to 3½ hours, US$5 to US$8
Izamal – 95 km, 2 hours, US$3.50, change buses at Hóctun
Mérida – 116 km, 2½ hours, US$6
Valladolid – 42 km, 30 to 45 minutes, US$1; frequent buses

These are 1st-class times; 2nd-class buses can be a bit slower.

Getting Around

Be prepared for walking at Chichén Itzá: from your hotel to the ruins, around the ruins, and back to your hotel, all in the very hot sun and humidity. For the Grutas de Balankanché, you can set out to walk early in the morning when it's cooler (it's eight km from Piste, less if you're staying on the eastern side of the ruins) and then hope to hitch a ride or catch a bus for the return.

A few taxis are available in Piste and sometimes at the Unidad de Servicios car park at Chichén Itzá, but you cannot depend upon finding one unless you've made arrangements in advance.

IZAMAL
Population: 40,000

In ancient times, Izamal was a centre for the worship of the supreme Mayan god Itzamná and the sun god Kinich Kakmó. A dozen temple pyramids in the town were devoted to these or other gods. Perhaps this Mayan religiosity is why the Spanish colonists chose Izamal as the site for an enormous and very impressive Franciscan monastery. As a site for the monastery's main church, the planners selected the platform of one of the major Mayan temples.

Today Izamal is a small, quiet provincial town with the atmosphere of life in another century. The occasional horse-drawn carriage clip-clopping through town reinforces this feeling. Its two principal squares are surrounded by impressive arcades and dominated by the gargantuan bulk of the monastery.

Convento de San Antonio de Padua
When the Spaniards conquered Izamal, they destroyed the major Mayan temple, the Popul-Chac pyramid and in 1533 they began to build from its stones one of the first monasteries in the hemisphere. The work was finished in 1561.

As you enter the centre of town, you can't miss the monastery, which dominates everything. The arcade, an architectural feature both useful and beautiful, was fully and abundantly used by Izamal's colonial designers in the monastery, in the Palacio Municipal, in the small market and in many other town buildings. The traditional yellow you see everywhere gives the town its nickname of Ciudad Amarilla.

The monastery's principal church is the Santuario de la Virgen de Izamal, approached by a ramp from the main square. Walk up the ramp and through an arcaded gallery to

---

HENEQUEN
Henequen, *(agave fourcroydes)*, also called sisal, is a common plant in Yucatán and indeed in most of Mexico. Its stalk grows almost two metres high in the wild, about one metre in cultivation, and has lance-shaped leaves up to two metres long and 10 to 15 cm wide, edged with thorns. The evil-smelling flowers are borne on a central stalk which grows straight upwards to heights of six metres. Agaves flower periodically but infrequently, some species only once in a century.

A cultivated henequen plant yields about 25 leaves annually from the fifth to the sixteenth year after planting. The leaves are cut off by a worker with a machete, taken to a factory, and crushed between heavy rollers. The pulpy vegetable matter is scraped away to reveal fibre strands up to 1½ metres in length, which are slightly stretchable and resistant to marine organisms.

Around Izamal and en route from Chichén Itzá to Mérida, you pass through the henequen fields that gave rise to Yucatán's affluence in the 19th century. Prosperity in these parts reached its high point during WW I when the demand for rope was great and synthetic fibres had not yet been invented.

Sometimes you can smell the greyish spikey-leafed henequen plants before you see them, as they emit a putrid, excremental odour. Once planted, henequen can grow virtually untended for seven years. Thereafter, the plants are annually stripped for fibre. A plant may be productive for upwards of two decades.

Although growing henequen for rope is still economically viable, synthetic fibres have significantly diminished profits. This decline has not been all that devastating for Mayan peasants, as the crop never employed a great many labourers to begin with. Those who worked during its heyday on the haciendas were badly exploited. ■

YUCATÁN

the Atrium, a spacious arcaded courtyard in which the fiesta of the Virgin of Izamal takes place each 15 August. Across the Atrium is the 12-metre-high church, which is very simple in design, without much decoration. A miraculous portrait of the Virgin hangs in the church; the Virgin of Izamal is patron saint of Yucatán. The original of the portrait was brought here from Guatemala in 1558, but was destroyed by fire in 1829 and replaced with a copy.

The monastery and church were restored and spruced up for the papal visit of John Paul II in August 1993. Entry to the church is free. The best time to visit is in the morning, as it may be closed during the afternoon siesta.

In various parts of the town are remnants of the other 11 Mayan pyramids. The largest is the temple of Kinich Kakmó; all are unrestored piles of rubble.

Places to Stay & Eat

Few travellers stay the night in Izamal. The small *Hotel Kabul* (☎ (995) 4-00-08), on Calle 31, facing the main plaza, will put you up in simple but fairly clean rooms without private bath for US$16 in one bed (one or two persons), or US$19 in two beds. Next door to the hotel is the *Cocina Económica La Reina Itzalana*, where the food is cheap and filling. Directly across the square are more cheap little loncherías and also the small market area.

Getting There & Away

There are direct buses several times daily from Mérida (72 km, 1½ hours, US$3) and from Valladolid (155 km, two hours, US$4). Coming from Chichén Itzá, you must change buses at Hóctun. If you're driving from the east, turn north at Kantunil, where the Cuota (toll road) ends.

Top: Cancún, Yucatán, Mexico (TB)
Left: Ferry to Isla Mujeres, Yucatán, Mexico (GE)
Right: Chichén Itzá, Yucatán, Mexico (GE)

Top: Convento de San Antonio de Padua, Izamal, Yucatán, Mexico (TB)
Left: Colonial House, Mérida, Yucatán, Mexico (GE)
Right: Religious wares, Mérida, Yucatán, Mexico (GE)

Mérida

Population: 600,000

The capital of the state of Yucatán is a charming city of narrow streets, colonial buildings, shady parks and Mayan pride. It has been the centre of Mayan culture in Yucatán since before the conquistadors arrived; today it is the peninsula's centre of commerce as well. If Cancún is Yucatán's cash register, Mérida is Yucatán's heart and soul.

Though it is the largest city in southeastern Mexico, the commercial Mérida of furniture factories, breweries, flour mills, auto dealerships and warehouses filled with sisal products, fruit, timber, tobacco and beef, is mostly on the outskirts. At the city's heart is a colonial street grid dotted with old mansions and churches. There are lots of hotels and restaurants of every class and price range and good transportation services to any part of the peninsula and the country. Mérida can be your base for numerous excursions into the Mayan countryside which surrounds it.

If Mérida has drawbacks, they are traffic pollution and heat. Noisy buses pump clouds of noxious fumes into the air; it's unpleasant but bearable. And Yucatán's high temperatures seem even higher in this city. Many buildings catch the heat and hold it well into the evening. Even these sensory assaults will do little to dampen your enjoyment of this interesting city, however.

Mérida seems busiest with tourists in high summer (July and August), and winter (December through March).

HISTORY

The Spaniards had to work hard to conquer Yucatán. Mayan forces put up such fierce resistance to the advance of Francisco de Montejo's conquistadors in the early 1530s that Montejo returned to his base in central Mexico utterly discouraged. But his son, also named Francisco de Montejo, took up the struggle and returned to found a Spanish colony at Campeche in 1540. From this base he and his army were able to take advantage of political dissension among the Maya, conquering Tihó (now Mérida) in 1542. By the end of the decade, Yucatán was mostly under Spanish colonial rule.

When Montejo's conquistadors entered defeated Tihó, they found a major Mayan settlement of lime-mortared stone which reminded them of Roman architectural legacies in Mérida, Spain. They promptly renamed the city after its Spanish likeness and proceeded to build it into the colonial capital and centre of control. Mérida took its colonial orders directly from Spain, not from Mexico City, and Yucatán has had a distinct cultural and political identity ever since.

With the conquest of Yucatán, the indigenous people became little more than slaves. With religious redemption as their rationale, the colonial governors and church leaders built their own little empires on the backs of the Indians. Harsh rule created resentments that would later explode.

When the Mexican War of Independence ended in 1821, the Spanish colonial governor of Yucatán resigned his post and the peninsula enjoyed a brief two years as an independent nation before it finally threw in its lot with Mexico, joining the union of Mexican states in 1823.

Spanish control, harsh as it was, had prevented certain abuses of power from becoming too much of a problem in Yucatán. With colonial rule removed, local potentates were free to build vast estates, or haciendas, based on the newly introduced cultivation of sugar cane and henequen. The lot of the indigenous peoples got even worse. Though the Indians were nominally free citizens in a new republic, their hacienda bosses kept them in debt peonage.

As the hacendados grew in power and wealth, they began to fear that outside forces (the government in central Mexico, or the USA) might covet their prosperity. The

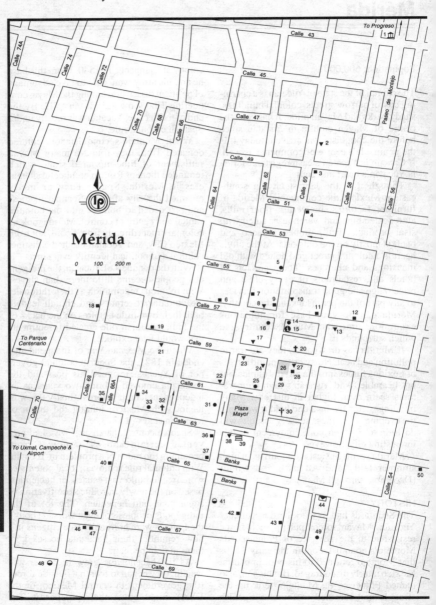

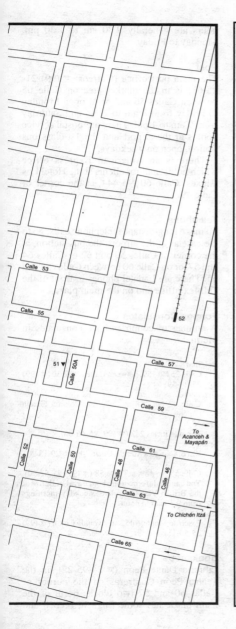

PLACES TO STAY

3 Hotel Los Aluxes
4 Hotel Trinidad Galería
6 Hotel El Castellano
7 Hotel Trinidad
9 Hotel Mérida Misión Park Plaza
11 Posada Toledo
12 Hotel Mucuy
18 Casa Mexilio
19 Hotel del Gobernador
28 Hotel Caribe
29 Gran Hotel
34 Hotel Margarita
35 Hotel Las Monjas
36 Casa de Huéspedes Peniche
37 Hotel Sevilla
40 Casa Bowen
42 Hotel México
43 Hotel Peninsular
45 Posada del Angel
46 Hotel Victoria
47 Casa Becil
50 Hotel Dolores Alba

PLACES TO EAT

2 Restaurant La Casona
8 Pop Cafetería & Restaurante Portico del Peregrino
10 Restaurant El Tucho
13 Restaurant Tikal
17 Ananda Maya
21 Lonchería Mily
22 El Louvre
23 Pizzería de Vito Corleone
24 Café-Restaurant Express
27 Restaurant Tiano's
38 Panificadora Montejo
51 Los Almendros

OTHER

1 Anthropology Museum (Palacio Cantón)
5 Parque Santa Lucia
14 Teatro Peón Contreras
15 Tourist Information Centre
16 Universidad de Yucatán
20 Iglesia de Jesús
25 Palacio de Gobierno
26 Parque Hidalgo
30 Cathedral
31 Palacio Municipal
32 Ex-Convento de las Monjas
33 Casa de los Artesanías
39 Casa de Montejo (Banamex)
41 Progreso Bus Station
44 Main Post Office
48 Terminal de Autobuses
49 Mercado Municipal
52 Railway Station

YUCATÁN

Méridan government organised armed forces and issued weapons to the soldiers, who were the same Indians being oppressed on the haciendas. Given the power to achieve their freedom, the Indians rebelled in 1847, beginning the War of the Castes.

Only Mérida and Campeche were able to hold out against the rebel forces; the rest of Yucatán came under Indian control. On the brink of surrender, the ruling class in Mérida was saved by reinforcements sent from central Mexico in exchange for Mérida's agreeing to take orders from Mexico City.

Though Yucatán is certainly part of Mexico, there is still a strong feeling of local pride in Mérida, a feeling that the Mayab (Mayan lands) are a special realm set apart from the rest of the country.

ORIENTATION

Be advised that house numbers may progress very slowly; you cannot know whether Calle 57 No 481 and Calle 56 No 544 are one block or ten blocks apart. Perhaps for this reason, addresses are usually given in this form: Calle 57 No 481 X 56 y 58 (between Calles 56 and 58).

INFORMATION
Tourist Office

There are information booths of minimal usefulness at the airport and the 1st-class bus station. Your best bet for information is the Tourist Information Centre (☎ (99) 24-92-90, 24-93-89), at the corner of Calles 60 and 57, in the south-west corner of the huge Teatro Peón Contreras, less than two blocks north of the Plaza Mayor.

Money

Casas de cambio, though they may charge a fee for changing money, offer faster, better service than banks. Try Finex (☎ (99) 24-18-42), Calle 59 No 498K, near the Hotel Caribe on Plaza Hidalgo. In addition, there are lots of banks along Calle 65 between Calles 60 and 62, the street one block behind Banamex/Palacio Montejo (that is, one block south of the Plaza Mayor). Banking

hours are generally 9.30 am to 1.30 pm, Monday to Friday.

Post

The main post office (Correos; ☎ (99) 21-25-61) is in the market area on Calle 65 between Calles 56 and 56A, open Monday to Friday from 8 am to 7 pm and Saturday from 9 am to 1 pm. There are postal service booths at the airport and the 1st-class bus station, open on weekdays.

There is an American Express office which holds mail for clients at the Hotel Los Aluxes, Calle 60 No 444, at the corner of Calle 49.

Telephone

To make long-distance telephone calls, go to the casetas at the airport, the bus station, at the corner of Calles 59 and 62 or Calles 64 and 57, or on Calle 60 between Calles 53 and 55. There are Ladatel phones in front of the TelMex office and on the main plaza.

Foreign Consulates

A number of countries have consulates in Mérida:

Belgium
  Calle 25 No 159, between Calles 28 & 30 (☎ (99) 25-29-39)
Denmark
  Calle 32 No 198 at Calle 17, Colonia Garcia Ginerés
France
  Avenida Itzaes 242 (☎ (99) 25-46-06)
Spain
  Km 6, Carretera Mérida-Uman (☎ (99) 29-15-20)
UK
  Calle 53 No 489, at Calle 58 (☎ (99) 21-67-99). You can get information about travel in Belize at the British Vice-Consulate, weekday mornings from 9.30 am to noon.
USA
  Paseo de Montejo 453, at Avenida Colón (☎ (99) 25-50-11)

Bookshops

Librería Dante Peón (☎ 24-95-22), in the Teatro Peón Contreras, at the corner of Calles 60 and 57 two blocks north of the main plaza, has some English, French and

German books as well as Spanish ones. It's open seven days a week. At the south-west corner of Parque Hidalgo, half a block north of the Plaza Mayor, is Hollywood (☎ 21-36-19), Calle 60 No 496, which has a selection of international newspapers, magazines and some novels and travel guides.

PLAZA MAYOR

The most logical place to start a tour of Mérida is in the main plaza, or Plaza Mayor. This was the religious and social centre of ancient Tihó. Under the Spaniards it was the Plaza de Armas, or parade ground, laid out by Francisco de Montejo the Younger. Surrounded by harmonious colonial buildings, its carefully pruned laurel trees provide welcome shade for those who come here to relax or socialise. On Sunday, the main plaza's adjoining roadways are off limits to traffic and hundreds of Méridans take their paseo in this municipal park.

Cathedral

On the east side of the plaza, on the site of a Mayan temple, is Mérida's huge, hulking, severe cathedral, begun in 1561 and completed in 1598. Some of the stone from the Mayan temple was used in the cathedral's construction.

Walk through one of the three doors in the Baroque façade and into the sanctuary. The great crucifix at the east end of the nave is Cristo de la Unidad, Christ of Unity, a symbol of reconciliation between those of Spanish and Mayan stock. To your right over the south door is a painting of Tutul Xiú, *cacique* (local ruler) of the town of Maní, paying his respects to his ally Francisco de Montejo at Tihó (Montejo and Xiú jointly defeated the Cocoms; Xiú converted to Christianity and his descendants still live in Mérida).

Look in the small chapel to the left (north) of the principal altar for Mérida's most famous religious artefact, a statue of Jesus called Cristo de las Ampollas, or the Christ of the Blisters. Local legend has it that this statue was carved from a tree in the town of Ichmul. The tree, hit by lightning, suppos-

edly burned for an entire night yet showed no sign of fire. The statue carved from the tree was placed in the local church where it alone is said to have survived the fiery destruction of the church, though it was blackened and blistered from the heat. It was moved to the Mérida cathedral in 1645.

The rest of the church's interior is plain, its rich decoration having been stripped by angry peasants at the height of anticlerical feeling during the Mexican Revolution.

Palacio de Gobierno

On the north side of the plaza, the Palacio de Gobierno houses the state of Yucatán's executive government offices; it was built in 1892 on the site of the palace of the colonial governors. Make your way past the armed guards to see the historical murals painted by local artist Fernando Castro Pacheco. The murals were completed in 1978 after 25 years of work. They were restored in 1993.

In vivid colours the murals portray a symbolic history of the Maya and their interaction with the Spanish. Over the stairwell is a painting of Mayan sacred corn, the 'ray of sun from the gods'. Overall, the murals suggest that despite the oppressive intrusion of the Europeans, the spirit of Mayan culture lives on. The palace is open every day from 8 am to 8 pm.

On Sunday at 11 am, there's usually a concert (jazz, classical pops, traditional Yucatecan) in the Salón de la Historia of the Palacio de Gobierno.

Palacio Municipal

Facing the cathedral across the square, the Palacio Municipal (Town Hall) is topped by a clock tower. Originally built in 1542, it has twice been refurbished, in the 1730s and the 1850s. Today the building also serves as the venue for performances of Yucatecan dances (especially the jarana) and music at the weekly Vaquería Regional, a regional festival held to celebrate the branding of the cattle on haciendas. Performances are on Monday evenings at 9 pm.

Every Sunday at 1 pm, the city sponsors a

YUCATÁN

re-enactment of a colourful mestizo wedding at the Palacio Municipal.

Casa de Montejo

From its construction in 1549 until the 1970s, the mansion on the south side of the plaza was occupied by the Montejo family. Sometimes called the Palacio de Montejo, it was built at the command of the conqueror of Mérida, Francisco de Montejo the Younger.

These days the great house shelters a branch of Banamex and you can look around inside whenever the bank is open (usually from 9 am to 1.30 pm, Monday to Friday). If the bank is closed, content yourself with a close look at the Plateresque façade, where triumphant conquistadors with halberds hold their feet on the necks of generic barbarians (who are not Maya, but the association is inescapable). Also gazing across the plaza from the façade are busts of Montejo the Elder, his wife and his daughter. The armorial shields are those of the Montejo family.

CALLE 60

A walk north from the Plaza Mayor along Calle 60 takes you past many of Mérida's churches, parks, hotels and restaurants and brings you finally to the beginning of Paseo de Montejo.

A block north of the main plaza is the shady refuge of the **Parque Hidalgo** (sometimes called the Parque Cepeda Peraza after a 19th-century general who collected a significant library).

At the far end of the park, several restaurants, including Café El Mesón and Tiano's, offer alfresco sipping and dining. Tiano's often has a marimba band in the evening, enjoyable whether you eat there or just sit nearby. The city sponsors free marimba concerts here on Sunday mornings at 11.30 am as well.

Just to the north of the parque rises the 17th-century **Iglesia de Jesús**, also called the Iglesia El Tercer Orden. Built by the Jesuits in 1618, it is the surviving edifice in a complex of Jesuit buildings which once filled the entire city block. Always interested

in education, the Jesuits founded schools which later gave birth to the Universidad de Yucatán, just a few steps farther to the north. General Cepeda Peraza's library of 15,000 volumes is housed in a building behind the church.

Directly in front of the church is the little **Parque de la Madre**, sometimes called the Parque Morelos. The modern madonna and child statue, which is a common fixture of town squares in this nation of high birth rates, is a copy of a statue by Lenoir which stands in the Jardin du Luxembourg in Paris.

Just north of the Parque de la Madre you confront the enormous bulk of the great **Teatro Peón Contreras**, built from 1900 to 1908 during Mérida's henequen heyday. Designed by Italian architect Enrico Deserti, it boasts a main staircase of Carrara marble, a dome with frescos by Italian artists imported for the purpose and the Tourist Information Centre, in its south-west corner.

The main entrance to the theatre is at the corner of Calles 60 and 57. A gallery inside the entrance often holds exhibits by local painters and photographers; hours are usually 9 am to 2 pm and 5 to 9 pm Monday to Friday, 9 am to 2 pm Saturday and Sunday. To see the grand theatre itself, you'll have to attend a performance. Perhaps the best and most interesting performance to attend is Yucatán y sus Raices (Yucatán & its Roots), a ballet folklorico show sponsored by the university and held each evening at 9 pm in the Teatro Peón Contreras.

Across Calle 60 from the Teatro Peón Contreras is the entrance to the main building of the **Universidad de Yucatán**. Though the Jesuits provided education to Yucatán's youth for centuries, the modern university was not established until the 19th century, when the job was done by Governor Felipe Carrillo Puerto and General Manuel Cepeda Peraza. The story of the university's founding is rendered graphically in a mural done in 1961 by Manuel Lizama. Walk in and ask for directions to the mural.

The central courtyard of the university building is the scene of concerts and folk performances every Tuesday or Friday evening at 9 pm (check with the Tourist Information Centre for performance dates and times).

A block north of the university, at the intersection of Calles 60 and 55, is the **Parque Santa Lucia**, with arcades on the north and west sides. When Mérida was a lot smaller, this was where travellers would get into or out of the stagecoaches which bumped over the rough roads of the peninsula, linking towns and villages with the provincial capital.

Today the park is the venue for orchestral performances of Yucatecan music on Thursday evenings at 9 pm and Sunday mornings at 11 am. Also here on Sunday at 11 am is the Bazar de Artesanías, the local handicrafts market.

To reach the Paseo de Montejo, walk 3½ blocks north along Calle 60 from the Parque Santa Lucia to Calle 47. Turn right on Calle 47 and walk two blocks to the paseo, on your left.

PASEO DE MONTEJO

The Paseo de Montejo was an attempt by Mérida's 19th-century city planners to create a wide European-style grand boulevard, similar to Mexico City's Paseo de la Reforma or Paris's Avenue des Champs-Elysées. Since this is Mérida, not Paris, the boulevard is more modest. But it is still a beautiful swath of green and open space in an urban conglomeration of stone and concrete.

As Yucatán has always looked upon itself as distinct from the rest of Mexico, the peninsula's powerful hacendados and commercial barons maintained good business and social contacts with Europe, concentrating on these to balance the necessary relations with Mexico City. Europe's architectural and social influence can be seen along the paseo in the surviving fine mansions built by wealthy families around the turn of the century.

Many other mansions have been torn down to make way for the banks, hotels and other high visibility establishments which always want prime places on the grand boulevards of the world. Most of the remaining mansions are north of Calle 37, which is three blocks north of the Anthropology Museum. Sidewalk cafés and restaurants south of Calle 39 can provide sustenance during your stroll along the avenue.

Two and a half blocks north along the paseo from Calle 47 brings you to the splendid white Palacio Cantón, home of Mérida's Anthropology Museum.

Anthropology Museum

The great white palace at the corner of Paseo de Montejo and Calle 43 is the Museo Regional de Antropología de Yucatán, housed in the Palacio Cantón. The great mansion was designed by Enrico Deserti, also responsible for the Teatro Peón Contreras. Construction took place from 1909 to 1911. When it was completed, the mansion's owner, General Francisco Cantón Rosado (1833-1917) moved in and lived here for a brief six years before he headed off to that great mansion in the sky.

After General Cantón's death his palace served as a school, as the official residence of the governors of the state of Yucatán and now as the Anthropology Museum. No building in Mérida exceeds it in splendour or pretension.

Admission to the museum costs US$5; free Sunday. It's open Monday to Saturday from 8 am to 8 pm, Sunday from 8 am to 2 pm. The museum shop is open from 8 am to 3 pm (2 pm on Sunday). Labels on the museum's exhibits are in Spanish only.

Exhibits on Mayan culture include explanations of the forehead-flattening which was done to beautify babies and other practices such as sharpening teeth and implanting them with tiny jewels. If you plan to visit archaeological sites near Mérida, you can study the many exhibits here – lavishly illustrated with plans and photographs – which cover the great Mayan cities of Mayapán, Uxmal and Chichén Itzá, as well as lesser sites.

PARQUE CENTENARIO

On the western edge of the city, 12 blocks from the Plaza Mayor, lies the large, verdant

Parque Centenario, bordered by Avenida de los Itzaes, the highway to the airport and Campeche. There's a zoo in the park which specialises in exhibiting the fauna of Yucatán. To get there, take a bus westwards along Calle 61 or 65.

FESTIVALS

Prior to Lent in February or March, Carnival features colourful costumes and nonstop festivities. It is celebrated with greater vigour in Mérida than anywhere else in Yucatán. During the first two weeks in October, the Christ of the Blisters (Cristo de las Ampollas) statue in the cathedral is venerated with processions.

PLACES TO STAY

Most of the cheap and middle-range hotels are within about six blocks of the plaza; the largest concentration of luxury hotels is along the Paseo de Montejo, 12 to 16 long blocks from the plaza. All Mérida hotels are expensive for what you get.

PLACES TO STAY – BOTTOM END

Prices for basic but suitable rooms in Mérida range from about US$15 to US$30 for a small but clean double room with fan and private shower only a short walk from the plaza. All hotels should provide purified drinking water, usually at no extra charge. (Sometimes the water bottles are not readily evident, so ask for agua purificada.)

Hotel Las Monjas (☎ (99) 28-66-32), Calle 66A No 509 at Calle 63, is one of the best deals in town. All 28 rooms in this little place have ceiling fans and running water (sinks or private baths with hot and cold water). Rooms are tiny and most are dark, but they are clean. Room No 12 is the best, quiet because it's at the back, light and cool because its windows provide good cross-ventilation. The price is US$14 to US$16 a double with fan, US$19 with air-con.

Hotel Margarita (☎ (99) 23-72-32), Calle 66 No 506, between Calles 61 and 63, is a favourite with foreigners because of its low price, convenient location and clean (if small) rooms with fan and running water for US$12 a single, US$14 a double (one bed) or US$17 (in two beds), US$20 a triple, US$25 a quad. Air-con is in some rooms for a few dollars more.

Hotel Mucuy (☎ (99) 28-51-93; fax 23-78-01), Calle 57 No 481, between Calles 56 and 58, has been serving thrifty travellers for more than a decade. It's a family-run place with 26 tidy rooms on two floors facing a long, narrow garden courtyard. Sra Ofelia Comin and her daughter Ofelia speak English; Sr Alfredo Comin understands it. Rooms with ceiling fan and private shower cost US$15/18/22 a single/double/triple.

Casa Bowen (☎ (99) 28-61-09), Calle 66 No 521B, near Calle 65, is a large old Mérida house converted to a hotel. The narrow courtyard has a welcome swath of green grass. Rooms are simple, even bare, and some are dark and soiled, but all have fans and showers for US$17 a double with fan, US$46 with air-con.

Casa Becil (☎ (99) 24-67-64), Calle 67 No 550C, between Calles 66 and 68 near the bus station, is a house with a high-ceilinged sitting room/lobby and small guest rooms at the back. With private shower and fan, the price is US$18 to US$22 a double. The family management tries hard to please.

Hotel Sevilla (☎ (99) 23-83-60), Calle 62 No 511, at the corner of Calle 65, offers a whisper of faded elegance, but most rooms are musty and dark. The price is not too bad: US$15/18/22 for a single/double/triple.

Hotel Trinidad (☎ (99) 23-20-33), Calle 62 No 464 between Calles 55 and 57, is decorated with modern Mexican paintings and the tiny courtyard is filled with plants. The hotel could use some paint. The guest rooms are all different, and range in price from US$20 for a small double with sink to US$43 a double for a large room with private bath and air-conditioning.

The Trinidad's sister hotel, *Hotel Trinidad Galería* (☎ (99) 23-24-63; fax 24-23-19), Calle 60 No 456, at the corner of Calle 51, was once an appliance showroom. There's a small swimming pool, a bar, art gallery and antique shop as well as presentable rooms with fans and private showers renting for similar rates.

Hotel Peninsular (☎ (99) 23-69-96), Calle 58 No 519 between Calles 65 and 67, is in the midst of the market district. You enter down a long corridor to find a neat restaurant and a maze of rooms, most with windows opening onto the interior spaces: it costs US$16/19/24 a single/double/triple with private bath and fan; add a few dollars for air-con.

Posada del Angel (☎ (99) 23-27-54), Calle 67 No 535 between Calles 66 and 68, is two blocks north-east of the bus station and is quieter than most other hotels in this neighbourhood. It's modern and convenient, and has a restaurant, but is a bit expensive at US$28 a double, US$34 with air-con.

PLACES TO STAY – MIDDLE
Mérida's middle-range places provide surprising levels of comfort for what you pay. Most charge US$35 to US$70 for a double room with air-conditioning, ceiling fan and private shower; and most have restaurants, bars and little swimming pools.

Hotel Dolores Alba (☎ (99) 21-37-45), Calle 63 No 464, between Calles 52 and 54, 3½ blocks east of the plaza, is one of the top choices in Mérida because of its pleasant courtyard, beautiful swimming pool and clean, comfortable rooms for US$30 a double (slightly more for air-conditioning).

Hotel Caribe (☎ (99) 24-90-22; fax 24-87-33), Calle 59 No 500, at the corner of Calle 60 on the Parque Hidalgo, is a favourite with visiting foreigners because of its central location, its rooftop pool, and its two restaurants. Most rooms have air-con and range in price from US$33 for a small single with fan to US$75 for a large double with air-con.

Gran Hotel (☎ (99) 24-77-30; fax 24-76-22), Calle 60 No 496, between Calles 59 and 61, is on the southern side of the Parque Hidalgo. Corinthian columns support terraces on three levels around the verdant central courtyard and fancy wrought-iron and carved wood decoration evoke a past age. All 28 rooms have air-con and cost US$46 to US$90 a double.

Casa Mexilio (☎ & fax (99) 28-25-05), Calle 68 No 495, between Calles 59 and 57, is Mérida's most charming pension, a beautifully restored and decorated house with comfortable rooms for US$60 a double, breakfast included.

Posada Toledo (☎ (99) 23-16-90; fax 23-22-56), Calle 58 No 487 at Calle 57, three blocks north-east of the main plaza, has a courtyard with vines, a dining room straight out of the 19th century and small, modernised rooms with fan or air-con overpriced at US$36/46 a single/double.

Hotel del Gobernador (☎ (99) 23-71-33), Calle 59 No 535, at Calle 66, is an attractive, modern hotel favoured by Mexican business executives. The price is good for what you get: US$60 to US$70 a double.

PLACES TO STAY – TOP END
Top-end hotels charge between US$70 and US$150 for a double room with air-con. Each hotel has a restaurant, bar, swimming pool and probably other services like a newsstand, hairdresser, travel agency and nightclub.

Holiday Inn Mérida (☎ (99) 25-68-77; in the USA (800) 465-4329), Avenida Colón 498 at Calle 60, half a block off the Paseo de Montejo behind the US Consulate General, is Mérida's one of Mérida's most luxurious establishments. Its 213 air-con rooms cost US$140.

For all-round quality, convenience and price, try the *Hotel Los Aluxes* (☎ (99) 24-21-99; fax 23-38-58; toll-free in USA (800) 782-8395), Calle 60 No 444, at Calle 49. This relatively new 109-room hotel has all the services, plus modern architecture and an intriguing name: *aluxes* (ah-LOO-shess) are the Mayan equivalent of leprechauns. Rates are US$100 a single/double, US$120 a triple.

The *Hotel Mérida Misión Park Plaza* (☎ (99) 23-9500; fax 23-76-65), Calle 60 No 491, at Calle 57, is half modern and half colonial in decor, comfortable without being particularly charming. Rates for the 150 air-conditioned rooms are US$85 for a single or double.

Hotel El Castellano (☎ (99) 23-01-00), Calle 57 No 513, between Calles 62 and 64, is a favourite with business travellers and tourists. Its 170 rooms cost US$82 for a single/double, US$125 for a triple/suite.

Hotel El Conquistador (☎ (99) 26-21-55; fax 26-88-29), Paseo de Montejo No 458, at Calle 35, has 90 rooms in a modern nine-storey structure. Rates are US$100 for a single/double, US$122 a triple.

The 90-room *Hotel Montejo Palace* (☎ (99) 24-76-44; fax 28-03-88), Paseo de Montejo 483-C and the older *Hotel Paseo de Montejo* (☎ (99) 23-90-33), Paseo de Montejo 482, face one another across the Paseo at Calle 41. Both hotels are under the same management and charge US$66 to US$100 a double.

Mérida's newest and most luxurious hotel is the 17-storey, 300-room *Hyatt Regency Mérida* (☎ (99) 25-67-22; fax 25-70-02), Avenida Colón and Calle 60, 100 metres west of Paseo de Montejo and about two km north of the Plaza Mayor. Rooms with all the comforts cost US$175 to US$195.

PLACES TO EAT

Mérida's restaurants are less numerous than Cancún's, but they are also less hyped, less expensive and more varied in cuisine. In Cancún it's expected that you want expensive lobster and shrimp at every meal; in Mérida you can order Yucatecan, Mexican, American, Italian, French, even Lebanese. The best restaurants are only moderately priced and the market eateries are cheap and good.

PLACES TO EAT – BOTTOM END

Walk two blocks south from the main plaza to Calle 67, turn left (east) and walk another two or three blocks to the market. Continue straight up the ramping flight of steps at the end of Calle 67. As you ascend, you'll pass the touristy Mercado de Artesanías on your left. At the top of the ramp, turn left and you'll see a row of market eateries with names like *El Chimecito, La Temaxeña, Saby, Mimi, Saby y El Palon, La Socorrito, Reina Beatriz* and so forth. Comidas corridas

here are priced from US$2.75 to US$4, big main-course platters of beef, fish or chicken with vegetables and rice or potatoes go for US$2.50 to US$4. The market eateries are open from early morning until late afternoon every day.

El Louvre (☎ 21-32-71), Calle 62 No 499, corner of Calle 61 at the north-west corner of the Plaza Mayor, has a loyal local clientele. The comida corrida costs US$6, though it's not what you'd call a gourmet treat. *Cafeteria Erick's*, just up the street, is even cheaper.

The *Lonchería Mily*, Calle 59 No 520 between 64 and 66, opens at 7 am and serves cheap breakfasts (US$2), a two-course comida corrida (US$3) and cheap sandwiches. It closes at 5 pm, and is closed all day Sunday.

For take-away food, try the *Pizzería de Vito Corleone* (☎ 23-68-46), Calle 59 No 508, at 62. This tiny eatery suffers from loud street noise, so many customers take their pizzas to the Parque Hidalgo instead. Pizzas are priced from US$4 to US$11, depending upon ingredients. Vegetarian varieties are available.

The best cheap breakfasts can be had by picking up a selection of pan dulces (sweet rolls and breads) from one of Mérida's several *panificadoras* (bakeries). A convenient one is the *Panificadora Montejo* at the corner of Calles 62 and 63, at the south-west corner of the main plaza. Pick up a metal tray and tongs, select the pastries you want and hand the tray to a clerk who will bag them and quote a price, usually US$2 or so for a full bag.

PLACES TO EAT – MIDDLE

Those willing to spend a bit more money can enjoy the pleasant restaurants of the Parque Hidalgo at the corner of Calles 59 and 60.

The least expensive, yet one of the most pleasant restaurants here, is the *Cafetería El Mesón* (☎ 21-92-32) in the Hotel Caribe. Meat, fish and chicken dishes are priced from US$5 to US$10, but sandwiches and burgers are less. El Mesón is open from 7 am to 10.30 pm.

Right next to El Mesón is *Tiano's* (☎ 23-71-18), Calle 59 No 498, a fancier version of El Mesón. In the evening the restaurant often hires a marimba group to entertain its patrons as well as the dozens of hangers-on in the square. Have sopa de lima, puntas de filete, dessert and a drink and your bill might be US$16. You can eat for less, though. Tiano's is supposedly open 24 hours a day, though you'll see it locked up tight from about midnight to 7 am.

Across Calle 60, facing the Parque Hidalgo, is an old Mérida standard, the *Café-Restaurant Express* (☎ 21-37-38), Calle 60 No 502, south of Calle 59. Busy with a loyal crowd of regulars and foreigners, Express is a bustling and noisy meeting place, but the food is okay, service is fast and prices are fair. Hours are 7 am to midnight daily.

For vegetarian meals, try *Amaro* (☎ 28-24-51), Calle 59 No 507, between Calles 60 and 62, open daily from 9 am to 10 pm. Yucatecan meals are served, as is Yucatecan beer, along with a few vegetarian dishes.

Pop Cafetería (☎ 21-68-44), Calle 57 between 60 and 62, is plain, modern, bright, air-conditioned, and named for the first month of the 18-month Mayan calendar. The menu is limited but adequate, with hamburgers, spaghetti and main-course platters such as chicken in mole sauce for US$4 to US$10. Breakfasts cost from US$3 to US$4.

Restaurant Tikal, Calle 57 No 485, next to the Hotel Flamingo, is small, nicely decorated, and moderate in price. Try the filling sopa de lima.

PLACES TO EAT – TOP END

Among the city's most dependable dining places is the *Restaurante Portico del Peregrino* (☎ 21-68-44), Calle 57 No 501, between Calles 60 and 62, right next to Pop. This 'Pilgrim's Refuge' consists of several pleasant, almost elegant traditional dining rooms (some are air-conditioned) around a small courtyard replete with colonial artefacts. Yucatecan dishes are the forte, but you'll find many continental dishes as well. Lunch (noon to 3 pm) and dinner (6 to 11 pm) are served every day and your bill for a full meal might be US$18 to US$24 per person.

La Casona (☎ 23-83-48), Calle 60 No 434 between Calles 47 and 49, is a fine old city house now serving as a restaurant. Dining tables are set out on a portico next to a small but lush garden; dim lighting lends an air of romance. Italian dishes crowd the menu, with a few Yucatecan plates to top it off. Plan to spend anywhere from US$12 to US$20 per person. La Casona is open every evening for dinner; on weekends, you might want to make reservations.

Los Almendros (☎ 21-28-51), Calle 50A No 493 between Calles 57 and 59, facing the Plaza de Mejorada, specialises in authentic Yucatecan country cuisine such as pavo relleno negro (grilled turkey with hot peppered pork stuffing), papadzul (tacos filled with egg smothered in a fiery sauce), sopa de lima (chicken broth with lime and tortillas) or Los Almendros' most famous dish, the zingy onion-and-tomato pork dish poc-chuc. Full meals cost US$10 to US$15. Some people are disappointed at Los Almendros because they go expecting delicacies; this is hearty food.

How about entertainment as you dine Yucatán-style? The *Restaurant El Tucho* (☎ 24-23-23), Calle 60 No 482 between 57 and 55, features Yucatecan specialties in a dining room fashioned to look like an enormous na, with thatched roof and bamboo walls. It's a place where the locals come for eating, drinking and singing, from 6 pm to midnight, seven days a week. Most main courses cost US$8 and a full meal can be yours for US$16 or US$18. Beware of the high prices for drinks.

ENTERTAINMENT

Though many visitors choose to enjoy a long dinner with drinks and conversation, or just to relax in the Plaza Mayor, others like to spend the evening at concerts or the cinema.

Concerts & Folklore

Proud of its cultural legacy and attuned to the benefits of tourism, the city of Mérida offers nightly folkloric and musical events in parks and historic buildings, put on by local performers of considerable skill. Admission is free to city-sponsored events. Check with the tourist office for the schedule.

Cinemas

Many English films, some of fairly recent release, are screened in Mérida with Spanish subtitles. Buy your tickets (usually about US$2) before showtime and well in advance on weekends. The popular *Cine Cantarell*, Calle 60 No 488, next door to the Restaurant Express, and *Cine Fantasio*, facing the Parque Hidalgo between the Gran Hotel and Hotel Caribe, are convenient. There's also the *Cine Premier*, at the corner of Calles 57 and 62 and the *Cinema 59*, Calle 59 between Calles 68 and 70.

THINGS TO BUY

From standard shirts and blouses to Mayan exotica, Mérida is *the* place on the peninsula to shop. Purchases you might want to consider include traditional Mayan clothing such as the colourful women's embroidered blouse called a huipil, a Panama hat woven from palm fibres, local craft items and of course the wonderfully comfortable Yucatecan hammock which holds you gently in a comfortable cotton web.

Guard your valuables extra carefully in the market area. Watch for pickpockets, purse-snatchers and slash-and-grab thieves.

Mérida's main market, the Mercado Municipal Lucas do Gálvez, is bound by Calles 56 and 56A at Calle 67, four blocks south-east of the Plaza Mayor. The market building is more or less next door to the city's main post office (Correos) and telegraph office, at the corner of Calles 65 and 56. The surrounding streets are all part of the large market district, lined with shops selling everything one might need.

The Bazar de Artesanías, Calle 67 at the corner of Calle 56A, is set up to attract tourists and their dollars. You should have a look at the stuff here, then compare the goods and prices with independent shops outside the Bazar.

Handicrafts

The place to go for high-quality craft and art items is the Casa de los Artesanías Estado de Yucatán on Calle 63 between 64 and 66; look for the doorway marked 'Dirección de Desarrollo Artesanal DIF Yucatán'. It's open Monday to Friday from 8 am to 8 pm, Saturday from 8 am to 6 pm, closed Sunday. This is a government-supported marketing effort for local artisans. The selection of crafts is very good, quality usually high and prices reasonable.

You can also check out locally made crafts at the Museo Regional de Artesanías on Calle 59 between Calles 50 and 48. The work on display is superlative, but the items for sale are not as good. Admission is free and it's open from Tuesday to Saturday from 8 am to 8 pm and Sunday 9 am to 2 pm, closed Monday.

Panama Hats

Panama hats are woven from jipijapa palm leaves in caves and workshops in which the temperature and humidity are carefully controlled, as humid conditions keep the fibres pliable when the hat is being made. Once blocked and exposed to the relatively drier air outside, the hat is surprisingly resilient and resistant to crushing. The Campeche town of Becal is the centre of the hat-weaving trade, but you can buy good examples of the hatmaker's art here in Mérida.

The best quality hats have a very fine, close weave of slender fibres. The coarser the weave, the lower the price should be. Prices range from a few dollars for a hat of basic quality to US$25 or more for top quality.

A store famous for its Panama hats is appropriately named Becal and is located at Calle 56 No 522. Another is El Becaleño, Calle 65 No 483, at the corner of Calle 56A, very near the post office. A third is La Casa de los Jipis, Calle 56 No 526, near Calle 65.

Hammocks

You will be approached by pedlars on the street wanting to sell you hammocks about every hour throughout your stay in Mérida. Check the quality of the hammocks on offer carefully. (See the aside on hammocks for more information.)

You can save yourself a lot of trouble by shopping at a hammock store with a good reputation. La Poblana (☎ 21-65-03), at Calle 65 No 492 between Calles 58 and 60, has a good reputation of long standing. Some travellers report slightly cheaper prices for good quality at El Aguacate, Calle 58 No 604 at the corner of Calle 73. El Campesino at Calle 58 No 548 between Calles 69 and 71 is even cheaper.

It's interesting to venture out to the nearby village of Tixcocob to watch hammocks being woven. The bus runs regularly from the Progreso bus station south of the main plaza at Calle 62 No 524, between Calles 65 and 67.

GETTING THERE & AWAY
Air

Mérida's modern airport is several km southwest of the centre off Highway 180 (Avenida de los Itzaes). There are car rental desks there. A Tourism Information office can help with questions and hotel reservations.

Most international flights to Mérida are connections through Mexico City or Cancún; the only nonstop international services are Aeroméxico's two daily flights from Miami and Aviateca's flights to Guatemala City. Domestic flights are operated mostly by smaller regional airlines, with a few flights by Aeroméxico and Mexicana.

Aerocaribe (☎ (99) 24-95-00, 23-00-02), Paseo de Montejo 476A, flies between Mérida and Cancún (morning and evening flights, US$75 one way, US$110 round-trip excursion), Chetumal, Mexico City, Oaxaca, Tuxtla Gutiérrez (for San Cristóbal de las Casas), Veracruz and Villahermosa.

Hammocks

In the sticky heat of Yucatán, most locals prefer sleeping in a hammock, where the air can circulate around them, rather than in a bed. The fine strings of Yucatecan hammocks make them supremely comfortable. Yucatecan hammocks are normally woven from strong nylon or cotton string and dyed in various colours; there are also natural, undyed versions.

Yucatán hammocks come in several widths. From smallest to largest, the names generally used are {sencillo} (about 50 pairs of end strings, US$12), {doble} (100 pairs, US$15 to US$25), {matrimonial} (about 150 pairs, US$25 to US$35) and {matrimonial especial} or {quatro cajas} (175 pairs or more, US$35 and up). You must check to be sure that you're really getting the width that you are paying for.

You will be approached by pedlars on the street wanting to sell you hammocks about every hour throughout your stay. Pedlars may quote low prices, but the quality of street-sold hammocks is mediocre at best. Check the particular hammock very carefully.

Look closely at the string. It should be sturdy and tightly and evenly spun. Check the end loops which should be fairly large and tightly wrapped in string. Many hammocks are made for sleepers of Mayan stature (ie, short). To make sure you get a hammock long enough for you, hold the hammock at the point where the end strings join the main body of the hammock; raise your hand as high as your head; the other end of the body of the hammock shoudl extend at least to the ground. In other words, the body of the hammock (not counting the end strings) should be as long as you are tall.

Open the hammock and look at the weave, which should be even, with few mistakes. Watch out for dirty patches and stains. Check the width. Any hammock looks very wide at first glance, but a matrimonial especial should be truly enormous, at least as wide as it is long and probably wider.

If you intend to sleep in a place without insect protection, be sure to buy one of the long tube-shaped mosquito nets to hang around your hammock. ■

YUCATÁN

Aerolineas Bonanza (☎ (99) 28-04-96, 24-62-28), Calle 56A No 579, between Calles 67 and 69, flies round trips twice daily from Mérida to Chetumal and once daily to Ciudad del Carmen.

Aeroméxico (☎ (99) 27-95-66, 27-92-77), Paseo de Montejo 460, has a few flights as well.

Aviacsa (☎ (99) 26-32-53, 26-39-54; fax 26-90-87), at the airport, flies nonstop to Cancún and Villahermosa, and direct to Tuxtla Gutiérrez, the airline's home base. They also have routes linking Tuxtla with Chetumal, Mexico City, Oaxaca and Tapachula.

Aviateca (☎ (99) 24-43-54) at the airport, flies to Tikal and Guatemala City several times a week.

Litoral (☎ toll-free (91-800) 2-90-20), based in Veracruz, flies to Ciudad del Carmen, Veracruz and Monterrey.

Mexicana (☎ (99) 24-66-33), Calle 58 No 500 has nonstop flights to and from Havana, Cancún and Mexico City.

Bus

The Terminal de Autobuses operated by the Unión de Camioneros de Yucatán is on Calle 69 between 68 and 70, about six blocks south-west of the main plaza. This is the main – though not the only – bus station in the city. If you're arriving from points east such as Cancún, Valladolid or Chichén Itzá, your Autobuses de Oriente Mérida-Puerto Juárez bus might make a stop, or even terminate the journey, at its garage on Calle 50 between Calles 65 and 67. The garage is six blocks east of the Plaza Mayor and about 12 blocks east of the Terminal de Autobuses.

At the Terminal de Autobuses, you'll find a bank, telegraph office, travel agency, Yucatán state tourism office, and Ladatel long-distance telephones.

A dozen different companies use the Terminal de Autobuses. Each company specialises in services to a certain part of the region or the country, but some companies' territories overlap. Shop around a bit before you buy your ticket, as fares, travel times and comfort can vary from one company to the next. Here's a quick rundown on the companies (their abbreviated name appears after the company name):

Autobuses de Oriente (ADO) – long-haul 1st-class routes to Campeche, Palenque, Villahermosa, Veracruz and Mexico City

Autotransportes Peninsulares (A Peninsulares) – frequent 1st-class buses to Chetumal

Autotransportes de Oriente Mérida-Puerto Juárez (A de O M-PJ) – frequent buses between Mérida and Cancún stopping at Chichén Itzá, Valladolid and Puerto Juárez (for Isla Mujeres boats); they also run buses to Tizimin and to Playa del Carmen (for Cozumel boats)

Autotransportes del Sur (A del Sur) – frequent buses to Uxmal, Kabah and Campeche and one bus a day to Villahermosa

Autotransportes del Caribe (A del Caribe) – nine buses daily to Ticul; also 1st and 2nd-class buses to Felipe Carrillo Puerto, Bacalar, Chetumal, Tulum and Akumal

Autotransportes del Sureste en Yucatán (A del Sureste) – one bus daily to Palenque and one to Tuxtla Gutiérrez

Expresso de Oriente – there are luxury buses Mérida-Valladolid-Cancún-Playa de Carmen-Tulum

Here's information on trips to and from Mérida; all buses are daily and all times are by 1st-class bus (2nd class may be slower):

Akumal – 350 km, six to seven hours; three 2nd-class buses daily by A de O M-PJ and three by A del Caribe

Bacalar – 420 km, 8½ hours; four 1st-class buses (US$12), four 2nd-class buses (US$10) by A del Caribe

Campeche – 195 km (short route via Becal), three hours; 250 km (long route via Uxmal), four hours; 26 1st-class buses (US$5) by ADO; 13 2nd-class buses (US$4) by A del Sur

Cancún – 320 km, 5½ to 6 hours; almost every 30 minutes 1st-class (US$8) by A de O M-PJ; 2nd-class buses (US$7) on the hour from 5 am to midnight (except no buses at 4, 7, 8, 9 and 10 pm) by A de O M-PJ; hourly deluxe buses (US$12) from 6 am to midnight by Expresso de Oriente

Chetumal – 456 km, 8 to 9 hours; seven 1st-class buses (US$12) by A Peninsulares and six 1st-class buses (US$12) by A del Caribe; four 2nd-class buses (US$10) by A del Caribe

Chichén Itzá – 116 km, 2½ hours; many 1st-class (US$6) and 2nd-class buses (US$5) by A de O M-PJ heading for Valladolid, Cancún, Playa del Carmen, etc. A special round-trip excursion bus by A de O M-PJ departs from Mérida at 8.45 am and returns from Chichén Itzá at 3 pm.

Felipe Carrillo Puerto – 310 km, 5½ to six hours; two 1st-class buses (US$9) by A del Caribe; others of this line may stop there as well. One 2nd-class bus (US$7) by A de O M-PJ.

Kabah – 101 km, two hours; six 1st-class buses (US$1.85) by A del Sur

Mexico City – 1550 km, 28 hours; six 1st-class buses (US$40) by ADO

Palenque – 556 km, 10 or 11 hours; one 1st-class bus (US$10) by A del Sureste directly to Palenque; some 1st-class ADO buses stop at Palenque as well. Many more will drop you at Catazajá, the main highway junction 27 km to the north of the town, from which you can hitchhike to the town.

Playa del Carmen – 385 km, seven hours; six 1st-class buses (US$6.50) and six 2nd-class buses (US$10) by A de O M-PJ

Progreso – leaves from another terminal; see below

Ticul – 85 km, 1½ hours; nine 2nd-class buses (US$2) by A del Caribe

Tizimin – 210 km, four hours; three 1st-class buses (US$5.50) by A de O M-PJ; or take a bus to Valladolid and change there for Tizimin

Tulum – 320 km, six hours; three 2nd-class buses (US$10) via Cobá by A del Caribe; three 2nd-class buses (US$11) via Cancún by A de O M-PJ take two hours longer

Tuxtla Gutiérrez – 1296 km, 20 hours; one 1st-class bus (US$23) by A del Sureste, or take a bus to Villahermosa and change there for Tuxtla

Uxmal – 80 km, 1½ hours; eight 2nd-class buses (US$2) by A del Sur, or take a bus bound for Campeche or beyond by the inland (longer) route and get off at Uxmal

Villahermosa – 700 km, 10 hours; 13 1st-class buses (US$17) by ADO; one 2nd-class bus (US$15) by A del Sur

If you take an all-night bus, don't put anything valuable in the overhead racks, as there have been several reports of gear being stolen at night.

For buses to Progreso and the ruins at Dzibilchaltún, go to the Progreso bus station 1½ blocks south of the main plaza at Calle 62 No 524 between Calles 65 and 67. Buses depart every 15 minutes on the run to the Dzibilchaltún access road (15 km, 30 minutes, US$1) and Progreso (33 km, 45 minutes, US$1.25).

Those heading to the Celestún flamingo region can choose from several departures a day from the Autotransportes del Sur station at Calle 50 No 531 at the corner of Calle 67.

To Río Lagartos or San Felipe Autotransportes del Noroeste buses depart three times daily from Calle 52 between Calles 63 & 65.

Train

Buses are preferable to trains in that they are faster and safer. Rail robberies in some areas (between Mérida, Campeche and Palenque in particular) have reached epidemic proportions. There are no *dormitorios* to lock on trains travelling this route – just vulnerable 1st and 2nd-class seating.

If you still want to get between Mérida and other points by rail, a train with no diner departs at midnight for Campeche, Palenque and ultimately Mexico City (two days journey). The station is at Calle 55 between Calles 46 and 48, about nine blocks northeast of the main plaza. Tickets should be bought several hours in advance.

Car

There are three ways to visit the old Mayan capital of Mayapán and the Puuc Route archaeological sites of Kabah, Sayil, Labná, Xlapak and Loltún: you can take a tour, take a bus to Kabah and walk many km (with the occasional hitchhike) in the hot sun, or you can rent a car.

Assume you will pay about US$60 per day for the cheapest car offered, usually a bottom-of-the-line Volkswagen or Nissan. If you can find others to share the cost, car rental is the best way to see the Puuc Route sites. The longer the rental, the less you'll spend per day for the car.

I can strongly recommend a small local car rental company, Mexico Rent a Car (☎ (99) 27-49-16, 23-36-37), Calle 62 No 483E between Calles 59 and 57, owned and operated by Alvaro and Teresa Alonzo and their daughter Teresa. They also have a desk on Calle 60 at the car park entrance next to the Hotel del Parque, just north of the Parque Hidalgo. Several friends of mine have used them for years with no complaints.

The big international car rental companies all have agencies in Mérida, the most active of which is Budget Rent-a-Car (☎ (99) 27-87-55), Paseo de Montejo Prolongación 497.

GETTING AROUND
To/From the Airport

Bus 79 ('Aviación') travels infrequently between the airport and city centre for US$0.40. Most arriving travellers use the

YUCATÁN

Transporte Terrestre minibuses (US$4.50) to go from the airport to the centre; to return to the airport you must take a taxi (US$12).

Bus

Most parts of Mérida that you'll want to visit are within five or six blocks of the Plaza Mayor and are thus accessible on foot. Given the slow speed of city traffic, particularly in the market areas, travel on foot is also the fastest way to get around.

The city's bus system is confusing at best, with routes meandering through the city, finally terminating in a distant suburban neighbourhood. For exact route information, ask at the tourist office.

The bus system is supplemented by minibus jitneys, which are easier to use as they run shorter and more comprehensible routes. The minibus (colectivo) you're liable to find most useful is the Ruta 10 (US$0.50) which departs the corner of Calles 58 and 59, half a block east of the Parque Hidalgo and travels along the Paseo de Montejo to Itzamná.

To walk from the Terminal de Autobuses on Calle 69, between Calles 68 and 70, to the Plaza Mayor, exit the terminal to the street in front (Calle 69), turn right and walk three blocks, passing the Church of San Juan de Dios and a park, to Calle 62. Turn left on Calle 62 and walk the remaining three blocks north to the plaza.

Around Mérida

The region around Mérida is the heartland of late Mayan civilisation, abounding in ancient ruins, colonial towns, traditional crafts and even some beaches. Using Mérida as your base you can see many of the wonders of Yucatán on day trips, or you can stay the night in most of the sites worth visiting.

Mérida's heat can be oppressive, even in the winter. When it gets too hot and especially on hot weekends, Mérida's citizens flock to the beaches at Progreso, a mere 33 km north of the city. Along the way, you might want to stop at the ruined city of Dzibilchaltún. Besides an interesting ruin or two, the site boasts a cool, clear cenote dedicated to swimming.

DZIBILCHALTÚN

This was the longest continuously utilised Mayan administrative and ceremonial city, serving the Maya from 1500 BC or earlier until the European conquest in the 1540s. At the height of its greatness, Dzibilchaltún covered 80 sq km. Archaeological research in the 1960s mapped 31 sq km of the city, revealing some 8500 structures. Today there is little for the casual visitor to see except a few ruined pyramids, a sacbé (ceremonial road) or two, the interesting little Temple of the Seven Dolls and the cenote swimming pool.

Dzibilchaltún (Place of Inscribed Flat Stones) is a large site, open from 8 am to 5 pm every day; admission costs US$4.50.

As you enter past the museum, the cenote is 100 metres directly ahead; the Temple of the Seven Dolls is about one km to the left .

While still a good distance away from the temple, note that you can see right through the building's doors and windows on the east-west axis. But when you approach, this view is lost. The temple's construction is such that you can't see through from north to south at all. I suspect that the rising and setting sun of the equinoxes 'lit up' the temple's windows and doors, making them blaze like beacons and signalling this important turning-point in the year. Thus the temple is impressive not for its size or beauty, but for its precise astronomical orientation and its function in the Great Mayan Time Machine.

The Temple of the Seven Dolls got its name from seven grotesque dolls discovered here during excavations; they may have been used in some healing rite.

On the walk back, note the Sendero Ecológico (Ecology Trail) which starts on the south side of the sacbé and winds through the scrub to rejoin the sacbé near the cenote.

It'll take you about 15 or 20 minutes to walk the trail.

The Cenote Xlacah, now a public swimming pool, is over 40 metres deep. In 1958, an expedition sponsored by the National Geographic Society sent divers down and recovered some 30,000 Mayan artefacts, many of ritual significance. The most interesting of these are now on display in the site's small but good museum. But enough history – plunge in and cool off!

Getting There & Away

Buses depart every 15 minutes on the run to the Dzibilchaltún access road (15 km, 30 minutes, US$1) on the right (east) side of the highway. It's five km from the highway to the entrance of the ruins along a sleepy country road and through a little village; the best time to hitch a ride is in the morning. From the site entrance, it's another 700 metres to the building housing the museum, admission ticket window and soft drinks stand.

PROGRESO

Population: 30,000

This is a seafarers' town, the port for Mérida and north-western Yucatán. The Yucatecan limestone shelf declines so gradually into the sea that a *muelle* (pier) 6.5-km long had to be built to reach the deep water.

This same gradual slope of land into water is what makes Progreso's long beach so inviting. The waters are shallow, warm and safe from such dangers as riptide and undertow.

Progreso is normally a sleepy little town, but on weekends, especially in summer, it seems as if all of Mérida is here.

History

After the founding of Mérida, the conquistador Francisco de Montejo advised his son that a road should be built to the coast, facilitating the export of goods. The port of Sisal, south-west of Progreso, served that function until the middle of the 19th century, when its shallow harbour and distance from Mérida proved inadequate for the needs of the growing henequen industry.

In 1840, local leaders suggested the site of Progreso, but the War of the Castes delayed the project until 1872 when it was established as a village. During the heyday of the henequen boom, Progreso prospered as Yucatán's most prominent port. A new harbour is scheduled for construction in the hope that cruise ships will dock here and Progreso will once again prosper.

Orientation

Progreso is long and narrow, stretched out along the seashore. If you want to move around the town and you don't have your own vehicle, you'll find yourself fighting the distances.

Though Progreso has an apparently logical street grid, it illogically is subject to two numbering systems fifty numbers apart. One system has the city centre's streets numbered in the 60s, 70s and 80s, another has them in the 10s, 20s and 30s. Thus you might see a street sign on Calle 30 calling it Calle 80 or on a map Calle 10 might also be referred to as Calle 60. I've included both systems on my map.

The bus stations are near the main square. It's six short blocks from the main square to the Malecón and the muelle.

Places to Stay

Progreso is looked upon as a resort, if a modest one, so rooms here tend to be a bit more expensive than in other Yucatecan towns. On Sundays in July and August, even the cheapest hotels fill up.

The best of Progreso's budget inns is the *Hotel Miralmar* (☎ (993) 5-05-52), Calle 77 No 124 at the corner of Calle 76, offering rooms with private shower, fan and one double bed for US$18, with two beds for US$21. Rooms on the upper floor are preferable – they're not as dungeon-like as the ground-floor rooms.

Several good lodging places are located

right on the Malecón facing the sea. *Hotel Playa Linda* (☎ (993) 5-11-57), Malecón at Calle 76, is a simple little two-storey place with rooms renting for US$20 a double with two beds. You get a private shower, a fan, and lounge chairs on the front terrace.

Three blocks east at the corner of Malecón and Calle 70 are two more hotels. *Tropical Suites* (☎ (993) 5-12-63) is the nicest I've mentioned so far, with tidy rooms with showers and fans going for US$22 to US$40 a double. Some rooms have sea views.

Hotel Real del Mar (☎ (993) 5-05-23), between Calles 70 and 72 behind the Restaurant Pelicanos, is an older hostelry which looks its age sometimes, but is still a good deal as it's right on the Malecón. Rooms with shower and fan cost US$20 a single/double in one bed, US$24 a double/triple in two beds, or US$28 for a suite.

Hotel Carismar (☎ (993) 5-29-07), Calle

71 No 151 between 78 and 80, has cheap rooms for US$19 a double with bath.

Places to Eat

Seafood is the strong point on the menus of Progreso's restaurants, of course. Note that if you come on a day trip to Progreso, you can often change clothes at the *vestidores* (changing cubicles) attached to most beachfront restaurants.

An all-purpose inexpensive eatery on the north side of the main square is *Restaurant El Cordóbes*, at the corner of Calles 81 and 80, open from early morning until late at night. Standard fare – tacos, enchiladas, sandwiches, chicken, etc – is served at good prices.

About the best prices you can find at an eatery on the Malecón are at *Morgan's*, Malecón between Calles 80 and 78, a Mexican beach restaurant where you can get

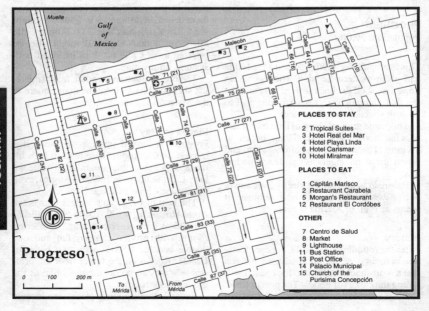

PLACES TO STAY
2 Tropical Suites
3 Hotel Real del Mar
4 Hotel Playa Linda
6 Hotel Carismar
10 Hotel Miralmar

PLACES TO EAT
1 Capitán Marisco
2 Restaurant Carabela
5 Morgan's Restaurant
12 Restaurant El Cordóbes

OTHER
7 Centro de Salud
8 Market
9 Lighthouse
11 Bus Station
13 Post Office
14 Palacio Municipal
15 Church of the
   Purisima Concepción

a full fish dinner for about US$12, everything included.

As you move eastward along the Malecón, restaurant prices rise. *Restaurant Carabela*, Malecón between Calles 68 and 70, is the spot for the young and hip beach crowd who come for the high-volume soft rock music (the bass notes shake the tables). Hamburgers are US$5, fish plates twice as much.

At the eastern end of the Malecón between Calles 62 and 60, almost one km from the muelle, stands *Capitán Marisco* (☎ 5-06-39), perhaps Progreso's fanciest seafood restaurant and certainly one of its most pleasant.

Getting There & Away

Both Dzibilchaltún and Progreso are due north of Mérida along a fast four-lane highway that's basically a continuation of the Paseo de Montejo. If you're driving, head north on the Paseo and follow signs for Progreso. Those travelling by bus must go to the Progreso bus station, 1½ blocks south of the main plaza in Mérida at Calle 62 No 524 between Calles 65 and 67.

Progreso is 18 km (20 minutes) beyond the Dzibilchaltún turn-off. A bus from Mérida to Progreso costs US$1.25 one way.

CELESTÚN

Famed as a bird sanctuary, Celestún makes a good beach-and-bird day trip from Mérida. Although this region abounds in anhingas and egrets, most birdwatchers come here to see the flamingos.

The town is located on a spit of land between the Río Esperanza and the Gulf of Mexico. Brisk westerly sea breezes cool the town on most days. The white sand beach is appealing, but on some days fierce afternoon winds swirl clouds of choking dust through the town. The dust makes the sea surfy and silty, and therefore unpleasant for swimming in the afternoon. Row upon row of fishing boats outfitted with twin long poles line the shore.

Given the winds, the best time to see birds is in the morning. Hire a *lancha* (boat) from the bridge on the highway one km east of the town. The rental should run to about US$16 for a 90-minute tour of the flamingo-inhabited areas.

Orientation

You come into town along Calle 11, past the marketplace and church (on your left/south) to Calle 12, the waterfront street.

Places to Stay

Hotels are few, and filled on weekends. A day-trip from Mérida is the best way to visit, but you can try for a room at these places:

Turn left (south) along Calle 12 from Calle 11 to find the *Hotel Gutiérrez* (☎ (99) 28-04-19, 28-69-78), Calle 12 No 22, at Calle 13, the top budget choice, with well-kept rooms with fan and bath costing US$20. *Hotel Maria del Carmen*, just south of it, is similar; enter from Calle 15.

Turn right (north) from Calle 11 along Calle 12 to find the *Hotel San Julio* (☎ 1-85-89), Calle 12 No 92, at Calle 9, where singles with fan and bath cost US$12 and doubles US$15.

Places to Eat

The junction of Calles 11 and 12 has many small restaurants, including the *Celestún*, *Playita*, *Boya* and *Avila*, most with sea views and seafood. The cheaper eateries, as always, are inland.

Getting There & Away

Buses run from Mérida's Autotransportes del Sur station on Calle 50 No 531 at Calle 67. They depart hourly on weekends until 2 pm and every two hours thereafter until 10 pm. The 92-km trip takes about 1½ to two hours and costs US$2.

YUCATÁN

Uxmal & the Puuc Route

La Ruta Maya continues southwards from Mérida, penetrating a region rich in ancient Mayan sites which have been restored and made accessible to the public. The towns of this region, Acanceh, Ticul and Oxkutzcab, provide views of how the Maya live today.

You cannot possibly visit all of these towns and ruins in a day trip from Mérida. Uxmal alone deserves most of a day, the Puuc Route sites another day. If time is short, go to Uxmal and Kabah. Otherwise, plan to stay overnight for at least one or two nights along the way. Lodgings at Uxmal are expensive; those in Ticul are cheap.

Ticul is also well known as the place to get excellent local handicrafts as well as being a good stopover on the way to Campeche.

After exploring the archaeological wealth

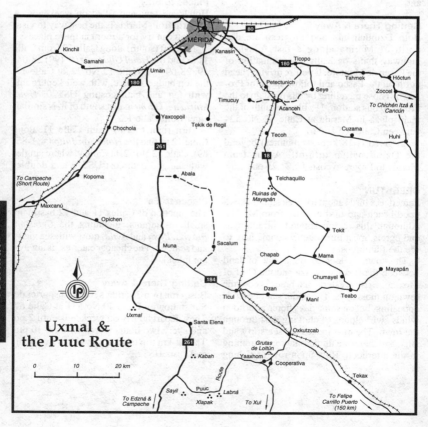

of this area, head south past Bolonchén de Rejón and Hopelchén to Cayal and the turn-off for the ruins of Edzná and finally to Campeche. If your goal is the Caribbean coast, go south-east from Ticul and Oxkutzcab to Felipe Carrillo Puerto, then north to the coast or south to Chetumal and Belize.

GETTING AROUND
Bus
Let's face it, the best way to see all there is to see in the area south of Mérida is by private car. Bus services to some points (Uxmal, Kabah, Ticul, Oxkutzcab) are frequent, but most of the Puuc Route sites are virtually impossible to reach by public transport, and to sites such as Mayapán, transport is fairly inconvenient – you'll spend a good deal of time waiting on country roads in the hot sun. If you decide to go by bus, plan to walk from one Puuc Route site to the next (say, between Kabah and Labná), with the occasional hitchhike. I've included exact distances between sites so that you'll know what you're in for.

Car
If you rent a car, plan on at least two days and preferably three, to see all there is to see. Spend the first night at Uxmal and continue to Kabah and the Puuc Route sites the next day. You can return to Mérida for the night, or to Uxmal, or go to Ticul. If you return via Yucatán State Highway No 18, you can stop for a visit to the ruins of Mayapán and a look at the pyramid in Acanceh. Those going directly to Campeche should take the shorter, faster route via Highway 180.

There are actually three major routes between Mérida and Campeche:

Fast Road to Campeche The westernmost route – the fastest route to Campeche – leaves Mérida by Avenida de los Itzaes, passes the airport and travels through the towns of Uman, Chochola, Kopoma and Maxcaná on its way to Campeche

To Uxmal via Muna The more interesting route to Campeche heads south-east at Uman to Uxmal and Kabah; after Kabah you can make a detour east to see the Puuc Route archaeological sites at Sayil, Labná, and Xlapak as well as the Grutas de Loltún.

It's 78 km from Mérida to Uxmal via Highway 180 south-west to Uman, then Highway 261 to Muna and Uxmal. Highway 261 continues south to Kabah and the junction with the road to the Puuc Route sites of Sayil, Xlapak and Labná. After the junction, Highway 261 continues south to the Grutas de Xtacumbilxunaan, the town of Bolonchén de Rejón and Hopelchén, where you turn to reach the ruins of Dzibalchén. From Hopelchén the highway heads west towards the turning for Edzná and beyond the turning, Campeche. This is a fairly well-travelled bus route and if you don't have your own car, this is probably the way you'll come.

The urban conglomeration of Mérida extends almost to the suburb of Uman, 17 km from the centre. At Uman you turn left and head south towards Muna. After 16 km there's a bend in the road and, on the right-hand (west) side of the road, the hacienda of Yaxcopoil.

The hacienda's French Renaissance-style buildings have been restored and turned into a museum of the 17th Century (open 8 am to 6 pm, Sunday 9 am to 1 pm; US$5). This vast estate specialised in the growing and processing of henequen. You can see much of what there is to see without paying the high museum admission fee.

Twenty-nine km south of Yaxcopoil is Muna, an old town with several interesting colonial churches, including the former Convento de la Asunción and the churches of Santa María, San Mateo and San Andrés. Another 16 km south of Muna is Uxmal; the highway passes the Hotel Misión Uxmal on the right and comes to the Hotel Hacienda Uxmal. Just across the highway from the hotel is the short entrance road (400 metres) to the ruins.

To Ticul via Acanceh The third, eastern-most route south goes via Acanceh and the ruins of the old Mayan capital city of Mayapán before reaching Ticul. Take Yucatán State Highway No 18 south-east via Kanasin, Acanceh and Tecoh to Mayapán, then on to the provincial town of Ticul, which has several cheap hotels. From Ticul you can go directly to Uxmal via Muna or go south-east to Oxkutzcab, then west to the Grutas de Loltún and the Puuc Route sites of Labná, Xlapak, Sayil and Kabah before heading north and west to Uxmal. Transport on this route is much more difficult without your own car. It might take the better part of a day to get from Mérida via the ruins of Mayapán to Ticul by bus. If you take this route you miss a visit to the hacienda of Yaxcopoil, but you get to see the ruins at Acanceh and Mayapán instead.

UXMAL

In 1840 the American explorer John L Stephens stood atop the Pyramid of the Magician at Uxmal and surveyed the ruins:

From its front doorway I counted sixteen elevations, with broken walls and mounds of stones and vast, magnificent edifices, which at that distance seemed untouched by time and defying ruin. I stood in the doorway when the sun went down, throwing from the buildings a prodigious breadth of shadow, darkening the terraces on which they stood and presenting a scene strange enough for a work of enchantment.

He later wrote about them in his book *Incidents of Travel in Central America, Chiapas & Yucatan*. Only Chichén Itzá and Tikal present as magnificent a picture as Uxmal.

History

Set in the Puuc Hills, which lent their name to the architectural patterns in this region, Uxmal was an important city during the Late Classic period (600-900 AD) of a region which encompassed the satellite towns of Sayil, Kabah, Xlapak and Labná. Although Uxmal means Thrice Built in Mayan, it was actually reconstructed five times.

That a sizable population flourished at all in this area is a mystery, as there is precious little water in the region. The Maya built a series of lime-lined reservoirs and cisterns

(chultunes) to catch and hold water during the dry season which must have been adequate.

First occupied in about 600 AD, the town was influenced by highland Mexico in its architecture, most likely through contact fostered by trade. This influence is reflected in Uxmal's serpent imagery, phallic symbols and columns. The well-proportioned Puuc architecture, with its intricate, geometric mosaics sweeping across the upper parts of elongated façades, is unique to this region.

Given the scarcity of water in the Puuc Hills, Chac the rain god was of great significance. His image is ubiquitous here in stucco monster-like masks protruding from façades and cornices.

There is much speculation as to why Uxmal was abandoned in about 900 AD. Drought conditions may have reached such proportions that the inhabitants had to relocate. One widely held theory suggests that the rise to greatness of Chichén Itzá drew people away from the Puuc Hills.

The first written account of Uxmal by a European came from the quill of the priest López de Cogullado in the 16th century. Thinking of Spanish convents, he referred to one building as the residence of Mayan virgins or nuns. The temple to this day is called the Nunnery Quadrangle.

The next influential European account of the site was written by Count de Waldeck in 1836 (see Palenque). In the hope of selling his work, the Count made Uxmal look like a Mediterranean ruin. Fortunately, misconceptions generated by Count de Waldeck were corrected by the great American archaeologist John L Stephens and his British illustrator Frederick Catherwood, who wrote about and drew the site with accuracy.

Uxmal was excavated in 1929 by Frans Blom. His was the first modern excavation and paved the way for others. Although much has been restored, there is still a good deal to discover.

Orientation & Information

As you come into the site from the highway,

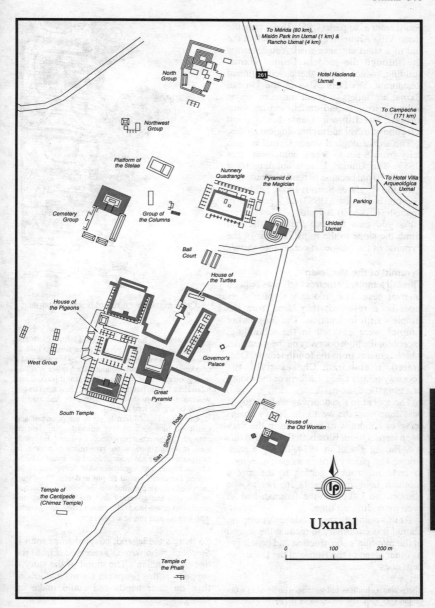

To Mérida (80 km),
Misión Park Inn Uxmal (1 km) &
Rancho Uxmal (4 km)

North
Group

261

Hotel Hacienda
Uxmal

To Campeche
(171 km)

Northwest
Group

Platform of
the Stelae

Nunnery
Quadrangle

Pyramid of
the Magician

To Hotel Villa
Arqueológica
Uxmal

Cemetery
Group

Group of
the Columns

Parking

Unidad
Uxmal

Ball
Court

House of
the Turtles

House of
the Pigeons

West Group

Governor's
Palace

Great
Pyramid

House of
the Old Woman

South Temple

San Simon Road

Temple of
the Centipede
(Chimez Temple)

Uxmal

0   100   200 m

Temple of
the Phalli

you'll enter a car park (US$1.25 per car); the Hotel Villa Arqueológica is to the left at the end of a short entrance road. You enter the site through the modern Unidad Uxmal building, which holds the air-conditioned Restaurant Yax-Beh. Also in the Unidad Uxmal are toilets, a small museum, shops selling souvenirs and crafts, and an auditorium. The Librería Dante has a good selection of travel and archaeological guides.

The archaeological site at Uxmal is open daily from 8 am to 5 pm; admission costs US$7. The Unidad Uxmal building stays open till 10 pm because of the 45-minute Luz y Sonido (Light & Sound) show, held each evening in English (US$3) at 9 pm and in Spanish (US$2.50) at 7 pm.

As you pass through the turnstile and climb the slope to the ruins, the rear of the Pyramid of the Magician comes into view.

Pyramid of the Magician

This tall temple, 39 metres high, was built on an oval base. The smoothly sloping sides have been restored; they date from the temple's fifth incarnation. The four earlier temples were covered in the rebuilding, except for the high doorway on the west side, which remains from the fourth temple. Decorated in elaborate Chenes style, the doorway proper takes the form of the mouth of a gigantic Chac mask.

The ascent to the doorway and the top is best done from the west side. Heavy chains serve as handrails to help you up the very steep steps. Queen Elizabeth II ascended this way during a visit in 1974, during a rainstorm. The plucky British monarch seemed to have no trouble getting to the top; a footman held an umbrella for her as she climbed, so I suppose the footman had an even more difficult time.

At this point in every guidebook covering Uxmal it is customary to recount the legend of the pyramid's construction and how it got its other name of the House of the Dwarf, so here goes:

There was a childless old woman who lived in a hut on the very spot now occupied by the pyramid. In her

Chac mask on corner of building, Uxmal

distress she took an egg, covered it with a cloth and laid it away carefully. Every day she went to look at it, until one morning she found the egg hatched and a creature born. The old woman called it her son and took good care of it, so that in one year it walked and talked like a man, but it also stopped growing. The old woman was more delighted than ever and said he would be a great lord or king.

One day she told him to go to the governor and challenge him to a trial of strength. Any feat of strength the governor performed, the dwarf did just as well, striking a blow at the governor's manhood. In exasperation, the governor ordered the dwarf to build a house higher than any other and to do it in one night, or else the dwarf would be put to death. The dwarf complied and the pyramid was the result. In a last test of strength the governor and the dwarf beat one another over the head with heavy clubs. Guess who won and became the new governor?

So there's the legend, adapted from John L Stephens, who wrote, 'I received it from the lips of an Indian'. The moral of the story, I suppose, is that people in Uxmal had lots of time on their hands and could make up strange legends.

From the top of the pyramid, survey the rest of the archaeological site. Directly west of the pyramid is the Nunnery Quadrangle. On the south side of the quadrangle, down a short slope, is a ruined ball court. Further south stands the great artificial terrace holding the Governor's Palace; between the palace and the ball court is the small House of the Turtles. Beyond the Governor's Palace and not really visible from the pyramid are remains of the Great Pyramid, and next to it are the House of the Pigeons and the South Temple. There are many other structures at Uxmal, but most have been recaptured by the jungle and are now just verdant mounds.

Nunnery Quadrangle

Archaeologists have not yet deciphered what this 74-room quadrangle was used for, but guess that it might have been a military academy, royal school or palace complex. The long-nosed face of Chac appears everywhere on the façades of the four separate temples which form the quadrangle. The northern temple, grandest of the four, was built first, followed by the south, then the east and the west.

Several decorative elements on the façades show signs of Mexican, perhaps Totonac, influence. The feathered serpent (Quetzalcóatl) motif along the top of the west temple's façade is one of these. Note also the stylised depictions of the na, or Mayan thatched hut, over some of the doorways in the northern building. The na motif alternates with stacks of Chac masks over the doors. Similar na depictions are over the doors of the southern building as well.

Ball Court

Pass through the corbelled arch in the middle of the south building of the quadrangle and continue down the slope to the ball court, which is much less impressive than the great ball court at Chichén Itzá.

House of the Turtles

Climb the steep slope up to the artificial terrace on which stands the Governor's Palace. At the top of the climb, on the right, is the House of the Turtles, which takes its name from the turtles carved on the cornice. The frieze of short columns or 'rolled mats' which runs around the top of the temple is characteristic of the Puuc style. Turtles were associated by the Maya with the rain god Chac. According to Mayan myth, when the people suffered from drought so did the turtles and both prayed to Chac to send rain.

Governor's Palace

When Stephens laid eyes on the Governor's Palace, he wrote:

There is no rudeness or barbarity in the design or proportions; on the contrary, the whole wears an air of architectural symmetry and grandeur; and as the stranger ascends the steps and casts a bewildered eye along its open and desolate doors, it is hard to believe that he sees before him the work of a race in whose epitaph, as written by historians, they are called ignorant of art...If it stood...in Hyde Park or the Garden of the Tuileries, it would form a new order...not unworthy to stand side by side with the remains of Egyptian, Grecian and Roman art.

The magnificent façade of the palace, nearly 100 metres long, has been called 'the finest structure at Uxmal and the culmination of the Puuc style' by Mayanist Michael D Coe. Buildings in Puuc style have walls filled with rubble, faced with cement and then covered in a thin veneer of limestone squares; the lower part of the façade is plain, the upper part festooned with stylised Chac faces and geometric designs, often lattice-like or fretted. Other elements of Puuc style are decorated cornices, rows of half-columns as in the House of the Turtles and round columns in doorways as in the palace at Sayil. The stones forming the corbelled vaults in Puuc style are shaped like boots.

Great Pyramid

Adjacent to the Governor's Palace, this 32-metre mound has been restored only on the northern side. There is a quadrangle at the top which archaeologists theorise was largely destroyed in order to construct another pyramid above it. This work, for reasons unknown, was never completed. At the top are some stucco carvings of Chac, birds and flowers.

House of the Pigeons

West of the great pyramid sits a structure whose roofcomb is latticed with a pigeon-hole pattern – hence the building's name. The nine honeycombed triangular belfries sit on top of a building which was once part of a quadrangle. The base is so eroded that it is hard for archaeologists to guess its function.

Places to Stay & Eat – bottom end

As there is no town, not even a village, at Uxmal, only the archaeological site and several top-end hotels, you cannot depend upon finding cheap food or lodging.

Campers can pitch their tents five km north of the ruins on Highway 261, the road to Mérida, at *Rancho Uxmal* (☎ in Ticul (997) 2-02-77). The rate is US$3 per person. Several serviceable guestrooms with shower and fan go for US$28 a double, expensive for what you get, but this is Uxmal. There's a restaurant. It may take you 45 to 55 minutes to walk here – in the hot sun – from the ruins, but there's some possibility of hitching a ride.

Other than the Rancho Uxmal, there's no cheap lodging in the area. If you don't want to return to Mérida for the night, make your way to Ticul.

The *Posada Uxmal Restaurant Nicté-Ha*, just across the highway from the road to the ruins, on the grounds of the Hotel Hacienda Uxmal, is a simple eatery open from 12.30 to 7 pm daily and offers sandwiches, fruit salads and similar fare at prices slightly lower than those at the Yax-Beh. Often staff will allow you to use the hotel's swimming pool after you've bought a meal.

Places to Stay & Eat – top end

The *Hotel Hacienda Uxmal* (☎ 4-71-42), 500 metres from the ruins across the highway, originally housed the archaeologists who explored and restored Uxmal. High ceilings with fans, good cross-ventilation and wide, tiled verandahs set with rocking-chairs make this an exceptionally

pleasant and comfortable place to stay. The beautiful swimming pool is a dream come true on a sweltering hot day.

Simple rooms in the annexe cost US$42 a single or double; the nicer rooms in the main building range from US$65 to US$120 a single, US$72 to US$130 a double. Meals are mediocre and moderately priced. You can supposedly make reservations in Mérida at the Mérida Travel Service in the Hotel Casa del Balam (☎ (99) 24-88-44), at the corner of Calles 60 and 57, but they seem not to know the correct room prices and have always told me the hotel is full, even if it isn't.

Hotel Villa Arqueológica Uxmal (in Mérida, ☎ (99) 24-70-53, Apdo Postal 449) is the closest lodging to the ruins. Run by Club Med, this attractive modern hotel offers a swimming pool, tennis courts, a good French-inspired restaurant and air-con guestrooms for US$65/75/90 a single/double/triple.

The *Hotel Misión Park Inn Uxmal* (in Mérida ☎ /fax (99) 24-73-08) is set on a hilltop two km north of the turn-off to the ruins. Many rooms have balcony views of Uxmal. Rooms with fan are priced at US$88 a single or double.

Getting There & Away

Air An airstrip is under construction near Uxmal. When it is finished routes from Cancún will be developed, making it possible for Cancúnites to visit Uxmal on a day excursion.

Bus From Mérida's Terminal de Autobuses it's 80 km (1½ hours) to Uxmal. Eight 2nd-class (US$2) buses of the Autobuses del Sur line make the trip daily and there are other buses as well. They'll drop you right at the turn-off to the ruins, only 400 metres away. For the return trip to Mérida, some buses depart from the car park at the archaeological site entrance; others must be flagged down on the main road. In late afternoon there may be standing room only.

If you're going to Ticul, hop on a bus

heading north, get off at Muna and get another bus eastwards to Ticul.

For buses to Kabah, the Puuc Route turn-off and points on the road to Campeche, flag down a bus at the turn-off to the ruins.

PUUC ROUTE

The ruins at Kabah, Sayil, Xlapak, Labná and the Grutas de Loltún offer a deeper acquaintance with the Puuc Mayan civilisation. The Palace of Masks at Kabah and El Palacio at Sayil are really worth seeing and if you're not prepared to make the rounds of all the Puuc sites I'd suggest that you visit at least these two. The Grutas de Loltún (Loltún Caves) are also impressive, especially if you enjoy visiting cool caves. You can then continue to Oxkutzcab and Ticul if you like.

If you make this excursion on Sunday, you will enjoy free admission to the archaeological sites.

Kabah

Heading south-east from Uxmal, 15 km brings you to the village of Santa Elena, where the highway turns south. Another 3.5 km brings you to the Zona Arqueológica Puuc and the ruins of Kabah. The highway passes right through the middle of the site, which is open from 8 am to 5 pm. Admission costs US$4, free on Sunday.

The temples here are presently under restoration, which will make them doubly impressive. Cold drinks and junk snacks are available.

Palace of Masks The Palace of Masks, set on its own high terrace, is truly an amazing sight, its façade covered in nearly 300 masks of Chac, the rain god or sky serpent. Unlike other Puuc buildings, the lower part of this façade is not severely plain; the decoration of masks extends from the base of the building all the way to the top. So Chacified is the façade that you enter some of the rooms by stepping on a Chac mask's hooked nose! Each of these mosaic masks consists of more than two dozen carved stones. The temple is unusual in having several series of rooms, with both front and back chambers.

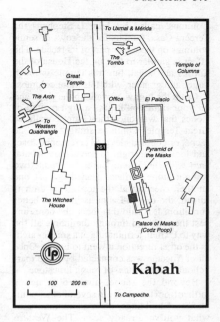

Kabah

The temple's Mayan name, Codz Poop (Rolled Mat) is explained in various ways by archaeologists and travel writers, none of them convincing. John L Stephens wrote:

To many of these structures the Indians have given names stupid, senseless and unmeaning, having no reference to history or tradition. This one they call Xcocpoop, which means in Spanish petato doblado, or a straw hat doubled up; the name having reference to the crushed and flattened condition of the façade and the prostration of the rear wall of the building.

Other Kabah Ruins To the north of the Palace of Masks is a small pyramid. Behind and to the left of the Palace of Masks is El Palacio, with a broad façade having several doorways; in the centre of each doorway is a column, a characteristic of the Puuc architectural style. El Palacio at Sayil is somewhat similar in design, but much larger and grander.

Walk around the northern side of El Palacio and follow a path to the Temple of

Columns, called by John L Stephens the Tercera Casa, famous for the rows of semi-columns on the upper part of its façade. The effect is similar to that on the House of the Turtles at Uxmal, but this temple is much larger and grander, with lots more columns.

Cross the highway, walk up the slope and on your right you'll pass a high mound of stones that was once the Gran Teocalli, or Great Temple. Continue straight on to the sacbé, or cobbled elevated ceremonial road, and look to the right to see a monumental arch with the Mayan corbelled vault (two straight stone surfaces leaned against one another, meeting at the top). This arch is ruined; the one at Labná is in much better condition. It is said that the sacbé here runs past the arch and through the jungle all the way to Uxmal, terminating at a smaller arch; in the other direction it went to Labná. Once all of Yucatán was connected by these marvellous 'white roads' of rough limestone.

Beyond the sacbé, about 600 metres farther from the road, are several other complexes of buildings, none as impressive as what you've already seen. The Western Quadrangle (Cuadrángulo del Oeste) has some decoration of columns and masks. North of the quadrangle are the Temple of the Key Patterns and the Temple of Lintels; the latter had intricately carved lintels of tough sapodilla wood. John L Stephens had them removed and shipped to New York for 'safekeeping', where they were destroyed in a fire shortly after their arrival. Luckily, Stephens' assistant Frederick Catherwood had made detailed drawings of the lintels before they were shipped.

Getting There & Away Kabah is 101 km from Mérida, a ride of about two hours, or just over 18 km south of Uxmal. Six 1st-class buses of the Autobuses del Sur line make the run daily, continuing to Campeche and returning along the same route; a one-way ticket costs US$2. To return to Mérida, stand on the east side of the road at the entrance to the ruins and flag down a bus. You may wish to try hitching as well (consider carefully the risks mentioned in the introductory Getting

Around chapter), because the buses are often full and won't stop. You may have the same problem of full buses if you stand on the west side of the highway and flag down a bus to take you to the Puuc Route turn-off, five km south of Kabah, or to other sites along Highway 261 farther south.

Many visitors come to Kabah by private car and may be willing to give you a lift southwards on the Puuc Route. You should offer to share fuel expenses as a courtesy. Those with cars would make this writer very happy if they offered rides to others, as transport along the Puuc Route is so difficult – and the sun on the road so hot.

Sayil

Five km south of Kabah a road turns east: this is the Puuc Route. Despite the interesting archaeological sites along this route, there is not much traffic and hitching can be difficult. The ruins of Sayil are 4.5 km from the junction with Highway 261, on the south side of the road. Sayil is open from 8 am to 5 pm daily; admission costs US$4, but is free on Sunday.

El Palacio Sayil is best known for El Palacio, the huge three-tiered building with a façade some 85 metres long that makes one think of the Minoan palaces on Crete. The distinctive columns of Puuc architecture are used here over and over, as supports for the lintels, as decoration between doorways and as a frieze above the doorways, alternating with huge stylised Chac masks and 'descending gods'.

Climb to the top level of the Palacio and look to the north to see several *chultunes*, or stone-lined cisterns, in which precious rainwater was collected and stored for use during the dry season. Some of these chultunes can hold more than 30,000 litres.

Should you visit the Palacio just before Easter, you can test a local superstition. John L Stephens, after his visit to Sayil (which he called Zayi), wrote that the Indians 'believed that the ancient buildings were haunted and, as in the remote region of Santa Cruz del

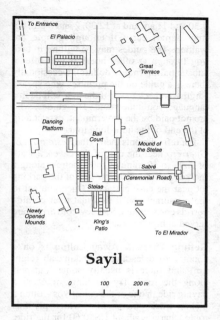

Sayil

0   100   200 m

---

than those at Kabah and Sayil, measuring only about 20 metres in length. It's decorated with the inevitable Chac masks, columns and colonnettes and fretted geometric latticework of the Puuc style. Immediately to the right is the rubble of what were once two smaller buildings.

If you trek along the remnant of an old 4WD road behind the palace, you may be rewarded with the sight of some brilliantly coloured tropical birds. The long-tailed motmot, or clock bird, is here in good number.

Labná

From the entrance gate at Xlapak, it's 3.5 km to the gate at Labná. The site here is open from 8 am to 5 pm; admission costs US$4.

El Arco Labná is best known for its magnificent arch, once part of a building which separated two quadrangular courtyards. It now appears to be a gate joining two small plazas. The corbelled structure, three metres wide and six metres high, is well preserved and stands close to the entrance of Labná. The mosaic reliefs decorating the upper façade are exuberantly Puuc in style.

If you look at the ornate work on the north-eastern side of the arch, you will make out mosaics of Mayan huts. At the base of either side of the arch are rooms of the adjoining building, now ruined, including upper lattice patterns constructed atop a serpentine design. Archaeologists believe a high roofcomb once sat over the fine arch and its flanking rooms.

Quiché, they said that on Good Friday of every year music was heard sounding among the ruins'.

El Mirador If you take the path southwards from the palace for about 400 metres you come to the temple named El Mirador, with its interesting rooster-like roofcomb once painted a bright red. About 100 metres beyond El Mirador by the path to the left is a stela beneath a protective palapa which bears a relief of a phallic god, now badly weathered.

Xlapak

From the entrance gate at Sayil, it's six km to the entrance gate at Xlapak (shla-PAK). The name means Old Walls in Mayan and was a general term among local people for ancient ruins, about which they knew little. The site is open from 8 am to 5 pm; admission is US$2.75, free on Sunday.

The ornate palace at Xlapak is smaller

El Mirador Standing on the opposite side of the arch and separated from it by the limestone-paved sacbé, is a pyramid with a temple atop it called El Mirador. The pyramid itself is poorly preserved, largely stone rubble. The temple, with its five-metre-high roofcomb, true to its name, looks like a watchtower. When John L Stephens saw El Mirador in 1840, it had a row of death's heads along the top and two lines of human figures beneath; over the centre doorway was a colossal seated figure in high relief.

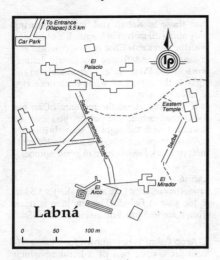

To Entrance
(Xlapac) 3.5 km

Car Park

El
Palacio

Eastern
Temple

Sacbé (Ceremonial Road)

Sacbé

El
Arco

El
Mirador

Labná

0   50   100 m

Palace & Chultún The palace, the first edifice you come to at Labná, is connected by a sacbé to El Mirador and the arch. One of the longest buildings in the Puuc Hills, its design is not as impressive as its counterpart at Sayil. There's a relief on the eastern corner on the upper level of a serpent gripping a human head between its jaws. Close to this carving is a well-preserved Chac mask. At Labná's peak there were some 60 chultunes (cisterns) in and around the city.

Grutas de Loltún (Loltún Caves)
From Labná it's 15 km eastward to the village of Yaaxhom, surrounded by lush orchards and palm groves which are surprising in this generally dry region. From Yaaxhom a road goes another four km to Loltún.

Loltún Caves, the most interesting *grutas* in Yucatán, provided a treasure trove of data for archaeologists studying the Maya. Carbon dating of artefacts found here reveals that the caves were first used by humans some 2500 years ago.

Loltún is open from 9 am to 5 pm daily, for US$7. To explore the 1.5-km labyrinth, you must take a scheduled guided tour at 9.30 and 11 am and at 12.30, 2 and 3 pm, but may depart early if enough people are waiting. The guides may be willing to take you through at other hours if you offer a substantial tip (a few dollars). Occasionally there is a guide on the premises who speaks English – check to see if the tour will be in a language you understand. The guides, who are not paid by the government, expect a tip at the end of the hour-long tour.

For refreshments there's the *Restaurant El Guerrero* near the exit of the caves, a walk of eight to 10 minutes (600 metres) along a marked path from the far side of the parking lot near the cave entrance. Once you get to the restaurant you'll find that their comida corrida costs about US$9. Icy-cold drinks are served at high prices.

Getting There & Away Loltún is on a country road leading to Oxkutzcab (eight km) and there is usually some transport along the road. Try hitching, or catch a paying ride in one of the colectivos – often a pickup truck or *camión* – which ply this route, charging about US$0.60 for the ride. A taxi from Oxkutzcab may charge US$7 or so, one way, for the eight-km ride.

Buses run frequently every day between Mérida and Oxkutzcab via Ticul.

If you're driving from Loltún to the Puuc Route site of Labná, drive out of the Loltún car park, turn right and take the next road on the right, which passes the access road to the restaurant. Do not take the road marked for Xul. After four km you'll come to the village of Yaaxhom, where you turn right to join the Puuc Route westwards.

UXMAL TO CAMPECHE
South of Uxmal and Kabah, Highway 261 leaves the Puuc Hills and heads straight for the border with the neighbouring state of Campeche. There is little except jungle until, 31 km south of Uxmal, you pass beneath the great arch over the roadway which marks the border between the two Mexican states.

Three km north of Bolonchén de Rejón, just off the highway, is the archaeological zone of Itzimté, with its many unrestored buildings in the Puuc style. This is the southernmost limit of the style; south of this point the ancient Mayan buildings are more elaborately decorated in the style known as Chenes, named for the many natural wells in the region. The suffix '-chén' is often found at the end of town names hereabouts.

Bolonchén de Rejón & Xtacumbilxunaan

Bolonchén ('Nine Wells', for the chultunes in the town square) is noted mostly as the town near the Grutas de Xtacumbilxunaan (or Xtacumbinxuna, as it's sometimes spelled), located about three km south of town. Follow Highway 261 south and watch on the right (west) for a small sign indicating the caves, which are 800 metres off the highway.

These Caves of the Hidden Girl get their unpronounceable Mayan name from a legend (of course): a girl was stolen from her mother by her lover and hidden in the cave. If this is true, the lovers left no trace of their tryst. In former centuries, the Nine Wells would fail each year during the dry season and the local inhabitants would make their way to this cave and go down several hundred metres into the earth through a narrow, claustrophobic system of tunnels to fill their small water jars.

Today you can visit the cavern by taking a 30 to 45-minute tour with the guide/caretaker for the price of a tip. The cave is 'open' whenever the caretaker is around, which is most of the time during daylight hours.

Edzná

Continuing west on Highway 261 from Hopelchén brings you, after 40 km, to the village of San Antonio Cayal and the junction with the road south to Edzná (20 km) .

Edzná, meaning House of Grimaces or House of Echoes, may well have been host to both, as there has been a settlement here since about 800 BC. Most of the carvings are of a much later date: 550 to 810 AD. Though a long way from the Puuc Hills, some of the architecture here is similar to Puuc style, but with local variations in design.

The refreshments stand to the left as you enter has icy-cold bottled drinks, which you will probably want in the intense heat. The site is open from 8 am to 5 pm daily, for US$5 admission.

Though the archaeological zone covers two sq km, the thing to see here is the main plaza, 160 metres long and 100 metres wide, surrounded by temples. Every Mayan site has huge masses of stone, but at Edzná there are cascades of it, terrace upon terrace of bleached limestone.

The major temple here, the 30-metre-high Temple of Five Levels, is to the left as you enter the plaza from the ticket kiosk. Built on a vast platform, it rises five levels from base to roofcomb, with rooms and some weathered decoration of masks, serpents and jaguars' heads on each level. A great central staircase of 65 steps goes right to the top. On the opposite (right) side of the plaza as you enter is a monumental staircase 100 metres wide, which once led up to the Temple of the Moon. At the far end of the plaza is a ruined temple that could well have been the priests' quarters.

Getting There & Away From Campeche's market, at the eastern end of Calle 53 across Avenida Circuito Baluartes Este, catch a 2nd-class village bus early in the morning headed for Edzná (66 km), which may mean a bus going to the village of Pich, some 15 km south-east of Edzná, or to Hool, about 25 km south-west. Either bus will drop you at the access road to the site. A sign just north of the junction says 'Edzná 2 km', but don't let it fool you. The ruins are just 500 metres beyond the sign, only about 400 metres off the highway. Coming from the north and east, get off at San Antonio Cayal and hitch or catch a bus 20 km south to Edzná.

When you leave you'll have to depend on hitching or buses to get you to San Antonio Cayal, from which you can hitch or catch a bus west back to Campeche or east and north to Hopelchén, Bolonchén and ultimately Uxmal.

Alternatively, guided tours (US$25 per

YUCATÁN

person) are set up by the larger hotels in Campeche if they have enough people.

TICUL

Ticul is a centre for weaving of fine huipiles, the traditional Mayan dresses with embroidered bodices. While you are here, you can pay homage to the best Yucatecan cooking by dining at the original Restaurant Los Almendros, which has branches in Mérida and Cancún.

Ticul's main street is Calle 23, sometimes called the Calle Principal, going from the highway north-east past the market and the town's best restaurants to the main plaza.

Places to Stay – bottom end

Hotel Sierra Sosa (☎ (997) 2-00-08; fax 2-02-82), Calle 26 No 199A, half a block north-west of the plaza, has very basic rooms for US$10 a single/double. A few rooms at the back have windows, but most are dark and dungeon-like. Be sure the ceiling fan works.

Similarly basic but more expensive is the *Hotel San Miguel* (☎ (997) 2-03-82), Calle 28 No 195, near Calle 23 and the market. Singles at the San Miguel cost US$11 with fan and bath, doubles US$12 to US$14.

Places to Stay – middle

Ticul's better hotels don't really offer too much more in the way of comfort and both are on the highway on the outskirts of town, an inconvenient two-km walk from the centre, but fine if you have a car.

Best in town is the new *Hotel Las Bougambillias* (☎ (997) 2-07-61), near the junction of the western end of Calle 25 and the highway to Muna and Mérida. The darkish rooms are simple but newer and cleaner than the competition's. Prices are US$19 for two in one bed, US$27 for two in two beds.

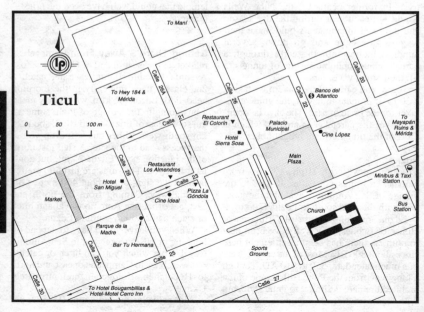

Top: Swimming in the Cenote Xlacah, Dzibilchaltún archeological site, Mexico (TB)
Left: Pyramid of the Magician, Uxmal, Yucatán, Mexico (TB)
Right: Tulum Ruins, Quintana Roo, Mexico (TB)

Top: Waterfall at Agua Azul, Chiapas, Mexico (JL)
Bottom: Cañón del Sumidero, Chiapas, Mexico (PW)

A hundred metres north-west of the Bougambillias on the opposite side of the highway is the older *Hotel-Motel Cerro Inn*. Set in more spacious, shady grounds, the Cerro Inn has nine well-used rooms with private shower and ceiling fan going for US$16 to US$20 a double.

Places to Eat – bottom end

Ticul's lively market provides all the ingredients for picnics and snacks. It also has lots of those wonderful market eateries where the food is good, the portions generous and the prices low. For variety, try out some of the loncherías along Calle 23 between Calles 26 and 30.

Should you want a sit-down meal, there's the cheap *Restaurant El Colorín* (☎ 2-03-14), Calle 26 No 199B, just close to the Hotel Sierra Sosa half a block north-west of the plaza. *Pizza La Góndola*, Calle 23 at Calle 26A. is tidy, with two-person pizzas cooked to order for US$5 to US$8.

Places to Eat – middle

Restaurant Los Almendros (☎ 2-00-21), Calle 23 No 207, between 26A and 28, is set up in a fortress-like town house with a large courtyard and portico. The air-con restaurant, open every day from 9 am to 8 pm, is fairly plain, but the food is authentically Yucatecan. The *combinado yucateco*, or Yucatecan combination plate, with a soft drink or beer, will cost less than US$10.

Getting There & Away

Ticul's bus station is behind the massive church off the main square. Numerous companies make the 85 km, 1½-hour run between Mérida and Ticul for US$3 to US$3.50. There are also three buses to Felipe Carrillo Puerto (US$7), frequent ones to Oxkutzcab (US$1), and five a day to Chetumal (12 hours, US$9).

You can catch a minibus (combi) from the intersection of Calles 23 and 28 in Ticul to Oxkutzcab (that's osh-kootz-KAHB), 16 km away and from Oxkutzcab a minibus or pickup truck to Loltún (eight km); ask for the

camión to Xul (SHOOL), but get off at Las Grutas de Loltún.

Minibuses to Santa Elena (15 km), the village between Uxmal and Kabah, also depart from the intersection of Calles 23 and 28, taking a back road and then leaving you to catch another bus north-west to Uxmal (15 km) or south to Kabah (3.5 km). You may find it more convenient to take a minibus or bus to Muna (22 km) on Highway 261 and another south to Uxmal (16 km).

To Felipe Carrillo Puerto Those headed eastwards to Quintana Roo and the Caribbean coast can go via Highway 184 from Muna and Ticul via Oxkutzcab to Tekax, Tzucacab and Peto. At Polguc, 130 km from Ticul, a road turns left (east), ending after 80 km in Felipe Carrillo Puerto, 210 km from Ticul, where there are hotels, restaurants, fuel stations, banks and other services. The right fork of the road goes south to the region of Lago de Bacalar.

From Oxkutzcab to Felipe Carrillo Puerto or Bacalar there are few services: very few places to eat (those that exist are rock-bottom basic), no hotels and few fuel stations. Mostly you see small typical Yucatecan villages with their *topes* (speed bumps), traditional Mayan na thatched houses and agricultural activity.

Getting Around

For getting around Ticul, the local method is to hire a three-wheeled cycle, Ticul's answer to the rickshaw – you'll see them on Calle 23 just up from the market. The fare is less than US$1 for a short trip.

MÉRIDA TO TICUL VIA ACANCEH & MAYAPÁN

The route south from Mérida via Acanceh and the ruins of Mayapán to Ticul and Oxkutzcab reveals a landscape of small Mayan villages, crumbling haciendas surrounded by henequen fields, a ruined Mayan capital city and of course the expected expanses of limitless scrubby jungle.

Those taking this route, whether by car or bus, should be careful to distinguish between

Ruinas de Mayapán, the ruins of the ancient city and Mayapán, a Mayan village some 40 km south-east of the ruins past the town of Teabo. The Ruinas de Mayapán are right on the main road (Yucatán state highway 18) between Telchaquillo and Tekit.

Getting Around

Buses and colectivos run fitfully along this route, but you should plan the better part of a day, with stops in Acanceh and Ruinas de Mayapán, to travel the route by public transport.

If you're driving, follow these directions carefully: leave Mérida on Calle 59, which is one-way eastward. When you reach a four-lane boulevard with railway tracks running in its centre, you've reached Circuito Colonias. Turn right onto this boulevard and go south until you reach a traffic roundabout with a fountain. Go three-quarters of the way around (you enter at 6 o'clock and exit at 9 o'clock) and head due east on the road marked for Kanasin, Acanceh and Tecoh.

Acanceh

The road enters Acanceh and goes to the main plaza flanked by a shady park and the church. To the left of the church is a partially restored pyramid and to the right of the church are market loncherías if you're in need of a snack. In the park, note the statue of the smiling deer; the name Acanceh means 'Pond of the Deer'. Another local sight of interest is the cantina Aqui Me Queda (I'm Staying Here), a ready-made answer for wives who come to the cantina to urge their husbands homeward.

Ruinas de Mayapán

One or two km past Telchaquillo (about 48 km from Mérida), look for a sign on the right-hand (west) side of the road indicating the Ruinas de Mayapán.

At the caretaker's hut 100 metres in from the road, pay the admission fee of US$2.50 and enter the site any day between 8 am and 5 pm. If you have camping equipment, the caretaker may grant you permission to camp near his hut. Facilities consist of a latrine and a well with a bucket.

History Mayapán was supposedly founded by Kukulcán (Quetzalcóatl) in 1007, shortly after the former ruler of Tula arrived in Yucatán. His dynasty, the Cocom, organised a confederation of city-states which included Uxmal, Chichén Itzá and many other notable cities. Despite their alliance, animosity arose between the Cocoms of Mayapán and the Itzaes of Chichén Itzá during the late 1100s and the Cocoms stormed Chichén Itzá, forcing the Itzá rulers into exile. The Cocom dynasty under Hunac Ceel Canuch emerged supreme in all of northern Yucatán and obliged the other rulers to pay tribute in cotton clothing, fowl, cacao and incense resin.

Cocom supremacy lasted for almost 2½ centuries, until the ruler of Uxmal, Ah Xupán Xiú, led a rebellion of the oppressed city-states and overthrew Cocom hegemony. Every member of the Cocom dynasty was massacred, except for one prince who had the good fortune to be away on business in Honduras. The great capital of Mayapán was utterly destroyed and was uninhabited ever after.

The Xiú victors founded a new capital at Maní, which remained the strongest Mayan city until the arrival of the conquistadors. But there was no peace in Yucatán after the Xiú victory. The Cocom dynasty recovered and marshalled its forces and frequent struggles for power erupted until 1542, when Francisco de Montejo the Younger founded Mérida. At that point the current lord of Maní and ruler of the Xiú people, Ah Kukum Xiú, offered to submit his forces to Montejo's control in exchange for a military alliance against the Cocoms, his ancient rivals. Montejo willingly agreed and Ah Kukum Xiú was baptised as a Christian, taking the unoriginal name of Francisco de Montejo Xiú. The Cocoms were defeated and – too late – the Xiú rulers realised that they had willingly signed the death warrant of Mayan independence.

Orientation The city of Mayapán was huge, with a population estimated at around 12,000; its ruins cover several sq km, all surrounded by a great defensive wall. Over 3500 buildings, 20 cenotes and traces of the city wall were mapped by archaeologists working in the 1950s and in 1962. The workmanship was inferior to the great age of Mayan art; though the Cocom rulers of Mayapán tried to revive the past glories of Mayan civilisation, they succeeded only in part.

Jungle has returned to cover many of the buildings, though you can visit several cenotes (including Itzmal Chen, a main Mayan religious sanctuary) and make out the large piles of stones which were once the Temple of Kukulcán and the circular Caracol.

Getting There & Away After visiting the ruins, head south again to Tekit, about eight km from the ruins (67 km from Mérida). Turn right and go through the town square to find the road marked for Oxkutzcab. Another seven km brings you to Mama, with its particularly fortress-like church. At Mama, the road forks: straight on to Oxkutzcab (27 km), right to Chapab and Ticul (25 km).

MÉRIDA TO CAMPECHE – SHORT ROUTE (HIGHWAY 180)

The short route from Mérida to Campeche is the fast way to go and if you simply buy a bus ticket from Mérida to Campeche, this is the route your bus will follow. If you'd prefer to go the long way via Uxmal and Kabah, you must ask for a seat on one of the less frequent long-route buses. If you'd like to stop at one of the towns along the short route, catch a 2nd-class bus.

Becal, Calkini & Hecelchakan

Becal, 85 km south-west of Mérida and just across the boundary in the state of Campeche, is a centre of Yucatán's Panama hat trade. The soft, pliable hats, called *jipijapa* by the locals, have been woven by townfolk from the fibres of the huano palm tree in humid limestone caves since the mid-19th century. The caves provide just the right atmosphere for shaping the fibres, keeping them pliable and minimising breakage. So devoted to hatmaking is Becal that the sculpture in the main square is composed of several enormous concrete hats tipped up against one another. As soon as you descend from your bus, someone is sure to approach you and ask if you want to see the hats being made; the guide expects a tip of course.

Jipi hats are of three general quality grades, judged by the pliability and fineness of the fibres and closeness of the weave. The coarse, open weave of large fibres is the cheapest grade, and should cost only a few dollars. Middle-grade hats have a finer, closer weave of good fibres and cost about US$20. Truly beautiful hats of the finest, closest weave may cost twice that amount.

Eight km south of Becal you pass through Calkini, site of the 17th-century Church of San Luis de Tolosa, with a Plateresque portal and lots of baroque decoration. Each year the Festival of San Luis is celebrated on 19 August.

Another 24 km brings you to Hecelchakan, home of the Museo Arqueológico del Camino Real, where you will find some burial artefacts from the island of Jaina, as well as ceramics and jewellery from other sites. The museum is open from Monday to Saturday from 9 am to 6 pm, closed Sunday. The Church of San Francisco is the centre of festivities on the saint's day, 4 October. From 9 to 18 August, a popular festival called the Novenario is held, with bullfights, dancing and refreshments.

From Hecelchakan it's another 77 easy km to the city of Campeche.

YUCATÁN

Campeche

The impressive walled city of Campeche with its ancient fortresses or *baluartes* propels the visitor back to the days of the buccaneers. Those who explore the region's ancient Mayan Chenes-style ruins of Edzná could find they have the sites all to themselves. With so much interest, why is Campeche the least-visited state in the Yucatán peninsula?

For all its attractiveness, Campeche is not particularly tourist-friendly. Hotels are few, often disappointing and expensive for what you get. The fine regional museum charges a very high admission price. The beaches, such as they are, can be less than clean and transport to Edzná can be haphazard.

Even so, the state has its attractions, and you should enjoy a short stay here.

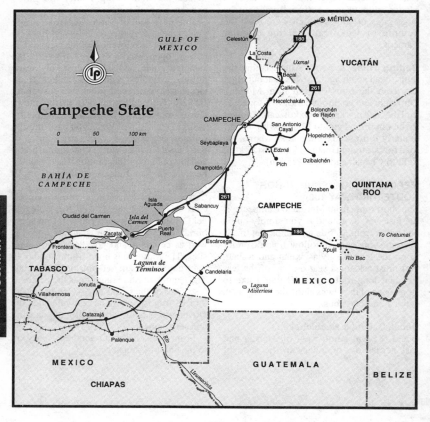

CAMPECHE

Population: 170,000

Filled with historic buildings, the centre of Campeche is quite appealing. Local people make their living fishing for shrimp or digging for oil, and the prosperity brought by those two activities is apparent in the town.

History

Once a Mayan trading village called Ah Kim Pech (Lord Sun Sheep-Tick), Campeche was invaded by the conquistadors in 1517. The Maya resisted and for nearly a quarter of a century the Spaniards were unable to fully conquer the region. Campeche was founded in 1531, but later abandoned due to Mayan hostility. Finally, by 1540 the conquistadors had gained sufficient control, under the leadership of Francisco de Montejo the Younger, to found a settlement here which survived. They named it the Villa de San Francisco de Campeche.

The settlement soon flourished as the major port of Yucatán. Locally grown timber, chicle and dyewoods were exported to Europe, as were gold and silver mined from other regions and shipped via Campeche. Such wealth did not escape the notice of pirates, who began their attacks only six years after the town was founded.

For two centuries, the depredations of pirates terrorised Campeche. Not only were ships attacked, but the port itself was invaded, its citizens robbed, its women raped and its buildings burned. In their most gruesome of assaults, in early 1663, the various pirate hordes set aside their jealousies to converge upon the city as a single flotilla, massacring many of Campeche's citizens in the process.

It took this tragedy to make the Spanish monarchy take preventive action, but not until five years later. Starting in 1668, 3.5-metre-thick ramparts were built. After 18 years of construction, a 2.5-km hexagon incorporating eight strategically placed baluartes surrounded the city.

Originally part of the state of Yucatán, Campeche became an autonomous state of Mexico in 1863. In the 19th century it fell into an economic decline brought on by the demise of mineral shipments to Spain. Independence, the freeing of Indians from plantation slavery, the devastation wrought by the War of the Castes and overall isolation put the port into a protracted decline.

Today, the hardwood timber and fishing industries are thriving and the discovery of offshore oil has led to a mini-boom in the city of Campeche.

Orientation

The old part of Campeche, enclosed by fragments of the sturdy walls, is where you'll spend most of your time. Though the baluartes stand, the walls themselves have been razed and replaced by streets which ring the city centre just as the walls once did. This is the Avenida Circuito Baluartes, or Circuit Avenue of the Bulwarks.

Besides the modern Plaza Moch-Cuouh, Campeche also has its Parque Principal, also called the Plaza de la Independencia, the standard Spanish colonial park with the cathedral on one side and former Palacio de Gobierno on another.

According to the compass, Campeche is oriented with its waterfront to the northwest, but tradition and convenience hold that the water is to the west, inland is east.

The ADO bus terminal is 1.7 km northeast of Plaza Moch-Cuouh along Avenida Gobernadores (Highway 180).

The railway station is three km east of the centre, south of Avenida Gobernadores on Avenida Héroes de Nacozari in the district called Colonia Cuatro Caminos.

The airport is east of the railway station at the northern end of Avenida López Portillo. To reach the air terminal you must go east to Avenida López Portillo, then north to the terminal, 3.5 km from Plaza Moch-Cuouh.

The central market, Mercado Pedro Sainz de Baranda, is at the junction of Calle 53 and Avenida Circuito Baluartes Este, just inland from the old city.

Information

Tourist Office The State Tourism Office

YUCATÁN

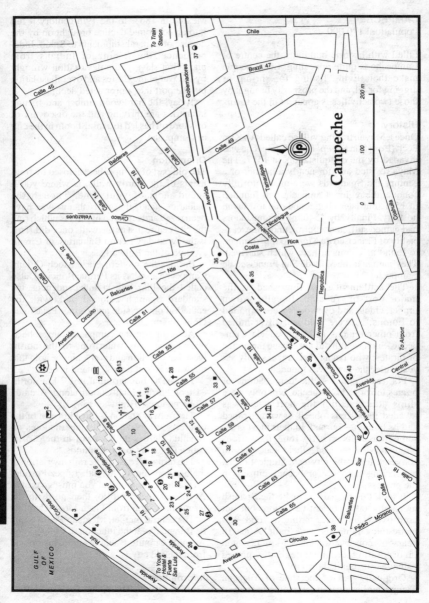

PLACES TO STAY

3	Ramada Hotel Campeche
4	Hotel Baluartes
14	Posada San Angel Inn
19	Hotel Reforma & Restaurant Marganzo
21	Hotel América Plaza
22	Hotel Roma
31	Hotel López
33	Hotel Colonial

PLACES TO EAT

15	Restaurant Los Portales
16	Restaurant-Bar Familiar La Parroquía
17	Restaurant del Parque
18	Café & Restaurant Campeche

23	Restaurant Miramar
24	Panificadora Nueva España
25	Cafetería y Nevería Continental

OTHER

1	Baluarte de Santiago & Jardín Botánico
2	Post Office (Edificio Federal)
5	Bancomer
6	Banco del Atlantico
7	Plaza Moch-Cuouh
8	Puerta del Mar
9	Baluarte de la Soledad
10	Parque Principal
11	Catedral de la Concepción
12	Mansión Carvajal
13	Banamex

20	Banco Mexicano
26	Baluarte de San Carlos
27	Banobras
28	Church
29	Cine Selem
30	Instituto de Cultura de Campeche
32	Ex-convento
34	Museo Regional de Campeche
35	Market
36	Baluarte de San Pedro
37	ADO (1st-Class) Bus Terminal
38	Baluarte de Santa Rosa & Tourist Office
39	Puerta de Tierra
40	Baluarte de San Francisco
41	Alameda
42	Baluarte de San Juan
43	IMSS Hospital

(☎ (981) 6-60-68, 6-67-67), is in the Baluarte de Santa Rosa, at the corner of Calles 14 and 67. The staff are very friendly and available Monday to Saturday from 8 am to 2.30 pm and 4 to 8.30 pm; closed Sunday.

Money Banks are open Monday to Friday from 9 am to 1 pm: Bancomer is across from Baluarte de la Soledad at Calle 59 No 2A, at Avenida 16 de Septiembre, Banco del Atlantico at Calle 50 No 406 and Banamex at Calle 10 No 15.

Post The central post office (☎ (981) 6-21-34), at the corner of Avenida 16 de Septiembre and Calle 53, is in the Edificio Federal near the Baluarte de Santiago at the north-western corner of the old town. Hours are Monday to Friday 8 am to 7 pm, Saturday 8 am to 1 pm and Sunday 8 am to 2 pm.

Walking Tour

Seven bulwarks still stand; four of them are of interest. You can see them all by following the Avenida Circuito Baluartes around the city on a two-km walk.

Because of traffic, some of the walk is not very pleasant, so you might want to limit your excursion to the first three or four baluartes described below, which house museums and gardens. If you'd rather have a guided tour, you can sign up for a city tour at either the Ramada Inn or Hotel Baluartes for US$18. We'll start at the south-western end of the Plaza Moch-Cuouh.

Close to the modern Palacio de Gobierno, at Circuito Baluartes and Avenida Justo Sierra, near the intersection of Calles 8 and 65 and a ziggurat fountain, is the **Baluarte de San Carlos**. The interior of the bulwark is now arranged as the **Sala de las Fortificaciones**, or Chamber of Fortifications, with some interesting scale models of the city's fortifications in the 18th century. You can also visit the dungeon, and look out over the sea from the roof. Baluarte de San Carlos is open from 9 am to 1 pm and 5 to 7.30 pm daily, for free.

Next, head north along Calle 8. At the intersection with Calle 59, notice the **Puerta del Mar**, or Sea Gate, which provided access to the city from the sea before the area to the north-west was filled in. The gate was demolished in 1893 but rebuilt in 1957 when its historical value was realised.

The **Baluarte de la Soledad**, on the north

YUCATÁN

side of the Plaza Moch-Cuouh close to the intersection of Calles 8 and 57, is the setting for the **Museo de Estelas Maya**. Many of the Mayan artefacts here are badly weathered, but the precise line drawing next to each stone shows you what the designs once looked like. The bulwark also has an interesting exhibition of colonial Campeche. Among the antiquities are 17th and 18th-century seafaring equipment and armaments used to battle pirate invaders. The museum is open 9 am to 2 pm and 3 to 8 pm Tuesday to Saturday, 9 am to 1 pm on Sunday, closed Monday. Admission is free.

Just across the street from the baluarte is the **Parque Principal**, Campeche's favourite park. Whereas the sterile, modernistic, shadeless Plaza Moch-Cuouh was built to glorify its government builders, the Parque Principal (Plaza de la Independencia) is the pleasant place where locals go to sit and think, chat, smooch, plot, snooze, stroll and cool off after the heat of the day, or have their shoes shined.

Construction was begun on the **Catedral de la Concepción**, on the north side of the plaza, shortly after the conquistadors established the town, but it wasn't finished for centuries.

The attractive, arcaded former **Palacio de Gobierno** (or Palacio Municipal) dates only from the 19th century.

Continue north along Calle 8 several blocks to the **Baluarte de Santiago**, at the intersection of Calles 8 and 51. It houses a minuscule yet lovely tropical garden, the **Jardín Botánico Xmuch Haltun**, with 250 species of tropical plants set around a lovely courtyard of fountains. Tours of the garden are given in Spanish every hour or so in the morning and evening, and in English at noon and 4 pm. The garden is open Tuesday to Saturday from 9 am to 8 pm and Sunday 9 am to 1 pm. Admission is free.

From the Baluarte de Santiago, walk east (inland) along Calle 51 to Calle 18, where you'll come to the **Baluarte de San Pedro**, in the middle of a complex traffic intersection which marks the beginning of the Avenida Gobernadores. Within the bulwark

is the **Exposición Permanente de Artesanías**, a regional exhibition of crafts, open Monday to Friday from 9 am to 1 pm and 5 to 8 pm. Admission is free.

To make the entire circuit, head south from the Baluarte de San Pedro along the Avenida Circuito Baluartes to the **Baluarte de San Francisco** at Calle 57 and, a block farther along at Calle 59, the **Puerta de Tierra**, or Land Gate. The **Baluarte de San Juan**, at Calles 18 and 65, marks the south-westernmost point of the old city walls. From here you bear right (south-west) along Calle 67 (Avenida Circuito Baluartes) to the intersection of Calles 14 and 67 and the **Baluarte de Santa Rosa**.

Museo Regional de Campeche

The Regional Museum (☎ 6-91-11) is set up in the former mansion of the Teniente del Rey, or King's Lieutenant, at Calle 59 No 36, between Calles 14 and 16. Architecture, hydrology, commerce, art, religion and Mayan science are all dealt with in interesting and revealing displays.

Hours are 8 am to 2 pm and 2.30 to 8 pm Tuesday to Saturday, 9 am to 1 pm Sunday, closed Monday. Admission is an unreasonable US$6.

Mansión Carvajal

Campeche's commercial success as a port town is evident in its stately houses and mansions. Perhaps the most striking of these is the Mansión Carvajal, on Calle 10 between Calles 51 and 53, mid-block on the left (west) side of the street as you come from the Plaza de la Independencia.

It started its eventful history as the city residence of Don Fernando Carvajal Estrada and his wife Sra María Iavalle de Carvajal. Don Fernando was among Campeche's richest hacendados, or hacienda-owners. The monogram you see throughout the building, 'RCY', is that of Rafael Carvajal Ytorralde, Don Fernando's father and founder of the fortune.

Other Sights

Walk through Campeche's streets – espe-

Mansión Carvajal

cially Calles 55, 57 and 59 – looking for more beautiful houses. The walk is best done in the evening when the sun is not blasting down and when the lights from inside illuminate courtyards, salons and alleys.

Forts

Four km south of the Plaza Moch-Cuouh along the coast road stands the Fuerte de San Luis, an 18th-century fortress of which only a few battlements remain. Near the fort, a road off to the left (south-east) climbs the hill one km to the Fuerte de San Miguel, a restored fortress now closed to the public. The view of the city and the sea is beautiful, but the walk uphill is a killer.

Getting There & Away To reach the Fuerte de San Luis, take a 'Lerma' or 'Playa Bonita' bus south-west along the coastal highway (toward Villahermosa); the youth hostel is out this way as well (see below).

Beaches

Campeche's beaches are not particularly inviting. The Balneario Popular, four km

south of the Plaza Moch-Cuouh along the coastal road just past the Fuerte de San Luis, should be avoided. A few km farther along is Playa Bonita with some facilities (restaurant, lockers, toilets) but water of questionable cleanliness and, at the weekends, wall-to-wall local flesh.

If you're really hard up for a swim, head south-west to the town of Seybaplaya, 33 km from Plaza Moch-Cuouh. The highway skirts narrow, pure-white beaches dotted with fishing smacks, the water is much cleaner, but there are no facilities. The best beach here is called Payucan.

Edzná Ruins

Should you want to visit the ruins at Edzná from Campeche, you can sign up for a tour at one of the larger hotels (about US$25), or you can do it on your own by bus. See the Uxmal to Campeche section in the previous chapter for details.

Places to Stay – bottom end

Youth Hostel Campeche's *Youth Hostel* (☎ (981) 6-18-02), on Avenida Agustín Melgar, is 3.5 km south-west of the Plaza Moch-Cuouh off the shore road; the shore road is Avenida Ruiz Cortines in town, but changes its name to Avenida Resurgimiento as it heads out of town toward Villahermosa. Buses marked 'Lerma' or 'Playa Bonita' will take you there. Ask the driver to let you off at the Albergue de la Juventud and you'll cross some railway tracks and pass a Coca-Cola/Cristal bottling plant before coming to the intersection with Avenida Agustín Melgar, near which the bus will drop you. Melgar is unmarked, of course. Look for the street going left (inland) between a Pemex fuel station and a VW dealership – that's Melgar. The hostel is 150 metres up on the right-hand side.

It is actually a university youth-and-sports facilities complex. To find the hostel section, walk into the compound entrance and out to the large courtyard with swimming pool, turn left and walk 25 metres to the dormitory building. The rate is less than US$4 per

YUCATÁN

person per night. There is a cafeteria which serves inexpensive meals.

Places to Stay – middle

Hotels The cheapest hotels – *Reforma, Castelmar, Roma* – are dumps. *Hotel Colonial* (☎ (981) 6-22-22), Calle 14 No 122, between Calles 55 and 57, offers much more comfort for just a bit more money. The hotel was once the mansion of Doña Gertrudis Eulalia Torostieta y Zagasti, former Spanish governor of Tabasco and Yucatán. The well-furnished rooms have fans and good showers with hot water. Price is US$20/25/30 a single/double/triple.

Hotel América Plaza (☎ (981) 6-45-88; fax 1 16 18), Calle 10 No 252, is a fine colonial house with large rooms overlooking the interior court costing a somewhat expensive US$33/36 a single/double with fan.

Posada San Angel Inn (☎ (981) 6-77-18), Calle 10 No 307, between Calles 55 and 53. The rooms remind one of a cell block, but they're modern and clean, with fan for US$30 a double, US$36 with air-con.

Hotel López (☎ 6-33-44), Calle 12 No 189, between Calles 61 and 63, is not as well kept as it should be to charge US$38 a double.

Places to Stay – top end

The best hotel in town is the 119-room *Ramada Hotel Campeche* (☎ (981) 6-22-33), Avenida Ruiz Cortines No 51. Prices are US$100/110/125 a single/double/triple.

Just south of the Ramada is its competition, the older but still comfortable *Hotel Baluartes* (☎ (981) 6-39-11). The Baluartes' well-used rooms are air-conditioned and comfortable, with sea views and cheaper at US$63/68 a single/double.

Places to Eat – bottom end

Among the best eateries is the *Restaurant Marganzo* (☎ 6-23-28), Calle 8 No 265, between Calles 57 and 59, facing the sea and the Baluarte de la Soledad. Breakfast costs US$2 to US$4, sandwiches US$4 to US$5; seafood is more than twice that much.

Cafetería y Nevería Continental (☎ 6-22-

66), Calle 61 No 2, at the corner of Calle 8, serves ice cream, cakes, desserts and drinks, but they have a few items from which to make a good, cheap lunch: filete de pescado, for example, or the hearty soup named caldo xochitl.

If you'd just like to pick up some sweet rolls, biscuits, bread or cakes, head for the *Panificadora Nueva España*, Calle 10 at the corner of Calle 61, which has a large assortment of fresh baked goods at very low prices.

The *Café y Restaurant Campeche* (☎ 6-21-28), Calle 57 No 2, opposite Parque Principal, is in the building which saw the birth of Justo Sierra, founder of Mexico's national university, but the restaurant is very simple, bright with fluorescent light bulbs and loud with a blaring TV set. The *platillo del día* usually costs less than US$4.

In the same block facing the plaza is the *Restaurant del Parque* (☎ 6-02-40), Calle 57 No 8, a cheerful little place serving fish, meat and shrimp. It opens early for breakfast.

Places to Eat – middle

Restaurant Miramar (☎ 6-28-83), corner of Calles 8 and 61, specialises in Campeche's seafood. Full meals cost between US$12 and US$20. It's open 8 am to midnight Monday to Friday, till 1 am Saturday, and 11 am to 7 pm Sunday.

Perhaps the best known restaurant in town is the *Restaurant-Bar Familiar La Parroquía* (☎ 6-18-29), Calle 55, between 10 and 12. The complete family restaurant-café-hangout, La Parroquía serves breakfasts priced at US$2.25 to US$3.50 from 7 to 10 am Monday to Friday and substantial lunch and dinner fare like chuleta de cerdo (pork chop), filete a la tampiqueña, shrimp cocktail or shrimp salad and even fresh pampano, for US$5 to US$11.

Entertainment

On Friday evenings at 8 pm (weather permitting) from September to May, the state tourism authorities sponsor *Estampas Turísticas*, performances of folk music and dancing, in the Plaza Moch-Cuouh. Other performances, sponsored by the city govern-

Campeche – Getting There & Away 395

ment, take place in the Parque Principal on Thursday, Friday and Saturday evenings at about 7 pm. Be sure to confirm these times and places with the tourist office.

Getting There & Away

Air The airport is west of the railway station at the end of Avenida López Portillo (Avenida Central), across the tracks about 800 metres away, or 3.5 km from Plaza Moch-Cuouh. You must take a taxi (US$5) to the city centre.

Bus Campeche's 1st-class ADO bus terminal is on Avenida Gobernadores, 1.7 km from Plaza Moch-Cuouh, or about 1.5 km from most hotels. The 2nd-class terminal is directly behind it. For village buses to Cayal, Pich and Hool (for Edzná), go to the market at the eastern end of Calle 53 across Avenida Circuito Baluartes Este.

Here's information on daily buses from Campeche:

Cancún – 512 km, nine hours; change at Mérida
Chetumal – 422 km, seven hours (US$16), three buses
Edzná – 66 km, 1½ hours; or take a faster bus to San Antonio Cayal (45 km) and hitch south from there
Mérida – 195 km (short route via Becal), three hours; 250 km (long route via Uxmal), four hours; 33 1st-class buses (US$8) by ADO round the clock; 13 2nd-class buses, US$7, by Autobuses del Sur
Mexico City – 1360 km, 21 hours (US$52), two buses
Palenque – 362 km, 5½ hours (US$13), one direct bus at 6.30 pm; many other buses drop you at Catazajá (Palenque turnoff), 27 km north of Palenque village
San Cristóbal de las Casas – 820 km, 14 hours; change at Villahermosa
Villahermosa – 450 km (US$17), 15 buses; they'll drop you at Catazajá (Palenque junction) if you like

Train The railway station is three km northeast of the city centre, south of Avenida Gobernadores on Avenida Héroes de Nacozari in the district called Colonia Cuatro Caminos. Buses departing from a stop to the right (west) as you leave the station will take you to the centre.

Around Campeche

ESCÁRCEGA
Population: 18,000

Most buses passing through Escárcega stop here to give passengers a refreshments break, but there is no other reason to stop in this town at the junction of highways 186 and 261, 150 km south of Campeche and 301 km from Villahermosa.

The town is spread out along two km of Highway 186 toward Chetumal. It's 1.7 km between the ADO and Autobuses del Sur bus stations. Most hotels are nearer to the Autobuses del Sur bus station than to the ADO; most of the better restaurants are near the ADO bus station.

Among the better hotels is the *Hotel El Yucateco* (☎ (981) 4-00-65), Calle 50 No 42-A, charging US$18 a double for a room with fan and private shower, a bit more with air-con.

There's also the *Hotel María Isabel* (☎ (981) 4-00-45), Avenida Justo Sierra No 127, 450 metres from Autobuses del Sur, 1200 metres from ADO. Rates are similar to El Yucateco

Hotel Escárcega (☎ (981) 4-01-86/7/8), on the main street, is the best place in town, one km from Autobuses del Sur, 550 metres from ADO.

ESCÁRCEGA TO CHETUMAL

Highway 186 heads due east from Escárcega through the scrubby jungle to Chetumal. Right on the border between the states of Campeche and Quintana Roo near the village of Xpujil, 153 km east of Escárcega and 120 km west of Chetumal, are several important Mayan archaeological sites: Xpujil, Becan, Chicanna and Río Bec.

Xpujil, Becan & Chicanna Ruins

These pristine unrestored sites, largely free of tourists, will fascinate true ruins buffs, but be forewarned that those expecting park-like sites such as Uxmal and Chichén Itzá will be

YUCATÁN

disappointed. Most of what you see here is jungle and rubble.

Orientation The village of Xpujil is the landmark, where the buses stop. The Xpujil ruins are visible from the highway; those of Becan are eight km west of Xpujil and 200 metres north of the highway. Chicanna, 2.5 km to the west of Becan, is only about 500 metres south of the highway. If you want to do all these ruins in a day, hop on an early bus from Escárcega, cajole the driver to drop you at Chicanna, go on to Becan, then Xpujil and wait in the village at Xpujil for a bus to take you onward to Chetumal, or return to Escárcega. If the driver won't stop (as is usual), you'll have to start your explorations in the village of Xpujil.

Xpujil The latticed towers of Xpujil's pyramid greet you as you explore the village. This temple is the only truly excavated building on the site. It is built in the Río Bec style (see below). There are two sculpted masks carved into the rear of the temple. New excavations are under way. The site flourished from 400 to 900 AD, though there was a settlement here much earlier.

Becan Becan means 'Path of the Snake' in Mayan. It is well named, as a two-km moat snakes its way around the entire city to protect it from attack. Seven bridges used to provide access to the city. Becan was occupied from 550 BC until 1000 AD.

Still to be excavated from Becan's profuse jungle cover are subterranean rooms and passages linked to religious ritual. Archaeologists have dug up some artefacts from Teotihuacán here, but still must determine whether they got here through trade or conquest. There's little to thrill the eye, though a few of the monumental staircases stimulate the imagination.

Chicanna Buildings at Chicanna are in a mixture of Chenes and Río Bec styles. The city flourished about 660 to 680 AD, when the eight-room 'palace' here was probably occupied by nobles. The palace's monster-mask façade symbolises Itzamná, the Mouth of the Serpent. Each inner room in the palace has a raised bench of stone; the other rooms show signs of having had curtains draped across their doorways for privacy.

Río Bec This site actually includes about 10 groups of buildings placed here and there in a site of 50 sq km. The sites are difficult to reach; a 4WD and guide are recommended.

Río Bec gave its name to the prevalent architectural style of the region characterised by long, low buildings that look as though they're divided into sections, each with a huge serpent-mouth for a door. The façades are decorated with smaller masks, geometric designs and columns. At the corners of the buildings are tall, solid towers with extremely small, steep steps, topped by small temples. Many of these towers have roofcombs as well.

ESCÁRCEGA TO PALENQUE

The 212-km ride from Escárcega to Palenque is unremarkable, but very hot. Upon leaving Escárcega and heading south-west, the fast, straight Highway 186 passes through regions aptly known as El Tormento (Torment) and Sal Si Puedes (Save Yourself if You Can).

By the time you reach Río Champon (or Chumpan), the traditional Mayan na with thatched roof and walls of sticks, wattle-and-daub or stone, has disappeared, giving way to board shacks with roofs of corrugated iron. As you enter the region of the Río Usumacinta the landscape becomes lush, the rich greenery a pleasant surprise after the semi-arid, riverless limestone shelf of Yucatán. But along with the lushness comes high humidity and no coolness.

About 184 km south-west of Escárcega you come to Catazajá, the junction with the road to Palenque, Ocosingo and San Cristóbal de las Casas. Turn left (south) for Palenque, 27 km south of the highway junction. If your goal is Villahermosa, continue straight on along Highway 186.

Yucatán's Caribbean Coast

The coast of Quintana Roo is among the fastest developing areas in Mexico. Despite the overbuilding of hotels in Cancún, developers are rushing to build more leisure palaces along the beaches of what is known rather romantically as the 'Cancún-Tulum Corridor'. A new, wider highway is planned to run along the corridor, inland from the old highway. When finished, it will bring the bustle of the city to this otherwise laid-back coast.

For the time being, however, there are still many places to enjoy. Small hotels stand alone on some stretches of beach. The Sian Ka'an Biosphere Reserve, south of Tulum, is protected from development. And it will be a few more years before Playa del Carmen, now a delightful, laid-back town, has the uptight money-grubbing fervour of Cancún.

GETTING AROUND
Interplaya runs shuttle buses up and down the coast between Cancún and Tulum every 20 minutes, stopping at major towns and tourist attractions. The fare depends upon the distance travelled. There are also regular intercity buses; see the Cancún section for details.

Distances shown below ('Km 328', etc) are as measured from the centre of Chetumal, capital of the state of Quintana Roo.

PUERTO MORELOS (Km 328)
Puerto Morelos, 32 km south of Cancún, is a sleepy fishing village known principally for its car ferry to Cozumel. There is a good budget hotel and travellers who have reason to spend the night here find it refreshingly free of tourists. A handful of scuba divers come to explore the splendid reef 600 metres offshore, reachable by boat.

Places to Stay & Eat
For good basic budget lodging, stay at the family-run *Posada Amor*, south of the centre. Rooms with fan and a clean shared bathroom cost US$36, single or double. Good meals are served in the cosy dining room.

North of the centre, the *Cabañas Puerto Morelos* (☎ (987) 1-00-04; in the USA (612) 441-7630) has two comfy apartments rented out by Bill and Connie Butcher, formerly of Minnesota. Rates for two persons are US$275 per week in summer, US$450 in winter. Write for reservations: Apdo Postal 1524, 77501 Cancún, Q Roo. *Los Arrecifes* (☎ (987) 1-01-12) has beachfront rooms for US$55 a double in summer, US$65 in winter.

The *Caribbean Reef Club* (☎ (987) 4-29-32; fax (98) 83-22-44; in USA (800) 322-6286) is a beautiful, very comfortable, quiet resort hotel right on the beach. Lots of water sports activities and helpful owners are the bonuses when you pay the rates: US$110 to US$140 from mid-December to late April, about 30% cheaper in summer.

For a fine moderately priced meal, try the *Doña Zenaida Restaurant*, on Avenida Javier Rojo Gómez, just south of the centre on the beach.

Getting There & Away
Interplaya buses drop you on the highway, two km west of the centre of Puerto Morelos. All 2nd-class and many 1st-class buses stop at Puerto Morelos coming from, or en route to, Cancún, 34 km (45 minutes) away. Buses generally come by every few hours during the day.

The car ferry (*transbordador*; ☎ in Cozumel (987) 2-08-27, 2-09-50) to Cozumel leaves Puerto Morelos daily. Departure times vary by the day of the week and from season to season.

Unless you plan to stay for awhile on Cozumel, it's hardly worth shipping your vehicle. You must get in line two or three hours before departure time and hope there's enough space on the ferry for you. Fare for the 2½ to four-hour voyage is US$55 per car,

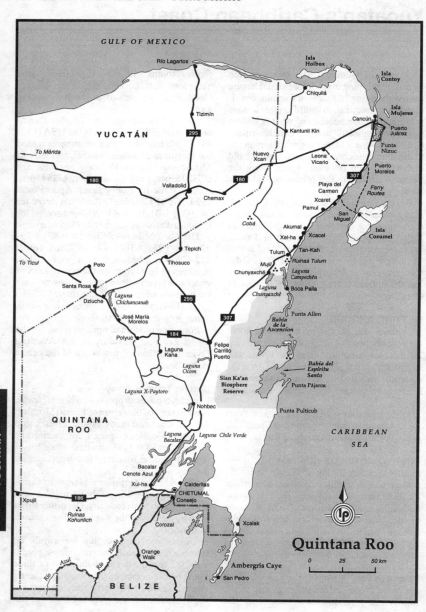

Quintana Roo

0   25   50 km

US$8 per person; you needn't have a car in order to steam over to Cozumel on this boat, of course. Note that rough seas often prevent the ferry from sailing. At times, it has remained in port for up to a week until the weather cleared.

Departure from Cozumel is from the dock in front of the Hotel Sol Caribe, south of town along the shore road. Be there several hours ahead of departure time in order to get in line.

PLAYA DEL CARMEN

For decades Playa (or Playacar, as it's also called) was just a simple fishing village on the coast opposite Cozumel. With the construction of Cancún, however, the number of travellers roaming this part of Yucatán increased exponentially. Now Playa has taken over from Cozumel as the preferred resort town in the area. Playa's beaches are better and nightlife groovier than Cozumel's, and the reef diving is just as good. On the beaches, tops are optional everywhere; nudity is optional about a km north of Playa town centre.

What's to do in Playa? Hang out. Swim. Dive. Stroll the beach. Get some sun. Catch the Interplaya shuttle to other points along the coast. In the evening, Avenida Quinta, the pedestrian mall, is the place to sit and have a meal or a drink, or stroll and watch others having meals and drinks. Early evening happy hour (5 to 7 pm), with two drinks for the price of one, is an iron rule. I found it impossible to order a single beer. The waiter automatically brought two.

Places to Stay

Playa del Carmen is developing and changing so fast, that almost anything written about it is obsolete by the time it's printed. Expect many new hotels by the time you arrive, and many changes in the old ones. The room prices given below are for the busy winter season. Prices are substantially lower in the off season.

Places to Stay – bottom end

The youth hostel, or *Villa Deportiva Juvenil*, is a modern establishment offering the cheapest clean lodging in town, but it's quite a walk to the beach and you sleep in single-sex dorm bunks. On the positive side, the hostel is cheap at US$5.50 per bunk.

Posada Lily, on Avenida Juárez (Avenida Principal) just a block inland from the main square, offers clean rooms with private shower and fan for US$22 a double. If it's full, try the *Hotel Dos Hermanos*, on Avenida 30 at Calle 4, for the same price. A half-block from the Dos Hermanos is the similar *Mom's Hotel* (☎ (987) 3-03-15).

Posada Sian Ka'an (☎ in Mérida (99) 29-74-22), on Avenida Quinta, has clean, simple rooms in semi-rustic buildings not far from the beach. It's a bit expensive for what you get: US$28 for a double without running water, US$46 for a double with private shower and fan.

Hotel El Elefante, on Avenida 10 at Calle 10, has undistinguished rooms with bath for US$38.

Places to Stay – middle

My favourite, *Hotel Maya Bric*, on Avenida Quinta between Calles 8 and 10, is a small hotel with big rooms, set around a swimming pool amidst flowering shrubs and coconut trees. Rates vary with the seasons, but range from US$28 in summer to US$55 or more in winter for a double with bath.

Hotel Costa del Mar (☎ (987) 3-00-58; fax 2-02-31; toll-free in USA (800) 329-8388) has clean, attractive rooms on the beach off Avenida Quinta at Calle 10, for US$55/75 a double with fan/air-con.

Hotel Delfín (☎ (987) 3-01-76), Avenida Quinta at Calle 6, is a newish concrete block building offering standard plain rooms with ceiling fan and tiled bathroom for US$36 to US$56 a double.

Cueva Pargo (☎ (987) 3-03-51) has a variety of cabañas at a variety of prices from US$35 a single, US$44 a double to US$90.

Blue Parrot Inn (☎ (987) 3-00-83; fax 3-00-49; toll-free in USA (800) 634-3547), on the beach at Calle 12, is the hip place to

YUCATÁN

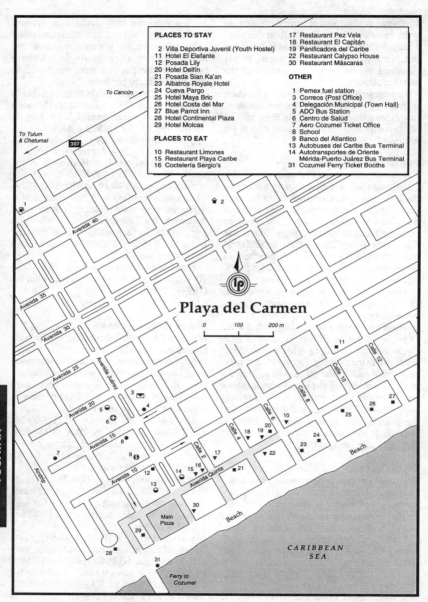

PLACES TO STAY

2 Villa Deportiva Juvenil (Youth Hostel)
11 Hotel El Elefante
12 Posada Lily
20 Hotel Delfín
21 Posada Sian Ka'an
23 Albatros Royale Hotel
24 Cueva Pargo
25 Hotel Maya Bric
26 Hotel Costa del Mar
27 Blue Parrot Inn
28 Hotel Continental Plaza
29 Hotel Molcas

PLACES TO EAT

10 Restaurant Limones
15 Restaurant Playa Caribe
16 Coctelería Sergio's
17 Restaurant Pez Vela
18 Restaurant El Capitán
19 Panificadora del Caribe
22 Restaurant Calypso House
30 Restaurant Máscaras

OTHER

1 Pemex fuel station
3 Correos (Post Office)
4 Delegación Municipal (Town Hall)
5 ADO Bus Station
6 Centro de Salud
7 Aero Cozumel Ticket Office
8 School
9 Banco del Atlantico
13 Autobuses del Caribe Bus Terminal
14 Autotransportes de Oriente
   Mérida-Puerto Juárez Bus Terminal
31 Cozumel Ferry Ticket Booths

To Cancún

To Tulum
& Chetumal

307

Avenida 40

Avenida 35

Avenida 30

Avenida 25

Avenida Juárez

Avenida 20

Avenida 15

Avenida 10

Airstrip

Playa del Carmen

0   100   200 m

Calle 12

Calle 10

Calle 8

Calle 6

Calle 4

Calle 2

Avenida Quinta

Main
Plaza

Beach

Beach

*CARIBBEAN
SEA*

Ferry to
Cozumel

YUCATÁN

stay. The thatch-roofed beach cabañas cost US$60 to US$95, depending upon facilities.

Albatros Royale Hotel (☎ (987) 3-00-01), Calle 6 near the beach, was new in 1993, with two-storey thatched stucco rooms with bath for US$50 to US$75.

Built above the ferry dock with sea views, the *Hotel Molcas* (☎ (987) 3-01-34; fax 3-00-71) charges US$60 to US$90 (depending upon the season) for its comfortable air-con double rooms.

Places to Stay – top end

Those seeking international-class luxury lodging will find the *Hotel Continental Plaza* (☎ (987) 3-01-00; fax 3-01-05; toll-free in USA (800) 882-6684) to their liking at US$140 to US$200 per room.

Places to Eat

Avenida Quinta is lined with restaurants, each offering bargain set-price meals. Stroll along and find a good one. All are open for lunch and dinner, some for breakfast.

Restaurant Playa Caribe, on Avenida Quinta seems to be a bit cheaper than the other places. A big, varied Mexican combination plate costs US$6.50. The nearby *Restaurant Pez Vela* on Calle 2 is another good choice. North-east of it, *Karen's Grill & Pizza* often has marimba music in the evenings, but is more expensive at US$10 to US$12 for a meal.

Coctelería Sergio's, Avenida Quinta and Calle 2, is simple, but has good food at cheap prices, like fish fillet for US$4.

Restaurant Calypso House, on Avenida Quinta, has good breakfasts for US$3 to US$4 (it opens at 7 am). Later on there are filling set-price meals for US$4 to US$8.

Of the more expensive places, the *Restaurant Máscaras*, on the main plaza, is the most famous and long-lived. The food is OK, but it's the company you come for. Drinks are expensive.

A better choice as far as the food is concerned is the *Restaurant Limones*, Avenida Quinta at Calle 6, where the atmosphere is more sedate than jolly, and the food is a bit more expensive but well worth the extra money.

For make-your-own breakfasts and picnics, there's the *Panificadora del Caribe*, on Avenida Quinta across the road from the Restaurant Calypso House.

Getting There & Away

Air Aero Cozumel (☎ (987) 3-03-50), part of Mexicana Inter, has an office next to Playa's airstrip. They fly little aircraft across the water from Cozumel to Playa in seven minutes every two hours from 8 am to 6 pm during the winter season. In summer there are usually four flights per day in each direction, departing from Cozumel at 9 and 11 am, and 3 and 5 pm, returning from Playa del Carmen 20 minutes later. The flight costs US$19 one way.

Bus Numerous companies serve Playa del Carmen (see map for terminal locations). Besides the Interplaya buses running up and down the coast every 20 minutes, there are Autotransportes Playa Express buses every 30 minutes, charging US$2.75 from Playa to either Tulum or Cancún.

Cancún – 65 km, one hour; six 1st-class (US$3), seven 2nd-class (US$2.75) by Autotransportes de Oriente M-PJ; Autotransportes del Caribe also has eight buses daily.

Chetumal – 315 km, 5½ hours; five 1st-class (US$12), and five 2nd-class (US$10) by Autotransportes del Caribe, stopping at Felipe Carrillo Puerto and Bacalar; Expresso de Oriente has luxury buses as well.

Cobá – 113 km, two hours; Autotransportes de Oriente and Expresso de Oriente have several 1st-class (US$2.50) and 2nd-class (US$2) buses daily on the route Tulum, Cobá, Valladolid.

Mérida – 378 km, eight hours; six 1st-class (US$8.50), six 2nd-class (US$7) by Autotransportes de Oriente M-PJ; these buses stop at Valladolid and Chichén Itzá. Six 1st-class buses by Expresso de Oriente and several more by A del Caribe buses to Mérida go via Oxkutzcab, Ticul and Muna.

Tulum – 63 km, one hour; lots of buses, including the Interplaya and Playa Express shuttles for US$2.75.

YUCATÁN

Valladolid – 213 km, four hours; the many Auto-transportes de Oriente buses to Mérida stop at Valladolid (US$9 1st-class, US$8 2nd-class), but it's faster to go on the *ruta corta* ('short route') via Tulum and Cobá (see Cobá), which is run by Expresso de Oriente as well.

Boats to Cozumel A variety of watercraft ply the seas between Playa del Carmen and Cozumel, taking between 30 and 75 minutes to make the voyage and charging US$5 to US$9 one way. Schedules, particularly in summer, may change, so buy a one-way ticket. That way, if your chosen boat doesn't materialise for a scheduled return trip, you can buy a ticket on another line.

Fastest boats are the waterjets *México* and *México III*, charging the top price, running about every two hours from dawn to dusk, but voyages may be cancelled at the last moment if the boat breaks down or if there aren't enough passengers. Note also that 'fast boat' emblazoned on ticket offices and billboards may not mean 'waterjet', and the 'fast boat' may actually be slower than the waterjet.

The next best boat is the *Playa del Carmen*, offering only slightly less in the way of comfort, speed and price.

The slowest, oldest, least comfortable but cheapest boats are the *Xel-Ha* and *Cozumeleño*, best avoided by those prone to seasickness.

COZUMEL
Population: 175,000

Cozumel ('Place of the Swallows') floats in the midst of the Caribbean's crystalline waters 71 km south of Cancún. Measuring 53 km long and 14 km wide, it is the largest of Mexico's islands. Cozumel's legendary Palancar Reef was made famous by Jacques Cousteau and is a lure for divers from all over the world.

Though it has that beautiful offshore reef, Cozumel does not have many good swimming beaches. The western shore is mostly sharp, weathered limestone and coral, and the eastern beaches are too often pounded by dangerous surf.

History
Mayan settlement here dates from 300 AD. During the Post-Classic period, Cozumel flourished both as a commercial centre and as a major ceremonial site. Maya sailed here on pilgrimages to shrines dedicated to Ixchel, the goddess of fertility and the moon.

Although the first Spanish contact with Cozumel in 1518 by Juan de Grijalva was peaceful, it was followed by the Cortés expedition in 1519. Cortés, en route to his conquest of the mainland, laid waste to Cozumel's Mayan shrines. The Maya offered staunch military resistance until they were conquered in 1545. The coming of the Spaniards brought smallpox to this otherwise surprisingly disease-free place. Within a generation after the conquest, the island's population had dwindled to only 300 souls, Mayan and Spaniards.

While the island remained virtually deserted into the late 17th century, its coves provided sanctuary and headquarters for several notorious pirates including Jean Lafitte and Henry Morgan. Pirate brutality led the remaining populace to move to the mainland and it wasn't until 1848 that Cozumel began to be resettled by Indians fleeing the War of the Castes.

At the turn of the century, the island's population, which was now largely mestizo, grew thanks to the craze for chewing gum. Cozumel was a port of call on the chicle export route and locals harvested chicle on the island. Although chicle was later replaced by synthetic gum, Cozumel's economic base expanded with the building of a US air force base here during WW II.

When the US military departed, the island fell into an economic slump and many of its people left. Those who stayed fished for a livelihood until 1961, when underwater scientist Jacques Cousteau arrived, explored the reef and told the world about Cozumel's beauties. A resort destination was born.

Orientation

It's easy to make your way on foot around the island's only town, San Miguel de Cozumel, where most of the budget lodgings are. Some of the middle-range places are here as well. For top-end hotels, take a taxi up or down the coast. The airport, two km north of town, is accessible only by taxi or on foot.

The waterfront boulevard is Avenida Rafael Melgar; on the west side of Melgar south of the ferry docks is a narrow but usable sand beach. Just opposite the ferry docks (officially called the Muelle Fiscal) on Melgar in the centre of town is the main plaza.

Information

Tourist Office The local tourist office (☎ (987) 2-09-72) is situated in a building facing the main square to the north of the Bancomer, on the 2nd floor. Opening hours are Monday to Friday from 9 am to 3 pm and 6 to 8 pm.

Money For currency exchange, the casas de cambio located around the town are your best bets for long hours and fast service,

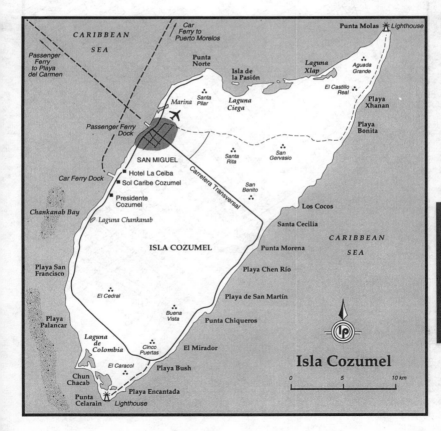

Isla Cozumel

YUCATÁN

San Miguel (Cozumel)

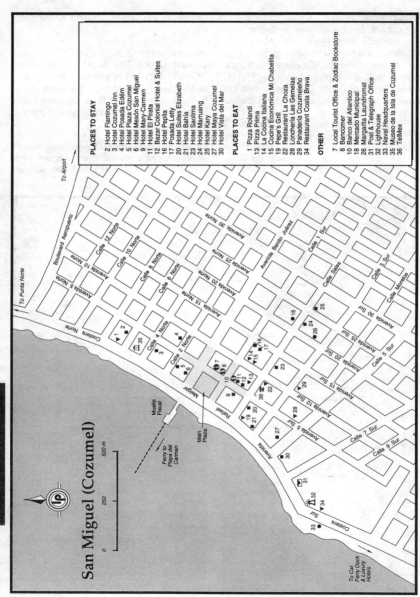

PLACES TO STAY

2 Hotel Flamingo
3 Hotel Cozumel Inn
4 Hotel Posada Edém
5 Hotel Plaza Cozumel
6 Hotel Mesón San Miguel
9 Hotel Mary-Carmen
11 Hotel El Pirata
12 Bazar Colonial Hotel & Suites
16 Hotel Pepita
17 Posada Letty
20 Hotel Suites Elizabeth
21 Hotel Bahía
23 Hotel Saolima
24 Hotel Marruang
25 Hotel Kary
27 Hotel Maya Cozumel
30 Hotel Vista del Mar

PLACES TO EAT

1 Pizza Rolandi
13 Pizza Prima
14 La Cocina Italiana
15 Cocina Económica Mi Chabelita
19 Pepe's Grill
22 Restaurant La Choza
28 Lonchería Las Gemelas
29 Panadería Cozumeleño
34 Restaurant Costa Brava

OTHER

7 Local Tourist Office & Zodiac Bookstore
8 Bancomer
10 Banco del Atlantico
18 Mercado Municipal
26 Margarita Laundromat
31 Post & Telegraph Office
32 Lighthouse
33 Naval Headquarters
35 Museo de la Isla de Cozumel
36 TelMex

though they may charge as much as 3.5% commission.

Bancomer and Banco del Atlantico, off the main plaza, change money only from 10 am to 12.30 pm, Monday to Friday, and the queues are long. Banpaís, facing the ferry docks, will change your travellers' cheques from 9 am to 1.30 pm Monday to Friday for a 1% commission.

Most of the major hotels, restaurants and stores will change money at a less advantageous rate when the banks are closed. ATMs, which issue cash dollars or pesos against your cash or credit card, are beginning to appear.

Post & Telecommunications The post and telegraph office (☎ (987) 2-01-06) is south of Calle 7 Sur on the waterfront just off Avenida Melgar. Hours are Monday to Friday from 9 am to 1 pm and 3 to 6 pm, and Saturday from 9 am to noon. Cozumel's postal code is 77600.

The TelMex telephone office is on Calle Salas between Avenidas 5 and 10 Sur. There are Ladatel phones in front, and they sell telephone debit cards in the office.

Bookshop The Zodiac Bookstore, on the south-east side of the plaza 40 metres from the clock tower, next to Bancomer, is open seven days a week selling English, French, German and Spanish books, and English and Spanish magazines and newspapers.

Laundry The clean and tidy Margarita Laundromat, Avenida 20 Sur 285, between Calle Salas and Calle 3 Sur, is open Monday to Saturday from 7 am to 9 pm, Sunday from 9 am to 5 pm, and charges US$2 to wash a load (40c extra if you don't bring your own detergent), US$1 for 10 minutes in the dryer. Ironing and folding services are available at an extra charge. Look for the sign reading 'Lavandería de Autoservicio'. There's also the Lavandería Express, Calle Salas at Avenida 10 Sur.

Island Museum
The Museo de la Isla de Cozumel, Avenida Rafael Melgar between Calles 4 and 6 Norte, has nautical exhibits covering the history of the island. It's open from 10 am to 6 pm for US$3.50; closed Saturday.

Activities
Scuba Diving For equipment rental, instruction and/or boat reservations, there are numerous dive shops on Avenida Melgar along San Miguel's waterfront. Generally, a two-tank, full-day scuba trip will cost US$65 to US$85 and an introductory scuba course in the neighbourhood of US$120.

The most prominent scuba destinations are: the five-km-long Palancar Reef, where stunning coral formations and a 'horseshoe' of coral heads in 70-metre visibility offer some of the world's finest diving; Maracaibo Reef, for experienced divers only, which offers a challenge due to its current and its aquatic life; Paraíso Reef, famous for its coral formations, especially brain and star coral; and Yocab Reef, shallow yet vibrantly alive and great for beginners.

Snorkelling You can go out on a boat tour for US$20 to US$30 or, far cheaper, rent gear for about US$8 and snorkel at the following places: Chankanab Bay, San Francisco Beach, La Ceiba Beach near the car ferry dock (where a plane was purposely sunk for the film *Survive*), Presidente Hotel and Palancar.

Glass-Bottom Boat You can enjoy the coral formations and aquatic life by taking a tour by glass-bottom boat. The boats are supposed to leave the car ferry dock area every day at 10 am, noon and 2 pm, but generally wait until they are filled. They cost US$10 to US$15, but if you don't come to Cozumel at the height of the tourist season you might try to bargain for a lower price.

Places to Stay – bottom end
Camping To camp anywhere on the island you'll need a permit from the island's naval authorities, obtainable 24 hours a day, for free, from the naval headquarters south of the post office on Avenida Rafael Melgar. Best

camping places are along the relatively unpopulated eastern shore of the island.

Hotels All rooms described below come with private bath and fan, unless otherwise noted.

Hotel Flamingo (☎ (987) 2-12-64), Calle 6 Norte No 81, off Melgar, is not the cheapest, but undoubtedly the best value for money. Run by an efficient señora, the 21 rooms go for US$25 to US$35 a double, depending upon the season.

Hotel Marruang (☎ (987) 2-16-78, 2-02-08) at Calle Salas 440 is entered from a passageway across from the municipal market. A clean room with one double and one single bed costs US$22 to US$28.

Hotel Cozumel Inn (☎ (987) 2-03-14), Calle 4 Norte No 3, has rooms for only US$20/27 a double with fan/air-con in summer.

Hotel Posada Edém (☎ (987) 2-11-66, 2-15-82), Calle 2 Norte 12, between Avenidas 5 and 10 Norte, is uninspiring but cheap at US$13/22 a single/double.

Posada Letty (☎ (987) 2-02-57), on Avenida 15 Sur near Calle 1 Sur, is among the cheapest lodgings in town at US$17 in summer, US$22 in winter.

Hotel Saolima (☎ (987) 2-08-86), Calle Salas 268 between Avenidas 10 and 15 Sur, has clean, pleasant rooms in a quiet locale for US$16/18 a single/double in summer.

Places to Stay – middle
Most middle-range hostelries offer air-conditioning and swimming pools. All have private bathrooms.

Hotel Vista del Mar (☎ (987) 2-05-45; fax 2-04-45), Avenida Melgar 45, at Calle 5 Sur, has a small swimming pool, restaurant, liquor store, rental car and travel agency. Some rooms have balconies with sea views. The price in summer is US$40 a double, rising to US$50 in winter.

Tried and true, clean, comfortable lodgings are yours at the *Hotel Mary-Carmen* (☎ (987) 2-05-81), Avenida 5 Sur 4, half a block south of the plaza. The 27 tidy air-con rooms cost US$40 a double in winter.

Equally pleasant and similarly priced is the *Hotel Suites Elizabeth* (☎ (987) 2-03-30), Calle Salas 44. Air-con bedrooms have kitchenettes here.

Hotel Pepita (☎ (987) 2-00-98), Avenida 15 Sur 2, corner of Calle 1 Sur, has well-maintained rooms around a delightful garden for US$25 in summer, US$35 in winter. Most rooms have two double beds, insect screens, fans and little refrigerators as well as the air-con.

Bazar Colonial Hotel & Suites (☎ (987) 2-13-87; fax 2-02-09), Avenida 5 Sur No 9, has studios and one-bedroom suites (some of which can sleep up to four people) with kitchenette, air-con and pretensions to decor for US$42 to US$50 a double in summer, US$50 to US$60 in winter.

The similar *Hotel Bahía* (☎ (987) 2-02-09), Avenida Melgar at Calle 3 Sur, is under the same management.

Hotel El Pirata (☎ (987) 2-00-51), Avenida 5 Sur 3-A, offers decent air-con rooms for US$30 a double in summer, US$40 in winter.

Hotel Maya Cozumel (☎ (987) 2-00-11; fax 2-07-18), Calle 5 Sur No 4, has good TV-equipped rooms and a pool for US$35/40/45 a single/double/triple in winter.

Hotel Kary (☎ (987) 2-20-11), Calle Salas at Avenida 25 Sur, is five blocks east of the plaza and a bit out of the way, but cheaper at US$22 to US$32 for a double with fan and US$29 to US$38 with air-con. There's even a pool.

Hotel Plaza Cozumel (☎ (987) 2-27-11; fax 2-00-66), Calle 2 Norte 3, just off Avenida Melgar a block north of the plaza, is a new, modern, comfortable hotel with a rooftop swimming pool, colour TV with satellite hook-up, and prices of US$57 in summer, US$88 in winter.

Hotel Mesón San Miguel (☎ (987) 2-03-23; fax 2-18-20), Avenida Juárez 2-B, on the north side of the plaza, has a little pool, blissful air-con, a restaurant, and 100 rooms with balconies. There's also a separate beach club with water sports facilities seven blocks from the hotel on the water. Rates are US$45/68 a double in summer/winter.

Places to Stay – top end

Several km south of town are the big luxury resort hotels of an international standard, which charge US$150 to US$300 for a room during the winter season. North of town along the western shore of the island are numerous smaller, more modest resort hotels, usually cheaper than the big places, but catering mostly to package tour groups.

South of town, the *Presidente Cozumel* (☎ (987) 2-03-22; fax 2-13-60), Carretera a Chankanab Km 6.5, is hard to miss with its 259 rooms, many with sea views, set amidst tropical gardens.

Sol Caribe Cozumel (☎ (987) 2-70-00; fax 2-13-01), Playa Paraíso Km 3.5 (Apdo Postal 259), Cozumel, Quintana Roo 77600, has 321 luxurious rooms and a lavish layout with tropical swimming pool complete with a large 'island'. For reservations at either hotel, call (800) 343-7821 in the USA.

Meliá Mayan Cozumel (☎ (987) 2-02-72; fax 2-15-99), Playa Santa Pilar, is a 200-room resort with a full list of water sport equipment. Another Meliá hotel, the *Sol Cabañas del Caribe* (☎ (987) 2-01-61, 2-00-17; fax 2-15-99) caters mostly to divers. For reservations, call (800) 336-3542 in the USA.

Places to Eat – bottom end

Cheapest of all eating places, with fairly tasty food, are the market loncherías located next to the Mercado Municipal on Calle Salas between Avenidas 20 and 25 Sur. All of these little señora-run eateries offer soup and a main course plate for less than US$4, with a large selection of dishes available. Hours are 6.30 am to 6.30 pm daily.

Lonchería Las Gemelas, Avenida 5 and Calle 5, is a cheap little mom-and-pop eatery open for all three meals every day. Try also the *Comida Casera Toñita*, Calle Salas between Avenidas 10 and 15 Sur, open from 8 am to 6 pm.

Restaurant Costa Brava, on Avenida Rafael Melgar just south of the post office, is among the more interesting – read funky – places to dine on the island. Cheap breakfasts (US$2 to US$3.50), and such filling dishes as chicken tacos, grilled steak and fried fish or chicken for US$3.50 to US$8, are served daily from 6.30 am to 11.30 pm.

Restaurant La Choza, Calle Salas 198, specialises in authentic Mexican traditional cuisine, which is not all tacos and enchiladas. Have the pozole, a filling, spicy meat-and-hominy stew. With a soft drink, you pay US$8 for a huge bowl.

The *Cocina Económica Mi Chabelita*, Avenida 10 Sur between Calle 1 Sur and Calle Salas, is a tiny, fairly cheap eatery run by a señora who serves up decent portions of decent food for US$5.50 or less. It opens for breakfast at 7 am and closes at 7 pm.

La Cocina Italiana, Avenida 10 Sur No 121, at Calle 1 Sur, has rustic wooden tables and rustic pizzas and pastas: US$7 to US$12 for a full meal.

Places to Eat – middle

My favourite is *Pizza Prima* (☎ 2-42-42), Calle Salas between Avenidas 5 and 10 Sur, open from 1 to 11 pm (closed Wednesday). The American owners produce home-made pasta and fresh pizza as well as excellent Italian specialties. Dine streetside, or upstairs on the patio, for about US$8 to US$14.

Pizza Rolandi, Avenida Rafael Melgar between Calles 6 and 8 Norte, serves good one-person (20-cm diameter) pizzas for US$7.50 to US$10. It's open from 11.30 am to 11.30 pm; closed Sunday.

Cozumel is so Americanised that it has its own sports buffs' watering hole, *The Sports Page* (☎ 2-11-99), a block north of the plaza at the corner of Calle 2 Norte and Avenida 5 Norte. A plate of fajitas costs US$12.

Places to Eat – top end

Cozumel's traditional place to dine well and richly is *Pepe's Grill* (☎ 2-02-13), Avenida Melgar at Calle Salas. Flaming shrimps, grilled lobster, caesar salad and other top-end items can take your bill to the lofty heights of US$40 or US$50 per person.

Entertainment

Nightlife in Cozumel is pricey, but if you

want to dance, the most popular disco is *Disco Neptuno*, five blocks south of the post office on Avenida Rafael Melgar. Cover charge is US$5, with drinks (even Mexican beer) for US$3 and up. Another hot spot, similarly priced, is *Disco Scaramouche* at the intersection of Avenida Melgar and Calle Salas. For Latin *salsa* music, try *Los Quetzales*, Avenida 10 Sur at Calle 1 Sur, a block from the plaza. It's open every evening from 6 pm.

Things to Buy

Along Melgar are boutiques selling jewellery made with black coral. Legitimate shops will probably not try to cheat you on quality, but beware the cut-price merchants who substitute black plastic for the real thing. True black coral is 'weathered', with gold-coloured streaks in it. It is very light – lighter than the plastic fakes – and true coral will not burn, as does plastic.

Getting There & Away

Air Cozumel has a surprisingly busy international airport, with numerous direct flights from other parts of Mexico and the USA. Flights from Europe are usually routed via the USA or Mexico City. There are nonstop flights on Continental (☎ (987) 2-02-51) and American (☎ (987) 2-08-99) from their hubs at Dallas, Houston, and Raleigh-Durham, with many direct flights from other US cities via these hubs. Mexicana (☎ (987) 2-02-63) has nonstops from Miami and direct flights from Mérida and Mexico City.

Aero Cozumel (☎ (987) 2-09-28, 2-05-03), with offices at Cozumel airport, operates flights between Cancún and Cozumel about every two hours throughout the day for US$50 one way. Reserve in advance.

Aero Cozumel also runs to and from Playa del Carmen (see that section).

Ferry For details on ferries from Playa del Carmen, see that section. Car ferries run from Puerto Morelos (see that section).

Getting Around

To/From the Airport The airport is about two km north of town. You can take a minibus from the airport into town for less than US$2, slightly more to the hotels south of town, but you'll have to take a taxi (US$4 or US$5) to return to the airport.

Bus & Taxi Cozumel's taxi drivers have a lock on the local transport market, defeating any proposal for a convenient bus service. A single bus leaves daily from the tourist booth on the plaza in town (near the ferry) at 11 am, heading south toward Chankanab Bay, returning at 5 pm. Fare is US$2. The walk from the Presidente Hotel south to Chankanab is about one km.

For other points on the island you will have to take a taxi. Fares in and around town are US$4 per ride, or roughly US$24 per hour. From the town to Laguna Chankanab is US$10.

Car & Motorbike Rates for rental cars are upwards of US$60 to $70 per day, all inclusive. You could probably haggle with a taxi driver to take you on a tour of the island, drop you at a beach, come back and pick you up, and still save money; keep this shocking fact in mind when you consider renting a car. If you do rent, observe the law on vehicle occupancy. Usually only four persons are allowed in a vehicle (say, a Jeep). If you carry more, the police will fine you.

Rented mopeds are popular with those who want to tour the island on their own. It seems that every citizen and business in San Miguel – hotels, restaurants, gift shops, morticians – rents mopeds, generally for US$30 to US$38 per day (24 hours), though some rent from 8 am to 5 pm for US$22. Insurance and tax are included in these prices. It's amusing that a 24-hour rental of two mopeds (for two people) almost equals the cost of renting a car (for up to four people) for the same period of time.

You must have a valid driving licence, and you must use a credit card to rent, or put down a hefty deposit (around US$60).

The best time to rent is first thing in the morning, when all the machines are there. Choose a good one, with a working horn, brakes, lights, starter, rear-view mirrors, and a full tank of fuel; remember that the price asked will be the same whether you rent the newest, pristine machine or the oldest, most beat-up rattletrap. (If you want to trust yourself with a second-rate moped, at least haggle the price down significantly.) You should get a helmet and a lock and chain with the moped.

When riding, keep in mind that you will be as exposed to sunshine on a moped as if you were roasting on a beach. Slather yourself with sunblock (especially the backs of your hands, feet and neck, and your face), or cover up, or suffer the consequences. Also, be aware of the dangers involved. Of all motor vehicle operators, the inexperienced moped driver on unfamiliar roads in a foreign country has the highest statistical chance of having an accident, especially when faced by lots of other inexperienced moped drivers. Drive carefully.

AROUND ISLA COZUMEL
In order to see most of the island (except for Chankanab Bay) you will have to rent a moped or bicycle, or take a taxi (see Getting Around). The following route will take you south from the town of San Miguel, then anticlockwise around the island.

Chankanab Bay Beach
This bay of clear water and fabulously coloured fish is the most popular on the island. It is nine km south of the town.

You used to be able to swim in the adjoining lagoon, but so many tourists were fouling the water and damaging the coral that Laguna Chankanab was made a National Park and put off limits to swimmers. Don't despair – you can still snorkel in the sea here and the lagoon has been saved from destruction.

Snorkelling equipment can be rented for about US$8 per day. Divers will be interested in a reef offshore; there is a dive shop, and scuba instruction is offered.

If you get hungry, there is a restaurant and snack shop on the premises. The beach has dressing rooms, lockers and showers, which

are included in the US$3.50 admission price to the National Park, open 9 am to 5 pm daily. The park also has a botanical garden with 400 species of tropical plants.

Getting There & Away There's one daily local beach bus which leaves San Miguel at 11 am, returns at 5 pm and costs US$2. The taxi fare from San Miguel to Chankanab Bay is about US$10.

San Francisco & Palancar Beaches
San Francisco Beach, 14 km from San Miguel, and Palancar Beach, a few km to the south, are the nicest of the island's beaches. San Francisco's white sands run for more than three km, and rather expensive food is served at its restaurant. If you want to scuba or snorkel at Palancar Reef you will have to sign on for a day cruise or charter a boat.

El Cedral
To see these small Mayan ruins, the oldest on the island, go 3.5 km down a paved road a short distance south of San Francisco Beach. Although El Cedral was thought to be an important ceremonial site, its minor remnants are not well preserved. The surrounding area is the agricultural heart of Cozumel.

Punta Celarain
The southern tip of the island has a picturesque lighthouse, accessible via a dirt track, four km from the highway. To enjoy truly isolated beaches en route, climb over the sand dunes. There's a fine view of the island from the top of the lighthouse.

East Coast Drive
The wildest part of the island, the eastern shoreline, is highly recommended for beautiful seascapes of rocky coast. Unfortunately, except for Punta Chiqueros, Chen Río and Punta Morena, swimming is dangerous on Cozumel's east coast due to potentially lethal rip tides and undertow. Be careful! Swim only in coves protected from the open surf by headlands or breakwaters. There are small eateries at both Punta Morena and Punta

YUCATÁN

Chiqueros and a hotel at Punta Morena. Some travellers camp at Chen Río.

El Castillo Real & San Gervasio Ruins

Beyond where the east coast highway meets the Carretera Transversal (cross-island road) that runs to town, intrepid travellers may take the sand track about 17 km from the junction to the Mayan ruins known as El Castillo. They are not very well preserved and you need luck or a 4WD vehicle to navigate the sandy road.

There is an equally unimpressive ruin called San Gervasio on a bad road from the airport. 4WD vehicles can reach San Gervasio from a track originating on the east coast, but most rental car insurance policies do not cover unpaved roads such as this. The jungle en route is more interesting than the ruins.

Punta Molas Lighthouse

There are some fairly good beaches and minor Mayan ruins in the vicinity of the north-east point, accessible only by 4WD vehicle or foot.

BEACHES ALONG THE COAST

Some of the world's most beautiful beaches lie between Cancún and Tulum.

Xcaret (Km 290)

Look for the Restaurant Xcaret on the east side of the highway; this marks the access road to this beautiful spot. Once a turkey farm, Xcaret has now been Disneyfied into what one might call Mayapark (entry US$15): several small Mayan ruins, a cenote for swimming, a beautiful inlet *(caleta)* filled with tropical marine life where you can swim with the dolphins (US$50); a restaurant and other amusements.

Pamul (Km 274)

Although Pamul's small rocky beach does not have long stretches of white sand like some of its Caribbean cousins, the palm-fringed surroundings are inviting. If you walk only about two km north of Pamul you will find an alabaster sand beach to call your own. The least rocky section is the southern end, but watch out for spiked sea urchins in the shallows offshore.

Giant sea turtles come ashore here at night in July and August to lay their eggs. Why they return to the same beach every year is a mystery not understood by zoologists. If you run across a turtle during your evening stroll along the beach, keep a good distance from it and don't use a light, as this will scare it. Do your part to contribute to the survival of the turtles, which are endangered: let them lay their eggs in peace.

Places to Stay & Eat *Hotel Pamul* offers basic but acceptable rooms with fan and bath for US$20 a single and US$30 a double. There is electricity in the evenings until 10 pm. The friendly family that runs this somewhat scruffy hotel and campsite also serves breakfasts and seafood at their little restaurant.

The fee for camping is US$7 for two people per site. There are showers and toilets.

Puerto Aventuras (Km 269.5)

The Cancún lifestyle spreads inexorably southward, dotting this recently pristine coast with yet more sybaritic resort hideaways. One such is the *Puerto Aventuras Resort* (☎ (987) 2-22-11), PO Box 186, Playa del Carmen, Q Roo, a modern luxury complex of hotel rooms, swimming pools, beach facilities and other costly comforts.

Laguna Yal-Ku (Km 256.5)

One of the secrets of snorkelling aficionados, Laguna Yal-Ku is not even signposted. Its dirt road turn-off is across from a stone-walled house with a windmill. The tiny lagoon is a good place to snorkel, filled with a delightful array of aquatic life. Best of all, you may have the lagoon to yourself.

Yal-Ku is basically for day trips, as there is little shade and not much in the way of decent places to pitch a tent. Bring your own refreshments and snorkelling gear.

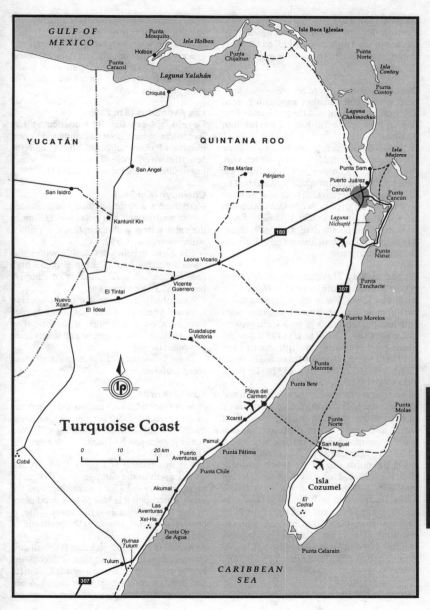

GULF OF MEXICO

Punta Mosquito
Isla Holbox
Isla Boca Iglesias
Holbox
Punta Chijaltun
Punta Norte
Isla Contoy
Punta Caracol
Punta Contoy
Laguna Yalahán
Chiquilá
Laguna Chakmochuk
YUCATÁN
QUINTANA ROO
Isla Mujeres
San Angel
Tres Marías
Pénjamo
Punta Sam
Puerto Juárez
Cancún
San Isidro
Punta Cancún
Kantunil Kin
Laguna Nichupté
180
Punta Nizuc
Leona Vicario
Punta Tanchacte
El Tintal
Vicente Guerrero
307
Nuevo Xcan
El Ideal
Puerto Morelos
Guadalupe Victoria
Punta Maroma
Punta Bete
Turquoise Coast
Punta Molas
Playa del Carmen
Xcaret
Punta Norte
San Miguel
Cobá
0   10   20 km
Puerto Aventuras
Pamul
Punta Fátima
Punta Chile
Isla Cozumel
Akumal
Las Aventuras
Xel-Ha
El Cedral
Ruinas Tulum
Punta Ojo de Agua
Tulum
Punta Celarain
307
CARIBBEAN SEA

YUCATÁN

Akumal (Km 255)

Famous for its beautiful beach, Akumal ('Place of the Turtles') does indeed see giant turtles come ashore to lay their eggs during the summer.

Beach Activities There are two dive shops here where you can rent snorkelling gear. The best snorkelling is at the north end of the bay; or try Laguna Yal-Ku, 1.5 km north of Akumal.

World-class divers come here to explore the Spanish galleon *Mantancero* which sank in 1741. You can see artefacts from the galleon at the museum at nearby Xel-Ha. The dive shops will arrange all your scuba excursion needs. Beginners' scuba instruction can be provided for less than US$120; if you want certification, the dive shops offer three-day courses. They will also arrange deep-sea fishing excursions.

Places to Stay The least expensive of this resort's three hotels is the *Hotel-Club Akumal Caribe Villas Maya*, where basic two-person air-conditioned cabañas with bath and the amenities of tennis and basketball courts cost US$90 to US$125 a double. Make reservations through Akutrame, ☎ (915) 584-3552, or toll-free outside Texas (800) 351-1622, PO Box 13326, El Paso, Texas 79913, USA.

The *Hotel Akumal Caribe* on the south end of the beach is an attractive two-storey modern lodge with swimming pool, boat rental and night tennis. Spacious air-con rooms equipped with refrigerators cost US$110. These can sleep six people.

On the north side of the beach you will find the cabañas of *Las Casitas Akumal* (☎ (987) 2-25-54) consisting of a living room, kitchen, two bedrooms and two bathrooms. Bungalows cost US$160 in the busy winter season, US$110 in summer. For reservations write to Las Casitas (in the USA ☎ (201) 489-6614; fax (201) 489-5070), 270 River St, Box 522, Hackensack, NJ 07602, USA.

Places to Eat Even the shade-huts near the

beach are expensive for light lunches and snacks, considering what you get. Just outside the walled entrance of Akumal is a grocery store patronised largely by the resort workers; if you are day-tripping here, this is your sole inexpensive source of food. The store also sells tacos.

Las Aventuras (Km 250)

Developers got the first chance at Las Aventuras, which now has a planned community of condominiums, villas, and the beautiful *Aventuras Akumal Hotel*, which has double rooms for about US$115.

Chemuyil (Km 248)

Here there's a beautiful sand beach shaded by coconut palms, and good snorkelling in the calm waters with exceptional visibility. Admission costs US$2.

Chemuyil is being developed, with some condos already built. During winter's high season there are a fair number of campers here (US$3.75 per person).

The cheap accommodation is spartan screened shade huts with hammock hooks. Enquire about availability at the bar; they cost US$20, and showers and toilets are communal.

Local fare is prepared at the bar, including some seafood.

Xcacel (Km 247)

Xcacel (shkah-CELL) has no lodging other than camping (US$7 per person), no electricity and only a small restaurant stall. You can enjoy this patch of paradise for a day-use charge of US$2.50.

For fine fishing and snorkelling, try the waters north of the campground. The rocky point leads to seas for snorkelling, and the sandy outcropping is said to be a good place to fish from. Swimming, like snorkelling, is best from the rocky point to the north end of the beach.

Xcacel offers good pickings for shell collectors, including that aquatic collector, the hermit crab. There are also some colourful and intricate coral pieces to be found. When beachcombing here, wear footgear.

Take the old dirt track which runs two km north to Chemuyil and three km south to Xel-Ha, and you may spy parrots, finches or the well-named clockbird (mot-mot) with its long tail.

Xel-Ha Lagoon (Km 245)

Once a pristine natural lagoon brimming with iridescent tropical fish, Xel-Ha (SHELL-hah) is now a Mexican national park with landscaped grounds, changing rooms, restaurant and bar. The fish are regularly driven off by the dozens of busloads of day-trippers who come to enjoy the beautiful site and to swim in the pretty lagoon.

Should you visit Xel-Ha? Sure, so long as you come off-season (in summer), or in winter either very early or very late in the day to avoid the tour buses. Bring your own lunch as the little restaurant here is over-priced. Entry to the lagoon area costs US$6 (children under 12 free); it's open from 8 am to 6 pm daily. You can rent snorkelling gear; the price is high and the equipment perhaps leaky.

Museum & Ruins The small maritime museum contains artefacts from the wreckage of the Spanish galleon *Mantancero*, which sank just north of Akumal in 1741. In 1958 Mexican divers salvaged guns, cannons, coins and other items. Admission costs US$1.

There is a small archaeological site on the west side of the highway 500 metres south of the lagoon entry road, open from 8 am to 5 pm for US$2. The ruins, which are not all that impressive, date from Classic and Post-Classic periods, and include El Palacio and the Templo de los Pájaros.

TULUM

The ruins of Tulum ('City of the Dawn', or 'City of Renewal'), though well preserved, would hardly merit rave notices if it weren't for their setting. And what a setting: the grey-black buildings of the past sit on a palm-fringed beach, lapped by the turquoise waters of the Caribbean.

Don't come to Tulum expecting majestic pyramids or anything comparable to the architecture of Chichén Itzá or Uxmal. The buildings here, decidedly Toltec in influence, were the product of Mayan civilisation in decline.

Tulum's proximity to the tourist centres of Cancún and Isla Mujeres make it a prime target for tour buses. To best enjoy the ruins, visit them either early in the morning or late in the day. The ruins are open from 8 am to 5 pm. There is a US$5 admission charge (plus US$10 for a video camera!); admission is free on Sunday.

History

Most archaeologists believe that Tulum was settled in the Early Post-Classic period (900-1200). When Juan de Grijalva's expedition sailed past Tulum in 1518, he was amazed by the sight of this walled city with its buildings painted a gleaming red, blue and white and a ceremonial fire flaming atop its seaside watchtower.

The ramparts that surround three sides of Tulum (the fourth side being the sea) leave little question as to its strategic function as a fortress. Averaging nearly seven metres in thickness and standing three to five metres high, the walls protected the city during a period of considerable strife between Mayan city-states.

The city was abandoned about three-quarters of a century after the Spanish conquest. Mayan pilgrims continued to visit over the years and Indian refugees from the War of the Castes took shelter here from time to time.

In 1842, John L Stephens and Frederick Catherwood visited Tulum by boat. They made substantial drawings and notes which, published in 1848, aroused the curiosity of the outside world. Subsequent expeditions were mounted, the most important being the 1916-22 investigations by the Carnegie Institute.

Orientation

There are two Tulums, Tulum Ruinas and Tulum Pueblo. The ruins are 800 metres south-east off Highway 307 along an access

YUCATÁN

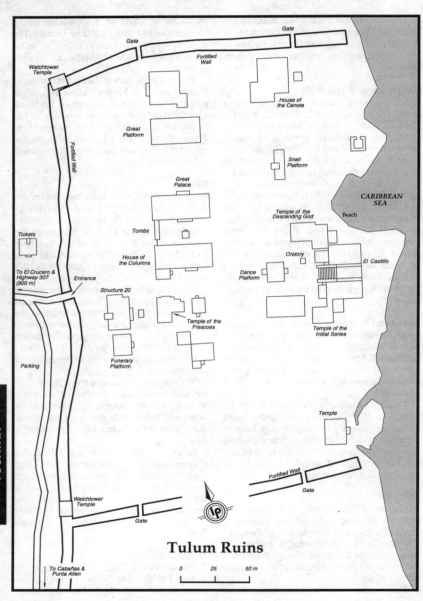

Tulum Ruins

road. The village *(pueblo)* of Tulum straddles Highway 307 about three km south of the Tulum Ruinas access road, or two km south of the Cobá road.

South of Tulum Ruinas, a road passes several collections of beachfront bungalows before entering the Sian Ka'an Biosphere Reserve. The road, unpaved, continues for some 50 km past Boca Paila to Punta Allen.

Tulum Pueblo has one lodging-place; no doubt more will open in the near future. The junction of Highway 307 and the Tulum Ruinas access road, called El Crucero, has several little hotels and restaurants. The bungalows south of Tulum can provide shelter and food as well.

Structure 20 & the Funerary Platform

As you enter the Tulum city gate, look to the first building on your right, Structure 20. The roof caved in about 1929, making it a bit difficult to envision what once was a royal palace. Fragments of paintings remain on the walls. Just to Structure 20's right is a Funerary Platform with a cross-shaped grave in its centre. Here archaeologists found skeletons and animal offerings, the latter to provide sustenance for the deceased on the journey to the next world.

Temple of the Frescoes

Thought initially to have been built about 1450, the temple has been added to on several occasions. Here you will see a carved figure very much in evidence at Tulum, the diving god. Equipped with wings and a bird's tail, this fascinating deity has been linked by some archaeologists with the Venus morning-star symbol of Quetzalcóatl. On the western façade are stucco masks thought to symbolise Quetzalcóatl in another form.

Inside the temple the best preserved of the greenish-blue on black murals may be seen through protective bars. The mural is painted in three levels demarcating the three realms of the Mayan universe: the dark underworld of the deceased, the middle order of the living and the heavenly home of the creator and rain gods.

Fresco from the Temple of the Frescoes, Tulum

Great Palace

To the left of the Temple of the Frescoes, as you face the sea, is the Great Palace. Smaller than El Castillo, this largely deteriorated site contains a fine stucco carving of a diving god.

El Castillo

Tulum's tallest building is a watchtower fortress overlooking the Caribbean, appropriately named El Castillo by the Spaniards. Note the serpent columns of the temple's entrance.

Look down to the north from El Castillo and you will see a good small beach, great for sunning and a refreshing dip. There's a bit of an undertow here, so swim with caution.

Temple of the Descending God

The Temple of the Descending (or Diving) God has a good stucco relief of a diving god above the door. If you ascend the inner staircase, you will see paint fragments of a religious mural.

Temple of the Initial Series

This restored temple is named for a stele now in the British Museum, which was inscribed with the Mayan date corresponding to 564

AD. At first this confused archaeologists, who had evidence that Tulum was not settled until some time later. Today, scholars believe that the stele was moved here from a city founded much earlier.

Places to Stay

El Crucero Right at the junction of Highway 307 and the Tulum access road are several hotels and restaurants, including the dismal *Motel El Crucero*, expensive at US$15 to US$20 a double. The restaurant and shop selling ice, pastries, snacks and souvenirs are more useful.

Facing the Motel El Crucero across the access road are the *Hotel Acuario* and *Restaurant El Faisan y El Venado*, which is newer but also overpriced at US$35 to US$50 a double.

Boca Paila/Punta Allen Rd South of the archaeological zone is a paradise of palm-shaded white beach dotted with collections of cabañas, little thatched huts of greater or lesser comfort, and simple wooden or concrete bungalows. Most of these places have little eateries at which you can take your meals, and some have electric generators which provide electric light for several hours each evening. There are no phones.

The cheapest way to sleep here is to have your own hammock, preferably with one of those tube-like mosquito nets to cover it; if you don't carry your own, several of the cheaper places will rent you what you need. If you have candles or a torch, it'll come in handy here. In the cheapest places you'll have to supply your own towel and soap.

Unfortunately, these lodgings are located some distance south of the ruins and there is no public transport along the road. Though you may occasionally be able to hitch a ride, you can depend only upon your own two feet to get you from your bungalow to the ruins, which may be up to seven km away.

I'll start by describing the places closest to Tulum ruins, then head south to describe the places farther and farther away.

Closest to the ruins are *Cabañas El Mirador* and *Cabañas Santa Fe*, on the beach about 600 metres south of the Tulum ruins parking lot. Of the two, the Santa Fe is preferable, though a bit more expensive, charging US$3 per person for a campsite, US$8 to hang your hammocks in a cabin, single or double.

One km south of the parking lot is *Cabañas Don Armando*, perhaps the best of the bottom-end cabaña places. For US$16 (single or double) you get one of 17 cabins built on concrete slabs, with lockable doors, hammocks or beds (you pay a deposit for sheets and pillows), mosquito netting, good showers and a good, cheap restaurant. Lighting in the rooms is by candles. This place is fun, right on the beach, and still only a 10-minute walk to the ruins.

The *Hotel El Paraíso* (☎ in Cozumel (987) 2-17-17), just 1.5 km south of the ruins, approaches a conventional hotel in its services. The newer rooms, with two double beds and private bath, cost US$40 to US$60. There's a nice little restaurant with a good sea view. There's electricity until 10 pm. *Gato's Cabañas*, 700 metres south, charge slightly less.

A road goes off to the right to join the main highway. South of this junction are *Cabañas Nohoch Tunich* and *Cabañas Mar y Sol*, five km south of the ruins. These are fairly rustic, charging US$16 a double. Just south the paved road gives way to a good sand track.

Osho Oasis Retreat (☎ (987) 4-27-72; fax 3-02-30 ext 174), Apdo Postal 99, Tulum, Q Roo 77780, is a resort for plain living and high thinking. There's a meditation hall and facilities for yoga, Zen, Kundalini and massage, as well as the beach. Cabañas cost US$30 to US$70 a double in high season; meals are US$7/6/14 for breakfast/lunch/dinner. *Cabañas de Anna y José*, two km farther south, has both older and newer cinder-block bungalows for US$38 to US$45 a double.

Just south is *Cabañas Tulum*, over seven km south of the ruins, where older concrete bungalows look out through palms to the sea and the beach. The rate is US$30 per night, single or double. The electric generator runs (if it's working) from dusk to 10 pm each evening.

Places to Eat

Tulum Ruinas The car park is surrounded by little souvenir stalls, with a few eateries. *Restaurant México*, on the left as you come into the car park from the highway, serves decent sandwiches for US$3.75, and fried chicken for US$5. Sometimes they have spaghetti or fish, and they always have cold beer and soft drinks.

The little restaurant right next door to the left of the Restaurant México is similar but not quite so nice. At the far end of the parking lot near the road to Punta Allen is the *Restaurant Garibaldi*.

El Crucero *Motel El Crucero* has a popular, very simple but somewhat expensive restaurant. Stick to the simpler items.

At the *Restaurant El Faisan y El Venado* across the street the surroundings are a bit more attractive, the food similar, the prices even higher.

Getting There & Away

Wait at El Crucero for an Interplaya or regular intercity bus.

TULUM TO BOCA PAILA & PUNTA ALLEN

The scenery on the 50-km stretch from Tulum Ruinas past Boca Paila to Punta Allen is the typically monotonous flat Yucatecan terrain, but the land, rich with wildlife, is protected as the Sian Ka'an Biosphere Reserve. The surfy beaches aren't spectacular, but there's plenty of privacy.

It's important to have plenty of fuel before heading south from Tulum as there is no fuel available on the Tulum-Punta Allen road.

Sian Ka'an Biosphere Reserve

Over 5000 sq km of tropical jungle, marsh, mangrove and islands on Quintana Roo's coast have been set aside by the Mexican government as a large biosphere reserve. During 1987 the United Nations appointed it a World Heritage Site – an irreplaceable natural treasure.

A trip into Sian Ka'an ('Where the Sky Begins') reveals thousands of butterflies as well as varied fauna: howler monkeys, foxes, ocelots, pumas, vultures, caimans (crocodiles), eagles, raccoons, giant land crabs and – if you're very lucky – a jaguar. Unrestored Mayan ruins are everywhere. Though small and mostly unimpressive, it's still a thrill to visit one of these quiet sites which has lain here unheeded for centuries.

Treks into the reserve are run from Cancún and Playa del Carmen. For details on the reserve, contact Amigos de Sian Ka'an (☎ (98) 84-95-83, 87-30-80), Plaza América, Avenida Cobá 5, Third Floor, Suites 48-50, Cancún, Q Roo 77500.

Boca Paila

Boca Paila is 25 km south of Tulum. One of the two hotels on the road to Punta Allen is *La Villa de Boca Paila*, where luxury cabañas complete with kitchens cost about US$90 per double, including two meals. The clientele is predominantly affluent American sport fishers. For reservations write to Apdo Postal 159, Mérida, Yucatán.

Ten km south of Boca Paila you cross a rickety wooden bridge. Beyond it is *El Retiro Cabañas* where you can hang hammocks or camp for a few dollars.

Punta Allen

Once a pocket of wealthy lobster fishers in a vast wilderness, Punta Allen suffered considerable damage from the ferocious winds of Hurricane Gilbert in 1988. The hurricane and overfishing have depleted lobster stocks, but a laid-back ambience reminiscent of the Belizean cayes gives hope for a touristic future.

Punta Allen does have some rustic lodgings. The *Cruzan Inn* (fax (983) 4-03-83) has cabañas with hammocks for about US$25 a double. The couple who run it prepare breakfast and lunch at a cost of US$6.50 per person and charge US$14 for dinner. They can arrange snorkelling and fishing expeditions, or visits to the offshore island of Cayo

YUCATÁN

Colibri, known for its bird life. To write for reservations, the address is Cruzan Inn, c/o Sonia Lillvik, Apdo Postal 703, Cancún, Quintana Roo 77500.

The *Bonefishing Club of Ascension Bay*, run by Jan Persson, specialises in guided fishing expeditions, but also has two rooms for rent in the house which is its headquarters. Family-style meals are served.

Let It Be Inn has three thatched cabañas with comforts such as private bath (with hot water) and sea-view porches hung with hammocks. For reservations write to Rick Montgomery, Let It Be Inn, Apdo Postal 74, Tulum, Q Roo 77780.

If you wish to camp on Punta Allen's beach, simply ask the Maya in front of whose house you would be sleeping for permission.

COBÁ

Perhaps the largest of all Mayan cities, Cobá, 50 km north-west of Tulum, offers the chance to explore mostly unrestored antiquities set deep in tropical jungles.

History

Cobá was settled earlier than Chichén or Tulum, its heyday dating from 600 AD until the site was mysteriously abandoned about 900 AD. Archaeologists believe that this city once covered 50 square km and held 40,000 Maya.

Cobá's architecture is a mystery; its towering pyramids and stelae resemble the architecture of Tikal, several hundred km away, rather than that of Chichén Itzá and other sites of northern Yucatán a quarter of that distance.

Some archaeologists theorise that an alliance with Tikal was made through marriage to facilitate trade between the Guatemalan and Yucatecan Maya. Stelae appear to depict female rulers from Tikal holding ceremonial bars and flaunting their power by standing on captives. These Tikal royal females, when married to Cobá's royalty, may have brought architects and artisans with them.

Archaeologists are also baffled by the network of extensive stone-paved avenues or *sacbeob* in this region, with Cobá as the hub.

The longest runs nearly 100 km from the base of Cobá's great pyramid Nohoch Mul to the Mayan settlement of Yaxuna. In all, some 40 sacbeob passed through Cobá. The sacbeob were parts of the huge astronomical 'time machine' that was evident in every Mayan city.

The first excavation was by the Austrian archaeologist Teobert Maler. Hearing rumours of a fabled lost city, he came to Cobá alone in 1891. There was little subsequent investigation until 1926 when the Carnegie Institute financed the first of two expeditions led by J Eric S Thompson and Harry Pollock. After their 1930 expedition not much happened until 1973, when the Mexican government began to finance excavation. Archaeologists now estimate that Cobá contains some 6500 structures of which just a few have been excavated and restored.

Orientation

The small village of Cobá, 2½ km west of the Tulum-Nuevo Xcan road, has several small, simple, cheap lodging and eating places. At the lake, turn left for the ruins, right for the upscale Villa Arqueológica Cobá hotel.

Cobá archaeological site is open from 8 am to 5 pm; admission costs US$5, free on Sunday.

Be prepared to do considerable walking – at least five to seven km – on jungle paths. Dress for heat and humidity, and bring insect repellent. It's also a good idea to bring a canteen of water; it's hot and there are no drinks stands within the site, only at the entrance. Avoid the midday heat if possible. A visit to the site takes two to four hours.

Cobá Group

Less than 100 metres along the main path from the entrance brings you to the Temple of the Churches, on your right, the most prominent structure in the Cobá Group. It's an enormous pyramid from the top of which there is a fine view of the Nohoch Mul pyramid to the north and shimmering lakes to the east and south-west.

Back on the main path, you pass through

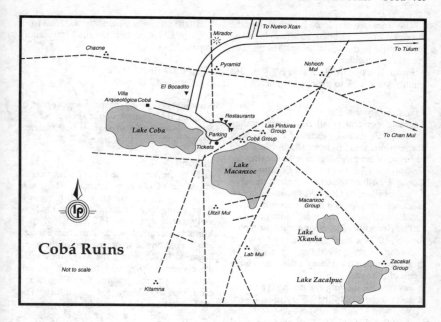

Cobá Ruins

Not to scale

the Juego de Pelota, or ball court, 30 metres farther along. It's now badly ruined.

Macanxoc Group

About 500 metres beyond the Juego de Pelota is the turning (right) for the Grupo Macanxoc, a group of stelae which bore reliefs of royal women thought to have come from Tikal.

Las Pinturas Group

One hundred metres beyond the Macanxoc turning, a sign points left toward the Conjunto de las Pinturas, or the Temple of Paintings. It bears easily recognisable traces of glyphs and frescoes above the door, and traces of richly coloured plaster inside.

You approached the Temple of Paintings from the south-west. Leave by the trail at the north-west (opposite the temple steps) to see several stelae. The first of these is 20 metres along beneath a palapa. A regal figure stands over two others, one of them kneeling with

his hands bound behind him. Sacrificial captives lie beneath the feet of a ruler at the base. Continue along the path past another badly weathered stele to the Nohoch Mul path, and turn right.

Nohoch Mul – The Great Pyramid

It's a walk of 800 metres to Nohoch Mul. Along the way, just before the track bends sharply to the left, a narrow path on the right leads to a group of badly weathered stelae. Farther along, the track bends between piles of stones – obviously a ruined temple – before passing Temple 10 and Stela 20. The exquisitely carved stela bears a picture of a ruler standing imperiously over two captives. Eighty metres beyond the stela stands the Great Pyramid.

At 42 metres high, the huge Great Pyramid is the tallest of all Mayan structures in the Yucatán Peninsula. Climb the 120 steps, observing that the Maya carved shell-like forms where you put your feet.

There are two diving gods carved over the doorway of the Nohoch Mul temple at the top, similar to the sculptures at Tulum. The view is spectacular.

From Nohoch Mul, it's a 1.4 km, 30-minute walk back to the site entrance.

Places to Stay & Eat

There are several small restaurants among the souvenir shops by the car park. The staff at the drinks stand right by the entrance tend to be surly, so buy your drinks at either the *Restaurant El Faisan* or the *Restaurant El Caracol*, both of which serve cheap meals.

In the village of Cobá, *Restaurant Lagoon* is nearest the lake, but the *Restaurant Isabel* and *Restaurant Bocadito* are more popular.

The Bocadito rents clean rooms with bath for US$10/14 a single/double

As for camping, there's no organised spot, though you can try finding a place along the shore of the lake.

For upscale lodging and dining the choice is easy: there's only the *Villa Arqueológica Cobá* (☎ in Cancún (98) 84-25-74; in the USA (800) 528-3100). The pleasant hotel has a swimming pool and good restaurant. Air-conditioned rooms cost US$70/80/90 a single/double/triple. Lunch or dinner in the good restaurant might cost US$20 to US$30.

Getting There & Away

Numerous buses trace the route between Tulum and Valladolid. Be sure to mention to the driver that you want to get out at Cobá junction; the road does not pass through the village.

Leaving Cobá is problematic, as most buses are full when they pass here. If you're willing to stand for the 50-km ride to Tulum or the 50 km to Nuevo Xcan (120 km to Valladolid), you have a better chance.

A more comfortable, dependable but expensive way to reach Cobá is by taxi from the car park at Tulum Ruinas. Find some other travellers interested in the trip and split the cost, about US$20 or US$30 round-trip, including two hours (haggle for three) at the site.

By the way, many maps show a road from Cobá to Chemax, but this road is virtually impassable.

FELIPE CARRILLO PUERTO
Population: 17,000

Now named for a progressive governor of Yucatán, this town was once known as Chan Santa Cruz, the dreaded rebel headquarters during the War of the Castes.

History

In 1849 the War of the Castes went against the Maya of northern Yucatán, who made their way to this town seeking refuge. Regrouping their forces, they were ready to sally forth again in 1850, just when a 'miracle' occurred. A wooden cross erected at a cenote on the western edge of the town began to 'talk', telling the Maya they were the chosen people, exhorting them to continue the struggle against the Whites, and promising the Maya forces victory. The talking was done by a ventriloquist who used sound chambers, but the people nonetheless looked upon it as the authentic voice of their aspirations.

The oracular cross guided the Maya in battle for eight years, until their great victory in conquering the fortress at Bacalar. For the latter part of the 19th century, the Maya in and around Chan Santa Cruz were virtually independent of governments in Mexico City and Mérida. In the 1920s a boom in the chicle market brought prosperity to the region and the Maya decided to come to terms with Mexico City, which they did in 1929. Some of the Maya, unwilling to give up the cult of the talking cross, left Chan Santa Cruz to take up residence at small villages deep in the jungle, where they still revere the talking cross to this day. You may see some of them visiting the site where the cross spoke in its little park, especially on 3 May, the day of the Holy Cross.

You can visit the **Sanctuario del Cruz Parlante** five blocks west of the Pemex fuel station on the main street (Highway 307) in the commercial centre of town. Besides the

Felipe Carrillo Puerto

0   100   200 m

PLACES TO STAY
5 Hotel Chan Santa Cruz
7 El Faisán y El Venado

PLACES TO EAT
7 Restaurant El Faisán y El Venado
8 Restaurant 24 Horas

OTHER
1 Santuario del Cruz Parlante
2 Correos (Post Office)
3 Banks
4 Cinema
6 Pemex
7 ADO Bus Station
9 Telegrafos
10 Santa Cruz Church/Balam Na
11 Ayuntamiento (Town Hall)

cenote and a stone shelter, there's little to see in the park, though the place reverberates with history.

Places to Stay & Eat

El Faisán y El Venado (☎ (983) 4-00-43), across from the Pemex station 100 metres south of the traffic roundabout, has 13 cheap rooms with private showers and ceiling fans. Prices are US$15/26 a single/double. They have a restaurant with surprisingly good food and service, too. The ADO bus station is on the south side of the restaurant. Just a few dozen metres to the south is the *Restaurant 24 Horas*, which is a bit cheaper.

Just off the main plaza is the *Hotel Chan Santa Cruz* (☎ (983) 4-01-70), with drab rooms around a courtyard priced similarly to those at El Faisan y El Venado.

Getting There & Away

Buses running between Cancún (224 km, four hours, US$8) and Chetumal (155 km, three hours, US$6) stop here, as do buses travelling from Chetumal to Valladolid (160 km, three hours, US$6). There are also a few buses between Felipe Carrillo Puerto and Ticul (200 km, 3½ hours, US$8); change at

Ticul or Muna for Uxmal. Bus fare between FCP and Tulum is US$3.75.

Note that there are very few services such as hotels, restaurants or fuel stations between Felipe Carrillo Puerto and Ticul.

LAGUNA BACALAR

Nature has set a turquoise jewel in the midst of the scrubby Yucatecan jungle – Laguna Bacalar. A large, clear fresh-water lake with a bottom of gleaming white sand, Bacalar comes as a surprise in this country of tortured limestone. For all its beauty, Bacalar has hardly been developed at all. While this preserves its beauty, it also makes it difficult to stop here for the night.

The small, sleepy town of Bacalar, just east of the highway some 125 km south of Felipe Carrillo Puerto, is the only settlement of any size on the lake. It's noted mostly for its old fortress and its swimming facilities.

The fortress was built over the lagoon to protect citizens from raids by pirates and Indians. It served as an important outpost for the Whites in the War of the Castes. In 1859, it was seized by Mayan rebels who held the fort until Quintana Roo was finally conquered by Mexican troops in 1901. Today,

YUCATÁN

with formidable cannon still on its ramparts, the fortress remains an imposing sight. It houses a museum exhibiting colonial armaments and uniforms from the 17th and 18th centuries. The museum is open daily from 8 am to 1 pm and has an admission charge of US$1.

A divided avenue runs between the fortress and the lakeshore northward a few hundred metres to the balneario, or bathing facilities. Small restaurants line the avenue and surround the balneario, which is very busy on weekends.

Costera Bacalar & Cenote Azul

The road which winds southward along the lakeshore from Bacalar town to Highway 307 at Cenote Azul is called the Costera Bacalar. It passes a few lodging and camping places along the way.

About 2.5 km south of Bacalar town is the *Mesón Nueva Salamanca*, Costera 51, with tidy little motel-type rooms for US$25 a double. There's no restaurant.

Hotel Laguna (☎ (983) 2-35-17 in Chetumal, (99) 27-13-04 in Mérida), 3.3 km south of Bacalar town along the Costera, is only 150 metres east of Highway 307, so you can ask a bus driver to stop here for you. Clean, cool and hospitable, it boasts a wonderful view of the lake, a swimming pool, a breezy terrace restaurant and bar. Rooms cost US$42 a single or double with fan, good cross-ventilation and private bath.

Only 700 metres past the Hotel Laguna along the Costera is a nameless little camping area on the shore run by a family who live in a shack on the premises. You can camp in the dense shade of the palm trees, enjoy the view of the lake from the palapas, swim from the grassy banks, all for US$6 per couple. Bring your own food and drinking water, as the nearest supplier is the restaurant at the Hotel Laguna.

The Cenote Azul is a 90-metre-deep natural pool on the south-western shore of Laguna Bacalar, 200 metres east of Highway 307. (If you're approaching from the north by bus, get the driver to stop and let you off here.) Being a cenote there's no beach, just a few steps leading down to the water from the vast palapa which shelters the restaurant. You might pay US$9 to US$15 for the average meal here. A small sign purveys the traditional wisdom: 'Don't go in the cenote if you can't swim'.

Getting There & Away

Coming from the north, have the bus drop you in Bacalar town, at the Hotel Laguna, or at Cenote Azul, as you wish; check before you buy your ticket to see if the driver will stop.

From Chetumal, catch a minibus from Combi Corner. Departures are about every 20 minutes from 5 am to 7 pm for the 39-km (40 minutes, US$3) run to the town of Bacalar; some northbound buses (US$2) departing from the bus station will also drop you near the town of Bacalar. Along the way they pass Laguna Milagros (14 km), Xul-ha (22 km) and the Cenote Azul (33 km), and all four of these places afford chances to swim in fresh water. The lakes are beautiful, framed by palm trees, with crystal clear water and soft white limestone-sand bottoms.

Heading west out of Chetumal, you turn north onto Highway 307; 15.5 km north of this highway junction is a turn on the right marked for the Cenote Azul and Costera Bacalar.

CHETUMAL

Population: 130,000

Before the conquest, Chetumal was a Mayan port for shipping gold, feathers, cacao and copper from this region and Guatemala to northern Yucatán. After the conquest, the town was not actually settled until 1898 when it was founded to put a stop to the illegal trade in arms and lumber carried on by the descendants of the War of the Castes rebels. Dubbed Payo Obispo, the town's name was changed to Chetumal in 1936. In 1955, Hurricane Janet virtually obliterated Chetumal.

During the rebuilding, the city planners laid out the new town on a grand plan with a grid of wide boulevards. In times BC (Before Cancún), the sparsely populated territory of Quintana Roo could not support such a grand city, even though Quintana Roo was upgraded from a territory to a state in 1974. But the boom at Cancún brought prosperity to all, and Chetumal is finally growing into its destiny as an important capital city.

Chetumal is also the gateway to Belize, and you may encounter groups of Belizeans coming to the 'big city' to shop.

Orientation

Despite its sprawling layout, the centre is easily manageable on foot. Once you find the all-important intersection of Avenida de los Héroes and Avenida Alvaro Obregón, you're within 50 metres of several cheap hotels and restaurants. The best hotels are only four or five blocks from this intersection.

The city's new bus station is three km north of the centre of town at the intersection of Avenida de los Insurgentes and Avenida Belice.

Information

A tourist information kiosk (☎ (983) 2-36-63) on Héroes at the eastern end of Aguilar, across from the market, can answer questions. Hours are 8 am to 1 pm and 5 to 8 pm. The state tourism authorities may be reached on ☎ 2-02-66.

For currency exchange, most banks are located along Héroes in the centre of town. For instance, there's a Bancomer (☎ (983) 2-02-05) at Héroes 6 and a Banamex (☎ (983) 2-27-10) at the intersection of Obregón and Juárez. Banking hours are 9.30 am to 1 pm, Monday to Friday.

The post office (☎ (983) 2-00-57) is at Plutarco Elias Calles 2A. The postal code for Chetumal is 77000.

The Guatemalan Consulate (☎ (983) 2-85-85) is at Avenida Chapultepec 354. It's open from 9 am to 2 pm Monday to Friday and offers quick visa service.

The Belizean Consulate (☎ (983) 2-49-08), was until recently at Obregón and Independencia.

Things to See

No one comes to Chetumal for sightseeing. Most of what's worthwhile in the area is outside of Chetumal (see Around Chetumal). The exception is the new, huge Museo Cultura Maya up from the tourist information kiosk, which should be open by the time you arrive.

Places to Stay – bottom end

Villa Juvenil Chetumal (☎ (983) 2-05-25), the youth hostel, on Calzada Veracruz near the corner with Obregón, is the cheapest place in town. It has a few drawbacks: single-sex dorms, 11 pm curfew, and a location five blocks east of the intersection of Héroes and Obregón. The cost is US$5 for a bunk in a room with four or six beds and shared bath. Breakfast costs US$3.75 and lunch or dinner US$4.50 in the cafeteria.

Hotel María Dolores (☎ (983) 2-05-08), Obregón 206 west of Héroes, above the Restaurant Sosilmar, is the best for the price, with tiny, stuffy rooms for US$11 a single and US$14 to US$17 a double with fans and private bath.

Hotel Ucum (☎ (983) 2-07-11), Avenida M Gandhi 167, is a large, rambling old place with lots of rooms around a bare central courtyard and a good cheap little restaurant. Plain, cheap rooms equipped with fan and private bath cost US$9 a single, US$14 a double, US$17 a triple.

Hotel Cristal (☎ (983) 2-38-78), Cristóbal Colón 207, between Juárez and Belice, is run by an energetic señora who offers clean rooms for US$11/16 a single/double with fan, US$22 a double with air-con.

Hotel Jacaranda (☎ (983) 2-03-20), on Obregón just west of Héroes, is plain and bright with fluorescent lights. Rates are US$12/16 a single/double, about US$3 or US$4 higher with air-con. Note that this hotel has many noisy rooms; choose carefully.

Want a very clean, quiet room with good cross-ventilation, fan, TV and private bath for only US$15/20 a double with air-con? Then find your way to the *Posada Pantoja* (☎ (983) 2-17-81), Lucio Blanco 95, one km

YUCATÁN

Chetumal

Circunvalación

To Bus Station,
Hotel Príncipe
& Calderitas

To Venus Bus
Station (Belize)

Belisario

General Felipe Ángeles

General Francisco J Mújica

Domínguez

Heriberto Lara

General

Felipe Carrillo Puerto

Carranza

Avenida Independencia

Avenida Primo de Verdad

Avenida Francisco I Madero

Avenida de los Héroes

16 de Septiembre

Calzada Veracruz

Juan Escuita

Cristóbal Colón

2

3

4

Avenida Benito Juárez

Avenida Belice

Avenida de los Héroes

Avenida

Avenida Miguel Hidalgo

Juan de la Barrera

Agustín Melgar

Francisco Márquez

Fernando Montes

Avenida

Mahatma Gandhi

5

6

7

8

9

10

11

Héroes de Chapultepec

Héroes de Chapultepec

13

Avenida Francisco I Madero

12

Lázaro Cárdenas

14

Avenida Plutarco Elías Calles

Avenida Benito Juárez

15

0   100   200 m

Ignacio Zaragoza

Cozumel

To Guatemalan Consulate,
Airport, Escárcega, Belize
& Cancún

16 17

18

19

Avenida Independencia

Avenida

22

20

21 23

24

25

26

Avenida Álvaro Obregón

Hidalgo

Reforma

Veracruz

Avenida de los Héroes

27

28

5 de Mayo

16 de Septiembre

Othon P Blanco

Miguel

Avenida

Calzada

Avenida

Bahía

29

Carmen Ochoa de Merino

Avenida

Avenida

Avenida

Boulevard

22 de Enero

Boulevard Bahía

BAHÍA DE CHETUMAL

YUCATÁN

PLACES TO STAY	
1	Posada Pantoja
2	Hotel Cristal
5	Hotel & Restaurant Ucum
8	Hotel Continental Caribe
13	Hotel Los Cocos
17	Hotel & Restaurant Jacaranda
19	Villa Juvenil Chetumal (Youth Hostel)
22	Hotel María Dolores & Restaurant Sosilmar
25	Hotel El Dorado
26	Hotel Caribe Princess

PLACES TO EAT	
6	Restaurant Pantoja
15	Restaurant El Taquito
18	Restaurant Campeche
21	Restaurant Pollo Brujo

23	Panadería La Muralla & Restaurant Campeche
24	Sergio's Pizzas & Maria's Restaurant

OTHER	
3	Museo Cultura Maya
4	Combi Corner (Minibus Stops)
7	Mercado (Market)
9	Tourist Information Kiosk
10	Hospital Morelos
11	Centro de Salud (Clinic)
12	Teléfonos de México
14	Correos (Post Office)
16	Banca Serfin
18	Taesa Airlines Office
20	Banamex
27	Banco Internacional
28	Banamex
29	Palacio de Gobierno

north-east of the tourist info kiosk in a peaceful residential area. Ask at the Restaurant Pantoja for directions.

Places to Stay – middle

The new *Hotel Caribe Princess* (☎ (983) 2-09-00), Obregón 168, has lots of marble and good air-con rooms for US$40 a double.

Hotel El Dorado (☎ 2-03-15), Avenida 5 de Mayo No 42, has large, tidy rooms for US$17/21/26 a single/double/triple with fan, US$30/35/38 with air-con.

Places to Stay – top end

Hotel Los Cocos (☎ (983) 2-05-44; fax 2-09-20), Avenida Héroes at Chapultepec, is the best in town, with a nice swimming pool set in grassy lawns, guarded car park and decent restaurant. Air-con rooms with TV, rich in nubbly white stucco, cost US$85 a single or double.

Two blocks north of Los Cocos along Héroes, on the right-hand side near the tourist information kiosk, is the *Hotel Continental Caribe* (☎ (983) 2-10-50; fax 2-16-76), Héroes 171. Its comfortable rooms overlook several swimming pools, a restaurant and bar, and cost US$48 a single,

US$58 a double; junior suites are US$70 a single, US$85 a double.

Places to Eat

Near the intersection of Héroes and Obregón is the quaint old *Restaurant Campeche*, in a Caribbean-style wooden building which may give way to the bulldozers and rampant modernisation at any moment. Until it does, you can enjoy cheap food in an old Chetumal atmosphere.

Next door is the *Panadería La Muralla*, providing fresh baked goods for bus trips, picnics, and make-your-own breakfasts.

Restaurant Sosilmar, next along Obregón west of Héroes below the Hotel María, is perhaps the cleanest and brightest. Prices are listed prominently; filling platters of fish or meat go for US$4 to US$6.

To the west of the Sosilmar is *Pollo Brujo*, a roast chicken place where you can roll your own burritos.

The family-owned and operated *Restaurant Pantoja*, on the corner of Avenida M Gandhi 164 and 16 de Septiembre 181, is a neighbourhood favourite which opens for breakfast early, and later provides a comida corrida for US$4.50, enchiladas for US$3, and meat plates such as bistec or liver and

YUCATÁN

onions (higado encebollado) for US$5. The nearby *Restaurant Ucum*, in the Hotel Ucum, also provides good cheap meals.

To sample the typical traditional food of Quintana Roo, head for the *Restaurant El Taquito*, Avenida Plutarco Elias Calles 220 at Juárez. You enter past the cooks, hard at work, to an airy, simple dining room where good, cheap food is served. There's a daily comida corrida for US$3.75.

Sergio's Pizzas (☎ 2-23-55), Obregón 182, a block east of Héroes, is actually a full-service restaurant. Look for the stained glass windows, enter the delightfully air-conditioned dining room, order a cold beer in a frosted mug or one of the many wines offered, and select a pizza priced from US$5 (small, plain) to US$20 (large, fancy). The pleasant wood-panelled dining room has paintings and soft classical music. Sergio's is open from 1 pm to midnight every day. *María's Restaurant*, right next door on the corner, is similar, with a menu of pizzas, steaks and continental dishes.

Getting There & Away

Air Chetumal's small airport is less than two km north-west of the city centre along Obregón and Revolución.

Aerocaribe (☎ (983) 2-66-75 at the airport) operates flights between Chetumal and Mérida, Cozumel and Cancún.

Aviacsa (☎ (983) 2-76-89, 2-76-76; at the airport 2-77-87) flies nonstop to Mexico City, and also to Tuxtla Gutiérrez. From Tuxtla you can fly to Mérida, Oaxaca, Tapachula or Villahermosa.

For flights to Belize City (and on to Tikal) or to Belize's cayes, cross the border into Belize and fly from Corozal.

Bus Chetumal's large new bus station is three km north of the city centre. The dominant company is Autotransportes del Caribe, but ADO buses stop here as well. For Belize, Batty's Bus Service runs from the Chetumal bus station; Venus Bus Lines runs from the intersection of Regundo and Calzada Vera-cruz, two km north of the centre.

Bacalar – 39 km, 45 minutes; nine 2nd-class (US$3.50)

Belize City – 160 km, four hours (express 3¼ hours); Venus has buses on the hour from 6 am to 6 am for US$10; Batty's has buses every two hours from 4 am to 6 pm for the same price.

Campeche – 422 km, seven hours; 1st-class buses (US$14) at 12.30 and 7 pm

Cancún – 382 km, seven hours; five 2nd-class (US$19) and seven 2nd-class (US$8.75)

Corozal (Belize) – 30 km, one hour with border formalities; see Belize City schedule, or catch a minibus for the 12 km ride to the border at Subteniente López (see Minibus).

Felipe Carrillo Puerto – 155 km, three hours; five 1st-class (US$8) and nine 2nd-class (US$7)

Kohunlich – 67 km, 1¼ hours; take a bus heading west to Xpujil or Escárcega. Get off just before village of Francisco Villa and walk nine km (1¾ hours) to site.

Mérida – 456 km, eight to nine hours; seven 1st-class (US$20) by A Peninsulares, and eight 1st-class by A del Caribe; nine 2nd-class (US$17) by A del Caribe

Muna (for Uxmal) – 375 km, seven hours; nine 2nd-class (US $18)

Playa del Carmen – 315 km, 5½ hours; five 1s- class (US$15), and seven 2nd-class (US$6)

San Cristóbal de las Casas – 700 km, 13 hours; one evening 2nd-class bus for US$26 by Auto-transportes del Caribe (who use the Transportes Lacandonia bus station in San Cristóbal)

Ticul – 352 km, 6½ hours; nine 2nd-class (US$15)

Tulum – 251 km, four hours; five 1st-class (US$12) and seven 2nd-class (US$10)

Valladolid – 305 km, five hours; two 2nd-class (US$12)

Villahermosa – 575 km, nine hours; two 1st-class (US$22) and one 2nd-class (US$18) at 1.15 pm

Xpujil – 120 km, two hours; three 2nd-class (US$6)

Minibus Not far from the tourist info kiosk are several minibus departure and arrival points. Volkswagen combi minibuses run from here to points in the vicinity of Chetumal such as Laguna Bacalar and the Belizean border at Subteniente López. Combi Corner, as I call it, is the intersection of Avenidas Primo de Verdad and Hidalgo, two blocks east of Héroes (four blocks north-east of the market).

AROUND CHETUMAL
Kohunlich Ruins

West of Chetumal along Highway 186 is rich sugar cane and cattle country; logging is still

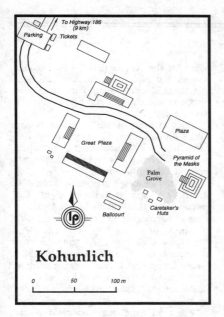

Kohunlich

0   50   100 m

important here as it was during the 17th and 18th centuries. The archaeological site of Kohunlich is only partly excavated, with many of its nearly 200 mounds still covered with vegetation. The surrounding rainforest is thick, but the archaeological site itself has been cleared selectively and is now a delightful forest park. Kohunlich's caretaker, Señor Ignacio Ek, may offer you a tour, after which a tip is in order. Otherwise, admission to the site costs US$4, and is open from 8 am to 5 pm daily. Drinks are sold at the site, but nothing else.

These ruins, dating from the late Pre-classic (100-200 AD) and Early Classic (AD 250-600) periods, are famous for the impressive Pyramid of the Masks: a central stairway is flanked by huge, three-metre-high stucco masks of the sun god. The thick lips and prominent features are reminiscent of Olmec sculpture. Though there were once eight masks, only two remain after the ravages of archaeology looters. The masks themselves are impressive, but the large thatch coverings which have been erected to protect them from further weathering also obscure the view; you can see the masks only from close up. Try to imagine what the pyramid and its masks must have looked like in the old days as the Maya approached it across the sunken courtyard at the front.

The hydraulic engineering used at the site was a great achievement; nine of the site's 21 hectares were cut to channel rainwater into Kohunlich's once enormous reservoir.

Getting There & Away At the time of writing, there is no public transport running directly to Kohunlich. To visit the ruins without your own vehicle, start early in the morning, and take a bus heading west from Chetumal to Xpujil or Escárcega, then watch for the village of Nachi-Cocom some 50 km from Chetumal. About 9.5 km past Nachi-Cocom, just before the village of Francisco Villa, is a road on the left (south) which covers the nine km to the archaeological site. Have the bus driver stop and let you off here, and plan to walk and hope to hitch a ride from tourists in a car; hold up this guidebook for the driver to see. (If you're the ones in the car, please pick up tourists on foot carrying a copy of this guide!)

To return to Chetumal or head westward to Xpujil or Escárcega you must hope to flag down a bus on the highway.

SOUTH TO BELIZE
Corozal, 18 km south of the Mexican/Belizean border, is a pleasant, sleepy, laid-back farming and fishing town, and an appropriate introduction to Belize. For details, see the Belize section.

A special 1st-class bus service goes directly between Chetumal's bus terminal and Flores (near Tikal) once daily (350 km, nine hours, US$35).

YUCATÁN

Tabasco

The state of Tabasco is a low-lying coastal area to the north of Chiapas, kept fertile by the huge rivers – Usumacinta, San Pedro, Grijalva, Tonalá – which slice through the state on their way to the Gulf of Mexico.

Unlike Chiapas to the south, which has a varied topography and climate, Tabasco is mostly hot and humid. It was in this unlikely part of the country that the Olmecs developed Mesoamerica's first great civilisation.

Besides its cultural wealth, Tabasco is noted for its mineral riches, particularly petroleum, which has brought great prosperity to the state capital, Villahermosa in recent years.

VILLAHERMOSA
Population: 250,000

Once just a way-station on the long, sweltering road from central Mexico to the savannas of Yucatán, Villahermosa was anything but a 'beautiful city' as its name implies. Its on the

banks of the Río Grijalva was pleasant enough, but its lowland location and high rainfall (150 cm annually) meant it was bathed in tropical heat and humidity every day of every year.

Today, courtesy of the Tabasco oil boom, Villahermosa is indeed a beautiful city with wide, tree-shaded boulevards, sprawling parks, fancy hotels (for the oilies) and excellent cultural institutions.

If you want to see everything here, you will have to stay at least one night. The Parque-Museo La Venta is one of Mexico's great archaeological exhibits, and will take you most of a morning. The excellent Regional Archaeological Museum deserves at least an hour or two. Half a day at Yumká's Nature Interpretive Center viewing wildlife can be enjoyed. The ruins of ancient Comalcalco are just a short bus ride from the city centre.

With even more time you can relax at beach sites like El Paraíso, El Limón, Pico

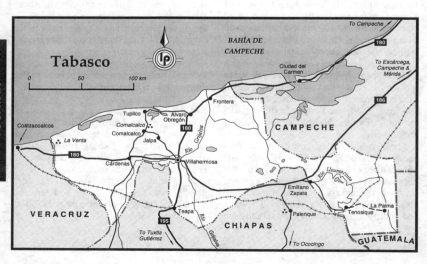

de Oro and Frontera. Although not on the Caribbean Sea, these beaches are pleasant enough and nearly free of tourists. The town of Teapa, an hour from Villahermosa, offers cave exploration, river swimming and a sulphur spa.

History

What is now called the state of Tabasco was once the home of the Olmecs, the first great Mesoamerican civilisation (1200-400 BC), whose religion, art, astronomy and architecture would deeply influence the civilisations that followed in its wake. The Olmec capital, La Venta, was situated in the western part of the state. The Chontal Maya who followed the Olmecs built a great ceremonial city called Comalcalco outside present-day Villahermosa. By the time the Spaniards landed, Comalcalco had already been long abandoned and lost in the jungle.

Cortés, who disembarked on the Gulf coast near present-day Villahermosa in 1519, initially defeated the Maya and founded a settlement called Santa María de la Victoria. The Maya regrouped and offered stern resistance until they were defeated by Francisco de Montejo, who pacified the region by

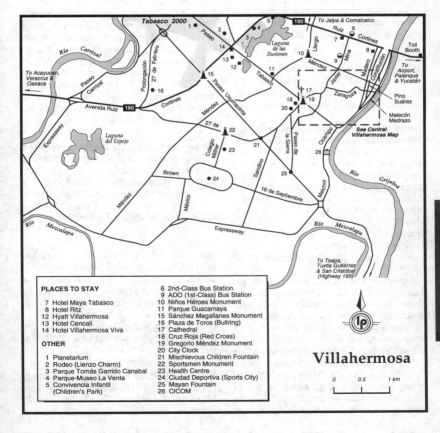

Villahermosa

YUCATÁN

PLACES TO STAY

7 Hotel Maya Tabasco
8 Hotel Ritz
12 Hyatt Villahermosa
13 Hotel Cencali
14 Hotel Villahermosa Viva

OTHER

1 Planetarium
2 Rodeo (Lienzo Charro)
3 Parque Tomás Garrido Canabal
4 Parque-Museo La Venta
5 Convivencia Infantil (Children's Park)
6 2nd-Class Bus Station
9 ADO (1st-Class) Bus Station
10 Niños Héroes Monument
11 Parque Guacamaya
15 Sánchez Magallanes Monument
16 Plaza de Toros (Bullring)
17 Cathedral
18 Cruz Roja (Red Cross)
19 Gregorio Méndez Monument
20 City Clock
21 Mischievous Children Fountain
22 Sportsmen Monument
23 Health Centre
24 Ciudad Deportiva (Sports City)
25 Mayan Fountain
26 CICOM

0   0.5   1 km

1540. However, this tranquillity was short-lived. The depredations of pirates forced the original settlement to be moved inland from the coast and renamed Villahermosa de San Juan Bautista.

After independence was won from Spain, various local land barons tried to assert their power over the area, causing considerable strife. The 1863 French intrusion under Maximilian of Hapsburg was deeply resisted here and led to regional solidarity and political stability. Nonetheless, the economy languished until after the Mexican Revolution, when exports of cacao, bananas and coconuts began to increase. Then, in the 1970s, US and British petroleum companies discovered oil, and Tabasco's economy began to revolve around the liquid fuel.

Orientation

Villahermosa is a sprawling city, and you will find yourself walking some considerable distances – in the sticky heat – and occasionally hopping on a minibus (combi) or taking a taxi.

Bottom-end and middle-range hotel and restaurant choices are mostly in the older commercial centre of the city which stretches from the Plaza de Armas, between Independencia and Guerrero, and Parque Juárez, bounded by streets named Zaragoza, Madero and Juárez. This section has been renovated in recent years and is known, because of those renovations, as the Zona Remodelada (Remodeled Zone) or, more poetically, as the Zona de la Luz (Zone of Lights). The zona is a lively place, busy with shoppers.

Top-end hotels are located on and off the main highway which passes through the city, named Avenida Ruiz Cortines. The Parque-Museo La Venta is also on Avenida Ruiz Cortines, several hundred metres north-west of the intersection with Paseo Tabasco.

The Central Camionera de Primera Clase (1st-Class Bus Station), sometimes called the ADO terminal (☎ (93) 12-89-00) is on Javier Mina, three long blocks south of Avenida Ruiz Cortines and about 12 blocks north of the city centre. The Central de Autobuses de Tabasco (2nd-Class Bus Station) is right on Avenida Ruiz Cortines near a traffic roundabout marked by a statue of a fisherman; the station is one block east of Javier Mina, four long blocks north of the 1st-class station, and about 16 long blocks from the centre.

Villahermosa's Rovirosa Airport (☎ (93) 12-75-55) is 13 km east of the centre on Highway 180, on the other side of the bridge across the Río Grijalva.

Information

Tourist Office The large, glitzy main Tabasco state tourist office (☎ (93) 16-36-23; fax 16-28-90) is in the governmental development known as Tabasco 2000, at Paseo Tabasco 1504, half a km north-west of the intersection with Ruiz Cortines. It's not very accessible except by car. Hours are 8.30 am to 4 pm Monday to Friday. The federal SECTUR office (☎ 16-28-91) is here as well. It's interesting that the tourist office is in an area convenient to bureaucrats but inconvenient to tourists.

Money There are at least eight banks within a five-block area of the Zona Remodelada, bounded by Aldama, Zaragoza, Madero and Reforma. Banamex (☎ (93) 12-89-94) is at the corner of Madero and Reforma; Bancomer (☎ (93) 12-37-00) is at the intersection of Zaragoza and Juárez. Banking hours are 9 am to 1.30 pm.

Post There's a small post office at the ADO bus station. The main post office (☎ (93)12-10-40), is on Saenz 131 at the corner of Lerdo de Tejada in the Zona Remodelada. Postal hours are Monday to Friday 8 am to 5.30 pm, Saturday 9 am to noon, closed Sunday. The telegraph office (☎ (93)12-24-94) is near the post office at Lerdo de Tejada 601.

Medical Services Unidad Medico Guerro Urgencias (☎ (93)14-56-97/98), on 5 de Mayo 44 at Lerdo de Tejada, is open 24 hours.

Laundry Super Lavandería Rex (☎ (93) 12-08-15), Madero 705 at Méndez, facing Restaurant Mexicanito, is open 8 am to 8 pm Monday to Saturday. A three-kg load costs US$8 for three hour service.

Acua Lavandería, next to the river on the corner of Madero and Reforma, is open every day but Sunday; they charge US$1 per kg for two-day service, US$1.50 per kg for same-day service and have no self-service.

Parque-Museo La Venta

History The Olmec city of La Venta, built on an island where the Río Tonalá runs into the Gulf some 129 km west of Villahermosa, was originally constructed in about 1500 BC, and flourished from 800 BC to 200 AD. Danish archaeologist Frans Blom did the initial excavations in 1925, and work was continued by Tulane and California Universities. M W Sterling is credited with having discovered, in the early 1940s, five massive heads sculpted from basalt.

When petroleum excavation threatened the site, the most significant finds were moved to Villahermosa and arranged as the Parque-Museo La Venta, a museum without walls in a lush green setting that enables you to picture these sculptures in their original Olmec city.

The park is a maze of paths with numbered artefacts set amidst jungle foliage. Three colossal Olmec heads, intriguingly African in their facial composition, were moved to the park. The largest weighs over 24 tonnes and stands more than two metres tall. It is a mystery how, originally, the Olmecs managed to move the basalt heads as well as religious statues some 100 km without the use of the wheel.

As well as the heads, you will see intricately carved stelae and sculptures of manatees, monkeys and, of course, the jaguar, totemic animal of the Olmecs.

Parque-Museo La Venta (☎ (93) 15-22-28) is open from 8 am to 4 pm, closed

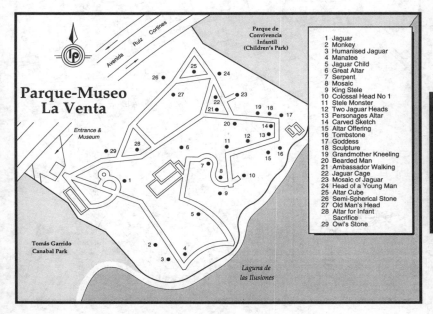

Parque-Museo La Venta

1 Jaguar
2 Monkey
3 Humanised Jaguar
4 Manatee
5 Jaguar Child
6 Great Altar
7 Serpent
8 Mosaic
9 King Stele
10 Colossal Head No 1
11 Stele Monster
12 Two Jaguar Heads
13 Personages Altar
14 Carved Sketch
15 Altar Offering
16 Tombstone
17 Goddess
18 Sculpture
19 Grandmother Kneeling
20 Bearded Man
21 Ambassador Walking
22 Jaguar Cage
23 Mosaic of Jaguar
24 Head of a Young Man
25 Altar Cube
26 Semi-Spherical Stone
27 Old Man's Head
28 Altar for Infant Sacrifice
29 Owl's Stone

YUCATÁN

YUCATÁN

Central Villahermosa

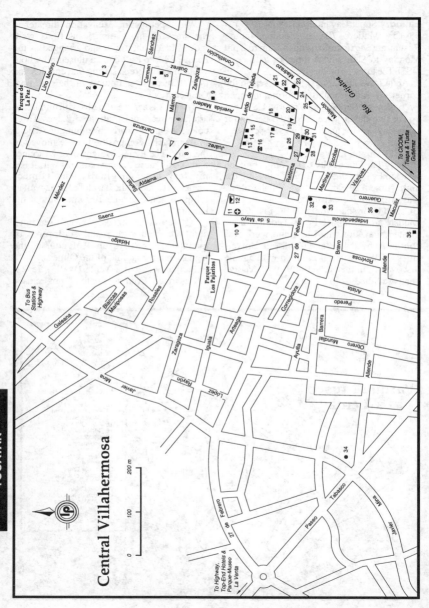

PLACES TO STAY

4	Hotel San Francisco
5	Posada Brondo
9	Hotel Palma de Mallorca
13	Hotel Tabasco
14	Hotel San Miguel
15	Hotel Oviedo
17	Hotel Oriente
18	Hotel Don Carlos
20	Hotel Madan
21	Hotel Buenos Aires
22	Hotel 'P' (Providencia)
24	Casa de Huéspedes Terecita
26	Hotel Miraflores
29	Hotel Madero
36	Hotel Plaza Independencia

PLACES TO EAT

1	Restaurant Vegetariano Pax
3	Restaurant Mexicanito
7	Aquarius Centro Vegetariano
8	Panificadora Los Dos Naciones
10	Restaurant Hong Kong
19	Restaurant Madan
25	Restaurant Shallymar
27	Rock and Roll Cocktelería
30	Restaurant Pimpollo
31	El Torito Valenzuela

OTHER

2	Super Lavandería Rex
6	Parque Juárez
11	Unidad Medico Guerro Urgencias
12	Post & Telegraph Office
16	Telephone Office
23	Acua Lavandería
28	Viajes Villahermosa
32	Patria es Primo Fountain
33	Palacio de Gobierno
34	Inter Ticket Office
35	Plaza de Armas

Monday; entry is US$1.75. Bring repellent as the mosquitoes can be vicious.

A small swarm of guides will approach you outside the gate and offer one hour tours for US$12 to US$16 (one to five people). To prearrange a tour in English, Italian or French, call Luis Carlos García's guide service at ☎ (93) 53-11-52. A guide is perhaps the best way to see the park as the signage is cryptic and map brochures usually nonexistent.

On the north-east side of Parque-Museo La Venta is the city's children's park, the Parque de Convivencia Infantil. Playgrounds, a small zoo and aviary keep the kids happy here from 9 am to 5 pm any day except Monday, when it's closed. Admission costs a few cents for adults, but is free for children under 12.

Behind Parque-Museo La Venta you can stroll along the Laguna de las Ilusiones in Tomás Garrido Canabal park, or climb up the circular stairway (200 steps) of the modern look-out tower.

Getting There & Away Though this world-famous open-air museum is the city's primary tourist attraction, and though all sorts of important places in this city are well marked, *there is not one single sign* to lead you to the parque, or to point out the entrance! The only way you know you've arrived is when you see the parque's name emblazoned on the wall (obscured by trees) by the entrance – and you won't see this until you are right there.

To reach Parque-Museo La Venta, some three km from the Zona Remodelada, catch any bus or combi heading north-west along Paseo Tabasco, get out before the intersection with Ruiz Cortines, and walk north-east through the sprawling Parque Tomás Garrido Canabal, a larger park which actually surrounds Parque-Museo La Venta. A taxi from the Zona Remodelada costs US$1.50.

CICOM & Regional Museum of Anthropology

The Center for Investigation of the Cultures of the Olmecs & Maya (CICOM) is a complex of buildings on the bank of the Río Grijalva one km south of the Zona Remodelada. The centrepiece of the complex is the Museo Regional de Antropología Carlos Pellicer Cámara, which is dedicated to the scholar and poet responsible for the preservation of the Olmec artefacts in the Parque-Museo La Venta. Besides the

YUCATÁN

museum, the complex holds a theatre, research centre, an arts centre and other buildings.

The Anthropology Museum (☎ (93) 12-32-02) is open 10 am to 3.30 pm every day; admission is US$1.75.

Just inside the front door, you're stopped in your tracks by the timeless gaze and regal expression of a massive Olmec head, one of those wonders from La Venta. The best way to proceed with your tour of the museum is to pay your respects to the head, turn left, take the lift to the 2nd (top) floor (3rd floor American style) and work your way down. Although the museum's explanations are all in Spanish, they are often accompanied by photos, maps and diagrams.

On the top floor, exhibits outline Mesoamerica's many civilisations, from the oldest stone-age inhabitants to the more familiar cultures of our millennium. Don't miss the codices by the window on the north side. These are copies of the famous painted books of the Maya; the originals are in repositories outside Mexico. The window here, by the way, offers a nice view of the river and Villahermosa's cathedral.

After you've brushed up on the broad picture, descend one flight to the 1st (middle) floor where the exhibits concentrate on the Olmec and Mayan cultures. Especially intriguing are the displays concerning Comalcalco, the ruined Mayan city not far from Villahermosa, which you may want to visit.

Finally, the ground floor of the museum holds various changing and travelling exhibits.

Getting There & Away CICOM is one km south of the city centre, or 600 metres south of the intersection of Malecón Madrazo and Paseo Tabasco. You can catch any bus or colectivo ('CICOM' or 'No 1') travelling south along Madrazo; just say 'CICOM?' before you get in.

Tabasco 2000 & Parque La Choca
The Tabasco 2000 complex is a testimonial to the prosperity the oil boom brought to

Villahermosa, with its modern Palacio Municipal, Omnimax cinema, chic boutiques in a gleaming mall, a convention centre and pretty fountains. If you are coming from the city centre, take a Tabasco 2000 bus along Paseo Tabasco.

Parque La Choca, just beyond the Tabasco 2000 complex, is the site of a state fair, complete with livestock exhibitions and a crafts festival in late April. It is also a pleasant place to picnic, has a swimming pool and is open Monday to Saturday from 7 am to 9 pm.

Yumká
Yumká (☎ /fax (93)13-23-90), 18 km east of the city (near the airport), is Villahermosa's attempt at ecotourism, a one-sq-km Nature Interpretive Center boasting spider monkeys, antelope, wildebeests, zebras, giraffes, elephants, white rhinos, water buffalo, ostriches, camels, caged jaguars, and maybe a crocodile. Though some metal fences partition the park, most animals are free to roam.

Named for the dwarf who looks after the jungle, the Yumká reserve is split into three sections: you begin with a half-hour stroll through the jungle, followed by an Asian and African Savannah tour by tractor-pulled trolley and finish up with a boat trip on the large lagoon. The obligatory guided tour takes 1½ to 2 hours. It's hardly a Kenya game drive, but if you fancy a dose of open space, greenery and a glimpse of the animal kingdom, go.

Yumká is open every day from 9 am to 5.30 pm. Admission costs US$5. Drinks and snacks are available at the front gate.

Getting There & Away On weekends, shuttles go between the Parque-Museo La Venta car park and Yumká every thirty minutes from 10 am to 4 pm. On weekdays, there are supposedly combis to Yumká from Parque La Paz on Madero, yet I could find only taxis, charging US$13 for the ride.

Places to Stay – bottom end
Camping It might be possible to set up a tent or caravan/trailer at the *Ciudad Deportiva* in

the southern part of the city. Ask at the field-house adjacent to the Olympic Stadium during the day. The Tamolte bus runs out here. There's trailer parking also at Parque La Choca on Paseo Tabasco north-west of Tabasco 2000, but no tents are allowed.

Hotels Most of Villahermosa's inexpensive hotels are conveniently located in the Zona Remodelada, but there is one relatively cheap choice near the 1st-class bus station. Keep street noise in mind when choosing accommodation in Villahermosa.

Hotel Palomino (☎ (93) 12-84-31) is on Javier Mina at Pedro Fuentes, across from the main entrance to the ADO (1st-class) bus station. Its location lets it get away with charging US$20 for a basic room (with fan and shower). It's sometimes noisy and you may be put on the 4th or 5th floor. The stairs can be lethal if you arrive on a late night bus in a semi-liquid state.

On Lerdo de Tejada between Juárez and Madero are three small, plain, cheap hotels all in a row. *Hotel San Miguel* (☎ (93) 12-15-00), in the mall off Madero at Lerdo 315, is perhaps the best of the lot, renting its plain rooms for US$11/15 a single/double, or US$20 for a double with air-con. *Hotel Tabasco* (☎ (93) 12-00-77), Lerdo 317, is a step down from the neighbouring San Miguel, but will do for US$11 a double. *Hotel Oviedo* (☎ (93) 12-14-55) at Lerdo 303, the worst of the lot, charges US$10 for a mediocre double.

Hotel Oriente (☎ (93) 12-01-21), Madero 425 near Lerdo, is simple and clean, and has its own good, cheap little restaurant on the ground floor. Rooms with private shower and ceiling fan go for US$11/15 a single/double.

For budget air-con rooms try the *Hotel San Francisco* (☎ (93) 12-31-98), at Madero 604 between Zaragoza and María del Carmen. A lift does away with the sweaty hike upstairs. Private baths are neat and tiled. It's pretty good for the price: US$16 for a double with one bed, US$20 with two beds.

Hotel Palma de Mallorca (☎ (93) 12-01-44/5), Madero 516 between Lerdo de Tejada and Zaragoza, is slightly more comfortable. Rooms with ceiling fan rent for US$16/21 a single/double, or US$25 with air-con.

The *Hotel Madero* (☎ (93) 12-05-16), Madero 301 between Reforma and 27 de Febrero, is in an old building with some character. The rooms are among the best at this price in the city, US$13/16 with ceiling fan and private shower. Air-con costs a few dollars more.

The cheapest beds are on Constitution. *Hotel Providencia* (☎ (93) 12-82-62), Constitución 210, between Lerdo and Reforma has tiny rooms, and even tinier baths that are often acceptably clean, and certainly well priced at US$8 per room. To find the hotel, look for the odd sign saying 'Hotel P', with an eye peering from a triangle. A few doors north of the Hotel Providencia, *Hotel Buenos Aires* (☎ (93) 12-15-55), Constitución 216, offers dispiriting rooms for US$8/10 a single/double, but it's being remodelled, so it may be worth a try.

Posada Brondo (☎ (93) 12-59-61), on Pino Suárez 411 between Carmen Sánchez and Mármol, has white, bright, clean rooms with TV and shower for US$15. For US$18 you get a room with a small couch, refrigerator, and perhaps a balcony. The lobby has the best maps of Villahermosa and Tabasco to be found.

Places to Stay – middle

Middle-range hotels are also in the Zona Remodelada. The well-situated *Hotel Miraflores* (☎ (93) 12-00-22/54), Reforma 304 just west of Madero, was renovated in 1991. Nicely appointed air-con rooms with bath are US$44/47.

Hotel Plaza Independencia (☎ (93) 12-12-99); fax 14-47-24), Independencia 123 near the Plaza de Armas, is a pleasant air-con hotel with TVs, private baths, and balconies (try for a room on an upper floor). A restaurant, bar, small pool and car park add to the hotel's appeal. Prices are US$44 a single, US$47 a double, US$53 a triple.

Hotel Madan (☎ (93) 12-16-50), Pino Suárez 105 just north of Reforma, has 20 nice, modern air-con rooms with bath in a conveniently located modern building. The hotel entrance is at the eastern end of the building on Pino Suárez; the western end on Madero houses the restaurant (see Places to Eat). A double costs US$43.

Hotel Don Carlos (☎ (93) 12-24-92), Madero 422 between Reforma and Lerdo, has air-con rooms with private baths, TV and telephones for US$48 a single or double, US$59 a triple. Though the lobby is lavish with mirrors and marble, the hotel has seen better days: the rooms are musty and the furniture creaky.

Choco's Hotel (☎ (93) 12-90-44), at the corner of Constitution and Lino Merino, needs redecoration, the rooms are cramped and the carpets worn, though every room has air-con and TV. The lobby is nice, as is the attached café. Rooms are available for US$44/48 a single/double.

For a moderately priced hotel near the bus stations, try the *Hotel Ritz* (☎ (93) 12-16-11), Madero 1013. This modernised three-storey building is one block south of Ruiz Cortines (Highway 180) and about five blocks east of both the 1st and 2nd-class bus stations. Air-con rooms with private baths are US$43/46 a single/double.

Places to Stay – top end
As an oil boom town, Villahermosa has no shortage of luxury lodgings. Three of the best hotels are located near the intersection of Paseo Tabasco and Avenida Ruiz Cortines (Highway 180), a pleasant 10-minute walk from Parque-Museo La Venta.

Poshest is the *Hyatt Villahermosa* (☎ (93) 15-58-08), south-west off Paseo Tabasco on the Laguna de las Ilusiones, south-east of Avenida Ruiz Cortines, with all the expected luxury services at US$141 a double.

The *Villahermosa Viva* (☎ (93)15-00-00; fax 15 30 73), at the intersection of Paseo Tabasco and Avenida Ruiz Cortines (Highway 180), is a two-storey motel-style white stucco building surrounding a large swimming pool. Comfortable rooms are US$82.

Another good option is the *Hotel Cencali* (☎ (93)15-19-96/97/99; fax 15-66-00),

Calle Juárez off Paseo Tabasco, next to the Hyatt (this is a different Calle Juárez from the one in the city centre!). The Cencali has tropical foliage, grassy lawns, a good restaurant, clean swimming pool, and pleasant modern air-con rooms with TV for US$77.

Holiday Inn Villahermosa (☎ (93)16-44-00; fax 16-44-99; toll-free in Mexico (800) 00-90-99), Paseo Tabasco 1407 in the Tabasco 2000 complex, is Villahermosa's newest luxury lodging, a modern slab-like building with comfortable rooms, a pool, restaurants and bars, and rooms for US$128.

Hotel Maya Tabasco (☎ (93) 12-11-11; fax 14-44-66) is a cool, safe haven four blocks north of the ADO bus station, a block west of the 2nd-class bus station and near the intersection of Javier Mina and Ruiz Cortines. Air-con rooms come with TV (satellite hookups). The hotel has a pool, lobby bar, two restaurants (Mexican and international), a disco, hairdresser and newsstand. The rate is US$77, single or double.

Places to Eat – bottom end
There are a number of good cheap eateries clustered around the 1st-class bus station on Javier Mina, but the main stem for cheap eateries is Avenida Madero. The pedestrian streets of the Zona Remodelada (Lerdo, Juárez, Reforma, Aldama) also have lots of snack and fast-food shops. Coffee drinkers beware! Most cheap places give you a cup of lukewarm water and a jar of instant coffee (sometimes decaf). If you need a quick early-morning shot of the good stuff, try KFC at Juárez 420, near Reforma.

El Torito Valenzuela, 27 de Febrero 202 at Madero, open from 8 am to midnight, is the most popular and convenient cheap taquería. Tacos made with various ingredients cost US$0.60 to US$1.80 apiece. Similarly varied tortas (sandwiches) go for twice as much. With its corner location, you can watch the busy street life as you munch.

Restaurant Pimpollo on Madero between Reforma and 27 de Febrero has quick service, and if you grab a table in the rear it's quiet. For breakfast you can have eggs and toast, hotcakes, or corn flakes for under US$2.50. They'll make you a hefty plate of chicken tostadas (US$2.75), or a four course comida corrida (US$4) for lunch or dinner.

Vegetarians have two equally tasteful options. Near Parque Juárez, *Aquarius Centro Vegetariano*, Zaragoza 513 between Aldama and Juárez, is open from 9 am to 9 pm; closed Sunday. Granola, yogurt and honey (US$1.50), a soyaburger (US$1.50), or its special sandwich (alfalfa, tomatoes, onions, avocado, cheese and beans on grain bread (US$2.25), can be enjoyed at the counter or in the patio courtyard. They also sell whole-wheat baked goods and vitamins.

Restaurant Vegetariano Pax, Méndez 719 between Castillo and Juan Alvarez, is a 10-minute walk from the Zona Remodelada. The karmically correct menu changes daily, though special orders may be possible. Try the 'taquitos de energia', vegetarian chili or cubanas for around US$2, or the veggie comida corrida for US$4.

Restaurant Mexicanito, Madero 704 north of Méndez, is a very plain little lonchería serves chilaquiles (red or green) with chicken or meat dishes for about US$4, and a variety of breakfasts for US$2.50 to US$3.50.

Always packed in the late afternoon is *Rock and Roll Cocktelería* on Reforma just east of Juárez. Here you may sample a cocktel (fish, tomato sauce, lettuce, onions and a lemon squeeze) with crackers for US$6.

At the Parque Los Pajaritos (Park of the Little Parrots), Zaragoza and 5 de Mayo, are two antojito stands where tacos are US$0.25 and tortas US$0.75. The food is OK, but it's the natural shade, big trees and the enormous cage of colorful birds that makes this park a relaxing snack stop. Somehow the breeze finds its way here and the fountain's quiet roar drowns out most city sounds.

If you're eating or drinking on the run, try *Jugos* next to the Hotel San Miguel on Lerdo for licuados or heaping fruit platters (US$1), or the *Panificadora y Pastelería* on Mármol facing the Parque Juárez, for sweet rolls, bread and pastries. Another useful bakery is the *Panificadora Los Dos Naciones*, at the corner of Juárez and Zaragoza.

Places to Eat – middle

Madero and Constitución have a number of suitable middle-range dining-places. *Restaurant Madan*, on Madero just north of Reforma, is bright, modern and air-conditioned, with a genuine espresso machine hissing in one corner. A full meal costs about US$10 though you can have a hamburger and beer for half that price. Hours are 8 am to 11.30 pm every day.

Restaurant Shallymar on Malecón Madrazo, just south of Reforma, specialises in seafood, which is not particularly cheap, but good if it's fresh. Expect to spend between US$15 and US$20 for a meal. Just north of Shallymar, *Los Faroles* on Malecón Madrazo past Reforma, is a nice patio place with brick arches, a river view and occasional live marimba. The menu bears all the Mexican favourites at prices which will bring your bill to US$10 or US$15.

Restaurant Hong Kong, 5 de Mayo 433, just off the Parque Los Pajaritos, is a fine Chinese restaurant on an upper floor with a six-page menu and subtle oriental decor. Start with eggrolls and wonton soup for US$4, then choose from curry dishes served with salad and rice for US$7, roast or steamed duck with Chinese vegetables, or a variety of chicken, fish, or beef dishes in black bean or oyster sauce for US$8.

Besides the dining rooms of the luxury hotels, there are several garden restaurants along Paseo Tabasco between the river and Avenida Ruiz Cortines. You may want to coordinate a visit at the Museo Regional de Antropología with lunch at the *Restaurant Los Tulipanes* in the CICOM complex, open from noon to 8 pm everyday. Seafood and steaks are their specialties and cost between US$10 and US$15. There is a pianist every afternoon and a Sunday buffet for US$16.

Entertainment

Teatro Esperanza Iris at the CICOM complex frequently hosts folkloric dance, theatre, comedy, and music performances.

For information on cultural goings-on, call the Instituto de la Cultura (☎ (93) 12-75-30) or ask at the tourist office or your hotel.

The so-called *planetarium* at Tabasco 2000 is in fact a circular cinema with Omnimax shows and good documentaries (sometimes in English) every night except Monday. Check times before heading out there.

Discos can be found in the Villahermosa Viva, Hyatt, Cencali and Maya Tabasco luxury hotels, open every evening except Sunday and Monday from about 10 pm. The newest *'Ku' disco*, near the junction of Sandino and Ruiz Cortines. has a good reputation. Cover charge at any of these is around US$10.

Getting There & Away

Air Villahermosa's Rovirosa Airport (☎ (93) 12-75-55) is 13 km east of the centre on Highway 180, on the other side of the bridge across the Río Grijalva.

Aerocaribe (☎ (93) 16-31-32), operated through the Mexicana Office (☎ (93) 12-83-49), Avenida de Los Rios 105, Tabasco 2000, flies daily to Mérida (1½ hours, US$123), Tuxtla (40 minutes, US$82), Oaxaca (two hours, US$139), Cancún (three hours, US$170). Mexicana has three flights to Mexico City (1½ hours, US$145)

Aviacsa (☎ 14-57-77) at Francisco Javier Mina 1025-D, has four flights a week to Mérida (US$88) and Cancún (US$132). They fly daily to Oaxaca (US$104), Tuxtla (US$68), and Mexico City (US$145).

Aeromexico (☎ (93) 21-15-28) at Avenida Carlos Pellicer Cámara 511, Plaza CICOM 2, has three flights a day to Mexico City (US$145). Litoral (☎ (93) 82-43-64; fax 82-43-63), is a small airline based in Monterrey that services Villahermosa, Veracruz, Tampico and Monterrey. Tickets are issued by Aeromexico.

Viajes Villahermosa Travel Agency (☎ (93) 12-54-56; fax 14-37-21), at 27 de Febrero 207, between Juárez and Madero, sells international and domestic tickets; the staff speak English and can arrange excursions. Hours are Monday to Friday 9 am to 7 pm, and Saturday 9 am to 1 pm.

1st-Class Bus The 1st-class (ADO) bus station, Javier Mina 297, has a small post office and a selection of little eating places. You can leave your luggage in the station for (US$0.20) per hour.

The two main 1st-class companies are ADO and Cristóbal Colón; UNO, the expensive luxury line, has buses to central Mexico. Villahermosa is an important transportation point, but many buses serving it are de paso, so buy your onward ticket as far in advance as possible.

All of the listings below are daily 1st-class:

Campeche – 450 km, seven hours; 11 ADO buses (US$15); they'll drop you at Catazajá (Palenque junction) for US$4.

Cancún – 915 km, 14 hours; three evening buses by ADO for US$30.

Chetumal – 575 km, nine hours; a 10.45 pm Cristóbal Colón Plus for US$22, and seven ADO buses for US$18.

Comalcalco – 53 km, 1½ hours; two Cristóbal Colón buses for US$3.50.

La Venta – 140 km, two hours; eight ADO buses for US$4.25.

Mérida – 700 km, 10 hours; 11 by ADO (US$20.75), one evening UNO for US$49.

Mexico City – 820 km, 14 hours; 19 ADO buses (US$30), one evening bus by Cristóbal Colón (US$32), and a Cristóbal Colón Plus for US$39; also three evening UNO buses for US$60.

Oaxaca – 700 km, 13 hours; one 6 pm bus by ADO (US$23), two by Cristóbal Colón for US$22.

Palenque – 150 km, 2½ hours; eight by ADO for US$5.50.

Playa del Carmen – 848 km, 14 hours; six ADO buses daily for US$28.

San Cristóbal de las Casas – 308 km, eight hours; all buses via Tuxtla by Cristóbal Colón (US$11).

Tapachula – 735 km, 13 hours; two evening buses by Cristóbal Colón for US$25.

Teapa – 60 km, one hour; five buses daily by Cristóbal Colón for US$1.75

Tenosique – 290 km, four hours; nine ADO buses for US$6.75.

Tuxtla Gutiérrez – 294 km, six hours; eight buses daily by Cristóbal Colón (US$9), an evening Plus bus for US$13.

Veracruz – 475 km, eight hours; 20 buses daily by ADO (US$15.50), one evening UNO bus for US$35.

2nd-Class Bus The 2nd-class Central de Autobuses de Tabasco bus station is on the north side of Avenida Ruiz Cortines (Highway 180) just east of the intersection with Javier Mina. It's about five blocks from the 1st-class bus station as the crow flies. Use one of the pedestrian overpasses to cross the highway.

A number of smaller companies serve local destinations within the state of Tabasco, but there are also 2nd-class buses run by Autobuses Unidos to Acayucan (four daily, US$6.50), Veracruz (one daily, US$13) stopping along the way at Catemaco (US$9), and to Mexico City (three daily, US$19). Buses to La Venta depart four times daily for US$3.75.

Train The nearest railhead is 58 km away at Teapa.

Car Dollar Rent A Car (☎ (93) 13-32-69; fax 16-01-63) is in the Holiday Inn Villahermosa at Paseo Tabasco 1407; Hertz (☎ (93)12-11-11) is in the Hotel Maya Tabasco at Avenida Ruiz Cortines 907.

Getting Around
To/From the Airport Transporte Terrestre minibuses charge US$5 per person for the trip into town; a taxi costs US$15. The 13 km trip takes about 20 minutes to the centre and 25 to 30 minutes to the top-end hotels. Buy your tickets from a counter in the terminal. From town to the airport a taxi is your only choice (US$15). Check to see if Yumká is running shuttles to/from town. If so, they may drop you at the airport entrance.

To/From the Bus Terminals From the 1st-class ADO bus station, it's generally about a 15-to 20-minutes walk to the recommended hotels. Figure around US$1.50 in the cheaper VW Beetle taxis for almost any ride in the city. Local bus fares are only a few cents.

As you exit the front of the ADO station, go left for two blocks to the corner of Mina and Zozaya, where buses stop en route to the Zona Remodelada and Madero, the main thoroughfare. If you are walking, go out the ADO station's front door, cross Mina and follow Lino Merino five blocks to Parque de la Paz on Madero, and turn right.

Bus & Minibus A dozen municipal (SEATA) bus routes link the centro with outlying areas of the city; but the green and white minibuses and combis are more useful than the larger city buses. The minibuses travel tortuous, twisting routes, but it is easy enough to get where you want as they bear the names of major landmarks scrawled in their windscreens. Catch a 'Palacio Mpal' minibus along Paseo Tabasco to get to Tabasco 2000 and the tourist office; 'Chedraui' for the big department stores on Javier Mina, 1½ blocks from the ADO station, and 'Centro' to get to the Zona Remodelada.

AROUND VILLAHERMOSA
Comalcalco Ruins
Comalcalco flourished during the Mayan Late Classic period between 500 and 900 AD, when the region's agricultural productivity prompted population expansion. The principal crop which brought Indian peasants from Palenque to this region was the cacao bean, which the Comalcalcans traded with other Mayan settlements. It is still the chief cash crop.

Comalcalco is open daily from 9 am to 5 pm; admission costs US$2.50.

Resembling Palenque in architecture and sculpture, Comalcalco is unique because it is built of bricks made from clay, sand and – ingeniously – oyster shells. Mortar was provided with lime obtained from the oyster shells.

As you enter the ruins, the substantial structure to your left may surprise you, as the pyramid's bricks look remarkably like the bricks used in construction today. Look on the right-hand side for remains of the stucco sculptures which once covered the pyramid.

YUCATÁN

In the northern section of the Acropolis are remains of fine stucco carvings.

Although the west side of the Acropolis once held a crypt comparable to that of Palenque's Pakal, the tomb was vandalised centuries ago and the sarcophagus stolen. Continue up the hill to the Palace, and from this elevation enjoy the breeze while you gaze down on unexcavated mounds.

Getting There & Away The 55-km journey takes about an hour. ADO runs buses at 12.30 and 8.30 pm daily for US$3.50. Ask the driver to get you to *las ruinas*.

YUCATÁN

Lowland Chiapas

The state of Chiapas has enormous variety, from the tropical lowland jungles of Palenque to the cool, foggy mountains of San Cristóbal de las Casas. For most of its long history Chiapas has been more intimately connected with Guatemala, culturally and politically, than with Mexico. Pre-Hispanic civilisations in the area spread across the modern international border, and for most of the colonial era Chiapas was governed from Guatemala.

PALENQUE
Population: 70,000
Altitude: 80 metres

Palenque is unique among ancient Mayan sites. Although not as expansive or massive

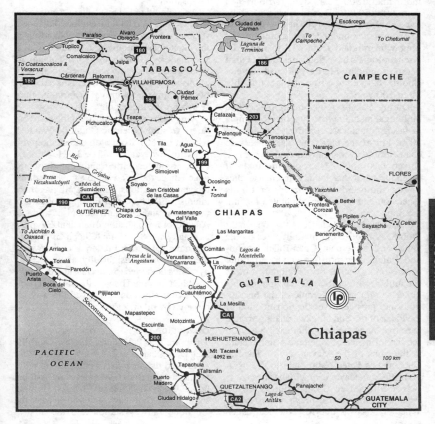

as Chichén Itzá and Uxmal, its setting – surrounded by emerald jungle – is superb, and its architecture and decoration exquisite.

History

Palenque means 'Palisade' in Spanish and has no relation to the ancient city's real name, which is still uncertain. It could be Nachan, (City of Snakes), or Chocan, (Sculptured Snake), or Culhuacán, Huehuetlapalla, Xhembobel Moyos, Ototium...no one knows for sure.

Evidence from pottery fragments indicates that Palenque was first occupied more than 1500 years ago. It flourished from 600 to 800 AD, and what a glorious two centuries they were! The city first rose to prominence under Pakal, a club-footed king who reigned from 615 to 683 AD. Archaeologists have determined that Pakal is represented by hieroglyphics of sun and shield. He lived to a ripe old age, possibly 80 to 100 years.

During Pakal's reign, many plazas and buildings, including the superlative Temple of Inscriptions, were constructed within the 20 sq km of the city. The structures were characterised by mansard roofs and very fine stucco bas-reliefs. Hieroglyphic texts at Palenque state that Pakal's reign was predicted thousands of years prior to his ascension and would be celebrated far into the future.

Pakal was succeeded by his son Chan-Balum, symbolised in hieroglyphics by the jaguar and the serpent. Chan-Balum continued Palenque's political and economic expansion as well as the development of its art and architecture. He completed his father's crypt in the Temple of the Inscriptions and presided over the construction of the Plaza of the Sun temples, placing sizable narrative stone stelae within each. One can see the influence of Palenque's architecture in the ruins of the Mayan city of Tikal in Guatemala's Petén region and in the pyramids of Comalcalco near Villahermosa.

Not long after Chan-Balum's death, Palenque started on a precipitous decline. Whether this was due to ecological catastrophe, civil strife or invasion has been disputed, but after the 10th century Palenque was largely abandoned. The ruins were overgrown with vegetation and lay undiscovered until the latter half of the 18th century.

Rediscovery of Palenque

It is said that Hernán Cortés came within 40 km of the ruins without any awareness of them. In 1773, Mayan hunters told a Spanish priest that stone palaces lay in the jungle. Father Ordoñez y Aguilar led an expedition to Palenque and wrote a book claiming that the city was the capital of an Atlantis-like civilisation.

An expedition led by Captain Antonio del Río set out in 1787 to explore Palenque. Although his report was then locked up in the Guatemalan archives, a translation of it was made by a British resident of Guatemala who was sufficiently intrigued to have it published in England in 1822. This led a host of adventurers to brave malaria in their search for the hidden city.

Among the most colourful of these adventurers was the eccentric Count de Waldeck who, in his 60s, lived atop one of the pyramids for two years (1831-33). He wrote a book complete with fraudulent drawings which made the city resemble great Mediterranean civilisations, causing all the more interest in Palenque. In Europe, Palenque's fame grew and it was mythologised as a lost Atlantis or an extension of ancient Egypt.

Finally, in 1837, John L Stephens reached Palenque with artist Frederick Catherwood. Stephens wrote insightfully about the six pyramids he started to excavate and the city's aqueduct system. His was the first truly scientific investigation and paved the way for research by other serious scholars.

Orientation

There are two Palenques, the town and the archaeological zone, 6.5 km apart. Most visitors to the area arrive either from Villahermosa and Tabasco, or from San Cristóbal de las Casas in highland Chiapas. Coming south from Highway 186, you'll pass the Palenque railway station and the airstrip before reaching a fork in the road, notable by the huge statue of a Mayan chieftain's head. Bear left at the statue for Palenque town (one km) or bear right for the ruins (5.5 km) within the national park. The road to the right toward the ruins also leads to the turn-off (left) for Nututum, Misol-Ha, Agua Azul and San Cristóbal de las Casas.

Most hotels and restaurants are in the town centre; the camping areas and several top-end hotels are located along the road to the ruins. There are also hotels and restaurants in La Cañada, a forested locality just to the left of the Mayan statue as you come in from the highway.

Though relatively small, the town of Palenque spreads for two km, with the Mayan statue at the western limit and the Hotel Misión Park Plaza at the eastern end. Most of the bus stations are clustered a few hundred metres east of the Mayan statue on the way into town; the walk to most hotels is 800 metres or less. The main road from the Mayan statue into town is Avenida Juárez, which ends at the town's main square, known simply as el parque (the park). Juárez is the centre of the commercial district.

With an average humidity of 78%, it's always sweltering in Palenque and there's rarely any breeze.

Information

Tourist Office Located in the Casa de la Cultura building on the corner of 20 de Noviembre and Jiménez, the tourist office (☎ (934) 5-08-28) has an English-speaking staff, reliable town and transit information and a few maps. Office doors are open Monday to Saturday 8 am to 2 pm and 5 to 8 pm.

Money Bancomer, 1½ blocks west of the park on Juárez, changes money between 10 and 11.30 am Monday to Friday. Banamex, 2½ blocks west of the park, does the exchange from 10.30 am to noon Monday to Friday. Some hotels, restaurants, travel agents and exchange shops in town will also change money, though at less favourable rates.

Post & Telecommunications The post office, just off the park on the left side of the Palacio Municipal is open Monday to Friday 9 am to 1 pm and 3 to 5 pm, and Saturday from 9 am to 1 pm.

You can place long-distance telephone calls from the ADO bus station. Person-to-person or collect (reverse-charge) calls are subject to a US$1.75 fee. There are a few long distance telephone shops on Juárez, near the banks. They offer a bit more privacy, and charge about US$4 per minute/US$10 per fax worldwide.

Bookshops Papelería y Novedades del Centro (☎ (943) 5-07-77), at Independencia 18 and Nicolás, is a small paper/bookshop attached to a cafe. Shelves hold a few English guidebooks, some Mayan literature and maps of Chiapas. There is a random magazine selection but you can find recent news sources or a Rolling Stone.

Laundry Lavandería Automática is a few steps uphill from the ADO bus station, across from the Hotel Kashlan.

Medical Services Palenque has a Hospital General across from the Pemex station near the Maya statue, a Centro de Salud Urbano (Urban Health Centre) next door, and various pharmacies. The Farmacia & Clinica Santa Fe, on Hidalgo at Javier Mina two blocks east of the park, is open 24 hours a day. Don't expect to see the lights on day and night, but feel free to wake the family in an emergency.

Palenque Ruins

The archaeological zone of Palenque is situated in a much larger reserve, the Parque Nacional Palenque. A new Visitors Centre at the entrance to the park holds a museum and other services.

Only 34 of Palenque's nearly 500 buildings have been excavated. As you explore the

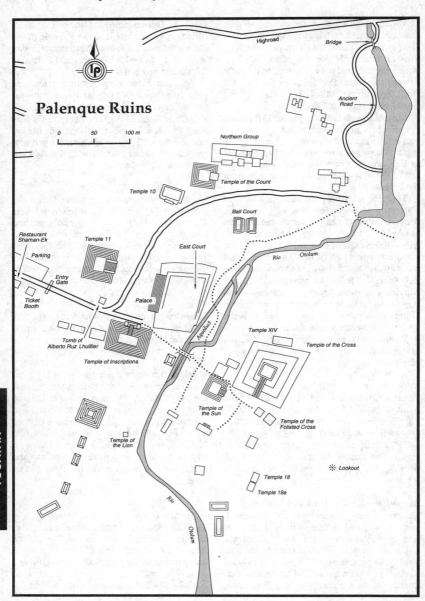

Palenque Ruins

0   50   100 m

Highroad

Bridge

Ancient Road

Northern Group

Temple of the Count

Temple 10

Ball Court

East Court

Río Otolum

Restaurant Shaman-Ek

Parking

Temple 11

Entry Gate

Ticket Booth

Palace

Tomb of Alberto Ruz Lhuillier

Temple of Inscriptions

Aqueduct

Temple XIV

Temple of the Cross

Temple of the Sun

Temple of the Foliated Cross

Temple of the Lion

Lookout

Temple 18

Temple 18a

Río Otolum

YUCATÁN

ruins, try to picture the grey edifices as bright red; at the peak of Palenque's power, the entire city was painted vermilion. Everything you see here was achieved without metal tools, pack animals or the wheel.

One of the prime times to visit the site is just after it opens, when a haze rises and wraps the ancient temples in a mysterious humid mist. The effect is best in the winter when the days are shorter.

The archaeological site is open from 8 am to 5 pm; the crypt in the Temple of Inscriptions – not to be missed – is only open from 10 am to 4 pm. Admission to the site costs US$5; parking in the car park by the gate costs US$0.20. There is no additional charge for entry to the crypt or the museum. Drinks, snacks and souvenirs are for sale in stands facing the car park.

Temple of Inscriptions After you enter the enclosure and walk along the path, look for a small stone structure on the left-hand side. This is the tomb of Alberto Ruz Lhuillier, the tireless archaeologist who revealed many of Palenque's mysteries between 1945 and 1952.

The magnificent pyramid on the right – the Temple of Inscriptions – is the tallest and most prominent of Palenque's buildings. Constructed on eight levels, it has a central staircase rising some 23 metres to a temple which crowns the structure; it once had a tall roofcomb as well. Between the doorways are stucco panels with reliefs of noble figures. On the temple's rear wall are three panels with a long inscription in Mayan hieroglyphs which gives the temple its name. The inscription, dedicated in 692 AD, recounts the history of Palenque and of the temple.

Ascend the 69 steep steps to the top for access to stairs down to the tomb of Pakal (open 10 am to 4 pm). This crypt lay undiscovered until 1952 when it was discovered by Alberto Ruz Lhuillier.

Although Pakal's jewel-bedecked skeleton and jade mosaic death mask were taken to Mexico City and the tomb recreated in the Museo Nacional de Antropología, the stone sarcophagus lid remains here. (The priceless

Stucco head found in the Temple of Inscriptions, Palenque

death mask was stolen from the Mexico City museum in 1985.) The carved stone slab protecting the sarcophagus includes the image of Pakal encircled by serpents, mythical monsters, the sun god and glyphs recounting Pakal's reign. Carved on the wall are the nine lords of the underworld. Between the crypt and the staircase, a snake-like hollow ventilation tube connected Pakal to the realm of the living.

Palace Diagonally opposite the Temple of Inscriptions is the Palace, an unusual structure harbouring a maze of courtyards, corridors and rooms. If you walk up to the tower (restored in 1955), you will see fine stucco reliefs on the walls.

Archaeologists and astronomers believe that the tower was constructed so that Mayan royalty and the priest class could observe the

YUCATÁN

sun falling directly into the Temple of the Inscriptions during the 22 December winter solstice.

Temples of the Cross Although Pakal had only the Temple of Inscriptions dedicated to him during his 68-year reign, Chan-Balum had four buildings dedicated to him, known today as the Temples of the Cross.

The Temple of the Sun's decoration includes narrative inscriptions dating from 642, replete with scenes of offerings to Pakal, the sun-shield king. The Temple of the Sun has the best preserved roofcomb of all the buildings at Palenque.

The smaller, less well-preserved Temple XIV next door also has tablets showing ritual offerings – a common scene in Palenque.

The largest of the buildings in this group is the Temple of the Cross, restored in 1990. Inside are sculpted narrative stones.

To the right of the Temple of the Sun stands the Temple of the Foliated Cross. Here the deterioration of the façade lets you appreciate the architectural composition, with the arches fully exposed. A well-preserved tablet carving shows a king with a sun-shield (most likely Pakal) emblazoned on his chest, corn growing from his shoulder blades and the sacred quetzal bird atop his head.

Other Ruins North of the Palace is the Northern Group, unrestored, and the ruins of a ball court. Crazy Count de Waldeck lived in one of the temples of the Northern Group – Temple of the Count, constructed in 647 AD under Pakal.

Jungle Walks You can hike on jungle paths just outside the ruins. Chances are you'll encounter howler monkeys barking in trees overhead. One path goes past the museum and across the river; another is outside the enclosure, about 250 metres back (on the left) along the road to Palenque town. Hidden in the jungle is the Cascada Motiepa, a scenic waterfall and pool which give off cooling zephyrs; bring mosquito repellent for any jungle trek, particularly in the rainy season (May to October).

Getting There & Away Colectivos Chambalu, at the corner of Hidalgo and Allende, and Colectivos Palenque, at the corner of Allende and 20 de Noviembre, operate combis (VW minibuses) between Palenque town and the ruins. Service is every 15 minutes (or when seats are full) from 6 am to 6 pm daily. The minibuses will stop to pick you up anywhere along the town-to-ruins road, which makes it especially handy for campers. Fare is US$0.30.

Organised Tours

Several companies in Palenque town operate transport and tour service to Palenque ruins, Agua Azul and Misol-Ha, Bonampak and Yaxchilán, and La Palma (to Guatemala), usually offering similar features at similar prices. Often there is a minimum number of passengers required. Here are the agencies:

Amfitriones Turísticos de Chiapas, on Allende between Avenida Juárez and Hidalgo (☎ (934) 5-02-10; fax 5-03-56)

Colectivos Chamula, at the corner of Hidalgo and Allende (☎ (934) 5-08-67)

Colectivos Palenque, at the corner of Allende and 20 de Noviembre

Shivalva Viajes Mayas, Merle Green 1A, La Canada (☎(934) 5-04-11; fax 5-03-92)

Viajes Aventura Maya, on Avenida Juárez, across from Banamex (☎(934) 5-07-98)

Viajes Misol-Ha, on Avenida Juárez 48 at Aldama (☎ (934) 5-09-11); fax 5-04-88)

Viajes Pakal-Kin, 5 de Mayo 7, half a block west of the park (☎ (934) 5-11-80)

Viajes Shumb'al, 5 de Mayo 105 in the Kashlan Hotel (☎ (934) 5-20-80; fax 5-03-90)

Viajes Toniná, Juárez 105, near Allende (☎ (934) 5 09 02)

YAX-HA, Juárez 123, next to Banamex (☎ (934) 5-07-98; fax 5-07-67)

Places to Stay – bottom end

Camping Campers can string a hammock or pitch a tent at the *Camping Mayabell*, on the southern side of the road to the ruins, within the national park boundaries. The Mayabell charges US$2.25 (per person or car). They've got toilets, showers, some shade, full hook-ups, snacks and drinks for sale, and a nearby waterfall. Mayabell is only two km from the ruins, though the walk is all uphill.

Camping María del Mar, three km from the ruins on the opposite side of the road, is similar but with less shade, at the same price.

Also possible is to camp on the banks of the Río Usumacinta, on the *Hotel Nututum Viva's* grounds, 3.5 km along the road from Palenque to San Cristóbal de las Casas. The fee is US$3 per person, US$2.75 per vehicle.

Hotels Hotels in town are cheaper than those on the road to the ruins, with the notable exception of the camping grounds.

Posada Charito (☎ (934) 5-01-21), 20 de Noviembre 15, two blocks south-west of the park, is quiet, well kept, and run by a friendly family. For US$10 you get a double with a shower, clean sheets, a ceiling fan, and a Gideon Bible (in Spanish) on your pillow.

The brand new *Caneck Youth Hostel*, on 20 de Noviembre (across from Posada Charito) has big, bright rooms with two to three beds each, wooden lockers big enough for the biggest backpack, and a private toilet and sink. All three floors have separate-sexed showers. Beds are US$6.

The *Hotel La Croix* (☎ (934) 5-00-14), Hidalgo 10, on the north side of the park, has a pretty courtyard with potted tropical plants and adequate rooms with fan and bath. Singles and doubles are US$13/16; La Croix is usually full by mid-afternoon.

Rock-bottom options are on Hidalgo, west of the park. *Casa de Huéspedes León*, between Abasolo and Independencia, rents dark rooms for US$6.50/8 for a single/double. The *Posada San Francisco*, between Allende and Aldama, isn't much better: basic, dingy doubles are US$11. Nicer is *Hotel Naj K'in* on Hidalgo 72, two blocks west of the park, a recently remodelled family-run place with middling rooms, nice bathrooms, hot water and fans. Rooms are US$11/16/23 for a single/double/triple.

Hotel Santa Elena, near the hospital, has breezy, pleasant, mahogany-panelled rooms with fan and shower for US$15; rooms with 4/8 beds go for US$26/50. Great rooftop views here. Also fairly near the bus stations is *Posada Santo Domingo* (☎ (934) 5-01-36), at 20 de Noviembre 119. They charge

US$10 for reasonably quiet, acceptable doubles with fan and private shower.

Hotel Avenida (☎ (934) 5-01-16), at Juárez 183 opposite the ATG bus station, lets you hear every thunderous unmuffled bus. In addition to lack of sleep (and hot water), you may have to contend with broken bathroom fixtures, but the camaraderie here is infectious. Singles/doubles cost US$13/15.

The quiet and friendly *Posada San Antonio*, three blocks north of the park on Independencia 42 at Velasco Suárez, has clean, indifferent rooms round a courtyard filled with plants and the family's laundry. Showers are cold. Singles/doubles/triples are US$8/11/15.

To find *Posada Bonampak* (☎ (934) 5-09-25) walk north (down the hill towards the market) on Allende. Just after Reforma, take a right onto Avenida Dr Belisario Domínguez; a few doors up on the left is Posada Bonampak. No frills here, but rooms are well kept and bathrooms nicely tiled. The back door opens into the jungle ravine. Doubles are US$13.

The *Hotel Regional* (☎ (934) 5-01-83), Juárez at Aldama, has adequate rooms with shower and fan around a small plant-filled courtyard priced at US$11/18/21. Also on Juárez, half a block west of the park, is *Hotel Misol-Ha* (☎ (934) 5-00-92), with serviceable, clean and bare rooms going for US$13/16/20, private shower and fan included.

La Posada (☎ (934) 5-04-37), behind Hotel Maya Tulipanes in La Cañada is a quiet backpackers' hangout with a courtyard/lawn, table tennis and a lobby wall covered with messages of peace, passion and travel. Average rooms with bath are US$13 a single and US$16 a double.

Places to Stay – middle

La Cañada is forested area near the Mayan statue, a 10-to 15-minute walk from the park.

Hotel La Cañada (☎ (934) 5-01-02) on Calle Merle Green (the unpaved main street, also called Calle Cañada) is a group of cottages surrounded by jungle, many with huge ceramic tubs. This was a favourite with

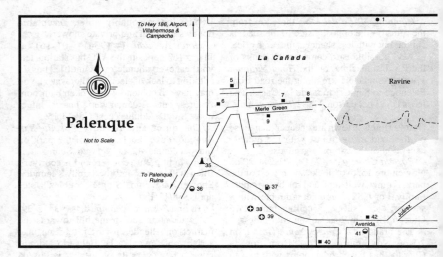

Palenque

Not to Scale

PLACES TO STAY

2 Posada San Antonio
3 Posada Bonampak
5 La Posada
6 Hotel Maya Tulipanes
7 Hotel Chablis
8 Hotel La Cañada
9 Hotel Xibalbas &
   Shivalvas Viajes
   Maya
10 Posada San Francisco
11 Casa de Huéspedes
   León
16 Hotel La Croix
19 Hotel Misión Palenque
   Park Plaza
21 Hotel Naj K'in
31 Hotel Misol-Ha
33 Hotel Casa de Pakal &
   Restaurant
   Castellano
34 Hotel & Restaurant
   Chan-Kah
40 Hotel Santa Elena
42 Hotel Avenida
48 Hotel Kashlan
49 Hotel Regional
58 Hotel Palenque
61 Caneck Youth Hostel
65 Posada Charito

PLACES TO EAT

12 Restaurnt Virgos
15 Restaurant Artemio's
20 Restaurant Maya
24 Pizzería Palenque
25 Restaurant Paisanos
26 Restaurant El
   Herradero
30 Restaurant La Kan-Ha
43 Restaurant La
   Francesa
45 La Tehuanita
46 Restaurant Ixchel
47 Restaurant Girasoles
51 Expendio de Pan
   Virginia
52 Pizzería Romanos
53 Cookshops
54 Tienda Naturista
   Escorpion
56 Taquerías
57 'Restaurant Row'
64 Restaurant Las Tinajas
66 Los Portales

OTHER

1 Market
4 Novedades del Centro
13 Post Office &
   Telegraph Office
14 Palacio Municipal
17 Farmacia Santa Fe
   (24 hours)
18 Clinica Santa Fe
22 Colectivos Chambalu
23 Anfitriones Turísticos
   de Chiapas
27 Banamex
28 Bancomer
29 Mercado de Artesanías
32 Farmacia Centro
35 Maya Head Statue
36 Cristóbal Colón Bus
   Station
37 Pemex Fuel Station
38 Hospital General
39 Centro de Salud
   (Clinic)
41 ATG Bus Station
44 ADO (1st-Class) Bus
   Station
50 Farmacia Principal
55 Church
59 Casa de la Cultura
60 Lavandería Automática
62 Tourist Office
63 Colectivos Palenque

YUCATÁN

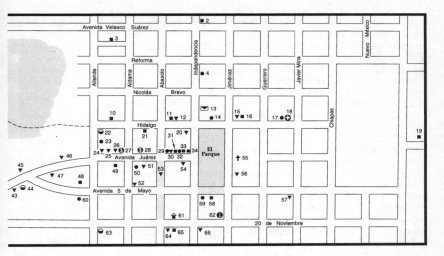

archaeologists working at the ruins and still maintains its legendary attraction with its good thatch-roofed restaurant and prices of US$25/36 for a single/double with fan, slightly more for air-con.

Sharing some of La Cañada's advantages is the nearby *Hotel Maya Tulipanes* (☎ (934) 5-02-01; fax 5-10-04), Calle Cañada 6. Air-con rooms go for US$26 a double; there is a small pool and nice restaurant.

Hotel Chablis (☎ (934) 5-04-46), near Hotel La Cañada, has a traditional Mexican restaurant, video bar, and appealing rooms going for US$23, US$29 with air-con. Across the road is *Hotel Xibalbas* (☎ (934) 5-04-11; fax 5-03-92), which has attractive rooms above Shivalva Travel Agency and in the modern A-frame next door. The US$25 doubles look into the forest.

In the town centre, try the *Hotel Kashlan* (☎ (934) 5-02-97; fax 5-03-09), Avenida 5 de Mayo 105 at Allende. Clean, bright and modern, the Kashlan offers its rooms with ceiling fan and shower for US$16/20 a single/double.

The *Hotel Palenque* (☎ (934) 5-01-88; fax 5-00-39), Avenida 5 de Mayo 15 at Independencia, is old but boasts a con-

venient location, pretty gardens and a small and often presentably clean swimming pool. Doubles are US$23, US$33 with air-con.

Hotel Chan-Kah (☎ (934) 5-03-18; fax 5-04-89), above the restaurant of the same name, is at the corner of Juárez and Independencia overlooking the park. Lots of extras here: a lift, insect screens, two double beds and a TV in each room, little balconies and frequent live music in the bar. Doubles are US$30, US$42 with air-con.

Around the corner near the park on Juárez, the *Hotel Casa de Pakal* has 14 small rooms with air-con and private bath. If you must have electric coolness, you will pay US$28 a double.

Readers with their own cars might want to consider staying at the new *Hotel El Paraíso* (☎ (934) 5-00-45), Carretera a las Ruinas Km 2.5, which, as the address indicates, is 2.5 km along the road to the ruins, on the right-hand side. Large, airy, clean, air-con rooms here with two double beds and gleaming tiled bathrooms cost US$36.

Places to Stay – top end

The *Hotel Misión Palenque Park Plaza* (☎ (934) 5-04-44; fax 5-03-00), Rancho San

YUCATÁN

Martín de Porres, Palenque, Chiapas 29960, located at the far eastern end of town along Avenida Hidalgo, is Palenque's top accommodation. It has aesthetic air-con rooms with a decor of wood, stone and stucco; well-kept gardens, a pool, restaurant and bar bring rates to US$97 a double. The hotel's minibus shuttles guests to the ruins.

The most attractive and interesting lodgings in Palenque are at *Chan-Kah* (☎ (934) 5-11-00; fax 5-04-89), three km from town on the road to the ruins. Handsome wood and stone modern cottages have a Mayan accent; the palapa-topped restaurant, enormous stone-bound pool, the lush jungle gardens and other accoutrements are lavish, but sparsely populated. Perhaps the reason is the high price (US$83 a double), the remoteness from town and the lack of air-conditioning.

South of town 3.5 km on the road to San Cristóbal is the *Hotel Nututum* (☎ (934) 5-01-00; fax 5-01-61), overlooking the Río Usumacinta just to the left of the road. The modern motel-style buildings are nicely arranged in spacious jungle gardens shaded by palm trees. Large air-con rooms with bath cost US$76 a double. You can also pitch your tent or park your camper here for US$3 per person and US$2.75 per vehicle. A swim in the hotel's river *balneario* costs US$1.

Hotel Plaza Palenque (☎ (934) 5-05-55; fax 5-03-95), a Best Western hotel 500 metres north of the Maya statue, has a pleasant but generic atmosphere, with 100 air-con rooms surrounding a garden and swimming pool, and a disco, bar, and restaurant. Doubles are US$82.

Places to Eat – bottom end

Cheapest fare in Palenque is at the open air cookshops on Abasolo (a pedestrian step-street) between Juárez and 5 de Mayo. Next cheapest comes from the taquerías along the eastern side of the park, in front of the church. Try *Los Faroles* or *Refresquería Deportista* for a plate of tacos at US$2 to US$3.

Restaurant Artemio's is a family-run place at the corner of Jiménez and Hidalgo, to the left of the church. Everything on the menu seems to cost between US$3 and US$6 whether it be filete, chicken, or traditional Mexican antojitos.

Another family-run place is the *Restaurant Las Tinajas*, 20 de Noviembre at Abasolo, only a few steps from the Posada Charito. The name means 'Earthen Jars', the building is quaintly woody, and tables set out on the small front terrace allow you to watch the street action as you eat. Breakfasts are US$3 to US$4, chimichangas, tacos, and quesadillas go for slightly less.

Sooner or later you'll probably drop into the *Restaurant Maya*, at the corner of Independencia and Hidalgo on the northwest corner of the park. This has been a popular meeting-place for travellers as well as locals 'since 1958', so the menu says. The food is típico and the hours long (7 am to 11 pm). Prices range from US$4 to US$10 for a full meal; the comida corrida costs US$4.50.

Park side, *Los Portales*, on the corner of 20 de Noviembre and Independencia (look for green polka-dotted pillars), has a typical menu; breakfast and antojitos go for about US$3, and thirst-quenching fruit shakes for US$1.75. Service is slow but friendly.

Several good cheap eateries are to be found along Avenida Juárez west of the park. *Restaurant La Kan-Ha*, Avenida Juárez 20 near Abasolo, serves breakfasts for US$3, chicken and meat dishes for a bit more. *Restaurante Paisanos*, on Juárez between Aldama and Allende, is a tidy, cheaper workers' place where everything seems to cost about US$3. The nearby *Restaurant El Herradero* is similar.

Pizzería Palenque on Juárez at Allende has surprisingly good pizzas ranging in price from a small cheese (US$5) to a large combination (US$12). *Pizzeria Romanos* on 5 de Mayo 63 at Aldama, has pizza, privacy, and promptness (20-minute service guaranteed). With just two tables, you can enjoy pasta (US$3), lasagna or eggplant parmesan (US$6), or one of their 14 pizza varieties (US$5 to US$13) in a small, pleasant atmosphere.

Restaurant Virgos on Hidalgo 5 offers

2nd-storey open-air dining one block west of the park. White pillars, a red tile roof, plants and occasional marimba set the scene, while caesar salads for two or Espagueti Virgo (spaghetti smothered with cheese) will please the palate for under US$5.

'Restaurant Row' is the name we give to 5 de Mayo at Mina, where you will find six food places lined up. Beside the cheap restaurants *Cenaduria*, *Capricornio* and *Shisho's*, there is a fruiterer and an ice cream shop.

There's a cluster of eating options around the bus stations. *Restaurant Girasoles*, two doors up from the ADO station on Juárez, serves daily soup, rice, meat, beans, and a drink for US$3.50. Across the street *Los Caminantes* has a patio restaurant overlooking the ravine, standard fare and prices, but nice atmosphere. *La Francesca*, next to ADO, serves ¼ bird, rice and salad for US$2.50. *Restaurant Ixchel* on Juárez across the street from ADO serves cheap, good and quick breakfasts and antojitos.

For natural food seek out *Tienda Naturista Escorpion* at the east end of Juárez, steps from the park.

Places to Eat – middle

The town's two best restaurants are 10 to 15 minutes' walk from the park, near the Mayan statue.

Hotel La Cañada has its own thatched restaurant with careful service and moderate prices. Most dishes are between US$5 and US$8. The restaurant maintains its tradition of attracting travellers with a serious interest in archaeology, who stay long after dinner discussing the ruins over cold beer or drinks.

The in-town *Restaurant Chan-Kah* faces the park at the corner of Independencia and Juárez. Stone pillars, wrought-iron grill-work, and a bit of jungle ambience make this an atmospheric place to dine. A popular choice here is the Mexican variety plate with an assortment of antojitos for US$5. Sometimes there is live music in the upstairs bar.

Things to Buy

Mercado de Artesanías, almost a block west of the park on Juárez, carries leather products, textiles, batiks and clothing. The prices are fair (though you can bargain) and it's possible to browse peacefully. The mercado is open every day 9 am to 2 pm, and 5 to 9 pm. If you're hammock hunting, bargain with the vendors on Juárez.

Getting There & Away

Air Palenque has a small airstrip north of town, used mostly for air taxi and charter flights. Occasionally there is short-hop scheduled service to and from Tuxtla Gutiérrez. Check with the tourist office or a travel agency in Palenque.

Bus There is less thievery on the bus than on the train, but some bus passengers have reported goods stolen. Don't leave anything of value in the overhead rack, and stay alert. Your gear is probably safest in the luggage compartment under the bus, but watch as it is stowed and removed.

The bus stations are all fairly close to one another, between the Maya statue and the centre of town. The 1st-class ADO is at the confluence of Avenida Juárez and 5 de Mayo. To spot the 1st and 2nd-class Auto-transportes Tuxtla Gutiérrez (ATG) and Transportes Fray Bartolomé de las Casas bus station, look for the Restaurant Pam-Pam. Both stations have left luggage (baggage check) rooms for (US$1 per piece per day).

The Cristóbal Colón bus station is next to Restaurant-Bar Hardy's, near the Maya statue. Autobuses Lagos de Montebello is behind the Hotel Maya Tulipanes in La Cañada. Transportes Lacandonia drop passengers near the market on Avenida Velasco Suárez.

It's a good idea to buy your onward ticket from Palenque a day in advance if possible. Here are some distances, times and prices:

Agua Azul Crucero – 60 km, 1½ hours; five 2nd-class buses (US$1.60) by ATG. These buses go on to Ocosingo, San Cristóbal and Tuxtla Gutiérrez; seats are sold to those passengers first. Tickets to Agua Azul go on sale 30 minutes before departure, and if all seats are sold, you must stand all

YUCATÁN

the way to the Agua Azul turn-off. It is easier to take a combi (see the Getting Around section).

Bonampak – 152 km, eight hours; Autobuses Lagos de Montebello (US$4.50) at 3 am, 9 am, 6 pm, 8 pm.

Campeche – 362 km, 5½ hours; three direct 1st-class buses (US$7) by ADO at 8 am, 9 pm or 10 pm, one 1st-class bus (US$14) at 2 pm by Cristóbal Colón. You can also catch a bus or combi, or hitchhike the 27 km north to Catazajá, on the main Villahermosa-Escárcega highway, and catch one of the buses which pass every hour or two.

Catazajá – 27 km, 30 minutes; six 1st-class buses (US$1) daily by ADO.

Chetumal – 487 km, seven hours; one 1st-class 8.30 pm bus (US$14) by ADO.

La Palma – 175 km, four hours; 10.30 am bus for US$5.25.

Mérida – 556 km, 11 hours; three 1st-class buses (US$18) by ADO at 8 am, 8 pm and 9 pm; a 1 am bus (US$14) by Cristóbal Colón.

Misol-Ha – 47 km, one hour; five 2nd-class buses (US$0.75) by ATG. (See Agua Azul Crucero, above.)

Mexico City – 1,020 km, 16 hours; one 6 pm 1st-class bus (US$18) by ADO; a 6 pm bus (US$43) by Cristóbal Colón.

Ocosingo – 85 km, two hours; six 1st-class buses (US$2.50) by ATG; two morning buses (US$4) by Cristóbal Colón.

San Cristóbal de las Casas – 190 km, 5½ hours; three Cristóbal Colón buses (US$6), six 2nd-class buses (US$4.50) by ATG.

Tuxtla Gutiérrez – 275 km, 7½ hours; three 1st-class buses (US$10) by Cristóbal Colón, three 2nd-class buses (US$8) by ATG.

Villahermosa – 150 km, 2½ hours; seven 1st-class buses (US$5) by ADO.

Getting Around

The train station is six km north of town. Taxis are available at the park and the bus stations. Colectivos run continuously to Palenque ruins – see the Getting There & Away section for Palenque ruins.

Several travel agents and colectivos operate excursions to Agua Azul and Misol-Ha, departing daily about 9 am, returning about 4 pm, and charging between US$6 and US$8 per person. Taking the organized tours, though more expensive than the bus, eliminates standing for hours on crowded buses and walking (perhaps with all your luggage) the 1.5 km in from the highway to (and back out from) Misol-Ha, and the 4.5 km walk downhill from the highway to Agua Azul proper – and then back uphill when it comes time to leave.

If you're interested in visiting the ruins at Bonampak or Yaxchilán, you will want to consider combi-and-boat tours. See those sections below for details.

RÍO USUMACINTA

The mighty Río Usumacinta snakes its way northwestwards along the border between Mexico and Guatemala. A journey along the river reveals dense rainforest, thrilling bird and animal life, and ruined cities such as Bonampak and Yaxchilán. You can visit these ruins by air if time is short and money plentiful, but a journey by car and boat is cheaper and much more exciting. You can also use tributaries of the Usumacinta as your waterways into El Petén, Guatemala's vast jungle province, with its stupendous ruins at Tikal. For details on three routes, see the Petén chapter in the Guatemala section.

BONAMPAK & YAXCHILÁN

The ruins of Bonampak – famous for its frescoes – and the great ancient city of

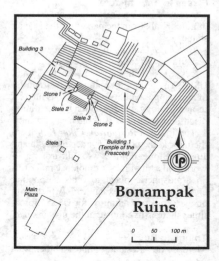

Bonampak Ruins

0   50   100 m

Building 3
Stone 1
Stele 2
Stele 3
Stone 2
Stele 1
Building 1 (Temple of the Frescoes)
Main Plaza

Yaxchilán are accessible on camping excursions from Palenque.

Bonampak and Yaxchilán have neither food nor water, so make certain you are well supplied; also bring insect repellent. Don't leave your gear unattended, as thefts have been reported. Finally, bring a torch (flashlight).

Taxis Aereos Ocosingo (☎ (967) 3-01-88), in Ocosingo on the Palenque-San Cristóbal road, runs air tours to Palenque, Yaxchilán, Bonampak and sometimes to Tikal in Guatemala. A one-day tour to Yaxchilán and Bonampak costs about US$100 per person (minimum four people).

The office is at the Ocosingo airstrip, just east of the market.

Bonampak

Bonampak, 155 km south-east of Palenque near the Guatemalan frontier, was hidden from the outside world by dense jungle until 1946. A young WW II conscientious objector named Charles Frey fled the draft and somehow wound up here in the Lacandón rainforest. Local Indians showed him the ruins, which they used as a sacred site. Frey revealed his findings to Mexican officials and archaeological expeditions were mounted. Frey died in 1949 trying to save an

One of a three panel lintel of Shield Jaguar, from Yaxchilán

expedition member from drowning in the turbulent Usumacinta.

The ruins of Bonampak lie around a rectangular plaza. Only the southern edifices are preserved. It was the frescoes of Building 1 that excited Frey: three rooms covered with paintings depicting ancient Mayan ceremonies and customs.

Unfortunately, 12 centuries of weather deterioration were accelerated when the first expedition attempted to clean the murals with kerosene. On the positive side, some restoration has been undertaken and reproductions installed for comparison.

Yaxchilán

Set above the jungled banks of the Usumacinta, Yaxchilán was first inhabited about 200 AD, though the earliest hieroglyphs found have been dated from 514 to 807 AD. Although not as well restored as Palenque, the ruins here cover a greater

extent, and further excavation may yield even more significant finds.

Yaxchilán rose to the peak of its prominence in the 8th century under a king whose name in hieroglyphs was translated as Shield Jaguar. His shield-and-jaguar symbol appears on many of the site's buildings and stelae. The city's power expanded under Shield Jaguar's son, Parrot Jaguar (752-70). His hieroglyph consists of a small jungle cat with feathers on the back and a bird superimposed on the head. Building 33 on the south-western side of the plaza has some fine religious carvings over the northern doorways, and a roofcomb which retains most of its original beauty.

The central plaza holds statues of crocodiles and jaguars. A lintel in Building 20 shows a dead man's spirit emerging from the mouth of a man speaking about him, and stelae of Maya making offerings to the gods.

Be certain to walk to Yaxchilán's highest

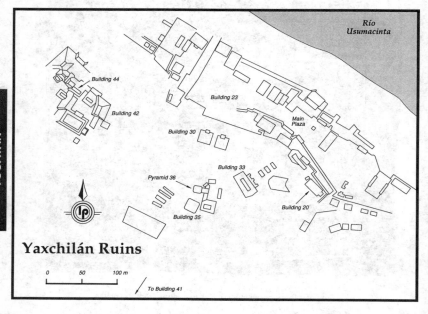

Yaxchilán Ruins

temples, which are still covered with trees and are not visible from the plaza. Building 41 is the tallest of these, and the view from its top is one of the highlights of a visit to Yaxchilán. Some tour guides do not want to make the effort to show you Building 41 – insist on it!

Getting There & Away
Various travel agencies in Palenque run two-day road and river tours to Bonampak and Yaxchilán (see Palenque – Organised Tours). A minivan takes you within 10 km of Bonampak and you walk the rest of the way. Tents are provided for overnight. The next morning, you are driven to the Río Usumacinta, where a motor boat takes you through the jungle to Yaxchilán. The rate is US$100 for the two-day venture, including transportation and all meals.

There are also one-day trips offered to Bonampak or Yaxchilán. Most travel agents charge US$50 to US$70 for a one-day excursion.

PALENQUE TO SAN CRISTÓBAL
According to Captain Dupaix, a Frenchman who trekked along La Ruta Maya in 1807:

Palenque is eight days' march from Ocosingo. The journey is very fatiguing. The roads, if they can be so called, are only narrow and difficult paths, which wind across mountains and precipices, and which it is necessary to follow sometimes on mules, sometimes on foot, sometimes on the shoulders of Indians, and sometimes in hammocks. In some places it is necessary to pass on bridges, or, rather, trunks of trees badly secured, and over lands covered with wood, desert and dispeopled, and to sleep in the open air, excepting a very few villages and huts.

Today the 85-km journey is considerably easier and faster, taking only about two hours by bus. It may take you longer, however, because the entire 190-km journey from Palenque to San Cristóbal de las Casas is dotted with interesting stopovers. Only 20 km from Palenque is the spellbinding tropical waterfall park of Misol-Ha, and another 36 km into the mountains are the many rapids and waterfalls at Agua Azul.

Ocosingo, 30 km beyond Agua Azul, is the nearest town to the seldom-visited Mayan ruins at Toniná, 14 km east of the town on a side road. From Ocosingo you will wind your way higher into the mountains, another 92 km past the Tzotzil and Tzeltal Mayan villages of Huixtán and Oxchuc to the Interamerican Highway, meandering through the Jovel Valley. Turn right (north) and after 12 km you're in San Cristóbal de las Casas.

Misol-Ha Cascades
About 20 km from Palenque, a waterfall plummets nearly 35 metres into a beautiful wide pool safe for swimming. The Misol-Ha cascade and its jungle surroundings are spectacular enough to be the setting for an Arnold Schwarzenegger epic.

The waterfall is 1½ km west by dirt road off Highway 199 and the turning is signposted. A fee of US$0.60 is charged.

Places to Stay & Eat You can set up a tent or hammock near the falls for US$5, or stay in one of their eight newly renovated cabins. Cabins are clean and comfortable with dark wood interiors, large bathrooms, hot water and furnished kitchenettes. Cabins with one double bed are US$20 to US$40, with two double beds US$40 to US$60. Rates vary with the seasons.

There is a small café near the entrance, but you're better off bringing food from Palenque.

Agua Azul Cascades
Just 50 km south of Palenque, and 4½ km off the highway, scores of dazzling turquoise waterfalls tumble over white limestone surrounded by jungle. Beyond the rapids, numerous pools of tranquil water offer a refreshing respite from the rainforest's sticky humidity.

On holidays the site is thronged with local families; at other times you will have few companions. Admission is US$1.75 per car, US$0.75 per person (on foot).

The temptation to swim is great but take extreme care. The current is deceptively fast, especially during the rainy season when the

YUCATÁN

'turquoise' waters, brown with silt, lower underwater visibility to zero so submerged trees and rocks are impossible to see. Use your judgment to identify slower, safer areas. Drownings are all too common here, as the crosses in the upper cascades show.

The falls stretch some distance up and down stream. Upstream, a trail takes you over some swaying, less-than-stable foot bridges and up through the jungle.

Warning An experienced female traveller reported that she was attacked above the falls, escaping only through a strategically aimed kick to the groin. Several travellers have also reported thefts at Agua Azul, even at gunpoint, so take care.

Places to Stay & Eat There are a few spots to hang your hammock or pitch a tent, but if you are looking for a decent bed, go back to Palenque. *Camping Agua Azul*, near the entrance, and *Restaurant Agua Azul*, next to the car park, rent hammocks and hammock space for a few dollars. You can leave your backpacks at Restaurant Agua Azul for US$1 per day. You'll find more solace and scenery if you camp upstream. Follow the trail up the left bank.

A five to ten-minute walk will bring you to *Camping Casablanca*. It's far from elegant but you can hang your hammock (US$2.50) or rent one (US$3.50) in its big hollow barn. Owner Geronimo guides three-hour (five km) hikes around the cascades for US$6 per person.

If you can gather another five minutes of walking energy, you'll find more pleasant camping at *José Antonio's*. It's the yellow house with white furniture and a Coca-Cola sign in front, a stone's throw from the water. There's a grassy lawn for tents, a palapa for hammocks, palm trees for atmosphere, and you're just steps from safe swimming. A night here will cost you about US$2.

There are several restaurants and food stalls next to the car park, but the food is overpriced and average. You would be much better off packing a picnic from Palenque.

Getting There & Away The Agua Azul junction, or *crucero* on Highway 199 is 45 km south of Palenque, 40 km north of Ocosingo, and 248 km north-east of San Cristóbal. (3½ hours by bus). The 4.5 km walk from the crucero to the falls is OK on the way down, but the sweltering heat makes it hard on the uphill trip back out. If you want to take the risk, hitching is possible but don't rely on it.

An easy way of visiting Agua Azul and Misol-Ha is a day trip from Palenque with transport laid on. Several travel agents in Palenque offer such trips, lasting about seven hours with typically three hours at Agua Azul and half an hour at Misol-Ha, for US$8 per person including entrance fees. Colectivos Chambalu and Colectivos Palenque in Palenque, charge US$6 for the 6½ hour trip. (For a list of Palenque travel agents, see Palenque – Organised Tours).

Alternatively you can travel by 2nd-class bus to the crucero and trust your legs and luck from there. Any bus between Palenque and San Cristóbal or Ocosingo will drop you there. The trip is about four hours from San Cristóbal (US$4), one hour from Ocosingo (US$1), and 1¼ hours from Palenque (US$1.50). Try to book ahead on these buses unless you want to stand. Catching a bus from the Crucero when you leave almost certainly means standing, to start with at least. Again, hitching is possible, but don't count on it.

Ocosingo
Population: 20,000

Ocosingo is a small mestizo and Tzeltal Indian valley town on the Palenque-San Cristóbal road. It's friendly but of no particular interest except as an access point for the Mayan ruins of Toniná, 14 km east.

Orientation & Information Ocosingo spreads downhill to the east of the main road. Avenida Central runs straight from the main road to the zócalo. Most of the bus stations are on Avenida 1 Norte, parallel to Avenida Central a block north.

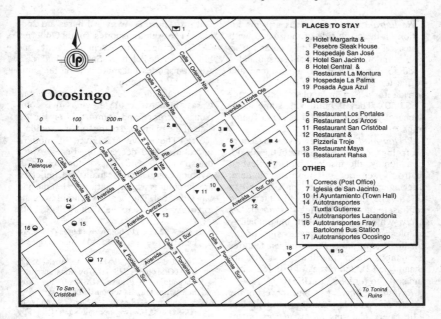

PLACES TO STAY

2 Hotel Margarita &
   Pesebre Steak House
3 Hospedaje San José
4 Hotel San Jacinto
8 Hotel Central &
   Restaurant La Montura
9 Hospedaje La Palma
19 Posada Agua Azul

PLACES TO EAT

5 Restaurant Los Portales
6 Restaurant Los Arcos
11 Restaurant San Cristóbal
12 Restaurant &
   Pizzería Troje
13 Restaurant Maya
18 Restaurant Rahsa

OTHER

1 Correos (Post Office)
7 Iglesia de San Jacinto
10 H Ayuntamiento (Town Hall)
14 Autotransportes
   Tuxtla Gutierrez
15 Autotransportes Lacandonia
16 Autotransportes Fray
   Bartolomé Bus Station
17 Autotransportes Ocosingo

To orient yourself on the zócalo, remember that the church is on the east side and the Hotel Central on the north side. The large market is three blocks east along Avenida 1 Sur Ote from the church.

None of the banks in town will change dollars or travellers' cheques, but this may change as Ocosingo edges onto the tourist map.

Places to Stay The *Hotel Central* (☎ (967) 3-00-39), Avenida Central 1, on the north side of the zócalo, has simple, clean rooms with fan and bath for US$14/20/26 a single/double/triple.

Hotel Margarita (☎ (967) 3-02-80) on Calle 1 Pte Norte, one block north-west of Hotel Central, charges US$20 a double. It's nothing elaborate but nicer than most hotels in town; rooms have fan and bath, there is a comfortable lobby downstairs and a restaurant upstairs.

Posada Agua Azul, at 1 Ote Sur 127, two blocks south of the church, has medium-size, average rooms around a courtyard which harbors a few tightly caged anteaters, hawks and macaws. Rooms are US$12/$20.

At the really cheap end there's *Hospedaje La Palma* on the corner of Calle 2 Pte and Avenida 1 Norte Pte, just down the hill from the ATG bus station. It's a clean family-run place, singles/doubles are US$5/US$10 with shared bathrooms. *Hotel San Jacinto* at Avenida Central 13, around the corner from the church charges US$5/11 for drab rooms with a shared bath. *Hospedaje San José* (☎ (967) 3-00-39), Calle 1 Ote 6, half a block north of the north-east corner of the zócalo, has small, dark, but clean rooms for US$8/13 a single/double.

Places to Eat Ocosingo is famous for its *queso amarillo* (yellow cheese), which comes in three-layered one-kg balls. The two outside layers are like chewy Gruyère, the middle is creamy.

Restaurant La Montura has a prime location on the north side of the zócalo, with tables on the Hotel Central's verandah as well as indoors. It has a sizable menu and is good for breakfast (fruit, eggs, bread and coffee for US$3), lunch or dinner (comida corrida for US$6 or a plate of tacos for US$2.50). They'll build you some sandwiches if you want to take a picnic to Toniná ruins.

Restaurant Los Portales, Avenida Central 19, facing the north-east corner of the zócalo, is a homey, old-fashioned place. Several matronly señoras will mother you here, offering traditional meals for US$3.50 to US$6. The Portales proves an interesting contrast to the neighbouring *Restaurant Los Arcos*, which is more modern, but not nearly so pleasant. On the opposite side of the zócalo, *Restaurant & Pizzería Troje* features the famous queso amarillo. Quesadillas are cheap (US$2), and pizzas of different sizes and sorts go for US$3 to US$10.

Restaurant Maya, two blocks west of the zócalo on Avenida Central is a tidy, bright little eatery featuring *platos fuertes* (main-course lunch or dinner platters) for US$3.50; fruit salads and antojitos are less. The *Restaurant San Cristóbal*, Avenida Central 22, near the Town Hall, is a simple lonchería where you have to ask what's cooking the day you visit. Nothing on the menu is more than US$3.

Pesebres Steak House, on Calle 1 Pte Nte above Hotel Margarita, has a nice breeze, super views and good dishes. If you're feeling carnivorous, order prime rib or filete mignon for US$8; if not, Mexican dishes and salads will run you less than US$4.

Restaurante Rahsa, two blocks southwest of the zócalo on Avenida 3 Sur Ote, is set down a walkway, beside a courtyard and provides the nicest dining atmosphere in Ocosingo. The restaurant has tall chairs, fresh flowers and fancy folded napkins on each table and a big wooden barrel of tequila in front of its wine rack. They serve seafood specialities baked in cognac and lemon for US$8, a spinach salad for US$3 and flavored local dishes for about US$5.

Getting There & Away All buses are 2nd-class. The Autotransportes Tuxtla Gutiérrez (ATG) terminal is on Avenida 1 Norte, one block from the Palenque-San Cristóbal road. Autotransportes Lacandonia is on the same street a little higher up.

Autotransportes Fray Bartolomé de Las Casas (in between the previous two companies for price and comfort) is on the far side of the main road at the top of Avenida 1 Norte. They have a mixture of modern microbuses and decrepit big buses. Autotransportes Ocosingo is at the corner of Avenida Central and the main road. Quickest are the combis which shuttle to Palenque and San Cristóbal. They leave when full from the top of Avenida Central and charge US$2.50.

Palenque – 82 km, 1½ hours; five buses (US$2.80) by ATG, two buses (US$3) by Autotransportes Fray Bartolomé de Las Casas.
San Cristóbal – 108 km, 2½ hours; six buses (US$2) by ATG, six buses (US$1.75) by Autotransportes Lacandonia, five buses (US$2.30) by Autotransportes Fray Bartolomé de Las Casas.
Tuxtla Gutiérrez – 193 km, 4½ hours; seven buses (US$4) by ATG, two morning buses (US$3) by Autotransportes Lacandonia, five buses (US$2) by Autotransportes Ocosingo.
Villahermosa – 232 km, six hours; two morning buses (US$3) by Autotransportes Lacandonia.

Toniná Ruins

Toniná was probably a city-state independent of both Palenque and Yaxchilán, though it declined when they did, around 800 AD. Dates found at the site range from 500 to 800 AD.

Toniná doesn't compare with Palenque for beauty or importance, but that may change as major excavations are under way which may uncover more significant structures. The ruins are open every day for US$3.

The track into the site goes past the small museum which holds quite a number of good stone carvings – statues, bas-reliefs, altars and calendar stones. Continue past the museum, over a stream and up to a flat area from which rises the terraced hill supporting the main structures. As you face this hillside, behind you are an outlying pyramid and the main ball court. The flat area contains a small ball court and fragments of limestone carvings. Some appear to show prisoners holding out offerings, with glyphs on the reverse sides.

The most interesting area of the terraced hillside is the right-hand end of its third and fourth levels. The stone facing of the wall rising from the third to fourth levels here has a zig-zag x shape, which may represent Quetzalcóatl, and also forms flights of steps. To the right of its base are the remains of a tomb, with steps leading up to an altar. Behind and above the tomb and altar is a rambling complex of chambers, passageways and stairways, believed to have been Toniná's administrative hub.

One level higher than the top of the 'Quetzalcóatl' wall is a tomb, covered in tin sheeting, thought to be of a ruler, buried with two others; lift the sheet to see the stone coffin beneath. To the left on the same level is a shrine to Chac, the rain god.

Getting There & Away The 14-km track from Ocosingo is unpaved and rough in spots, but crosses pleasant ranchland with lots of colourful birds.

If you have your own vehicle, follow Calle 1 Ote south from the Ocosingo church. Before long it curves left and you pass a cemetery on the right. At the fork, a couple of km further on, go left. At the next fork, the site is signposted to the right. Finally a sign marks the entry track to Toniná at Rancho Guadalupe on the left. From here it's another km to the site itself.

Without your own vehicle, you have the option of a taxi (about US$25 a round trip, with a one-hour wait at the ruins), hitching (maybe six vehicles an hour pass Toniná), trying to pick up one of the passenger trucks from the Ocosingo market, or a bus of Carga Mixta Ocosingo from their yard near the market. There appear to be two or three buses to Guadalupe (near the ruins), and back each day. The trip costs US$1 and takes about 45 minutes. The Rancho Guadalupe sometimes puts people up for the night or allows them to camp.

For a minibus day trip to Toniná from San Cristóbal de las Casas, with English speaking guides, contact Sexto Sol (☎ & fax (967) 8-43-53) on Real de Guadalupe 24-D in San Cristóbal. A one-day tour costs US$29.

Highland & Pacific Chiapas

Beautiful, rugged, backward, impoverished and rich in potential – that's Chiapas. Much of the land is still farmed by traditional Mayan methods. But the Mayans are being pushed off their traditional lands by developers, oil prospectors and rich cattle ranchers from central Mexico.

Fearful of the adverse economic effects which might come with NAFTA (the North American Free Trade Agreement), Chiapas' Indians revolted in January 1994. Armed rebels of a group calling itself the Zapatista National Liberation Army (EZLN) seized several towns and villages briefly, kidnapped government officials and destroyed government offices. Upwards of 100 people were killed in the fighting. The revolt underlines Chiapans' traditional resentment against the powers-that-be in Mexico City.

VILLARHERMOSA TO TUXTLA GUTIÉRREZ

Highway 195, the road into the Chiapan mountains, leaves Villahermosa to the southeast, passing CICOM, following Avenida Melchor Ocampo, then heading out of the city to pass through vast banana groves. The road is fairly fast, with wide bends.

At Teapa, 60 km from Villahermosa, you bear right toward Pichucalco rather than enter the town of Teapa proper. Five km past the Teapa turn-off, on the left-hand side, is the Balneario El Azufre (Sulphur Baths), as you can tell by the odour when you descend into the valley to cross a stream and the stink of sulphur rises to meet you.

Just past the bridge over the stream a large sign announces your entry into the state of Chiapas, 'Siempre México, Siempre Mexicano' (Always Part of Mexico, Always Mexican). The sign and the sentiment may have more to do with the central government in Mexico City than with the Chiapan people, who have been ambivalent throughout history about their links with the lands to the west of the Isthmus of Tehuantepec.

Upon entering Chiapas, the road climbs into the mountains through incredibly lush, beautiful countryside. It's still hot and muggy here, with typical tropical scenes on every side: gigantic ceiba trees, banana groves, Brahma cattle grazing contentedly, and jungle verdure everywhere.

The road passes through a beautiful river gorge (cañón). After passing through the village of Ixhuapan you'll notice that the air is definitely lighter, cooler and less humid.

About 150 km from Villahermosa is the small mountain town of Rayón (population 8500), which has a very basic eatery for travellers and a spartan hostelry for emergencies. Ten km past Rayón is a lookout (mirador) named El Caminero. The view would be beautiful but for the mist and fog.

At Rincón Chamula it is clear by the local people's dress that you've entered Maya country. Besides wearing the traditional clothing, the villagers sell it to travellers at little open-air stands by the roadside.

Pueblo Nuevo (population 10,000) is at 1200 metres altitude, deep in the beautiful mountain country, but still the road climbs. Past the junction with the road to Simojovel the countryside becomes drier, but it's still very mountainous.

The village of Bochil (population 13,000), 215 km from Villahermosa at an altitude of 1272 metres, is inhabited by Tzotzil Maya. It has two hotels: the tidy Hotel Juárez on the main road, and the more modest Hotel María Isabel set back a bit from the road. There's also a Pemex fuel station, the only one for many km.

After travelling 264 km from Villahermosa on Highway 195, you come to the junction with Highway 190. Turn left to go directly to San Cristóbal de las Casas (34 km), or right to Tuxtla Gutiérrez (50 km).

Heading toward Tuxtla Gutiérrez, after a few km the road rounds a bend to reveal a breathtaking panorama: you are clinging to a mountainside with a broad valley spread out below. The highway descends the steep slope by a series of switchbacks, then strikes out dead straight across the wide, warm, fairly dry Río Grijalva valley, also called the Central Depression of Chiapas, at 500 to 1000 metres altitude. Next stop is Tuxtla, the capital city of Chiapas, 294 km south of Villahermosa.

TUXTLA GUTIÉRREZ
Population: 300,000
Altitude: 532 metres

Tuxtla Gutiérrez is towards the west end of Chiapas' hot, humid central valley. Many travellers simply change buses in Chiapas' state capital as they head straight through to San Cristóbal de las Casas. But if you're not in a hurry this clean, surprisingly lively and prosperous modern city has several things worth stopping for – among them probably Mexico's best zoo (devoted solely to the fauna of Chiapas), and easy access to motorboat trips through the 1000 metre-deep Cañón del Sumidero.

History
The name Tuxtla Gutiérrez comes from the Nahuatl word *tuchtlán*, meaning 'where rabbits abound'. The conquistadors pronounced tuchtlán as Tuxtla (TOOSHT-lah), and in the 19th century the family name of Joaquín Miguel Gutiérrez was added. Gutiérrez was a liberal politician, Governor of Chiapas, and leading light in Chiapas' early 19th-century campaign not to be part of Guatemala.

San Cristóbal was capital of the state until 1892, when the title went to Tuxtla Gutiérrez – apparently because of hostility in San Cristóbal toward Mexico's dictator Porfirio Díaz.

Orientation
The centre of Tuxtla Gutiérrez is the large Plaza Cívica or zócalo, with the cathedral on its south side. The city's main east-west artery, here called Avenida Central, runs across the zócalo in front of the cathedral. As it enters the city from the west the same road

is Blvd Dr Belisario Domínguez; to the east it becomes Blvd Ángel Albino Corzo.

The Cristóbal Colón 1st-class bus station is two blocks west of the zócalo's north-west corner. The main 2nd-class bus station, Autotransportes Tuxtla Gutiérrez (ATG), is on 3 Sur Ote just west of 7 Ote Sur; from the south-east corner of the zócalo, that's four blocks east, one south, one more east, and one south. The last block is pedestrian only, through a small market.

Street Numbering System The central point for Tuxtla's street-numbering system is the corner of Calle Central and Avenida Central beside the cathedral. East-west streets are called Avenidas – 1 Sur, 2 Sur, etc as you move south from Avenida Central, and 1 Norte, 2 Norte, etc moving north. North-south streets are called Calles – 1 Pte, 2 Pte and so on going west of Calle Central; 1 Ote, 2 Ote, etc to the east.

It all gets a bit complicated with the addition (sometimes) of secondary names: each Avenida is divided into a Pte part (west of Calle Central) and an Ote part (east of Calle Central) – thus 1 Sur Ote is the eastern half of Avenida 1 Sur. Likewise Calles have Norte and Sur parts: 1 Pte Nte is the northern half of Calle 1 Pte.

Information
Tourist Office The Chiapas tourist information office (☎ (961) 3-51-86) is 1.75 km west of the zócalo, on the ground floor of the Edificio Plaza de las Instituciones, the building beside Bancomer. The office is open 9 am to 8 pm everyday.

Money Banamex, at the corner of 1 Pte and 1 Sur, and Bancomer, at the corner of Avenida Central Pte and 2 Pte, do foreign exchange Monday to Friday 10 am to noon. Banco International, on Calle Central Norte on the west side of the zócalo, will exchange money during all banking hours at a snail-like pace.

Post & Telecommunications The main offices are on a pedestrians-only block of 1

YUCATÁN

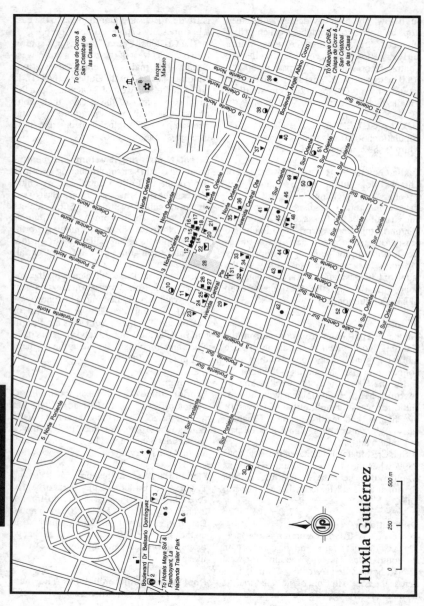

Tuxtla Gutiérrez

PLACES TO STAY		49	Casa de Huéspedes Muñiz	7	Museo Regional de Chiapas
1	Hotel Bonampak, Balam Restaurant & Aerocaribe		**PLACES TO EAT**	8	Botanical Garden
12	Posada del Rey			9	Centro de Convivencia Infantil
14	Hotel Casablanca	3	Pizza Villa Loma	10	Cristóbal Colón Bus Station
15	Hotel Plaza	11	Restaurant Jow Hua		
16	Hotel Estrellas	20	Restaurant La Parcela	13	Viajes Miramar
17	Hotel Mar-Inn	23	La Boutique del Pan	22	Post Office
18	Hotel María Dolores	24	Meson Manolo	25	Mexicana
19	Hotel Fernando	29	Restaurant Flamingo	28	Zócalo (Plaza Cívica)
21	Hotel Catedral	32	Trattoria San Marco	30	ADO Bus Station
26	Hotel Esponda	33	La Soya Naturismo	31	Cathedral
27	Gran Hotel Humberto	35	Restaurant Forteza	38	Transportes Cañon del Sumidero
34	Hotel Regional San Marcos	37	Restaurant Las Pichanchas	39	Parque 5 de Mayo
36	Hotel María Eugenia	47	Pizza Real Restaurant	42	Market
40	Hotel Balum Canan			44	Transportes Chiapa-Tuxtla
41	Hotel La Posada		**OTHER**	45	Caseta Las Tortugas
43	Hotel Olimpo			50	ATG Bus Station
46	Casa de Huéspedes Ofelia	2	Tourist Office	51	Autotransportes Nha-Bolom Bus Station
48	Hotel San Antonio	4	Aviacsa		
		5	Plaza de la Solidaridad	52	Bus to Zoo
		6	Solidarity Monument		

Norte Ote, just off the east side of the zócalo. The post office is open 8 am to 6 pm Monday to Saturday for all services, and 9 am to 1 pm on Sunday for stamps only; Tuxtla's postal code is 29000.

Telegram, telex, and fax services are available from 9 am to 8 pm Monday to Friday and 9 am to 5 pm Saturday. The American Express representative, Viajes Marabasco (☎ (961) 2-69-98) at Plaza Bonampak, Local 14, on Blvd Belisario Domínguez across the road from the tourist office, has a client mail service.

There are Ladatel phones on the west side of the zócalo, in the Cristóbal Colón bus station, and by the Choco Centro shop behind the east end of the cathedral. One of those outside Choco Centro takes credit cards. Caseta las Tortugas on 5 Ote Sur 214, between 1 and 2 Sur Ote, is a small telephone shop which will place local or international calls for you; the owner speaks English and is most helpful.

Laundry Gaily II Central de Lavado at 1 Sur Pte 575, between 4 and 5 Pte Sur, charges US$4 for a four kg load if you wash, US$7 if they wash. Hours are 8 am 2 pm, and 4 pm to 8 pm Monday to Saturday.

Plaza Cívica
Tuxtla's lively zócalo, the Plaza Cívica, occupies two blocks, with San Marcos cathedral facing it across Avenida central at the south end.

Zoo
Chiapas, with its huge range of environments, claims the highest concentration of animal species in North America – among them several varieties of big cats, 1200 types of butterfly and 641 bird species. You can see a good number of them in Tuxtla's excellent Zoológico Miguel Alvárez del Toro (ZOOMAT), where they're kept in relatively spacious enclosures in an hillside woodland area just south of the city.

Among the creatures you'll see are ocelot, jaguar, puma, tapir, red macaw, boa constrictor, the monkey-eating harpy eagle (aguila

YUCATÁN

Red Macaw

arpia) and some mean-looking scorpions and spiders.

The zoo is open 8 am to 5.30 pm daily except Monday and entry is free. It has a bookshop. To get there take a 'Cerro Hueco' bus (US$0.20) from the corner of 1 Ote Sur and 7 Sur Ote. They leave about every 20 minutes and take 20 minutes to get there. A taxi – easy to pick up in either direction – costs US$1.50.

Parque Madero Complex

This museum-theatre-park area is 1.25 km north-east of the city centre. If you don't want to walk, take a colectivo along Avenida Central to Parque 5 de Mayo at the corner of 11 Ote, then a combi north along 11 Ote.

The **Museo Regional de Chiapas** has splendid archaeological exhibits, colonial history, costume and craft collections all from Chiapas, plus often interesting temporary exhibitions. Hours are 9 am to 4 pm daily except Monday. Next door is the 1200-seat **Teatro de la Ciudad**. Nearby there's a shady **botanical garden**, with many species labelled, open 9 am to 6 pm daily except Monday; entry is free.

Also in Parque Madero are a public swimming pool (US$0.35) and an open-air children's park, the **Centro de Convivencia Infantil**, which adults may enjoy too. It has models and exhibits on history and prehistory, a mini-railway, pony and boat rides and mini-golf.

Places to Stay – bottom end

Camping *La Hacienda Hotel* (☎ (961) 2-79-86), Blvd Belisario Domínguez 1197, on the west edge of town beside a roundabout, has a pool, cafeteria and all hook-ups for US$10 a double.

Hotels Tap water in the cheaper hotels is 'al tiempo' (not heated) but, since this is a hot town, it is not cold either.

The cleanest real cheapie is the *Albergue CREA Youth Hostel* (☎ (961) 2-12-01) at Blvd Ángel Albino Corzo 1800, just under two km east of the zócalo. For a bed in a small, clean separate-sex dormitory you pay US$2.75 (plus US$1.75 deposit for sheets) and you don't need a Youth Hostel card. From the zócalo take a colectivo east along Avenida Central. The hostel is on the right beside a yellow footbridge.

Closest to the bus station is the *Casa De Huéspedes Muñiz* at 2 Sur Ote 733 (across from the north end of the bus yard). Rooms are bearable, bathrooms are shared; singles/doubles are US$8.50/10. On the same block at 2 Sur Ote 643, the *Casa de Huéspedes Ofelia* (☎ (961) 2-73-46), has no sign but '643' is visible above its doorway if you look hard. Rooms are fanless but clean and cost US$3.50/5 for a single/double. An average room at *Hotel La Posada* (☎ (961) 2-29-32), 1 Sur Ote 555, costs US$5/6.50 for shared bathroom and US$24 for a large triple with bath. .

Closer to the city centre, and slightly more expensive are the hotels on 2 Norte Ote, near the north-east corner of the zócalo. *Hotel Casablanca* (☎ (961) 1-03-05), half a block off the zócalo at 2 Norte Ote 251, is bare and basic, but exceptionally clean for the price; rooms with fan and shower are US$11/15, a single with shared bath is US$5.50. On 2 Norte Ote 229, at 2 Ote Norte, is the *Hotel Plaza* (☎ (961) 3-83-85), its fancy mirrored lobby is deceptive, rooms are no better than anywhere on the block, though a bit larger and cost US$11/15.

Across the street, *Hotel María Dolores* and *Hotel Estrellas*, at 2 Ote Norte 304 and 322, have indifferent rooms for US$8/11. Two blocks east at 2 Norte Ote 515, *Hotel Fernando* has spacious decent rooms with big windows for US$10.

The *Hotel San Antonio* (☎ (961) 2-27-13) at 2 Sur Ote 540, is an amicable place – it's a modern building with a small courtyard and clean rooms for US$10/13. Surprisingly, the rambling *Hotel Olimpo* (☎ (961) 2-02-95) at 3 Sur Ote 215 charges the same rates for small, muggy rooms, but it's clean and with bath.

For the travelling foursome who enjoy space, check out the *Hotel Catedral* (☎ (961) 3-08-24) at 1 Norte Ote 367 between 3 Ote Sur and the post office. They have enormous quadruples – two large rooms with a double bed in each are partitioned by a hallway. Bathroom, fans, hot water and cleanliness are included for US$18, doubles are US$11.

Hotel Regional San Marcos (☎ (961) 3-19-40; fax 3-18-87)), 2 Ote Sur 176, at Avenida 1 Sur one block from the zócalo, is reasonable value at US$16/20 for a moderately sized clean room, attached baths are prettified with tiles.

Hotel Esponda (☎ (961) 3-67-84), 1 Pte Nte 142, a block from the zócalo, has middling fan-cooled rooms with big bathrooms for US$21/25 a single/double. The *Hotel Mar-Inn* on 2 Norte Ote 341 has 60 well-kept rooms, with wide plant-lined walkways and a roof that seems to trap in humidity. Singles and doubles are US$20/30.

Places to Stay – middle

Gran Hotel Humberto, Avenida Central Pte 180 at 1 Pte Nte, a block west of the zócalo, has bright, spotless rooms with air-con, TV,

phone and vast showers. Singles/doubles are US$36/45.

The best downtown hotel is *Hotel María Eugenia* (☎ (961) 1-01-85), Avenida Central Ote 507, three blocks east of the zócalo. The hotel has attractive air-con rooms for US$64/76 and a nice restaurant.

Hotel Bonampak (☎ (961) 3-20-50), Belisario Domínguez 180, 1.75 km west of the zócalo, is among the city's oldest 'luxury' hotels. Rooms in the main block and on the grounds (in bungalows) are US$63/71. A pool, tennis and jai-alai court, and bar add to its attractiveness. There's a copy of Chiapas' famous Bonampak prisoner mural in the lobby which is more vivid than the original.

About 1.25 km further west is *Hotel Maya Sol* (☎ (961) 5-06-34), Belisario Domínguez 1380, set back from the busy road and draped in greenery; attractive air-con rooms go for US$52/64; there's a coffee shop, restaurant and pool.

Places to Stay – top end

Tuxtla's most luxurious hostelry is the *Hotel Flamboyant* (☎ (961) 5-08-88; fax 5-00-87), Belisario Domínguez Km 1081, four km west of the zócalo. The Disco Sheik (get it?) out front looks like a mosque. Rooms are priced at US$112.

Places to Eat

Every fourth doorway in Tuxtla is a taco/torta shop. The cheapest quick bite you'll find is at one of the taco joints in the pedestrian alley on your right as you exit the ATG station. The going rate is US$0.30 a taco, but the taco fumes are likely to inspire vegetarian thinking.

Among the prettiest, fanciest panaderías (bakery/pastry shop) is *La Boutique del Pan*, 2 Pte Nte 173, two blocks west and around a corner from the zócalo.

If you want a bag of granola, swing by *La Soya Naturismo* at 2 Ote Sur 132, just off Avenida Central. They sell vitamins, healthy snacks and health care products.

Enjoy pizza at the *Trattoria San Marco*, which has tables under red and white awnings. Twenty varieties of pizzas come in

YUCATÁN

five sizes for US$5 to US$16, sandwiches on baguettes, salads and papas relleñas (potatoes with filling) are about US$4, and they serve sweet, savory crepas. Next door, *Cafe Plaza* has a simpler menu, but good breakfasts (yogurt, fruit, cereal and coffee) for US$3.

If you're looking for a big meal at a little price, try *Pizza Real Restaurant* on 2 Sur Ote 540 in front of Hotel San Antonio, where a five course comida corrida is US$1.75. *Restaurant La Parcela*, on 2 Ote Norte behind the Post Office, serves hotcakes, huevos or seven tacos for under US$2, or a four-course comida corrida for US$2.75.

Meson Manolo, half a block west of the zócalo on Avenida Central Pte has a steady stream of customers; menu options are a huevos ranchero breakfast for US$2.50, tacos or quesadillas for US$3, or meaty dishes for US$4 to US$6.

It's worth making the short trek six blocks east to the *Restaurant Las Pichanchas* (☎ 2-53-51) at Avenida Central Ote 857 (look for a sign with a black pot on a pink background and the words 'Sientase Chiapaneco'). This open-air, plant-filled courtyard restaurant has a long menu of local specialities. Try the chipilín, a cheese-and-cream soup on a maize base; and for dessert, chimbos, made from egg yolks and cinnamon. In between you could go for any of six types of tamales, vegetarian salads (beetroot and carrot), or more substantially, a steak. There is live marimba music and Chiapas folk dances all evenings but Monday.

The *Restaurant Flamingo*, down a passage at 1 Pte 17, is a quiet, slightly superior place with air-con. An order of three tacos or enchiladas is US$4.50, and meat and fish dishes are US$7.50 to US$11.

As for a good comida corrida (US$6), one of the best for the money is served in the dining room of the *Hotel María Eugenia* on Avenida Central Ote, three blocks east of the zócalo.

Restaurant Jow-Hua, 1 Norte Pte 217, 1½ blocks from the zócalo (around the corner from the Hotel Esponda), has a Cantonese comida corrida for US$9 to US$17.

Entertainment

There's live music in the zócalo Sunday nights. If its dancing you're after, Tuxtla's best disco is *Colors* in the Hotel Arecas at Belisario Domínguez Km 1080, just west of the Hotel Flamboyant. Friday is the busiest– drinks are US$1.75 and entry is about US$8. You can look for live music in the hotels. *Disco Sheik* at the Hotel Flamboyant is reputed to be fun, as is the singles bar in the *Hotel Bonampak*.

Getting There & Away

Air Mexicana and Aviacsa fly to/from Mexico City (US$130) three times daily. Aviacsa and Aerocaribe fly to Oaxaca (US$81), Cancún (US$158), Mérida (US$111), Villahermosa (US$70), and Tapachula (US$76).

Mexicana (☎ (961) 2-54-02) is on Avenida Central Pte 206, a block west of the zócalo. Aerocaribe (☎ (961) 1-14-90) is in Bungalow 414 in the Hotel Bonampak at Blvd Belisario Domínguez 180, but you can also book through Mexicana. Aviacsa (☎ (961) 2-80-81) is at Avenida Central Pte 1144, 1.25 km west of the zócalo.

Tuxtla has two airports. Aeropuerto San Juan, 35 km west of the city handles the bigger jets, and at present is used only by Mexicana. Aviacsa and Aerocaribe use Aeropuerto Terán (☎ (961) 2-29-20), two km south of Highway 190 from a signposted turning, about five km west of the zócalo.

Viajes Miramar (☎ (961) 2-39-83; fax 3-04-64), next to Hotel Del Rey on 1 Ote Norte 310, sells domestic and international air tickets; the staff speak some English. Hours are Monday to Friday 9 am to 2 pm and 4 pm to 7 pm, and Saturday 9 am to 2 pm.

Bus Cristóbal Colón, at the corner of 2 Norte Ote and 2 Pte Norte, two blocks north-west of the zócalo, is the major 1st-class bus line serving Tuxtla.

ADO, at the corner of 9 Pte Sur and 5 Sur Pte, about 1¼ km west of the zócalo then five blocks south, has limited service. The aging 2nd-class buses of Autotransportes Tuxtla Gutiérrez (ATG) congregate in a yard on 3 Sur Ote 712, half a block west of 7 Ote Sur, nearly a km south of the zócalo. Much newer 2nd-class buses are used on the San Cristóbal run by Autotransportes Nha-Bolom from 8 Ote Sur 330, two blocks east then half a block north of the ATG station.

Chiapa de Corzo – 12 km, 20 minutes; Transportes Chiapas-Tuxtla microbuses leave 3 Ote Sur, near the corner of 3 Sur Ote, every 15 minutes from 5 am to 7 pm for US$0.50.

Ciudad Cuauhtémoc (Guatemalan border) – 255 km, four hours; two buses (US$8) by Cristóbal Colón, one evening ATG bus for US$5.

Comitán – 168 km, 3½ hours; five Cristóbal Colón buses (US$5), hourly buses by ATG (US$3.75).

Mérida – 995 km, 16 hours; one evening Cristóbal Colón bus (US$33), two Cristóbal Colón Plus buses (US$46), a lunchtime ATG bus for (US$25).

Mexico City – 1000 km, 19 hours; three afternoon Cristóbal Colón buses (US$38), a 6 pm Cristóbal Colón Plus (US$48), two evening ADO buses (US$38).

Oaxaca – 550 km, 10 hours; two Cristóbal Colón buses (US$17), one Cristóbal Colón Plus bus (US$21), one ATG bus for (US$12).

Palenque – 275 km, six hours; six Cristóbal Colón buses (US$7), a midnight Cristóbal Colón Plus bus (US$11), one 1 am ATG bus for US$7.

San Cristóbal de las Casas – 85 km, two hours; hourly buses (US$2.75) by Cristóbal Colón, ATG (US$2), and Autotransportes Nha-Bolom (US$2).

Tapachula – 456 km, seven hours; five Cristóbal Colón buses (US$12), five ATG buses for US$9.

Villahermosa – 294 km, six hours; six Cristóbal Colón buses (US$8.75), one midnight Cristóbal Colón Plus (US$13), three ATG buses for US$8.

Car Rental companies include Budget (☎ (961) 5-13-82) at Blvd Belisario Domínguez 2510; Dollar (☎ (961) 2-89-32) at 5 Norte Pte 2260; and Gabriel Rent-a-Car (☎ (961) 2-07-57) at Belisario Domínguez 780, 500 metres west of the Hotel Bonampak, and Hertz in the Hotel Bonampak.

Getting Around

To/From the Airport Transportes Terrestre combis (☎ (961) 2-15-54) runs to/from the Aeropuerto San Juan for Mexicana flights to/from Mexico City (US$3.25 per person). They'll drop you anywhere in the city. Going to the airport you can board a bus at the Gran

Hotel Humberto two hours before takeoff. For Aeropuerto Terán you will need a taxi; to/from the city centre costs US$3.

Local Transport All colectivos (US$0.30) on Belisario Domínguez-Avenida Central-Blvd Albino Corzo run at least as far as the tourist offices and the Hotel Bonampak in the west, and 11 Ote in the east. Official stops are marked by the blue 'Ascenso/Decenso' signs but they'll sometimes stop for you elsewhere. Taxis are abundant and rides within the city usually cost US$1.50.

AROUND TUXTLA GUTIÉRREZ
Cañón del Sumidero

The Cañón del Sumidero is a daunting fissure in the countryside a few km east of Tuxtla Gutiérrez, with the Río Grijalva (also called the Río Grande de Chiapas) flowing north through it. When the Chicoasén Dam was completed at the canyon's northern end in 1981, the canyon became a long, thin reservoir. Fast passenger launches speed along its 35-km length trip between sheer walls rising to heights of 900 to 1200 metres. The two to three-hour ride can cost as little as US$6 – a bargain for a crocodile's-eye view of some of Mexico's most awesome scenery.

Highway 190, going east from Tuxtla Gutiérrez, crosses the canyon mouth about 10 km from central Tuxtla, shortly before Chiapa de Corzo on the east bank of the Grijalva, where the boat trip starts.

The fast, open fibreglass launches leave from the embarcadero on the Río Grijalva at Chiapa de Corzo, operating between roughly 8 am and 4 pm. A round trip of an hour each way and maybe a half-hour stop at the far end costs US$50 for a boat that will hold 8 to 10 people (about US$6 each). If you don't have enough people to fill a boat, relax; even on weekdays you shouldn't have to wait more than a half-hour or so. Noontime is the busiest. Bring a layer or two of warm clothing and something to shield you from the sun.

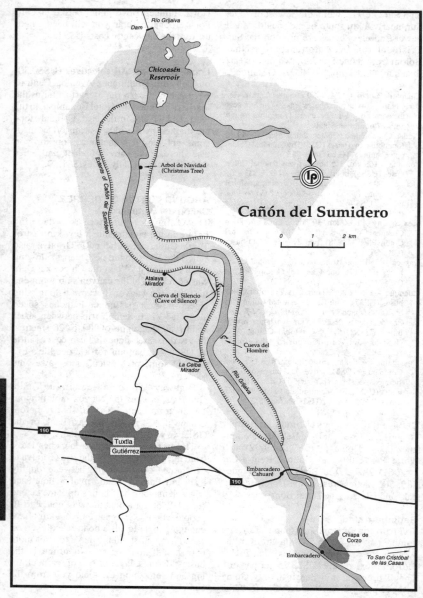

Cañón del Sumidero

Chiapa de Corzo

Chiapa de Corzo is the starting point for trips to the Cañón del Sumidero. Its large main plaza is called Plaza General Ángel Albino Corzo. Buses stop on 21 de Octubre, the street running east from the top end of the zócalo.

For boats into the canyon, walk down the left side of the zócalo (5 de Febrero) and straight on for a couple of blocks until you reach the *embarcadero* on the river front.

Places to Eat By the embarcadero are eight restaurants with almost identical menus and deafening music. All are equally overpriced.

More appealing is the friendly *Restaurant Jardines de Chiapa*, in a garden off Avenida Francesca, one block south of the zócalo. *Restaurant Los Corredores*, on the corner of Avenida Francesca and 5 de Febrero, serves a coffee, egg, toast and fruit breakfast for US$2, or seafood options of pescado fritó (fried fish), pescado or camarones empanizado (breaded fish of shrimp) for US$6.

El Campanario is half a block off the zócalo (off La Mexicanidad) on Coronel Urbina. There is an international menu, a beautiful garden, winsome staff and good seafood for US$6 to US$8.

Getting There & Away From Tuxtla, Transportes Chiapas-Tuxtla microbuses run every fifteen minutes between 3 Ote Sur, near the corner of 3 Sur Ote, and a yard on 21 de Octubre, half a block east of the Chiapa de Corzo zócalo. Fare for the 12-km, 20-minute trip is US$0.50.

Cristóbal Colón, at 21 de Octubre 26, runs 1st-class buses daily from San Cristóbal to Chiapa de Corzo (US$2.25, 1½ hours). The Cristóbal Colón terminal is a white building east of the zócalo on 21 de Octubre. Autotransportes Tuxtla Gutiérrez (ATG), a little farther up the same street at No 284, runs buses the same route every half-hour for US$1.75.

El Aguacero

Río de la Venta's El Aguacero waterfall makes for good swimming and an off-the-beaten-track day trip, though it can be busy with locals and picnickers on weekends. A three-km road leading to the falls goes north off Highway 190, between Ocozocoautla and Cintalapa, 53 km west of Tuxtla. At the roads end, descend 800 steps. Rodolfo Figueroa buses (US$1.50) leaving from 4 Pte Sur between 8 and 9 Sur Pte every 15 minutes, will get you to the road junction.

SAN CRISTÓBAL DE LAS CASAS

Population: 70,000
Altitude: 2100 metres

San Cristóbal (cris-TOH-bal; 'Jovel' to the locals), a tranquil colonial town in a temperate, pine-clad mountain valley, doesn't have many major postcard-type 'sights' but rewards generously those who have the time to get acquainted with it. The area is endlessly intriguing to explore, surrounded by mysterious Indian villages and endowed with abundant good-value accommodation, food to suit all tastes, and easy-to-find good company.

The numbers of visitors, hotels, restaurants and glossy shops have all risen sharply in recent years. Nevertheless, the highland light retains its unrivalled clarity, the quiet Tzotzil and Tzeltal Indians from nearby villages still brighten the streets with their pink, turquoise, black or white costumes, and on cool evenings woodsmoke still lingers calmly over the town.

History

The Maya ancestors of the Tzotzils and Tzeltals moved to these highlands after the collapse of lowland Maya civilisation. The Spaniards arrived in 1524, and Diego de Mazariegos founded San Cristóbal as their regional headquarters four years later.

For most of the colonial era San Cristóbal's Spanish citizens made their fortunes – usually from wheat – at the cost of the Indians, who lost their lands and suffered diseases, taxes and forced labour. Early on, the church gave the Indians some protection against colonists excesses. Dominican monks arrived in Chiapas in 1545 and made

YUCATÁN

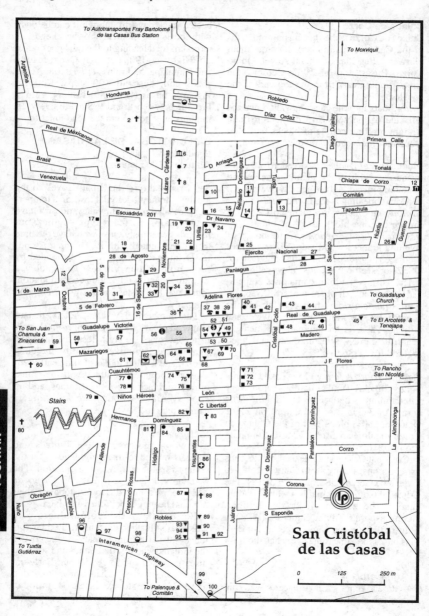

YUCATÁN

San Cristóbal
de las Casas

0   125   250 m

PLACES TO STAY

4	Posada El Candil
5	Casa de Glady's
16	Hotel Plaza Santo Domingo
17	Hotel Parador Mexicanos
20	Hotel Posada Caridad
21	Posada Santo Domingo
22	Hotel Casa Mexicano
25	Posada El Cerrillo
26	Hotel Rincón Del Arco
27	La Posadita
28	Posada Jovel
29	Hotel Flamboyant Español
30	Posada del Sol
31	El Paraíso
35	Hotel Posada Diego de Mazariegos
38	Hotel Real del Valle
39	Hotel San Martín
41	Posada Santiago
42	Casa de Huéspedes Margarita
43	Hotel Don Quijote
44	Posada Tepeyac
47	Posada Casa Real
48	Posada Virginia
57	Posada Yaxchilán
59	Hotel Mansión del Valle
64	Hotel Ciudad Real
65	Hotel Santa Clara
66	Posada San Cristóbal
70	Hotel Los Angeles
72	Casa de Huéspedes Lupita
73	Hotel Palacio de Moctezuma
76	Hotel Fray Bartolomé de las Casas
78	Posada Mayo
79	Posada Los Morales
85	Hotel D'Monica & Restaurant Unicornio
87	Posada Lucella
90	Posada Lupita
91	Hotel Capri
92	Posada Vallarta
94	Posada Insurgentes

PLACES TO EAT

13	El Zorro
14	La Casa del Pan
15	La Parrilla
18	Jardín de Canton
19	Restaurant Las Estrellas
24	Cafetería Jardín Colonial
32	Café-Restaurant El Teatro
33	Café Olulu
34	La Salsa Verde
45	La Taberna (Restaurant & Bar)
49	Restaurant Flamingo
50	Restaurant París México
51	Restaurant Fulano's
53	Restaurant Los Arcos
54	Restaurant El Faisán
58	El Taquito
61	El Circo Restaurant
63	La Galería
67	Restaurant Tia Maty
68	Restaurant La Mansión del Fraile
69	Restaurant Langosta
71	Comedor Familiar Normita II
74	Cafetería San Cristóbal
75	Restaurante Tuluc
82	Madre Tierra Restaurant & Panadería
89	Cafetería y Lonchería Palenque
93	Restaurant Chamula
95	Tikal Restaurant

OTHER

1	Combis to San Juan Chamula, Zinacantán & Tenejapa
2	Church
3	Market
6	City Museum
7	Sna Jolobil Gallery
8	Santo Domingo Church
9	La Caridad Church
10	J'pas Joloviletic
11	Church
12	Na Bolom
23	Librería Chilam Balam
36	Cathedral
37	Sexto Sol
40	Casa de las Imagenes
46	Centro Cultural El Puente
52	Casa de Cambio Lacantún
55	Zócalo (Plaza 31 de Marzo)
56	Tourist Office
60	La Merced Church
62	Post Office
77	Centro de Investigaciones Ecológicas del Sureste
80	Hill & Church of San Cristóbal
81	El Carmen Church
83	San Francisco Church
84	Bellas Artes Auditorium
86	Hospital
88	Santa Lucía Church
96	ATG Bus Station
97	Colectivos to Tuxtla Gutiérrez
98	Transportes Lacandonia Bus Station
99	Cristóbal Colón Bus Station
100	Autotransportes Nha-Bolom Bus Station

YUCATÁN

San Cristóbal their main base. Bartolomé de las Casas (after whom the town is now named), appointed bishop of Chiapas that year, and Juan de Zapata y Sandoval, bishop from 1613 to 1621, are both fondly remembered.

San Cristóbal was the state capital from 1824, when Chiapas joined independent Mexico, to 1892, when Tuxtla Gutiérrez took over. The road from Tuxtla Gutiérrez wasn't paved until the 1940s.

Orientation

San Cristóbal is easy to walk around with straight streets rambling up and down several gentle hills. The Interamerican Highway (Highway 190) passes along the south side of town, and just off it are the main bus stations. From these terminals, walk north (slightly uphill) to the zócalo (Plaza 31 de Marzo), which has the cathedral on its the north side. From the Cristóbal Colón terminal it's just six blocks up Insurgentes to the zócalo; from ATG it's five blocks up Allende, then two to the right along Mazariegos.

Places to stay and eat are scattered all around town, but there are concentrations on Insurgentes, Real de Guadalupe, and Madero, going east from the zócalo.

Information

Tourist Office San Cristóbal's helpful tourist office (☎ (967) 8-04-14) is in the north end of the Palacio Municipal, on the west side of the zócalo. Hours are 8 am to 8 pm Monday to Saturday, 9 am to 2 pm Sunday. The notice board in front is plastered with flyers of the current happenings; there's a message board inside and they will hold mail.

Money Several banks on and near the zócalo exchange foreign currency only from 9 to 11 am. It's quicker and easier to use their ATMs. Or change cash or traveller's cheques at Casa de Cambio Lacantún (☎ (967) 8-25-87), Real de Guadalupe 12-A, half a block from the zócalo, where rates are only about 50 pesos per dollar worse than at the banks. The minimum transaction is US$50 and

hours are 8.30 am to 2 pm and 4 to 8 pm Monday to Saturday, 9 am to 1 pm Sunday.

Post & Telecommunications The post office (☎ (967) 8-07-65) is on the corner of Cuauhtémoc and Crescencio Rosas, one block west and one south of the zócalo. It's open 8 am to 7 pm Monday to Friday, 9 am to 1 pm Saturday, Sunday and holidays. San Cristóbal's postal code is 29200. For telegrams go to Diego de Mazariegos 29, 2½ blocks west of the zócalo.

There are Ladatel phones on the west side of the zócalo and in the Cristóbal Colón and ATG bus stations. Sexto Sol, half a block east of the zócalo on Real de Guadalupe 24-D, can place calls and send faxes for you.

Bookshops La Pared, in the Centro Cultural El Puente, Real de Guadalupe 55, has a large selection of used books in English and Spanish, mostly paperbacks which you can buy, sell, trade or rent.

Librería Chilam Balam has a good selection of history and anthropology books, and some novels and guidebooks in English, German, and French. Their larger shop is on Utrilla 33 at Dr Navarro (diagonally opposite La Caridad Church); a smaller shop is on Insurgentes 18 at León. Librería Soluna, at Real de Guadalupe 13-B, less than a block east of the zócalo has a decent English section.

The 14,000 books at Na Bolom comprise one of the world's biggest collections on the Maya, and includes many other aspects of Chiapas and Central America. Those interested can use the library Tuesday to Saturday from 9 am to 1 pm.

Laundry Lavasec, at Crescencio Rosas 12 just north of Hermanos Domínguez, open Monday to Saturday 8 am to 6 pm, will wash and dry three kg for US$3.25, and has same day service if you drop it off by 10 am. *Lavasor* has a drop-off/pick-up shop on Real de Guadalupe 26, between Utrilla and Juárez. Same day service costs US$3 for four kg; hours are 8 am to 10 pm daily.

Zócalo

Officially called Plaza 31 de Marzo, this old Spanish centre of town was used for markets until early this century. Today it is a fine place to sit, watch the town life happen around you, or enjoy a meal in the central kiosk.

The cathedral, on the north side, was begun in 1528 but completely rebuilt in 1693. Its gold leaf interior has a baroque pulpit and altarpiece,

The Hotel Santa Clara on the south-eastern corner was the house of Diego de Mazariegos, the Spanish conqueror of Chiapas. It's one of the few non-ecclesiastical examples of the Plateresque style in Mexico.

Santo Domingo Church

North-west of the centre, opposite the corner of Lázaro Cárdenas and Real de Mexicanos, Santo Domingo is the most beautiful of San Cristóbal's many churches – especially when its pink façade is floodlit at night. The church and the adjoining monastery were built from 1547 to 1560. The church's baroque façade was added in the 17th century. There's plenty of gold inside, especially on the ornate pulpit. Chamulan women conduct a daily crafts market around Santo Domingo and La Caridad church (1712) immediately to its south.

El Carmen & Bellas Artes

El Carmen church stands at the corner of Hidalgo and Hermanos Domínguez. Formerly part of a nunnery (built in 1597), it has a distinctive tower (1680) resting on an arch, erected to replace one destroyed by floods 28 years earlier. Next door is the Casa de Cultura, containing an art gallery, library, and the Bellas Artes auditorium.

Weavers' Cooperatives

Sna Jolobil (a Tzotzil name meaning Weavers' House) is on Lázaro Cárdenas 42 across from Santo Domingo Church and **J'pas Joloviletic** is on Utrilla 43, just past La Caridad Church. Sna Jolobil has 650 women in its organisation, J'pas Joloviletic

about 850, all backstrap-loom weavers from 20 nearby Tzotzil and Tzeltal villages. The co-ops were founded to foster this important folk art for income and to preserve Indian identity and tradition. The weavers aim to revive forgotten techniques and designs, and to continue to develop dyes from plants, dirt and tree bark.

Each Chiapas highland village has its own distinctive dress. Most of the seemingly abstract designs are in fact stylised snakes, frogs, butterflies, dog pawprints, birds, people, saints and so on.

Sna Jolobil is open from 9 am to 2 pm and 4 to 6 pm daily except Sunday; J'pas Joloviletic is open Monday to Saturday 9 am to 1 pm and 4 to 7 pm, Sunday 9 am to 1 pm. In both showrooms you can see huipiles, shawls, sashes, ponchos and hats. Prices range from a few dollars for smaller items up

Weaver with a backstrap loom

to US$500 for the finest huipiles and ceremonial garments.

Na Bolom

A visit to Na Bolom, a house on Guerrero 33 on the corner of Chiapa de Corzo, six blocks north of Real de Guadalupe, is one of San Cristóbal's most fascinating experiences. For many years it was the home of Danish archaeologist Frans Blom, who died in 1963, and his wife the Swiss anthropologist and photographer Gertrude (Trudy) Duby-Blom, who died in 1993 at age 92.

The couple shared a passion for Chiapas and particularly for its Indians. While Frans explored, surveyed and dug at ancient Mayan sites including Toniná, Chinkultic and Moxviquil, Trudy devoted much of her life to studying the tiny Lacandón Indian population of eastern Chiapas. She worked for the Lacandóns' well-being, but also attracted criticism for shielding the Lacandóns too zealously from change.

The house, whose name is Tzotzil for 'Jaguar House' as well as a play on the owner's name, is full of photographs, archaeological and anthropological relics and books, a treasure-trove for anyone with an interest in Chiapas. Visits are by informal guided tours, conducted in English and Spanish, Tuesday through Sunday at 4.30 pm (US$3.25). Following the tour, a lengthy film is shown on the Lacandón and Trudy Blom's work.

Centro Cultural El Puente

'El Puente' (☎ /fax (967) 8-22-50), on Real de Guadalupe 55, 2½ blocks east of the zócalo is an information and cultural centre buzzing with locals, artists and interested travellers, open every day but Sunday from 8 am to 10 pm. El Puente has a gallery with continual exhibitions and a media room busy nightly with films, lectures, music or theater (English or Spanish). The Centro's *Café El Puente* serves vegetarian meals.

Centro Bilingüe, the language school, has two offices. Spanish classes are given in Centro Cultural El Puente (☎ /fax (967) 8-37-23) on Real de Guadalupe 55, and

English is taught at Insurgentes 57 (☎ (967) 8-41-57).

One-on-one lessons are US$7.50 per hour, three-on-one lessons are US$5.25 per person per hour.

Homestay programs offer 15 hours of instruction (three hours per day, five days a week), at least three hours of homework every day, homestay for a full week (seven days, double occupancy) and include three meals a day (every day except Sunday). A homestay with one-on-one instruction is US$184, three-on-one is US$151 per week. If you study for more than one week, it's a bit cheaper. For US$119, you can sign up for 'lunch/breakfast with Spanish', a five-day program which includes a meal and three hours of lessons each day.

City Museum

The Museo de Arqueología, Etnografía, Historia y Arte, located next to the Santo Domingo church, deals mainly with the history of San Cristóbal. All explanatory material is in Spanish. Hours are Monday to Saturday 10 am to 5 pm, and entry is US$3.

Market

The flavor of outlying Indian villages can be sampled at San Cristóbal's busy market, between Utrilla and Belisario Domínguez, eight blocks north of the zócalo, open till late afternoon daily except Sunday. Many of the traders are Indian villagers for whom buying and selling is the main reason to come to town.

The Indians generally keep their distance from the mestizo population, the result of centuries of exploitation. But they can be friendly and good-humoured (and hard bargainers!)

San Cristóbal & Guadalupe

The most prominent of the several small hills over which San Cristóbal undulates are the Cerro (Hill) de San Cristóbal in the southwest quarter of town, reached by steps up from Allende, and the Cerro de Guadalupe, seven blocks east of the zócalo along Real de Guadalupe. Both are crowned by churches and afford good views. There's an amazing crucifixion sculpture made entirely of vehicle number plates behind the San Cristóbal church; but there have been reports of attempted rapes here too.

Grutas de San Cristóbal

The grutas (caves) are in fact a single long cavern nine km south-east of San Cristóbal, among lovely pine woods a five-minute walk south of the Interamerican Highway. The first 350 metres or so of the cave have a wooden walkway and are lit. You can enter for US$0.75 from 9 am to 5 pm daily. To get there take an ATG bus west and ask for 'Las Grutas' (US$0.30). Camping is allowed, and there are horses for hire.

Huitepec Ecological Reserve & Pro-Natura

The Reserva Ecológica Huitepec is a two-km interpretive nature trail on the slopes of Cerro Huitepec, about 3.5 km out of San Cristóbal on the Chamula road. The ascent, rising through various vegetation types to rare cloud forests, takes about 45 minutes. It's open from 9 am to 4 pm daily except Monday.

Pro-Natura, an independent organisation staffed by volunteers and funded by donations, offers tours for US$2. Its office is at Maria Adelina Flores 2 (☎ (967) 8-40-69).

Activities

Horse Riding Various travel agents and hotels can arrange rides to surrounding villages or the caves. Try to find out about the animals before you commit yourself: are they horses or just ponies, fiery or docile, fast or slow? Will there be a guide?

Casa Margarita, Posada Jovel and Posada Del Sol charge about US$16 for a three-to five-hour ride. José Hernández (☎ (967) 8-10-65) at Elías Calles 10, (a dirt road two blocks north-west of Na Bolom), off Huixtla just north of Chiapa de Corzo, hires horses cheaper at US$12 a ride. The Rancho San Nicolás campground (☎ (967) 8-18-73) also provides mounts.

Bicycle Rentals Gante, at 5 de Mayo 10-B near 5 de Febrero, rents mountain bikes for US$6 a day; included in the price is a lock, key and map. It's a good way to explore the city and surrounding country.

Organised Tours

Travel agents, hotels, and individuals offer tours to nearby Indian villages. They rarely go anywhere you couldn't reach under your own steam, though they may be able to offer information or combinations of destinations that you couldn't manage easily.

Some of the most interesting tours are the small groups (three to eight people) led by Mercedes Hernández Gómez, a fluent English speaker who grew up in San Juan Chamula. You can find Mercedes at 9 am near the kiosk in the zócalo, twirling a colourful umbrella. Tours are US$10 and generally last 5 to 6 hours, traveling by public bus and foot. We have also had good reports of the tours led by Alex and Raul, who you can find in front of the main cathedral next to the zócalo daily at 9.30 am. They offer similar tours for the same price, but also give city tours. If you want to prearrange a special tour you can call them at (☎ (967) 8-37-41).

Travel agents in San Cristóbal offer day trips further afield for those who are short of time. Average prices (with four people) are: Indian Villages (five hours, US$18), Cañón del Sumidero (eight hours, US$30), Lagos de Montebello-Chincultik ruins-Amatenango Del Valle (nine hours, US$27). Palenque ruins-Agua Azul-Misol-Ha (13 hours, US$40) and Toniná (six hours, US$28).

Several travel agents are:

Sexto Sol (☎ & fax (967) 8-43-53) Real de Guadalupe 24-D, half a block east of the zócalo.
Viajes Blanquita (☎ & fax (967) 8-03-80) in Centro Cultural El Puente, Real de Guadalupe 55, 2½ blocks east of the zócalo.
Viajes Pakal (☎ & fax (967) 8-28-19), at the corner of Hidalgo and Cuauhtémoc.

Festivals

In spring, Semana Santa (Holy Week, before

Easter), with processions on Good Friday and the burning of 'Judas' figures on Holy Saturday, is followed by the Feria de la Primavera y de la Paz (Spring & Peace Fair) with more parades, bullfights and so on. Sometimes the celebrations for the anniversary of the town's founding (31 March) fall in the midst of it all too!

Also look out for events marking the feast of San Cristóbal (17 to 25 July), the anniversary of Chiapas joining Mexico in 1824 (14 September), National Independence Day (15 and 16 September), the Day of the Dead (2 November), the Feast of the Virgin of Guadalupe (10 to 12 December) and preparations for Christmas (16 to 24 December).

Places to Stay – bottom end

Camping The *Rancho San Nicolás* camping and trailer park (☎ (967) 8-00-57) is two km east of the zócalo: go east along León for a km after it becomes a dirt track. It's a friendly place with a grassy lawn, apple trees, horses grazing and hot showers. Cost is US$3 per person in a tent, US$6 in a cabin, US$5 to US$7 per person in a caravan or camper with full hook-ups.

Hotels & Casa de Huéspedes Several cheap hostelries are dotted along Insurgentes, the street leading from the Cristóbal Colón bus station to the zócalo. Many are dingy and uncared for. Better deals can be found along Real de Guadalupe, which heads east off the zócalo.

Insurgentes Posada Insurgentes (☎ (967) 8-24-35), Insurgentes 73, 1½ blocks north of the bus station, has unadorned but clean rooms, shared baths, and caged macaws in the courtyard for US$8/US$10 a single/double. Just opposite on Insurgentes 46, *Posada Lupita*, is plain to the point of severity; rates are US$5/8 for a single/double.

Posada Lucella (☎ (967) 8-09-56), Insurgentes 55, directly across from the Santa Lucia Church, has OK doubles for US$8.50, US$10.50 with private bath.

Posada San Cristóbal (tel(967) 8-19-07) at Insurgentes 3, near the zócalo, has airy, colorful rooms, set around a pleasant courtyard; singles and doubles are US$13/US$16.

Hotel Fray Bartolomé de las Casas (☎ (967) 8-09-32), Niños Héroes 2 at Insurgentes, two blocks south of the zócalo, has cleanliness, character and a variety of rooms for US$13/16.

Posada Vallarta (☎ (967) 8-04-65), half a block east off Insurgentes at Hermanos Pineda 10 (the first street to the right as you go up Insurgentes) has clean and modern-ish rooms with private baths and balconies for US$15/18 a single/double.

Real de Guadalupe Casa de Huéspedes *Margarita* (☎ (967) 8-09-57), Real de Guadalupe 34, 1½ blocks east of the zócalo, has long been a popular budget travellers' halt and a good meeting place. A *dormitorio* bed is (US$5), doubles, triples, or quadruple rooms are between (US$14 and US$20). The Margarita will hold mail for you.

Just beyond the Margarita is the *Posada Tepeyac* (☎ (967) 8-01-18), Real de Guadalupe 40, a modest, clean place. With common bath, singles/doubles are US$6.50/US$10; doubles with private bath cost US$13. Rooms at the back are lighter. A few doors up from Posada Tepeyac on the opposite side of Real de Guadalupe, next to El Puente is *Posada Casa Real*, humble, clean and US$5 a bed.

Elsewhere Undoubtedly the best deal in town is at *Bed and Breakfast* (☎ (967) 8-04-40), Madero 83, five blocks east of the zócalo. Clean dorm beds (US$3.25), singles (US$5), and rooms with private baths (US$8/11) all include breakfast of egg/beans/tortilla and coffee. For US$0.30 you can use the kitchen.

The *Posada Jovel* (☎ (967) 8-17-34) at Paniagua 28 between Cristóbal Colón and Santiago, attracts backpackers with its friendly owners and atmosphere and prices of US$6.75/10 with shared bath, US$8.50/11.75 with private bath. They serve a nice breakfast. If that's full, try the next-door *La Posadita* at Paniagua 30; rooms are off a bright courtyard and cost US$6.50/8 for a single/double with private bathrooms.

Posada Del Sol (☎ (967) 8-04-95), on Primera de Marzo 22 at 5 de Mayo, three blocks west of the zócalo, has caged birds, '70s decor and dangling light bulbs; asking price is US$8/10 with shared bathroom, US$11/15 with private bath.

For a hint of the '60s, try the easygoing *Casa de Gladys* at Real de Mexicanos 16. This colonial house looks a bit like university housing with its purplish courtyard, hanging hammocks and peace posters. Dorm beds are US$5 and coffee and purified water are free. The nearby *Posada El Candil* (☎ (967) 8-27-55), Real de Mexicanos 7, 1½ blocks west of Santo Domingo church, has bright, clean, simple rooms without baths for US$6.50 a single, US$11 for doubles.

Casa de Huéspedes Lupita, Juárez 12 between León and Felipe Flores has dowdy, average rooms. Five blocks north, *Posada El Cerrillo* at Belisario Domínguez 27, just north of Ejercito Nacional, is elemental, but has a pleasant courtyard.

Posada Santo Domingo, three blocks north of the zócalo on 28 de Agusto, between 20 de Noviembre and Utrilla, is among the cleanest, and also has a courtyard. *Hotel Posada Caridad*, on Escuadrón 201, across from La Caridad park, has standard rooms and a good central location.

Places to Stay – middle

Insurgentes A block and a half up from the Cristóbal Colón bus station, *Hotel Capri* (☎ (967) 8-00-15), Insurgentes 54, has modern, clean, and fairly quiet rooms round a narrow flowery courtyard for US$21/25. Don't confuse it with Posada Capri, a block down on the other side of the street.

Hotel Plaza Santo Domingo (☎ (967) 8-19-27) on Utrilla 35, across from La Caridad church, has an interesting past: over the years it has served as a hospital, a convent and a prison. Built atop of a maze of tunnels, this structure now encompasses refined rooms, lovely courtyards and a good restaurant.

Doubles/triples/quadruples are US$25/31/38; the hotel adds a 10% tax.

Zócalo & Around Back in the 16th century, the *Hotel Santa Clara* (☎ (967) 8-08-71), Avenida Insurgentes 1 (the south-east corner of the zócalo) served as the home to Diego de Mazariegos, the Spanish conqueror of Chiapas. Amenities here include sizable, comfortable rooms, a pleasant courtyard brightened by caged red macaws, a restaurant, a bar/lounge, and heated pool. Singles/doubles are US$33/43.

Hotel Ciudad Real (☎ (967) 8-18-86), Plaza 31 de Marzo 10, on the south side of the zócalo, is a colonial mansion with a covered courtyard. Rooms are pleasant, through rather small, and top floors are the most quiet. Rates are US$40/50/60 for one, two, or three people. Prices are identical at *Hotel Los Angeles*, half a block east of the zócalo on Madero.

West of the Zócalo The *Hotel Mansión del Valle* (☎ (967) 8-25-82; fax 8-25-81), Diego de Mazariegos 39, 3½ blocks west of the zócalo, is a comfortable renovated old house. Rooms are average, have TV and go for US$33/43.

El Paraíso (☎ (937) 8-08-85), 5 de Febrero 19, three blocks west of the zócalo, has a cheery courtyard with leather sunchairs to relax in. It's a subtle, amiable atmosphere with fine rooms (US$28/33 for a double/king) and an attached bar and restaurant serving Swiss and Mexican dishes.

Hotel Parador Mexicanos (☎ (967) 8-00-55) at 5 de Mayo 38, just south of Escuadrón 201, has big comfortable rooms flanking its garden-cum-drive, at the end of which is a tennis court. A lobby lounge, restaurant and pleasant verandahs make it fair value at US$21/25.

Posada Los Morales (☎ (967) 8-14-72) at Allende 17 has a dozen bare white-washed two-person bungalows for US$20 a night. The location is superb: the bungalows are built on a slope in a maze of gardens. Each has a fireplace, bathroom and gas stove.

YUCATÁN

Some bungalows are cleaner and brighter than others, so check out a few.

East of the Zócalo *Hotel Don Quijote* (☎ (967) 8-09-02; fax 8-03-46) on Cristóbal Colón 7, between Real de Guadalupe and Adelina Flores, is among the brightest and newest in the area. Colourful maps and traditional costumes embellish the walls; rooms and the upstairs restaurant are pleasing, and it has a laundry service, travel service and free morning coffee. Rooms are comes to US$20/25.

Hotel Rincón Del Arco (☎ (967) 8-13-13; fax 8-15-68) is in San Cristóbal's oldest neighborhood, 2½ blocks from Na Bolom on Ejercito National 66 at Guerrero. Rooms have ceramic fireplaces, telephones and TV. The 2nd-storey balconies have fabulous city views. The restaurant serves three meals a day and entertains with nightly marimba. Singles are US$40, doubles are US$50.

Hotel Real del Valle (☎ (67) 8-06-80), Real de Guadalupe 14, half a block east of the zócalo, has ordinary clean rooms grouped around a courtyard. Doubles with bath go for US$30. *Hotel San Martín* (☎ (967) 8-05-33) next door at No 16 has a narrow courtyard with tiers of bright but basic rooms for US$20/25.

Posada Virginia, just south of Real de Guadalupe at Cristóbal Colón 1, has comfortable rooms with bathrooms for US$16 a double. The nearby *Posada Santiago* (☎ (967) 8-00-24), Real de Guadalupe 32 near Colón, is a friendly, decent place where carpeted, ordinary rooms with private baths are US$18.

Hotel Palacio de Moctezuma (☎ (967) 8-03-52; fax 8-15-30), Juárez 16 at León, is a pleasant place with flowery courtyards and modern rooms for US$24/26.

Places to Stay – top end
Hotel Casa Mexicano (☎ (967) 8-06-98; fax 8-26-27), 28 de Agusto at Utrilla, with its sky lit garden, fountains, plants, and traditional art and sculptures, exudes colonial charm. Rooms are agreeable, have views of the courtyard and cost US$65/70; suites with a jacuzzi are US$90.

The *Hotel Posada Diego de Mazariegos* (☎ (967) 8-05-13), occupies two fine buildings on Utrilla one block north of the zócalo. The main reception is in the western building, at 5 de Febrero 1. Rooms are tastefully furnished and most have a fireplace and TV. The hotel has a restaurant, bar and a few shops. Rates are US$63/73.

Places to Eat
Vegetarian & Cafés *Madre Tierra Restaurant* (Mother Earth), Insurgentes 19 at Hermanos Domínguez, is a vegetarian's oasis in the land of carnes and aves. The menu is eclectic and appetising with filling soups, wholemeal sandwiches, brown rice dishes, pasta, pizzas and salads. Most everything on the menu is between US$1.75 and US$4. Excellent whole-wheat bread is served with all meals. The *Panadería Madre Tierra* next door is a wholefood bakery selling breads, muffins, cookies, cakes, quiches, pizzas and frozen yogurt.

La Casa del Pan at Dr Navarro 10, two blocks east of Utrilla, serves a 'feel-great breakfast' of fruit, granola, yogurt, muffins and organic coffee, and a veggie comida corrida of soup, rice, beans, quesadilla, beverage and dessert, each for US$5. You may dine in the calming courtyard or the inside restaurant where they sell a variety of tasty grain breads, bagels, brownies and cookies. Hours are 7 am to 10 pm; closed Monday.

Café El Puente, in the Centro Cultural El Puente at Real de Guadalupe 55, serves a delicious waffle breakfast, a peanut butter-honey-banana-raisin sandwich, along with vegetable soup with warm wheat bread or brown rice with salad all for under US$2.50. El Puente is ideal for a leisurely café mocha or a cup of tea.

Probably the best coffee in town, and good cakes too, are served in the little *Cafetería San Cristóbal*, on Cuauhtémoc just off Insurgentes. The clientele is mainly Mexican men who bring along chess sets and newspapers to relax. If atmosphere is crucial for your coffee hour, stop by the jungle-like courtyard of *Cafetería Jardín Colonial* on the corner of Utrilla and Dr Navarro. The menu is típico, yet coffees and cappuccinos are above average.

The walls of the *Restaurant Las Estrellas* on Escuadrón 201 6B, across from La Caridad park, are covered with beautiful batiks (for sale, of course). Its menu includes pesto dishes, veggie quiches and rice plates for US$2.25, and pasta with garlic bread or pizza for US$3. Service is friendly and fast.

Cactus Crazy, four blocks west of the zócalo on Guadalupe Victoria 59-A, is a spirited place with travellers' messages scribbled on the walls between painted cactuses, cowboy hats and vultures. A hefty breakfast of eggs, beans, tortillas and coffee is US$1.75; burritos and chicken and meat dishes are under US$3. With its thumping reggae and jazz, it can get lively after dusk.

Under a yin/yang signpost at 28 de Agosto 19, between 5 de Mayo and 16 de Septiembre, is the entrance to *Jardín de Cantón*, a Chinese restaurant that opens into a jungle garden lavishly decorated with Chinese lamps, gourds, bamboo, hundreds of plants in tin containers and an enormous tree. Order chop suey, lo mein, or vegetable and tofu dishes for about US$5, or fried rice for US$2. There is a vegetarian comida corrida for US$6. Hours are 1.30 pm to 9 pm; it's closed Sunday.

Restaurant París México at Madero 20, one block east of the zócalo, is an artsy little café serving French and Mexican specials daily for US$5, crepas for US$3, and great coffee.

International Upstairs at Hidalgo 3, a few doors from the zócalo, *La Galería* has perhaps the most restful ambience in town with its soft music wafting through the green courtyard. Built in 1540, this building was inhabited at various times by Diego de Mazariegos, Francisco de Montejo, and various bishops of Chiapas. Today bow-tied waiters will serve you breakfast, luncheon soups and salads for US$3, or a beef filet in mushroom sauce for about US$6. English movies are shown nightly in the video bar,

and there's often folk, salsa or Mexican music in the courtyard.

The *Casa Margarita*, at Real de Guadalupe 34, is a popular, pricey little restaurant with a reliable mixture of western, Mexican and vegetarian options. Most meals are between US$4 and US$7.

Another popular eatery is *Restaurante Tuluc* at Insurgentes 5, a block and a bit from the zócalo. It can be hard to get a table here at dinner time. Two good choices, both around US$5, are the tasty filete Tuluc, a beef filet rolled round cheese and spinach, with bacon and beans on the outside; and pescado Veracruzana, fish in tomato sauce. The Tuluc scores with its 6.15 am opening time, allowing for breakfast before an early morning bus.

El Circo Restaurant at Crescencio Rosas 7, half a block from the zócalo, specialises in Italian food. Under its circus roof, you can sample ravioli, lasagna, pesto tagliolini, or pesto with four cheeses for US$6 and top it off with tiramisu and an expresso. El Circo is open from 1 pm to 11 pm, has live music Wednesday through to Saturday and is closed Sunday.

La Pérgola, in Plaza Xaman on 20 de Noviembre 4, has a quiet courtyard atmosphere and a stylish counter/bar. They have an international menu, with vegetarian options. Lasagnas, pizzas, and chicken or meat dishes run between US$4 and US$6, while you can get a good salad or vegetarian burger for US$2.50.

La Taberna, 3½ blocks from the zócalo at Real de Guadalupe 73, has great pizzas cooked in wood ovens for US$4 to US$7 (see Entertainment).

Further down Insurgentes is a trio of cheap favorable places. *Cafetería & Lonchería Palenque* at Insurgentes 40 serves orthodox Mexican fare; for US$3 you'll get a good meal. *Restaurant Chamula*, Insurgentes 69, is a bit cramped but has good meat, chicken and enchilada plates, or a comida corrida for US$4. The *Tikal Restaurant*, a block from the highway, is the most pleasant of the three with its Guatemalan decor, quiet music and rack of *National Geographic* magazines.

They serve generous spaghettis (such as Genovesa, with cheese, nutmeg and spinach), and good guacamole with totopos, all at (US$2.50). Meat dishes and burgers are a bit more.

Café-Restaurant El Teatro, upstairs at Primero de Marzo 8, near 16 de Septiembre, is among the few top-ranking restaurants in town. The menu, based on French and Italian cuisine, lists chateaubriand, crepes, fresh pasta, pizzas and desserts. Expect to spend US$6 to US$12 for a full dinner here.

Restaurant Flamingo, *Restaurant Fulano's* and *Restaurante Langosta* are all on Madero. Flamingo and Fulano's are respectable, with similar menus and fair prices: spaghetti and salads are about US$2.50, pizzas and main dishes are twice that. Langosta distinguishes itself with shish kebab, rice and beans for US$7 and live marimba music daily after 2 pm.

Mexican One block from the zócalo, *Restaurant La Mansión del Fraile*, Insurgentes 10 at the corner of J F Flores, is a long, high-beamed, tile-roofed room with colonial mountain town ambience. Try the tasty anafres, (sizzling cheese or meat platters, US$12 for two), or mole Jovel (chicken in rich brown sauce, US$4.50).

Several cheaper workaday Mexican eateries are strung around the zócalo. *Restaurant Tía Maty* and neighbouring *Restaurant Casa Blanca*, on Insurgentes one block south of the zócalo, serve a variety of antojitos for US$1 to $3. *Restaurant Los Arcos* just off the zócalo on Madero, has a four-course corrida comida for US$4.

At the humbler *El Taquito*, on the corner of Diego de Mazariegos and 12 de Octubre, tacos are half the price and still good. You can also enjoy filete al queso a la parrilla (grilled meat filete with a cheese topping) for US$5, or fruit cocktail with granola and honey for US$2. *La Parrilla* at the corner of Belisario Domínguez and Dr Navarro, open from 6.30 pm to midnight Sunday to Friday, serves excellent carnes and quesos al carbón (char-grilled meats and cheese). A dinner, drink and desert will cost about US$10.

The *Comedor Familiar Normita II*, on the corner of J F Flores and Juárez, has been around a while. It's been painted and spruced up (hence II). The cooking remains local and good. Pozole, a soup of maize, cabbage, pork, radishes and onions costs US$2 or US$2.75, and Plato Típico Coleto, a local mixed grill with pork sausage, chops, frijoles and guacamole for US$5, are specialities, but there is plainer fare for US$2 to US$3.

El Zorro on Comitán, three blocks east of La Caridad church, is a casual Mexican restaurant; a small bar and grill take up the front room, and a pleasant restaurant and band area (live music on Saturday nights) are in the back room. The menu includes tacos (US$0.75), quesadillas (US$2), sincronizadas (US$2.75) and burgers (US$5).

Entertainment

San Cristóbal is an early-to-bed town, and conversation in cafés, restaurants or rooms will most likely occupy many of your evenings. However there are films, cultural events, concerts and rowdy music scenes to be relished if so motivated. Check the notice boards in front of the tourist office and in El Puente for scheduled events.

Centro Cultural El Puente, on Real de Guadalupe 55 has cultural programs, films, concerts or conferences nightly.

The *Casa de las Imagenes* at Belisario Domínguez 11, just north of Real de Guadalupe, is an art gallery cum bookshop cum café with a cinema showing interesting international films.

There are fairly regular musical and theatrical performances at the *Casa de Cultura/Bellas Artes* at the corner of Hidalgo and Hermanos Domínguez.

A handful of restaurants have regular live music. *La Galería* has a piano bar, occasional folk music, and a video bar showing English-language movies nightly. *El Circo* has folk or Latin American music Wednesdays and Thursdays, and reggae/salsa on Friday and Saturday nights after 9 pm. *Casa Margaritas* and *El Zorro* occasionally have live shows, and *Cactus Crazy* advertises 'super-cool music', though it's rarely live.

If you are a musician or enjoy a party, drop by *La Taberna* at Real de Guadalupe 73, 3½ blocks west of the zócalo. A fun local band plays nightly, though any musician is welcome to perform between sets, longer if the crowd claps sincerely. Happy-hour specials begin at 7, two-peso beers are served at 9.30 (if you have the change), and the wood-oven-baked pizzas are great.

San Cristóbal's *Cinema Santa Clara* is at 16 de Septiembre 3, near 28 de Agusto. Nightly films and Saturday matinees are US$2. There are two discos – *Crystal* and *Princess* – on opposite sides of the Interamerican Highway, about half a km in the direction of Comitán from the bottom of Insurgentes.

Things to Buy
Chiapas' Indian crafts are justifiably famous and there are now hosts of shops in San Cristóbal selling them. The heaviest concentrations are along Real de Guadalupe (where prices go down as you go away from the zócalo) and Utrilla (towards the market end). La Galería at Hidalgo 3, has beautiful and expensive crafts.

Textiles – huipiles, rebozos, blankets – are the outstanding items, for Tzotzil weavers are some of the most skilled and inventive in Mexico (see the Weaving Cooperatives section). Indian women also sell textiles in the park around Santo Domingo. You'll also find some Guatemalan Indian textiles and plenty of the appealing and inexpensive pottery from Amatenango del Valle (animals, pots, jugs, etc) in San Cristóbal. Leather is another local speciality.

You can even buy black ski-mask hooded Subteniente Marcos dolls, effigies of the popular leader of the Zapatista Liberation Army.

Always bargain unless prices are labelled (though there's no harm in trying even then), and don't imagine that apparently meek Indians are any softer than anyone else when it comes to commercial transactions.

Getting There & Away
Tuxtla Gutiérrez is 85 km west, Comitán is 85 km south-east. The Guatemalan border at Ciudad Cuauhtémoc (165 km) is 80 km beyond Comitán. The road to Ocosingo (100 km), Agua Azul (155 km) and Palenque (210 km) turns north off the Interamerican 12 km south-east of San Cristóbal. For Villa-hermosa (300 km), you turn north off the Interamerican between Tuxtla Gutiérrez and San Cristóbal, onto Highway 195.

Air Scheduled flights come no nearer than Tuxtla Gutiérrez, though this may change as there is talk of a new airport (by '95?). Travel agents in San Cristóbal can make domestic and international bookings for you.

Bus A new Central de Autobuses is planned in the south of the town but for the moment each company has its own terminal. Cristóbal Colón is at the junction of Insurgentes and the Interamerican Highway. The main 2nd-class lines are: Autotransportes Tuxtla Gutiérrez (ATG) on Allende half a block north of the Interamerican Highway; Transportes Lacandonia on the Interamerican Highway between Hidalgo and Crescencio Rosas (1½ blocks west of the Cristóbal Colón); Autotransportes Nha-Bolom on the Interamerican Highway half a block east of Cristóbal Colón; and Auto-transportes Fray Bartolomé de las Casa on Avenida Soloman González Blanco, the continuation of Utrilla, 300 metres north of the market.

Autotransportes Tuxtla Gutiérrez (ATG) is overall the best equipped 2nd-class company, but it's still nothing to write home about. Transportes Lacandonia calls some of its services '1st class'. They aren't, though they're better than normal 2nd-class.

For transport to highland villages near San Cristóbal see the Around San Cristóbal section. Other bus departures from San Cristóbal include:

Chetumal – 700 km, 13 hours; one Cristóbal Colón Plus evening bus (US$25), and a Transportes Lacandonia '1st-class' bus for US$19.

Chiapa de Corzo – 70 km, 1½ hours; ATG (US$1.75) every half-hour.

Ciudad Cuauhtémoc (Guatemalan border) – 165 km, three hours; eight buses by ATG (US$3.60). Take an early bus if you hope to get any distance into Guatemala the same day.

Comitán – 83 km, 1½ hours; one Cristóbal Colón bus (US$3.25), one Plus (US$6), and 15 ATG buses for US$1.75.

Huatulco – 520 km, 11 hours; two Cristóbal Colón buses for US$17.

Mérida – 770 km, 15 hours; one ATG Plus at 6 pm (US$32), and three 1st-class buses (US$30) by Autotransportes Lacandonia.

Mexico City – 1085 km, 21 hours; one Cristóbal Colón bus (US$30), three buses by ATG (US$36), one ATG Plus (US$50).

Oaxaca – 718 km, 12 hours; one Cristóbal Colón 5 pm bus for US$18.

Ocosingo – 108 km, three hours; several ATG buses (US$2.50), and 12 Autotransportes Lacandonia buses running every half-hour for US$3.

Palenque – 190 km, 5½ hours; eight Cristóbal Colón 1st-class buses (US$6), five ATG buses (US$5) and three Mundo Maya buses (US$4.75) .

Tapachula – 485 km, nine hours via Arriaga; one Cristóbal Colón 1st-class bus (US$7.50), one ATG for US$5.

Tonalá – 265 km, 5½ hours; buses every half-hour between 6 am and 10 pm for US$5.50.

Tuxtla Gutiérrez – 85 km, two hours; 1st-class Cristóbal Colón buses every hour (US$2); ATG and Nha-Bolom buses (US$2) run all day; Mundo Maya has six buses for US$2.

Villahermosa – 300 km, eight hours; 1st-class Cristóbal Colón buses (US$10) at noon and 6 pm daily, one 7 am Autotransportes Lacandonia for US$7.

Getting Around

For buses to the Indian villages near San Cristóbal, see Around San Cristóbal. Taxis are fairly plentiful. One stand is on the north side of the zócalo.

Car Budget (☎ (976) 8-18-71) is in Auto Rentas Yaxchilán at Diego de Mazariegos 36, 2½ blocks from the zócalo. Hours are Monday to Saturday 8 am to 2 pm and 3 to 8 pm. At busy periods you may need to book a few days in advance. The cheapest, a VW Sedan, is around US$40 with unlimited mileage, insurance and taxes included.

AROUND SAN CRISTÓBAL

There are many interesting villages to visit near San Cristóbal. Note that it can be dan-gerous to walk between villages because of robbers. Play it safe and ride.

Indigenous Peoples

Of Chiapas' approximately 3.2 million people, an estimated 600,000 are Indians, descendants of the people who were here before the Spaniards came. The Indians are second-class citizens in economic and polit-ical terms, with the least productive land in the state. Some have emigrated into the eastern jungle to clear new land, or to cities farther afield in search of jobs. Those who remain showed their feelings in the rebellion of 1 January 1994.

Despite these problems, traditional festi-vals, costumes, crafts, religious practices and separate languages help Indian self-respect survive. Indians remain suspicious of out-siders and are often resentful of interference – especially in their religious practices. Nev-ertheless they may also be friendly and polite if you treat them with respect. Spanish is no more than a second language to them.

The Indian people that travellers are most likely to come into contact with are the 150,000 or so **Tzotzils** who occupy an area of 50 km from east to west and 100 km from north to south, with San Cristóbal at its center. You may also encounter the strongly traditional **Tzeltal** people, some 200,000-strong, who inhabit the region north-east and south-east of San Cristóbal, including Amatenango del Valle, Acatenango, Ten-ejapa, Cancuc, Oxchuc, Abasolo, Bachajón, Chilón and Yajalón. These Indians guard their traditions fiercely; approach them with respect.

Other Chiapas Indians include about 80,000 **Chols** who live in the villages of Tumbalá, Tila and Salto de Agua, on the north side of the Chiapas highlands, east and west of Palenque, with a further 20,000 or so in neighbouring Tabasco; about 25,000 **Tojolabals** (also called Chañabals) live in south-east Chiapas, near Comitán, and some 25,000 **Zoques**, who used to inhabit western Chiapas, but were dispersed by the 1981 Chichonal eruption. An estimated 20,000 Mexican **Mames** reside near the

YUCATÁN

Lacandónian man

Guatemalan border between Tapachula and Ciudad Cuauhtémoc.

There are still a few hundred **Lacandóns**, Mexico's most untouched Indian people, and the last true inheritors of ancient Maya traditions, in the eastern Chiapas rainforest. They speak a language related to Yucatán Maya which they themselves call 'Maya'. The past four decades have wrought more changes in Lacandón life than the previous four centuries.

Photography

In some villages, particularly those nearest San Cristóbal, you may be greeted with wariness, the result of centuries of oppression and the desire to preserve traditions from interference. Cameras are at best tolerated – and sometimes not even that. The San Cristóbal tourist office displays a sign stating that photography is banned in the church and during festivals at Chamula, and banned completely at Zinacantán. A tale circulated for years that two tourists were killed for taking photos in the Chamula church. Whether or not it's true, it's certainly evidence of the hostility that can be aroused by insensitive behaviour. If in any doubt at all, ask before taking a picture.

San Juan Chamula

The Chamulans have always defended their independence fiercely: they put up strong resistance to the Spaniards in 1524 and launched a famous rebellion in 1869. Today they are one of the most numerous of the Tzotzil groups – 40,000 strong – and their village 10 km north-west of San Cristóbal is the centre for some unique religious practices. A big sign at the entrance to the village says it is strictly forbidden to take photos in the church or anywhere rituals are being performed.

A sign on the church door tells visitors to ask at the 'tourist office', also on the plaza, for tickets (US$1) to enter. If the sense of intruding doesn't overwhelm you, the atmosphere inside is extraordinary. The rows of burning candles, the thick clouds of incense, the chanting worshippers kneeling with their faces on the pine-needle carpeted floor, are all reminiscent of an Asian temple as of anywhere else. Among the candles stand Pepsi and Coke bottles – offerings to the spirits of the ancestors buried nearby.

The Chamulans believe that Christ rose from the cross to become the sun. Christian festivals are interwoven with older ones: the pre-Lent Carnival celebrations, which are among the most important and last several days in February or March, also mark the five 'lost' days *(uayeb)* of the ancient Mayan Long Count calendar (see Facts about the Region under Vague Year). Other festivals include ceremonies for San Sebastián (mid to late January); Semana Santa; San Juan, the village's patron saint (22 to 25 June); and the annual change of village leadership posts (30 December to 1 January).

Zinacantán

This Tzotzil village, centre for roughly 15,000 Zinacantecos, is 11 km north-west of San Cristóbal. The road to it forks left off the Chamula road, then down into the valley. Zinacantán has two churches. Photos are banned altogether here.

YUCATÁN

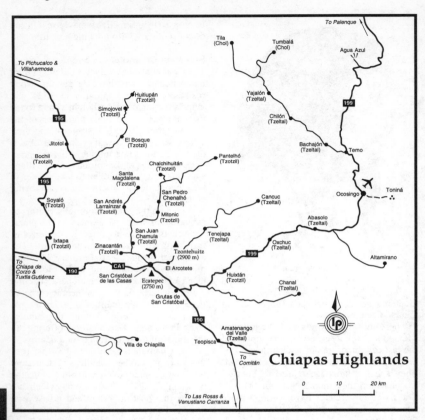

Chiapas Highlands

The men wear very distinctive red-and-white striped tunics (which appear pink), and flat, round, beribboned palm hats. Unmarried men's hats have longer, wider ribbons. A market is usually held only at fiesta times. The most important celebrations are for the patron saint, San Lorenzo, between 8 and 11 August, and for San Sebastián in January.

Zinacantecos venerate the geranium which, along with pine branches, is offered in rituals to bring a wide range of benefits. The crosses dotting the Zinacantán countryside mostly mark entrances to the abodes of the important ancestor gods or of the Señor de la Tierra (Earth Lord), all of whom must be kept happy with offerings at appropriate times.

Tenejapa

Tenejapa is a Tzeltal village 28 km north-east of San Cristóbal, set in a pretty valley with a river running through it. There are about 20,000 Tenejapecos in the surrounding area. Early Sunday mornings a busy market fills the main street (round behind the church). More interesting than what's on sale in the market are the people's costumes.

Tenejapa has a few comedores in the main

street and one basic posada, the *Hotel Molina*, but it's not always open. The main festival is for the village's patron saint, San Ildefonso, on 23 January.

Amatenango del Valle

The women of this Tzeltal village, 37 km south-east of San Cristóbal down the Interamerican Highway, are renowned potters. Amatenango pottery is still fired by the pre-Hispanic method of burning a wood fire around the pieces, rather than putting them in a kiln.

Amatenango's patron saint, San Francisco, is fêted on 4 October.

Other Villages

Intrepid Mayaphiles might want to make visits to some more remote villages.

San Andrés Larráinzar is a hilltop Tzotzil and mestizo village 28 km north-west of San Cristóbal (18 km beyond San Juan Chamula). A turn-off uphill to the left, 10 km after San Juan Chamula, leads through spectacular mountain scenery to San Andrés. The patron saint's day is 30 November. A weekly Sunday market is held and the people seem less reserved towards outsiders than those of other villages. People from Santa Magdalena, another Tzotzil village a few km north, attend the San Andrés market; their ceremonial huipiles are among the finest of all Chiapas Indian garments.

The plaza at **Mitonic**, a small Tzotzil village a few hundred metres left of the Chenalhó road, 23 km beyond San Juan Chamula, has both a picturesque ruined 16th century church and a more modern working one. The patron saint, San Miguel, is honoured from 5 to 8 May.

San Pedro Chenalhó is a Tzotzil village in a valley with a stream running through it; it's 1500 metres high, 27 km beyond and quite a descent from Chamula. It's the centre for about 14,000 people in the surrounding area. There's a weekly Sunday market. The main fiestas are for San Pedro (27 to 30 June), San Sebastián (16 to 22 January) and Carnival.

Huixtán, 32 km from San Cristóbal and the centre for roughly 12,000 Tzotzils, was one of the main pre-Hispanic Tzotzil centres. Huixtán has a 16th-century church. **Oxchuc**, 20 km beyond Huixtán, is a small Tzeltal and mestizo town dominated by the large colonial church of San Tomás.

Getting There & Away

There are paved roads to San Juan Chamula, Zinacantán, Amatenango del Valle, and most of the way to Tenejapa. Reaching the other villages mentioned involves long stretches of pretty rough dirt track, but buses make it along them and so can a VW sedan (slowly).

Bus and colectivo schedules are geared to getting villagers into town early and back home not too late.

Combis for San Juan Chamula and Zinacantán depart from the north-west corner of the San Cristóbal market every 20 minutes or so (US$0.75). For Tenejapa they leave about every half-hour; the hour ride costs US$1. Return services from Tenejapa start getting scarce after noon. To Amatenango de Valle, take a Comitán bus (see San Cristóbal – Getting There & Away), the fare is US$1.

Transportes Fray Bartolomé de las Casas (see San Cristóbal – Getting There & Away) runs buses to Chenalhó (US$1.50, 2½ hours), and to San Andrés Larraínzar (US$1.25, 2½ hours.

COMITÁN

Population: 84,000
Altitude: 1630 metres

Comitán is a pleasant town, the jumping-off point to the Lagos de Montebello, and the last place of any size before the Guatemalan border at Ciudad Cuauhtémoc.

The first Spanish settlement in the area, San Cristóbal de los Llanos, was established in 1527. Today the town is officially called Comitán de Domínguez, after Belisario Domínguez, a local doctor who was also a national senator during the presidency of Victoriano Huerta. Domínguez had the cheek to speak out in 1913 against Huerta's record of political murders and was himself murdered for his pains.

Orientation

Comitán is set amidst hills, so you'll find yourself walking up and down, down and up – with your gear. The wide and attractive main plaza is bounded by Avenida Central on its west side and 1 Sur Pte on the south. The street numbering scheme resembles that of Tuxtla Gutiérrez in its complexity and confusion.

The 1st-class Cristóbal Colón bus station is on the Interamerican Highway, which passes through the western edge of the town, about 20 minutes' walk from the town centre. To reach the zócalo, turn left out of the bus station and along the highway, take the first right, (downhill along 4 Sur Pte but it's not marked), go six blocks (up and down hills), then turn left on to Avenida Central Sur and go three blocks. Alternatively, taxis outside

the terminal will charge US$1.30 for the short trip to the zócalo.

The 2nd-class Autotransportes Tuxtla Gutiérrez (ATG) is at 4 Sur Pte 55, between Avenida 3 and Avenida 4 Pte Sur; for the zócalo go left out of the entrance on 4 Sur Pte 3½ blocks, at Avenida Central Sur go three blocks north.

Linea Comitán-Montebello serves Lagos de Montebello; they go from Avenida 2 Pte Sur 17-B between Calles 2 and 3 Sur Pte, two blocks west and 1½ south of the zócalo.

Information

Tourist Office There's a tourist office (☎ (963) 2-00-26) in the Palacio Municipal on the north side of the zócalo, open 9 am to 8 pm Monday to Saturday, and 9 am to 2 pm on Sunday.

Money Bancomer is on the south-east side of the zócalo. Banamex is a block south at the corner of Calles 2 Sur Ote and 1 Ote Sur.

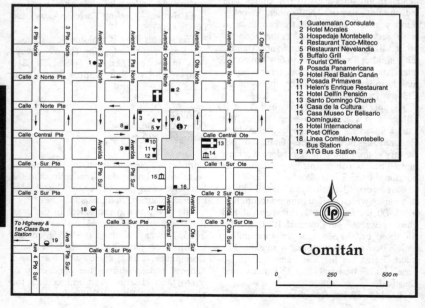

1 Guatemalan Consulate
2 Hotel Morales
3 Hospedaje Montebello
4 Restaurant Taco-Miteco
5 Restaurant Nevelandia
6 Buffalo Grill
7 Tourist Office
8 Posada Panamericana
9 Hotel Real Balún Canán
10 Posada Primavera
11 Helen's Enrique Restaurant
12 Hotel Delfín Pensión
13 Santo Domingo Church
14 Casa de la Cultura
15 Casa Museo Dr Belisario Domínguez
16 Hotel Internacional
17 Post Office
18 Linea Comitán-Montebello Bus Station
19 ATG Bus Station

Comitán

0   250   500 m

Post & Telecommunications The post office is on Avenida Central Sur between 2 and 3 Sur, 1½ blocks south of zócalo. Hours are Monday to Friday 8 am to 7 pm, Saturday 8 am to 1 pm). There's a Ladatel phone at the south-west corner of the zócalo, and a Lada caseta on 2 Sur Pte, half a block west of Avenida Central Sur.

Foreign Consulates The Guatemalan Consulate (☎ (963) 2 26 69) is at Avenida 2 Pte Nte 28, open 8 am to 1 pm and 2.30 to 4.30 pm Monday to Friday. Visas (for those who need them) cost US$10 and take about half an hour to get.

Things to See
On the east side of the zócalo, **Santo Domingo church** dates from the 16th century. The adjacent **Casa de la Cultura**, on the south-eastern corner of the zócalo, includes an exhibition gallery, auditorium, and museum.

Casa Museo Dr Belisario Domínguez, the family home of the martyr-hero, has been turned into a museum that provides fascinating insights into the medical practices and the life of the professional classes in turn-of-the-century Comitán. The museum is at Avenida Central Sur 29, half a block south of the zócalo. It's open from 10 am to 6.45 pm Tuesday to Saturday. Admission costs US$0.50.

Places to Stay – bottom end
Comitán has several cheap posadas with small, often dingy rooms, most of them OK for a night. *Posada Primavera*, Calle Central Pte 4, only a few steps west of the zócalo, charges US$5.25 per bed for rooms with sinks, but without bath or windows; doubles are US$6.75. The *Hospedaje Montebello* (☎ (963) 2-17-70), a block further at Calle 1 Norte Pte 10, has acceptable rooms around a courtyard for US$5/10 a single/double. *Posada Panamericana*, at the corner of Calle Central Pte and Avenida 1 Pte Nte, has dark downstairs cubicles for US$4, and upstairs brighter, breezier rooms for US$8.

Posada Las Flores (☎ (963) 2-33-34), 1 Pte Nte 15, half a block north of Calle 2 Nte, has rooms round a quiet courtyard; beds are rented for US$6 each. Its less comfortable neighbour, *Posada San Miguel* charges US$3.25 per bed; it's clean but you get what you pay for here.

Places to Stay – middle
Hotel Delfín Pensión (☎ (963) 2-00-13), Avenida Central on the west side of the zócalo, has spacious rooms with private baths (hot water intermittent). Back rooms are modern and overlook a leafy courtyard. Singles/doubles are US$15/18.

The *Hotel Morales* (☎ (963) 2-04-36), Avenida Central Norte, 1½ blocks north of the zócalo, resembles an aircraft hangar with small rooms perched round an upstairs walkway. With private baths, rooms are US$18.

The *Hotel Internacional* (☎ (963) 2-01-10), a block south of the zócalo on Avenida Central Sur 16 at Calle 2 Sur, has clean, bright but no-frills rooms for US$20/25.

Comitán's most polished place is *Hotel Real Balún Canán* (☎ (963) 2-10-94), a block west of the zócalo at Avenida 1 Pte Sur 7. Prints of Frederick Catherwood's 1844 drawings of Mayan ruins decorate the stairs and the small rooms are comfortable with TV and phone. The rate is US$46 a double.

Places to Eat
Several reasonable cafés line the west side of the zócalo. Prime among them is *Helen's Enrique Restaurant*, in front of the Hotel Delfín. With a porch and pretensions to decor, Helen's serves buttered biscuits with beans and cheese for US$3, antojitos, fried chicken, pizza, or huevos rancheros for a bit more. Main dishes cost between US$4 and US$7. *Restaurant Acuario*, *Restaurant Yuly*, and *Restaurant Vicks*, in the same row, are more basic and cheaper.

Restaurant Nevelandia, on the north-west corner of the zócalo, has tacos for US$0.30 to US$0.75, antojitos, spaghetti and burgers for around US$3, and meat dishes typically for US$6.

YUCATÁN

The friendly, colorful *Taco-Miteco*, on Avenida Central Norte 5 near the zócalo, serves 13 varieties of tacos for US$0.50 each, quesadillas or veggie queso for US$2, and a 'super-breakfast' of juice, coffee, eggs, toast and chilaquiles for US$3.

For a festive meal under wagon wheel chandeliers head for the *Buffalo Grill* on Central Nte 4, near 1 Nte Pte. Live music and yards of beer (US$2.25), complement the atmosphere. The US$6 large buffalo pizza has a bit of everything on it; tacos and quesadillas are about US$2.50, while chicken and meat specials run about US$6.

For a more expensive meal amid international-style surroundings go to the Hotel Real's Balún Canán, where *El Escocés Restaurant* is open until 11 pm and the *Grill Bar* until 1 am.

Getting There & Away

Comitán is 85 km south-east down the Interamerican Highway from San Cristóbal, and 80 km north of Ciudad Cuauhtémoc. Buses are regularly stopped for document checks by immigration officials, both north and south of Comitán, so keep your passport handy.

For directions to the Cristóbal Colón, ATG and Linea Comitán-Montebello terminals, see the Orientation section above. Departures include:

Ciudad Cuauhtémoc (Guatemalan border) – 80 km, 1½ hours; three 1st-class buses (US$2.50) by Cristóbal Colón; six 2nd-class buses (US$1.75) by ATG.

Mexico City – 1168 km, 21½ hours; one 1st-class bus (US$36) and one 1st-class Plus (US$46) by Cristóbal Colón.

Palenque – 275 km, seven hours; one morning bus by Linea Comitán-Montebello for US$5.

San Cristóbal de las Casas – 83 km, 1½ hours; three morning locals, one evening direct and a dozen buses de paso by ATG for US$2.75.

Tapachula – 260 km, seven hours (via Motozintla); two direct morning buses, and one 2 pm (only to Motozintla, combi to Tapachula) 2nd-class bus (US$5.75) by ATG.

Tuxtla Gutiérrez – 170 km, 3½ hours; nine 1st-class buses (US$5) by Cristóbal Colón and three 2nd-class buses (US$4) by ATG.

LAGOS DE MONTEBELLO

The temperate forest along the Guatemalan border south-east of Comitán is dotted with about 60 small lakes – the Lagos or Lagunas de Montebello. The area is beautiful, refreshing, not hard to reach, quiet and eminently good for hiking. Some Mexican weekenders come down here in their cars, but the rest of the time you'll see nobody except the few resident villagers and a small handful of visitors. There are two very basic hostelries, a campground and a restaurant. And at one edge of the lake district are the rarely visited Mayan ruins of Chinkultic. A number of Guatemalan refugee camps are in and around the lakes area.

Orientation

The paved road to Montebello turns east off the Interamerican Highway 16 km south of Comitán, just before the town of La Trinitaria. Running first through flat ranch and ejido land, it passes the track to Chinkultic after 30 km, entering the forest and Montebello National Park five km further on. At the park entrance (no fee) the road splits. The paved section continues four km ahead to the Lagunas de Colores, where it dead-ends at two small houses 50 metres from Laguna Bosque Azul. To the right (east) from the park entrance a dirt road leads past tracks to several more lakes, then to the village and lake of Tziscao (nine km).

Chinkultic

These dramatically sited ruins lie two km along a track leading north off the La Trinitaria-Montebello road, 27 km from the Interamerican Highway at the village of Hidalgo. A sign, 'Chinkultic 3', marks the turning. Doña María at La Orquidea restaurant, half a km further along the road, has a map and book on Chinkultic.

Chinkultic was on the extreme western edge of the ancient Mayan area. Dates carved here extend from 591 to 897 AD – the last of which is nearly a century after the latest dates at Palenque, Yaxchilán and Toniná. These years no doubt span Chinkultic's peak period, but occupation is thought to have

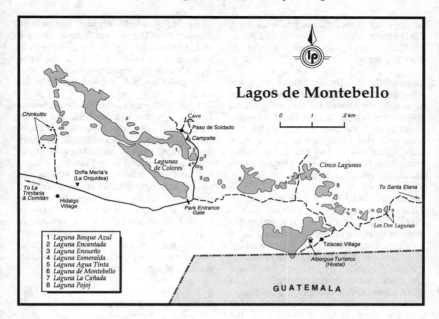

Lagos de Montebello

0   1   2 km

1 Laguna Bosque Azul
2 Laguna Encantada
3 Laguna Ensueño
4 Laguna Esmeralda
5 Laguna Agua Tinta
6 Laguna de Montebello
7 Laguna La Cañada
8 Laguna Pojoj

Chinkultic

Cave
Paso de Soldado
Campsite

Lagunas de Colores

Cinco Lagunas

Doña María's (La Orquidea)

To La Trinitaria & Comitán

Hidalgo Village

Park Entrance Gate

To Santa Elena

Los Dos Lagunas

Tziscao Village

Albergue Turístico (Hostal)

GUATEMALA

YUCATÁN

started in the late Pre-Classic (around 200 AD) period and continued until after 900. Of the 200 mounds scattered over a wide area, few parts have been cleared, but still it's worth the effort.

The track from the road brings you first to a gate with a hut on the left. Here take the path to the left, which curves round to the right. On the overgrown hill to the right of this path stands one of Chinkultic's major structures, called simply E23. The path leads to a long ball court where several stelae lie on their sides under thatched shelters. Other stelae – some carved with Mayan-looking human figures – lie in the vicinity.

Follow the track back to the hut and turn left, passing what could be a car parking area, soon after which you can spot a few stone mounds in the undergrowth to the right. The hillside ahead of you shortly comes into full view and on it the partly restored temple called El Mirador. The path goes over a stream and steeply up to El Mirador, from

which there are good views of the surrounding lakes and down into a big 50-metre-deep cenote.

Lakes

Lagunas de Colores The paved road straight on from the park entrance leads through the Lagunas de Colores, so called because their colours range from turquoise to deep green. The first of these, on the right after about two km, is Laguna Agua Tinta. Then on the left come Laguna Esmeralda followed by Laguna Encantada, with Laguna Ensueño on the right opposite Encantada. The fifth and biggest of the Lagunas de Colores is Laguna Bosque Azul, on the left where the road ends. One of the two small houses here sells drinks and food, and there's a lakeside campsite.

Two paths lead on from the end of the road. Proceeding straight on for 800 metres brings you to the gruta – a cave shrine where locals make offerings to ward off illness and so on (take a torch/flashlight with you). Taking the path to the left, you reach Paso de Soldado, a picnic site beside a small river after 300 metres.

Laguna de Montebello About three km along the dirt road towards Tziscao (which turns right at the park entrance), a track leads 200 metres left to Laguna de Montebello. This is one of the bigger lakes, with a flat, open area along its shore where the track ends. About 150 metres to the left is a stony area which is better for swimming than the muddy fringes elsewhere.

Cinco Lagunas A further three km along the Tziscao road another track leads left to these 'five lakes'. Only four of them are visible from the road, but the second, La Cañada, on the right after about 1.5 km, is probably the most beautiful of all the Montebello Lakes – it's nearly bisected by two rocky outcrops. The track eventually reaches the village of San Antonio and, amazingly, is a bus route.

Laguna Pojoj A further km along the Tziscao road, a track to the left leads to this lake one km off the road.

Laguna Tziscao This comes into view on the right a further km along the road. Continue on to the junction for Tziscao village on the right. The village has pleasant grassy streets, friendly people and a hostel.

Places to Stay & Eat
Half a km past the Chinkultic turn-off, you can camp or rent a cabin at *La Orquidea*, a small restaurant on the left of the road. The owner, Señora María Domínguez de Castellanos, better known as Doña María, has helped Guatemalan refugees by buying a nearby farm and turning it over to them. For the cabins, which have electric light but no running water, you pay US$3; meals are a bit less.

Inside the national park, camping is officially allowed only at Laguna Bosque Azul (no fee), the last and biggest of the Lagunas de Colores, where the paved road ends.

There are toilets and water here. *Bosque Azul Restaurant*, at the Laguna Bosque Azul car park, serves eggs (US$2), chiles rellenos or meaty dishes (US$4), and drinks, chips and fruit. Outside the restaurant, local cowboys wait, eager to guide you (by horse) to the caves (US$3).

Tziscao village has a hostel – the *Albergue Turístico* – where you pay US$3 per person for a dormitory bunk or a wooden cabaña, or camp for US$1. The hostel lies on the shore of one of the most beautiful lakes – you can rent a rowing boat – and Guatemala is just a few hundred metres away. Entering the village, turn right beside a corner store soon after you come level with a small church on the hill, and follow the track down towards the lake, then round to the left. The señora will cook up eggs, frijoles and tortillas (US$2) and there's a fridge full of refrescos. The toilets seem to be in permanent desperate need of a good clean.

Getting There & Away
It's possible to make a whirlwind tour of Chinkultic and the lakes in a day from San Cristóbal – either by public transport or tour, but if you prefer a pace that enables you to absorb something of your surroundings, it's better to stay at the lakes or at least at Comitán.

Buses and combis to the Lagos de Montebello go from the yard of Linea Comitán-Montebello in Comitán. One or the other leaves every 20 or 30 minutes up to about 5 pm. Vehicles have a number of different destinations so make sure you get one that's going your way.

Most people head initially for Chinkultic, Doña María's (La Orquidea), Lagunas de Colores, Laguna de Montebello or Tziscao. The last vehicle to Tziscao (1¼ hours, US$2) is at about 2 pm. By combi it's 45 minutes to Doña María's; a local bus can take up to 1½ hours (US$1.75). It's the same fare to the Chinkultic turnoff or Lagunas de Colores.

Returning to Comitán, the last bus leaves Lagunas de Colores at 4.30 pm. There's a steady trickle of vehicles through the lakes area, making hitching possible.

MOTOZINTLA

The small town of Motozintla lies in a deep valley in the Sierra Madre 70 km south-west of Ciudad Cuauhtémoc. A good road leads to it from the Interamerican Highway a few km north of Ciudad Cuauhtémoc, then continues down to Huixtla near the Chiapas coast near Tapachula – a spectacular, unusual trip. Be sure to carry your passport as there are immigration checks along the way.

GUATEMALAN BORDER – CIUDAD CUAUHTÉMOC

Ciudad Cuauhtémoc is just a few houses and a comedor or two, but it's the last/first place in Mexico on the Interamerican Highway (Highway 190). Comitán is 80 km away, San Cristóbal is 165 km. Ciudad Cuauhtémoc is the Mexican border post; the Guatemalan post is three km south at La Mesilla. If your bus from Comitán or San Cristóbal isn't going on to La Mesilla, there are taxis (US$2), combis and trucks (US$0.50) across the no-man's-land.

If yours is a passport which requires only a tourist card (see Facts for the Visitor), you can get it at the border. If you need a visa, obtain it in advance at the Guatemalan Consulate in Comitán.

There's no bank at this border. Individual money changers operate here but they give you fewer quetzals than a bank would.

Getting There and Away

Cristóbal Colón runs two 1st-class buses daily each way between Ciudad Cuauhtémoc and Comitán (US$2.50, 1½ hours), San Cristóbal de las Casas (US$3.50, three hours) and Tuxtla (US$8, five hours). At the time of writing, departures from the border are 6 am, 12.30 pm and 3.30 pm. It is often easier to use one of the twenty or so daily 2nd-class buses of ATG, or other buses en route to Comitán.

Guatemalan buses depart La Mesilla for main points inside Guatemala like Huehuetenango (84 km, 1½ hours), Quetzaltenango (also known as Xela, 174 km, 3½ hours) and Guatemala City (349 km, seven hours). Lago de Atitlán (245 km, five hours) and Chichicastenango (244 km, five hours) both lie a few km off the Interamerican Highway. Before boarding a bus at La Mesilla, try to find out when it's leaving and when it reaches your destination. This could save you several hours of sitting in stationary buses.

THE SOCONUSCO

Along the Pacific coast of Chiapas is the hot, fertile plain known as the Soconusco, 15 to 35 km wide, which has quite heavy rainfall from June to October, especially in July and August. Inland and parallel to the coast is the range of the Sierra Madre de Chiapas, mostly between 1000 and 2500 metres but higher in the south where the Tacaná volcano on the Guatemalan border reaches 4092 metres.

Coastal Chiapas, a rich source of cacao, was conquered by the Aztecs at the end of the 15th century and became their empire's most distant province, under the name Xoconochco. Soconusco was the first part of Chiapas to be subdued by the Spaniards, lying as it did on Pedro de Alvarado's route to conquer Guatemala in 1524.

Arriaga

Arriaga, where the Juchitán-Tapachula road meets the Tuxtla Gutiérrez-Tapachula road, has a few suitable lodgings and restaurants, but no good reason for you to stop.

For some reason, quite a few buses end their runs in Arriaga. Happily, the same number start their runs here. The new Centro de Autobuses houses all the 1st and 2nd-class buses serving Arriaga. Departures include:

Juchitán – 135 km, two hours; three 1st-class buses daily by Cristóbal Colón (US$3.30); many 2nd-class buses by Sur and Fletes y Pasajes/Transportes Oaxaca-Istmo.

Mexico City (TAPO) – 900 km, 16 hours, one afternoon Cristóbal Colón bus (US$34), and a Plus at 6.30 pm (US$43), 2nd-class buses daily by Fletes Y Pasajes/Transportes Oaxaca-Istmo.

Oaxaca – 400 km, seven hours; a 10 pm bus by Cristóbal Colón (US$13), a few 2nd-class buses daily by Sur and Fletes Y Pasajes/Transportes Oaxaca-Istmo.

Salina Cruz – 175 km, three hours; several buses daily by Cristóbal Colón for US$6.25, and by Sur.

San Cristóbal de las Casas – 240 km, five hours; buses every 30 minutes (via Tuxtla) by Cristóbal Colón (US$6.50), several by ATG for US$6.

Tapachula – 245 km, 3½ hours; seven buses daily by Cristóbal Colón (US$8), and by Sur and ATG.

Tonalá – 23 km, 30 minutes; Transportes-Arriaga-Tonalá microbuses every few minutes for US$0.75.

Tuxtla Gutiérrez – 155 km, three hours; every hour by Cristóbal Colón (US$4.50), 2nd-class buses daily by ATG.

Tonalá

Twenty-three km south-east of Arriaga on Highway 200, Tonalá has only marginally more intrinsic appeal but is the jumping-off point for the laid-back beach spot of Puerto Arista. A tall pre-Hispanic stele in the Tonalá main plaza appears to depict Tláloc, the central Mexican rain god. There's also a small regional museum at Hidalgo 77, with some archaeological pieces found in the region.

The tourist office (☎ (966) 3-01-01) is on the ground floor of the Palacio Municipal (look for its clock), on the Hidalgo side of the zócalo. It's open 9 am to 3 pm and 6 to 8 pm Monday to Friday, and 9 am to 2 pm Saturday.

Tonalá has no great accommodation deals. If you're heading for Puerto Arista, go straight there if you can.

Puerto Arista

Puerto Arista, 18 km south-west of Tonalá, is a half-km collection of palm shacks and a few more substantial buildings in the middle of a 30-km grey beach. The food's mostly fish, you get through a lot of refrescos, and nothing else happens except the crashing of the Pacific waves...until the weekend, when a few hundred Chiapanecos cruise in from the towns, or until Semana Santa and Christmas, when they come in the thousands, and the residents make their money for the year.

Usually the most action you'll see is when

an occasional fishing boat puts out to sea, or a piglet breaks into a trot if a dog gathers the energy to bark at it. Mosquitos and sand fleas seem to be the only relentless energetic beings in town. The temperature's usually sweltering if you stray more than a few yards from the shore, and it's humid in summer.

The sea is clean here but don't go far from the beach: there's an undertow, and rip tides known as *canales* can sweep you a long way out in a short time.

TAPACHULA
Population: 220,000

Most travellers come to Mexico's southernmost city only because it's a gateway to Guatemala; though for ruins buffs, Izapa, 11 km east, is worth a visit.

Tapachula is a busy commercial centre, overlooked by the 4092-metre Tacaná volcano to its north-east, the first of a chain of volcanoes stretching down into Guatemala.

Orientation
Bus stations are scattered north-east and north-west of the zócalo.

Information
Tourist Office The tourist office (☎ (962) 6-54-70; fax 6-55-22) is at Avenida 4 Nte 35, a few doors north of Hospedaje Colonial, on the 3rd floor, and has few customers.

Money Several banks around the city centre will change dollars and quetzals, but for a little extra commission. The Casa de Cambio Tapachula at the corner of Calle 3 Pte and Avenida 4 Nte is quicker and open longer – 7.30 am to 7.30 pm Monday to Saturday and 7 am to 2 pm Sunday.

Post & Telephone The post office is several blocks from the centre at the corner of Calle 1 Ote and Avenida 9 Nte and is open 8 am to 6 pm Monday to Friday, 8 am to noon Saturday. Tapachula's postal code is 30700.

There are Lada casetas on Calle 17 Ote, 1½ blocks west of the Cristóbal Colón bus

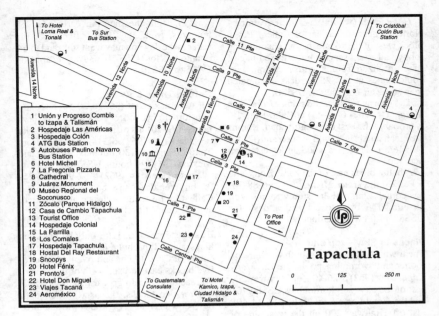

Tapachula

1 Unión y Progreso Combis to Izapa & Talismán
2 Hospedaje Las Américas
3 Hospedaje Colón
4 ATG Bus Station
5 Autobuses Paulino Navarro Bus Station
6 Hotel Michell
7 La Fregonia Pizzaria
8 Cathedral
9 Juárez Monument
10 Museo Regional del Soconusco
11 Zócalo (Parque Hidalgo)
12 Casa de Cambio Tapachula
13 Tourist Office
14 Hospedaje Colonial
15 La Parrilla
16 Los Comales
17 Hospedaje Tapachula
18 Hostal Del Ray Restaurant
19 Snoopys
20 Hotel Fénix
21 Pronto's
22 Hotel Don Miguel
23 Viajes Tacaná
24 Aeroméxico

station, and in the Farmacia Monaco across from Hotel Don Miguel on Calle 1 Pte.

Foreign Consulate The Guatemalan Consulate (☎ (962) 6-12-52) is at Calle 2 Ote 33, between Avenidas 7 and 9 Sur. It's open 8 am to 4 pm Monday to Friday. Visas are issued quickly.

Soconusco Regional Museum
The Museo Regional del Soconusco on the west side of the zócalo has some archaeological and folklore exhibits, including some finds from Izapa. Entry is US$3.25.

Places to Stay – bottom end
The friendly *Hospedaje Las Américas* (☎ (962) 6-27-57), at Avenida 10 Nte 47 north of the zócalo, has singles with fans and private bathroom for US$6.50/8 a single, double. The *Hospedaje Colón*, on Avenida Central Nte, a couple of doors north of Calle

9 Ote, has small, noisy, mosquito-inhabited rooms with fans for US$10/13.

The *Hospedaje Colonial* (☎ (962) 6-20-52), at Avenida 4 Nte 31, half a block north of Calle 3 Pte, has clean, bright rooms with private baths along a balcony for US$6.50 per person. Ring the bell to enter.

Around the corner (one block west) from the Cristóbal Colón bus station is the *Hospedaje Chelito* (☎ (962) 6-24-28), at Avenida 1 Nte 107 between Calle 15 Pte and 17 Pte. Rooms are clean, pink and pretty. For a black and white TV, fan and private bathroom you pay US$15, for US$20 you get a color TV and air-con. Attached is a small café.

Places to Stay – middle
The *Hotel Santa Julia* (☎ (962) 6-31-40), Calle 17 Ote 5, next door to the Cristóbal Colón 1st-class bus station, has clean singles/doubles with TV, telephone and private bath for US$29/32.

Hotel Fénix (☎ (962) 5-07-55), Avenida 4 Norte 19 near the corner of Calle 1 Pte, a block west of the zócalo, has an encouraging lobby and room service but a mixed bag of medium-sized rooms within. Some fan-cooled ones at US$25 are less dilapidated than some air-con ones at US$30.

The nearby modern and pricier *Hotel Don Miguel* (☎ (962) 6-11-43) at Calle 1 Pte 18, is probably the best city centre hotel. Rooms are clean and bright with air-con and TV for US$46/56. There's a good little restaurant here too.

A half a block east of the zócalo, on Calle 5 Pte 23, the *Hotel Michell* (962) 6-88-74) has comely 2nd and 3rd-storey rooms with air-con, TV, big closets and a desk for US$35/44 for a single/double.

Places to Stay – top end

The town's two top hotels, both with air-con rooms and swimming pools, are the *Motel Kamico* (☎ (962) 6-26-40), on Highway 200 east of the city (singles/doubles US$60/70), and the *Hotel Loma Real* (☎ (962) 6-14-40), just off Highway 200 on the west side of town, where rooms are US$75.

Places to Eat

Several restaurants line the south side of the zócalo. *Los Comales* serves antojitos for US$3, meat dishes US$4 to US$7, a filling comida corrida for US$5 and a breakfast of eggs, coffee and juice for US$3. *La Parrilla*, across the street at Avenida 8 Norte, is probably better value, and open 24 hours. There's a big choice of good meat dishes for about US$5, and breakfast for US$3. *Pronto's*, on Calle 1 Pte between Avenidas 4 and 2 Norte, is also open 24 hours but is a bit dearer.

If the sun is in, you may want to sit out on the sidewalk cafe of *La Fregonia Pizzaría*, the pedestrian extension of Calle 5 Pte, half a block west of the zócalo. Pizzas, pastas, burgers and antojitos are all between US$3 and US$6.

Breakfast at *Hostal Del Rey Restaurant*, Avenida 4 Norte 17 near Calle 3 Pte, with its quiet music, waiters in pink bow ties and cummerbunds, and pretty decor, is a nice

way to begin the day. An early meal of hotcakes, fruit, eggs and coffee is US$4. Later in the day you may want soup and salad or antojitos for US$3.50, or aves or carne for US$6 to US$10.

Getting There & Away

Air Aeroméxico (☎ (962) 6-20-50) has daily nonstop flights to/from Mexico City (1½ hours, US$70). Its office is at Avenida 2 Nte 6. Aviacsa (☎ (962) 6-31-47) flies to/from Tuxtla Gutiérrez (30 minutes, US$77) and Mexico City (2½ hours, US$70).

Viajes Tacaná (☎ (962) 6-87-95; fax 6-35-02) on Avenida 4 Nte 8, between Calle 1 and Calle Central, sells Aviacsa, Aeroméxico, and Mexicana tickets.

Bus Cristóbal Colón is the only 1st-class bus line serving Tapachula. Its terminus is at the corner of Calle 17 Ote and Avenida 3 Norte, five blocks east and six north of the zócalo. To reach the zócalo go west (left) along 17 Ote for two blocks, then six blocks south (left) down Avenida Central Norte and three west (right) along Calle 5 Pte.

The main 2nd-class bus stations are Sur, at Calle 9 Pte 63, a block west of Avenida 12 Norte; Autotransportes Tuxtla Gutiérrez (ATG), at the corner of Calle 9 Ote and Avenida 3 Norte; and Autobuses Paulino Navarro, on Calle 7 Pte 5, half a block west of Avenida Central Norte.

Buses to/from the Guatemalan border are covered in the Talisman & Ciudad Hidalgo section. Other departures include:

Arriaga – 245 km, 3½ hours; eight buses (US$9) by Cristóbal Colón, three afternoon buses (US$6) by ATG, buses every 30 minutes by Autobuses Paulino Navarro (US$6).

Comitán – 260 km, seven hours (via Motozintla); three buses (US$12) by ATG; several by Paulino Navarro (US$13).

Juchitán – 380 km, six hours; three buses by ATG (US$12), several daily by Sur.

Mexico City – 1150 km, 20 hours; six regular Cristóbal Colón buses (US$43) and two afternoon Plus buses (US$53).

Oaxaca – 650 km, 11 hours; two Cristóbal Colón buses (US$43), and one evening Plus (US$21), and one 2nd-class evening by Sur.

Salina Cruz – 420 km, seven hours; two buses daily by ATG (US$14).

San Cristóbal de las Casas – 350 km, eight hours; 15 buses by Cristóbal Colón (via Tuxtla) for US$14, three by ATG for US$7.

Tonalá – 220 km, three hours; eight 1st-class buses daily by Cristóbal Colón (US$7), three by ATG (US$5.50), several by Sur.

Tuxtla Gutiérrez – 400 km, seven hours; 15 buses by Cristóbal Colón (US$12), six buses by ATG (US$10), two by Sur.

Train The station lies just south of the intersection of Avenida Central Sur and Calle 14. Only masochists, the dull-witted and the hopelessly adventurous take the train.

Getting Around

Tapachula airport is 18 km south of the city off the Puerto Madero road. Transportes Terrestre (☎ (962) 6-12-87) at Avenida 2 Sur 40-A charges US$3.25 to the airport and will pick you up from any hotel in Tapachula. A taxi is US$7.

AROUND TAPACHULA
Izapa Ruins

If this site was in a more visited part of Mexico it would have a constant stream of visitors, for it's not only important to archaeologists as a link between the Olmecs and the Maya but interesting to walk around. It flourished from approximately 200 BC to 200 AD. The Izapa carving style – typically seen on stelae with alters placed in front – is derived from the Olmec style and most of the gods shown are the descendants of Olmec deities, with their upper lips grotesquely lengthened. Early Maya monuments from lowland north Guatemala are similar.

Northern Area Most of this part of the site has been cleared and some restoration has been done. There are a number of platforms, a ball court, and several of the stelae and altars whose carvings provide Izapa's main interest for archaeologists. The platforms and ball court were probably built some time after Izapa was at its peak.

Southern Area This area is less visited than the northern area. Go back about 1.75 km along the road towards Tapachula and take a dirt road to the left. Where the vehicle track ends, a path leads to the right. There are three areas of interest – you may have to ask the caretaker to find and explain them, as they are separated by foot trails that are less than obvious. One is a plaza with several stelae under thatched roofs. The second is a smaller plaza with more stelae and three big pillars topped with curious stone balls. The third has just one item – a carving of the jaws of a jaguar holding a seemingly human figure.

Getting There & Away Izapa is 11 km east of Tapachula on the road to Talismán. You can reach it by the combis of Unión y Progreso which depart from Calle 5 Pte, half a block west of Avenida 12 Nte in Tapachula. The main (northern) part of the site is marked on the left of the road. The second (southern) part lies less than one km back towards Tapachula on the other side of the road.

TALISMÁN & CIUDAD HIDALGO (GUATEMALAN BORDER)

The road from Tapachula to Guatemala heads 20 km east past Izapa ruins to the border at Talismán bridge, opposite El Carmen, Guatemala. A branch south of this road leads to another border crossing at Ciudad Hidalgo (38 km from Tapachula), opposite Ciudad Tecún Umán. Both crossings are open 24 hours.

At the time of writing it was possible to obtain Guatemalan visas as well as tourist cards at the border, but check in advance. There's a Guatemalan Consulate at Ote 10 in Ciudad Hidalgo, as well as the one in Tapachula. The Guatemalan border may make various small charges as you go through, and insist that you pay for your tourist card in US dollars or quetzals, so get some before you leave Tapachula.

Getting There & Away

Combis of Unión y Progreso shuttle between Tapachula and Talismán every few minutes. The fare is US$0.75. A taxi from Tapachula to Talismán takes 20 minutes and costs US$3.

Autobuses Paulino Navarro makes the 45-minute journey between Tapachula and Ciudad Hidalgo every hour for US$1.

There are two daily Cristóbal Colón 1st-class buses from Talismán to Mexico City for US$43.

For information on the border crossing, see the Guatemala section.

Glossary

Abrazo – embrace, hug. In particular, the formal, ceremonial hug between political leaders.

Alux, aluxes – Mayan for gremlin, leprechaun, benevolent 'little people'

Apartado Postal – post office box, abbreviated *Apdo Postal*

Ayuntamiento – often seen as *H Ayuntamiento* (*Honorable Ayuntamiento*) on the front of Town Hall buildings, it translates as 'Municipal Government'.

Barrio – district, neighbourhood

Billete – banknote (unlike in Spain where it's a ticket)

Boleto – ticket (bus, train, museum, etc)

Caballeros – literally 'horsemen', but corresponds to 'gentlemen' in English; look for it on toilet doors

Cacique – Indian chief; also used to describe provincial warlord or strongman

Cafetería – literally 'coffee-shop', it refers to any informal restaurant with waiter service; it is not usually a cafeteria in the American sense of a self-service restaurant

Callejón – alley or small, narrow or very short street

Camión – truck; bus

Casa de cambio – moneychanger. In Mexico it offers exchange rates comparable to or better than banks and is much faster to use.

Caseta de larga distancia – long-distance telephone station, often shortened to *caseta*

Cazuela – clay cooking pot, usually sold in a nested set

Cenote – large natural limestone cave used for water storage (or ceremonial purposes) in Yucatán

Cerveza – beer

Chac – Mayan god of rain

Chac-mool – Mayan sacrificial stone sculpture

Chapín – a citizen of Guatemala; Guatemalan

Charro – cowboy

Chingar – literally 'to rape' but in practice a word with a wide range of colloquial meanings similar to the use of 'to screw' or 'to fuck' in English.

Chultún – artificial Mayan cistern found at Puuc archaeological sites south of Mérida

Churrigueresque – Spanish baroque architectural style of the early 18th century, with lavish ornamentation; named for architect José Churriguera

Cigarro – cigarette

Cocina – literally 'kitchen', also seen as *cocina económica* (economical kitchen) or *cocina familiar* (family kitchen). It's a cookshop, a small, basic restaurant usually run by one woman, often located in or near a municipal market; see also *lonchería*

Colectivo – jitney taxi or minibus (usually a *combi*, or Volkswagen minibus) which picks up and drops off passengers along its route

Completo – full up, a sign you may see on hotel desks in crowded cities

Conquistador – Spanish explorer-conqueror of Latin America

Correos – post office

Curandero – Indian traditional healer

Damas – ladies, the usual sign on toilet doors

Dzul, dzules – Mayan for foreigners or 'townfolk', that is, not Maya from the countryside

Ejido – in Mexico, communally owned Indian land taken over by landowners but returned to the original owners under a program initiated by President Lázaro Cárdenas

Encomienda – Spanish colonial practice of putting Indians under the 'guardianship' of landowners, practically akin to medieval serfdom

Estación ferrocarril – railway station

Ferrocarril – railway

Galón, galones – US gallons (fluid measure; sometimes used in Guatemala)

Gringo/a – male/female European or North American visitor to Mexico

Gruta – cave

Guayabera – man's thin fabric shirt with pockets and appliquéd designs on the front, over the shoulders and down the back; worn instead of a jacket and tie

Guardarropa – cloakroom, place to leave parcels when entering an establishment

Hacienda – estate; also 'Treasury', as in *Departamento de Hacienda*, Treasury Department

Hay – pronounced like 'eye', meaning 'there is', 'there are'. You're equally likely to hear *no hay*, 'there isn't' or 'there aren't'.

Henequen – agave fibre used to make rope, grown particularly around Mérida in Yucatán

Huipil – woven white dress from the Mayan regions with intricate, colourful embroidery

IMSS – Instituto Mexicana de Seguridad Social, the Mexican Social Security Institute; it operates many of Mexico's larger public hospitals. In Guatemala the corresponding institution is the IGSS.

IVA – the *impuesto al valor agregado* or 'ee-vah' is a value-added tax which can be as high as 15% and is added to many items in Mexico

Kukulcán – Mayan name for the Aztec-Toltec plumed serpent Quetzalcóatl

Larga distancia – long-distance telephone, abbreviated as Lada; see also Caseta de larga distancia

Lavandería – laundry; a *lavandería automática* is a coin-operated laundry (laundromat)

Leng – colloquial Mayan term for coins (Guatemalan highlands)

Libras – pounds (weight; sometimes used in Guatemala)

Lista de correos – poste restante or general delivery; literally 'mail list,' the list of addressees for whom mail is being held, displayed in the post office

Lonchería – from English *lunch*; a simple restaurant which may in fact serve meals all day (not just lunch). You often see loncherías near municipal markets.

Lleno – full (fuel tank)

Machismo – maleness, masculine virility. An ever-present aspect of Mexican society.

Manzana – apple; also a city block. A *supermanzana* is a large group of city blocks bounded by major avenues. Ciudad Cancún uses manzana and supermanzana numbers as addresses.

Mariachi – small ensemble of street musicians; strolling mariachi bands often perform in restaurants

Mestizo – people of mixed blood (Spanish and Indian); the word now more commonly means 'Mexican'

Metate – flattish stone on which corn is ground

Millas – miles (distance); sometimes used in Guatemala

Montezuma's revenge – Mexican version of 'Delhi-belly' or travellers' diarrhoea

Mordida – 'little bite,' or small bribe that's usually paid to keep the wheels of bureaucracy turning. Giving a *mordida* to a traffic policeman may ensure that you won't have a bigger traffic fine to pay.

Mudéjar – Moorish architectural style

Mujeres – women

Onzas – ounces (weight); sometimes used in Guatemala

Palacio de Gobierno – building housing the executive offices of a state or regional government

Palacio Municipal – Town Hall, seat of the corporation or municipal government

Palapa – thatched roof; palm leaves are used for thatch

Parada – bus stop, usually for city buses

Pisto – colloquial Mayan term for money, quetzals (Guatemalan highlands)

Pie, pies – foot, feet (unit of measure; sometimes used in Guatemala)

Pinchazo – automobile tyre repair shop (Guatemala)

Plateresque – 'silversmith-like'; the architectural style of the Spanish renaissance (16th century), rich in decoration

Plazuela – small plaza

PRI – Institutional Revolutionary Party. The controlling force in Mexican politics for more than half a century.

Propino, propina – a tip, different from a *mordida*, which is really a bribe

Puro – cigar

Quetzalcóatl – plumed serpent god of the Aztecs and Toltecs

Rebozo – long woollen or linen scarf covering the head or shoulders

Retablo – ornate gilded, carved decoration of wood in a church

Retorno – 'return'; in Cancún, a U-shaped street which starts from a major boulevard, loops around and 'returns' to the boulevard a block away

Sacbé, sacbeob – ceremonial limestone avenue or path between great Mayan cities

Sanatorio – hospital, particularly a small private one

Sanitario – literally 'sanitary'; usually means toilet

Serape – traditional woollen blanket

Stelae – standing stone monuments, usually carved (sing. *stele*)

Supermercado – supermarket, ranging from a corner store to a large, American-style supermarket.

Taller – shop or workshop. A *taller mecánico* is a mechanic's shop, usually for cars. A *taller de llantas* is a tyre-repair shop (Mexico)

Teléfono monedero – coin-operated telephone (Guatemala)

Templo – in Mexico, a church; anything from a wayside chapel to a cathedral

Tequila – clear, distilled liquor produced, like pulque and mezcal, from the maguey cactus

Tex-Mex – Americanised version of Mexican food

Típico – typical or characteristic of a region; particularly used to describe food

Topes – speed-break ridges found in many Mexican towns, indicated by a highway sign bearing a row of little bumps

Viajero – traveller

Vulcanizadora – automobile tyre repair shop (Mexico)

War of the Castes – bloody Mayan uprising in Yucatán during the mid-19th century

Zócalo – Aztec for 'pedestal' or 'plinth', but used to refer to a town's main plaza

Menu Translator

Antojitos

Many traditional Mexican dishes fall under the heading of *antojitos* ('little whims'), savoury or spicy concoctions that delight the palate.

burrito – any combination of beans, cheese, meat, chicken or seafood seasoned with salsa or chilli and wrapped in a flour tortilla

chilaquiles – scrambled eggs with chillis and bits of tortillas

chiles rellenos – *poblano* chillis stuffed with cheese, meat or other foods, dipped in egg whites, fried and baked in sauce

enchilada – ingredients similar to those used in tacos and burritos wrapped in a corn tortilla, dipped in sauce and then baked or fried

machaca – cured, dried and shredded beef or pork mixed with eggs, onions, cilantro and chillis

papadzul – corn tortillas filled with hard-boiled eggs, cucumber or marrow seeds, and covered in tomato sauce

quesadilla – flour tortilla topped or filled with cheese and occasionally other ingredients, and then heated

queso relleno – 'stuffed cheese', a mild yellow cheese stuffed with minced meat and spices

taco – a soft or crisp corn tortilla wrapped or folded around the same filling as a burrito

tamale – steamed corn dough stuffed with meat, beans, chillis or nothing at all, wrapped in corn husks

tostada – flat, crisp tortilla topped with meat or cheese, tomatoes, beans and lettuce

Sopas (Soups)

chipilín – cheese and cream soup on a maize base

gazpacho – chilled vegetable soup spiced with hot chillis

menudo – popular soup made with the spiced entrails (tripe) of various four-legged beasts

pozole – hominy soup with meat and vegetables (can be spicy)

sopa de arroz – not a soup at all but just a plate of rice; commonly served with lunch

sopa de lima – 'lime soup', chicken stock flavoured with lime

sopa de pollo – bits of chicken in a thin chicken broth

Huevos (Eggs)

huevos estrellados – fried eggs
huevos fritos – fried eggs

huevos motuleños – local dish of the Yucatecan town of Motul: fried eggs atop a tortilla spread with refried beans, garnished with diced ham, green peas, shredded cheese and tomato sauce, with fried bananas (platanos) on the side

huevos rancheros – ranch-style eggs: fried, laid on a tortilla and smothered with spicy tomato sauce

huevos revueltos estilo mexicano – 'eggs scrambled Mexican-style' with tomatoes, onions, chillis and garlic

huevos revueltos – scrambled eggs; *con chorizo* (chor-REE-so) is with spicy sausage, *con frijoles* is with beans

Pescado, Mariscos (Seafood)

The variety and quality of seafood from the coastal waters of Yucatán and Belize is excellent. Lobster is available along Mexico's Caribbean coast and in Belize, particularly on the cayes. Campeche (Mexico) is a major shrimp fishing port, with much of its catch exported.

All of the following types of seafood are available in seafood restaurants most of the year. Clams, oysters, shrimp and prawns are also often available as *cocteles* (cocktails).

abulón – abalone
almejas – clams
atún – tuna
cabrilla – sea bass
camarones gigantes – prawns
camarones – shrimp
cangrejo – large crab
ceviche – raw seafood marinated in lime juice and mixed with onions, chillis, garlic, tomatoes, and *cilantro* (fresh coriander leaf)
dorado – dolphin
filete de pescado – fish fillet
huachinango – red snapper
jaiba – small crab
jurel – yellowtail
langosta – lobster
lenguado – flounder or sole
mariscos – shellfish
ostiones – oysters
pargo – red snapper
pescado al mojo de ajo – fish fried in butter and garlic
pescado – fish after it has been caught (see *pez*)
pez espada – swordfish
pez – fish which is alive in the water (see *pescado*)

sierra – mackerel
tiburón – shark
tortuga or *caguama* – turtle
trucha de mar – sea trout

Carnes y Aves (Meat & Poultry)

asado – roast
barbacoa – literally 'barbecued', but by a process whereby the meat is covered and placed under hot coals
biftec de res – beefsteak
biftec, bistec – any cut of meat, fish or poultry
birria – barbecued on a spit
borrego – sheep
cabro – goat
carne al carbón – charcoal-grilled meat
carne asada – tough but tasty grilled beef
carnitas – deep-fried pork
chicharrones – deep-fried pork skin
chorizo – pork sausage
chuletas de puerco – pork chops
cochinita – suckling pig
codorniz, la chaquaca – quail
conejo – rabbit
cordero – lamb
costillas de puerco – pork ribs or chops
guajolote – turkey
hígado – liver
jamón – ham
milanesa de res – crumbed beefsteak
milanesa – crumbed, breaded
patas de puerco – pig's feet
pato – duck
pavo – turkey, a fowl native to Yucatán, which figures prominently in Yucatecan cuisine
pibil – Yucatecan preparation: meat is flavoured with *achiote* sauce, wrapped in banana leaves and baked in a pit oven, or *pib*
poc-chuc – slices of pork cooked in a tangy sauce of onion and sour oranges or lemons
pollo – chicken
pollo asado – grilled (not roast) chicken
pollo con arroz – chicken with rice
pollo frito – fried chicken
puerco – pork
tampiqueño, tampiqueña – 'in the style of Tampico', a style of cooking meats often using a spiced tomato sauce
tocino – bacon or salt pork
venado – venison

Frutas (Fruit)

coco – coconut
dátil – date
fresas – strawberries, but also used to refer to any berries
guayaba – guava
higo – fig

limón – lime or lemon
mango – mango
melón – melon
naranja – orange
papaya – papaya
piña – pineapple
plátano – banana (suitable for cooking)
toronja – grapefruit
uva – grape

Legumbres, Verduras (Vegetables)

Vegetables are rarely served as separate dishes, but are often mixed into salads, soups and sauces.

aceitunas – olives
calabaza – squash, marrow or pumpkin
cebolla – onion
champiñones – mushrooms
chícharos – peas
ejotes – green beans
elote – corn on the cob; commonly served from steaming bins on street carts
jícama – a popular root vegetable which resembles a potato crossed with an apple; eaten fresh with a sprinkling of lime, chilli and salt
lechuga – lettuce
papa – potato
tomate – tomato
zanahoria – carrot

Dulces (Desserts, Sweets)

flan – custard, crème caramel
helado – ice cream
nieve – Mexican equivalent of the American 'snow cone': flavoured ice with the consistency of ice cream
paleta – flavoured ice on a stick
pan dulce – sweet rolls, usually eaten for breakfast
pastel – cake
postre – dessert, after-meal sweet

Other Foods

achiote – a sauce of chopped tomato, onion, chillis and *cilantro* (fresh coriander leaf) used widely in Yucatán
azúcar – sugar
bolillo – French-style bread rolls
crema – cream
guacamole – mashed avocados mixed with onion, chilli sauce, lemon, tomato and other ingredients
leche – milk
mantequilla – butter
mole poblano – a popular sauce in Mexico made from more than 30 ingredients, including bitter chocolate, chillis and many spices; often served over chicken or turkey

pimienta negra – black pepper
queso – cheese
salsa – sauce made with chillis, onion, tomato, lemon
  or lime juice and spices
sal – salt

At the Table

copa – glass
cuchara – spoon
cuchillo – knife
cuenta – bill
menú – menu; sometimes, fixed price meal, as in
  menú del día
plato – plate
propina – the tip, 10 to 15% of the bill
servilleta – table napkin

taza – cup
tenedor – fork
vaso – drinking glass

Café (Coffee)

café sin azúcar – coffee without sugar. This keeps the
  waiter from adding heaps of sugar to your cup,
  but it doesn't mean your coffee won't taste sweet;
  sugar is often added to and processed with the
  beans.
café negro or *café americano* – black coffee with
  nothing added except sugar, unless it's made with
  sugar-coated coffee beans
café con leche – coffee with hot milk
café con crema – coffee with cream served separately
nescafé – instant coffee

Index

ABBREVIATIONS

B – Belize   G – Guatemala   M – Mexico

MAPS

Altun Ha Ruins (B) 264
Antigua Guatemala (G) 114

Belize 227
Belize City (B) 241
   Central Belize City 244-245
Belize's Cayes (B) 251
Belmopan (B) 287
Benque Viejo del Carmen (B) 298
Bonampak Ruins (M) 452

Campeche (M) 390
Campeche State (M) 388
Cancún (M) 320
   Ciudad Cancún (M) 316
Cañón del Sumidero (M) 468
Carretera al Atlantico (G) 174
Caye Caulker (B) 252
Chetumal (M) 424
Chiapas (M) 441
Chiapas Highlands (M) 484
Chichén Itzá (M) 344
Chichicastenango (G) 138
Chiquimula (G) 182
Cobá Ruins (M) 419
Cobán (G) 177
Comitán (M) 486
Copán (Honduras) 190
   Around Copán 188
Copán Ruinas (Honduras) 192
Corozal Town (B) 270

Dangriga (B) 274

El Petén (G) 205
Esquipulas (G) 184

Felipe Carrillo Puerto (M) 421
Flores-Santa Elena (G) 207

Guatemala 84
Guatemala City North (G) 96
Guatemala City South (G) 98
Guatemala's Highlands (G) 112
Guatemala's Pacific Slope (G) 163
Guatemala, Belize & Yucatán 14-15

Huehuetenango (G) 157

Isla Cozumel (M) 403
   San Miguel (Cozumel) (M) 404
Isla Mujeres (M) 328
   Isla Mujeres Town (M) 331

Kabah (M) 379
Kohunlich (M) 427

Labná (M) 382
Lago de Atitlán (G) 126
Lago de Petén Itzá (G) 212
Lagos de Montebello (M) 489

Mérida (B) 354-355
Mountain Pine Ridge (B) 293

Ocosingo (M) 457
Orange Walk Town (B) 268

Palenque (M) 442-443
Palenque Ruins (M) 446
Panajachel (G) 129
Placencia (B) 278
Playa del Carmen (M) 400
Progreso (B) 370
Puerto Barrios (G) 200
Punta Gorda (B) 281

Quetzaltenango (G) 147

Central Quetzaltenango 150
Quintana Roo (M) 398
Quiriguá Ruins (G) 195

Retalhuleu (G) 165

San Cristóbal de las Casas (M) 470
San Ignacio (B) 290
San Pedro (B) 256
Santa Lucía Cotzumalguapa (G) 167
Sayil (M) 381

Tabasco (M) 428
Tapachula (M) 493
Ticul (M) 384
Tikal (G) 214-215
Tizimin (M) 340
Tulum Ruins (M) 414
Turquoise Coast (M) 411
Tuxtla Gutiérrez (M) 462

Uaxactún (G) 222
Uxmal (M) 375
Uxmal & the Puuc Route (M) 372

Valladolid (M) 338
Villahermosa (M) 429
   Central Villahermosa 432
   Parque-Museo La Venta (M) 431

Xunantunich Ruins (B) 297

Yaxchilán Ruins (M) 454
Yucatán Peninsula, North (M) 336, 338

Zaculeu Ruins (G) 158

TEXT

Map references are in **bold** type.

Abaj Takalik (G) 166
Acanceh (M) 26, 373, 374, 386

accommodation 66-67
Agua Azul Cascades (M) 455-456
Aguilar, Jerónimo de 18

Ah Cacau (G) 216
air travel 72-77
   departure tax 77
   glossary 74-75

Mayan route tickets 72
  regional 80
  to/from Belize 235
  to/from Guatemala 108
  to/from Mexico 313
  within Belize 235
Akumal (M) 412
Alta Verapaz (G) 88, 173
Altun Ha (B) 264-265, **264**
Alvarado, Pedro de 19, 143
Amatenango del Valle (M) 485
Ambergris Caye (B) 250, 255-262
Antigua Guatemala (G) 19, 66, 113-124, **114**
  entertainment 123-124
  getting there & away 124
  information 116-117
  language courses 119-120
  orientation 115-116
  places to eat 122-123
  places to stay 120-122
  shopping 123-124
  sights & activities 117-119
architecture, Mayan 25-28
  celestial plan 25
  styles 26-28
Arévalo, Juan José 86, 88
Arévalo, Marco Vinicio Cerezo 87, 88
Arriaga (M) 491-492
Aztecs 18

Baboon Sanctuary (Bermudian Landing) (B) 263-264
Bacalar (M) 421
Baja Verapaz (G) 173
Balankanché Caves (M) 348
Balneario El Azufre (M) 460
Banana Bank Lodge (B) 286
bargaining 43
Bliss, Baron (B) 243
Barrios, Justo Rufino 85
Becal (M) 387
Becan (M) 395-396
Belize 226-299, **14-15, 227**
  business hours 233
  climate 232-233
  economy 229
  embassies 231-232
  food 234
  geography 228-229
  government 229
  history 226-228
  language 230
  media 234
  money 232
  people 229-230
  post 233

telephone 233-234
  tourist offices abroad 233
  visas 231-232
Belize Barrier Reef (B) 250
Belize City (B) 240-249, **241, 244-245**
  entertainment 249
  getting around 249
  getting there & away 249
  information 240-242
  orientation 240
  places to eat 248-249
  places to stay 243-248
  sights & activities 242-243
Belize Zoo (B) 285-286
Belmopan (B) 286-288, **287**
Benemerito (M) (G) 223
Benque Viejo del Carmen (B) 206, 297-299, **298**
Bernoulli, Dr Gustav 216
Bethel (G) 223
Big Creek (B) 277
Bilbao (G) 168
Biotopo Cerro Cahuí (G) 212
Biotopo del Quetzal (G) 175-176
Biotopo Monterrico-Hawaii (G) 172
Blom, Frans 374, 474
Blue Creek (B) 284
Blue Hole (B) 253, 258
Blue Hole National Park (B) 273
boat travel 81
  to/from Belize 235
  within Belize 238-239
Boca Paila (M) 416-418
Bochil (M) 460
Bolonchén de Rejón (M) 373, 383
Bonampak (M) 223, 452-455, **452**
books 50-54
  culture, art & architecture 53-54
  history 53
  Mayan life & culture 50-51
  travel guides 51
  travelogues 51-53
border crossings 78
British Honduras 228
bullfight 30
bus travel 80
  to/from Belize 235
  to/from Guatemala 108-110
  to/from Mexico 313
  within Belize 236-237
  within Guatemala 111

Cabrera, Manuel Estrada 85
Cahal Pech (B) 289-290
Cakchiquel 137

Calakmul Biosphere Reserve (M) 21, 206, 263
Calendar Round 26, 34
Calkini (M) 387
Calzones 28
Campeche (M) 66, 389-395, **390**
  entertainment 394
  getting there & away 395
  history 389
  information 389-391
  orientation 389
  places to eat 394
  places to stay 393-394
  sights & activities 391-393
Cancún (M) 313, 315-327, **316, 320**
  entertainment 325-326
  getting around 327
  getting there & away 326-327
  information 317-318
  orientation 315-317
  places to eat 324-325
  places to stay 319-323
  shopping 326
  sights & activities 318-319
Cañón del Sumidero (M) 467, **468**
car & motorbike travel 77-78, 81
  within Belize 237-238
  within Guatemala 91, 111
  within Mexico 313-314
Caracol (B) 17, 291, 294
Cardamom 180
Carrera, Rafael 85
Carretera al Atlantico (G) 173, **174**
Carretera al Pacífico (G) 162
Casas, Bartolomé de las 19, 173
Castillo de San Felipe (G) 197
Catazajá (M) 396
Catherwood, Frederick 374
Cauac Sky 195
Caye Caulker (B) 250-255, 258, **252**
Caye Chapel (B) 262
Ceibal (G) 223-224
Celestún (B) 371
Cenote Azul (M) 422
Cenote Dzitnup (Xkakah) (M) 337
Cenote Zací (M) 337
Central Farm (B) 288-289
Cerros (B) 263, 271
Chac 345
Champerico (G) 166
Champoton (M) 18
Chan Chich Lodge (B) 265-266
Chan Santa Cruz (M) 302, 420
Chankanab Bay Beach (M) 409

Chechem Ha Mayan Cave (B) 294
Chemuyil (M) 412
Chenes 17, 27, 303
Chetumal (M) 422-426, **424**
Chiapa de Corzo (M) 469
Chiapas (M) 304, 441-496, **441**
  climate 309
Chicanna (M) 395-396
Chichén Itzá (M) 17, 26, 27, 66, 343-351, **344**
  Cenotes, Sacred 347
Chichicastenango (G) 137-142, **138**
chicle (M) 402
Chimaltenango (G) 125
Chinkultic (M) 488-489
Chiquibul River (B) 291
Chiquimula (G) 181-183, **182**
Chochola (M) 373
Chols 482
CIA 86
Cinco Lagunas (M) 490
Ciudad Cuauhtémoc (M) 160, 491
Ciudad Hidalgo (M) 162, 495-496
Ciudad Tecún Umán (G) 162
Ciudad Vieja (G) 124
climate, regional 44-46
climbing 65

Coatepeque (G) 164
Cobá (M) 28, 66, 418-420, **419**
Cobán (G) 176-179, **177**
Cockscomb Basin Wildlife Sanctuary (B) 276-277
Cocom Lineage 18
Cocoms 19
Comalcalco Ruins (M) 429, 439-440
Comitán (M) 485-488, **486**
Copán (Honduras) 17, 27, 66, 186-194, **188, 190**
Copán Ruinas (Honduras) 191, **192**
Copán Valley 16
Córdoba, Hernández de 329
Corozal (B) 427
Corozal Town (B) 269-272, **270**
Cortés, Hernán 18
Costera Bacalar (M) 422
Cozumel (M) 19, 402-409, **403, 404**
Crooked Tree Wildlife Sanctuary (B) 263, 265
Cuatro Caminos (G) 145
Cuchumatanes Range (G) 88
culture, Mayan 28-31

customs 42
cycling 82
  within Belize 238

dance 29-30
Dangriga (B) 273-276, **274**
Dem Dats Doin (B) 283
dinosaur bones (G) 88
diving
  Akumal (M) 412
  Ambergris Caye (B) 257
  Cancún (M) 319
  Caye Caulker (B) 253
  Cozumel (M) 405
  Isla Mujeres (M) 330
Drinks 68-70
Duby-Blom, Gertrude 474
Dzibilchaltún (B) 368-369

ecology 21
Edzná (M) 66, 383-384, 393
Ekbalam (M) 339-340
El Aguacero (M) 469
El Carmen (G) 162-164
El Cedral (M) 409
El Cruce (G), see Puente Ixlu
El Estor (G) 197
El Florido (G) 193
El Mirador 16
El Naranjo (G) 223
El Petén (G) 18, 88, 205-224, **205**
El Remate (G) 211-213
El Tormento (M) 396
El Zarco Junction (G) 164
electricity 50
Elías, Jorge Serrano 87
enredo 28
entertainment 70
Escárcega (M) 395
Escuintla (G) 171
Esperanza Culture 17
Esquipulas (G) 183-186, **184**
Estanzuela (G) 181

fajas 29
Felipe Carrillo Puerto (M) 385, 420-421, **421**
festivals 46-48
Finca El Baúl (G) 168-169
Finca Las Ilusiones (G) 169-170
flora & fauna 21-24
Flores (G) 20, 206-211, 272, 293, **207**
food 67-68
Frontera Corozal (M) 223
Fuentes Georginas (G) 154-155

Gallon Jug (B) 266

Gallows Point Caye (B) 262
Gálvez, Mariano 85
Garifunas (Garinagus) 202, 230
Garrafón National Park (M) 329
Georgeville (B) 294
Glover's Reef (B) 258
Grijalva, Juan de 402
Grutas Actun-Can (G) 208
Grutas de Lanquín (G) 179
Grutas de Loltún (Loltún Caves) (M) 382
Guanacaste Park (B) 286
Guatemala 84-224, **14-15, 84**
  business hours 92
  climate 92
  economy 88-89
  embassies 90-91
  food 94
  geography 87-88
  government 88
  history 85-87
  media 93
  money 91-92
  people 89
  post 92-93
  telephone 93
  visas 90
Guatemala City (G) 19, 95-111, **96, 98**
  entertainment 107
  getting around 110-111
  getting there & away 108-110
  history 95
  information 99-101
  orientation 95-97
  places to eat 106-107
  places to stay 104-106
  sights & activities 101-104
Guzmán, Jacobo Arbenz 86, 88

Half Moon Caye (B) 258, 262
hammocks 67, 365
Hattieville (B) 285
health 54-63
Hecelchakan (M) 387
henequen 305, 351
Hidden Valley (B) 291
Hidden Valley Falls (B) 294
Highlands, Guatemalan (G) 112-161, **112**
hiking 65
hitching 81
Hol Chan Marine Reserve (B) 258
holidays 46-48
Hopelchén (M) 373
Hopkins (B) 276
Huehuetenango (G) 156-160, **157**

huipiles 28, 31
Huixtán (M) 485
human sacrifice 31
Hummingbird Highway (B) 273
Hurricane Gilbert 327, 329, 417
Hurricane Hattie 285
Hurricane Janet 269

Independence (B) 277
Indian Church (B) 266
Interamerican Highway 88, 113
Isla Contoy Bird Sanctuary (M) 334
Isla Holbox (M) 343
Isla Mujeres (M) 327-334, **328, 331**
itineraries, suggested 41-42
Itzaes 17, 216
Iximché (G) 28, 125-127
Izamal (M) 351-352
Izapa Ruins (M) 495
Iztapa (G) 171-172

Kabah (M) 66, 379-380, **379**
Kaminaljuyú (G) 17, 26, 103-104
Kanasin (M) 374
King 18 Rabbit 187, 195
King Bird-Jaguar 17
King Great Jaguar Paw 213
King Jade Sky 195
King K'ucumatz (G) 32, 143
King Pacal 17
King Yax Moch Xoc 213
Kohunlich Ruins (M) 426-427, **427**
Kopoma (M) 373
Kukulcán, see Quetzalcóatl
K'umarcaaj (G) 28, 143

La Democracia (G) 170-171
La Ermita Valley (G) 95
La Mesilla (G) 113, 160
La Mordida 78
La Palma (M) 223
La Venta 16
La Venta, Parque-Museo (M) 431, **431**
Labná (M) 17, 381-382, **382**
Lacandóns 483
Lago de Amatitlán (G) 172
Lago de Atitlán (G) 125-134, **126**
Lago de Izabal (G) 197
Lago de Petén Itzá (G) 18, 20, 206, **208**
Lagos de Montebello (M) 488-491, **489**
Laguna Bacalar (M) 421-422
Laguna de Montebello (M) 490
Laguna Tziscao (M) 490

Lagunas de Colores (M) 489-490
Lago de Izabal (G) 197
Lamanai (B) 266-267
Landa, Friar Diego de 19-20
language 36-40
    courses 65, 119-120, 149
    Mayan 39-40
    Spanish 36-39
Las Aventuras (M) 412
laundry 50
León Carpio, Ramiro de 87
Lighthouse Reef (B) 258
Likín (G) 171-172
Lívingston (G) 202-204
Long Count 17, 34-35
Lord Water 216
Los Encuentros (G) 127
Los Vahos (G) 153-154
Lubaantun (B) 283

Macal River Valley (B) 289
Maler, Teobert 216
Mames (M) 482
Mango Creek (B) 277
Mantancero galleon (M) 412
Maps 51
Maruba (B) 264-265
Maskall (B) 264
Maudslay, Alfred P 216
Maxcaná (M) 373
Maya Biosphere Reserve (G) 21, 206, 263
Maya Centre (B) 276
Maya, the
    culture 50-51
    history 13-21
    people 24-25
    religion 31-33
Maya, the, in Mexico 482-483
    architecture, see architecture, Mayan
    economy 304-305
    geography 303-304
    government 304
    history 302-303
    people 305
Maya-Toltec 17
Mayan Calendar System 33-36
Mayan Counting System 35-36
Mayan ruins
    Abaj Takalik (G) 166
    Acanceh (M) 26, 373, 374, 386
    Aguateca (G) 224
    Altun Ha (B) 264-265, **264**
    Becan (M) 395-396
    Bilbao (G) 168
    Bonampak (M) 223, 452-455, **452**
    Cahal Pech (B) 289-290

Caracol (B) 17, 291, 294
Ceibal (G) 224-224
Cerros (B) 263, 271
Chechem Ha Mayan Cave (B) 294
Chicanna (M) 395-396
Chichén Itzá (M) 17, 26, 27, 66, 343-351, **344**
Chinkultic (M) 488-489
Cobá (M) 28, 66, 418-420, **419**
Comalcalco Ruins (M) 429, 439-440
Copán (Honduras) 17, 27, 66, 186-194, **192**
Cuello (B) 267
Dos Pilas (G) 224
Edzná (M) 66, 383-384
El Castillo Real (M) 410
El Cedral (M) 409
Finca El Baúl (G) 168-169
Finca Las Ilusiones (G) 169-170
Grutas de Loltún (Loltún Caves) (M) 382
Isla Mujeres (M) 327-334, **328, 331**
Itzimté (M) 382
Izapa (M) 495
Kabah (M) 66, 379-380, **379**
Kaminaljuyú (G) 17, 26, 103-104
Kohunlich (M) 426-427, **427**
K'umarcaaj (G) 28, 143
La Venta, Parque-Museo (M) 431, **431**
Labná (M) 17, 381-382, **382**
Lamanai (B) 266-267
Lubaantun (B) 283
Mayapán (M) 18, 19, 28, 373, 374, 385, 386-387
Monte Alto (G) 170
Nim Li Punit (B) 283
Nohmul (B) 268
Palenque (M) 17, 27, 66, 441-452, **442-443, 446**
Quiriguá (G) 17, 66, 194-197
Río Bec (M) 396
San Gervasio (M) 410
Santa Rita (B) 271
Sayil (M) 66, 380-381, **381**
Tamarindito (G) 224
Tikal (G) 16, 17, 27, 66, 213-220, **214-215**
Toniná (M) 458-459
Tulum (M) 28, 413-417, **414**
Uaxactún (G) 16, 26, 66, 221, **222**
Uxbenka (B) 284
Uxmal (M) 17, 66, 372, 374-379, **372, 375**
Xlapak (M) 66, 381

Xpujil (M) 395-396
Xunantunich (B) 296-297, **297**
Yaxchilán (M) 452-455, **454**
Zaculeu (G) 158-159, **158**
Zona Arqueológica El Rey (M) 318
Mayapán (M) 18, 19, 28, 373, 374, 385, 386-387
Mazatenango (G) 166
media 54
Melchor de Mencos (G) 206, 221, 299
Mérida (B) 19, 65, 313, 353-368, **354-355**
  entertainment 363-364
  getting around 367-368
  getting there & away 365-367
  history 353-356
  information 356-357
  orientation 356
  places to eat 362-363
  places to stay 360-362
  shopping 364-365
  sights & activities 357-360
mestizos 20, 305
Mexico 302-496, **336, 338**
  business hours 310
  climate 309
  embassies 306-308
  food 311-312
  media 311
  money 308-309
  post 310
  telephone 310-311
  tourist offices 309-310
  visas 306-308
Mexico Cave (B) 258
Misol-Ha Cascades (M) 455
Mitonic (M) 485
Mixco Viejo 28
Modesto Méndez (G) 197
Momostenango (G) 155-156
money 42-43
Montejo Xiú, Francisco de 19
Montejo, Francisco de (El Adelantado) 19, 353, 429
Montejo, Francisco de (El Mozo) 19
Monterrico (G) 172
Morazán, Francisco 85
Motagua Valley (G) 89
Motozintla (M) 491
Mount Hope (B) 288
Mountain Pine Ridge (B) 290, 293-296, **293**
music 29-30

na 16, 26
Nebaj (G) 144

New River (B) 266
New River Lagoon (B) 266
Nim Li Punit (B) 283

Ocosingo (M) 456, **457**
Olmecs 16, 186
Ontario Village (B) 288
Orange Walk (B) 267-269, **268**
Oxkutzcab (M) 374, 385

Pacific Highway (G) 88
Pacific Slope (G) 88, 162-172, **163**
Painted Books 20
Palancar Beach (M) 409
Palenque (M) 17, 27, 66, 441-452, **442-443, 446**
Palmetto Reef (B) 258
Pamul (M) 410
Panajachel (G) 66, 128-134, **129**
Pantí Medicine Trail (B) 291, 294
Payucan (M) 393
Peto (M) 385
photography 54
Pichucalco (M) 460
Pipiles (G) 223
Placencia (B) 277-280, **278**
Playa del Carmen (M) 399-402, **400**
Polguc (M) 385
Popol Vuh 32, 53
post 48-49
Progreso (B) 369-371, **370**
Pueblo Nuevo (M) 460
Puente Ixlu (El Cruce) (G) 211, 221
Puerto Arista (M) 492
Puerto Aventuras (M) 410
Puerto Barrios (G) 198-202, **200**
Puerto Morelos (M) 397-399
Puerto San José (G) 171-172
Punta Allen (M) 416-418
Punta Arena (B) 258
Punta Celarain (M) 409
Punta Gorda (B) 280-283, **281**
Punta Molas (M) 410
Puuc Route (M) 17, 27, 372, 379-374, **372**

Quechquémitl 28
Quetzalcóatl (Kukulcán) 17, 18, 27, 345
Quetzaltenango (G) 146-153, **147, 150**
Quiché (G) 19, 136-144
Quiché Maya 173
Quiriguá (G) 17, 66, 194-197, **165**

Rabinal Maya 173
Rayón (M) 460
Retalhuleu (G) 164-166, **165**
Rincón Chamula (M) 460
Río Bec 17, 27, 396
Río Bravo Conservation Area (B) 21, 206, 263
Río Champon 396
Río de la Pasión 223
Río Dulce 202-203
Río Frio 291
Río Frio Caves (B) 294
Río Grijalva 467
Río Hondo 180-181
Río Lagartos 341-342
Río Motagua 88, 195
Río Motagua Valley (G) 173
Río On 291, 294
Río San Pedro 223
Río Usumacinta 223, 396, 452
Rockstone Pond (B) 264

safety 63-64
Sal Si Puedes (M) 396
Salamá (G) 173-175
San Andrés Larráinzar (M) 485
San Antonio (B) 284
San Antonio Aguas Calientes (G) 124
San Benito, see Flores
San Cristóbal de las Casas (M) 66, 455, 469-482, **470**
San Felipe (M) 342-343
San Francisco Beach (M) 409
San Francisco El Alto (G) 155
San Ignacio (Cayo) (B) 66, 289-293, **290**
San José Succotz (B) 297
San Juan Chamelco (G) 179
San Juan Chamula (M) 483
San Lucas Tolimán (G) 134
San Miguel Chicaj (G) 175
San Pedro (B) 255-262, **256**
San Pedro Carchá (G) 179
San Pedro Chenalhó (M) 485
San Pedro Columbia (B) 283
San Pedro Cut (B) 258
San Pedro La Laguna (G) 135-136
Santa Catarina Palopó (G) 134
Santa Cruz del Quiché (G) 142-144
Santa Elena, see Flores
Santa Lucía Cotzumalguapa (G) 166, **167**
Santa María de Jesús (G) 125
Santiago Atitlán (G) 134-135
Sayaxché (G) 223-224
Sayil (M) 66, 380-381, **381**

Semuc-Champey (G) 179-180
Serrano (G) 88
Seybaplaya (M) 393
Shipstern Wildlife Reserve (B) 263
Shipyard (B) 266
shopping 70-71
Sian Ka'an Biosphere Reserve (M) 417
Sibun River (B) 273
Sisal (B) 369
Sittee River (B) 276
Sittee River Village (B) 276
Smoke Imix 187
Smoke Monkey 187
snorkelling, see diving
Soconusco (M) 491-492
Sololá (G) 127-128
South Water Caye (B) 276
Southern Cayes (B) 276
Southern Highway (B) 276-277
Spaniards in Central America 18
Spanish Lookout Caye (B) 262
St George's Caye (B) 262
St Herman's Cave (B) 273
Stephens, John L 183, 187, 195, 216, 374
Subteniente López (M) 272

Tabasco (M) 303-304, 428-440, 428
    climate 309
Talismán (M) 162, 495-496
Talking Cross 302-303, 420993
Tapachula (M) 492-495, 493
Tayasal, see Flores
Teakettle Village (B) 288
Teapa (M) 460
Tecoh (M) 374
Tecpán Guatemala (G) 125
Tecún Umán (G) 143, 162
Tekax (M) 385
telephone 49

Tenejapa (M) 484-485
Tenochtitlán (M) 19
Teotihuacán (M) 17
theft 64, 93
Ticul (M) 374, 384-385, 384
Tikal (G) 16, 17, 27, 66, 213-220, 214-215
Tikal National Park (G) 216
time 50
tipping 43
Tizimin (M) 340-341, 340
Tobacco Caye (B) 276
Todos Santos Cuchumatán (G) 160-161
Tojolababals 482
Toltecs 17
Tonalá (M) 492
Tonalamatl 34
Toniná (M) 458-459
Totonicapán (G) 145-146
tours 79
train travel 81
Tres Cocos Cut (B) 258
Tula 17
Tulum (M) 28, 413-417, 414
Turneffe Islands (B) 258, 262
Tuxtla Gutiérrez (M) 313, 461 462
Tzeltals (M) 482
Tzolkins 34
Tzotzils (M) 482
Tzucacab (M) 385

Uaxactún (G) 16, 26, 66, 221, 222
Ubico, Jorge 86
Uman (M) 373
United Fruit Company 198, 199
Unitedville (B) 288
Utatlán, see K'umarcaaj
Uxmal (M) 17, 66, 372, 374-379, 372, 375

Vaca Falls (B) 291
Vado Hondo (G) 193
Vague Year 16, 26, 34
Valladolid (M) 66, 335-339, 338
Villahermosa (M) 313, 428, 429, 432
Volcán Agua (G) 124, 125
Volcán Pacaya (G) 125
Volcanoes (G) 125

War of the Castes 356, 302, 420
water sports 65
Western Highway (B) 288
women travellers 63
work 64-65

Xcacel (M) 412-413
Xcaret (M) 410
Xel-Ha Lagoon (M) 19, 413
Xibalba 26, 31, 32
Xiús 18, 19
Xlapak (M) 66, 381
Xpujil (M) 395-396
Xtacumbilxunaan (M) 373, 383
Xunantunich (B) 296-297, 297

Yal-Ku Lagoon (M) 410
Yax Pac (G) 187
Yaxchilán (M) 17, 223, 452-455, 454
Yucatán Peninsula, see Mexico
Yumká (M) 434

Zacapa (G) 181
Zaculeu (G) 158-159, 158
Zapatista National Liberation Army (EZLN) 460
Zapotecs 16
Zinacantán (M) 483
Zoques (M) 482
Zunil (G) 154

508

Thanks

Thanks to the many travellers who wrote in with comments about our last edition, and with helpful tips and interesting stories:

Maranne & Oliver Allard (F), Vicente Alvarez (D), Henry Anderson (C), Helle Andreasen (Dk), Elisabeth Annat (UK), Alvaro Argueta, Sue Ashley (NL), Karen Baldwin (UK), Pochi Balladelli (I), Steve Scot Basil (USA), Hugo Baur (CH), Mrs Bird (UK), Heinz Broecker (D), J Bruyniks (NL), Bruce Burford (UK), Sung Byun (USA), Iwen Chiu (USA), Richard Colbey (UK), Giovanni Costato (I), Kaela M Curtis (USA), Karin E Czulik (USA), Antoine de Champs (F), Leo de Rooij (NL), Michele Deakin (C), Philippe Delacombaz (CH), Annika Dellholm (S), Bruce Docking (USA), Debbi Dolan (USA), A Dyer (C), Ake S Ericson (S), Rosa Escarpenter (Sp), Bastian Fischer (D), Alan Flippen (USA), Bill Frechette (USA), Karl Frey (A), Manuel Garica Lozano, Rob Garner (UK), Lorena Garver (USA), David & Leslie Gold (C), Tom Harding, David Heaton (UK), Hans Heintze (NL), Freddie Heitman (USA), Wes Hill (USA), Marc Hogenhout (NL), Michelle Hollings (UK), Marga Hop (NL), Alexander Hribar (D), Anne Huxtable (Aus), John Israel (USA), Ian Jackson (UK), J Jacobsen (C), Malcolm Keir (UK), Peter Kelly-Detwiler, Petra Kern (CH), Walter Kirchdorfer (D), Christy Lanzal (USA), J G Leemhuis (NL), Arlene Lew (C), Jill Livingston (USA), Karen Lock (USA), Chris Loggers (USA), Fred Lohmann (USA), Sandra & James Macdonald (C), Anders Magnusson (S), Donna Mattson, Deirdre McDade (C), Malcolm McFall (Irl), Ann McLemore, Murray Melbin (USA), Steve Miles (UK), Ramon Mireles (USA), Martha Mora Weese, Hedwig Neefs (NL), Sheila O'Connell (USA), David O'Gorman, Tom Owens (USA),Christine Pavon (USA), Helen Pearson (UK), Benjamin Perez, Anthony Peters (USA), Kevin Phillips (UK), Scott Posner (USA), Ariane Ribbeck (D), Wendy Rodewall (USA), P V Roermund (NL), Jens Rohark (D), S Romanengo (USA), Amy Rothstein (USA), Julie Rugg (UK), David Saxon (USA), Howard Scotland (USA), Pickett Scott (USA), D R Shreve (USA), Dwayne Shreve (USA), Karen Silver (USA), Ami Silverman (USA), Amy Smith (USA), John & Sheila Stauber (USA), John Steedman (UK), Andrea Sutphin (USA), Sarah Taines (USA), Karin Taraschewski (D), Mark Teitelbaum (USA), Rob Tulleken (NL), Tomas Turecki (CZ), Thijs Turksema (NL), Sergio Valdes, Vincent van Hove (NL), Emily van Weiler (NL), Susan Waite (USA), Michael Wakefield (UK), Bonnie Waldman (USA), Jane Walton (USA), Fred Wambolt (USA), Simon Watson-Taylor (UK), Nicholas Wellington (USA), Ed Wilde (USA), Dave Worley (USA), Roberta Yamada (USA), Simon W Zayler (UK)

A – Austria, C – Canada, CH – Switzerland, CZ – Czechoslovakia, Dk – Denmark, D – Germany, F – France, Irl – Ireland, I – Italy, NL – Netherlands, Sp – Spain, S – Sweden,

PLANET TALK
Lonely Planet's FREE quarterly newsletter

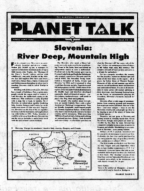

We love hearing from you and think you'd like to hear from us.

When...is the right time to see reindeer in Finland?
Where...can you hear the best palm-wine music in Ghana?
How...do you get from Asunción to Areguá by steam train?
What...is the best way to see India?

For the answer to these and many other questions read PLANET TALK.

Every issue is packed with up-to-date travel news and advice including:

- *a letter from Lonely Planet founders Tony and Maureen Wheeler*
- *travel diary from a Lonely Planet author - find out what it's really like out on the road*
- *feature article on an important and topical travel issue*
- *a selection of recent letters from our readers*
- *the latest travel news from all over the world*
- *details on Lonely Planet's new and forthcoming releases*

To join our mailing list contact any Lonely Planet office (address below).

LONELY PLANET PUBLICATIONS
Australia: PO Box 617, Hawthorn 3122, Victoria (tel: 03-819 1877)
USA: Embarcadero West, 155 Filbert St, Suite 251, Oakland, CA 94607 (tel: 510-893 8555)
TOLL FREE: (800) 275-8555
UK: 10 Barley Mow Passage, Chiswick, London W4 4PH (tel: 081-742 3161)
France: 71 bis rue du Cardinal Lemoine – 75005 Paris (tel: 1-46 34 00 58)

Also available: Lonely Planet T-shirts. 100% heavyweight cotton (S, M, L, XL)

Guides to the Americas

Alaska – a travel survival kit
Jim DuFresne has travelled extensively through Alaska by foot, road, rail, barge and kayak, and tells how to make the most of one of the world's great wilderness areas.

Argentina, Uruguay & Paraguay – a travel survival kit
This guide gives independent travellers all the essential information on three of South America's lesser-known countries. Discover some of South America's most spectacular natural attractions in Argentina; friendly people and beautiful handicrafts in Paraguay; and Uruguay's wonderful beaches.

Baja California – a travel survival kit
For centuries, Mexico's Baja peninsula – with its beautiful coastline, raucous border towns and crumbling Spanish missions – has been a land of escapes and escapades. This book describes how and where to escape in Baja.

Bolivia – a travel survival kit
From lonely villages in the Andes to ancient ruined cities and the spectacular city of La Paz, Bolivia is a magnificent blend of everything that inspires travellers. Discover safe and intriguing travel options in this comprehensive guide.

Brazil – a travel survival kit
From the mad passion of Carnival to the Amazon – home of the richest ecosystem on earth – Brazil is a country of mythical proportions. This guide has all the essential travel information.

Canada – a travel survival kit
This comprehensive guidebook has all the facts on the USA's huge neighbour – the Rocky Mountains, Niagara Falls, ultramodern Toronto, remote villages in Nova Scotia, and much more.

Central America on a shoestring
Practical information on travel in Belize, Guatemala, Costa Rica, Honduras, El Salvador, Nicaragua and Panama. A team of experienced Lonely Planet authors reveals the secrets of this culturally rich, geographically diverse and breathtakingly beautiful region.

Chile & Easter Island – a travel survival kit
Travel in Chile is easy and safe, with possibilities as varied as the countryside. This guide also gives detailed coverage of Chile's Pacific outpost, mysterious Easter Island.

Colombia – a travel survival kit
Colombia is a land of myths – from the ancient legends of El Dorado to the modern tales of Gabriel Garcia Marquez. The reality is beauty and violence, wealth and poverty, tradition and change. This guide shows how to travel independently and safely in this exotic country.

Costa Rica – a travel survival kit
Sun-drenched beaches, steamy jungles, smoking volcanoes, rugged mountains and dazzling birds and animals – Costa Rica has it all.

Eastern Caribbean – a travel survival kit
Powdery white sands, clear turquoise waters, lush jungle rainforest, balmy weather and a laid back pace, make the islands of the Eastern Caibbean an ideal destination for divers, hikers and sun-lovers. This guide will help you to decide which islands to visit to suit your interests and includes details on inter-island travel.

Ecuador & the Galápagos Islands – a travel survival kit
Ecuador offers a wide variety of travel experiences, from the high cordilleras to the Amazon plains – and 600 miles west, the fascinating Galápagos Islands. Everything you need to know about travelling around this enchanting country.

Hawaii – a travel survival kit
Share in the delights of this island paradise – and avoid its high prices – both on and off the beaten track. Full details on Hawaii's best-known attractions, plus plenty of uncrowded sights and activities.

Mexico – a travel survival kit
A unique blend of Indian and Spanish culture, fascinating history, and hospitable people, make Mexico a travellers' paradise.

Peru – a travel survival kit
The lost city of Machu Picchu, the Andean altiplano and the magnificent Amazon rainforests are just some of Peru's many attractions. All the travel facts you'll need can be found in this comprehensive guide.

South America on a shoestring
This practical guide provides concise information for budget travellers and covers South America from the Darien Gap to Tierra del Fuego.

Trekking in the Patagonian Andes
The first detailed guide to this region gives complete information on 28 walks, and lists a number of other possibilities extending from the Araucanía and Lake District regions of Argentina and Chile to the remote icy tip of South America in Tierra del Fuego.

Also available:
Brazilian phrasebook, **Latin American Spanish** phrasebook and **Quechua** phrasebook.

Lonely Planet Guidebooks

Lonely Planet guidebooks cover every accessible part of Asia as well as Australia, the Pacific, South America, Africa, the Middle East, Europe and parts of North America. There are five series: *travel survival kits*, covering a country for a range of budgets; *shoestring guides* with compact information for low-budget travel in a major region; *walking guides*; *city guides* and *phrasebooks*.

Australia & the Pacific
Australia
Bushwalking in Australia
Islands of Australia's Great Barrier Reef
Fiji
Melbourne city guide
Micronesia
New Caledonia
New Zealand
Tramping in New Zealand
Papua New Guinea
Bushwalking in Papua New Guinea
Papua New Guinea phrasebook
Rarotonga & the Cook Islands
Samoa
Solomon Islands
Sydney city guide
Tahiti & French Polynesia
Tonga
Vanuatu
Victoria

South-East Asia
Bali & Lombok
Bangkok city guide
Cambodia
Indonesia
Indonesia phrasebook
Laos
Malaysia, Singapore & Brunei
Myanmar (Burma)
Burmese phrasebook
Philippines
Pilipino phrasebook
Singapore city guide
South-East Asia on a shoestring
Thailand
Thai phrasebook
Vietnam
Vietnamese phrasebook

North-East Asia
China
Beijing city guide
Cantonese phrasebook
Mandarin Chinese phrasebook
Hong Kong, Macau & Canton
Japan
Japanese phrasebook
Korea
Korean phrasebook
Mongolia
North-East Asia on a shoestring
Seoul city guide
Taiwan
Tibet
Tibet phrasebook
Tokyo city guide

Middle East
Arab Gulf States
Egypt & the Sudan
Arabic (Egyptian) phrasebook
Iran
Israel
Jordan & Syria
Middle East
Turkish phrasebook
Trekking in Turkey
Yemen

Indian Ocean
Madagascar & Comoros
Maldives & Islands of the East Indian Ocean
Mauritius, Réunion & Seychelles

Mail Order

Lonely Planet guidebooks are distributed worldwide. They are also available by mail order from Lonely Planet, so if you have difficulty finding a title please write to us. US and Canadian residents should write to Embarcadero West, 155 Filbert St, Suite 251, Oakland CA 94607, USA ; European residents should write to 10 Barley Mow Passage, Chiswick, London W4 4PH; and residents of other countries to PO Box 617, Hawthorn, Victoria 3122, Australia.

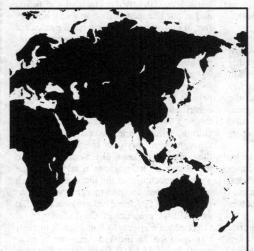

Indian Subcontinent
Bangladesh
India
Hindi/Urdu phrasebook
Trekking in the Indian Himalaya
Karakoram Highway
Kashmir, Ladakh & Zanskar
Nepal
Trekking in the Nepal Himalaya
Nepali phrasebook
Pakistan
Sri Lanka
Sri Lanka phrasebook

Africa
Africa on a shoestring
Central Africa
East Africa
Trekking in East Africa
Kenya
Swahili phrasebook
Morocco, Algeria & Tunisia
Arabic (Moroccan) phrasebook
South Africa, Lesotho & Swaziland
Zimbabwe, Botswana & Namibia
West Africa

Central America & the Caribbean
Baja California
Central America on a shoestring
Costa Rica
Eastern Caribbean
Guatemala, Belize & Yucatán: La Ruta Maya
Mexico

North America
Alaska
Canada
Hawaii

Europe
Baltic States & Kaliningrad
Dublin city guide
Eastern Europe on a shoestring
Eastern Europe phrasebook
Finland
France
Greece
Hungary
Iceland, Greenland & the Faroe Islands
Ireland
Italy
Mediterranean Europe on a shoestring
Mediterranean Europe phrasebook
Poland
Scandinavian & Baltic Europe on a shoestring
Scandinavian Europe phrasebook
Switzerland
Trekking in Spain
Trekking in Greece
USSR
Russian phrasebook
Western Europe on a shoestring
Western Europe phrasebook

South America
Argentina, Uruguay & Paraguay
Bolivia
Brazil
Brazilian phrasebook
Chile & Easter Island
Colombia
Ecuador & the Galápagos Islands
Latin American Spanish phrasebook
Peru
Quechua phrasebook
South America on a shoestring
Trekking in the Patagonian Andes

The Lonely Planet Story

Lonely Planet published its first book in 1973 in response to the numerous 'How did you do it?' questions Maureen and Tony Wheeler were asked after driving, bussing, hitching, sailing and railing their way from England to Australia.

Written at a kitchen table and hand collated, trimmed and stapled, *Across Asia on the Cheap* became an instant local bestseller, inspiring thoughts of another book.

Eighteen months in South-East Asia resulted in their second guide, *South-East Asia on a shoestring*, which they put together in a backstreet Chinese hotel in Singapore in 1975. The 'yellow bible' as it quickly became known to backpackers around the world, soon became *the* guide to the region. It has sold well over half a million copies and is now in its 7th edition, still retaining its familiar yellow cover.

Today there are over 130 Lonely Planet titles in print – books that have that same adventurous approach to travel as those early guides; books that 'assume you know how to get your luggage off the carousel' as one reviewer put it.

Although Lonely Planet initially specialised in guides to Asia, they now cover most regions of the world, including the Pacific, South America, Africa, the Middle East and Europe. The list of *walking guides* and *phrasebooks* (for 'unusual' languages such as Quechua, Swahili, Nepali and Egyptian Arabic) is also growing rapidly.

The emphasis continues to be on travel for independent travellers. Tony and Maureen still travel for several months of each year and play an active part in the writing, updating and quality control of Lonely Planet's guides.

They have been joined by over 50 authors, 60 staff – mainly editors, cartographers & designers – at our office in Melbourne, Australia, at our US office in Oakland, California and at our European office in Paris; another five at our office in London handle sales for Britain, Europe and Africa. Travellers themselves also make a valuable contribution to the guides through the feedback we receive in thousands of letters each year.

The people at Lonely Planet strongly believe that travellers can make a positive contribution to the countries they visit, both through their appreciation of the countries' culture, wildlife and natural features, and through the money they spend. In addition, the company makes a direct contribution to the countries and regions it covers. Since 1986 a percentage of the income from each book has been donated to ventures such as famine relief in Africa; aid projects in India; agricultural projects in Central America; Greenpeace's efforts to halt French nuclear testing in the Pacific and Amnesty International. In 1994 $100,000 was donated to such causes.

Lonely Planet's basic travel philosophy is summed up in Tony Wheeler's comment, 'Don't worry about whether your trip will work out. Just go!'.